National Intelligencer Newspaper Abstracts 1843

Joan M. Dixon

HERITAGE BOOKS
2006

HERITAGE BOOKS
AN IMPRINT OF HERITAGE BOOKS, INC.

Books, CDs, and more—Worldwide

For our listing of thousands of titles see our website
at
www.HeritageBooks.com

Published 2006 by
HERITAGE BOOKS, INC.
Publishing Division
65 East Main Street
Westminster, Maryland 21157-5026

Copyright © 2004 Joan M. Dixon

All rights reserved. No part of this book may be reproduced or transmitted in any form or by any means, electronic or mechanical, including photocopying, recording or by any information storage and retrieval system without written permission from the author, except for the inclusion of brief quotations in a review.

International Standard Book Number: 978-0-7884-3133-1

NATIONAL INTELLIGENCER NEWSPAPER
WASHINGTON, D C
1843

TABLE OF CONTENTS

Daily National Intelligencer
  Washington, D C, 1843---1

Army and Navy Intelligence/Chronicle—135; 175; 224; 238; 297-298; 333
Army Orders—225; 321-323
Ass'n of American Geologists & Natural Historians—210; 219

Cincinnati fire disaster—109-110
Coincidences--309
Columbian Horticultural Society—269

Commencements: Academy of the Visitation, Gtwn, D C—347-348
                         Balt Academy of the Visitation—337
                         Georgetown College, D C—340-341; 344
                         Howard University at Cambridge—391-392
                         St John's College, N Y—369-370

Debts due—177-178
Delinquent lands in Alleghany Co, Md—116-118
Hodijah Baylies—223-224

Loss of the frig Missouri—448-449
Loss of the schnr Grampus—377-378
Loss of the steamer Pegasus—380-381

Loss of the steamer Sarah Barnes—498
Manuscript of the Revolutionary War—381
Marine Corps-orders-215

Medical Society of D C—20
Midshipmen—297
Mr Weir's picture of the Embarcation of the Pilgrims—562-563

Mutiny on a Texian sloop-of-war--212
Mutiny on the brig Somers—2; 4; 17-18; 34
Napoleon's Tomb—461

Naval Court Martial—63
Navy Orders—225-226; 378
New Guide to Washington City—534

Officers of the: Boston—361
                  Brandywine—246-247
                  Columbus—368
                  Columbus 74—31-32
                  Congress—32; 548
                  Decatur—362
                  Fairfield—32
                  Independence—476
                  Levant—403
                  Lexington—387
                  Macedonian—352-353
                  Margaret Hugg—163
                  Missouri—352-353
                  Preble—399
                  Somers—234
                  Vandalia—234; 388
                  Yorktown—51; 362

Ordinaries & Taverns in Washington City—488-497
Passengers on the Great Western—228; 306
Passengers on the Hibernia—236-237

Passengers on the steamboat Ohio—396-397
Promotions-Army—123-125
Promotions-Marine Corps—127

Promotions-Navy—127; 336
Public sale of land for Canal scrip—217-218
St Patrick's Day volunteers—154

Street smoking—165
Texian prisoners; 90-92; 223
Texians killed & wounded—133

Treaty between U S & Chippewa Indians—182-183
Typographical Society—22
View of Hanover, Va—425

Visit to Santa Anna in 1839—9
Washington City-tax sale—418-422
Washington Corp—292-293

Will of Horace Appleton Haven, of N H—534

Index--575

PREFACE
Daily National Intelligencer Newspaper Abstracts
1843
Joan M Dixon

The National Intelligencer & Washington Advertiser is hereafter the Daily National Intelligencer. It was the first newspaper printed in Washington, D C; Samuel H Smith, the originator. The same was transferred to Jos Gales, jr on Aug 31, 1810; on Nov 1, 1812, the paper was under the firm of Jos Gales, sr, & Wm W Seaton. The Library of Congress has microfilm of the paper from the first issue of Oct 31, 1800 thru Jan 8, 1870, the final paper. The Evening Star Newspaper of Jan 10, 1870 reports: The Intelligencer is discontinued: the proprietor, Mr Alex Delmar, says that having lost several thousand dollars, & being in poor health, he has resolved to discontinue its publication.

Included in the abstracts are advertisements; appointments by the President; Hse o/Rep petitions; passed Acts; legal notices; marriages; deaths; mscl notices; social events; tax sales; military promotions; court cases; deaths by accident; prisoners; & maritime information-crews. Items or events which might be a clue as to the location, age or relationship of an individual are copied.

No attempt has been made to correct the spelling. Due to the length of some articles, it was necessary to present only the highlights of same. Chancery and Equity records are copied as written.

The index contains <u>all</u> surnames and *tracts of lands/places*. Maritime vessels are found under barge, boat, brig, frig, schn'r, ship, sloop, steamboat, tugboat, yacht or vessel.

ABBREVIATIONS:
AA CO	ANNE ARUNDEL COUNTY
CO	COMPANY/COUNTY
CMDER	COMMANDER
CMDOR	COMMODOR
D C	DISTRICT OF COLUMBIA
ELIZ	ELIZABETH
ELIZA	ELIZA
MONTG CO	MONTGOMERY COUNTY
PG CO	PRINCE GEORGES CO
WASH	WASHINGTON
WASH, D C	WASHINGTON, DISTRICT OF COLUMBIA

BOOKS IN THE NATIONAL INTELLIGENCER NEWSPAPER SERIES: 1800-1805/1806-1810/1811-1813/1814-1817/1818-1820/1821-1823/1824-1826/1827-1829/1830-1831/1832-1833/1834-1835/1836-1837/1838-1839/1840/1841/1842/1843/1844/1845/1846/
SPECIAL: CIVIL WAR 2 VOLS, 1861-1865

Dedicated to the memory of my G G Grandparents
George McLaughlin b 1803 Ireland d 1850 Balt, Md
Mrd in 1827, Ireland
Mary A McCadden b 1810 Ireland d 1853 Balt, Md

> DAILY NATIONAL INTELLIGENCER NEWSPAPER
> WASHINGTON
> 1843

MON JAN 2, 1843
The King of France has presented Wm Norris, our celebrated locomotive engine manufacturer, a gold medal, & a gold box ornamented with diamonds, besides giving him an order for the construction of several locomotives.

John M Donn, successor to Boteler & Donn, will continue the House-Furnishing Business at the old stand. --J M Donn

Maj T S Brown, late of the U S Corps of Engineers, has been appointed Chief Engineer of the N Y & Erie Railroad.

Hon Arthur P Bagby was on Dec 19th re-elected a Senator of the U S for the State of Alabama, for the term of 6 years from Mar 4 next, when his present term of service will expire.

Disastrous fires in N Y on Thu night: broke out in the hat & fur store of Messrs Swift & Nichols, at 158 Water st & Fletcher; consumed the wholesale shoe dealer store occupied by Calvin W Howe-131 Maiden Lane; both these stores were owned by Howe; also consumed-156 occupied by Sawyer & Hobby, mathematical instrument makers, & Silas Smith, brush manufacturer. The stores were owned abroad. 154 Water occupied by J D Philips & Co, fur dealers, destroyed. Store occupied by Smith Wright, Lyon & Co, with a large stock of saddlery on hand was consumed. Another fire occurred soon after in a grocery, 118 Broad st, occupied by Richd Fitzpatrick. Adjoining bldgs occupied by Mr G Foster, as a grocery; J Lynch, a barber; Carman & Bohomon, carpenters, & several families, all destroyed.

Govn'r Seward dismissed David Moulton from the ofc of Sheriff of Oneida Co as published in the Albany Journal. Moulton came to Wash to demand from the Pres, by the authority of the Govn'r, a criminal then in D C; that while here, he agreed with the man not to arrest him, & to secure the discontinuance of the suit by the prosecutor; that he received for this $180, of which $80 was to be retained for payment of his own expense, & the rest to be given to the prosecutor; & on his return he demanded & received payment from the State Treas of his expenses for duties which he had not only not performed, but bargained, for a pecuniary consideration, not to perform. These reasons the Govn'r thinks abundantly sufficient to justify his dismissal.

Land scrip for sale. Apply to John Carroll Brent, City Hall.

The proprietor of the Metropolis will be pleased to receive such of his fellow citizens as may be disposed to exchange salutations with him on Mon next. Egg Nogg served up at the shortest notice. –A R Jenkins, Proprietor of the Metropolis.

Naval Board of Inquiry-assembled this morning: Mutiny on board the brig **Somers**. From the N Y Evening Post of Fri. Capt Mackenzie taxed Spencer with having made communication to Mr Wales, which he admitted, but said it was a joke. He was confined & put in double irons, with orders to the guard to take his life if he attempted to speak to any of the crew. The lockers of Mr Philip Spencer were searched & a razor case was found with a paper with Greek characters, which was translated by midshipman H Rogers. It was a list of the crew; those certain & uncertain; those to be retained & those to be destroyed; those to keep watch & those who were to commit the murder, with many other particulars. The appearance of Cromwell & Small was observed. After the Divine service on Sun, by the management of Saml Cromwell, the top-gallant mast was carried away; those men mentioned in Spencer's manuscript, wherever stationed, collected at the topmast. Elisha Small was likewise arrested & put in irons. Mackenzie thought he would see what effect he could produce on the crew, & proceeded to detail such an account as he thought best of the conspiracy which he had discovered. Some men wept & some appeared horror-struck. Spencer & 2 others were deprived of tobacco. Everything seemed to be growing worse. Master Wilson was arrested & ironed, with McKinley & Grun. The ofcrs presented a communication to Capt Mackenzie, stating that they were convinced that Spencer, Small, & Cromwell were engaged in mutiny; that it would be impossible to convey them safely to the U S; & the safety of their own lives required that those three be put to death. Mackenzie put on his full uniform, & communicated to Spencer his fate, giving him 10 minutes to write any communication he might please for any of his relations. They then told Cromwell & Small their fate. Spencer refused to write any letter, but wished his father & mother all happiness. He said, also, it would kill his poor mother; this was the first time Capt M knew Spencer had a mother. Capt M said it would have hurt him more if he had succeeded in his plan. He also confessed he had the same project on board the ship **John Adams** & the ship **Potomac**. He was furnished, at his own request, with a Bible & Prayer-book; after upwards of an hour had elapsed, they were led out. After dinner the bodies were lowered, & preparation made for burying them. This was done. Mackenzie suggested that the thanks of the Navy Dept should be given to all the ofcrs for their support of him, taking all the responsibility of the execution on himself. He praised Mr Wales also, & Sgt Garty, who was on board sick in his hammock, but got up & performed duty until the termination of the mutiny. He recommended that Garty should be promoted to a 2nd lieutenancy in the marines; that several petty ofcrs should be appointed boatswains, & that his nephew, O H Perry, should be placed on the list to receive the vacancy occasioned by Spencer's death.

Servants for sale: for a term of years. One has 13 years & the other 11 years to serve. No restriction as to where the purchaser may wish to carry them. –Wm H Richards, corner 7th st & Md ave

Hon John P Booth, Judge of the 6th Judicial Crct of Alabama, resigned his office Dec 20.

I take this method of informing all those indebted to me that their accounts will be rendered between Jan 1 & Jan 13, 1843 to make settlement. Just received from N Y 100 kegs of Goshen Butter, of the first quality. –Robt Cruit, F st, between 14th & 15th sts.

Mrd: on Dec 27, by Rev Mr Mathews, Mr John Connelly to Miss Rebecca Mudd, all of Wash City.

Died: on Jan 1, after a lingering & painful illness, in her 72nd year, Mrs Mary Legare, the excellent mother of Hugh S Legare. Her funeral is tomorrow at 12 o'clock from his residence, Count de Menon's Bldgs.

Died: on Dec 30, at her residence in Wash City, of consumption, Mr Julia A McComb, w/o David McComb, in her 28th year.

New Auction & Commission Store to open Jan 3, 1843: in the House lately occupied by Mr Waring, on 7th st, nearly opposite the store of Messrs Pittman & Phillips. –David S Waters, Auctioneer

Restaurant at the Capitol: in the basement story of the Capitol on the left hand side, lately occupied by Mr Pettibone as a Restaurant. Bar will be well stocked with Wines & Liquors. –Jno West

Saml De Vaughan has just received his supply of fresh Swedish Leeches, of a very superior quality. Country physicians can be supplied as usual, by the dozen or hundred.

Circuit Court of Wash Co, D C. Matthew Hornung has filed his petition for the benefit of the Bankrupt Law: hearing on the first Mon of Feb next. Same for John T Bishop. –Wm Brent, clk

Circuit Court of Wash Co, D C. About 10 days ago, a verdict was rendered by a jury against Lambert S Beck, constable, muleting him in damages to the amount of $125, for personal injuries inflicted upon Polly Williams, a colored woman, residing in the 1st Ward of Wash City, by which she was prevented from attending to her business as a laundress for some time, & had a doctor to pay for surgical services.

Circuit Court of Wash Co, D C. On Wed last, Mr Henry Ould, of Gtwn, was admitted as an atty & cnslr of this Court.

The Farmers & Mechanics' Bank of Gtwn have brought suit for slander against Jos N Fearson, of Gtwn. The alleged slander or libel is contained in an advertisement which Mr Fearson lately published in the Gtwn Advocate.

TUE JAN 3, 1843
The printing & bleaching establishment of Mr Isaac Saunders, at the head of the Cove, in Providence, took fire on Tue last. Insurance was in the amount of $71,900.

Naval Board of Inquiry-assembled Dec 29, 1842: Mutiny on board the brig **Somers**. The narrative of Capt Mackenzie, dated U S brig **Somers**, N Y, Dec 19, 1842: to Hon Abel P Upshur, Sec of the Navy: [6½ cols.] Abstracts: 1-Chas Lambert, apprentice, had been guilty of theft in stealing sinnet for a hat from Ward M Gagely; & Henry Waltham, the ward room steward, had stolen brandy from the ward room mess, & given it to Mr Spencer. 2-Waltham told Danl McKinley where 3 bottles of wine could be found. 3-Mr Wales detected Chas A Wilson attempting to draw out a hand-spike from under the launch, with an evident purpose of felling him. 4-Ofcrs who received my [Mackenzie] letter: Lt Guert Gansevoort, Passed Assist Surgeon R W Leecock, Purser H M Hickskell, Actg Master M C Perry, Midshipman Henry Rodgers, Midshipman Egbert Thompson, Midshipman Chas W Hays. 5-When told of his fate, Cromwell was completely unmanned, protested his innocence, & invoked the name of his wife. 6-Small said, I have nobody to care for me but my poor old mother, & I would rather that she should not know how I have died." 7-Spencer said he deserved death for this & many other crimes. There are few crimes that I have not committed. I have wronged my parents; this will kill my poor mother! This may injure my father. 8-Cromwell's last words were, "Tell my wife I die an innocent man; tell Lt Morris I die an innocent man!" 9-The three were hanged. Spencer was laid out dressed in complete uniform, except the sword, which he had forfeited his right to wear. The two seamen were also laid out with neatness. 10-Cromwell admitted he had been in a slaver, & had been an inmate of Moro Castle at Havana. 11-Spencer's body was place in a coffin. The bodies of the 2 sailors were sewed up in their hammocks. 12-After prayers, the bodies were consigned to the deep. 13-Noble conduct of Purser H M Hieskeil & of Passed Assist Surgeon R W Leecock, for services which they so freely yielded beyond the sphere of their regular duties. Leecock was indeed in no condition to go to sea when he joined the **Somers**. He had recently returned in the ship **Dolphin** from the coast of Africa, where his constitution had been completely shattered by a fever contracted in the river Nunez. 14-Mr J W Wales has rendered to the American Navy a memorable service. 15-Sgt Michl H Garty –I will only say that his conduct was worthy of the noble corps to which he has the honor to belong. 16-I recommend that boatswain's mates Oliver B Browning & Wm Collins, & capt of the forecastle Chas Stewart, may be appointed boatswains in the navy; that the gunner's mates Henry King & Andrew Anderson, & quartermaster Chas Rodgers, be appointed gunners, & Thos Dickerson a carpenter in the navy.

The Balt Patriot annonces the death of the venerable & highly esteemed Dr Nathl Potter, late Prof in the Univ of Md. He died suddenly yesterday by strangulation, brought on my severe coughing, to which he had been subject for some time. On the preceding day he seemingly enjoyed his usual health, & was attending to the duties of his profession.

A person named McLean, another one of the party concerned in the murder of Maj Floyd, perpetrated some time since near St Louis, has been tried at that city, & found guilty of murder in the first degree. Sentence has not been passed upon him or upon Johnson, who was convicted a few weeks ago.

Butter, Butter-good fresh Pennsylvania Roll Butter for sale cheap: apply at Connolly's Farmers' Hotel, corner of 8th & D sts. –Jas Leibey, of Newburg, Cumberland Co, Pa.

Petition of Wm H Tuck, adm d b n C T A of Levin Boone, filed in a cause pending in PG Co Crt, as a Crt of Equity, for the appointment of a trustee under the will of Jos Pope, dec'd, on the application of Susan Osbourn. The ptn states that, upon the ptn of Susan Osbourn, such proceedings were had that a sale of the real estate of the said Jos Pope was made & ratified by the Court; that the Auditor stated an account of the proceeds, in which Eliz Soper, Colmore Pope, Jos Pope, & Saml Marshall are each entitled to $346.07, under the will of the dec'd; that said sums remain in the hands of the trustee, & under the control of the Court. That, before the commencement of the proceedings, Levin Boone has purchased from the said Eliz, Colmore, Jos & Saml, their interest in the said land of Jos Pope, dec'd, & paid them the purchase money, as will appear by the receipts filed with the ptn. The petitioner, as administrator of Levin Boone, claims to be substituted in their places as to the said fund, & prays that the trustee pay the money to him, with a due proportion of interest. The ptn states that Colmore Pope, Jos Pope, & Saml Marshall removed many years since to the State of Ky, but the petitioner does not know whether they are now alive; if alive they still reside there, or that if dead, he does not know whethere they left heirs or legal reps, or their names or places of residence. It is ordered that said dfndnts appear in this Court on or before the first Mon in Jul next.
–John Stephen, John B Brooke, clerk of PG Co Crt.

Mrd: on Dec 29, at Bohemia, Cecil Co, Md, by Rev Mr Wiley, Philip Hamilton, of N Y C, to Rebecca, d/o the Hon Louis McLane.

Mrd: on Jan 1, by Rev Henry Bean, Chas K Stellwagen, of Phil, to Miss Eliza S, y/d/o Jas Tucker, of Wash City.

Died: on Jan 1, of consumption, Miss Eliz T Queen. Her funeral will be from the residence of her aunt on 4½ st, at 10 a m this morning.

Died: on Dec 28, in PG Co, Md, Mr Nathan Walker, at the advanced age of 86 years. He was an affectionate husband, an indulgent father, & a kind master.

Died: on Dec 28, at Brooklyn, Rev Thompson S Harris, Chaplain U S Navy.

Died: on Dec 28, at Balt, Mrs Mgt Smith, wid/o the late Hon Robt Smith, in her 79th year.

Died: on Dec 24, at the residence of her son, Lt Col R E De Russy, at Old Point Comfort, Va, in her 78th year, Madame Madileine E Bessiere De Russy, relict of Thos de Russy, of Saint Malo, France, & for many years a resident in the U S.

Circuit Court of Wash Co, D C. Richd W Griffith has filed his petition for the benefit of the Bankrupt Law: hearing on the first Mon of Feb next. –Wm Brent, clk

WED JAN 4, 1843
The Staunton Spectator learns from an authentic source that the books & records of *Greene Co, Va*, stolen from the clerk's ofc of that county about 12 months ago, have been recently found by a fox-hunting party, in a cave in the side of a mountain.

A quarrel took place at Nashville on Dec 25 between 2 young men, named Sturdivant & Armstrong, in which the former drawing a pistol, & his brother interposing to prevent him from shooting, the pistol discharged & the contents passed through Sturdivant's own hand into the breast of his brother, killing him instantly.

A Jew banker, M Cohn, of Antwerp, has been nominated knight of the Spanish order of Isabella. The country in which a Jew some scores of years back could not set his foot without incurring the risk of being burnt alive now decorates him with an order.

Senate: 1-Ptn from J G Hudson, asking that the Sec of War may be authorized to settle the conflicting claims in relation to the Pea Patch Island. 2-Ptn from the widow & heirs of John P Chandonai, a half breed Indian, asking compensation, etc. [Etc as copied.] 3-Ptn from Geo Reber, administrator of Wm H Hunter, asking remuneration for expenses incurred. 4-Cmte on the Post Ofc & Post Roads: House bills for the relief of Saml L Rose & others, & for the relief of Barent Striker, without amendment. 5-Cmte of Claims: adverse report on the claim of J B McKoun; which was ordered to be printed. 6-Resolved, that the report of Lt Wilkes to the Sec of the Navy, relating to the Territory of Oregon, be printed, & that the charts of Columbia river & the waters of Admiral's Inlet &Paget Sound be engraved. 7-Cmte of Private Land Claims: to inquire into confiming to Absalom Link a certain tract of land lying in Missouri, & that the papers on file be referred to the same cmte. 8-Cmte on Private Land Claims: to inquire into confirming to Martin Fenwick, of Missouri, a certain tract of land in Missouri, & that the papers on file be referred to the same cmte. 9-Cmte on Private Land Claims: to inquire into making an appropriation for the benefit of the heirs of W A Slacum, & that the ptn & papers on file be referred to the said cmte.

Boots & Shoes makers, corner of Pa ave & 10th st. —John Mills & Co

For sale: tract of land containing about 200 acs, above the Little Falls' Bridge, on the Leesburg Turnpike Road: improvements consist of an enclosure of the entire tract, & a good new log-cabin, well adopted for a commodious kitchen, on a beautiful site for a residence. Apply to my brother, Basil E Gantt, who resides in the vicinity, or to Wm O Slade, of Wash City. —John Gantt, Fairfax Co, Va

In N Y, on Sun week, Theodore Mackey, a boy, was killed by a fire engine. He slipped & fell, while having hold of the drag rope, & the engine passed over his head. He died on the way to the hospital.

Mr Geo Savage will thankfully receive donations for the benefit of the widow Hill & her fatherless children. -Local News

Hse/o Reps: 1-Ptn of David C Eastman, of Fayette Co, Ohio, praying Congress to obtain a likeness of Madison Washington, & to place it in the Library of Congress. 2-Ptn of Christopher Cray for a pension. 3-Ptn of Eliz Rawson, wid/o of Jos Rawson, for renewal of 5 years' pension. 4-Ptn of Chas Weldon, of Ohio, for compensation for supplies furnished the army in Florida. 5-Ptn of Nathl Sawyer, S Schooley, Chas D Dana, & others, citizens of Hamilton Co, Ohio, praying the establishment of a national exchequer, to deal in exchanges. 6-Ptn of D Raymond, C Fletcher, M Allen, & others, of Hamilton Co, Ohio, in favor of the exchequer reported by the cmtes of Congress with amendments. 7-Ptn of Heman Blodgett & others, of Genesee Co, N Y, praying Congress to pass into law the plan of an exchequer, recommended by the Executive at the opening of the present Congress. 8-Ptn of Jos French & 49 others, citizens of Barnstead, N H, for a mail route from Gilmanton Iron Works to Manchester, N H. 9-Ptn of Ephraim Tibbets & 51 others, citizens of said Gilmanton Iron Works; of Jas Knox & 70 others, citizens of Pembroke; of R T Leavitt & 117 others, citizens of Pittsfield; & of J G Gilley & 129 others, citizens of Manchester; all praying for the establishment of a mail route from Gilmanton Iron Works to said Manchester. 10-Ptn of Thos D Morrison, of N H, for remuneration.

<u>Washington Assemblies: the first Assembly will take place on Jan 12, 1843.</u>
Managers:

Hon W P Mangum	Ch Lee Jones
Hon Wm Cost Johnson	J Mandeville Carlisle
Hon Caleb Cushing	Dr J M Thomas
Com Lewis Warrington	Richd Wallach
Gen Geo Gibson	Richd S Hill
Gen Alex Hunter	P Kearney, U S A
Fletcher Webster	Wm May, U S N

Wash Corp: 1-Ptn from Wm J Bronaugh: referred to the Cmte of Claims. Same for the ptn of John France. 2-Cmte of Claims: asked to be discharged from further consideration of the ptn of Thos J Fletcher. 3-Ptn of Jas Wormley, for relief, Cmte of Claims recommended its indefinite postponement.

Mrd: on Jan 1, in Balt, by Rev Mr Hamilton, Mr Jacob Green, of that city, to Miss Ann Garland, y/d/o the late Alexander Howison, of Prince Wm Co, Va.

Mrd: on Dec 27, at Hadley, Mass, by Rev D Huntington, Rev S G Bulfinch, of Wash, to Miss Caroline, d/o the Hon Chas P Phelps, of Hadley.

Died: on Dec 28, Wm Bernard, infant s/o Dr Wm P Johnston, of Wash City.

Female teacher wanted, anxious to procure a teacher in his family, of middle aged lady qualified to teach the higher branches of an English education, including instrumental & vocal music & drawing, together with the French language. Apply to the subscriber, John B Mullikin, Queen Anne, PG Co, Md.

Military Civic Ball: First Annual Ball of the Independent Grays will be held at the Assembly Room of the Union Hotel, Gtwn, on Jan 17, 1843, being the Anniversary of the formation of the Company.

Managers:

Capt C Smith	Capt Middleton	Capt Hanly
Capt John Mason, jr	Capt Williams	Capt Snyder
Capt R France	Capt McCauley	Capt Hawkins
Capt Buckingham	Capt Duvall	

Cmte of Invitation & Reception:

Capt Smith	Richd Fulslove	Sergeant Garrett
Lt Wright	John Mehegan	Saml McAtee
Ensign Kidwell	Lt Hill	A L Settle
Surgeon Lauck	Pioneer Bronaugh	R Wilburn

Cmte on Refreshments:

Lt Kidwell	C E Upperman	Chas A Newton
Cpl Adams	Cpl Sedgwick	Jos L Semmes
Chas S Jones	John E Carter	

Cmte on Decorations:

Sargeant Ridgway	Wm H Semmes	Jas A Crow
Wm Herron	Wm Waugh	Geo Harvey

Tickets $2-to be had at the Drug Stores of J L Kidwell & G M & J L Sothoron, Gtwn; & at the Stores of Farquhar & Morgan, R L Patterson, & J P McKean, Washington; of F Reilly, Navy Yard, & at the door on the night of the Ball. Gentlemen who desire invitation tickets for Ladies will please notify the Cmte thereof. No Servants will be admitted under any circumstances, except those engaged by the Company. Lloyd Williams' Cotillion Band is engaged for the occasion.

For rent: 2 story frame house on I st at 7th: rent $150 per annum. Also, the 2 story brick house on 13th & E sts: rent $150 per year. –J Fugitt & Co, Centre-market space

Orphan's Court of Wash Co, D C. Letters of administration on personal estate of Richd Hendley, late of said county, dec'd. -John Richd Hendley, adm

Orphan's Court of Wash Co, D C. Case of the administrator of John Forsyth, dec'd. Jan 31st set for the settlement of said estate. –Ed N Roach, Reg/o wills

Wm Slater, Brush Maker, from Greenwich St, N Y, has opened the store adjoining the Railroad Ofc, on Pa ave, Wash.

Circuit Court of Wash Co, D C. John P Vantyne has filed his ptn for the benefit of the Bankrupt Law: hearing on the first Mon of Feb next. –Wm Brent, clk

THU JAN 5, 1843

A visit to Santa Anna in 1839. The huts, though poor, were clean; no windows, subdued light came through the leafy canes. We arrived at Manga de Clava, the property of Santa Anna; the house is pretty, slight looking, kept in nice order. The Señora de Santa Anna, tall & thin, was dressed to receive us, in clear white muslin, with white satin shoes, & with very splendid diamond earrings, brooch, & rings. She introduced her dght, Guadalupe, a miniature of her mother. Gen Santa Anna arrived, in modest clothes, with one leg, apparently somewhat of an invalid. He spoke of his leg which is cut off below the knee. He speaks of it frequently, like Sir John Ramorny of his bloody hand. After breakfast the Señora dispatched an ofcr for her cigar case-which was gold with a diamond latch-offered me a cigar, which I having declined, she lighted her own, a little paper cigarito, & the gentlemen followed her good example. The lady informs us that the practice of ladies smoking has become unfashionable among the genteel society of Mexico, being confined mostly to elderly ladies who cannot give it up; & being voted vulgar, will probably not survive another generation. DISCIPLINE OF THE MALE PENITENTS. We went to the church of St Augustin where there were about 150 men, enveloped in cloaks & sarapes, their faces concealed. A monk mounted the pulpit & the discourse appeared like a preparation for the execution of a multitude of condemned criminals. The organ struck of the Miserere, & the church was plunged in darkness. Suddenly we heard the sound of scourges descending upon the bare flesh. It was sickening. At the end of half an hour a little bell is rung, & the voice of the monk is heard calling upon them to desist, but such was their enthusiasm that the horrible lashing continued louder & fiercer than ever. They say that the church floor is frequently covered with blood after one of those penances, & that a man died the other day in consequence of his wounds.

H P Karl has just finished at his manufactory, on the south side of Pa ave, between 12th & 13th sts, a new & fine-toned piano forte, which he now offers for sale. He had much experience as a manufacturer of Piano Fortes in Germany. To those who purchase Pianos made by him in Wash City, he pledges himself to keep them in perfect tone for one year, free of all charge.

For rent: a very comfortable & commodious house in Gtwn, in complete order. Inquire of Saml McKenney.

Wm Pratt, of Boston, died on Thu at his father's residence in Summer st, in consequence of an accidental fall upon the ice on Sat last.

Richd Henry Marshall appointed Assoc Judge for the 5th judicial district of Md, vice Shriver, resigned. Geo W Paschal elected a Judge of the Supreme Court of Arkansas for 8 years.

Hse/o Reps: 1-Cmte on Accounts to inquire into the allowing to the widow of Hon Jas W Williams & Richd W Haberhsam, dec'd, both late of this House, their usual mileage. Resolution amended by limiting its provision to the time of the death of the gentleman referred to. 2-Cmte of Claims: made a report upon the ptn of Chas Waldron, with a bill for his relief. Same cmte made an unfavorable report upon the ptn of Jos H Waring. 3-Cmte on Foreign Affairs: made a report upon the ptn of John Randolph Clay, late Sec of Leg of the U S at the Crt of Vienna, & reported a bill for his relief. 4-Cmte on Revolutionary Pensions: made a report upon the ptn of Jacob White, with a bill for his relief. 5-Ptn of Chas Noyrit, of Natchitoches, La: referred. 6-Ptn of Jas Pepper, of the Parish of Madison, La: referred. 7-Ptn of the widow & heirs of Robt N Kelly, late receiver of the land ofc at Opelousas, La: referred. 8-Ptn & documents of Mrs Drusilla Giesey, wid/o Valentine Giesey, late superintendent of the Cumberland Road, praying to be refunded the amount of a judgment recovered in the court of Fayette Co, Pa, against the estate of the said superintendent for work done on the Cumberland Road. 9-Ptn of Jane Dade, of Alexandria, for a further appropriation of land to meet the claims of military land warrants granted for Revolutionary services in the Virginia line. 10-Memorial of Horatio S & Mary Ann Fitch, legal reps of Wm Lyle, praying compensation for the Revolutionary services of said Lyle. 11-Ptn of Fred'k L French, for compensation for services as master's mate. 12-Ptn of Geo Whipple & 160 others, of Lorain Co, Ohio, for the repeal of all laws of the U S for the establishment & regulation of slavery. 13-Ptn of H C Taylor & 162 others, legal voters of Russia, Lorain Co, Ohio, for the repeal of the 21st rule. 14-Ptn of Lydia R Finney & 250 others, ladies of Russia, Lorain Co, Ohio, for the repeal of the 21st rule of the Hse/o Reps.

Z D Gilman informs his customers that their bills with him will be presented during this & next month.

Senate: 1-Ptn from Richd Pollard, late Charge d'Affaires at Chili, asking remuneration for loss sustained in consequence of the depressed state of commercial credit. 2-Ptn from R Sands & others, citizens of the U S, asking that the Post Ofc law affecting the transmission of newspapers otherewise than by mail may be repealed. 3-Ptn from Capt Thos S Easton, asking an examination be made into his invention for the mode of preventing the explosion of steam boilers. 4-Cmte on Finance: joint resolution authorizing the Sec of the Treas to settle the liabilities of the sureties of Gordon S Boyd, late Receiver of public moneys at Columbus, Mississippi, with amendments. 5-Cmte on Finance: House bill for the relief of Isaac & Thos S Winslow; for the relief of Burr & Smith; for the relief of Ferdinand Seebars, without amendment.

The partnership existing under the firm of Lambright & Crandell is this day dissolved by mutual consent. Persons indebted to make payment to Geo Lambright. –Geo Lambright, Jos Crandell

Farm for rent: 3 miles from Washington on the north road leading from Wash to Bladensburg, known as P Packard's dairy & garden farm, containing about 200 acs, with 4 small but convenient dwlg houses, 2 barns, with cellars under them. Call on Capt Saml Wroe, corner of H & 5th sts, Wash, whom I have duly authorized to lease or rent the same. –Philip Smallwood, Howard District, Anne Arundel Co, Md.

Sugar Plantation for sale: on the west bank of the Mississippi river, in Louisiana, about 17 miles above New Orleans: it has cleared land of about 625 arpens: dwlg house; kitchen;about 10 cabins; one large sugar house & purgery.
–Robt B Corbin, Caroline Co, Va; or H C Cammack, New Orleans.

Died: on Dec 18, at the residence of her husband, in Sullivan Co, Tenn, Nancy Anne McClellan, the w/o the Hon Abraham McClellan, a member of Congress from that State. When Col McClellan left home to take his seat at the present session, he left Mrs McClellan in fine health, & the bereavement has fallen suddenly & painfully. The mail which bore to him the melancholy intelligence of her sickness, was followed, in a few days, by the news of her death. Mrs McClellan was descended from one of the patriotic pioneers of the West, who left behind him a numerous respectable family. She was a native of Tenn, where her father, at an early period of its history, & when she was yet a child, lost his life in its defence against the Indians. She was married when very young to Col McClellan, & their union had lasted nearly 34 years. Together they had toiled through the trials of life; & in all its stages her bright example of Christian faith & ardent devotion in the discharge of all the duties of a wife & mother had cheered the path of her husband.

For sale: As agent for the heirs of the late Hon John Forsyth, I offer at private sale the dwlg house in Wash City, lately occupied by the family of the dec'd, & now by the Navy Dept as a depot for charts, & naval instruments. Apply to R S Chew.

FRI JAN 6, 1843
Firemen's Ins Co of Wash & Gtwn, meeting on the 2nd inst. Directors elected for the ensuing year:
John D Barclay & Saml Redfern, from the Union Fire Co
Jacob Gideon & Andrew Rothwell, from the Perseverance Fire Co
Saml Burche & Jos W Beck, from the Columbia Fire Co
Richd Barry & Abel G Davis, from the Navy Yard
Geo Shoemaker, from the Western Star Fire Co
John Myers & Chas E Eckel, from the Vigilant Fire Co
-Alex'r McIntire, Sec

I propose to commence in Jan, 1843, the publication of the Army & Navy Chronicle & Scientific Repository; this is in place of the Army & Navy Chronicle which has been discontinued. –Wm Q Force

Naval Court of Inquiry-assembled Dec 30, 1842: Mutiny on board the brig **Somers**. Jas W Wales, the purser's steward on board the **Somers** was sworn in: was informed of a mutiny on board on the night of Nov 25. Mr Spencer & I were alone when he said he was leagued with about 20 of the brig's company to take her, murder all her ofcrs, & commence piracy. I could not make any reply. He commenced talking to Small in Spanish; I did not understand the language. The name of the topman was Benj F Green; Green was an apprentice on board. Mr Wales was called again on Dec 31. Lt Gansevoort was the next witness called. He was on board the **Somers** during her late cruise as first lt-the only lt on board. He stated the names of the ofcrs on board: Cmder Mackenzie; Dr Leecock; Purser Hieskell; Sailingmaster Perry; Midshipmen Henry Rodgers, Egbert Thompson, C H Hays, Philip Spencer, & Acting Midshipmen Delande & Tillotson, clerk O H Perry. Lt Gansevoort was recalled on Jan 3. He said that Small addressed the crew: "Messmates & Shipmates, I never murdered any body, but I said I would; now, see what words will do. Take warning by me." The Cmder gave the order to fire. I called out "whip!" & the men were run up to the mainyard. The Cmder asked me how I though it would do to give 3 cheers. I told him I though it would do well; it might show who were wrong & who were right. Circumstances that led Gansevoort to think that an attempt would be made to rescue the prisoners: McKee, McKinley, Green, Goldenham, & Sullivan & some others I had seen passing looks with Spencer. Court adjourned.

Lots at auction: deed of trust from Mrs Henrietta Shryock to Chas W Boteler, dated Sep 28, 1839: sale of lot 8 in sq 308, & all of sq 353, in Wash City.
–Robt W Dyer & Co, aucts

Fire at Norfolk: Sat last by which a large brick bldg, on Wide-Water st, occupied as 2 distinct grocery stores, was, with its contents, destroyed. Mr Jas B Gray & Mr J Hendren are the suffers, who were but partially insured. A detachment of sailors from the U S ship **Pennsylvania**, under the command of Lt John R Tucker, reached the shore with the engine of the ship, & actively engaged in extinguishing the fire.

A couple of weeks since the dwlg-house of Mr Henderson Bell, in Graham township, Indiana, was burnt, & his sister, a child about 4 years old, perished in the flames. Mr Bell himself was so severely injured that he died on Sun night, & 2 others of his children are yet deemed to be in a critical situation. Thus 3 have perished; members of a respectable & much respected family.

Maj John Taylor was thrown fom his sulley on Dec 15, while returning to Tallahassee, Fla, from a visit to one of his children, & was so much injured that he died in a few hours. He was a native of Va, but had lived in Fla about 14 years. He was in his 63rd year.

On Mon last Mr Jos Abell, a farmer residing near Camden, N J, was found by his wife in a dying state, lying in some hay in his own barn. He had been with some companions the previous afternoon. He had a sum of money missing, but it could have dropped from his pocket. He had bruises, but not enough to cause his death. He might have fallen. He was 25 or 30 years of age, much respected by his friends & beloved by his family. –Phila Inquirer

Mrd: on Dec 26, at Harrisburg, Pa, by Rev J F Mesick, John P Frazer, of Wash City, to Catharine Mary, d/o John A Stehley, of the former place.

Died: on Wed night, Mrs Hannah Morfit, formerly of Norfolk, Va. Her funeral will be from the house of her son, Henry M Morfit, on N J ave, tomorrow at 3 p m.

Died: on Dec 26, in her 60th year, Mrs Ann D Hall, consort of Thos Hall, of PG Co, Md. She had a complicated disease for many years. She was beloved by all her acquaintances. She left a husband & 8 children to survive her irreparable loss.

Died: on Dec 30, in PG Co, Md, at the residence of J B Mullikin, Mrs Maria E Cox, in her 38th year, relict of the late Fleet Cox, of Westmoreland Co, Va. As a teacher, she was very favorable known in Va & Md.

Died: on Dec 30, in Chas Co, Md, Elias P Matthews, a native & citizen of Md, in his 48th year. No one held a higher place in the esteem of his acquaintances, or a larger share in the affections of his friends.

Died: on Dec 2, at the *Oaks*, near Charlotte, St Mary's Co, Md, Mrs Clarissa Keech, w/o Mr Jas Keech, in her 62nd year. She lived to see a large family of sons & dghts arrive at full maturity of life. To them she has left the rich inheritance of a good name, the remembrance of a pious & devoted parent, & their best, kindest, & most constant friend.

Stolen, from the house of the subscriber, a red Morocco pocket-book, containing $18 in notes & about $5 in silver. Return the pocket-book & the thief is welcome to the money & no questions asked. –Rachael Combs

Senate: 1-Ptn from Wm Depeyster & Henry N Cruger, asking compensation for a slave sent away by order of the commanding ofcr, with a party of emigrating Seminole Indians. 2-Cmte on Finance: adverse report on House bill for the relief of Noah Brown & others, ofcrs & crew of the American private armed brig **Warrior**. 3-Cmte of Claims: House bills, without amendment, for the relief of Peter Lienberger; for the relief of John B Dulaney; for the relief of Jas M Morgan; for the relief of Cornelius Wilson & Jas Canter; for the relief of the legal reps of Capt Saml Shannon, dec'd. 4-Cmte on Public Lands: House bill for the relief of Elisha Moreland, Wm M Kenedy, Robt J Kenedy, & Mason E Lewis, without amendment. 5-Bill for the relief of Benj Murphy, of Arkansas, was read a third time & passed.

Eliza Reynolds has opened a School on 8th st, between G & H sts, & respectfully solicits a share of public patronage. All the branches usually taught in a preparatory school will be attended to, & no efforts spared essential to the advancement of the pupils..

Hse/o Reps: 1-Resolved, that the Cmte on Revolutionary Claims inquire into allowing to the heirs of Geo Yates, dec'd, compensation for his services as a surgeon's mate in the war of the Revolution-it was adopted. 2-Cmte on Private Land Claims: received the bill for the relief of John N Howard. 3-Cmte on Indian Affairs: report in the case of Geo C Johnston, with a bill for his relief. 4-Cmte on Invalid Pensions: adverse report on case of Geo Raines, of Va: to lie on the table.

$150 reward for runaway negro man John, about 23 years of age.
--John Blakiston, Chaptico, Md

SAT JAN 7, 1843
Hse/o Reps: 1-Bills passed-for the relief of:

John Core	Danl Dunham	Boyd Reilly
Saml B Tuck	David Allspach	John E Hunt & others
Thos D Gilson	Conrad House	Geo Randall & others
Jos R Chandler	Robt G Ford	Heirs of Philip
Jonathan Britton	Catharine Wilson	Renault

Heirs, or assignees of the heirs, of Isaac Todd, & Jas McGill

2-Ptn of Gervis Foot, asking relief for losses sustained in consequence of the Gov't not fulfilling a contract made with him: referred. 3-Cmte on Naval Affairs: report on the ptn of Wm Fabre, with a bill for his relief; read a third time & passed.

Senate: 1-The Pres of the Senate laid before the body a report from the Sec of the Treas, stating that a previous appropriation would be necessary to enable him to carry into effect the act of Aug, 1842, for the relief of Danl Hays, John Henderson, & others. 2-Ptn from A Adams & other mechants, asking a remission of certain duties: referred. 3-Ptn from Mary Ann Boyd, asking a pension: referred. 4-Ptn from Jas S Conway, praying to be released from a judgment obtained against him by the U S: referred. 5-Ptn from Alonzo Smith, asking a revival of the bounty land act: referred. 6-Ptn from W McPherson, asking a pension for injuries received while in the service of the U S: referred. 7-Cmte on the Judiciary: House bills for the relief of John P Skinner & the legal reps of J S Green. 8-Same cmte: Relief of the reps of Alexander McComb, Robt Jennings, & the heirs & legal reps of Jas Rody, dec'd, sureties of Saml Champlin, late paymaster in the U S army. 9-Same cmte: bill for the relief of John McKeon, with a report. 10-Cmte on Pensions: adverse report on the ptn of Mary Fenton. Same cmte: report with a bill for the relief of Saml Davy.

Mrd: on Dec 27, at Wicomico House, Chas Co, Md, by Rev Mr Davis, Dr Catesby Graham Brown, of PG Co, Md, to Miss Mary Truman, 2nd d/o the Hon John T Stoddert.

Circuit Court of Wash Co, D C. Jas A Ratcliff has filed his ptn for the benefit of the Bankrupt Law: hearing on the first Mon in Feb next. Same for Thos B Addison, & Wm R Nicholls. –Wm Brent, clk

Orphan's Court of Chas Co, Md. Letters of administration on the personal estate of Chas S Locke, late of said county, dec'd. -F Stone, administrator of C S Locke

Murder was committed in the town of Greenfield, in this county, on Fri last. A man by the name of Berage beat his father-in-law, Thos Holland, aged 90 years, in such a brutal manner that he expired on Sun. -Detroit Advertiser

Naval: The U S schnr **Grampus**, Lt Cmder Van Brunt, from a cruise in the West Indies, & 8 days from Stirrop Key, Bahamas, arrived at Norfolk on Tue. Ofcrs & crew all well.

By virtue of 2 writs of fieri facias, issued by Benj K Morsell, one of the J Ps for Wash Co, D C, & to me directed, I shall offer for public sale, for cash, on Jan 14, opposite the Centre Market-house, one heavy gold guard chain, seized & taken as the property of Geo W Macrae, & will be sold to satisfy a judgment due John L Faut. –Lambert S Beck, Constable

A letter from the postmaster at Penn Yan, Yates Co, announces the death, on Dec 28, of the Hon Joshua Lee, one of the most distinguished citizens of that place, & widely known heretofore as a member of Congress & the State Leg. –Albany Argus

MON JAN 9, 1843
Govn'r Porter has signed the death-warrant of the brothers, Patrick & Bernard Flanagan, convicted in the court of Cambria Co of the murder of an aged female named Eliz Holder. They are to be executed in the jail-yard at Ebensburg, on Mar 3 next, between the hours of 10 & 2.

Accident in Charleston on Christmas. Saml O'Neal, age about 12 or 13 years, was killed near the corner of Meeting & Chalmers sts in the following manner: He was on horseback, & encountered a number of boys burning fire crackers; one of the missiles was flung at the horse, exploding as it struck him. The animal plunged forward & threw his rider, who held by the stirrup, dragging him until the victim had his head fractured by repeated kicks from the horse. He was taken up lifeless.

Died: on Fri last, in his 81st year, Lewis Edwards, formerly of Petersburg, Va, but for the last 33 years a resident of Wash City.

Senate: 1-Report of Col Thos Bullit: Jun 23, 1832, his heirs were allowed 6,666 2/3rd acres for a service of 3 years. For these warrants, $8,333.33 in scrip was issued. Feb 14, 1838, he was allowed 2,703 acres for a service of 2 years & 2 months over 6 years. These warrants are outstanding, amounting in scrip to $3,379.75. Thos Bullit was deputy adjutant general, but held no rank in the army, &, being a staff ofcr, was not entitled to the bounty. He died in 1778, & his heirs, not being entitled to the bounty by the laws of Virginia, petitioned the Assembly of that State for its allowance by special resolution; but the claim was rejected by vote of the Hse of Delegates, as appears by the journals of that body for Jun 18, 1784. It did not become a good claim until the U S began to satisfy the bounties. Proceedings of the Va Assembly in 1776-7, & of the Continental Congress in 1777, to wit: Resolved that Thos Bullit, Deputy Adj Gen, have the rank of Colonel in the Continental Establishment. [See Jrnl of Congress of 1777-8, Feb 22, page 117, vol 2.] He served as a Captain in the war of 1755, & distinguished himself in battle at the taking of Fort Du Quesne, & by his bravery, coolness, & intrepidity, saved the remnant of the army & baggage. He was the only ofcr out of 8 who escaped, all the others being either killed or taken prisoners. –Wileman Thomas, one of the heirs of Thos Bullit: Jan 7, 1843

Hse/o Reps: 1-Cmte on Private Land Claims instructed to inquire into granting 160 acres of bounty land to John McGinnis, of Mercer Co, Pa, a sldr of the last war, who enlisted on Mar 1, 1813, for the period of for & during the war, & served in the corps of artillery, & was discharged on Mar 17, 1815; & that said cmte report by bill or otherwise. 2-Cmte on Judiciary: to which was referred the ptn of John Rowlett for a law to continue the copy-right of his tables of discount & interest, reported a bill supplementary to the act of May 24, 1828, to continue a copy-right to him: committed to a Cmte of the Whole House. 3-Ptn of J Barratt & 160 other citizens of Middletown, Conn, & its vicinity, for a reduction of letter-postage in U S mail. 4- Hse resumed the motion to reconsider the vote by which the bill for relief of the heirs of Philip Ranault had been passed. 5-Resolved: the map of the western boundary of Missouri, made out by Seth Lea, with the report of said survey, be printed, provided the printing of said map shall not exceed $6 per hundred copies. 6-Communication from the Treas Dept, asking for an appropriation to carry into effect the act of Aug 9, 1842, for the relief of David M Hughes, Chas Shipman, & John Henderson. Laid on the table. 7-Ptn of Geo O'Brien, for indemnification for losses sustained by his father Richd O'Brien, Consul Gen of the Barbary Powers, previous to 1800.

Stevens Thompson Mason, well known by having been Govn'r of Michigan at a very early age, died in N Y on Wed last, after a very short illness. He acted as Govn'r of Mich at age 19, having been appointed by Gen Jackson as Sec of the Territory. He married in N Y & removed there, & practiced law; but death cut short his career when only 31 years of age. His father, Gen Mason, was with him when he died. He also leaves a young wife & children.

Naval Crt of Inquiry in the case of the Somers: examined-Midshipman Perry, Dr Leecock, & Midshipman Rodgers. Following is a translation of the paper that was written in Greek characters, & found in Mr Spencer's locker.

Certain:
P Spencer	McKinley	
E Andrews	Wales	

Doubtful:
Wilson, +	Green, +	Sullivan
McKee, +	Godfrey	Howard
Warner, +	Van Velson	Gallia, +

To be kept, nolens volens
Sibley	Dickinson	Clark
Scott	The Doctor	Nevera
Van Brunt	Gannabrantz	Velsor
Smith	Strammer	Corning
Whitmore	Rodman	

Wheel-McKee
Arm Chest-McKinley
Cabin-Spencer, Small, Wilson
War room-Spencer
Steerage-Spencer, Small, Wilson

Explanatory notes: "Those on the list of doubtful who are marked with a cross will probably be inducted to join before the project is carried into execution. The remainder will probably join when the thing is done-if not, they must be forced. If any not marked down wish to join after it is done, we will pick out the best, & dispose of the rest." All of the names except E Andrews were of persons on board the **Somers**-there was no one bearing that name on board. [+ used for the cross symbol.]

Fire on Dec 23 consumed the valuable mills a mile west of Clarksburg, Va, on West Fork river, belonging to Mr Jas A Duncan. The loss is estimated, by the Clarksburg Scion, at $15,000. No insurance. On Dec 18, the dwlg-house of Mr Saml Jackson, in Middletown, Marion Co, Va, with all his furniture, was destroyed by fire. The fire, we understand from the paper published in that place, originated from the curtains around a bed, which were accidentally set on fire with a candle.

TUE JAN 9, 1843
Senate: 1-Ptn from J R & John Gregory & Co, merchants in New Orleans City, asking remuneration for certain money sent by mail to N Y C, & lost therein. 2-Ptn from Wm A Bradley & others, of D C, in relation to the incorporation of a gas light company in said District. 3-Ptn from John R Williams, asking that a certain tract of land should be patented to him. 4-Cmte on Military Affairs: Hse bill for the relief of Thos Copeland, without amendment. 5-Cmte of Claims: adverse report on the bill for the relief of Dexter Hungerford. Same cmte: a report on the ptn of Saml Guie. Same cmte: Hse bill for the relief of John Jackson, without amendment. Same cmte: Hse bill for the relief of Saml Hambleton, without amendment, & recommending a passage. 6-Cmte on Revolutionary Claims: adverse report on the ptn of Ezekiel Wade. Same cmte: unfavorable report on the ptn of Lucretia Haymaker.

Supreme Court of the U S: Jan 9, 1843: met at the Capitol: present-
The Hon Roger B Taney, Chief Justice
Assoc Justices:
Smith Thompson   Henry Baldwin
John McLean   John Catron
John M Krum, of Missouri, & John Hogan & John Lorimer Graham, were admitted attys & counselors of this Court.

Died: Jan 7, in Wash City, Michael, s/o Mary M & Michael R Shyne, aged 6 months.

Died: Jan 3, of pneumonia, Mrs Mary Briscoe, in her 64th year. On Fri, Jan 6, of the same disease, her husband, Richd Sothoron Briscoe, aged 74. They were for more than 35 years residents of Wash City, & died respected by all who knew them. Their remains have been removed to the family burying-place in Chas Co, Md.

Died: on Fri last, in his 81st year, Lewis Edwards, formerly of Petersburg, Va, but for the last 33 years a resident of Wash City.

Died: on Jan 8, after a long illness, Mrs Ellen Thomas, w/o the late Jos Thomas, aged 65 years & 36 days. She was a native of this part of the District before it was laid out as the District of Columbia, & a resident nearly ever since, leaving many relatives & friends to lament her irreparable loss; but they can rejoice that her death was not without hope. Her funeral is this day at 1 p m, from her late residence on 11th st south, near the steamboat wharf.

Sale of very handsome furniture: order of Orphan's Court of Wash Co, D C. Sale on Jan 10, at the late residence of Col Jas Thomas, dec'd, on Louisiana ave, near the Bank of Wash: Hair seat sofa, parlor chairs, maple chairs; Carpets, rugs, fireirons & fenders, 3 parlor stoves; Mahg sideboard, dining & breakfast tables; Window curtains & ornaments; Set ivory knives & forks, nearly new; China & dinner ware & cut glass; Silver ladles, table, dessert & tea spoons; Traveling trunks, lot of clothing; Mahg bureaus, wardrobes, clothes presses; Rush seat & other chairs; Washstands, toilet sets, writing table; Magh & other bedsteads; Best feather beds, mattresses & bedding; Chamber carpets, rugs, dressing glasses; Kitchen furniture, copper saucepans; Bottles wines, such as Madeira, Sherry, Claret, & Sauterne; Qrtr cask of good Brandy, Jamaica Spirits, & superior old whiskey. -Robt W Dyer & Co, aucts

WED JAN 11, 1843
Cases before the U S Supreme Court on Jan 10, 1843.
#1-Thos Hammond's adm et al, appellants, vs Gen Geo Washington's execs.
#5-Wm Rector's adm, plntf in error, vs the U S. The plntf having failed to appear, this writ of error to the Circuit Court of the U S for the Dist of Missouri was, on motion of the Atty Gen, dismissed.
#7-The U S appellant, vs Domingo Acosta.
#9-Jonathan Strout et al, appellants, vs Jas Foster et al.

Died: on Mon last, suddenly, at her residence near Wash City, Mrs Eliz Hutchinson, consort of John Hutchinson, in her 36th year. Her funeral is at her residence on 7th st, near the first toll-gate, at 3 p m.

Died: on Jan 10, Mrs Eliz Shanks, aged 85 years. Her funeral is this day, from the house of her son, her late residence, at 3 p m. The friends & connexions of the family are invited to attend without further notice, at the corner of 18th & E sts.

The Hon Albert Gallatin was on Tue last elected Pres of the N Y Historical Society, vice the Hon Peter Augustus Jay, who declined re-election.

Orphan's Court of Wash Co, D C. Letters testamentary on the personal estate of Eliz T Queen, late of said county, dec'd. -Henry Queen, Jas MacDaniel, excs

Meeting of the Medical Society of the Dist of Col was held on Jan 9: following elected ofcrs: Dr F May, Pres
V Ps: Dr McWilliams & Dr Causin
Dr Sewall, Corr Sec   Dr J C Hall, Treas
Dr Borrows, Rec Cor   Dr Miller, Librarian
Examiners:
Dr Worthington   Dr Young   Dr J F May
Dr Lindsly   Dr Thomas
-Jos Borrows, Rec Sec

Cumberland Civilian: Col C M Thruston, having taken charge of one of the large Mining Companies in the Frostburg district, has resigned the Presidency of the Mineral Bank of Md, & R T Lowndes, has been chosen in his stead.

St Matthew's Church: evening service on Jan 15, at half past 6 o'clock. For the the benefit of the Male Orphan Society recently established at St Matthew's Chr. Several of the most talented professors of music in this country have generously proffered their gratuitous aid in the holy cause: among these gentlemen are Messrs La Mauna, from Italy, & Hewitt, of Wash City, with several other professors, in union with Signor Daunas & the choir of St Matthew's Church.
–J P Donelan, Rector of St M Chr

Died: Jan 7, in Wash City, Michael, s/o Mary M & Michael R Shyne, aged 6 months.

The venerable patriarch [says the Minerve] Alexis Chenet, a native of Acadia, died at St Denis, on Dec 12th, at the advanced age of 106 years. He was one of those who saw, at any early age, all his countrymen driven from their birth place, & carried to those British colonies now the U S. He was himself put on board an English frig, & served 12 years as a seaman. He obtained his discharge in England & came to Canada in hope to fine some of his family. Having fixed his residence at St Denis at age 25, in 1761, he cut the first tree with his own hands, & cleared the fourth concession of this parish. He has left 9 children & 71 grandchildren. –Montreal Herald

Jos N Robbins, while fixing a belt in the mill of Mr Peter Lawson, in Dracutt, last evening, was caught in the same and killed. He was 23 years of age, of excellent character. He married about 6 months ago a young woman of this city. We learn that he was a native of Acton in this county. –Lowell Courier

Mrd: In Locke, Cayuga Co, N Y, on Nov 22, by Levi Henry, Seth Stevens, of Hartford, Cortland Co, to Miss Sylvia Heath, d/o Benj Heath, of the former place. This marriage took place after a 19 years courtship. Mr Stevens is a man of 61 years, & the fair bride is 51.

Information wanted: of Henry Burford, formerly of Wash, who was in the U S Army in 1837, under the command of Capt Trenor, at Fort Smith, Ark. It is requested to make known to the subscriber his present place of residence, as all his relatives in this city are anxious to hear from him on account of some important business in which he is interested. –Philip Otterback, Wash [The Litle Rock Gaz, in Ark, & the St Louis Argus, in Mo, will confer a great favor by giving the above 3 insertions, & send their bills to the subscriber for payment. –P Otterback]

Senate: 1-Cmte on the Judiciary: bill for the relief of Richd Henry Wilde: referred. 2-Cmte on the Judiciary, to whom was referred the bill to indemnify Maj Gen Andrew Jackson for damage sustained by him in the discharge of his official duty: report the bill with an amendment. The fine of $1,000 imposed upon Maj Gen Andrew Jackson by the Hon Dominick A Hall, be, & the same is hereby, restored, & that the Sec of the Treas be directed to pay to Maj Gen Andrew Jackson the sum of $1,000 with interest at 6%, thereon from the day of its payment by him, out of any moneys in the Treas not otherwise appropriated. 3-Bill for the relief of Walker Kingsley: to be engrossed. 3-Bill for the relief of Wm Debuys, postmaster at New Orleans: to be engrossed. 4-Bill for the relief of Eliz Monroe: to be engrossed.

Hse/o Reps: 1-Revolutionary Pensions: ptn of Isaac Ogg, a citizen of Hamilton Co, Ohio, a sldr in Gen Wayne's army, praying for a pension: referred. 2-Ptn of Onslow Stearns & 347 citizens of Hillsborough Co, N H, & principally of the towns of Nashua & Nashville, praying for the repeal of the bankrupt law. 3-Ptn of Jas Haly, of Pittsburg, praying Congress for compensation for an improvement made by him in the mode of casting cannon & shot. 4-Ptn of Geo Wallis, praying compensation for cattle killed by the Sac, Fox, & Iowa Indians. 5-Ptn of Robt B Williams & others, of Boston, for the establishment of a national foundry & yard for the erection of steamships of war on the lands of the U S near the Navy Yard at Charlestown, Mass. 6-Ptn of Jane Hanson, of Ill, praying to be allowed a pension. 7-Ptn of Elisha Morrill, atty of John Peters & Sarah Farnum, for title to land. 8-Ptn of E A Hibbard, of Winchester, Va, agent for the Balt Clipper & Sun, asking leave to convey newspapers on railroads without hinderance from the Post Ofc Dept. 9-Ptn of the heirs of Jas Greer, praying for compensation for inventing a highly useful mode of boring gun barrels. 10-Ptn of Jos L Righter, Jonathan F Updegraff, & 82 men, & of Jane Robinson & Eliz Heaton, & 97 women, of Mount Pleasant, Ohio, against the annexation of Texas, & the admission of any new slave State, & of any abridgement of the right of petition. 11-Ptn of Wm Robinson, Isaac Waterman, & 72 other men, & of Julia Ann Job, Rebecca F Updegraff, & 82 other women, for the abolition of slavery in D C & the Territories of the U S & the domestive slave trade. Rejected under the 21st rule.

Boarding: house is located on Missouri ave, near the Railroad Depot: always commanded a full share of patronage. Will rent several rooms or the whole house & furniture, on very low terms. –Mary Ann Pierce

Circuit Court of Wash Co, D C. Augustus G Tibbets, a bankrupt, has filed his ptn for his discharge & certificate: hearing on Apr 10. Same for John Drill; same for Wm H Yates; same for Wm Padgett; same for Thos L Fitzhugh. Same for Richd H Gordon, with hearing on Mar 26. –Wm Brent, clk

At the annual meeting of the Typographical Society, held on Jan 7, the following were elected ofcrs: Ferdinand Jefferson, Pres
Geo Cochran, V P   Jas Wimer, Rec Sec
Wm J Delano, Corr Sec   Michl Caton, Treas

Obit-died: on Jan 4, after 2 days severe illness, at his late residence, [Waverley House, in N Y C,] Stevens Thomson Mason. Mr Mason was a native of Va, & was the only s/o Gen John Thomson Mason, of Ky. Having retired from political life, he went about a year since to N Y C, where he had numerous friends, as well as connexions to whom he was allied by marriage. Mr Mason left behind him a young & devoted wife & 3 children &, besides these, a father & 2 sisters.

Wash Corp: 1-Cmte referred the ptn of Geo Collard, for permission to erect a fence around his coal & wood yard, asked to be discharged from the further consideration of the same: discharged accordingly. 2-Cmte of Ways & Means: asked to be discharged from further consideration of the ptn of C Colton, editor of the True Whig, respecting the publication of the Corporation laws, in that paper.

THU JAN 12, 1843
The Mass Hse of Delegates on Sat elected Mr Danl P King, [Whig,] of Danvers, Speaker of the House.

Hse/o Reps: 1-Cmte on the Public Lands: adverse report upon the ptn of A H Evans. 2-Cmte on Naval Affairs: report on ptn of Anne W Angus, wid/o Saml Angus, with a bill for her relief. 3-Cmte on Revolutionary Pensions: report on ptn of Eliz Gresham, wid/o Capt Geo Gresham, with a bill for her relief. 4-Cmte on Revolutionary Pensions, report on ptn of Eliz Powers, wid/o Timothy Powers, with a bill for her relief. Same cmte, an adverse report on the ptn of Mary Ripley, wid/o Jabez Ripley.

Earthquake at Cincinnati on Jan 4, 1843. At the residence of Dr Gana, on the corner of Franklin & Broadway, the shaking stopped a mantel clock, threw a parrot from her roost, & so alarmed some German domestics that they thought the world was really about to end. –Jos Ray [It appears that the earthquake felt in Cincinnati on Jan 4, was also felt in Columbia, S C.]

Senate: 1-Memorial of Horatio Greenough, sculptor, on the subject of the statue of Washington, suggesting the propriety of a change in position. He moved its reference to the Joint Cmte on the Library, stating that the memorial was a paper of much merit & interest, as every thing coming from the hands or pen of that distinguished artist is. He moved that the memorial be printed. 2-From John Grant, asking permission to sue the U S for damages sustained in a certain contract with the Engineer Dept for removing a bar in the harbor of Mobile. 3-Cmte on Commerce: bill for relief of Rufus & Chas Lane. 4-Cmte on Commerce: adverse report on Hse bill for relief of the owners, master, & crew of the schnr **Martha**, of Eastport, in the State of Maine. 5-Adverse report on ptn of Sarah Brown. 6-Adverse on Hse bill for relief of Saml Billings, owner of the fishing schnr _____.[Blank] 7-Hse bill for relief of the owners, master, & crew of schnr **Joanna**, of Ellworth, Maine. 8-Cmte on the Dist of Col: Hse bill for relief of Casper W Wever, without amendment. 9-Cmte on Naval Affairs: asking to be discharged from the further consideration of the bill for the relief of Allen Rogers, & it be referred to the Cmte of Claims. 10-Cmte on Commerce: adverse report on Hse bill for the relief of Owen Prentiss, of Stonington, cmder of the schnr **Lilly**. 11-Same Cmte, on Hse bill for the relief of Isaac Champlin & others, owners of the schnr **Buffalo**. 12-Cmte on the Judiciary: adverse on the ptn of the sureties of Wm Linn, late receiver of public moneys at Vandalia, Ill, praying to be relieved from liabilities on certain conditions. 13-Adverse report on Hse bill for relief of Graham A Neill. 14-Cmte on Finance: bill for relief of John Gandford. 15-Hse bill for relief of Saml D Ross & others: laid on the table. 16-Hse bill for relief of Barent D Stryker: laid on the table. 17-Bill for relief of Henry Gardiner & others, directors of an assoc called the New England Mississippi Land Co, was, after some remarks from Messrs Benton, Tappan, Berrien, King, & others, made a special order of the day for Jan 16. 18-The joint resolution for relief of Gordon D Boyd was rejected.

The Whig paper, the Winchester Republican, has passed from the hands of Mr Wm Towers, its late publisher, into those of Robt H Gallaher, who is now the publisher.

From Mexico: Vera Cruz, Dec 19, 1842. New has arrived here, from the west, of the occupation of Monterey, a town in Calif, by Cmdor Jones, of the frig **United States** & corvette **Cyane**. He held the town about 2 days & then gave it up, declaring that he took it in consequence of a report that war was declared by the U S against Mexico. Mr W E Dryden, with 7 other Americans, who had been confined nearly 12 months in Chihuahua, have been liberated by the Mexican Gov't through the interposition of the U S Minister.

Dr John Brockenbrough superseded in the ofc, which he has filled for a great many years, of Pres of the Bank of Virginia, & Jas W Pegram elected by the stockholders of the Bank to take his place.

Naval-The ship **Alkmar**, from Port Mahon, arrived at Norfolk on Tue last, having on board as passengers Dr John O'Conner Barclay, U S Navy, & Midshipmen C H Baldwin, R C Duvall, W B Browne, C H Oakley, & a number of seamen, invalids from the Mediterranean Squadron.

John Ashworth & Jas Bruff, indicted for burglariously entering the house of Judge Jones [near Phil] on Nov 16 last, & also for having committed an assault on the Judge with intent to kill, had their trial on Fri in Phil. Verdict of guilty against both prisoners. Sentenced by Judge Doran to 10 years in the Eastern Pen.

Mrd: on Jan 10, by Rev Wm B Edwards, Mr Christopher Atz to Miss Ellen Ann Robinson, both of Wash City.

Red Springs for sale: deed of trust executed by Philip Rogers, dated May 25, 1835, in the Clerk's Ofc of the County Crt of Alleghany. Sale Mar 10 next: property contains 1,100 acres, more or less, bounded on one side by the *Sweet Spring Tract*. Also for sale, for cash, the following slaves, to wit: Billy Cook, Billy Blacksmith, Billy Lewis, Albert, Jim Right, Big Jim, Armstead, Harrison, Spencer, Violet, Esther, Hannah, & Rachel, with the increase of the females since date of said deed. Also, all the stock & household & kitchen furniture conveyed to us by said deed. Title to the above is believed to be indisputable. –John Crow, P Guerrant, trustees

Died: yesterday, in Gtwn, of pneumonia, after a sickness of 12 days, Peregrine Warfield, s/o Albert G & Louisa Ann Meriwether, aged 2 years, 6 months & 4 days. His funeral is today at 1 o'clock today, from his father's residence, First st, Gtwn.

Died: on Jan 9, Zophia Leona Stanislaus, infant d/o Leon & Henrietta Gawronski.

Cnstbl's sale: virtue of a writ of fieri facias, issued by T C Donn, one of the J Ps for Wash Co, D C: sale on Jan 19 opposite the Centre-market House, one gold watch & key, seized & taken as the property of Wm B Scasscar, & will be sold to satisfy a judgement due Chas W Boteler, jr. –L S Beck, cnstbl

Circuit Court of Wash Co, D C. Wm Tyler filed his ptn for the benefit of the Bankrupt Law: hearing on the first Mon in Feb next. –Wm Brent, clk

Circuit Court of Wash Co, D C. Wm E Moran, a bankrupt, has filed his ptn for his discharge & certificate: hearing on Apr 10. Same for bankrupts: Jas Morss, jr; Nathan Hammond; Wm McGrath; John T Wright; & for Wm Handy. –W Brent, clk

FRI JAN 13, 1843
On Fri last, Mr Jas Howell, an aged & respectable citizen of Jefferson Co, Va, was drowned in fording the Shenandoah river. It is supposed that his horse fell, thereby throwing him from his saddle in the midst of the current.

Senate: 1-Ptn from John Hutchins for a pre-emption. 2-Ptn from Thos M Somerall, asking confirmation of a certain entry of land. 3-Ptn from Robt Elliot, asking confirmation of a certain tract of land. 4-Ptn from Zachariah Dixon, asking the right of pre-emption to 160 acres of land. 5-Ptn from Wm Downing, register of a land ofc in Mississippi, asking to be reimbursed for a sum of money paid in clerk hire. 6-Cmte of Claims, without amendment: the bill for the relief of Wm G Saunders. 7-Cmte on Public Lands: a bill to revive the bill of Mary Tucker. 8-Cmte on Public Lands: Hse bill for the relief of Jos Hoover, A Guthrie, & Edmund Ogden. 9-Cmte of Claims: adverse report on the bill for the relief of Teackle Savage, administrator of Bolitha Laws. 10-Cmte on the Judiciary: adverse report on claims of David Haley. 11-Mr King moved to reconsider the joint resolution for relief of the sureties of J Gordon Boyd, late receiver of public moneys at Columbus, Miss, & that it be referred to the Cmte on Finance. 12-Senate bills considered as in Cmte of the Whole; were severally engrossed: bills from the Hse for the relief of: Isaac & Thos Winslow. Relief of Burr & Smith. Relief of Ferdinand Seibert. Relief of Elisah Moreland, Wm M Kenedy, Robt J Kenedy, & Mason E Lewis. Relief of Peter Lionberger. Relief of John R Dulany. Relief of Jas M Morgan. Relief of Cornelius Wilson & Jas Canter. Relief of the legal reps of Capt Saml Shannon, dec'd. Relief of the owners, ofcrs, & crew of the armed brig **Warrior** or their legal reps, was, on motion of Mr Evans, indefinitely postponed.

The Guardians of the Gtwn School will meet on Jan 18, to elect a teacher of the said school, at an annual salary of $500. Application for the same are invited to be made up to the evening on which the election is held. –Jeremiah Orme, sec

Hse/o Reps: 1-Memorial of Wm W Street, asking compensation for the services of steamboat **Phenix**, while engaged in the transportation of troops & military supplies on the Chipolas & Apalachicola rivers, in Fla, under a written contract with H R Wood, Colonel of the 11th Regt of Florida Militia: referred. 2-Remonstrance of Alanson Peake & 25 others, of Jefferson Co, N Y, against the repeal of the bankrupt law: referred. 3-Cmte of Claims: made a report upon the ptn of Geo A Wilson, with a bill for his relief. 4-Ptn of R K Moulton, of Brooklyn, N Y, in relation to the fine imposed on Gen Jackson: referred. 5-Ptn of John McClintock & others, citizens of Portsmouth, N H, praying indemnity for French spoliations on American commerce prior to 1800: referred.

U S Circuit Court for the Southern Dist of N Y: application from the widow of Cromwell for a warrant to arrest Cmder Mackenzie & Lt Gansevoort on a charge of murder, Judge Betts on the following day delivered an opinion declining to grant the warrant-on the ground, first, that it is exceedingly questionable whether the civil courts have jurisdiction in this case; &, secondly, because the present is not a proper time for such a proceeding, the case being under examination before a tribunal.

The trustees of the Cottage Academy, Montg Co, Md, on taking leave of Mr F S Sandford, [who, having resigned as Principal, is on the eve of his departure,] cannot withhold the expression of their entire satisfaction with the management of the school whilst under his direction, & deeply regret the loss of his highly valuable services as an instructor. We congratulate him on the propect before him, & on his appointment as Principal of the Washington Academy, Va, where his services will command a more adequate reward than he has been enabled to obtain in this institution. -R Y Brent, Jon Prout, trustees

News reached the city yesterday from Balt of the death of our respected fellow-citizen Francis S Key, [whilst on a professional visit to that city,] created a very painful sensation. The Supreme Court suspended its sitting on the occasion; & resolutions were adopted at a meeting of the Bar expressive of their sensibility to the loss of one of their most esteemed brethren which they have thus sustained.

The dwlg of Job Eastman, Town Clerk of Norway, Oxford Co, Maine, was burned on Dec 4, with all its contents. Mrs Eastman, aged 70 years, seized her husband, whose advanced age rendered him extremely feeble, & bore him through the snow to a place of safety. The town records of 50 years past were destroyed.

The remains of Bolivar were disinterred at Santa Martha, in New Granada, on Nov 20, & delivered up to the commissioners of Venezuela. By them they were conveyed to Caraccas & delivered to the authorities of Venezuela, amid great pomp & ceremony, to be deposited in the cathedral. The final ceremonies took place on Dec 16.

Fire on Wed in the direction of **Meridian Hill**, burned the country house owned by Mr Paul Kinchy, near **Holmead's Burial Ground**; dwlg & out bldgs were totally destroyed. [Jan 16 newspaper: We now learn that the fire originated in & destroyed the large barn attached to the dwlg, which was in the occupancy of Mr Henry Johnson. The dwlg was not injured. We learn that 4 horses & a colt, 5 fine cows, 3 hogs, & the whole crop of hay were totally destroyed. Mr Kinchy has offered $100 for the apprehension of the diabolical persons who were guilty of this foul act of incendiarism.]

Dissolution of partnership by mutual consent existing under the firm of Easby & Hanly. Easby to settle accounts. –Wm Easby, Edw Hanly. The Lime & current business will be cont'd at the old establishment by Wm Easby.

Sale: by virtue of deed of trust from Chas T Iardella, to me, recorded in liber W B, #83, one of the land records for Wash Co, D C, sale on Jan 25, at the store situated on the corner of 12th st & Pa ave, the entire stock of goods, drugs, medicines, & fixtures contained. –Walter Lenox, trustee -R W Dyer & Co, aucts

Circuit Court of Wash Co, D C. Wm A Batchelor, a bankrupt, has filed his ptn for his discharge & certificate: hearing on Apr 10. –Wm Brent, clk

SAT JAN 14, 1843

A letter from Columbus, Ga, dated Jan 6, gives an account of a rencontre between Gen McDougald & Col B Hepburn, which resulted in the death of the latter gentleman: "One of those appalling tragedies for which this place has been notorious ever since its settlement, was acted here this morning. Col Burton Hepburn was shot dead by Gen McDougald [brother of the candidate for Congress, & formerly Pres of the Planters & Mechanics' Bank of this place,] in McD's ofc, the old Insurance Bank."

Passed at the Third Session of the 27th Congress. Annuities & Grants: to Josiah H Webb-$25; to Rachael Dohrman-$100; to Eliz C Perry-$200.

Law Notice: the subscribers have formed a partnership to practise law. They will attend all the courts held in the city & in the counties of Goochland & Louisa. Ofc on Governor st, next door to Jos Mayo. -Peachy R Grattan, Henry Coalter Cabell, Richmond, Va

L F Whitney, Pa ave, between the Railroad Depot & 3rd st, is prepared to accommodate a mess of members of Congress, or persons visiting the city, with pleasant rooms.

Senate: 1-Ptn from Jos Cable & others, citizens of Carrollton, Ohio, asking that Amos Kendall, late Postmaster Gen, be saved from losses arising out of a suit instituted against him by Stockton & Stokes: referred. 2-Ptn of Richd Patten was taken from the files & referred to the Cmte on Naval Affairs. 3-Cmte on Pensions: adverse report on Hse bill for the relief of Carter B Chandler. Also, on Hse bill for the relief of Richd Marsh. Also, an unfavorable report on the bill for the relief of Andre Spear, wid/o John Spear. Also, on the ptn of Jonathan Brown. Also, the Hse bill for the relief of Mary Williams, wid/o Jacob Williams, with an amendment. 3-Cmte on Pensions: adverse reports on the following Hse bills: a bill for the relief of Eliz Dawkins; a bill for the relief of John Peake. Also, from the same cmte, Hse bill granting a pension to Robt Poindexter, of Ky, with an amendment. 4-Cmte on the Judiciary: a bill for the relief of John Wharney, without amendment. 5-Cmte on Naval Affairs: without amendment, Hse bill for the relief of Benj I Totten. Also, Hse bill granting to Jas Lowe $1,000 & a section of land. 6-Cmte on Naval Affairs: an adverse report on Hse bill for the relief of Mary Crawford. Also, from the same cmte, a bill for the relief of Wm Allen, with an amendment. 7-The Senate proceeded to consider, as in Cmte of the Whole, the bill for the relief of John P Skinner & the legal reps of Isaac Green; when, after considerable debate, the further consideration was postponed.

J B Perrault, late cashier of the Citizens' Bank of New Orleans, has disappeared from that city, leaving his bank account minus some $50,000 or $60,000.

Supreme Crt of the U S: Fri, Jan 13, 1843. Mr Legare, the Atty Gen of the U S, speaks of the melancholy task of conveying the loss which society & the profession have sustained in the death of the late Francis Scott Key.

Lexington [Ky] Intell of Dec 30th: the Hon Thos M Hickey, departed this life yesterday, after an illness of some months. His death has caused a chasm which cannot be readily filled.

MON JAN 16, 1843
Dr Barker, of Lynn, Mass, died very suddenly on Sun, says the Boston Democrat, from the effects of mortification in a body upon which he was performing a post mortem examination. The Dr had a slight wound on one of his fingers, were the infection, it is supposed, took its instantaneous & deadly effect.

Hse/o Reps: 1-Cmte on the Public Lands: was referred a bill from the Senate for the relief of Eliz Munroe, reported the same without amendment. 2-Ptn of B B Whittemore & others, citizens of Amherst, N H, praying for the repeal of the bankrupt law. 3-Resolved that the Sec of War furnish to this Hse a copy of the report of T B W Stockton of his survey of the harbor, at the mouth of Gallen river, [New Buffalo,] in Mich. 4-Cmte on Military Affairs: adverse report in the case of the heirs of Lt Noah Wiseman. Also, an adverse report on the ptn of Edw Ward & others, members of Capt Dimock's company of artl. 5-Cmte on Naval Affairs: report upon the ptn of Mary Barry, wid/o Thos Barry, late a master in the U S Navy, with a bill for her relief. 6-Bill for the relief of the heirs of Philip Ranault was, after a brief consideration, postponed. 7-Ptn of 106 citizens of Cayuga, N Y, praying that the fine imposed upon Gen Jackson be refunded to the widow & children of John Harris: referred. 8-Memorial of Jos H Walters, of Brunswick Co, N C, praying to be allowed & paid the amount of damage he alleges he has sustained in his rice plantation in consequence of the operations of the Gov't for the improvement of the navigation of Cape Fear river: referred. 9-Ptn & documents of Margaretta Boss, the wid/o Danl C Boss, who was wounded in battle whilst in the sevice of the U S, during the late war with Great Britain, asking a pension: referred. 10-Letter from Isaiaff Lukens, of Phil City, claiming compensation for a clock & bell manufactured by him for the use of the Gov't: referred. 11-Ptn of Clayton H Page & 122 citizens of Burlington Co, N J, asking an appropriation for the purpose of establishing buoys in the south channel of New Inlet, near Tuckerton, N J.

Madison [Ia] Banner of Sat week: we record the death of 2 children of Mr Henderson Bell, dec'd, whose condition we noticed in the Banner 2 weeks ago. They were injured by the fire which occasioned the death of their father, his child, & sister; & thus, by that midnight, 5 members of the family had perished.

Orphan's Court of Wash Co, D C. Ordered that the adminisrator [J L Edwards,] on the personal estate of Lewis Edwards, late of said county, give notice required by law to the creditors of said dec'd, by advertisement, once a week for 3 weeks, in the Nat'l Intell. –Ed N Roach, Recordder of Wills.

Orphan's Court of Wash Co, D C. Letters of administration on the personal estate of Clorinda A Thorne, late of Wash Co, dec'd, have been granted to Noah Drummond by said court. –Noah Drummond, adm

Noah Beauchamp, some time since convicted of the murder of Geo Mickelberry, was hung at Rockville, Ind, Jan 6. A large collection of people were at the execution.

Mr Jas Meeks, one of the most efficient of the Albany police, committed suicide at Hudson a few days since.

Jos E Hover, of Phil, has manufactured an excellent black ink, that flows freely, leaves no sediment, & is well adapted to steel pens. Orders to be addressed to: Jos E Hover, 105 North 3rd st, Phil.

Circuit Court of Wash Co, D C. Saml Scott, a bankrupt, has filed for his discharge & certificate: hearing on Apr 10 next. –Wm Brent, clk

A soldier of the Revolution is gone. Bartlette Cox, of Cumberland Co, Va, died a few weeks ago, aged 101 years. He enjoyed fine health, & attended to his little farm until a few months before his death. He has left an aged widow & several children to mourn their loss. He entered the Revolutionary war soon after the commencement, & served throughtout, & was in several severe engagements under Gen Washington & others. He lived an honest life, & died perfectly at peace with his Maker. He was the last old soldier in Cumberland, & he is gone. –Richmond Whig

TUE JAN 17, 1843
European papers: The will & 4 codicils of the late Hannah Waldo, late of Worthing, in the county of Sothampton, England, widow, the relict of Peter Waldo, has passed the seal of the Prerogative Court to John Hawkins, the sole executor. This lady, who had attained the age of nearly 90, & whose charity knew no bounds whilst living, bequeathed to numerous charities. The personal property of the dec'd has been sworn under L80,000. She was the last of the family of the Waldos, which is considered to be the oldest family in England, having come over to this country in the time of Wm the Conqueror. The original name is stated to have been the Waldos or Waldenses. The last lady of that name died at Clapham about 2 years since, at age 92, leaving property to an immense amount.

European papers: Died lately, aged 108, at Rumney Iron Works, England, Mrs Joyce Jones. She was the mother, grandmother, great-grandmother, & great-great-grandmother of 105 children. Her youngest son is living–73 years old. She lived 80 years in Dowlais, the 6 last years with her grand-dght, Mrs Watkin Morris, Castle Inn, Rumney. This extraordinary woman lived in 4 Kings & 1 Queen's reign. –Welshman

Valuable property for sale on James River, in Chas City County, Va. In consequence of recent events, the pressing demands of my creditors, I will sell a part or the whole of my landed estate in the above county, consisting of 2 plantations, joining each other, the one, my late residence, known as *Weyanoke*, the other the late residence of my brother Jas, both of which are in a high state of improvement. Both have good comfortable dwlgs, with all necessary out-bldgs. –John Minge, Petersburg

Exparte Ptn-in PG Co Court. Martha Young for a commission under the act of descent on the land of Eleanor Young. Com'rs have refused to take the land in the proceedings mentioned at the valuation of the com'rs, thereupon, this Jan 11, 1842, adjudged & ordered, by the authority of this Court, that the same shall be sold. –Clem Dorsey [Jno B Brooke, clerk, in pursuance of the above decree, the com'rs in this case will proceed to sell, at the court house, Upr Marlboro, PG Co, Md, on Feb 4, the premises referred to in the above order. –Jas Mullikin, R C Bowie, G W Bowie]

Supreme Court of the U S. Jan 16, 1843. 1-John W O Leveridge, of N Y, was admitted as atty & counselor of this Court. Case #224: John Buchanan et al appellants vs, Edwin Upshaw.

Senate: 1-Ptn from Waity A Spencer, in behalf of herself & others, widows of ofcrs & sldrs of the Revolution, praying for the revival of the pension act of Jul 7, 1838. 2-Ptn from Isaac Hopkins, asking indemnity for property destroyed during the Revolutionary war. 3-Memorial of Sarah A Bacon, of Norwich, Conn, wid/o Fred'k A Bacon, late passed midshipman in the U S Navy. Mr Huntington said this young ofcr was ordered to join the Exploring expedition, & was on board the ship **Sea Gull** when she was lost, & with his brother ofcr, Passed Midshipman Reid, & all the crew perished. The navy lost a valuable ofcr. His widow & only child survive him. 4-Ptn from Scott Campbell, asking for the money & land granted in the treaty of Washington, Sep 29, 1837. 5-Ptn from Christopher Doughty, a sldr of the Revolution, asking an increase of pension. 6-Ptn from John F Delaplane, of N Y, asking the repeal of the bankrupt law. 7-Ptn from Mary E Zantzinger, wid/o Maj Zantzinger, asking a pension in consideration of the claims of her late husband. 8-Ptn from A G Stewart, administrator of Capt Wm Walker. 9-The papers in the case of Alex Cummings were taken from the files & referred to the Cmte on the Post Ofc & Post Roads. 10-Thos M Isett had leave to withdraw his papers. 11-Cmte on Naval Affairs: Bill for the relief of Richd Patten. Adverse reports on Hse bills for the relief of Lloyd J Bryan & of Nancy Tompkins. 12-Cmte on Naval Affairs: asking to be discharged from the ptn of John Bosworth, & that it be referred to the Cmte on Pensions. 13-Cmte on Naval Affairs: hse bill for the relief of Robt Ramsey, with an amendment. Adverse report on Hse bill for the relief of Susan Brum. 14-Cmte on Patents: bill for the relief of Chas M Keller. 15-Cmte of Claims, without amendment, the following Hse bills: relief of John Coxe. Relief of John E Hunt & others. Relief of Thos D Gilson. Relief of Robt G Ford. With an amendment, Hse bills for the relief of Geo Randall, John E Haskell, & Elisha H Holmes. Adverse report on Hse bill for the relief of Conrad House. The Senate then took up from the table the bill for relief of Jos Nourse, & ordered the same to be engrossed. The bill for relief of Thos Fillebrown, jr; which bill was cousin german to that which the Senate had just disposed of, & which had been also laid on the table: was lost by the casting vote of the Chair.

The U S Mediterranean Squadron: U S ship **Columbus 74**, frig **Congress**, sloop **Fairfield** & sloop **Preble**, sailed from Mahon for Genoa on Nov 12-all well. Ofcrs attached to the **Columbus 74**, bearing the broad pennant of Com C W Morgan.

Capt W A Spencer   Cmder S B Wilson

Lts-10:
J M Watson Q P Griffin C F M Spottswood
J R Goldsborough B F Sands H N Harrison
A H Kilty D B Ridgely
T H Page G H Scott

1st Master, L Maynard Fleet Surgeon, B F Bache
2nd Master, H Cadwallader Surgeon, J F Brooke
Assist Surgeons-3: S W Kellogg; I Hastings; H Morson
Purser, J N Todd Chaplain, P G Clarke
1st Lt Marines, E L West Prof Math, J McDuffie
2nd Lt Marines, J D Simms Cmdor Sec, F Schley

Passed Midshipmen-6:
W M Caldwell J N Brown
F K Murray E P Nichols
H Rolando T L Kinlock

Midshipmen-23:
J M Bradford G D Chenoweth G S Simms
M Duralde R Summers E T Andrews
L Paulding W H Parker E C Grafton
L McDougall D Coleman S Phelps
C Comegys A G Cook J L Ferguson
C S Bell G H Bier E Johnston
C K Graham G King A W Habersham
J D Daniels W G Hoffman

Boatswain, J Shannon Carpenter, Patrick Dee
Gunner, Chas Cobb Sailmaker, J G Gallagher

Capt's Clk, J C Spencer, jr　　　　　　　Master's Mate, Thos Shanton
Com's Clk, Mr Sutherland

Ofcrs attached to the frig **Congress**: Capt Philip T Voorhees
Lts:
Boyle	Gilliss	Bache
Browning	Jenkins	D D Porter

Actg sailingmaster, S C Barney　　　　　Purser, Cahoone
Surgeon, Smith　　　　　　　　　　　　Chaplain, Jackson
Lts Marines-2: Brooke; Grayson
Assist Surgeons-2: Jackson; Baxter
Prof of Math, J Pierce　　　　　　　　　Passed Midshipman, J C Howell
Midshipmen-19:

Nelson	Eaton	Luce	Bayard
Crosby	McCorkle	J B Smith	Mercer
Simpson	Holmes	G Harrison	De Kraft
Calhoun	Ashmead	Erind	W Smith
Riley	Fillebrowne	Upshur	

Capt's Clk, Tilton　　　　　　　　　　　Gunner, City
Purser's Clk, Flemming　　　　　　　　Carpenter, Gill
Boatswain, Bock　　　　　　　　　　　Sailmaker, Blackford

Officers attached to the ship **Fairfield**:
Cmder, Abraham Bigelow
Lts: C G Hunter, Malancthon Smith, W Leigh, S Dod, E Lanier

Acting Master, Trenchard　　　　　　　Purser, Forrest
Surgeon, J V Smith
Midshipmen:

Tatnall	Cuyler	Murphy	Langhorne
Corbin	Davis	Collins	

Prof of Math, Beechler　　　　　　　　Capenter, White
Boatswain, W Forrester　　　　　　　　Sailmaker, Burdine
Gunner, Arnold

Ofcrs attached to the ship **Preble**:
Cmder W C Nicholson
Lts:
Tilton	Handy	Frailey	W R Gardner

Acting Master, Ronckendorff　　　　　Passed Midshipman, E G Beale
Surgeon, Sickles

Midshipmen:
Phelps   Madrigan   Stout   Barrett

Capt's Clerk, Rich   Carpenter, Jenkins
Gunner, Craig   Sailmaker, Bruce

Died: in Sep last, on board the U S frig **Constellation**, lying in Hong Kong bay, [China,] Lt Levin Handy, U S Navy, in his 29th year.

Died: on Jan 2, in Greeneville, Tenn, Wm Dickson, in his 68th year. He was born in the county of Antrim, Ire, but emigrated to this country in 1791, & located himself as a merchant in the village of Greeneville in 1796, & was the same year appointed Postmaster under Gen Washington's Administration, & has been continued as such, through every change of parties, until his death. [East Tenn Miscellany]
[By the death of Wm Dickson the Editors of the Nat'l Intell have lost an old & valued subscriber, whose character universal report, as well as their own intercourse with him, had taught them highly to respect. Mr Dickson has been more than 42 years a subscriber to this paper; had ever been conscientiously exact in the payment of his subscription; & had actually paid his account up to the 5th day of the month preceding his decease. –Nat Intel.]

Died: on Jan 15, in Wash Co, D C, of consumption, Frank Piles, in his 77th year.

Died: on Jan 7, at her residence, in Jeffersonton, Culpeper Co, Va, after a long & painful illness, Mrs Eliz Luckett, w/o Thos Luckett, in her 55th year. She has left a husband & 6 children to mourn their loss

A fire, which destroyed property to the amount of $14,000, occurred in the village of Rome, Oneida Co, N Y, last Thu. It broke out in the brick store owned by Seth R Roberts, & occupied by Peter Van Patten, dry goods merchant, & H S Roberts, bookseller & stationer. The bldg & contents were consumed.

Hses & lots for sale: I am authorized to sell 4 houses in Northern Liberties, & 12 unimproved bldg lots. Call me at the Drug & Seed Store, corner of E & 7th sts. –J F Callan

Obit: died: on Dec 10 last, in Huntingdon, Carroll Co, Tenn, Maj Pleasant Henderson, late of Chapel Hill, in this State, nearly 87 years of age. He was a native of Granville Co, for many years a resident of Rockingham, then of Chapel Hill, & finally of the county where he died. Coming of age about the beginning of the Revolution, he was much involved in the scenes that ensued. He bore the commissions first of Sgt, then of Lt, & then of Maj Gen, Greene's army. He was an ofcr in command of the troops that guarded the Com'rs who ran the dividing line between Tenn & Ky in 1779; a duty of great peril, as nearly the whole extent was occupied by hostile savages. He was the companion & friend of Danl Boone in many of his adventures in the early settlement of Ky. His elder brother, Richard, had at one time a fee simple right for nearly the whole of the former state, which was afterwards compromised for the **Henderson Reserve**, & finally lost to his heirs by some kind of legal chicanery. Major Henderson was the private secretary of Gov A Martin, & for nearly 30 years chief clerk of the Hse of Commons in this state. Conceit, presumption, & selfishness were strangers in his nature. Often, too, he has been the medium of intercession with the college authorities & procured the restoration of delinquents. Many times have his purse & table afforded the means of education to young men whom some adverse change in affairs was about to draw home. All these things are too well known in N C to be forgotten soon. "

WED JAN 18, 1843
Public sale: on Feb 7, at the head of Frazier's, the residence of the late John Baptist Kerby, near the Potomac river, & adjoining the farm called **Blue Plains**, formerly owned by the late Capt Wm Marbury, a few miles above Alexandria, on the east side of the river, one seine, supposed to be 200 fathoms long & 30 feet deep, the greater part new net, with good lines & cork, together with one seine chest.
--Geo Kerby, Agent

The brig **Somers**: letter to a friend by Mr R H Dana, author off "Two Years before the Mast", who went on board the ship **North Carolina**, & heard part of the trial going on there, & thence proceeded to the **Somers**. In the ships of the line, frigs,or sloops of war which I have visited, there is a great appearance of protection, defence, & imposing authority connected with the after end of the ship. There is a poop deck, a cabin built about the main deck, with doors & windows looking forward, a marine, with a bayonet & loaded musket, at the door, another at the gangway, & others on guard at various parts of the ship, clear roomy decks, & plenty of ofcrs about, & the qrtrs of ofcrs furnished with arms, & well guarded. But you must make a revolution in all your ideas upon these particulars to judge of the **Somers**. You would hardly believe your eyes if you were here to see, as the scene of this dreadful conspiracy, a little brig, with low bulwarks, a single narrow deck, flush fore & aft, & nothing to make the ofcrs' qrtrs but a long trunk house, or companion, raised a few feet above the deck, to let light & air in below, such as you many have seen in our smaller packets which ply along the seaboard. Half a dozen resolute conspirators could have swept the deck, & thrown overboard all that opposed them before aid could come from below. The ofcrs' qrtrs & the cabin are on the same floor with the berth deck of the crew, separated only by bulkheads. In short, no one, at all acquainted with nautical matters, can see the **Somers** without being made feelingly aware of the defenceless situation of those few ofcrs, dealing with a crew of 90 persons, of whom some were known to be conspirators, while, of the rest, they hardly knew upon whom to rely for active & efficient aid in time of danger.

Senate: 1-Credentials of Chas G Atherton, Senator elect from N H, for 6 years, from Mar 3, 1843, were presented. 2-Ptn from the wid/o Pollerescky, a Revolutionary ofcr, for a pension. 3-Ptn from May Krug, asking that a pension may be granted, she being the wid/o a dec'd Revolutionary sldr. 4-Ptn from the heirs of Danl Truheart, asking indemnity for property destroyed during the Revolution. 5-Cmte on Pensions: Hse bills, without amendment, for the relief of John Hicks, & the relief of John Javins. 6-Cmte on Indian Affairs: bill for the relief of Jos Bryan, Harrison Young, & Benj Young. 7-Bill for the relief of Saml Dicey was passed. 8-Bill for the relif of Jos Nourse was taken up on its passage, when there appeared for the passage of the bill 22 ayes, noes not counted. 9-Cmte on Military Affairs: bill for the relief of Boyd Reilly.

Nashville Banner: the Hon Robt L Caruthers declines consenting to be a candidate for re-election to Congress.

J M Duffield, editor of the Natchez Courier, has been elected Major of the city of Natchez.

Circuit Court of Wash Co, D C. Wm Devereux, a bankrupt, has filed his ptn for his discharge & certificate: hearing on the first Mon of May. Same for Geo M Phillips. –Wm Brent, clk

Circuit Court of Wash Co, D C. Geo W Robinson has filed his ptn for the benefit of the Bankrupt Law: hearing on the first Mon of Mar next. Same for Benj P Smith. –Wm Brent, clk

Hse/o Reps:: 1-Cmte of Claims: adverse reports upon the ptns of Jas Davis, Henry P Russell, administrator of Saml Russell, & Rebecca McCann, wid/o Arthur McCann. Same cmte, reported the following bills, viz: bill for the relief of the legal reps of Robt A Kelly, & a bill for the relief of the legal reps of Alex'r Mitchell. 2-Cmte of Claims, to which was referred the bill from the Senate for the relief of J R Vienne, reported the same without amendment. 3-Cmte of Claims, made a report upon the ptn of Sarah Eveleth, with a bill for the relief of the legal reps of Wm S Eveleth, dec'd. 4-Letter from the Sec of War, transmitting a certified copy of all the papers to be found in the War Dept relative to the arrest & trial by court-martial of E L Louallier under the order of Gen Jackson in Mar, 1815. 5-Ptn of Allen Denny & others, citizens of Will Co, Ill, in relation to the 16th section: referred. 6-Ptn of Moses G Buck & 81 others, citizens of Maine, for additional duties on sawed lumber, fire-wood, hemlock bark, & spars.

Died: on Jan 7, Catharine Augusta, infant d/o Wm Smith, aged 10 months.

Died: on Dec 29, at his late residence in Pomonkey, Chas Co, Md, Henry Brawner, aged 68 years.

Detention on the Railroad not far from Beltsville: the evening train from Balt, with the Northern mail, was detained & did not arrive in Wash City until 6 a m. It is no light matter to have the passengers kept 12 hours on the road, in winter, in some cases, subject to the cold, & without the comforts of a good meal & a blazing fire. Conductor-Capt Slack. A steer rushed down before the locomotive, which, passing over it, threw the locomotive, tender, & baggage cars off the track; the engine wheels buried in the mud. No person injured. Great praise is due Capt Slack. Chas B Calvert came early to their assistance with his force of men & oxen, & by whose personal & laborious assistance [continued from 7 until 3] they are most largely indebted for success in freeing the track from incumbrance, & in continuing the journey. Mr Calvert also tendered to the passengers the hospitalities of his house.

Died: on Dec 26, at ***Retirement***, his residence in Harrison Co, Va, Mr Benj Reeder, in his 98th year. He emigrated from Md to Morgantown, which section of country he has for many years represented in the Leg of Va, with honor to himself & credit to his constituents. He was appointed Marshal of the Western Dist of Va, which ofc he held nearly 30 years, with increased honor to himself. He was removed during the administration of Gen Jackson for opinion's sake only. Since then he has lived a retired life in Harrison Co, surrounded & beloved by numerous descendants. His last hours were cool, collected, & resigned. He departed this life a Christian, in the full expectation of a blessed eternity.

THU JAN 19, 1843
Orphan's Court of Wash Co, D C. Letters testamentary on the personal estate of Maria Gant, dec'd. Claims to be exhibited on or before Jan 10 next. –E G Bell, exc

Washington Assemblies: Ball will take place on Jan 26. Subscribers will procure their tickets from Mr Fischer. Managers:

Hon W P Mangum	Chas Lee Jones
Hon W C Johnson	J M Carlisle
Hon Caleb Cushing	Richd Wallach
Com Lewis Warrington	Dr J M Thomas
Gen Geo Gibson	Richd S Hill
Gen Alex'r Hunter	R Kearney, U S A
Fletcher Webster	Wm May, U S N

Handsome & fashionable furniture at auction: on Dec 23, at the residence of Mrs F Durmitt, on B st south, between 10th & 11th sts, her household & kitchen furniture, which is of the very best & most fashionable kind, nearly new, having been in use about 6 months; amongst which are: Mahg, hair seat, & maple case seat chairs
Mahg hair seat sofa; Pair of marble top pier tables
Marble top center table & sideboard
Dining & breakfast tables, coquette sofa, pair girandoles

Plated candlesticks, astral & hall lamps
Blue moreen & muslin window curtains & ornaments
White china dinner set, china tea set
Cut glass tumblers, jellies, etc, ivory handle knives
1 doz silver forks, silver table & tea spoons & ladle
superior Brussels & ingrain parlor carpets & rugs
hat rack, lounge, case seat chairs
marble top dressing & other bureaus
dressing tables, mahg & maple bedsteads
best feather beds & hair mattresses
washstands, toilet sets -R W Dyer & Co, aucts

For rent: a 4 story dwlg, the late residence of Jas McCormick, jr, situated on N J ave, fronting the Capitol square. For further information, apply next door to Jane Adams, or at the Bank of Washington.

Public Notice: I forewarn all persons from crediting any person or persons on my account, without written order with my signature thereon, as I will not pay any bills or accounts so created. –R McGregor, PG Co, Md.

PG Co-Crt of Equity, Jan Term, 1843. Wm H Piles vs Lucy Mullen & Ellen Mullen. Object of the bill is to obtain a decree requiring the dfndnts, Lucy Mullen & Eliza Mullen, as the heirs of Jos Mullen, dec'd, to convey by deed to the cmplnt a parcel of land in PG Co, called **Lanham's Delight**, containing 80 acs. The bill states that on Apr 11, 1842, the cmplnt purchased of the said Jos Mullen [a colored man] the said parcel of land, with a written agreement with the said Jos in regard to the purchase, whereby Jos bound & obliged himself & his heirs to convey the said land to the cmplnt whenever the cmplnt should be prepared to pay the sum of $300 & interest thereon, the purchase money agreed to be paid for the land. Cmplnt is now prepared to pay the purchase money & interest. The said Jos Mullen has since departed this life intestate, leaving as his heirs-at-law a dght, Lucy Mullen, who resides in PG Co, & another dght, Eliza Mullen, who many years since removed from Md to Ohio, & has not since been heard of, & is supposed to have died intestate & unmarried. Cmplnt is anxious to secure the deed to the land. The 2nd Mon in Oct next is set to answer this bill of cmplnt. –C Dorsey -John B Brooke, clk of PG Co Crt [Md]

Hse/o Reps: 1-Ptn of Israel Goodridge & others, for the allowance of bounty on the fishing schnr **Blooming Youth**. 2-Ptn of Wm Appleton & Co & 60 others, merchants of Boston, for the passage of a law giving the right of drawback on foreign fabrics & products exported to Canada & other British provinces. 3-Ptn of 100 inhabitants of Wesley township, Washington Co, Ohio, praying Congress to authorize the issue of two hundred millions of Gov't stock upon the plan of Mr W Cost Johnson.

Circuit Court of Wash Co, D C. Hanson Barnes has filed his ptn for the benefit of the bankrupt law: hearing on the first Mon in Mar next. –Wm Brent, clk

Senate: 1-Ptn from Thos Jefferson Dant, asking that the bankrupt law may be so modified as to give mechanics a lien on their labor. 2-Ptn from Wm Morrow, asking remuneration from Congress for a violation by the U S agent engaged on the Arsenal in D C. 3-Cmte on Public Lands: asked to be discharged from the further consideration of the ptn of Wm Downing, & that it be referred to the Cmte of Claims. 4-Cmte on Revolutionary Claims: bill from the Hse/o Reps for the relief of the heirs & legal reps of the Baron De Kalb.

Circuit Court of Wash Co, D C. Leon R Gawronski, a bankrupt, has filed his ptn for his discharge & certificate: hearing on the first Mon in May next. –Wm Brent, clk

Annual Meeting of the American Colonization Soc met at the Capitol last evening. Speakers were: Mr Wise; Senator Miller; Rev Mr Andrews; Z C Lee; & Mr Penrose

Mrd: on Jan 3, by Rev Mr Jorden, Wm Biscoe to Miss Jane Y Barber, d/o Dr Luke T Barber, all of St Mary's Co, Md.

Mrd: on Jan 17, by Rev John C Smith, Geo Stettinius to Miss Caroline V Lalanne, all of Wash City.

Mrd: on Tue last, at the residence of Gen John H Eaton, by Rev Mr French, pastor of the Episc Church, Mr John Brockenborough Randolph, of the U S Navy, to Miss Mgt Rosa Timberlake, of Wash City.

Died: on Jan 18, John Wells, jr, in his 52nd year. His funeral will be today at 3 p m.

Died: on Wed, at the residence of her brother-in-law, Griffith Coombe, after an illness of 5 days, Miss Eliza Pleasonton. Her funeral will be today at 3 p m.

Died: on Jan 18, Mary Louisa, d/o Fred'k & Eliza Cudlipp, aged 17 months & 13 days. Her funeral is at 10 a m, on Fri, from his residence.

Mr John Murphy, printer & publisher of Balt, has just issued a printed volume of 321 pages, being a biographical sketch of the Most Rev John Carroll, first Archbishop of Balt, with select portions of his writings, edited by John Carroll Brent, from the memoranda of the late Danl Brent, Consul for the U S at Paris. It contains what is said to be an admirable engraved likeness of the subject of the sketches.
-Balt Patriot

The accounts due at the ofc of the Nat'l Intell in the state of N C have been placed in In the hands of Mr Israel E James, who with his assistants, Jas K Whipple & Henry Platt, are authorized to collect the same for the proprietors.

FRI JAN 20, 1843
Senate: 1-Ptn from John Golder, of N Y C, praying the authority of Congress to issue an amount of credit checks, not to exceed twenty-six millions. 2-John Goode was allowed to withdraw his papers from the files of the Senate. 3-Cmte on Military Affairs: act for relief of the heirs or assignees of Isaac Todd. 4-Cmte of Claims: bill for relief of Johnson Patrick: without amendment. Same cmte: bill for relief of John Drysdale: without amendment. 5-Cmte of Claims: bill for relief of Duncan L Clinch. 6-Cmte of Claims, Hse bill, with an amendment, for relief of Asahel Lee, Harry Lee, & Lemuel Lee. 7-Bills to be engrossed: bill for relief of Saml Hambleton. Relief of the adms of John Jackson. Relief of Dexter Hungerford, of Watertown, Jeff Co, N Y. Bill for relief of the reps of Alex'r Macomb, Robt Jennings, & the heirs & legal reps of Jas Roddy, dec'd, sureties of Saml Champlin, late a paymaster in the U S army, was passed over informally. 8-Bill from the Hse for relief of Thos Copeland was taken up, & indefinitely postponed. 9-Bill for relief of Wm De Peyster & Henry W Cruger was taken up, &, after having been explained by Mr Crittenden, was ordered to be engrossed. 10-Cmte on Private Land Claims: bill for relief of the heirs of Philander Smith, & Jas Young. Same cmte: unfavorable report upon the ptn of Jacob Haas. 11-Cmte on Naval Affairs: joint resolution for the relief of Francis M Lewis. Same cmte: reported upon the case of Mary Neale, with a joint resolution for her relief. 12-Cmte on Revolutionary Pensions: report upon the case of Jacob Miller, with a bill for his relief. Same cmte: reported a bill granting a pension to David Munn, & a bill for the relief of Saml Edgecombe. Same cmte: adverse reports on the cases of March Farrington, Sutherland Mayfield, Benj Watson, Wm Scott, & Hugh Wallace Wormley. Same cmte: made a report upon the ptn of Nancy Wilson, with a bill for her relief. 13-Cmte on Invalid Pensions: adverse report upon the ptn of Peter W Short. Same cmte: adverse report on the ptn of Jas Stevens.

Levin Handy: cut off in the meridian of a promising life, terminated at age 29 years, in the midst of a career, a Lt in the U S Navy. He first opened his eyes at Snowhill, Worcester Co, Md; at age 9 years was removed to this city with his father, Saml Handy, who had then become associated with one of the Depts of Gov't. Descended from a line of Revolutionary ancestry, on both sides, of high rank. Levin received, through the kind regard of the lamented Southard, an appointment as acting Midshipman in the U S Navy. He gradually rose to the grade of passed midshipman, & from thence was enrolled as Lt. In service 14 years, commencing in the Pacific, now on the Brazils, then with the coast survey, again on the Floridas, or that last, which has so unexpectedly & fatally terminated in the China seas. He has left sorrowing brothers, a heart-broken wife, & an aged father. --J M B

Mr Geo Hamilton, publisher of the Natchitoches [La] Reporter, died at that place on Dec 29, in his 28th year.

Died: on Dec 6, at Key West, Fla, Mr Chas Seabrook Finley, s/o the late Capt Finley, of this place.

Horrible Cruelty & Death. Hartford [Conn] Review of Jan 14$^{th/}$ On Jan 3, a lad named Gillet, about 14 years of age, who lived with a man named Viets for some months, from Granby, died from long exposure to extreme cold. He was forced by Viets to ride the horse all the way to a store in that city, some 18 miles distant. A legal investigation into the treatment he received from Viets will be had. -Tribune

On Jan 9, in Paint Township, Ohio, Constable Jas Stafford, while in the discharge of his official duty, shot Mr Jos Carroll, who lived but 5 or 10 minutes after receiving the wound. The altercation having originated in an attempt on the part of the ofcr to levy upon the property of the dec'd, he was legally acquitted of all blame in the matter, it being deemed a justifiable homicide.

Mr Lafayette Peirce, of Hinsdale, was instantly killed on Mon last, by being caught in a water wheel in Mr Tilden's tannery. He has left a family to mourn him.
–Lenox [Mass] Eagle

The creditors of Wm Ogden Niles, whose claims accrued previous to May 8, 1839, are hereby notified to file their claims, duly proved, on or before May 1 next.
–T G Hill, trustee

Hse/o Reps:: 1-Ptn of Peter Yates & others, citizens of Milwaukie, in the Territory of Wisconsin, for an appropriation for a harbor at that place. 2-Ptn of Lewis Gordon, a disabled seaman, praying for a pension. 3-Ptn of Josiah Blatchfond & others, citizens of Mass, praying for the erection of buoys on certain rocks & shoals near Cape Ann. 4-Ptn of Adeline Hews, for a grant of money due Wm Watts, a surgeon of the army of the Revolution, as his heir at law. 5-Ptn of Henry Switzer & 160 others, of Jeffersonville, Indiana, praying an appropriation to improve the navigation of the Western waters. 6-Memorial of Eli White & Son, & sundry other persons interested in the manufacture of hats, complaining of so much of the late tariff as lays a duty of 25% "on all hatters' furs," which were always before imported free of duty, while on foreign manufactured hats it imposes only 35%, & on foreign unfinished hats only 25%.

Prince George will stand the ensuing season at my farm near Good Luck Post-ofc, PG Co, Md, 15 miles from Wash City. Terms: $25 the season for blood mares, & $10 the season for common. Pasturage furnished at $3 per month; grain fed for .25 per day. No liability for accidents or escapes. 50 cents in each case to the groom.
–G W Duvall

Wash Corp: 1-Cmte of Claims: bill for the relief of Wm Thomas: passed. 2-Ptn from Owen McCue: referred to the Cmte of Claims. 3-Cmte of Claims: reported bill for the relief of John France: passed. Same cmte: asked to be discharged from the further consideration of the ptn of W J Bronaugh; but, before the question was taken thereon, the ptn was ordered to lie on the table. 4-Ptn of A H Young, praying permission to erect a frame bldg within 24 feet of a brick one: referred to the Cmte on Improvements. 5-Ptn of D W Oyster, praying to be refunded a certain amount paid erroneously for a stall in Centre Market: referred to the Cmte of Claims. 6-Ptn of John A Donohoo & others, praying that the curb may be set & footway paved on 1st st east, in sq 575: referred to the Cmte on Improvements.

We have been requested by Mr John N Trook, a letter carrier in the City Post-ofc, who was the "principal sufferer" alluded to in our late notice, to say that the statement lately made in the Balt Sun, that there is another defaulting clerk in our City Post-ofc besides the absconding defaulter Adams, is incorrect, & unjust toward him [Mr Trook] & the other carriers & clerks employed in that ofc. We make this correction as an act of justice to Mr Trook, & regret that the erroneous statement published in the Balt Sun has been copied into the Patriot & other newspapers. The statement published in the Nat'l Intell was accurate in every particular, as we are assured by a respectable & intelligent gentleman attached to the City Post-ofc.

Circuit Court of Wash Co, D C. Lambert S Beck has filed his ptn for the benefit of the Bankrupt Law: hearing on the first Mon in Mar next. –W Brent, clk

SAT JAN 21, 1843
On Wed last the **largest steamboat** in the world was launched from the ship-yard of Wm H Brown, at the foot of 12th st, East river, N Y. She was built for the Troy Steamboat Co, & is intended to ply between N Y & Troy. Her extreme length on deck is 330 feet, breadth of beam, exclusive of guards, 30 feet & 6 inches, dept of hold 9 feet 9 inches. She will be, it is supposed, the fastest boat ever built.

Senate: 1-Ptn from Chas L Williamson, asking for a pension. 2-By Mr Crafts: asking the withdrawal of the papers on file relating to the claim of Jos Edson. 3-Cmte on Pensions: bill for the relief of John T Wiley. Relief of Nancy Hambright, wid/o Capt John Hambright, dec'd. Relief of Jas Sweetman. Relief of Thos King. Also, an adverse report on Hse bill for the relief of Gideon A Perry. Same cmte: asking that the bill for the relief of Martha Damarine be laid on the table, the petitioner having died pending the time the bill was before the Hse. Also, asking to be discharged from the further consideration of the ptn of John Bosworth, & that it be referred to the Cmte on Naval Affairs, it being in that service he received a wound. He would, for the second time, move its reference to that cmte. 4-Cmte on Pensions: favorable reports on the following Hse bills, & recommending their passage: bill for the relief of Jos Nimblett. Bill granting a pension to Israel Thomas.

Also, unfavorable report on the Hse bill for the relief of the wid/o Capt Wm Royall, dec'd. 5-Cmte on the Judiciary: Hse bill, with an amendment, & recommending its passage, for the relief of Jos W Reckless. An act supplementary to the act of May 24, 1828, to continue a copyright to Jno Rowlet. Hse bill for the relief of Richd Coke, Robt Anderson, & Geo W Southall. 6-Cmte on Military Affaris: unfavorable report on the ptn of Mary A Boyd. 7-Cmte on Pensions: adverse report on the ptn of Wm A Davis. Also, on the memorial of Chas Larrabee. 8-Cmte of Claims: adverse report on the Hse bill for the relief of Saml B Tuck. 9-An act for the relief of the reps of Alexander Macomb, Robt Jennings, & the heirs & legal reps of Jas Roddy, dec'd, sureties of Saml Champlin, late a paymaster in the U S army: passed. 10-Bill for the relief of Richd Henry Wilde was taken up.

P A Southall, the bearer of dispatches from Washington to Gen Waddy Thompson, our Minister at Mexico, arrived in New Orleans on Jan 9, & sailed then in the U S revenue cutter **Woodbury**, for Vera Cruz.

Orphan's Court of Wash Co, D C. Executors of Jas Walker, dec'd, appointed Feb 7 next, for final settlement. -Ed N Roach, reg/o wills

Case lately brought by Mr Saml Harris, in the Balt Co Crt, against the Phil, Wilmington, & Balt Railroad Co, to recover damages alleged to have been sustained by the plntf in consequence of his child [a small boy] having been run over & killed by the cars, was decided on Wed last in a verdict of $1,125 damages to the plntf.

Bethel S Farr, a member of the St Louis Bar, was shot by Mr Leo D Walker, with a pistol, on Jan 6, in a street affray. He died a day or 2 afterwards. The matter is before the grand jury, in session in St Louis.

Orphan's Court of Wash Co, D C. Letters of administration on the personal estate of Geo Webster, late of said county, dec'd. –Jas Marshall, adm

Circuit Court of Wash Co, D C. Geo W Craig has filed his ptn for the benefit of the Bankrupt Law: hearing on the first Mon of Mar next. –Wm Brent, clk

Foreign Ofc, London, Dec 6. The Queen has appointed Wm Pitt Adams, now Sec to her Majesty's Legation to the Mexican Republic, to be her Majesty's Charge d'Affaires & Consul Gen to the Republic of Peru. The Queen has appointed Percy Wm Doyle, now first Attache to her Majesty's Legation to the Mexican Republic.

Died: on Jan 10, at his residence in Spottsylvania Co, Va, Mr John Pratt, in his 82nd year. His long journey through life was distinguished by its usefulness & the practice of every virtue, & its termination by the Christian humility, resignation, & calmness of the closing scene.

Balt Sun, dated at Reisterstown, in Balt Co, Md, on Jan 18. The dwlg of Miss Henrietta Israel, 3 miles s w of this place, was consumed by fire yesterday, & herself & a little boy, the only inmates of the house, perished in the flames. The fire appeared to be the work of incendiary & murderer, as it was generally believed the lady had a considerable amount of money by her, bequeathed by a deceased uncle; also that she was very careful to have her property well secured by locks, all of which were found unlocked; only about $170 in silver was found, a great part of which was melted so much as to render it uncurrent.

Hse/o Reps: 1-Cmte of Claims: Ptn of D & J Wilkinson, with a bill for their relief. Bill for the relief of Andrew Fisher. Bills for the relief of Gamaliel E Smith & W W Street. 2-Cmte on Commerce: bill for the relief of Saml Hoffman. 3-Cmte on Invalid Pensions: bill from the Senate for the relief of Saml Dicy, reported the same without amendment. 4-Bill for the relief of the heirs of Philip Renault came up again on the question of its final passage, the vote which had been reconsidered. Further consideration postponed until this day four weeks. 5-Ptn of Andrew F Tyler, of Morgan Co, Ohio, who lost his health while in the U S army, praying a pension. 6-Ptn of Edw Dexter, of Providence, R I, praying indemnity for the capture of the schnr **Betsey** by the French privateer Cisalpine in 1798. 7-Cmte on Commerce: memorial of Benj Rich & others, of Boston, on the subject of the imprisonment of free colored seamen in certain Southern ports of this Union. Resolved: the seizure & imprisonment, in any port of this Union, of free colored seamen, citizens of any of the States, & against whom there is no charge, is a violation of the 2nd section of the 4th article of the Constitution of the U S.

Richmond Compiler of yesterday. Announce the death of Mr T W White, Editor of the Southern Lit Messenger. He died yesterday morning. He was the head of an interesting family.

Supreme Crt of the U S, Jan 20, 1843. Geo Armstrong, of Ky, was admitted as atty & counselor of this Court. #16: Lessee of John Mercer et ux, plntfs in error, vs, W C Selden. Argument in this cause was continued by Gen Jones for the plntf in error.

MON JAN 23, 1843

Hse/o Reps: 1-Ptn of Christopher Doughty, a sldr of the Revolution, now in the 89th year of his age, praying Congress for a pension for his services in the Revolutionary war: referred. 2-Ptn of Jacob Wilt, of Lehigh Co, Pa, a sldr of the Revolutionary war, praying for a pension: referred.

On Tue week, Mr Isaiah Wells, of Ashtabula Co, Ohio, was removing a large oak saw-log near the saw mill of Mr Newbury, when the log became disengaged from its fastenings, & passed over his body, causing his death in about 40 minutes.

A sailor belonging to the ship **Alabama** fell from the rigging yesterday into the river, & would have perished but for the exertions of a tar named Temple, who plunged in & succeeded in saving the life of a human being. --New Orleans Crescent

Mrd: on Jan 19, by Rev Horace Stringfellow, Mr Geo W Holtzclau, of Fauquier, Va, to Eliz Ann, 2nd d/o Almon Baldwin, of Wash City.

Died: on Jan 14, John Thos Wagler, in his 24th year, leaving a widow & 2 children to mourn his loss.

Died: on Jan 18, Mary Genevieve, infant d/o Wm C Orme.

Senate: 1-Cmte on Revolutionary Pensions: made a report on the ptn of Jane McGuire, wid/o Maj Thos McGuire, dec'd, with a bill for her relief. 2-Cmte on Invalid Pensions: reported a bill for the relief of Samson Brown. Same cmte: reported a bill for the relief of Wm Patterson.

Orphan's Court of Wash Co, D C. Letters of administration on the personal estate of Richd S Briscoe, late of said county, dec'd. --Geo Fletcher, adm

Circuit Court of Wash Co, D C: in Chancery. Seth Hyatt, administrator of Wm Whelan vs Patrick Delany's excs & devisees. Jas M Carlisle, trustee, sold all that part of lot 23, in sq 254, in Wash City, of which Patrick Delany died seised, with the improvements; & at such sale Abraham Butler became the purchaser for $1,000; & that Butler had complied with the terms of the sale: ratify same. --Wm Brent, clk

Fatal accident on last Fri near the Railroad depot in Wash City, by which a sober & industrious man, Lloyd Hayes, a fireman in the employment of the Balt & Wash Railroad Co, was struck upon the stomach by the short pole attached to the car, while he was under the platform, trying to connect the 2 cars, preparatory to their departure from this city the next morning. It does not appear that any blame is attached to the engineer Shipley, who was assisting the dec'd to connect the cars. Mr Hayes died from the effects of the internal injury in about 3/4^{ths} of an hour after he was struck. He only spoke twice & said, "I am very much mashed." "Lord, have mercy upon me." He has left a widow & one child, the former arrived in this city last Sat morning, overwhelmed with distress.

TUE JAN 24, 1843
Senate: 1-Ptn from Jas L Smith, praying the establishment of an additional executive dept of the Gov't, having superintendence of agriculture & education. 2-Ptn from Jas Gee, a sldr of the last war, asking for a pension. 3-Ptn from Saml Dexter, asking indemnity for spoliations made by the French prior to 1800. 4-Ptn from A J Ramsey & others, purchasers of public lands in Louisiana, asking for relief in consequence of their patents having been withheld. 5-Mr Walker moved to recommit the bill for the

relief of Gorham Worth, on which an unfavorable report had been made, to the Cmte on the Judiciary. Agreed to. 6-Cmte on Public Lands: Hse bill, with an amendment, for the relief of Jas B Sullivan, of Rapides Co, La. 7-Cmte on Pensions: Hse bill for the relief of Saml M Asbury, with amendments. Same cmte: adverse report on the hse bill for the relief of Saml Neely.

Mrd: on Jan 17, by Rev Mr Mudd, at Oakland, the seat of Chas A Pye, Chas Co, Md, Dr Wm I Digges to Miss Rebecca Jane, y/d/o Edw I Heard, of Louisiana.

Mrd: on Jan 19, by Rev John P Donelan, Mr Peter Gallant to Miss Amelia Hoburg, all of Wash City.

Memory of Francis Scott Key: remarkable from youth for the quickness & brilliancy of his intellect; allied by marriage to one of the most honorable & honored families of Md; devoted every Sabbath to the ofcs of religion-title of a *Sabbath School Teacher*. It was during the late war, when a British fleet had penetrated to the very Capitol of our country, & while approaching the outworks & fort which guard a sister city, that young Key, then detained on board an English ship of war, beheld, as the twilight closed upon the invading forces, the flag of his country waving above the fortress of attack, & when the night set in, was taunted by the threat & boast of the invaders that ere morning that flag would be struck to the prowess of its enemies. The dawn broke & he caught the first glance of that yet unconquered ensign still there, waving over the free & brave. At this moment of rapture he wrote a song which has become the brightest gem of our literature.

Died: on Sun, at the Washington Navy Yard, Joanna L, w/o Dr Jos Hopkinson, of the U S Navy, in her 23rd year. Her friends & those of her family are requested to attend her funeral from her late residence, at the Navy Yard, at 10 a m this morning, without further notice.

Hse/o Reps: 1-Ptn of Geo B Williamson, asking to be relieved from liability for money collected by him as postmaster at Wainsborough, Ga, & which was destroyed by fire with the ofc. 2-Ptn of Stephen Mathews & 72 other citizens of Lake Co, Ohio, praying Congress to regulate the currency. 3-Ptn of Danl Branch & 36 others, praying for the abolition of slavery in D C. Same persons against the admission of Texas into the Union. 4-Ptn of David Stevens, praying for bounty land. 5-Ptn of Uriah Loomis for a pension. 6-Ptn of Richd C French & 63 other inhabitants of Fall River Mass, praying the removal of the Seat of Gen Gov't to some place north of the Ohio river. 7-Ptn of Andrew Hicks & others, praying the erection of a light-house at the harbor of Westport Point, Mass. 8-Ptn of Wm Porter, jr, & 301 legal voters of the town of Lee, Mass; the ptn of Danl N Dewey & 92 others, citizens of Williamstown, Mass, for the repeal of the bankrupt law, to take effect from the commencement of this session of Congress. 9-Ptn of Wm B Crews, asking compensation for services rendered the U S. 10-Ptn of 48 citizens of Scioto Co,

Ohio, praying that a pension may be allowed to Danl Wolford, a sldr of the late war, for wounds received in the service of his country. 11-Memorial of Edw Carrington & Co, & others, ship owners & merchants of Providence, R I, asking for such action in relation to the present commercial treaties & arrangements of the U S with foreign Gov'ts, as may secure a just reciprocity to the navigation of this country.

Agency at Washington for the prosecution of claims before Congress & the several Depts of Gov't. Will prepare all kinds of legal instruments. --Chas S Wallach, ofc in the basement of the west wing of City Hall.

Supreme Court of the U S: Jan 23, 1843. #1: Thos Hammond's adm, etc, vs, Gen Geo Washington's exc. Appeal from the Circuit Court of the U S for Alexandria. Mr Justice Daniel delivered the opinion of the Crt, reversing the decree of the Circuit Court with costs, & remanding the same to the said Crt to be preceeded in conformably to the opinion of this Crt. #58: Arthur Bronson, cmplnt, vs, John H Kinzie et al. Case was submitted to the Crt on the record & printed argument of Mr Arnold for the cmplnt. #20: Robt Morris, appellant, vs, Henry Nixon's excs et al.

Handsome furniture at auction: Jan 27, at the house lately occupied by the Chevalier de Nordin, a few doors west of the War Ofc, on Pa ave, the furniture in the house: Scarlet velvet mahg sofa & chairs; Marble top pier tables, Mantel & pier glasses, mantel ornaments; Astral & other lamps; Carpets & rugs; curtains & ornaments; Heavy silver forks & spoons, [King's pattern;] Dinner table; Dinner & breakfast china, cut glass, knives & forks; Sideboard, bureaus, washstands, bidets, bathing tub; Feather bed & bedding; lot of coppers & kitchen furniture. -R W Dyer & Co, aucts

Phil, Jan 21, 1843. Surgeon W P C Barton, Chief of the Naval Bureau of Medicine & Surgery at Wash, has sent me a copy of a circular printed Nov 24, 1842. In it is stated that on board our ships of war, the liquors procured for the sick are promiscuously stowed amongst the boxes of liquor belonging to the messes of ofcrs, & have too much & too long been considered a stock from which all felt at liberty to borrow-whether with the intention of returning or not, avails nothing-but with the positive result of a general ommision to do so. Response of Jas Biddle, Capt U S Navy: How is it possible that Surgeon W P C Barton can have any personal knowledge of the service afloat. It is well known that during the war he refused to go to sea. It is well known that during the war he was employed professionally to attend the army recruits in this city. It is well known that without going to sea, & without going to the frontier, he received during the war pay both from the army & the navy. Since the peace he has made one cruise-not exceeding 6 months-in the frig **Brandywine** to the West Indies. During the period therefrom, of 31 years, from 1811 to 1842, he has served on board ship 6 months & no more. How, then, I repeat, is it possible for Surgeon W P C Barten to know anything of the service afloat. --Jas Biddle

City Hotel, N Y: Chester Jennings has taken this house & it will be opened Feb 1. The Croton water is introduced on every floor. Mr Willard is associated with him.

WED JAN 25, 1843
New Orleans, Jan 15. It is now rendered certain that Mr Geo B Ogden did not meet his death by drowning, but that his body was thrown into the canal after life was extinct. It is palpable enough that he died at the hands of assassins. –Picayune

Dade's Massacre: letter dated Washington, Dec 16, 1842. Colonel: in my operations in Florida it was my good fortune to take from the Seminole Indians the double barreled gun used by your gallant relative, the late Maj Dade, in the battle in which he & his companions so gloriously fell. At the first onset our troops were nearly surrounded. The fugitives were rallied by the celebrated chief Hopatte-Hadjo. Though the gun is a national trophy, the proper depository of it is, in my opinion, the family of the dec'd. I have not been able to learn whether Maj Dade left children. If he did, & they still live, I desire that it be presented to them. If not, I beg of you to present it in my name to his nearest male relative. –Th Jesup, to Col John B Dade, Wash. Letter from J B Dade: dated Washington, Jan 10, 1843. Dear Gen: Permit me to introduce to you my son-in-law, Mr Edw Smith, who will hand you this. Maj Dade left a widow & 2 small children; one of his children has since died, & the mother & remaining one, [a dght, I believe,] now reside in Florida. The next nearest relative is an only borhter, Dr Laurence S Dade, who is a resident of King Geo Co, Va. May I ask that you will designate to which of these branches of his family I shall give the gun. –J B Dade

Miss Mathieu has established herself at Mr Favier's, on 19th st, near Pa ave, for the purpose of ironing, plaiting, & fluting collars, cuffs, of muslin & lace.

Hse/o Reps: 1-Cmte on Revolutionary Pensions: report on the ptns of Maria Fowler & Mary Rhinevault, with bills for their relief. 2-Cmte on Revolutionary Pensions: discharged from the further consideration of the ptns of Levi Turner, Jane Floyd, Joel Tiffany, Eunice Everson, Oliver Thompson, & Mgt Gould: & they were ordered to lie on the table. 3-Cmte on Public Lands: act to revive the act for the relief of Mary Tucker, reported the same without amendment. 4-Cmte of Claims: adverse reports on the ptns of John Monroe, of Va, Isaac Carmack, Wm Rice, Geo Delft, & Chas Coleman. 5-Cmte on the Public Lands: made a report on the ptn of Benj Pegg. 6-Cmte on the Post Ofc & Post Roads: adverse report on the ptn of Farley D Thompson. 7-Ptn of John S Kimball & others, citizens of Maine, asking that additional duties may be imposed on wood, bark, lumber, & lime. 8-Ptn of Peter McWilliams, late a private in company E of the 2nd Artl, asking for relief. 9-Ptn of Sarah Scovel, for a pension. 10-Memorial of Robt Rogers & 51 other citizens of Bristol, R I, praying the adoption of measures by Congress which will place the navigating interests of the country upon a more equal footing with foreign Powers.

Circuit Court of Wash Co, D C. Wm Mullin, Jas Thomas, Isaac S Lauck, & John Espy, have each filed their ptn for the benefit of the Bankrupt Law: hearing for each on the first Mon in Mar next. –Wm Brent, clk

Senate: 1-Ptn from Saml Dewey, for a pension. 2-Ptn from Laurent Millandon, asking for the confirmation of certain sales of the public lands. 3-Ptn from Bailie Peyton, of New Orleans, praying the sanction of the award of certain arbitrators between him & the Gov't. 4-Papers presented relating to the claim of Jos Watson. 5-Cmte on Military Affairs: a bill for the relief of Mary W Thompson. 6-Resolved: that the Sec of War be directed to communicate to the Senate a copy of the contract made with John Grant for dredging the channel of Choctaw Pass, in Oct, 1836. 7-Bill for the relief of Richd Henry Wilde was read a 3rd time: "Shall this bill pass?"

Laws of the U S passed at the 3rd session of the 27th Congress. 1-Act for the relief of Cornelius Wilson & Jas Canter. That the Sec of War cause to be made up a pay roll for the services of Wilson & Canter, privates in the company of volunteer militia from N C, commanded by Capt Wm W Pedru or J J Bryan, raised by a requisition of Gen Winfield Scott on the Gov't of said State of N C, dated Apr 11, 1838, to aid him in removing the Cherokee Indians west of the Mississippi, allowing them the same pay, pro rata, which was allowed the other privates of said company from the time they arrived at the place of rendezvous to the time of their rejection for insufficiency of health, including pay & rations for travel each way to & from the place of rendezvous, & certify the same to the Sec of the Treas, who is hereby required & directed to pay the amount thereof to Wilson & Canter, or to their legal reps. 2-Act for the relief of Elisha Moreland, Wm M Kennedy, Robt J Kennedy, & Mason E Lewis: who were deprived of their respective rights of pre- emption to their improvements in Madison Co, Ala, to which they were entitled under the act of Congress of May 29, 1830, by the location of a reservation for a Cherokee Indian named Challenge, under the treaty of 1819, & the confirmation thereof by an Act of Congress passed for his relief, be, & they hereby are, authorized to enter each one qrtr section of any unappropriated public land, not improved or settled, within the Huntsville land district, in Ala, or any adjoining district, by paying therefore the then minimum price per acre. 3-Act for the relief of John R Delany: Sec of Treas to pay the amount of judgment rendered on Mar 26, 1839, in the Circuit Court of Hamilton Co, Tenn, wherein John Cornell was plntf, & Jos Powell, John R Delany, Thos J Caldwell, & Reuben Roddy were dfndnts, & which judgment has been paid by the said John R Delany; together with all costs incurred in said suit, including atty's fees. 4-Act for the relief of Snow Y Sears: Sec of Treas to pay Sears, of Barnstable, Mass, master mariner, or his atty, the sum of $400, on account of a fine of that amount remitted to said Sears, by the Sec of Treas, on Sep 24, 1841, & which was paid into the Treas before the remission of the same could take effect. 5-Act for the relief of Joshua Drew: Sec of Treas to pay to Drew, of Duxbury, Mass, the sum of $240, being the amount of a fine collected from him by the collector of the port of New Orleans, for a supposed violation of the law relative to return seamen. 6-Act for the

relief of the legal reps of Capt Saml Shannon, dec'd. Sec of War to examine & audit the accounts of Shannon, dec'd, as assist paymaster of the U S army, according to the principles of justice & equity, & report to the next session of Congress.
7-Act for the relief of Ferdinand Leibert: Sec of the Treas to settle & adjust the claim of Leibert, of New Orleans City, liquidating partner of the firm of Fibreman & Leibert, for the amount paid as the penalty on a debenture bond for 33 bales of Texas cotton shipped on Apr 17, 1839, in the British ship **Robert Bruce**, in all respects as if the amount paid by him, as penalty for not producing the consular certificate of the lading of the cotton, had not been transferred or paid into the Treas of the U S. 8-Act for the relief of Isaac & Thos S Winslow: that the collector of the port of N Y is required to pay to them $754.91, to indemnify them for duties exacted from them upon a quantity of gin which was improperly landed by the custom house ofcrs, from the brig **Amphitrite**, on Jun 1, 1837, at the port of N Y, & which was destroyed by fire a few hours after, before the same was entered at the custom house, & while in the custody of said ofcrs, & upon which the insurance against loss by fire was prevented by the irregular conduct of said ofcrs. 9-Act for the relief of Burr & Smith: Sec of Treas to refund to Ephraim Willard Burr & Nathl P Smith, of Warren, R I, merchants in company, $216.07, being duties paid to the collector of N Y on 7 casks of oil imported into N Y, & afterwards reshipped to said Warren, & re-exported therefrom with a view to obtain the benefit of drawback, in May, 1840. 10-Act for the relief of Peter Lionberger: Sec of Treas to pay Lionberger $100, for the value of a horse of the said Lionberger, which died while in the service of the U S, in 1813, for want of sufficient forage.

Died: on Jan 19, at the Convent of the Visitation of the B V Mary, Gtwn, D C, Sister Mary Doloris, in her 22nd year, 5th dght of Cmdor Stephen Cassin.

Wash Corp: 1-Ptn of Danl Paullin, praying to be indemnified for certain damages sustained by the sinking of his vessel in the canal: referred to the Cmte of Claims. 2-Ptn from Jos Harbaugh & 4 others, remonstrating against the erection of a market house on the public square at the junction of N Y & Mass ave: read & laid on the table. 3-Memorial from Danl Gold: against the erection of the market house. 4-Ptn of Jos Fowler & 10 others, residents of the northern part of the city, praying that 9th st may be improved before a market house is erected: referred to the Cmte on Improvements. 5-Cmte of Claims: asked to be discharged from the further consideration of the ptn of Hugh Terry: which was agreed to.

Wash City Orphan Asylum meeting Jan 19: following chosen managers for the present year:

Mrs Hawley	Mrs Larned	Mrs Stone
Mrs Laurie	Mrs R S Coxe	Mrs Tucker
Mrs Brown	Miss Richd Smith	Mrs Luce
Mrs Lear	Mrs Markoe	Mrs Dr Washington
Mrs Henderson	Mrs Gadsby	Miss A C Smith

Miss Bingham   Miss Van Ness

Money wanted. S W Handy informs those indebted to him that he will be in the city on Tue of each week, with his books, to attend to the settlement of his accounts. He will be found at Miss Mary G Handy's, opposite Fuller's Hotel. All persons indebted are respectfully invited to call & pay, as his books must be closed.

Circuit Court of Wash Co, D C. Jas H Blake, a bankrupt, has filed his ptn for his discharge & certificate: hearing on the first Mon in May next. –Wm Brent, clk

THU JAN 26, 1843
P F Ravesies & E B Drake: Auctioneers & Commission Merchants, Mobile, Ala.
References: Hon Jno Henderson, M C, from Mississippi
Hon B G Shields, M C, from Alabama   Mr Chas B Jones, Linden, Ala
Gen N Stewart, Atty at Law, Mobile   Messrs Kissam, Bryce, & Jones, N Y
F P Duconge, New Orleans   Mr John M Chapron, Phil
Jas Stewart, Louisville, Ky   Dr E Strudwick, Hillsborough, N C
Jas R Lyle, Cincinnati   Hon Elisha Young, Green Co, Ala
Wm Pannill, Petersburg, Va   Hon C C Langdon, Mobile, Ala
Messrs Dewing & Edmonds, N Brookfield, Mass
Hon Jas Martin, Atty at Law, Mobile, Ala
John T Lomax, Atty at Law, Demopolis, Ala

Circuit Court of Wash Co, D C. Jas J Randolph, a bankrupt, has filed his ptn for his discharge & certificate: hearing on the first Mon in May next. –Wm Brent, clk

Senate: 1-Ptn from the heirs of Joshua Raymond, who state that their father owned 2 vessels out of New London, which were taken with their cargoes prior to 1800 by a French privateer, & that their father was a soldier of the Revolution until the end of the war. They ask indemnity for the property taken, & that the widow of said Raymond may be placed on the pension list. 2-Ptn from Jos Warren Cross & 63 others, of West Boylstown, Mass, upon the subject of peace, deprecating the evils of war, & recommending a reference in the last resort to some third Power, & praying that in all future treaties an article may be inserted to that effect. 3-Ptn from McKean Buchanan, praying indemnity for losses sustained in consequence of an order of a U S ofcr prohibiting the issue of certain bills of exchange. Also, asking that he may be allowed a per centage on certain bills of exchange drawn by him for the relief of the U S. 4-Ptn from D G Skinner. [No other details.] 5-Cmte on Commerce: asking to be discharged from the further consideration of the memorial of Bailie Peyton, of New Orleans, & that it be referred to the Cmte on the Judiciary, as it involved a mere legal question. 6-Bill for the relief of Chas J Jenkins & Wm W Mann, assignees of John M Kinne was taken up.

Lot at auction: deed of trust from Walter Humphrey to Richd G Briscoe, recorded in liber W B #86, folios 463 thru 465, one of the land records of Wash Co: sale on the premises of lot 7 in square 487, with the improvements. –R W Dyer & Co, aucts

Circuit Court of Wash Co, D C. Wm H McClean has filed his ptn for the benefit of the Bankrupt Law: hearing on the first Mon in Mar next. Same for Jas W Davidson. –Wm Brent, clk

Household furniture, carriage, & horse, at auction by order of the Orphan's Court of Wash Co, D C; at the late residence of Mr R S Briscoe, dec'd, on I st, between 20th & 21st sts. The house is for rent. –Robt W Dyer & Co, aucts

Mutiny of the brig **Somers**: we learn that the Pres of the U S, without waiting to learn the decision of the recent Court of Inquiry, has ordered a Court Martial to convene at the Navy Yard at N Y for the trial of Cmder Mackenzie & the ofcrs of the **Somers**, for the execution of Spencer, Cromwell, & Small. This decision was in compliance with the demand of Mackenzie & his brother ofcrs; & will of course terminate the proceedings in this case, as all interference by the civil authority will now be unconstitutional, even if the civil courts originally had jurisdiction in the case.

Hse/o Reps: 1-Bill reported for the relief of Richd Sneed.

List of ofcrs attached to the U S sloop of war **Yorktown**, in the Pacific Ocean, Dec, 1842:

John S Nicholas, Cmder   Chas F McIntosh, 3rd Lt
Percival Drayton, 1st Lt   Miles K Warrington, Acting Master
C W Pickering, 2nd Lt   Wm L Van Horn, Surgeon
Thos [2 lines of information missing.]
Midshipmen:
Henry K Stevens   Robt Savage   Henry H Key
Paul Shirley   Richmond Aulick
H A Colborn   H G D Brown
A P Warley   Simeon S Bassert

Edw Cavendy, Boatswain   Wm Ward, Sailmaker
John Martin, Gunner   Julius Vanstenburg, Master's Mate
Jas McDonnell, Carpenter

Mr Archibald B McGrew, Register & Recorder of Westmoreland Co, Pa, committed suicide on Thu by hanging himself to one of the rafters of his barn. Mr McGrew was in easy circumstances; he was honest, industrious, & moral, was surrounded by affectionate relations, & was generally beloved by his neighbors.
Difficult to assign any cause for the suicide.

FRI JAN 27, 1843
Fruit trees for sale. –John Douglas, Florist & Seedsman, opposite the State Dept.

For rent, the store-house at present occupied by Mr Thos Jewell, situated in Gtwn, on the north side of Bridge st, in the center of the town, & has been used as a dry goods store for the last 35 years. Inquire of the subscriber, at the Lumber yard, Water st, or of Thos Jewell, on the premises. –John Pickrell

Blooded colt at auction: on Sat next, opposite the Centre Market. –D S Waters, auct

Wash Co, D C, to wit: I hereby certify that Benj Bryan brought before me as an estray a sorrel horse. –Jas Marshall, J P Notice: owner to come forward, prove property, pay charges, & take him away. –Benj Bryan

Senate: 1-Cmte on Foreign Affairs: Hse bill for the relief of Edwin Bartlett, late consul of the U S at Lima, Peru, without amendment. Also, with an amendment, Hse bill for the relief of the legal reps of Danl Brent, dec'd, late consul of the U S at Paris. Also, from the same cmte, without amendment, & recommending that they be indefinitely postponed, Hse bills for the relief of Alex'r H Egerett, & for the relief of John A Smith. 2-Cmte on Naval Affairs: adverse report on the ptn of Chas G Ridgely. Same cmte: adverse report on the ptn of Chas L Williamson. 3-Cmte of Claims: asking to be discharged from the further consideration of Hse bill for the relief of Garret Vleit, & that it be referred to the Cmte on Public Lands. Same cmte: Hse bill for the relief of the legal reps of Francis Pellier, & recommending that it be indefinitely postponed. Same cmte: Hse bill for the relief of Allen Rogers, without amendment, & recommending its passage. Same cmte: asking to be discharged from the further consideration of the bill for the relief of Scott Campbell, & that it be referred to the Cmte on Indian Affairs. 4-Resolved: that the Cmte on Private Land Claims to inquire into the claim of Jos Barrow, sen, of Indiana, sole heir of Pierce Barrow, who was entitled to 400 acs of land under the act of Congress of Aug 29, 1788, & Mar 3, 1791, & also of satisfying the claim of said Jos Barrow, sen, to a military right for land located on White River, joining the land of Abraham King Kendall, confirmed by the Gov't prior to 1806. 5-Passed over informally: bill for the relief of Alex'r Macomb, Robt Jennings, & the heirs & legal reps of Jas Roddy, dec'd, sureties of Saml Champlin, late a paymaster in the U S army. 6-Bill to indemnify Maj Gen Andrew Jackson for damages sustained in the discharge of his official duty. 7-Cmte of the Whole: ordered to be engrossed for a 3rd reading: a bill for the relief of Wm Russell & others. 8-Act for the relief of Saml Billings, owner of the fishing schnr **Lurana**: postponed. Same for relief of the owners, master, & crew of the schnr **Joanna**, of Ellsworth, Maine: postponed An act for the relief of the owners, master, & crew of the schnr **Martha**, of Eastport, Maine: postponed.

The Hon Wm L Goggin, of Va, was suddenly called home by the news of the serious illness of his lady.

J E Scheel, professor of music & the science of harmony, will be happy to receive a few more pupils of the piano forte who are somewhat advanced on that instrument. References can be made at Mrs Chambers' store, Pa ave, between 9th & 10th sts, or to the Rev Pastor of the English Lutheran congregation at his residence corner of F & 11th sts.

Biography of Col Richd M Johnson, with an appendix, containing highly important & interesting papers in connexion with his public life. --Wm Emmons, Washington, Jan 21, 1843

Mrd: Jan 25, by Rev Mr Rich, Mr Saml B Goddard, of Wash City, to Miss Clara Ballard, of Concord, N H.

Jacob A Bender, Bricklayer, informs that he still continues to carry on the bricklaying business in all its various branches. Numerous bldgs in Washington were erected under his superintendence for the last 26 years. He can be found at his residence on E st, east of the Gen Post Ofc Dept.

Extensive fire on Mon at Petersburg, Va, destroyed the lumber houses of H Boisseau, Chas Kent, Roper & Noble, & Barton & Marsh, all of them wooden bldgs, & mostly insured.

Fire on Wed week at Charlotee Court Hse, Va, destroyed part of that beautiful village. It destroyed all the bldgs from Capt Smith's tavern to Mr Dupuy's store, except one. A part of the tavern was also consumed.

Chas M Keller will deliver a course of 5 lectures on the properties of Steam & the Steam Engine: on Jan 28, at the Apollo Hall. Admittance 25 cents for each lecture, & for the whole course $1.00.

Hse/o Reps: 1-Memorial of David Taylor, G F Norris, & J K Rogers, Cherokee claimants under the treaty of 1835 & 1836, praying the adoption of such speedy measures as shall render effectual the 17th article of said treaty. 2-Cmte of Claims: adverse report on the ptn of Jos M Hernandez. Same cmte: adverse reports on the ptns of Jno Metcalf, Aaron Adams, Wm Barnes, A G Monroe, Henry Putman, & Patrick Shepherd. 3-Cmte on Claims: report on the ptn of Jno Hodgkin, with a bill for his relief. 4-Cmte on the Post Ofc & Post Roads on the case of S & M Rich, sureties of Jno F Moore, dec'd, late postmaster at Gaines' Cross Roads, in Ky, with a bill for their relief.

Circuit Court of Wash Co, D C. Saml Ball, & Paul Stevens, have each filed their ptn for the benefit of the Bankrupt Law: hearing on the first Mon in Mar next.
--Wm Brent, clk

Appointments by the Pres:
Custom House Ofcrs:
Collectors:
Hugh Nelson, Petersburg, Va, vice J W Campbell, dec'd.
Geo Royster, Teche, La, vice John W Dough, dec'd.
Surveyors:
Danl Foster, Beverly, Mass, vice S D Turner, who did not qualify.
Wm P Porter, Richmond & Petersburg, Va, vice J H Battie, resigned.
Oliver Harris, St Louis, Missouri, vice E R Hopkins, dec'd.
Naval Ofcr:
Joel B Sutherland, Phil, vice Alex'r Ferguson
Appraiser:
Ernest Morphy, New Orleans, vice A H Inskeep.
Land Ofcrs:
Register:
Albert W Parris, Muscoday, Wisc, vice J D Weston, resigned.
Receivers:
Robt B Semple, Tallahassee, Florida, vice Henry Washington, resigned.
Moses H Kirby, Lima, Ohio, vice Wm Blackburn, whose commission expires.
John H McRae, Grenada, Mississippi, vice Jas A Girault, resigned.

Supreme Court of the U S: Jan 26, 1843. R S Caruthers & Milton Brown, of Tenn, were admitted attys & counselors of this Court. #20: Thos Morris, appellant, vs Maria Nixon, et al.

Meeting of the Vestry of Trinity Parish, Wash, Jan 24, 1843, on the recent death of Francis S Key, a member of the vestry. Resolutions were proposed by A O Dayton & adopted. --E S Childs, Register

SAT JAN 28, 1843
Senate: 1-Ptn from Patrick Keon, of Jefferson Co, asking an alteration of the naturalization laws. Also, from H F Pomert,of Oswego, praying that he may be permitted to import certain timber from Canada free of duty. 3-Cmte on Pensions: adverse report on the ptn of Jas Gee. Same cmte: Hse bill, with an amendment, for the relief of Esther Augur. Same cmte: Hse bill, without amendment, & recommending its passage, for the relief of Benj Truslow. Same cmte: a bill for the relief of Nancy Polenesky. 4-Bill from the Hse for the relief of Eliz Hawkins: this bill had been reported on adversely by the Cmte on Pensions, yet since that period positive & well authenticated testimony had been received, which would be supplied. The bill was then ordered to be recommitted. 5-Bill from the Hse for the relief of

Barent Striker: ordered to a 3rd reading. 6-Bill for the relief of Henry M Shreve & to authorize the purchase of his patent for a snag boat: was introduced.

Many persons are in the habit of using German silver tea & table spoons without being aware of their poisonous composition. German silver is composed of copper, arsenic, & nickel, & that it oxidizes very rapidly in contact with any acid, & that slow particles are taken into the stomach which imperceptibly act as a slow but sure poison. –Nashvile Banner

Hse/o Reps: 1-Memorial of S D Walker & 100 citizens of Balt, embracing mercantile firms & persons of all parties, praying Congress to issue 200,000,000 of stock to be divided among the States, & also a memorial signed by Chas Baltzell & 1,000 other citizens of Balt, embracing all parties & various pursuits of business; which were referred to the select cmte on that subject.

Horrid tragedy enacted in the lower part of Anne Arundel Co, Md, on Wed. It seems that an ill feeling had existed between Capt Jos Owens, of West river, & his son, growing out of a law suit, which ended by the father shooting the son, inflicting a wound which caused almost instant death. The father was immediately arrested & taken to Annapolis, where he was committed to jail to await his trial. Capt Owens was, at the time of the occurrence, & is now, partially insane, which probably induced him to commit the rash act. -Clipper [Apr 29th newspaper: trial at Annapolis concluded on Wed last-verdict of the jury: guilty of murder in the 2nd degree. Sentenced to 7 years in the Penitentiary.]

The beautiful town at Culpeper Court-hse, Va, has been visited with a severe affliction. The Bell Tavern, Maj Lightfoot's, Mrs Rosson's, Mrs Thompson's, with a house owned by Mr Ficklen, were all destroyed by fire on Tue last. The village has never witnessed such a scene before. –Fredericksburg Herald

Circuit Court of Wash Co, D C. Jos B Ford, a bankrupt, has file his ptn for his discharge & certificate: hearing on the first Mon in May next. –Wm Brent, clk

Mrd: on Jan 25, in Richmond, Va, at the residence of Dr Brockenbrough, by the Rev Mr Norwood, the Hon Albert S White, Senator of the U S from Indiana, to Harriet W, 3rd d/o Thos Mann Randolph, of Tuckahoe.

Died: on Jan 12, after a protracted illness, Mr Bernard Aldworth, in his 29th year.

Died: on Jan 24, at Balt, Mrs Ann Groc, aged about 76 years, an exemplary Christian, a kind friend, an amiable lady.

Died: on Jan 26, at the residence of her dght, Miss Ann Carroll, of Montg Co, Md, Mrs Eliz Carroll, in her 89th year. Her illness, which terminated in her death, was of long continuance, & her sufferings were borne throughout with singular fortitude & resignation.

Died: on Jan 25, Mrs Ann Lydane, consort of Patrick Lydane, in her 26th year.

France: a d/o Louis Philippe, the Princess Clementine, is to be married to the Prince of Saxe Cobourg.

From Europe: 1-Maj Gen Drummond, Admiral Sir John Longford, & Vice Admiral Evans are dead. The first served under Sir John Moore in Spain, & at the battle of Waterloo. He was the director-general of that royal artl, & had been 49 years in the army. 2-Dreadful disaster. On Dec 21, the ship **Scotland**, of N Y, experienced heavy gales which carried overboard her cmder, Capt Robinson, the 2nd mate, Mr A Palmer, the steward, J Simpson, [a boy,] & 2 seamen.

MON JAN 30, 1843

Hse/o Reps: Bills passed: 1-Relief of John Patten, jr owner of the fishing schnr **Credit**, & the master & crew of said vessel. Relief of Abner Lowell & others, owners of the fishing schnr **William**. Relief of Wm Ellery, owner of the fishing schnrs **Savo & Ida**, & others. Relief of John H Russell & others, owner, master, & crew of the fishing schnr **Lucy Ann**. Relief of Mary Bradstreet & Amos Tappan. Relief of Knott Martin the 3rd, & Arnold Martin, owners of the fishing schnr **Only Son**, & others. Relief of Barnabas Baker & others, owners of the fishing schnr **Union**, of Dennis, Mass. Relief of Joshua Knowles, jr, & owners & the crew of the fishing schnr **Garnet**. 2-Bill for relief of Thos Weaver & Jacob Heyberger, sureties of the Norristown & Valley Railroad Co: laid aside, objection being made. Same for the relief of the legal reps of Alex'r Wilson. Also, same for the relief of Danl Homans. 3-Ptn from Wm Guthridge, of Alexandria, a disabled seaman, praying for a pension. 4-Memorial of Nathl S Ruggles & other merchants of Newport, R I, asking Congress to make such change in our commercial arrangements with foreign Gov'ts as shall give to the navigation of the U S such terms of reciprocity as shall most conduct to the public welfare. 5-Memorial of the pastor, session, & trustees of the Presbyterian Church of Elizabethtown, N J, praying indemnity for property destroyed in the Revolution. 6-Cmte on Commerce: bill for the relief of Rebecca Guest. 7-Cmte on Private Land Claims: adverse report on the ptn of Henry J T Moss. 8-Cmte on Patents: ptn of Saml K Jennings for a renewal of his patent for the discovery of the speedy generation & convenient application of heat to the human body: made a favorable report. 9-Cmte on the Public Bldgs: to which was referred the ptn of John Skirving for renumeration for furnaces furnished by him for warming the Treas bldg: made a favorable report thereon. 10-Cmte on Invalid Pensions: adverse reports on the ptns of Jos Bowlen & Geo Pool. 11-<u>Bills passed: relief of</u>-

Chas Waldron	B O Tayloe	Anne W Angus
John Randolph Clay	Geo C Johnston	Eliz Gresham
Jacob White	Jas Gray	Eliz Powers

Geo A Winslow	Saml Edgecomb	D & J Wilkinson
Jeremiah Kimball	Jacob Miller	Andrew Fisher
J R Vienne	Nancy Wilson	Gamaliel E Smith
Wm Street	Mary Rhinevault	John Skirving
Saml Hoffman	Richd Sneed	Lgl reps of Andrew Mitchell
Saml Dicey	S & M Rich	
Jane McGuire	John Hodgkin	Lgl reps of W B Eveleth
Wm Patterson	Thos H Brown	
Maria Fowler	Saml K Jennings	
Benefit of Mary Pike; & of Francis M Lewis	Benefit of Mary Neale Pension: David Munn	
Mary Barry, widow & adms of Thos Barry		

News from Texas of the death of Col Mathew Caldwell, who was one of the oldest settlers of Texas, signed the declaration of her independence, & was an active partisan ofcr in many of her struggles against both the Mexicans & Indians. He commanded the spy company attached to the unfortunate Santa Fe expedition, & since then commanded the Texians at the battle of the Salado, in which Gen Woll was defeated. He died at Gonzales, of pleurisy. [No date-current item.]

Lt A D Downes has been appointed to the command of the U S schnr **Grampus**. Army & Navy Chron

For rent, the dwlg over the store of the subscriber. –R C Washington

Deaths from drowning. On Tue last the sloop **General Lewis** was capsized in a squall while on her way from Northport, L I, to N Y C. Those lost were Platt Brush, Doris Bunce, & ___ Onderdonk, the latter supposed to be the son of Bishop Onderdonk, of N Y. A like casualty occurred on the same day in the Alleghany river, near Pittsburg: lost were Van Orsdallan, Jos Moon, & John Cornelius.

The subscriber wishes to purchase 50 negroes for the New Orleans market. Himself or agent can be found at the conrer of 7th & Mass ave. –Thos Williams

Circuit Court of Wash Co, D C. Chas H Metteregger, a bankrupt, has filed his ptn for his discharge & certificate: hearing on Apr 10 next. –W Brent, clk

The fine family mansion at "***Elk Island***," the estate of Randolph Harrison, on the James River, was consumed by fire on Tue last, while the severe gale of wind prevailed. The bldg cost some $40,000 & was insured for $10,000.

The family mansion of John D Bowling, Chas Co, Md, was entirely consumed by fire on Fri last, with nearly every article of furniture & the wardrobe of the family, who barely escaped with their lives. Estimated loss $5,000.

Baffled in her former application to Judge Betts for the arrest of Mackenzie & Gansevoort on a charge of murder, the widow of Cromwell [the mutineer] yesterday made a similar application to Judge Lynch, in the Crt of Sessions. Judge Lynch refused to grant the warrant desired for the same reasons which influenced Judge Betts. –Tribune

The ofc of the Gtwn Advertiser was totally desgroyed by fire on Sat, together with all the printing materials. Proprietor-John T Crow.

Died: on Jan 29, in his 73rd year, Nicholas Harper, nearly 30 years a clerk in the Treas Dept. He served many years in the Navy of the U S, & shared liberally in the esteem & confidence of Cmdors Barry, Decatur, & Tingey, Capt McNeil, & many other ofcrs, who witnessed his conduct in the West Indies in the frig **United States**, & afterwards in the frig **Boston** in the Mediterranean, at the blockade of Tripoli. Mr Harper was a native of Ireland; & in 1798, in the abortive struggle for liberty in that ill-fated land, took an active part; was engaged in several bloody contests, in all of which he behaved bravely. At the battle of Vinegar Hill he was wounded, & at Enniscorthy, while advancing on the enemy, two of his brothers were shot down, one on each side of him, one 22 & the other 26 years of age. As a man, a patriot, & a Christian, Mr Harper did honor to the country of his birth, as well as that of his adoption. His funeral is on Jan 30, from Gallabrun's to St Patrick's Church, the place of interment, at 3 p m.

Mr Lea, a hog drover from Ky, was murdered on his return home, a few days ago, in the mountain region of Virginia, by 2 men who traveled with him the principal part of the day on which he was murdered. He had been shot by a pistol in the back part of his head; he fell from his horse, grasping for air. The robbers rifled his pockets, & were in the act of riding off when they were brought to a stand by the appearance of 2 mountaineers who happened to be close by hunting game in the woods. Mr Lea told them what had happened, just before he died. The hunters marched the robbers to the village jail. –Milton Chronicle

TUE JAN 31, 1843
Circuit Court of Wash Co, D C. Chas Huntt, a bankrupt, has filed his petition for his discharge & certificate: hearing on Apr 10 next. –W Brent, clk

Marshal's sale: writ of fieri facias, on judgment of condemnation, issued from the Clerk's ofc of Wash Co, D C: sale on Feb 7, in front of Mr Peter Vonesson's stable, on Congress st, Gtwn, D C, the following property, viz: Omnibus, 2 horses, gear complete, one bay horse, & a lot of gear, or 2 sets of harness, seized & levied upon as the property of one John Francis, late of said county, & sold to satisfy Judicials #9, to March term of said Court, 1843, in favor of Peter Vonesson & Jas P Gannon. –Alex'r Hunter, Marshal of D C

Senate: 1-Memorial from Sarah Williamson, appealing from the construction put on the pension act of Jul 7, 1838, as contrary to the spirit of that law. 2-Ptn from Farly D Thompson, asking to be relieved from a certain judgment obtained against him while acting as postmaster. 3-Cmte on Claims: Hse bills, with amendment, for the relief of Jas S Calhoun, & further to continue in force the act for the payment of horses & other property lost in the military service of the U S. Same cmte: without amendment, Hse bill for the relief of Richd Rush & for the relief of Danl S Skinner. Also, an adverse report on the bill for the relief of Jas Taylor. 4-Cmte on Public Lands: a bill for the relief of John Hutchins. 5-Cmte on Public Lands: a bill for the relief of John R Williams.

The subscriber, not desiring to occupy the house in which he now resides, in Washington, longer than to Mar 1, 1843, offers the same for sale or rent, together with the adjacent ofc, & lot of ground on which both the dwlg house & ofc stand, being lot 16 in sq 489, on 5th st & Judiciary sq. The title is unquestionable. For terms apply to H H Dent, at his ofc on 4½ st, near the City Hall. -W D Merrick

Died: on Jan 23, in Winchester, Va, Mrs Miranda Collins, in her 39th year, w/o the Rev John A Collins, of the Balt Conference of the Meth Episc Chr. The dec'd had long been afflicted with a pulmonary complaint. In the important relations of dght, wife, & mother, she had probably few equals, & possibly no superiors. To her bereaved husband & their 5 sons, the loss is truly great.

Hse/o Reps: 1-Ptn of Eliz Raymond, Louisa Raymond, Sarah Flint, Rebecca Fowler, Molly Verguson, Mary Mack, Eunice Clark, Anna Chapel, Lucretia Dodge, widows of sldrs of the Revolution, & each upwards of 80 years of age, whose husbands died before the passage of any pension law, & thus they were deprived of the support enjoyed by many more favored in this respect, praying in view of their infirmities & advanced age, & the services rendered by their husbands in the struggle of the Revolutionary war, that the act of Jul 7, 1838, may be revived or relief speedily granted in some other way. 2-Memorial signed by R T Bentley, Basil Brooke, & 41 other citizens of Montg Co, Md, asking for the relief of the States. Same for Geo R Carroll & 35 citizens of Balt. Same for J F Garrard & citizens of Wash Co, Ohio. 3-Ptn of E W Clarke & 64 inhabitants of Oswego, N Y, praying that the punishment of flogging may be prohibited in the U S naval service. 4-Memorial of Rufus S Reed & divers other citizens of Erie Co, Pa, praying the adoption of the Exchequer plan submitted to Congress by the Administration. 5-Ptn of John L Reed & 17 other electors of Lorain Co, Ohio, for the abolition of slavery in the Dist of Columbia. 6-Memorial of Thos McLellan & others, citizens of Maine, praying for indemnity on account of French spoliations prior to 1801. 7-Ptn of Aaron P Grenon & others, citizens of Maine, praying for a revision of the tariff so as to impose a specific duty upon wood, brought from the North American colonies.

Submarine telescope: invention of Mrs Sarah P Mather, of Brooklyn. She has added an important improvement, which enables one standing on the deck of a vessel to view the under part of the hull as distinctly as one sees his own face in a mirror.
–N Y Com Adv

WED FEB 1, 1843
R Finley Hunt, Surgeon Dentist, from Phil, has removed his ofc to north side of Pa ave, between 9th & 10th sts, Washington, where he is prepared to perform all operations in Dental Surgeryy. [Testimonial signed: Dr Wm J A Birkey, s e corner of 8th & Locust sts, Phil, Pa.]

Hse/o Reps: 1-Cmte on the Judiciary: bill from the Senate to authorize the settlement of the account of Jos Nourse, reported the same with a recommendation that it do not pass. 2-Cmte on Private Land Claims: reported a bill to confirm Eliz Burriss, her heirs or assigns, in their title to a tract of land. 3-Same cmte: made a report on the ptn of the heirs & reps of John Peters, dec'd, with a bill for the relief of the parties. 4-Cmte on the Post Ofc & Post Roads: to which was referred the bill from the Senate entitled "An act for the relief of Wm De Buys, postmaster at New Orleans," reported the same with an amendment. 5-Ptn of Reuben Drake & 33 other inhabitants interested, praying for the establishment of a post route from Natchitoches to Monroe, La.

In Illinois, Jas Semple, Richd M Young, & John M Robinson have been elected Justices of the Supreme Court. Of the 2 last, the first now is, & the other lately was, a Senator of the U S.

Supreme Court of the U S: Jan 30, 1843. Wm Kinney, of Va, & P J Smith, of Fla, were admitted attys & counsellors of this Court. #27: F F Vidal et al, appellants, vs, the Execs of Stephen Girard. Jan 31, 1843: A P Bagby, of Alabama, was admitted an atty & counsellor of this Court. #27 was continued.

On Fri last a coroner's inquest was held at Phil on the body of Jas Hart, who committed suicide by throwing himself head foremost into a rain water cask in the yard of his residence, & suffocating. He was almost 53 years of age, & said to be in good circumstances. The cause of the act is attributed to great distress of mind & pain occasioned by hernia. Verdict,"voluntary suicide."

Reward for lost coral & gold bracelet: lost on Jan 30 between the residence of Gen John H Eaton & Mrs Abercrombie's boarding house, on 11th st. Finder may leave it at the house of Gen Eaton or at this ofc.

The Perserverance Fire Co will give $50 reward for any information which will lead to the detection of the villains who cut their Hose at the fire on Tue last.
–Saml Bacon, Capt of Hose

Senate: 1-Ptn from citizens of Phil city & county, in relation to the release of Amos Kendall. 2-Ptn from Patrick Gray, asking compensation for a horse killed in the Black Hawk war. 3-Documents presented in the cases of Wm C Murphy & Aaron Payne. 4-Ptn from Alvin C Goell, praying compensation for improvement in projectiles & military engineering. The memorialist states that he has, at great expense & loss of time, made various improvements in projectiles; that the Gov't has become possessed of his patent without affording any remuneration; & that he has suffered manifest injustice at the hands of the U S ofcrs at the arsenal, where he was directed by the Sec of War to make experiments in his machinery, by the obstructions wantonly thrown in his way, & vexatious opposition in the prosecution of his designs, for which he appeals to the justice & magnanity of Congress for relief. 5-Additional evidence presented in the claim of Eliz Dawkins. 6-Cmte on Pensions: bill granting a pension to David Welsh. 7-Cmte on Pensions: recommending that the bill from the Hse for the relief of Tirzah Hunt be indefinitely postponed.

The members of the Columbia Fire Co take this method to thank their worthy Pres Jas Adams, for his kindness & generosity in having refreshments prepared for them at his dwlg, on their return from the fire yesterday morning, which was so acceptable after their exertions. [The fire was in the stables called the "National Livery Stables," occupied by Messrs Walker & Kimmell, on C st.]

Mrd: on the 26th ult, by Rev J P Donelan, Jeremiah G Matlock to Sarah E Ames, both of Wash City.

Died: on Jan 31, at the residence of his son, Lt M F Maury, in Wash City, Mr Richd Maury, in his 77th year. His funeral is this day at 12 o'clock.

Died: on Jan 27, in his 39th year, Wm Bradford Stockton, one of the aids-de-camp of the Govn'r of N J, s/o the late Hon Richd Stockton, & brother of Capt Stockton of the Navy. At the breaking out of the Indian war in Florida, Mr Stockton was a resident of Glynn Co, Ga, & at the first report of arms he, with a small number of his friends & neighbors, hastily formed themselves into a company of cavalry, marched with the utmost speed to the banks of the Withlacoochee, & volunteered their services to Gen Clinch. They were the first body of volunteers which marched to his support, & during the whole of that perilous campaign rendered the most efficient services. Mr Stockton was recommended to the notice of the General, by whom he was appointed his aid-de-camp. After the close of the campaign he was elected by the citizens of Glynn Co to the Senate of Georgia. His health broken by the exposure of the campaign in Florida, compelled him soon to abandon his residence in the South, & to return to his native place, Princeton, N J, where he has continued to live respected & beloved by all who knew him.

Died: yesterday, in Wash City, after a long & painful illness, Mr Emanuel Longston, stonecutter, in his 28th year. His funeral is this afternoon at 3 p m.

Died: on Jan 19, in Fayette Co, Pa, after a lingering illness, in her 35th year, Mrs Mgt Ann Moore, consort of the Rev S P Moore, & d/o Mr Jas Glenn, of Wash City, leaving a disconsolate husband & 4 infant children to mourn their irreparable loss.

THU FEB 2, 1843
I wish to employ a competent person to take charge of a small School, in the immediate vicinity of my residence in Chas Co, Md. The children that will attend this school are small, & will at present require elementary instruction only.
–Wm D Merrick

For sale or rent, the 3 story brick house on Pa ave, a few doors east of 4½ st, at present occupied by Mrs Arguelles. Possession on Feb 24. Apply to Geo Watterston, Capitol Hill. Also: the subscriber will sell the farm on which he resides, on the south side of the Eastern Branch of the Potomac, about 2 miles from Wash City. –C B Hamilton

For rent, a very commodious brick dwlg house on 12th st, between C & D sts. Apply to Mrs Mary Alexander, on Pa ave, between 12th & 13th sts.

Patent Ofc: 1-Ptn of Zebulon Parker, of Licking, Ohio, praying for the extension of patent granted to Zebulon Au_ten Parker for an improvement in the percussion & re-action Water Wheel, for 7 years from the expiration of said patent, which takes place on Oct 19, 1843. 2-Ptn of Isaac Knight, of Balt, Md, praying for the extension of a patent granted to him for an improvement in Railroad Carriages for 7 years from the expiration of said patent, which takes place on Mar 18, 1843. –Henry L Ellsworth, Com'r of Patents

Senate: 1-Cmte on Finance: asking to be discharged from the further consideration of the ptns of John Golden & F Parment. 2-Cmte on the Post Ofc & Post Roads: Hse bill, with an amendment, for the relief of Peters, Moore & Co. 3-Bill introduced for the relief of Jamison & Williamson.

Hse/o Reps: 1-Mr Foster introduced to the Hse the Hon G W Crawford, member elect from the State of Georgia [vice R W Habersham, dec'd,] who was qualified & took his seat. 2-Cmte of Claims: to inquire into paying John Phagan for services he rendered the U S, under the direction of the Sec of War, in Florida among the Seminole Indians. 3-Ptn of John Odia & other citizens of Boston, praying that a national foundry & yard, for the erection of steam ships of war, may be established on the extensive lands of the U S in Boston harbor, opposite the navy yard. 4-Ptn from Danl Weed, & other citizens of Ipswich, Mass, praying for the diminution of the present rates of postage. 5-Memorial of Philip Greely & others, citizens of Maine, in relation to existing commercial arrangements with foreign countries.

Appointments by the President: 1-Jos S Murphy re-appointed Surveyor & Inspector of the Revenue at Wilmington, N C. 2-Wm G Flood re-appointed Register of the Land Ofc at Quincy, Ill. 3-Saml Leech re-appointed Receiver of Public Moneys at Quincy, Ill.

Died: on Tue last, in Gtwn, D C, John McCobb, the y/s/o Thos B & Mary Dashiell, in the 3rd year of his age.

Died: on Feb 1, Mary Eliz, only d/o Jas & Martha Leckie, aged 2 years. Friends are invited to attend her funeral today, Thu, at 3 p m.

On Jan 10, Geo Washington Brocks, aged 12 years, convicted in the U S District Court of the Southern District of Alabama of robbing the mail; was received in the pen of Alabama for the term of 2 years.

Henry German, a resident of Chester Co, Pa died last week of the "Glanders." He was bleeding a horse afflicted with that disease, when the poisonous virus entered his system through a small wound in his hand. He suffered very much.

FRI FEB 3, 1843
Lost: taken from the house of the Hon Mr Wickliffe, on the evening of Jan 31, a black cloth cloak with velvet collar & facings, & lined throught with black worsted stuff. Please send it to the house of the Misses Harrison, E st, second house west of 10th, & receive his own.

Senate: 1-Papers on file in relation to claim of Capt Shreve be & again referred. 2-Cmte of Claims: Hse bill for relief of Andrew Fisher, without amendment. 3-Cmte of Claims: Hse bill for relief of Wm W Street, without amendment. 4-Cmte on Private Land Claims: Bill to grant a tract of land to Villeneure Le Blanc, in consideration of the benefit derived to the public lands from his services in draining up the mouth of False river. 5-Cmte on Private Land Claims: bill for relief of the heirs of Wm Fisher. Same cmte: discharged from the further consideration of the ptn of Wm Gwinn. 7-Cmte on Patents: bill for the relief of Robt B Lewis.

Naval Court Martial to assemble on board the U S ship **North Carolina**, at N Y: members of the Court being 11 Capts & 2 Commanders. Capt Downes, Pres

Capt Read	Capt Smith	Capt Gwinn
Capt Bolton	Capt Storer	Capt Wyman
Capt Turner	Capt McKeever	Cmder Ogden
Capt Sloat	Capt Page	Cmder Shubrick

Wm H Norris, of Balt, Judge Advocate

Mrd: on Feb 2, at St John's Church, Gtwn, by Rev Mr Butler, Capt Bladen Dulany, of the U S Navy, to Caroline R, d/o Maj Chas J Nourse, of the District of Columbia.

The Freemen's Vigilant Total Abstinence Society will hold their meeting at F st Presby Chr [Dr Laurie's] on this evening. –E Brooke, sec

Circuit Court of Wash Co, D C. 1-Douglas Vass has filed his ptn for the benefit of the Bankrupt Law: hearing on the first Mon in Mar next. 2-Same for Wm Espey. –Wm Brent, clk

SAT FEB 4, 1843
Hse/o Reps: 1-Bill reported-An Act for the relief of Geo Mayfield. 2-Cmte on Foreign Affairs: bill for the relief of Seth Sweetser. 3-Cmte on Revolutionary Pensions: reported a bill for the relief of Hannah Jenkins, wid/o Jas Jenkins. 4-Cmte on Revolutionary Pensions: made a report on the case of John Carey, a free colored man, the servant of Gen Washington in the old French war, as also in the war of the Revolution, granting him a pension. 5-Cmte on Military Affairs: to which was referred the bill from the Senate entitled "An act for the relief of Wm De Peyster & Henry N Cruger, reported the same with amendments. 6-Cmte on Revolutionary Pensions: reported a bill for the relief of Patrick Masterson. 7-Cmte of Claims: made a report on the claim of Saml Weller, with a bill for his relief. Same cmte: reported a bill for the relief of Robt C Jennings, Jas Rody, & Robt C Jennings. Same cmte: made an adverse report upon the case of Jos E Caro. Same cmte: made adverse reports on the ptns of Saml T Anderson & Lund Washington. 8-Cmte on Commerce: made a report on the ptn of Jeremiah & Moses Noble, owners & crew of the schnr **Privado**, with a bill for their relief. 9-Cmte on Commerce: adverse report on the ptn of Adam McCulloch. 10-Cmte on Invalid Pensions: adverse reports on the cases of John H Lincoln, Lewis Gordon, & John R Bold. 11-Cmte on Indian Affairs: made an adverse report on the ptn of Mgt C Murray. 12-Cmte on Invalid Pensions: adverse report on the case of Job Wood. 13-Cmte on Commerce: made a report on the ptn of Benj Fearing & others, with a bill for the relief of the owners of the schnr **Joseph**, of Wareham. 13-Cmte of the Whole: the bill granting a pension to John Carey was read a 3rd time & passed. 14-Cmte of the Whole: be discharged from the further consideration of the bill for the relief of Jas C Watson, of Ga.
15-Ptn of Col Hugh W Dobbin, praying compensation for services during the late war with Great Britain. 16-Memorial of Jas Ingersoll & 47 others, merchants of Boston, on the subject of the lumber & molasses trade. 17-Memorial of Windsor Fay & others, of Boston, in reference to the drawback on rum. 18-Ptn of Wm McCabe, of Clark Co, Ill, praying to be paid for a horse lost in the service of the U S.

Circuit Court of Wash Co, D C. Edw Smith has filed his ptn for the benefit of the Bankrupt Law: hearing on the first Mon of Mar next. –Wm Brent, clk

The house of Luther Campbell, about half a mile south of the village of Rush, N Y, was consumed by fire on Jan 25. Mr Campbell was considerably burnt about the face & hands in attempting to rescue a child. His son, about 15 years old, went in to get some furniture, as it is supposed, but was unable to make his way out, & became a sacrifice in the effort.

Senate: 1-Cmte on Naval Affairs: Hse bill for the relief of Mrs Anne W Angus without amendment, & recommending that it be indefinitely postponed. 2-Cmte on Pensons: adverse reports on Hse bills for the relief of John Farnham; for the relief of Jonathan Britton; for the relief of the heirs & legal reps of Wm Lomax.

Orphan's Court of Wash Co, D C. Letters testamentary on the personal estate of Nicholas Harper, late of Wash Co, dec'd. -Patrick Tracy, exc

Died: Feb 2, Marian Theresa, d/o Peter & Rowena Callan, aged 4 months & 19 days.

Supreme Court of the U S: Feb 2, 1843. #28: Robt Porterfield, vs, Wm Clarke's heirs & devisees.

Appointment by the Pres: Wm G Hammond re-appointed Surveyor of the Revenue at Newport, R I.

Laws of the U S passed at the 3rd Session of the 27th Congress. 1-An Act to revive the act for the relief of Mary Tucker: that the act approved on Feb 27, 1842, be revived & continued in force for the term of 12 months from the passage of this act. 2-Act for the relief of the administrator of John Jackson: Sec of the Treas authorized to enter credits of $100. & $650. to the account upon the books of the Treas Dept against Capt John Jackson, dec'd, so as to stop interest upon $100 of any balance that may stand against him on said books, from Apr 27, 1836, & upon $650 of said balance, from May 19, 1836. 3-Act for the relief of Saml Hambleton: that the Sec of the Navy is authorized to cause to be settled the account of Saml Hambleton for ofc rent & clerk hire while he was on duty as purser in the navy yard at Pensacola, in 1826 thru 1829; &, in such settlment, to cause to be allowed to him at the rate of $600 a year for clerk-hire, & $350 for house rent & ofc rent, from Aug 21, 1826, until sufficient accommodations were put up by the Gov't at the said navy yard for the accommodation of the purser with house & ofc room. 4-Act for the relief of Eliz Munroe, of Boon Co, Missouri: that she or her legal rep, upon the surrender, at the proper land ofc, to be cancelled, of the certificate for the east half of the s w qrtr of section #31, township #58, range #21, entered for her by mistake at the land ofc at Fayette, Mo; &, upon the surrender of said certificate, shall be, & they are hereby, authorized to enter 80 acs of land upon which she has located & made her improvements, & which she, at the time of said entry, supposed she was locating: Provided, that the land upon which she settled shall not, previous to the date of this act, have been sold by the U S. Approved, Jan 28, 1843.

Pension Agency: the subscriber for the last 2 years has been engaged in the examination of claims for Revolutionary services in the Pension Ofc. –Henry H Sylvester

MON FEB 6, 1843
Hair cuts @ 25 cents & shaves @ .12½ cents is the uniform practice. You can get the same for just half the sum, & warranted to be inferior to none in the District. Shop is at the corner of 6th st & Pa ave. Started in the spring of 1842, by me & me alone. –Jas A Ratcliffe

Naval Court Martial: Court read this paper: The undersigned beg leave to state to the Court Martial assembled for the trial of Cmder Alex'r Slidell Mackenzie, that they have been employed by the relatives of acting Midshipman Philip Spencer, one of the persons for the murder of whom Cmder Mackenzie is upon trial, to attend the trial & take part therein, as such counsel, if permitted by the Court. [They want to exam & cross-exam the witnesses.] -B F Butler, Chas O'Conner REPLY of the Court: "The Court, after mature deliberation, are of opinion that the above paper be put on record, and decide that the application contained in it be not granted."

Circuit Court of Wash Co, D C. Henry B Foster: Jas Nokes: Nelson R Robertson: have filed for the benefit of the Bankrupt Law: hearing for each one will be on the first Mon in Mar next. –Wm Brent, clk

The sword actually used by Gen Washington during the Revolutionary war will be presented to Congress tomorrow at 12 o'clock, in the Hse/o Reps, by a member of the Va delegation. It is presented at the request of the reps of Gen Washington, in whose possession it has been.

The Nashville Whig announces the death, on Jan 25, of Robt Woods, a member of the well-known firm of Yeatmen, Woods & Co. Mr Woods was a native of Western Va, but has been for many years a citizen of Nashville. He stood alike eminent & respected as the successful merchant, the honest banker, & the sincere & devoted philanthropist & Christian.

On Fri night a marine, named Griffith, serving on board the ship **Independence**, lying in N Y harbor, having been refused leave of absence, jumped overboard with the intention of swimming to the shore. The tide was too strong for him, & he was swept away in spite of all the efforts of a boat's crew to save him.

Died: on Sat last, Mr Wm Worthington, in his 68th year. His funeral will be from his late residence, at half past one o'clock this afternoon.

On Feb 3, Jas Hannahan, formerly a dry goods & grocery merchant, at Warwick, Orange Co, N Y, age about 40 years, was found hanging by the neck with a silk handkerchief, which had been first appended to a pile of shingles in the lumber-yard of Messrs Centine & Co, corner of Clarkson & Wests sts. He had been unfortunate in business, at least as far as could be learned. He has left a wife & 3 small children. –Evening Post

Hse/o Reps: Bills passed, viz: 1-Bill granting a pension to John Cary. 2-Bill for the relief of the legal reps of W T Smith. 3-Relief of Thos Weaver & Jacob Heyberger, sureties of the Norristown & Valley Railroad. 4-Bill for the relief of John Skirving. 5-Bill for the relief of John McGinnis. 6-Bill to confirm Eliz Barnes, her heirs & assigns, to their title to a tract of land. 7-Bill for the relief of the legal reps of John Peters. 8-Bill for the relief of Seth Sweetser. 9-Bill for the relief of Hannah Jenkins, wid/o Jas Jenkins. 10-Relief of Nancy Williams. 11-Relief of Ephraim D Dickson. 12-Relief of Patrick Masterson. 13-Memorial of Chas Gibbons & 37 others, citizens of Phil, praying Congress to create a national stock of two hundred millions of dollars, to be distributed among the States & Territories, & the Dist of Col, by an equitable allotment, on the basis of representation. 14-Memorial of Harry McLaughlin, & 32 other citizens of Centre Co, Pa, of a similar import. 15-Ptn of the surviving children of Winifred Tomlinson, for a pension. 16-Ptn of Abram Keen, for a pension. 17-Ptn of Frances Crafton, for a pension. 18-Ptn of D G Dorrance & others, citizens of Oneida Co, N Y, asking for the passage of the Exchequer plan by the present Congress. 19-Ptn of Paul L Clerc & 109 other inhabitants of the parishes of Terrebenne, St Mary, & Assumption, praying for a post route from Houama to Dutch Settlement, Louisiana. 20-Ptn of Geo S Wahusly & 14 others, & Henry O McEmery & 133 others, praying for a post route direct from Natchitoches to Monroe, Louisiana. 21-Ptn of Aaron Blinn & others, of Columbia Co, N Y, praying a renewal of the pension act for the benefit of the widow of Revolutionary ofcrs & sldrs. 22-Memorial signed by C M Thruston & 200 citizens of Cumberland, Md, praying Congress to issue two hundred millions of Gov't stock, to be divided for the relief of all the States & Territories. Also, a memorial of similar import, signed by Washington Keith & a large number of other citizens of Pa.

TUE FEB 7, 1843
Trustee sale of valuable real estate: decree in #1777 on the equity docket of Fred'k Co Court: sale on Mar 11 at the tavern of Mr Gilbert, in Fred'k, the FARM on which Mr Wm Eader has resided for a number of years, lying on the Balt turnpike, about 1 mile from Fred'k, containing about 222 acs; improvements are a log dwlg hse, brick barn, & outbldgs. Also, between one & two hundred acres of Woodland, on the south side of the Balt turnpike, 4 miles from Fred'k. Also, a lot of ground, fronting on Market st, near the Farmers' & Mechanics' Bank. –G M Eichelberger, trustee

Circuit Court of Wash Co, D C. Jacob Staub; : Thos Lumpkin; & Jas W Brown: have filed their ptns for the benefit of the Bankrupt Law: hearing for each on the first Mon in Mar next. –Wm Brent, clk

Senate: 1-Ptn from Saml James, a Revolutionary sldr, asking a renewal of his pension. 2-Cmte on Public Lands: bill for the relief of Jos Robey. 3-Ptn from John Howell & others, asking to be relieved from a judgment obtained against them as sureties of Thos J Wilson, late postmaster at Trenton. 4-Ptn from Jos W Kirk, in relation to an invention which he claims to be of great value in taking snags from the Western rivers. He asks Congress to purchase his patent, or to appropriate a small sum to test its efficacy. 5-Ptn from Jacob Waggoner, asking to be allowed to change a certain tract of land. 6-Ptn of John Rodgers & others, Cherokee Indians, on the subject of their claims against Gov't. 7-Ptn from Geo E Payne, in relation to the settlement of certain claims.

Hse/o Reps: 1-Cmte of Claims: favorable report with a bill for restoring Amos Kendall to his personal liberty. 2-Cmte of Claims: adverse reports in the cases of Wm Clendening & Ira Carpenter. 3-Cmte of Claims: a favorable report on the case of Geo Harrison, with a bill for his relief. 4-Cmte on Indian Affairs: adverse report on the case of Caleb Atwater. 5-Cmte on Invalid Pensions: adverse reports on the ptns of Thos W Drewry, Jno R Knott, reps of Wilfred Knott, Catharine H T Johnson, & Dan Stevens.

Orphans Crt of Chas Co, Md. Letters testamentary on the personal estate of Henry C Bruce, late of said county, dec'd. -John R Fergusson, exc

Circuit Court of Wash Co, D C. Thos B Addison, bankrupt, has filed his ptn for his discharge & certificate: hearing on the first Mon in Jun next. –Wm Brent, clk

The steam Flouring Mill & New Foundry bldgs of Henry Wise, near Fredericktown, East Bethlehem township, in Wash Co, Pa, were burnt to the ground on Jan 26: loss is very heavy. The fire is supposed to be the work of an incendiary.

WED FEB 8, 1843
Hse/o Reps: 1-Memorial of Mrs S J Jackson, wid/o Pierce Jackson, asking for a pension. 2-Ptn of Timothy Dever, for a pension. 3-Ptn of John N Snassey & 42 other inhabitants of Arrington, Maine, for an increase of duties on lumber, wood, bark, & fish. Like ptn of Timothy Nye & 44 other inhabitants of Bucksport, Maine.

Fires in Balt: warehouse at the corner of Pratt st & Cheapside, occupied by Messrs A M Fenby & Co, was destroyed on Sun last. On Mon night fire occurred in the dry-good store of Mr H Diffenderffer, on Balt st, near Gay st, which spread through the premises.

Hse/o Reps: Mr Saml T Washington, a citizen of Kanawha Co, Va, presents in his name & on his behalf, to the Congress of the U S, the sword worn by Geo Washington, first as a Colonel in the Colonial service of Va, in Forbee's campaign against the French & Indians, & afterwards during the whole period of the war of Independence as Cmder-in-Chief of the American Army. It is plain couteau, or hanger, with a green belt & silver guard. On the upper ward of the scabbard is engraven, "J. Bailey, Fish Kill." It is accompanied by a buckskin belt, which is secured by a silver buckle & clasp, whereon are engraven the letters "G. W." and the figures "1757." These are all of the plainest workmanship, but substantial & in keeping with the man & with the times to which they belonged. The decorum of the Hse had kept every man in his seat while the addresses were in delivery, but no sooner had the adjournment been announced, & the Speaker left the chair, than there was a simultaneous rush from all qrtrs to obtain a nearer view of the memorials: every hand was outstretched to touch them. Letter from Saml T Washington, with the Sword & Cane presented to Congress. Coal's Mouth, Kanawha Co, Va: Jan 9, 1843. My Dear Sir: with this, you will receive the war-sword of my grand-uncle, Gen Geo Washington, & the gold headed cane bequeathed to him by Dr Benj Franklin. These interesting relics I wish to be presented, through you, my dear sir, to the Congress of the U S, on behalf of the nation. Congress can dispose of them in such manner as shall seem most appropriate, & best calculated to keep in memory the character & services of those two illustrious founders of our Republic. I am, with esteem, yours, Samuel T Washington. /To Hon Geo W Summers, Hse/o Reps. Letter from Col Geo C Washington: Gtwn-Jan 3, 1843. Gen Washington, by his will, made disposition of his swords in the following words: "To each of my nephews, William Augustine Washington, George Lewis, George Steptoe Washington, Bushrod Washington, & Samuel Washington, I give one of the swords, or couteaux, of which I may die possessed; & they are to choose in the order they are named. These swords are accompanied with an injunction not to unsheath them for the purpose of shedding blood, except it be for self-defence, or in defence of their country and its rights; and in the latter case, to keep them unsheathed, and prefer falling with them in their hands to the relinquishment thereof." I often heard my father say that he would have preferred the sword selected by Col Saml Washington, from the fact that it was used by the Gen during the Revolutionary war. The cane presented to Congress was the property of the philosopher & patriot Benjamin Franklin. By a codicil to his last will & testament [Franklin,] we find it thus disposed of: "My fine crab-tree walking stick, with a gold head, curiously wrought in the form of the cap of Liberty, I give to my friend, & the friend of mankind, Gen Washington. If it were a scepter, he has merited it and would become it." Gen Washington, in his will, devises this cane as follows: "Item. To my brother, Charles Washington, I give and bequeath the gold-headed cane left me by Dr Franklin in his will." Capt Samuel Washington was the only son of Chas Washington, the devisee from whom he derived, by inheritance, this interesting memorial; and, having transmitted it to his son, Saml T Washington.

Mr Wm Cook, who shipped a large quantity of stock on board the boat **Ohio Belle** last week, for New Orleans, & accompanied them, accidentally stepped off the boat, on Sun, just below Madison, Ind, & was drowned. He had connexions in Bourbon & Nicholas Counties, Ky. -Ibid

Died: on Feb 1, at Greencastle, Pa, the Hon David Fullerton, in his 72nd year. He formerly represented in Congress the district in which he resided, & afterwards for several years represented his county in the State Leg, discharging his public duties always faithfully & most conscientiously.

Died: on Feb 2, in Gtwn, D C, after an illness of 2 weeks, Richd Pierce, in his 24th year. He was one of Nature's noblemen-an honest man.

Died: on Jan 28, at Romney, Va, in his 73rd year, Dr Robt Newman. As a physician, he was eminently successful, & commanded for a long period of years, the entire confidence of the mass of the community in which he lived.

Senate: 1-Adverse report on the bill for the relief of Thos H Brown. 2-Papers on file belonging to the claim of John W Skidder: asked to withdraw same. 3-Cmte on the Post Ofc & Post Roads: Hse bill, with an amendment, for the relief of S & M Ritchie. 4-Cme of Claims: Hse bill for the relief of D & J Wilkinson, with a recommendation that it be indefinitely postponed.

Appointments by the President: P S Loughborough, Atty of the U S for the district of Ky, reappointed.
Consuls:
Saml McLean, of Missouri, for Cien Fuegos, in the Island of Cuba.
Jas McHenry, of Phil, for Londonderry.
Chas H Delavan, of N Y, for Sydney, Nova Scotia, vice John J D'Wolf, resigned.
A M Green, of Va, for Galveston.
Robt B Campbell, of Ala, for Havana.
Chas Nichols, of Pa, for Amsterdam.
Elisha Hathaway, jr, for Hobart Town, in Van Diemen's Land.
John P Adams, of Balt, for Laguaura, vice Benj Renshaw, dec'd.

Supreme Court of the U S: Feb 7, 1843. B W Bonney & Wm Coventry H Waddell, of N Y, were admitted attys & counselors of this Court. #12: McClurg, Parry & Higby, vs Kingsland, Lightner & Co. In error to the Circuit Court U S for Pa. Opinion of this Court: affirms the judgment of the said Circuit Court in this cause with costs. #74: Wm Nelson, a petitioner in bankruptcy. On a certificate of division of opinion between the Judges of the Circuit Court U S for Ky. Mr Chief Justice Taney delivered the opinion of this Court, dismissing this cause for the want of jurisdiction. #29: J C C Bell et al, plntfs in error, vs Mathias Bruen.

Circuit Court of Wash Co, D C. Ignatius Chutkowski, a bankrupt, has filed his ptn for his discharge & certificate: hearing on the first Mon in Jun next. –W Brent, clk

THU FEB 9, 1843
Having sold out my entire property in the Grocery corner of E & 7th sts to Mr Wm Anderson, the business will hereafter be carried on at the same place, at the most reduced prices for cash. –W B Burger

For rent: 2 story brick house, north side of Bridge st, Gtwn, near the bridge.
–Saml McKenney

Persons requiring bread will find a comfortable loaf prepared for them this morning, on application at Geo Krafft's Bakery, corner of Pa ave & 18th st.

Public sale of valuable land: decree of Montg Co Court as a Court of Equity: in the case of Allen B Davis vs John Brewer, administrator of Elhanan W Reinhart & others: sale on the premises, on Mar 4, the farm in said county, 2 miles n w of Tennally town, containing 167 acs of land, more or less, being the lands sold by the cmplnt to the late Elhanan W Reinhart, & formerly owned by Adam Young. Improvements are a comfortable frame dwlg, a large barn, & an orchard.
–Richd I Bowie, trustee

Worcester Co Court, Nov Term, 1842. In the matter of the ptn of John C Stevenson for the division of the real estate whereof Jos Stevenson died seized. The com'rs made return that the same is not susceptible of division without loss & injury to all parties. Notice to be given to John C Stevenson, Jas S Stevenson, & Joel L Stevenson, & Mary B Stevenson, Nancy Stevenson, Lydia J Stevenson, & Esther G Stevenson, parties entitled to elect to take said estate at the valuation, & who are absent, out of the State of Md, that May 2 next is appointed for said parties to appear & make their election. –Gordon M Handy, clk

Circuit Court of Wash Co, D C. Jas H Upperman, a bankrupt, has filed his ptn for his discharge & certificate: hearing on the first Mon in Jun next. –Wm Brent, clk

Circuit Court of Wash Co, D C. Jos S Potter has filed his ptn for the benefit of the Bankrupt Law: hearing on the first Mon of Mar next. –Wm Brent, clk

Columbian Lyceum: lecture this evening at half past 7 o'clock, by J E Norris.
–John T Mickum, Jas Overstreet, John T Pardy, Lecture Cmte

FRI FEB 10, 1843
Meeting of the Stockholders of the steamboat **Phenix** on Feb 13, at 11 a m, at the ofc in Alexandria. -Stephen Shinn, treasurer

A splendid Gold Medal will be presented to the Hon Geo N Briggs, of Mass, by the Freeman's Vigilant Total Abstinence Society, as a mark of their high regard for his labors in the cause of total abstinence. The medal will be presented by the Hon Thos F Marshall at the Apollo Hall, on Feb 10. Doors open at 6 p m.

For New Orleans, the splendid bark **Parthian**, Capt G W Allen, will sail from Richmond about Mar 1. For steerage or cabin passage, having elegant state room accommodations, apply to A C Pleasants, Richmond, Va.

Notice. To prevent further advantage being taken of my children, I forewarn all persons from receiving nine notes, dated Nov 1, 1839, drawn in favor of Peter Brady, for $450, as I am determined not to pay any person except my children, who are the only persons authorized to receive the same. --R M Beall

Yesterday, a white man, Jas Bevan, recently escaped from the work-house, called at the dwlg of a respectable gentleman on 7th st to beg victuals. He was kindly fed in the kitchen & the ungrateful fellow stole a silver spoon & made his way to the street. He was followed by Silas Moore, constable, & arrested. He confessed the theft & was committed for trial at the next Criminal Court.

$100 for my pointer dog Lara, of a yellow color, who disappeared a few days ago. --Chas Lee Jones

On Fri at Eaton square, Pimlico, at a house now being finished for the Earl of Denbigh, it appears that a large cornice had just been fixed against the side of the bldg by the bricklayers, which fell, causing the acaffolding to give way, & 3 men fell 40 feet. The Countess of Denbigh, who was passing at the time, witnessed the scene, & was so affected that she was instantly conveyed home, & we regret to say, that her ladyship expired before the day closed. The Countess was *enceinte*, & has had 11 children. The poor men were conveyed to St George's Hospital. -Chronicle

Hse/o Reps: 1-Cmte of Claims: made a report on the ptn of Matilda Drewry, one of the legal reps of Capt Wm Smallwood Tillan, with a bill for the relief of the said legal reps. Same cmte: made an unfavorable report on the case of Clark Allen. 2-Cmte on the Judiciary: to which was referred the bill from the Senate entitled "An act for the relief of Richd Henry Wilde," reported the same without amendment. 3-Cmte on Private Land claims: made a report on the ptn of Jas Pepper, with a bill for his relief.

Orphan's Court of Wash Co, D C. Letters of administration, with the will annexed, on the personal estate of Francis S Key, late of said county, dec'd. --Jno A Smith, adm, with the will annexed

Senate: 1-Ptn from Mary Gordon. 2-Cmte on Public Lands: bill for the relief of John Wagoner. Also, a bill for the relief of Richd Dewit & Ira J Price, with amendments. Also, asking to be discharged from the further consideration of the memorial of David Irvin & others, & that they have leave to withdraw their papers. Also, from the same cmte, Hse bill for the relief of Garret Vleit, with amendments. 2-Cmte on Commerce: adverse reports on the following bills from the Hse with a written report on each: for the relief of the owners, master, & crew of the schnr **Cod Hook**, of Blue Hill, Maine. For the relief of the owners of the schnr **Three Brothers**. For the relief of John Patten, owner of the fishing schnr **Credit**. For the relief of Levi Eldridge & others. For the relief of Mary Broadstreet, Amos Tappan, & others. For the relief of John H Russell & others, as owners, master, & crew of the fishing schnr **Lucy Ann**. For the relief of Wm Ellery, owner of the fishing schnr **Sevo & Ida**, both of Gloucester, Mass, & others. For the relief of Barnabas Baker, jr, & others, owners of the fishing schnr **Union**, of Dennis, Mass. For the relief of Joshua Knowles, jr, & others, owners of the fishing schnr **Garnet**. Also, from the same cmte, an adverse report on the ptn of Jas Hall & Thos Curtis. Also, from the same cmte, Hse bill for the relief of Knott Martin & Arnold Martin, owners of the fishing schnr **Only Son**, without amendment, & recommending its passage. 3-Cmte of Claims: Hse bills for the relief of Teakle Savage, administrator of Bolitha Laws; & for the relief of the legal reps of Francis Peilicer, without amendment, & recommending that they be indefinitely postponed. 4-Hse bill for the relief of the legal reps of Wm S Eveleth, without amendment, & recommending its passage. 5-Cmte on Finance: Hse bill for the relief of Wm Selden, Treas of the U S, with an amendment; which, on motion, was considered in Cmte of the Whole, & ordered to a 3rd reading. 6-Cmte on Private Land Claims: House bill, without amendment, for the relief of the heirs of Philander Smith & Jas Young. Also, from the same cmte, asking to be discharged from the further consideration of the ptn of Wm Wynn, asking to be confirmed in his title to certain lands. 7-Cmte on Naval Affairs: asking to be discharged from the further consideration of the memorial of McKean Buchanan, a purser in the navy, with a written report. Also, to be discharged from the further consideration of the ptn of Thos Ragsdale, & that he have leave to withdraw his papers. 8-Cmte on Military Affairs: bill for the relief of John Moore. 9-Cmte on Indian Affairs: Hse bill for the relief of Geo C Johnson, without amendment. 10-Cmte on Finance: a joint resolution authorizing the Sec of the Treas, to settle, on certain conditions, the liabilities of the sureties of Gordon S Boyd, with an amendment. 11-Bills indefinitely postponed: relief of Dexter Hungerford, of Watertown, N Y. Relief of Orrin Prentiss & others, of Stonington, Conn. Relief of Isaiah Champlin. 12-Cmte of the Whole: bill for the relief of Caspar W Wever: ordered to be read a 3rd time. 13-Bill from the Hse for the relief of the reps of Alex'r Macomb, Robt Jennings, & others, sureties of Saml Champlin, late a paymaster in the army, was passed.

Naval Court Martial: opinion of the Court in the mutiny on board the brig **Somers**. Cmder Mackenzie was not bound to risk the safety of his vessel, & jeopardy the lives of the young ofcrs & the loyal of his crew, in order to secure to the guilty the forms of trial, & that the immediate execution of the prisoners was demanded by duty & justified by necessity. The conduct of Cmder Mackenzie & his ofcrs was prudent, calm, & firm, & that he & they honorable performed their duty to the service & their country. –Chas Stewart, Pres of the Court -Ogden Hoffman, Judge Advocate

Louisiana Chronicle of Jan 21: Jas Fort Muse, an old & highly respected citizen of the parish of Point Coupee, was crushed to death a few days since by a tree falling upon him.

A son of Mr Rufus Soule, of Lisbon, Maine, was killed there last Fri by a horse which he was leading to water. The lad slipped down on the ice and the horse stepped on his head, fracturing his skull.

Mrd: on Feb 8, in Wash City, by Rev Dr Hawley, Francis A Worthington, of Chillicothe, Ohio, to Jane Taylor, eldest d/o Maj Mann P Lomax, late of U S Army.

Mrd: by the Rev Mr O'Flannagan, Mr Clement I Sewell to Miss Sarah E Graves, both of Gtwn, D C. [No date-current item.]

Mrd: on Feb 9, at Mr S Hyatt's, by Rev Mr Rich, Mr Christopher H Brashears, of PG Co, Md, to Miss Jane Giller, of Wash City.

Died: on Jan 15, at Guines, Island of Cuba, Benj F Allan, s/o the Hon Chilton Allan, of Winchester, Ky, in his 33rd year. The dec'd was a young man of bright promise, endowed by nature with high capacities, improved & adorned by assiduous cultivation.

SAT FEB 11, 1843
Hse/o Reps: 1-Memorial of Isaiah Hooker & 62 other citizens of Pa, praying the issue of 200,000,000 of stock by Gov't to be divided among all the States for their relief. 2-Memorial of M R Bartlett, regarding currency. 3-Ptn of Jas Dallas, & 35 other citizens of Champagne Co, Ohio, praying for the passage of a law for the relief of the States according to the plan proposed by the Hon W Cost Johnson. 4-Ptn of Wm Wheatly, clerk of the penitentiary in D C, praying the allowance of compensation for certain services rendered to the institution.

Circuit Court of Wash Co, D C. Alfred Taylor, & Jas M Cutts, & Jacob Colclazer, have filed their ptns for the benefit of the Bankrupt Law: hearing on the first Mon in Mar next. –Wm Brent, clk

Senate: 1-Cmte on Pensions: Hse bill for the relief of Judd White, without amendment. 2-Cmte of Claims: asking to be discharged from the further consideration of the ptn of Israel Kitcham. Also, same cmte: adverse report on the ptn of Nimrod Farrow & Richd Harris. 3-Cmte on the Judiciary: asking to be discharged from the further consideration of Hse bill for the relief of Thos Weaver & Jacob Haymaker, sureties of the Norristown & Valley Railroad Co, & that it be referred to the Cmte on Finance. 4-Cmte on Pensions: Hse bill for the relief of Jas Gray, with amendment. 5-Cmte on Military Affairs: a bill for the relief of F A Kerr. Same cmte: a bill for the relief of the legal reps of Wm W Walker. 6-Cmte on Pensions: adverse reports on Hse bills for the relief of Eliz Whiteman & of Wm Patterson; also, on House bill for the relief of Samson Brown, with written reports with each case. Also, asking to be discharged from the further consideration of the ptn of Eliz Hilleman, on the ground that she was entitled to relief from the Dept. 7-Cmte on Commerce: a joint resolution to authorize an experiment to test the ability of an invention of Jos W Kirk, as a Mississippi boat fender. 8-Mr Young, on leave, introduced a bill for the relief of John W Skidmore. 9-Bill for the relief of the heirs of Wm Fisher, was considered in Cmte of the whole, & ordered to be engrossed. 10-Following bills that were passed: bill for the relief of Caspar W Wever. Bill for the relief of Wm Selden & others.

The undersigned, a cmte appointed by the Antrim parish, are desirous of receiving proposals for the bldg of an Episcopal Church at Halifax Court-house, Va, to be completed within the present year. –J Grammer, C H Cabaniss, Wm Holt, Cmte: Halifax Court-house, Va

Valuable Fairfax Farm for sale: two deeds of trust from Geo Beard to the undersigned, dated Feb 8, 1839, & Mar 16, 1840, recorded in the County Court of Fairfax, Va: the farm called **Red Hill**, owned & occupied by Geo Beard, containing about 400 acs: in an excellent state of improvement. It is situated about 7 miles from Gtwn, 10 from Wash, in the immediate vicinity of the late Dr Mathew Ball, Com Thos Ap C Jones, & adjoining the land formerly owned by Rev Wm Maffit & others. Maj Beard, who resides on the premises, will show the farm. –T R Love, trustee

Dissolution of the partnership by mutual consent, the Saddle, Harness, & Trunk Business, heretofore existing between Richd W Polkinhorn & Danl Campbell. Danl Campbell will continue the business.

Died: on Jan 24, at his father's residence, in Upper Marlborough, Wm Fowler, in his 32nd year.

Died: on Feb 9, after a protracted illness, Mrs Eliz Edwards McIntire, consort of Alex'r McIntire, in her 45th year. The dec'd was the oldest d/o the late Joshua John Moore, one of the oldest settlers of Wash City. Her funeral is on Sun next, at 1 o'clock *precisely*. Residence on 19th st, between G & H sts.

Died: on Jan 31, near Rockville, Montg Co, Md, at the residence of her mother-in-law, in her 29th year, after a short illness, Mrs Charlotte Prather, consort of Mr

Singleton Prather, & d/o the late Mr Thos Crusselle, of Wash City. The dec'd emigrated from Wash City a few years ago to Decatur, Ill, & but lately returned on a visit to her relatives & friends, when she was struck by the hand of death. She has left a husband, 3 children, & numerous relatives to mourn her untimely death.

Miss S M Peale, Portrait Painter, at Mr Johnson's, E st, between 10th & 11th sts.

For sale: N J Peach & Ornamental Trees. Call at the store of Tucker & Son.
-Enoch Tucker

MON FEB 13, 1843
Drowned, on Fri last, in the Eastern Branch of the Potomac, not far from the residence of Capt Jos Johnson, a colored man named Jeff or Jeffry.

Wash Corp: 1-An act for the relief of John France: that the fine imposed on John France by judgment of J D Clark for an alleged violation of the law in relation to the sale of lottery tickets, be, & the same is remitted: provided he pay the costs of prosecution. 2-Act for the relief of Henry Neale: that the fines imposed on Henry Neale by several judgments of Saml Drury, dated May 10, 1842, for an alleged violation of law respecting hackney carriages, together with the costs of prosecution, be, & the same are hereby, remitted.

Orphans Court of Chas Co, Md. Letters of administration on the personal estate of Philip A L Contee, formerly of said county, latterly of Alexandria, D C, dec'd.
--Josias Hawkins, adm

Orphan's Court of Wash Co, D C. Letters of administration on the personal estate of John Kincaid, late of the State of Louisiana, dec'd. --Clement Cox, adm

On Thu last a wagoner, named McGee, was run over & crushed to death by his wagon a short distance from Finksburg, Carroll Co, Md, on his way from Balt. He was a single man, about 23 years of age, the s/o a widow woman who resides in Franklin Co, Pa.

Arthur McGonagle, a respectable citizen of Pottsville, was crushed between a loaded car & a post in that city, on Sat last, & so severely injured that he died the next day.

Mr John Thomas, master & owner of the schnr **Florida**, while passing down the bay from Balt on Mon, encountered a squall of wind which caused the main boom to strike his head, knocking him overboard. The body was soon recovered & taken on shore, where, in a few minutes, life became extinct.

Abraham C Skillman, of Mercer Co, N J, age 15 years, lost his hand on Jan 28, by its being caught in a machine for threshing clover.

Mr Wm F Allen, a Jersey pilot, belonging to the N J pilot boat **Savannah**, was lost overboard on Sunday during the heavy easterly gale. All attempts to save him proved ineffectual. –Jour Com

The woolen factory, owned & occupied by Mr Benj Kent, situated on the line of Chester & Lancaster Counties, in Pa, was burn down on Jan 24. The dwlg of Mr Kent, separated from the factory by a public road, was also consumed with nearly all the furniture. Loss from $7,000 to $8,000.

Hse/o Reps: 1-Memorial of Danl Heively & 122 citizens of Pa, praying for an issue of Gov't stock to the amount of the indebtedness of the States. Also, from John S Hust & 40 others on the same subject. 2-Memorial of Hall J Kelly, agent of Chas Bulfinch & others, in relation to claims to certain lands in the Territory of Oregon. 3-Ptn of Matthew Tucker, of Mass, for a naval pension.

A stray bull came to the farm of Jas Moore [called the ***Mooreland Farm***] about the middle of Jan last. The owner is requested to come forward, prove property, pay charges, & take him away. –Wm Murrey, for Jas Moore

Circuit Court of Wash Co, D C. John J Wilkins has filed his ptn for the benefit of the Bankrupt Law: hearing on the first Mon in Mar next. –Wm Brent, clk

TUE FEB 14, 1843
For rent: the residence of the late F S Key, on C st, next to Maj Selden's. Inquire of J A Smith, at the City Hall.

Trustees sale of valuable mill property & land: deed of trust, dated Apr 6, 1841, from John P Smart to the undersigned, as trustees for the benefit of Geo Rust, jr, & John Richardson, recorded in Loudoun Co, in liber P P P P, folio 116: sale in front of the Court-house in Leesburg, Va, on Mar 13. The ***Big Spring Mills***, on the banks of the Potomac: attached to the mills are 40 acres of land. The ***Goshen Farm***, containing 442 acres of land, with the Ferry attached, known as ***Edwards' Ferry***. On it there are a comfortable dwlg house, dairy, fine well of water, & stabling. –Wm B Tyler, Thos Rogers, trustees

Public sale: by a deed dated May 13, 1841, by Robt Speiden to the subscriber: sale in front of the premises on Mar 15 next, all the estate & interest of the said R Speiden in: Lot #6 in sq 15 in Wash City, fronting 54 feet on K st & 75 feet on 26th st, with the cooper's shop, bldgs, & other improvements thereon. Also, the implements of trade belonging to the said shop. –W Redin, trustee

Houses for sale: subscriber wishes to sell or rent 2 frame houses on H st, between 10th & 11th sts; one on N st, near the Twenty Bldgs, & one in an eligible part of the

Northern Liberties. The last memtioned house is now in building, & will probably be enclosed in 5 or 6 weeks; its sale would be preferred after it shall be finished. Also, several valuable lots of ground, on Capitol Hill & in the Northern Liberties. Apply to Thos M Milburn, on B st north, between 10th & 11th sts west.

The subscribers will sell or rent the Hotel Stand at present occupied by them, & formerly kept by Mr Richd D Burroughs, in Upper Marlborough, PG Co, Md, including the furniture. –Saml Y Harris & Co.

From Florida: Gen Abram Eustis, U S A, & Lt Col E A Hitchcock, U S A, came passengers to Savannah in the ship **St Matthews**. The former ofcr is on his way to visit his family in Beaufort district, the latter to join his regt, near Tallahassee.

Died: yesterday, in his 23rd year, Edw Preble, s/o Jas Leander Cathcart, of Wash City. His funeral is on Feb 15, at 3 p m, which the friends & acquaintances of the family are respectfully invited to attend.

Died: on Sun last, of a short attack of croup, aged 9 months & 6 days, Susan Watts, child of Philip Kearny, U S A, & of Diana Kearny.

Mrd: on Sun last, by Rev John P Donelan, Mr Simeon D Bronson to Miss Julia Ann Thomas, d/o Capt Wm Thomas, all of Wash.

Phil, Feb 11. The affair involving the suspected abduction of a young lady of Southwark, has had an awful termination. Mr Mahlon Hutchinson Heberton, the alleged abductor, fell last evening, shot by the hand of the brother of the latter when he arrived by the ferry boat **John Fitch**, at Camden. The brother who committed the deed was Singleton Mercer, a clerk in the store of Messrs Carson & Newbold, south wharves. Mercer was taken into custody immediately. –Gaz [Newspaper of Feb 15: Mercer was about age 20 years & a book-keeper in the mercantile house of Messrs Carson & Newbold, 52 So wharves, & had enjoyed the confidence of his employers. The body of Mercer was brought to this city, & conveyed to the residence of his mother, in 9th st, above Arch, from which place his funeral will take place. Miss McNeal, who keeps a house of bad repute in Pine st, near 12th, gave information to Mr Mercer that his dght was at her house. She is about 16 years of age, very pretty, & generally reputed to be of rather weak intellect. Since the death of Heberton, Mr & Mrs Mercer have been of the most acute character.]

Wm McL Cripps has finished his new warehouse, & is now prepared to continue his business on a more extensive scale than formerly. His furniture will be made up after the latest N Y fashions & in the best manner. Please call at the old stand on 11th st, near Pa ave. –W M C

For rent, a 2 story brick house, on G st, near 11th st, nearly opposite the Methodist Falls Church, now occupied by Maj J W Williams. Apply at Mr John France's Lottery & Exchange Ofc, Pa ave, between 12th & 13th.

WED FEB 15, 1843
Hse/o Reps: 1-Cmte of Claims: adverse report on ptn of John J Bulow. 2-Cmte of Commerce: reported the following bills, viz: bill for relief of the owners & crew of the schnr **Blooming Youth**; the schnr **Seppican**; & the schnr **Florilla**. 3-Cmte on Commerce: bills from the Senate: An act for the relief of Wm Russell & others, & an act for the relief of the owners & crew of the schnr **Twin**: reported the same without amendment. 4-Cmte on Public Lands: adverse report on ptn of Cadwallader Wallace. 5-Cmte on the Judiciary: referred the memorial of Jos Hoyt: reported that the cmte be discharged from consideration thereof. 6-Ptn of Geo Daracott & 103 others, legal voters of Boston, in favor of the Exchequer plan. 7-Memorial & ptn of Geo S King & 80 other citizens of Pa, for relief by the creation of U S stock. 8-Memorial of Jesse McConkey, J B Haines, & Saml Moresson, & 41 others, citizens of the southern part of Lancaster Co, Pa, praying the issue of U S stock. 9-Ptn of Zenas Darnall & 32 others, called themselves the "Amity Assoc," asking Congress to grant them the pre-emption right to a township of land in the interior of the late purchase west of Iowa Terr. 10-Additional papers in the case of Jona Shafer, of Wash Co, Md. 11-Ptn of Fred'k Guliand & 29 citizens of Greene, Chenango Co, N Y, praying that Congress adopt the Exchequer, or plan of Finance, as recommended by the Pres. 12-Ptn of Chas R Allen, praying the allowance of an account attached to said ptn. 13-Memorial of sundry citizens of Cincinnati, in favor of the plan of the Hon W C Johnson for the relief of the State. 14-Ptn of R Mattison & 59 others of Oswego Co, N Y, for the passage of a law granting jury trial to all persons claimed as fugitive slaves; & that all persons be presumed free until shall be proved otherwise. 15-Ptn of Rev David Strang & 99 persons of Associate Congregation of York & Covington, N Y, praying for the repeal of all laws allowing or demanding labor on the Lord's day. 16-Ptn of Hester L Stevens, J C Chumesero, & 200 other citizens of Rochester, N Y, praying for the abatement, as nuisances, of all such establishments within the District as are used as places for purchasing, enchaining, incarcerating, & selling "certain two-legged unfeathered animals" of the same species as the owners of these establishments. 17-Memorials of Ezekiel Rambo, Jos Gardner, & 102 others, citizens of Chester Co, Pa, asking Congress to pass a law authorizing the issue of $200,000,000 of Gov't stock, to be divided among the States, etc. 18-Ptn of Geo Daracott & 103 others, legal voters of Boston, in favor of the Exchequer plan. 19-Resolved, that the Sec of Treasury be directed to communicate to this Hse the amount of the defalcation of Jesse Hoyt, late collector of the port of N Y, & also what means, if any, have been adopted for the recovery of the same, together with the names of the sureties of said Hoyt.

Dissolution of the copartnership existing between John Mills & Jas Johnson, trading under the firm of John Mills & Co, dissolved by mutual consent. –John Mills, Jas

Johnson. John Mills will continue the business at the old stand, corner of Pa ave & 10th st, where boots & shoes may be purchased extremely low for cash.

Died: on Feb 14, in his 29th year, Mr V P Ray, after a long & excruciating attack of cancer, leaving a wife & 3 small children to lament the loss of a kind & indulgent parent. His funeral will be from his late residence on F st, opposite the Union Hotel, at 3 p m today.

Died: on Feb 14, Mr John Radcliff, in his 28th year. His funeral is this Wed at 3 p m, at the residence of his brother, on Md ave, near the Long bridge. The friends of the family are invited to attend.

Died: on Feb 10, at the residence of her nephew, Maj Wm D Nutt, in Alexandria, D C, Miss Linna Deakins, in her 69th year. The disease which terminated her earthly existence was of a protracted & exceedingly painful nature, but was born with that calmness which Christianity alone can inspire.

Died: on Jan 25, in Guilderland, N Y, in his 88th year, John Vanderpool, one of the few remaining sldrs who served his country in the Revolutionary war. He accompanied Montgomery in the important expedition to Quebec, & on different occasions was actively employed in repelling aggressions on the frontiers of the State of N Y.

Died: on Feb 4, in Watervleit, N Y, Fred'k Damp, in his 102nd year.

Capt Moses Barlow & his son, Cromwell Barlow, both of Newport, R I, were drowned in Narragansett Bay on Tue of last week by the sinking of a bay sloop.

The brig **Raymond**, Capt Levenseller, from New Orleans, bound to N Y, went ashore on Feb 10, near Great Egg Harbor bar. The capt, first mate, & 5 seamen were drowned.

Elijah M Amos, of Knoxville, Crawford Co, Ga, was accidentally killed on Feb 1, when his horse took fright, & ran away with the sulky in which he was riding. Mr A was dragged near a mile entangled to the sulky. He was about 43 years of age & had been a resident of Knoxvill since the early settlement of the county; was a highly respected & influential member of the community, & for many years Clerk of the Superior Court of the county, & Postmaster at Knoxville at the time of his death. -Messenger

The hero of the frig **Constitution** is no more. Cmdor Isaac Hull died at his residence in Phil City, on Feb 13, aged 68 years. He received an appointment as Lt in the U S Navy in 1798, having been in the service of his country 45 years.

Nashville [Tenn] Banner says: John Somerville, the venerable & worthy cashier of the Union Bank of Tenn, resigned his place & Jas Corry, at present cashier of the Bank of North America, Phil, has filled the appointment. Mr Somerville has spent the last 30 years of his life in the banking institution of this city, & resigns on account of advanced age.

Senate: 1-Ptn from Capt Saml Mabson, late of the army, for a pension. 2-Ptn from Wm Williams, asking commutation for his bounty land. 3-Cmte on Naval Affairs: adverse report on Hse bill for the relief of Mary Barry. 4-Cmte of Claims: adverse report on the ptn of Wm Dawsing. 5-Cmte on Foreign Affairs: Hse bill for the relief of John Randolph Clay, Sec of Leg at the Court of Vienna, without amendment, & recommending its passage. 6-Cmte of Claims: following Hse bills without amendment: bill for the relief of Chas Waldron; relief of Geo A Winslow; relief of Jos R Chandler. 7-Cmte on Public Bldgs: Hse bill for the relief of John Skirving. 8-Cmte of the Whole: bill for the relief of Wm Fisher. 9-Consideration taken of the bill to grant a tract of land to Villeneuve Le Blanc, in consideration of the benefit derived to the public lands from his services in damming up the mouth of Fall river: bill was lost by a large majority. 10-Cmte on Naval Affairs: bill for the relief of the heirs of Robt Fulton. 11-Cmte on the Judiciary: asking to be discharged from the further consideration of the ptn of Lewis Lambert, & that it be referred to the Cmte on Public Lands. 12-Cmte on Pensions: adverse report on the bill from the Hse for the relief of Maj Thos Harrison.

Supreme Court of the U S: Feb 14, 1843. #25: John Lloyd vs Geo S Hough. In error to the Circuit Court of the U S for Alexandria. Mr Justice Daniel delivered the opinion of this Court, affirming the judgment of the said Circuit Court in this cause with costs. #32: M A Connor, plntf in error, vs Henry Bradley & wife.

THU FEB 16, 1843
Supreme Court of the U S: the case of #34, we are informed, will be called today. It is the case of Jewell vs Jewell, from S C, & involves a question of marriage between a Catholic woman & a Jew, who, after living 15 years together, & bearing 8 children, separated, & Jewell married a Jewess, & died intestate, leaving 2 families. The contest is, which is legitimate? The parties are highly respectable, & the event of the suit momentous. The legal requisites of a valid marriage will be discussed.

Circuit Court of Wash Co, D C. Saml M Bootes has filed his ptn for the benefit of the Bankrupt Law: hearing on the first Mon of Apr next. –Wm Brent, clk

Senate: 1-The credentials of the Hon W H Hayward, Senator elect from N C for 6 years from & after Mar 4 next, were presented. Also the credentials of the Hon Silas Wright, Senator elect from N Y for 6 years from & after Mar 4 next. 2-Ptn from Jas Wilson, asking for an increase of pay for the services performed by him as porter at the Capitol gate. 3-Ptn from Eliz Raymond, wid/o Joshua Raymond, for a pension.

4-Ptn of R Drake & R G Quarles, asking to be allowed to purchase such lands as they reclaim at a reduced price. 4-Cmte of Claims: unfavorable report on the ptn of Chas Dehault Delassus, of Missouri. Also, from the same cmte: adverse report on the ptn of Wm Morrow. 5-Cmte on Private Land Claims: a bill for the relief of the heirs & legal reps of Madame de Lusser. Same cmte: Hse bill confirming the claim of the heirs of Jos Thompson, sen, to a tract of land in Missouri. 6-Cmte on Pensions: asking to be discharged from the further consideration of the ptn of Seneca Thomas. Also, from the same cmte, same for the ptn of Sarah Williamson. Also, on Hse bills for the relief of Prudence Couch, & a bill granting a pension to David Munn. 7-Cmte on Naval Affairs: Hse bill for the relief of Jas Mount, without amendment, & recommending that it be indefinitely postponed. 8-Senate took up the bill for the relief of Chas J Jenkins & W M Mann, assignees of John M Kinne.

Laws of the U S: passed at the 3rd Session of the 27th Congress. 1-An Act for the relief of J R Vienne: Sec of State to pay J R Vienne, of La, one of the assistant marshals employed in taking the recent census of the inhabitants of the parish of Orleans, & New Orleans City, the sum of $418.09, that being the balance due to him for said service. 2-Act for the relief of Saml Dicy: Sec of War to place the name of Saml Dicy, of N H, on the roll of invalid pensioners, & pay him at the rate of $6 per month; to commence on Jun 29, 1842, & during his natural life. 3-Act for the relief of John P Skinner, & the legal reps of Isaac Green: they are released from the payment of the balance of $5,341.75, remaining unpaid on a judgement recovered at the May Term, 1839, of the Circuit Court of the U S for the Vermont district, by the U S, against Thos Emmerson & the said John P Skinner, & Isaac Green, sureties on the official bond of the said Emmerson, late pension agent, for the sum of $13,690.91, it appearing that the amount due to the U S by said Emmerson might have been detained from him with out resorting to said sureties, if legal proceedings had been adopted against him the proper ofcrs of the U S, & that said ofcrs, though requested by said sureties to commence & prosecute such proceedings, neglected & refused so to do: Provided, that nothing in this act shall be construed to discharge the said Emmerson from liability under said judgment. 4-Act for the relief of Barent Stryker: the Postmaster Gen is authorized to pay to Stryker, at & after the rate of $490 a year, for carrying the mail on route #923, in the State of N Y, for the time that he has carried or may hereafter carry the mail on said route under his present contract; & that the Postmaster Gen be further authorized to relet the said #923 at any time before the expiration of the contract of the said Barent Stryker. 5-Act for the payment of 7 companies of Georgia militia, for services rendered in 1840 & 1841. That the Sec of War cause to be paid to the companies of Capts Johnston, Henderson, Knight, Jones, & North, for services rendered in 1840, according to the muster rolls of said companies now on file in the War dept, made out & verified by Capt J Brown, of the U S army; & that he cause to be paid, also, the companies of Capts Jernigan & Sweat, for services rendered in 1841, according to the muster rolls of said companies now on file in the War Dept, as verified by Assist Adj Gen W W S Bliss, of the U S army; & that the laws & regulations applicable to the payment of the volunteers & militia of the U S govern in the payment of these companies; & that the sum of $19,399.87 be, & hereby is, appropriated for the purpose of making said payments, out of any money in the Treas not otherwise appropriated.

Soapstone land at auction: at the Auction Rooms on Bridge st, a lot of land, containing 63 acs, more or less, near the Fred'k road, above Gtwn, D C. This land has 2 hills composed almost entirely of soapstone. Mr John O'Harra or Mr Godfrey Conrad, both residing at Tennallytown, will show the land. –Henry Hazel
-Ed S Wright, auct

Public sale of valuable lands & water power: about 160 acs of land, 4 miles from the Centre Market, adjoining the lands of Capt Wm G Sanders & M Shepperd. The tract is in D C. Also, a tract of 89 acs, about 6 miles from Wash, in PG Co, Md; also a mill-seat a mile & a half from the Capitol. The lands will be offered on Mar 11 next, on the tract adjoining the lands of Capt Wm G Sanders & M Shepperd, near Rock Creek chr. –Geo Attwood Digges, near Bladensbrug, Md

By writ of fieri facias, issued by B K Morsell, Justices of the Peace for Wash Co, D C, I offer at public sale on Mar 17: lot #6 in sq 322, at the corner of west 12th & north C sts; seized & taken as the property of David Monroe, & will be sold to satisfy a judgment due Lloyd Cooper. -L S Beck, constable

Supreme Court of the U S: Feb 15, 1843. $33: E K Cartwright vs Alex'r T Howe et al. In error to the Circuit Court of the U S for Wash, D C. This matter in controversy in this case having been settled, this writ of error was dismissed with costs. #32: M A Conner, plntf in error, vs Henry Bradley et ux. Concluded by Mr Brent for the plntf in error. #26: Chas McKnight, appellant, vs Laurence B Taylor. Cause was argued by Messrs Semmes & Jones for the appellant, & by Mr Bradley for the appellee.

U S ship **Erie**, off Cape Cod on a cruise to the South Pacific: Feb 9. 1843. List of ofcrs attached to the ship: Thos J Manning, Lt Commanding; Geo Hurst & R W Meade, Lts; Wm E LeRoy, Actg Master; J Rutledge, J P Decatur, Passed Midshipmen; J H Norris, Purser; Wm Grier, Assist Surgeon; A N Smith, Geo N Ranson, W O Grain, Stanwix Gansevoort, Midshipmen; J A Manning, Capt's Clerk; Alfred Heigerty, Boatswain.

W W Corcoran offers for sale lots 7, 8, 12, 14, & 19, of the tract of land immediately opposite Gtwn-about 4 acs. Also, the Stone Quarries, #1 to 43, extending from the aqueduct nearly to the Falls bridge. The lands will be divided into 20 or 30 ac lots.

FRI FEB 17, 1843
Hse/o Reps: 1-Cmte on Private Land Claims: report on the ptn of J Eper Cowan, with a bill for the relief of the legal reps of Antoine Vasques & others. 2-Cmte on

Revolutionary Pensions: reported bills for the relief of Ebenezer Dewey, John Rose, & allowing a pension to Fred'k Hopkins. 3-Cmte on Invalid Pensions: reported a bill for the relief of John P Schuyler. Same cmte: adverse report on the ptn of Richd B Bramfield; & ptn of Horace B Abbey; & ptns of John Bull, jr, Simon Kenton, John Dixon, Christopher Lambert, John Owen, Empson Hamilton, & Sarah Pratt. 4-Cmte on Commerce: adverse report on memorial of Chas H Russell & Chas Potter. 5-Cmte on Indian Affairs: act for the relief of Benj Humphrey, reported with an amendment. 6-Cmte on Post Ofc & Post Roads: reported a bill for the relief of Jas H Jenkins. 7-Cmte on Naval Affairs: reported a bill giving a pension to John Wolfendena: referred to the Cmte of the Whole. Mr Wolfenden has been 40 years in service, & last year was honorably discharged, & allowed to retire to the naval asylum at Phil. He could have retired earlier, but refused to leave the service while the Maine boundary was unsettled. His cmder gave him a high character, & there was a highly complimentary letter to Mr W from the Sec of the Navy, Mr Upshur. The object of the present bill was merely to allow Mr W to receive the amount now paid him in another form, in the form of a pension, instead of being supported at the naval asylum. The pension would enable him to live among his friends & relatives in N C. The bill was read a 3rd time & passed. 8-Additional papers in the case of Henry Holbrook, of Somerset Co, Md. 9-Ptn of Jared Coffin & others, of Nantucket, Mass: regarding commercial treaties & arrangements of the U S with foreign nations. Same for the ptn of Jos Grinnell & others, of New Bedford, Mass.

To The Public: Nathan Morden & his 2 sons, Jas & John Morden, emigrated from Fauquier Co, Va, to Ky, some 30 years ago. The undersigned would be very thankful for any information as to their where-abouts, or any one of them. Address- Wm Jett, Amissville, Rappahannock Co, Va.

Senate: 1-Ptn from Wm K Weston, asking that a certain bond deposited by him in the War Dept be cancelled. 2-Cmte on Public Lands: adverse report on ptn of Lewis Lambert. 3-Cmte on Pensions: Hse bill granting a pension to Nancy Williams, wid/o David Williams, one of the captors of Maj Andre, & recommending its passage. 4-Cmte on Indian Affairs: bill for the relief of the legal reps of Nat Pryor, dec'd, & recommending its passage. 5-Cmte of Claims: bill for the relief of Capt J Throckmorton. Also, asking to be discharged from the further consideration of the memorial of Juan Quavre, asking remuneration for property taken by the British force in 1814, at Cat island, in consequence of his refusing to pilot their vessels into Lake Borgne.

More on the late Cmdor Hull. Cmdor Hull was the 3rd on the list of Post Capts- Cmdor Barron & Cmdor Stewart were before him. His commission of Capt bears date Apr 23, 1806, one day after Cmdor Stewart's. Cmdor Hull was, we believe, a native of Connecticut, where he married & spent much of his time when not on public duty. He was about 68 years of age, though his personal appearance would have led to the belief that he was much younger. Before entering the navy, he made

2 voyages to England, one to Ireland, one to Rotterdam, 2 to Lisbon, 2 to Cadiz, & 10 voyages to the West Indies. He commenced his nautical career when 12 years of age, 56 years ago, & went on board a prize taken by his father from the British during the Revolution, when the enemy had possession of N Y. On Mar 9, 1798, he entered the navy as a lt. While 1st Lt of the frig **Constitution**, under Cmdor Talbot, in May, 1800, in the *quasi* French war, he cut out a French letter of marque from Porte Platte, [St Domingo,] with a small sloop. This was achieved without the loss of a man. In 1804 he commanded the brig **Argus**, & rendered service in the Tripolitan war, in the storming of Tripoli, & the reduction of Derne. In 1812 he commanded the **Constitution**, & escaped from a British squadron under Cmdor Broke.

By virtue of an order of distress for house rent from Sarah Polkinhorn, I shall offer at public sale, all the household & kitchen furniture in the house over the store of Mr Winters, & next door to Messrs Polkinhorn & Campbell's, Pa ave. The property is as follows: one pair of card tables, a dressing bureau, a sofa, a mahg sideboard, tables, a dressing bureau, a sofa, a mahg sideboard, window curtains & ornaments, 7 chairs, a washstand, bowl, & pitcher, 2 fire-fenders, 3 pictures, 4 spittoons, a large pine talbe, 2 carpets, 1 hearth rug, a stair carpet & rods, 1 cushioned chair, 5 bracket lamps, one lot of glass ware, 3 waiters, 2 grates & fixtures. –John Waters, bailiff

Extract of the Judgment of the Supreme Court. #492: U S vs Nourse. On Dec 20, 1830, the accounts exhibited by both parties were referred by the Court to auditors, who, on Jan 4, 1831, reported that the dfndnt, for specified services which he rendered the U S, & for which he had received no compensation, was justly entitled to $23,582.72. This report having been duly considered by the Court, was confirmed & made absolute. #9 Peters, 28. The Court determined that the said Jos Nourse was entitled to compensation for the extra services he had rendered to the Gov't, & appointed auditors to ascertain the value of his services & compensation. The report of the auditors allowed to the cmplnt a commission of 2½ % on the sum of $943,308.83 disbursed by him, leaving a balance due to him from the U S. The report was confirmed, & the injunction made perpetual. The District Judge had full jurisdiction over it: he pronounced his final decree against the U S. The District Court then had complete jurisdiction over the case, & its decision is final

Wash News: Inquest was held yesterday, before Thos Woodward, Coroner, at the Alms-house, on the body of Maria Hersch, a German, aged 37 years, who died very suddenly at a private house in Wash City a few days ago, & who was interred in the Alms house grave yard, under circumstances which led the neighbors to suspect that all was not right. After a post morten examination by Dr A McWilliams, jr, & Dr A Holmead, jr, the Jury were of the opinion that the death was caused by apoplexy. The inquest was held to allay some excitement & to prevent unjust suspicions.

SAT FEB 18, 1843
Senate: 1-Cmte on Pensions: adverse reports on the following Hse bills: for the relief of Patrick Masterson; for the relief of Jane McGuire, wid/o Maj Thos McGuire, dec'd; & for the relief of Mary Elder. Same cmte: Hse bill for the relief of Jeremiah Kimball. Same cmte: Hse bill for the relief of Solomon Emerson, & for the relief of Lyman N Cook, without amendment, & recommending their passage. 2-Cmte on Pensions: bill for the relief of Asahel Brainard. Same cmte: Hse bill for the relief of Eliz Gresham, wid/o Geo Gresham, recommending its passage. Also, asking to be discharged from the further consideration of the ptn of the wid/o the late Richd Zantzinger, & that it be referred to the Cmte on Military Affairs. Also, from the same cmte: adverse reports on the following Hse bills, recommending that they be indefinitely postponed, with a written report in each case: for the relief of Eliz Harris; relief of Henry Freeman; relief of Leah Tenure; relief of Geo Hammill; granting a pension to Jos Watson. 3-Cmte on Pensions: Hse bill for the relief of Eliz Powers. 4-Mr Barrow asked the Senate to gratify him by taking up 2 bills for the relief of residents of Tennessee, namely, a bill for the relief of Nancy Hambright, & one for the relief of Thos King. They were taken up & considered in Cmte of the Whole & ordered to a 3rd reading.

Mr Edw Ruffin, of Va, the able editor of the Farmers' Register, has been appointed by the Govn'r of S C to conduct the Agricultural Survey of that State, ordered by the Legislature at its late session.

The Navy Dept has purchased the beautiful yacht **On-ka hye**, built by the Messrs Stevens, of N Y. She has been placed under the command of Lt W C Whittle, with the same name as before, & is to be employed, we presume, as a dispatch baot between Pensacola & Chagres, agreeably to the intimation announced in connexion with the schnr **Wave**, under the command of Lt John A Davis. A new military post has been ordered to be established at the junction of Raccoon creek with the river Des Moines, to be garrisoned by Capt J Allen's company 1st dragoons, & one company of the 1st infantry. The position lately occupied at the Sac & Fox agency is to be vacated. The name of the new post is not yet decided upon.

Appointments by the Pres: 1-Wm P Pelletier, Surveyor & Inspec of the Revenue at Swansborough, N C, vice Martin Frasure, dec'd. 2-Robt Benguerel, Receiver of Public Moneys for the district of lands subject to sale at Opelousas, La, vice Geo M Smith, dec'd.

From Mexico. The Texian prisoners were at work at Perote. Mr Van Ness had been taken to the city of Mexico & was at work upon the streets.

The schnr **Samuel Phillips**, Capt Prettyman, of Vienna, from Gtwn, D C to N Y, with a cargo of flour, went ashore about 12 miles north of Barnegat, on the night of Feb 5. The flour, which is insured, would probably be saved in a damaged state.

MON FEB 20, 1843
Mr John Martin, a Revolutionary sldr, died at Augusta, Ga, on Feb 14, at the advanced age of 105 years.

Accident on Lake Phelps a few days ago took the lives of the 8 & 11 year old sons of Josiah Collins. They went out on the lake in a boat with 2 negro boys, the boat upset, & all 4 boys drowned. –Raleigh Star

Alexandria Boarding School will be resumed on Feb 20th. –Caleb S Hallowell & Brother

For sale, a small brick house on the corner of Mass ave & 4th st. Apply to Jas A Burche.

The house of the undersigned, at Monticello, Va, was entered on or about Dec 29 last, and between 10 & 12 hundred dollars were stolen there-from. There was in the amount one $500 Treas note, issued by the Treas in favor of S McClellan, Navy Agent at Balt, dated Mar 29 or Apr 28, 1842. This note was disbursed by Mr McClellan on May 11, 1842, & so endorsed on the back. –U P Levy, Monticello, Va

The last Marlborough Gaz notices the death of a female servant of Robt H Lanham, who died on Sun last at the advanced age of 111 years, having been born in the year 1732.

For rent: the hse at present occupied by the Hon John Leeds Kerr, on 13th st, between G & H sts north, will be for rent after Mar 1. Apply to the subscriber, corner of 14th & L sts. –W W Billing

Hardware, Hardware. Richd M Waring & Co opened opposite Brown's Hotel, one door east of Boteler & Donn's, where they will keep a general assortment of goods in their line, which they will sell low for cash or to punctual customers.

Orphans Court of PG Co, Md: Feb 14, 1843. Ordered that Jonathan T Walker, administrator of Nathan Walker, late of PG Co, dec'd, give notice as required by law. –Phil Chew, Reg [Said notice followed: letters testamentary on the personal estate of Nathan Walker, dec'd. –Jona T Walker, administrator of Nathan Walker]

Senate: 1-Ptn from Rose Howe, [late Rose Bailly,] of Ill, praying the relinquishment of the reversionary interest of the U S in 2 sections of land reserved to the dghts of Mo-nee by her last husband, Jos Bailly, by the treaty with the Pottawatamies of the Prairie & Kenkakee bands, made at Camp Tippecanoe on Oct 20, 1832. 2-Cmte on Finance: bill for the relief of Benj Adams & Co, & others. Same cmte: unfavorable report on the Hse bill for the relief of S Morris Waln. Also, an adverse report on the bill for the relief of Geo P Pollen & Robt Colgate. 3-Cmte on the Post Ofc & Post Roads: bill for the relief of John W Skidmore & recommending its passage. 4-Cmte on Naval Affairs: a bill granting a pension to Wm McPherson. Same cmte: bill for the relief of John Wolfenden. 5-Cmte on the Judiciary: on leave given, reported a bill for the relief of Jos & Wm Wilcox. 6-Memorial signed by Andrew Shriver, one of the most substantial & intelligent Democrats in Md, & 213 other citizens of all parties, of Carroll Co, Md, praying Congress to issue 200,000,000 of stock, to be divided among all the States & Territories. Similar prayer by R M Magrew, John K Sapping, & 114 other citizens of Harford Co, Md. Like prayer of Jno A Bailey & 67 citizens of Posey Co, Indiana, of all parties. Memorial of Aaron Gregg & 84 other citizens of Carmichael, Pa, making a similar request. Same for the memorial of Edwin Mitchell & John Lloyd & 250 other citizens of Phil, of all parties, praying for the same. 7-Memorial of D Jarvis, F Shipley, J Culbertson, H B Wellman, & 210 other citizens, of all parties, of Massilon, Ohio, praying for the issue of 200,000,000 stock. Also, for the same, the ptn of Jas Lane & 50 other citizens of Bedford Co, Pa. 8-Ptn of Chas Van Loon & 74 voters of Cayuga Co, N Y, praying the repeal of the law respecting the recapture of fugitive slaves, & the enactment of a law granting them the right of trial by jury. 9-Ptn of J Frothingham & others, artists of the city of Boston, praying an alteration in the duties on imported pictures.

Circuit Court of Wash Co, D C. Jas B Davis, a bankrupt, has filed for his discharge & certificate: hearing on the first Mon of May next. –W Brent, clk

The funeral of the late Cmdor Isaac Hull took place on Fri at Phil. The citizen soldiery, under the command of Gen Cadwallader, formed a handsome military display, & the ofcrs of the Army & Navy turned out in considerable force.

Orphan's Court of Wash Co, D C. Letters of administration, with will annexed, on the personal estate of Isaac Ball, late of said county, dec'd. –Mary Ball, admx w a

TUE FEB 21, 1843
Mrd: on Feb 1, in Columbus, Ga, by Rev Mr D Cairns, Richd P Spencer to Laura Jane, eldest d/o Wm P Younge, all of that place.

Mrd: on Jan 31, by Rev Mr Murphy, Bennett F Gwynn, eldest s/o Capt John H Gwynn, to Eleanor G Edelin, 4th d/o Raphael C Edelin, all of PG Co, Md.

Mrd: on Feb 16, at Exeter, near Leesburg, Loudoun Co, Va, by Rev E R Lippitt, John Augustine Washington, of Mount Vernon, to Eleanor Love, only d/o Wilson Cary Selden.

Hse/o Reps: 1-Ptn of Israel Dille & 52 other citizens of Licking Co, Ohio, praying the passage of the Pres' plan of an Exchequer. 2-Ptn of Richd Stillwell & 94 other citizens of Muskingum Co, Ohio, praying a change of the place of holding the Jul terms of the Circuit & Dist Courts of the U S for the Dist of Ohio from Cincinnati to Columbus. 3-Ptn of Arthan Tappan & 56 legal voters of Brooklyn, N Y, against any law of Congress sustaining slavery in D C. 4-Ptn of Hosea Illaley, Geo W Otis, & other citizens

Senate: 1-Ptn from Hall Jackson Kelly, asking to be allowed to purchase land from the Indians in the Oregon Territory for a permanent settlement. 2-Ptn from Gilbert Buckingham & 225 others, citizens of Henry & Whiteside counties, in Ill, praying for a tri-weekly mail route from Peoria to Albany. 3-Cmte on Pensions: adverse reports on the following Hse bills: relief of Anna Jones; relief of Catharine Wilson; relief of Maria M Brooks. 4-Ptn of Mary Crafton, for a pension under the act of Jul 7, 1838. Also, the ptn of Mary Gafford, for a pension under the same act. 5-Memorial & ptn of Wm Postlethwaite & 80 others, citizens of Somerset Co, Pa, regarding the U S issuing stock to the amount of $200,000,000. Also, the memorial of Saml W Pearson & 54 other citizens of Somerset Co, of similar tenor.

Died: on Feb 17, in N Y, Mary McEvers, w/o John R Livingston, jr, & d/o the late Chas McEvers.

Shandy Hall for sale: beautiful estate on the Rappahannock river, Richmond Co, Va: contains 1,200 acs of bottom or flat land; the larger mansion would accommodate a large family. There are numerous houses, barns, ice houses, & overseer's houses. I have now about 3,000 bushels of oysters laid along the shore, which is about 100 yards from the mansion. I shall be at *Shandy Hall* all Apr, & about Jul 1. –Aug Neale, Phil P S Reference may be had to Hon J Taliaferro, of Congress, Wm H Taylor, Dr John Mayo & Taliaferro Hunter, of the neighborhood.

For sale: a thorough bred Maltese Jack, imported by an ofcr of the navy. He may be seen at the farm of Danl F Dulany, sen, Fairfax Co, Va, on the Middle Turnpike road, 8½ miles from Alexandria. For further information address the subscriber at Fairfax Court-house, Va. –J H Dulany

Died: on Feb 20, in Wash City, of a painful & lingering illness, which he bore with unsurpassed patience & Christian fortitude, Capt Edmund Hanly, in his 39th year. In his demise, his widow & children have been deprived of a kind & affectionate husband & father, & our city of one of her most useful, enterprising, & patriotic citizens. His funeral will be from his late residence, corner of G & 20th sts, on Wed, at 2 p m.

Died: on Feb 19, in Wash City, in her 50th year, Mrs Ann Hepburn, consort of Mr Peter Hepburn, after a lingering illness, which she bore with Christian fortitude, leaving a disconsolate husband & 6 children, besides a large circle of friends & acquaintances to mourn their irreparable loss.

The Texas Times publishes the following list of Texian prisoners recently captured by the Mexicans at the town of Mier.

Ofcrs:

Wm W Fisher	John Sinnickson	John R Baker
Thos J Green	Wm J McMoth	Wm M Eastland
T W Murray	Claudius Buster	Wm Ryon
R F Brenham	Chas H Reese	Esven Cameron
Wm M Shepherd	J G W Pierson	F M Gibson
Chas A Clarke	Thos W Cox	G B Crittenden
John M Shipman	A A Lee	Wm A Clopton
Israel Canfula	F W Douglass	T S Smith

Non-Commissioned Ofcrs:

John P Wyatt	J D Cocke	Zaccheus Wilson
J R Johnson	J J Blonto	R W Turner
J N M Thompson	Ferge Anderson	Wm H Frensley
W H Van Horne	A S Boark	
R G Waters	Henry Whaling	
T H Nelson		

Privates:

Thos Brannon	G Lewis	Peter A Ackerman
Thos J Dellon	Jas M McMichen	Jas H Neely
Jeremiah Leechan	Jas Trumbull	Edw D Wright
John Mills	J Y Peacock	Lawson F Mills
P H Lurk	S H Walker	Thos Senabough
R Willoughby	Matthew W Alexander	Henry Jourcay
D H E Busby	W P Stapp	J Harvy
T R Alexander	Wilson N Vandyke	Danl Davis
Thos Owen	H Bridyn	W Miller
John B Benny	Isaac Zumalt	J Watts
J Joops	Geo W Bush	David Overton
R H King	W E Millen	C Davis
J Young	D R Hallowell	A B Hanne
Asa Hill	Benoni Middleton	M C Wing
R H Oats	W B Middleton	T W T Harrison
Allen S Holderman	J L Shepherd	Jas N Jonny
John Fitzgerald	Francis Riley	S Goodman
R S Beard	Willis Coplan	Wm Morus
Wm J Martin	S McDade	E Smith
C Isom	Owen R Willis	O C Phelps
A W B C Byron	T A Thompson	J Philips
C M Roberts	J J Humphreys	W S Beard
W Oldham	John Hay	G N Downs
S Mcfall	C K Gleason	A S Hammond
W H Moore	G Lord	F Brey

T Davis	S G Benner	W Reese
S McClelland	H Muiller	John Ewen
W B Coddy	W A A Wallace	Wm Mitchell
John Res	G W Urahem	J C Wilson
Pat Maher	P Rockeyfellow	J H Livergood
J J Simons	W Kaigler	J F Smith
J Calvert	B Z Boon	Leonidas Saunders
W Clark	Sullivan J Holffer	John Hawk
Wm Moore	Fr White	C M McMahan
Alex Mathews	J C Groyceau	J A Santburg
Adam Moser	W H Roan	C Hill
D C Hourie	W Jones	A J Dewis
P F Bowman	J S Cash	J Wilson
Wm Wism	Wm Tompson	Wm Parker
J S Jatem	Patrick Usher	D H Van Vichten
A B Laforge	J J Morehead	R H M C Smith
D McDonaluo	J McMullin	R Brown
J Arthur	T Colville	D Smith
H D Heddenburg	Wm Dunbar	J B Neely
J Grubs	Wm Gibson	R H Dunhan
John McGurly	R B King	Wm Davis
E B Jackson	M M Rogers	Thos W Bell
Levi Williams	John Jonny	P D Randolph
E G Coffman	T L James	W R Davis
J S White	H Woodland	W J Wilson
E H Pius	E F Esk	Sandford Rice
M R Pilley	C S Kelley	A F Barns
H V Novel	H H Roberts	F Whitehurst
P R Dougherty	Jas Burke	P M Maxwell
Alex'r Armstrong	Jos D McCutcheon	
John Lacy	Leonidas D F -Edwards	
J E Dusenbery	J Barney	
R W Harris	E R Porter	S A Barney
W J Runyan	W M Allwood	J L D Blackburn
R P Boswell	C McLaughlin	Lorenzo D Rice
Carter Sargent	J H Ewrey	M McCouly
Wm Sargent	G P Pillart	Wm Bailey
Saml Lyons	A McKinnel	Stanly Lockerman
Jas Barber	David Allen	D H Gettis
Lyn Bobo	Wm Ripley	R Beal
Henry D Weeks	W Y Scott	Nathl R Mallon
W H Kuykendall	J O Rice	J Jeancy
J D Malby	Lewis Hayes	Edw Y Kehue
Jeffrey Hill	J Hill	Wm H Sellers

Galbert R Brush   J C Armstrong   J M Ogden
B Bluse   C Hensly

Fearful calamity at Troy, N Y, occasioned by a land-slide: Feb 17, 5½ p m. It occurred in the immediate vicinity of the terrible avalance of 1837, about 4 p m this afternoon, covering acres of ground at the base of hill, & crushing to stone some 10 or 12 houses, nearly all occupied. The names of the families that have perished are Birdsall, Day, Kelley, & some others that I cannot now recollect. [Newspaper of Feb 24: Occupants of the houses destroyed are: Wm Brazell, teamster; W H Kilfoile, teamster; Zebulon P Birdsall, painter; Wm Purdy, mason; & Chas Dumbleton. The following dead bodies taken out, according to the Common Council: Mrs Mathew Grenin & child; Mr Wm Brazell & 2 children; Michl Donn; Thos Keely & wife; Edw Dumbleton, a lad; a child of Jas Caldwell; 2 children of Danl E Day; Miss Ann Wilber; a child of Mrs Gardner; & Miss Jane Sanford. The following persons were taken out alive: Mrs Kilfoile, one arm broken; a child of K P Birdsall; Jane McCollom; Mrs Gardner; 2 children, names not ascertained; Jas Barnett & wife. Mrs Dunn is missing, supposed to be in the ruins.]

WED FEB 22, 1843
Mr B W Hall, residing 4 miles from Balt on the Harford road, one of the Dirs of the Balt & Phil Railroad Co, was killed on Sun last, by an accident on the Portsmouth & Roanoke Railroad, near Wilmington, N C. We do not have the particulars of the accident. –Balt Patriot [Feb 23rd newspaper: Mr Hall was the only person killed. Several other passengers received considerable injury. The accident was caused by the breaking of an axletree of the passenger car.]

The "Last of the Barons" is actually received & for sale at the Cheap Literary Depot, Pa ave, a few doors east of 4½ st. The price is only 25 cents, & Harper's edition, upwards of 200 pages. –Wm B Zieber

Letters from Boston from the Sandwich Islands, overland, to Oct 30. The whaling ship **George**, of New Bedford, Mass, arrived there with the scurvy on board. The capt, chief mate, & 6 men had died, & not one of the survivors was able to manage the helm. They tried to reach the harbor of Honolulu, but could go no further than to make the island when some of the Missionaries went on board & anchored the ship.

The dwlg of Mr Philip Dugan, about 6 miles from Chestown, Md, was consumed by fire on Feb 10, & his wife, a young lady, lost her life in the flames. Mr Dugan was aroused from his sleep by the fire & smoke, & instantly tried to rescue his wife, but was unable to succeed. The entire household effects were destroyed.

Pittsburg [Pa] Chronicle says: a rencontre took place in Henderson Co, near Pleasant Exchange, on Feb 5, between Mr Henry Morris & Mr Reuben Morgan, in which the latter was shot through by the former with a rifle, & died without speaking a word. Morgan has left a wife & helpless family of children. Morris is in jail awaiting trial.

Nashville, Tenn, Feb 11. Payne, Kirby, & Carroll, the first convicted of murder in Franklin Co, the second of the same offence in White Co, & the last of the same offence in Sumner Co, were yesterday executed by hanging, on the common near the Murfreesborough Turnpike. An immense crowd gathered.

Sldr of the Revolution gone. Gen Robt Porterfield, one of the few remaining sldrs of the Revolution, & the oldest ofcr of his rank, perhaps, left in Va, died at his residence in Augusta, on Feb 13, in his 91st year. He entered the war of the Revolution, we believe, as an ensign, & came out of it with the rank of capt; serving part of the time in the South, where he was taken prisoner, & afterwards in the North, under the immediate command of Gen Washington. He also served a tour of duty as brig gen during the late war, & was an acting magistrate of the county for more than 50 years, during which he twice held the ofc of high sheriff. –Staunton [Va] Spectator

J U Shilt, a well known commission merchant of Mobile, was found dead on Feb 8 in his ofc. He had been missing for some 24 hours from home, & when found, he was sitting in a chair at his desk stiff & cold.

Headqrtrs Nat'l Blues: You are ordered to meet at the Armory this morning, at 9 a m, with knapsacks, fully armed & equipped, for parade. By order. L J Middleton, Capt

At last Nelson Court, Mr Egbert Johnson was murdered by Wm Chick, both of Lovingston, & both were young men. The cause grew out of a fracas which took place between them. Chick fled the country. –Lynchburg Virginian

Military funeral for the late Edmund Hanly, takes place this afternoon at 2 p m. The Union Guards embraced an invitation to attend the funeral of the late commander of that company. Resolutions will be entered on the journal & a copy sent to the family of the dec'd. –Saml E Douglass, sec

Juvenile Dinner: the Junior Artillerists of Wash, will give a dinner on Feb 22, at C Buckingham's room. Cmte of Invitation & Reception:

| Capt F H Williams | Lt L Beeler | Sgt J West |
| Lt B F Beers | Sgt J Buckingham | Pvt J Tucker |

Tickets 50 cents; to be had at the stores of W A Williams, Geo Savage, the Temperance Hotel, & at the door on the day of the dinner.

Senate: 1-Adverse report on the ptn of Mark Tristoe, late postmaster at Warsaw. 2-Cmte on Naval Affairs: the bill from the Hse for the relief of the heirs of Robt Fulton, with an amendment, & recommending its passage. 3-Cmte on Indian

Affairs: adverse report on the ptn of Campbell Scott; also, on the Hse bill for the relief of the adms of Wm H Hunter, with written reports in each case. 4-Cmte on Pensions: Hse bill for the relief of Maria Fowler, & recommending its indefinite postponement, on the ground that the Dept had granted the relief. The report was concurred in. Also, an adverse report on the ptn of Aaron Page. 5-Cmte on Revolutionary Claims: adverse report on the ptn of Benj Harrison. Also, same cmte, Hse bill for the relief of Henry Hoffman, with a report. Also, asking to be discharged from the further consideration of the ptn of Isaac Hopkins. 6-Cmte on Naval Affairs: bill for the relief of Chas E Sherman, with an amendment. 7-Cmte on pensions: adverse report on the ptn of Jacob Miller. 7-Bill for the relief of Chas J Jenkins & Wm W Mann, assignees of John McKinne, was taken up & was decided in the negative. 8-Resolved, That the Sec of War to communicate to the Senate the copy of any contract entered into by Robt Fulton with the U S Gov't in 1814 or 1815, for the furnishing or fitting out of one or more steamboats for the use of the Gov't, the amount of money advanced to him in virtue of the said contract, & how far the same has been fulfilled or complied with on the part of the said Fulton; also, a statement of the account of the Fulton, as the same appear on the books of the Treas.

Died: on Feb 10, at *Oakley*, her late residence in St Mary's Co, Md, in her 51st year, Eliz, relict of S Gough, & d/o the late Judge John R Plater, of Md.

Columbia Artl to meet at the armory for parade, today, at 8 a m. –J Holohan, O S

Mechanical Riflemen, you are ordered to meet at the Armory this day, at 12 o'clock, for parade, fully armed. –W A Kennedy, 1st Sgt

Members of the Perserverance Fire Co to meet at the Engine house this day, at 12 o'clock, in citizen's dress, to attend the funeral of Edmund Hanly, late Pres of the Union Fire Co. –Geo S Gideon, sec

THU FEB 23, 1843
For sale, a small brick house on the corner of Mass ave & 4th st. It is a desirable place for a retail store. For terms apply to Jas A Burch.

Senate: 1-Ptn from Ellen Dixon, wid/o a dec'd surgeon, asking for a pension. 2-Cmte on Finance: Hse bill for the relief of Rebecca Guest, & recommending its indefinite postponement. 3-Cmte on Pensions: Hse bill for the relief of Saml Edgecombe, recommending its indefinite postponement, with a report. 4-Cmte on Revolutionary Claims: an adverse report on Hse bill for the relief of Wm T Smith. Also, from the same cmte, an adverse report on Hse bill for the relief of Joshua W Newcomb.

Hse/o Reps: 1-Bill from the Senate entitled "An act for the relief of the heirs of Wm Fisher," without amendment. 2-No objection being made, the bill for the relief of Aschel Brainard was passed.

The undersigned takes this method to inform his friends that he has closed his work of the last season, & is now ready to enter into contract for bldg or other jobbing, to be done in the best workmanlike manner; also, acting as architect in his own business. --Balaam Birch

FRI FEB 24, 1843
Senate: 1-Memorial from Ann Chew, Mary Hopper, & others, remonstrating against the annexation of Texas & Florida to the Union. 2-Cmte of Claims: Hse bills, without amendment, & with a recommendation that they pass, for the relief of the legal reps of R T Spence, & for the relief of Saml Weller. Same cmte: adverse reports on the following bills from the Hse: for the relief of John Hodgkin, & for the relief of the legal reps of Lt T W Smith.

Cobourg [Upper Canada] Star: a few days ago the house of Wm Cottingham, at Williamstown, near that place, was destroyed by fire, & 4 of his children & 2 female servants were burnt to death.

Letter in N Y papers that Elijah White, who went out as U S agent to Oregon, & took with him a large party of emigrants, writes, under date of Aug 17, that his party had increased to 112, although they had lost 2-one by sickness & the other by an accident. They stated with 19 wagons & their journey had been slow & tedious; but they had passed 2/3rd of the way, & were in excellent health & spirits.

Hse/o Reps: 1-Cmte on Revolutionary Claims: adverse report in the case of the heirs of Capt John Winston. 2-Cmte on the Library, made a report, with a joint resolution for removing & placing Greenough's statue of Washington, under the supervision of Greenough. 3-Cmte of Military Affairs: adverse report on the ptn of Chas Madis. 4-Cmte of Claims: adverse reports on the cases of: John W Webb & others, heirs of Jos Webb, dec'd; Ephraim T Gilbert, John Burke, Elijah S Bell, John Chaffee, John W Crane, & Jas J Pattison. Same cmte: adverse reports on the cases of John S Gatewood, Thos McCoy, Timothy Cook, & Guy Carpenter. 5-Cmte on the Judiciary: reported a bill for the relief of Langtry & Jenkins, & their assigns. Same cmte: made an adverse report on the ptn of Manual Cruzat. 6-Cmte on Revolutionary Claims: made adverse reports on the cases of the Pastor & Session of the First Presby Church at Elizabethtown, N J; the heirs of Jos Young, dec'd; the heirs of John Hopper, dec'd; & the Trustees of the Presby Church at Yorktown, Westchester Co, N Y. 7-Cmte of the Whole: discharged from the further consideration of the bill for the relief of John P Schuyler: read a 3rd time & passed. 8-Cmte of Claims: adverse reports on the ptns of Henry Disbrow & Geo Fisher. 9-Cmte on the Dist of Col: adverse report on the ptn of Josiah Lukins. 10-Memorial of

Jas C Atler & a number of citizens of New Windsor, Carroll Co, Md, for Congress to issue $200,000,000 in stock. 11-Ptns of Maria Evrit, of Hudson, N Y, & Polly Thomas, of Clavenack, N Y, praying an extension of the widows' pension act. 12-Memorial of Geo Grogan & a number of citizens of Alleghany Co, Md, praying Congress to issue $200,000,000 in stock. 13-Ptn of Geo W Campbell, Saml K McIlhenny, & 112 other citizens of Mississippi, praying the establishement of a stage mail line between Louisville, Miss, via Macon, in that State, to Clinton, Ala. 14-Cmte on Public Expenditures: report on certain payments from the Treas to Chas J Catlett, intended as a supplement to the report upon the same subject made at the last session of Congress. 15-Cmte on Military Affairs: reported a joint resolution to present a sword to Gen Duncan L Clinch. 16-Cmte on Revolutionary Pensions: bill for the relief of Jno Everly. 17-Cmte on Invalid Pensions: bill for the relief of Lathrop Taylor, of Jas Maines, & of Geo Whetton, with reports. Same cmte: adverse reports on the cases of Jos McRhea, Chauncey G Storm, Geo Armstrong, & Fielding Pratt. 18-Cmte on Invalid Pensions: referred the bill from the Senate entitled "An act granting a pension to Wm McPherson," reported the same without amendment. Same cmte: adverse report on the case of Peter McWilliams. 19-Cmte on Revolutionary Claims, made adverse reports upon the cases of: which several reports were laid on the table:

Heirs of Lt Wm Lewis, dec'd
Reps of Isaiah Younglove
Heirs of Joel Haraway
Heirs of Capt Saml Jones
Heirs of Capt Jos Michaux
Heirs of Benj Harrison, jr
Heirs of Capt Mark Thomas
Heirs of Thos Jett
Geo Purcell
Eleazer Butler
Heirs of Geo Yates
Heirs of Capt Reuben Fields
Chas W Macomber
Heirs of Maj Jno W Brant
Heirs of Philip Courtney
Heris of Wm Meredith
Heirs of Harvey Whiting
Reps of Jno Spencer
Reps of Thos Abbott
Heirs of Jno Jennings
Adm of Danl Royer & the heirs of Saml Royer
Adeline Hughes & other heirs of Wm Watts
Mgt Freeman, wid/o Constant Freeman
Jane Dade & other heirs of Capt Wm Rumsey
Jonathan Shafer, heir of Christian Orendorff
Heirs of Tarleton Woodson, Thos Gordon, Wm Tabb, & other heirs of Thos Cheeseman

Geo S Curson, bearer of despatches for Mexico, arrived at New Orleans on Feb 12, & proceeded to Balize to procure a passage to Vera Cruz.

Cobourg [Upper Canada] Star: a few days ago the house of Wm Cottingham, at Williamstown, near that place, was destroyed by fire, & 4 of his children & 2 female servants were burnt to death.

A complimentary benefit will be given Mr Jos Whipple, this evening, by the members of the Freemen's Vigilant Total Abstinence Society, in consideration of his expenses in a recent Temperance tour to N Y, & for his furtherance of the cause of Total Abstinence. The Hon Thos F Marshall will deliver his valedictory address. Messrs May, Murphy, & Lebar, of N Y, vocalists, will favor the society with their company. Tickets 12½ cents each; to be had at Cammack's, Beers', & Savage's. –E Brooke, sec

Ladies who have not received their invitations to the Beneficial Civic & Military Ball, will please send their names to Mr J B Philips or J P McKean, or either of the undersigned. –Jos B Tate, John P Stallings, H D Cooper

Wanted immediately. A middle aged woman to nurse a baby. None need apply but such as can bring the best testimonials of ability, morals, & good temper. –Col Burche's

Circuit Court of Wash Co, D C. Wm Kehoe has filed his ptn for the benefit of the Bankrupt Law: hearing on the first Mon in Apr next. –Wm Brent, clk

The subscriber lost from his pocket, in Wash City, on Feb 21, by some strange casualty, or something worse, the sum of $1,501.41, consisting of bank notes & drafts. Of the drafts, one was dated Jan 9, 1843, drawn by Walter Wood in favor of John B Lawson on Neale & Luckett, of Balt, endorsed by said John B Lawson. Another draft, drawn by Walter H Mitchell at sight, on Thompson & Spalding, of Balt, in favor of Wm Ferguson & Brother, & by them endorsed. Another draft, drawn by Saml Cox, on Thompson & Spalding, of Balt, in favor of Wm Ferguson & Bro, & by them endorsed. I will give $200 reward for the recovery of the money, or $300 for the recovery of the money & the conviction of the thief. –Wm Ferguson

Supreme Crt of the U S: Feb 20, 1843. #34: S J Jewell et al, plntfs in error, vs Benj Jewell et al. Argument in this cause was concluded by Mrs Legare for the plntfs in error. Feb 21, 1843. #37: B McKenna, plntf in error, vs C B Fish. Feb 22, 1843. #30: Thos E Ellis et al, vs M D Taylor's adm, in error to the U S Circuit Court for Alabama. The judgment of the said Circuit Court was affirmed, with costs, & 6% damages.

Died: on Feb 22, at the residence of Mr John Mason, jr, in Wash City, John Navarre Macomb, aged 18 months, s/o John & Czarina Macomb.

Died: at the residence of Col Kearney, of the army, Miss Mary Ann Fallon. A long life, passed in the exercise of all the best affections of the Christian character & in the enjoyment & consolation of a pure & religious hope, she met the summons of her Saviour with a meekness & resignation inspired by a deep & holy reliance on his favor & protection. –K [No date-current item.]

Died: on Feb 22, at Annapolis, Md, Somerville Pinkney. He lived beloved, & died in the prime of life, lamented by all who knew him.

SAT FEB 25, 1843

Laws of the U S passed at the 3rd Session of the 27th Congress. 1-Act for the relief of Casper W Wever: Sec of Treas to pay Wever $1,500, in full for his claim for compensation for services rendered by him in superintending the improvement of Pa ave, under the act of Congress of Feb, 1833. 2-Act for the relief of the reps of Alex'r Macomb, Robt Jennings, & the heirs & legal reps of Jas Roddy, dec'd, sureties of Saml Champlin, late a paymaster in the U S army. That Robt Jennings, & the heirs & legal reps of the late Alex'r Macomb & Jas Roddy be, & they are hereby, discharged from their liabilities on bond to the U S, in which the said Macomb, Roddy, & Jennings were sureties for Saml Champlin, formerly a paymaster in the U S army, & from any judgment obtained by the U S on said bond, against all or any of the said sureties, or their reps. 3-Act for the relief of Wm W Street: Sec of Treas to pay to Street $625, for five days' use of his steamboat in the transportation of Florida militia, in Oct, 1837. 4-Act for the relief of Wm De Buys, pastmaster at New Orleans. De Buys is authorized to retain, out of any sums in his hands, or which may come to his hands on account of rents arising from boxes or other private receptacles for letters in his ofc, the sum of $648.72; to reimburse him for money expended by him in repairs & fixtures for the post ofc in New Orleans city, between Jul 26, 1841, & Jan 1, 1842.

$25 reward for runaway negro woman Matilda, aged about 26 years.
–John H Waring, living near Nottingham, PG Co, Md.

Harvard Univ: Plan & objects of the law dept. Law library consists of 6,000 volumes. No examination & no particular course of previous study are necessary for admission; but the student is expected to produce testimonials of a good moral character. He also gives a bond of $200 to the Steward, with a surety resident in Mass, for the payment of College dues; or deposites, at his election, $150 with the Steward, at the commencement of each year. The price of board varies from $2.25 to $3.50 per week, & of room rent from .75 to $1.25 per week. –Simon Greenleaf, Royal Prof of Law, Cambridge, Mass

$15 for runaway negro man Arthur, about 21 years old. Deliver him to me at my residence in Culpeper Co, Va, near the town of Jefferson. –Pickett Withers

We regret to learn that Com Porter, the representative of our country at Constantinople, is in very delicate health. An extract from a private letter, received by his nephew, residing in Balt, from his sister, says: "Your uncle is at present in very feeble health, & we are apprehensive that he will not survive the present season." -Clipper

Hse/o Reps: 1-Bill for the relief of Gen Andrew Jackson. Maj Gen Andrew Jackson was in the defence of the city of New Orleans. A fine of $1,000 was imposed upon him by the Hon Dominick A Hall, in 1815. The Sec of Treas is directed to pay to Maj Gen Jackson the sum of $1,000 with interest, at 6%, from the day of its payment by him, out of any moneys in the Treas not otherwise appropriated. [The fine was for contempt of court.] 2-Ptn of Jacob T Stern & others, citizens of Pa, asking Congress to exert its power towards the abolition of all provisions of the Constitution & laws which sanction or sustain slavery. 3-Ptn of Hannah Parkman & others, of Hudson, N Y, praying an extension of the widows' pension act of Jul, 1838. 4-Ptn of Archibald Green & 73 citizens of Cayuga Co, N Y, for the repeal of the law of 1793, authorizing the capture of fugutive slaves. 5-Ptn of Lutellus Lindley & sundry citizens of Fayette Co, Pa, in favor of the proposition to issue scrip to the amount of $200,000,000, for the relief of the States. 6-Ptn of Milton Green, A Metcalf, & 36 others, citizens of Guernsey Co, Ohio, in favor of the measure proposed for the relief of the States. 6-Memorial of John Talbott, D W Whitehead, John Young, & 289 others, voters of Perry Co, Ohio, for the issue of $200,000,000 in stock for the relief of the States. 7-Ptn of Belinda Corner & 27 women of Ohio, setting forth that, according to a law of Congress, the vilest man may seize either of them or their children with out any warrant, & carry them to the land of manacies & despair; that there is no nation of Europe where the like violence & inhumanity would be perpetrated with impunity; that a dog or goose could be taken from the petitioners without a trial by jury. And praying they may be as well protected by law as the women of Europe; & if Congress have not power to grant such protection, that they may at least receive as much as a dog or a goose.

Bloomsbury for sale: valuable estate, the residence of Mrs Rebecca Somerville. It is 7 miles from Balt, 4 miles from Ellicott's Mills, 1 mile south of Catonsville, on the Balt & Fred'k turnpike road, & adjoins the farm of John Glenn. It contains 900 acs of land: improvements include the dwlg of brick, rough-cast, 80 feet front, & 40 feet deep, with porticos in front & rear. It commands a most extensive view of the city of Balt & of the river & bay. The stable, carriage house, & out houses are of stone, as is the barn, which is 80 feet by 50 feet. There is a valuable Tavern; 2 other stone dwlgs, with a Smith shop, Wheelwright's shop; all under rent to good tenants. Any further information may be had of John Glenn, in Balt. The subscriber, residing on the property, will be pleased to show it. –W T Somerville

The partnership existing between the subscribers under the firm of Phillips & Lansdale, is this day dissolved by mutual consent. The accounts of the firm will be left in the hands of Jas B Phillips for settlement. –Jas B Phillips, Enoch Lansdale

Valuable Potomac farm for sale: virtue of a deed of trust from Chas C Jett & Mary W his wife, dated Oct 12, 1838, & recorded in the ofc of the County Court of Westmoreland, Va: sale on Mar 25, in said county, the farm on which Gen

Washington was born, called *Wakefield*, containing 1,336 acs: farm is between Pope's & Mattox creek, in a high state of improvement. There is on the premises a small dwlg house with the necessary out-houses attached to it; overseer's house, & barns. I will also offer, at the same time & place, for cash, 25 likely negroes, consisting of men, women, boys, & girls. The title to the property is believed to be indisputable, but I shall convey such only as is vested in me as Trustee. –Patrick G Robb, trustee. [This is followed by: The undersigned will be pleased if any gentleman who may wish to purchase the farm *Wakefield*, offered for sale by Dr Robb, as Trustee, will visit him previous to the day of sale, when the farm can be visited & examined. The negroes offered for sale are also valuable, & offer strong inducements to purchasers. –Chas C Jett]

Foreign News: Mr Drummond, private Sec to Sir Robt Peel, was shot in the vicinity of Charing Cross, on Jan 20th. He died in the course of 5 days afterwards. The assassin, Danl McNaughton, is a native of Scotland, & it appears he mistook Mr Drummond for Sir R Peel, his intended victim. Opinions are various as to his insanity. His trial has been postponed.

Appointments by the Pres: Land Ofcs: 1-Thos W Newman reappointed Register at Washington, Mississippi. 2-John Bartow reappointed Register at Genesee, Mich. 3-Isaac D G Nelson appointed Receiver at Fort Wayne, Ind, vice Saml Lewis, dec'd.

Bradford Thompson, a highly respectable & wealthy citizen of Russell Co, Ala, was killed by his horse, near his residence at Sand Fort, a week or two ago. While with several of his neighbors, he was in pursuit of a buck, & his horse became unmanageable & ran at full speed, until the rider was jostled from the saddle, & dashed against a tree. He never again spoke, & lived only a few hours.

MON FEB 27, 1843
At Pelham, Westchester Co, N Y, on Tue last, Abraham Devoe loaded a fowling piece and went to the residence of his aunt, Mary Lecor, age 76 years, & deliberately shot her dead. He was taken into custody & said that he had been commanded to do so to atone for a grievous sin that he had committed.

Senate: 1-Hse bills considered in Cmte of the Whole, & passed: bill for the relief of John Core; relief of Thos D Gilson; relief of John E Hunt & others; relief of Robt G Ford; relief of Geo Randall, John C Haskell, & Elisha H Holmes; relief of Wm False. 2-Cmte on Pensions: asking to be discharged from the further consideration of the Hse bill for the relief of Asa Davis, & the bill granting a pension to Isaac Plummer. Also, from the same cmte, an adverse report on Hse bill for the relief of John Cary. 3-Cmte on Naval Affairs: adverse reports on Hse bills in favor of Frances M Lewis, wid/o Wm Lewis, & in favor of Mary Neale. Same cmte, an unfavorable report on the ptn of Ellen Dix. 4-Cmte of Pensions: adverse reports on Hse bills for the relief of Abraham Vanhorn, & for the relief of Nancy Byrd, wid/o Baylor Byrd. 5-Cmte on Pensions: adverse report on Hse bill for the relief of Geo Roushe. Also, asking to be discharged from the consideration of the bill for the relief of Jas Trimble, & that it be referred to the Cmte on Public Lands. 6-Cmte on Private Lands Claims: Hse bills, without amendment, for the relief of the legal reps of John Peters, dec'd, & for the relief of John McGinnis, a sldr in the late war. 7-Bills considered in Cmte of the Whole & finally passed: relief of Mary Crawford; of Benj J Totten; of John Warry; of Mary Williams, wid/o Jacob Williams; of Jos Horer & Abelard Guthrie; of Wm G Saunders; of Wm Allen, of Portland, Maine. Act granting to Jas Lowe $1,000 & a section of land. 8-Bills indefinitely postponed: relief of David W Haley; of Alice Usher; of Ardle Spear, wid/o John Spear, late an invalid pensions. Also, relief of Richd Marsh; of Carter B Chandler. Also of a bill granting a pension to John Peak. Also of a bill granting a pension to Robt Poindexter, of Ky. 9-Cmte on Revolutionary Claims: adverse reports on the 3 following memorials: from the legal reps of Chas M Thurston; from the heirs of Wm Williams; from the heirs of Brighton Payne. Also, same cmte, adverse report on Hse bill for the relief of Silvia Underwood. 10-Cmte on Military Affairs: asking to be discharged from the further consideration of the ptn of Alvin C Goell.

New Orleans, Feb 16, 1843. Mr Lavergne, Pres of the Consolidated Bank, made way with himself yesterday. He visited the family burying place in the rear of Algiers, where he stabbed himself with a sword cane or ponlard. He was brought over to the city & expired about 1 o'clock. -Bee

Sir Chas Bagot expired at his residence in Kingston on Feb 9. He was in brief service as Govn'r Gen of the Canadas. He was the first Minister from Great Britain to the U S after the restoration of peace between his country & the U S by the Treaty of Ghent, & resided here in that capacity 2 or 3 years with his consort. [Mar 1 newspaper: We are most happy to learn that the annunciation by a Rochester paper of the death of Sir Chas Bagot was incorrect. The latest dates represent him as being decidedly convalescent.]

Died on Feb 21, in Boston, Peter Oxenbridge Thacher, Judge of the Municipal Court of Suffolk Co, aged 66 years. The immediate cause of his death was more a general decay of the vital powers than any particular disease.

Hse/o Reps: 1-Memorial of Danl Engel & 114 citizens of Carroll Co, Md, praying Congress to issue 200,000,000 of stock for the relief of the States. Similar prayer of A G Catlett & a large number of other citizens of Wellesville, Ohio. The memorial of Dr Thos Lawson & 98 other citizens of Wellesville, Ohio, for the same. 2-Ptn of the widow of John Anderson. 3-Ptns from the following for the issue of 200,000,000 of stock for the relief of the States: Jas Adison & 108 other citizens of the town of Beaver, Pa. John Deckey & 138 other citizens of Brown Co, Pa. John G Deckey, of Bridgewater, Beaver Co, Pa. Thos Thornly, of Fallston, Beaver Co, Pa. John Push, of New Brighton, Beaver Co, Pa. T McClelland & 16 other citizens of Beaver

Co, Pa. 4-Ptns presented to the Hse/o Reps: by John Quincy Adams: Moses S F Tobey & others of Wareham, Mass, in favor of the Exechequer bill. Jabin Hatch & others of norther Pa. Against the repeal of the bankrupt law. S Lyons & 5 others, same prayer. W Fordham & 12 others, same prayer. S P Williams & 108 members of the annual conference of the Meth Episc Church in N H. Abolition of slavery under the jurisdiction of the nation. J Wolfenden & 43 Pa pensioners, navy asylum: for relief. Amy Collins Taft, Erie Co, N Y. Not to annul the late treaty with Great Britain. Nathl Swasey & others of Bath, Maine. To repeal the territorial Florida law of May 5, 1841. Amasa Soule & others of Maine. Abolition of slavery & no new slave state to be admitted. W R Rogers & 9 others of Maine: measures for the peaceable dissolution of the Union. S C Thomas & 14 others, South Chenango. To prohibit Sunday mails. Jas Mason, Jas Blair, John McDowell, John Snodgrass, & Saml Bennett: all followed by others, all the same prayer-to prohibit Sunday mails. Mary J Downer & others of Oneida Co, N Y. Appoint a cmte to investigate the condition of slaves. Cynthia Delong & others of Oneida Co, N Y. Repeal of fugitive slave act of Feb, 1793.

On Tue night the dwlg of Mr Nicholas Larzelere, in Abington Township, Montg Co, Pa, was destroyed by fire, & one of his children, a boy about 8 years of age, & a domestic, Sarah Weeks, perished in the flames. It is supposed they suffocated before the flames reached them.

Foreign Item. Dorothy & Sukey Adams, two old maiden sisters, aged 79 & 76, who had lived together from infancy, died last week at Petersfield, within 6 hours of each other.

Sale of furniture, books, clothing: order of the Orphan's Court of Wash Co, D C: on Mar 2. Sale of part of the personal estate of the late Capt J D Woodside & Nicholas Harper. –Robt W Dyer & Co, aucts

Yesterday Mr Richd Reid, of this place, a carriage-spring maker by trade, went out from town for the purpose of gunning. In taking the gun from the buggy in which he had carried it, the cock accidentally struck, & the muzzle being towards his body the whole discharge entered his breast, & he was immediately killed. [Copied from the Alexandria Gaz of Sat.] He has left a wife & children to mourn his premature death. The remains of the unfortunate Mr Reid were brought to this city for interment yesterday. He was a member of the Order of Odd Fellows, & they turned out in great numbers to attend the funeral.

$100 reward for runaway negroboy Dennis Lowe Harrison, about 16 years old. –A H Wells, near Bladensburg, PG Co, Md.

TUE FEB 28, 1843

Died: on Feb 13, at his residence in Augusta Co, Va, Gen Robt Porterfield, in his 91st year, one of the few surviving ofcrs of the Revolution. He was appointed by the Cmte of Safety, in Fred'k Co, & State of Va, in 1776, a 2nd lt in Capt Peter Brian Bruin's company of Continental troops; that company joined the main army under Gen Washington at Middlebrook, N J, & was ordered to join the 11th Va Continental regt commanded by Col Danl Morgan. He served the campaign in 1777 as lt, in 1778 as lt & adjutant, & the campaign in 1779 as capt & aid-de-camp to Gen Wm Woodferd; & in Dec, 1779, the Va troops were ordered to the South, where he accompanied Gen Woodferd as his aid-de-camp. The Gen, his aid-de-camp, & the greater part of the Va troops were captured at Charleston, S C. Gen Porterfield commanded a brig of militia in the last war with Great Britain; his brig was principally encamped at Mount Holly, in Va. He was a great patriot & gallant sldr; an honest & upright man. The author of these few lines knew him well; York, N J, & Pa, the campaigns of 1777, 1778, & 1779, under the command of Gen Washington; was his messmate [in a small open log-hut] during the winter of 1777-78, at Valley Forge, Pa. He has left 3 children, 13 or 14 grand-children, & 3 or 4 great grand-children, together with numerous friends, to lament his loss.
–Feb 24, 1843. –P S [The Richmond [Va] Whig will please copy the above.]

Obit-died: on Feb 1, in Kanawha Salines, Va, Col David Ruffner, aged 76 years. Col Ruffner emigrated from Shenandoah in 1797. Within a few months he was re-appointed a magistrate, an ofc which he had held in Shanandoah for some years previous to his removal. He continued in the active discharge of the duties of that ofc for nearly 47 years, up to the time of his death. He was elected to a seat in the Legislature within less than a year after his first arrival in the county. Without having enjoyed the advantages of early education, he attained, by his own strong common sense & by a good use of late occurring opportunities, to a degree of general intelligence that would do credit to a man of liberal education.
–Kanawha Republican

Cloverseed from Pa now landing & for sale by R L Jackson & Bro. [Local ad.]

$5 reward will be given by the subscriber to any one who will give information of the *drunken, loafing rowdies,* who threw stones & broke the lamps & glass on Pa ave on Sun night. –John A Donohoo

Mrd: on Wed last, by Rev John C Smith, Mr Andrew Smith to Mrs Matilda Brown.

Mrd: on Feb 21, by Rev John P Donelan, Mr Wm Becker to Miss Mary E Stiner, all of Wash City.

Died: on Feb 23, full of years, Mrs Mgt Miller, wid/o the late Robt Miller, of Wash City.

Died: on Feb 13, at Neabsco, Prince Wm Co, Va, in her 6th year, of croup, Virginia, eldest d/o Wm & Virginia Davies, of Louisville, Ky.

Died: on Feb 25, in Wash City, in her 71st year, Mrs Alice Bird.

Died: Sat last, in Wash City, Miss Eliz Brown, d/o the late Dr Gustavus Richd Brown, of Md. Her funeral is today at 10 a m, from Mr Griffith's, on F, near 7th st.

Died: on Jan 31, in Germantown, Stockes Co, N C, at the residence of C H Nelson, Mrs Maria Moore, consort of Mr John L Moore, late of Wash, D C.

Died: on Tue last, at Elkwood, Jefferson Co, Va, Benj Forrest, infant s/o Mr John Jas Abell.

Circuit Court of Wash Co, D C. Wm W Street; Jonathan Elliot; Geo Brown [colored]; have filed their ptns for the benefit of the Bankrupt Law: hearing on the first Mon in Apr next. –Wm Brent, clk

The wife of Jonathan Leveridge, a respectable mechanic of Newark, N J, while laboring under derangement of mind caused by the Miller doctrine, on Fri, administered arsenic to herself & 2 of her children, one aged 3 years & the other 12 months. She had sent her 3 oldest children to her aunt's, in the neighborhood. One of the children died at 12 o'clock, the other at 2 o'clock, & the wife died about 6 o'clock. [See below.]
+
At a Millerite meeting in Providence, last week, the minister got the audience worked up to such a pitch, that they were every moment looking for the end of all things, which he told them would be announced by the sound of a trumpet.

Circuit Court of Wash Co, D C. Wm W Street; Jonathan Elliot; Geo Brown [colored]; have filed their ptns for the benefit of the Bankrupt Law: hearing on the first Mon in Apr next. –Wm Brent, clk

Senate: 1-Cmte on Pensions: asked to be discharged from the further consideration of the following ptns: ptn of the wid/o Philip King, a Revolutionary sldr. Ptn of Joshua Raymond, a sldr of the Revolution. Ptn of Mary Spencer & Mary Field. Ptn of the wid/o Jos Thompson & Jno Gould. 2-Cmte on Pensions: Hse bill for the relief of Danl Penhallow, & recommending its passage. Same cmte: adverse report on the ptn of John Bosworth. 3-Cmte on Private Land Claims: Hse bill for the relief of the legal reps of Antoine Vasques & others. Same cmte: adverse report on Hse bill for the relief of Eliz Burriss, her heirs or assigns, in their title to a tract of land. 4-Cmte on the Judiciary: bill for the relief of Jno Grant. 5-Cmte on Finance: adverse report on Hse bill for the relief of Saml Hoffman. 6-Cmte of the Whole: bill for the relief of Richd Patten. Bill for the relief of C M Keller.

WED MAR 1, 1843
Hse/o Reps: 1-Cmte on Commerce: made a report on the memorial of Ferguson & Rice, with a bill for their relief. Cmte of Claims: made a report on the case of Jos Nock, accompanied by the following resolution: Resolved, that the claims of Jos Nock, for damages occasioned by the annulment of his contract for furnishing locks & keys for the use of the U S mail, be, & it hereby referred to the Solicitor of the Treas, & that the said Solicitor is authorized to examine said claim; & report to the next Congress what gain, in his opinion, Mr Nock would have realized upon his contract in addition to what he has received, if he had been permitted & required to furnish locks & keys, according to the terms of his contract, sufficient with those delivered & paid for, to supply the entire U S mail for 5 year from & after Apr 1, 1841, & that the said Solicitor have power to take testimony relative to the expenses of manufacturing such locks & keys as Nock contracted to deliver, including the cost of labor, use & hazard of capital, & the wear of locks & machinery. 3-Cmte of Claims: adverse report on the ptn of Benj Bentley. 4-Cmte on Commerce: made a report on the ptn of John Morse, for fishing bounty, with a bill for the relief of the owners of the boat **Ann**. 5-Cmte on the Post Ofc & Post Roads: was referred the ptn of J & P Voorhees, reported a joint resolution to authorize the Postmaster General to settle with said persons. 6-Ptn of Jas Currie, jr, & 50 other citizens of N Y C, praying Congress to adopt some measure to enable the indebted States to fulfill their engagements. 7-Ptn of Geo Warfield & a number of other citizens of Carroll Co, & Howard district, in A A County, in favor of the issue of $200,000,000 Gov't stock for the relief of the indebted States. Ptn of Henry Keefer & 130 other citizens of Carroll Co, Md, for the same purpose.

Died: on Mon last, in Wash City, Miss Mary Davies, sister of the late Mrs Anne Blagden. Her funeral will be from the First Presby Church, 4½ st, today at 2 p m.

Died: on Feb 28, Mrs Mgt Dalton, in her 60th year, after a lingering & painful illness, which she bore for nearly 26 months with Christian patience & resignation. Her funeral is at Mr Thos Adams', corner of F & 12th sts, tomorrow, at 3 p m.

Senate: Cmte on Patents: Hse bill, without amendment, for the relief of Saml K Jennings. 2-Cmte on Public Bldgs: without amendment, Hse bill for the relief of John Skirving. 3-Cmte on Private Land Claims: Hse bills, & recommending their passage: relief of Hugh Riddle, of N Y; of John Darlin; of Mary McGee, & Susan Price, heirs at law of Geo Neilson. 4-Cmte on Indian Affairs: adverse report on the ptn of Saml Bingham. Also, asking to be discharged from the further consideration of the ptn of Benj Crawford. 5-Cmte on Finance: Hse bill authorizing the Sec of the Treas to refund to David Natkinson & Co, certain duties paid on goods imported into N Y. 6-Bills considered in the Cmte of the Whole, & passed: Relief of Duncan L

Clinch; relief of Mary W Thompson, wid/o the late Lt Col Thompson, of the U S Army; relief of Danl G Skinner, of Ala; relief of John R Williams.7-Bill for the relief of Jas Taylor & for other purposes was considered in Cmte of the Whole & indefinitely postponed. 8-Bill granting a pension to David Welsh was taken up, &, after having been considered in Cmte of the Whole, was ordered to be engrossed.

Appointment by the Pres: David McGahey, Receiver of Public Moneys for the district of lands subject to sale at Palestine, Ill, vice Augustus C French, whose commission has expired.

The coroner held an inquest on Mon, at N Y C Hospital, on the body of Dr Henry Mead, aged 65, native of Connecticut. The dec'd was formerly Alderman of the 13th ward: a man of wealth & fashion, a practicing physician in this city; of genius & enterprise, being the first that ever manufactured porcelain or china ware in this country, in which he engaged at Jersey City; the first who ever made pins here, & the first that ever refined camphor in this country. He lost his wife some 4 years since. He had become reduced greatly in circumstances & was very destitute. He went to the hospital on Fri to lodge. He became delirious & was attacked with convulsions on Sat, refused medicine, & died about 3 a m on Sun. –N Y Jrnl of Commerce

Hon Henry A Wise has been nominated to the Senate by the Pres of the U S, to be Minister Plenipotentiary & Envoy to France.

Gen Mirabeau B Lamar, Ex-Pres of Texas, & Gen H McLeod, cmder of the Texian Santa Fe Expedition, arrived at New Orleans in the last Galveston packet, on thier way to visit their friends in Georgia.

Wooster [Ohio] Democrat: Gen Reasin Beall died on Feb 20th at his mansion, half a mile from this town. Gen Beall stood as a patriarch in the midst of his descendants. He was 73 years of age. The disease which terminated his existence was inflammation of the lungs with which he was confined about 10 days.

Circuit Court of Wash Co, D C. Louisa Ballard has filed her ptn for the benefit of the Bankrupt Law: hearing on the first Mon in Apr next. –Wm Brent, clk

On Sun night, the dwlg of the Hon Danl Webster, Sec of State, was burglariously entered, & several silver & plated articles stolen therefrom. On the same night or morning, Mr John Davidson, of Gtwn, was robbed of several silver articles in a similar manner. In the course of the same day, Mr Alison Naylor, who resides in 13th st, between F & G, was also robbed of several silver articles. It is to be hoped that the police ofcrs & the auxiliary guard will unite their endeavors to ferret out & arrest these daring burglars.

Wash Corp: Feb 27, 1843. 1-Ptn of Thos Goddard was referred to the Cmte of Claims. 2-Cmte of Claims, reported without amendment, the bill for the relief of Eliza Bell: read a 3rd time & passed. Same cmte: reported a bill for the relief of W H Yates: read a 3rd time & passed. 3-Cmte of Common Council: bill for the relief of Benj F Wright was taken up: read a 3rd time & passed. 4-Ptn of Jos Milburne, praying remission of a fine: referred to the Cmte of Claims. 5-Ptn of Jas Young, jr, & Wm Young, praying remission of a fine: referred to the Cmte of Claims. 6-Cmte of Claims: bill for the relief of Wm J Bronaugh, reported the same without amendment, & recommend that it be indefinitely postponed: which report was agreed to. 7-Ptn of Wm A Bradley & others, on the subject of Ward boundaries, was laid on the table. 8-Bill for the relief of Wm Thomas was taken up: read a 3rd time & passed. 9-Cmte on Improvements: ptn of Thos Gallaher & others, reported a bill authorizing a gravel footwalk from G to H st on 4th st west: read a 3rd time & passed.

THU MAR 2, 1843
Circuit Court of Wash Co, D C. John Larkin Dorsey; & Henry Miller: have each filed their ptn for the benefit of the Bankrupt Law: hearing on the first Mon in Apr next. –Wm Brent, clk

Genius of Liberty Ofc, Leesburg, Va: We shall sell this ofc on Mar 28: consists of 2 presses, 4 founts of type, fancy & job type. Terms cash. –Geo Richards

The Hon Ruel Williams, one of the Senators in Congress from Maine, has sent in his resignation to the Leg of that State.

Died: on the 10th ult, at *Oakley*, her late residence, in St Mary's Co, Md, in her 51st year, Eliz, relict of S Gough, & d/o the late Judge John R Plater, of Md.

Died: on the 18th ult, at his residence, in Howard District, A A Co, Maj Henry Welling, in his 67th year, beloved & respected by all who knew him.

Died: on the 26th ult, at Alexandria, in his 87th year, Edman Yeates, a native of England, late of Phil.

Died: on Mar 1, Wm Edw, infant s/o Robt W & Sarah R Bates, aged 2 months & 3 days. His funeral is this day at 1 p m.

Senate: 1-Cmte on Pensions: adverse reports on the following bills: relief of John P Schuyler; relief of Eliz Dawkins; Hse bill for the relief of John Everly. 2-Cmte on Claims: Hse bill, without amendment, for the relief of the legal reps of Robt A Kelly. 3-Cmte on Military Affairs: bill for the relief of Mrs Zantzinger, wid/o Capt Zantzinger, of the U S Army. 4-Cmte on Pensions: hse bill for the relief of Josiah Westlake, of Nancy Wilson, & of Robt Layton's children. 5-Cmte of the Whole: indefinitely postponed: relief of Jos W Reckless; relief of Gideon A Perry; relief of

Saml B Tuck; relief of Benj Evans; relief of Saml Neely; relief of Mrs Anne W Angus; relief of Jos Robey; relief of Thos H Brown; relief of S & M Riche; relief of D & J Wilkinson. 6-An Act for the relief of the owners, master, & crew of the schnr **Codhook**, of Blue Hill, Maine. 7-Act for the relief of Levi Eldredge & others. 8-An Act for the relief of the owners of the schnr **Three Brothers**. 9-Act for the relief of John Patten, jr, owner of the fishing schnr **Credit**, & the master & crew of said vessel. 10-Act for the relief of Wm Ellery, owner of the fishing schnrs **Sevo & Ida**, both of Gloucester, Mass, & others. 11-Act for the relief of John H Russell, & others, as owners, master, & crew of the fishing schnr **Lucy Ann**. 12-Act for the relief of Mary Broadstreet, Amos Tappan, & others. 13-Act for the relief of Barnabas Baker, jr, & others, owners of the fishing schnr **Union**, of Dennis Mass. 14-Act for the relief of Joshua Knowles, jr, & others, owners & crew of the fishing schnr **Garnet**. 15-Act for the relief of Teakle Savage, administrator of Bolitha Laws. 16-Act for the relief of the legal reps of Francis Pellicer. 17-Act for the relief of John Farnham. 17-Acts for the relief of the heirs & legal reps of Wm Lomax: relief of Alex'r H Everett; relief of Jno A Smith; relief of Wm Paterson; relief of Eliz Whiteman; relief of Sampson Brown; relief of Geo E Johnson; relief of Mary Barry, wid/o Thos Barry; relief of Maj Thos Harrison; relief of Prudence Couch. 18-Acts granting a pension to Patrick Masterson; Mary Elder; David Munn; Leah Tenure; Henry Freeman; Eliz Harris, Geo P Pollen, Robt Colgate, & S Morris Walen; Jane McGuire, wid/o Maj Thos McGuire; Mrs Ann Royal, wid/o Capt Wm Royal.

Mrd: on Tue last, at the residence of the Postmaster Gen, by the Rev Septimus Tuston, Chaplain of the U S Senate, Robt C Wickliffe to Miss Ann R Dawson, d/o the Hon J B Dawson, Rep in Congress from Louisiana.

Teacher wanted: trustees of the Elkton Academy are desirous of engaging a Principal to take charge of the institution on Apr 1 next. Apply to Col A Whann, Postmaster, Trustee, Elkton Acad, Cecil Co, Md.

Col John Cox re-elected Mon last, Mayor of Gtwn, to serve for the ensuing 2 years.

The flour mill of Mr Geo Platt, at Stanton, Del, was consumed by fire on Thu night, together with 200 barrels of flour, & a quantity of grain.

Hse/o Reps: 1-Cmte on Commerce: made a report on the ptn of John B Hodges, of Balt, with a bill for his relief. 2-Cmte on Private Land Claims: made an adverse report on the ptn of Ellen Duval, in behalf of her late husband, E W Duval. 3-Conference Cmte: made a report in the case of Jas F Calhoon. 4-Cmte on Roads & Canals: reported a bill to authorize an experiment to test the utility of an invention of a snag fender by Jos W Kirk, which bill was committed to a Cmte of the Whole House on the state of the Union. 5-Cmte on Expenditures in the Navy Dept: reported the following resolution: That the Sec of the Navy to report to this Hse the number of persons who were under the command of Lt J T McLaughlin, attached to the Florida squadron during the year commencing Oct 9, 1842, or for such time as he was in actual command of the squad, & also the average number of persons who were on the sick list during that period. 6-Cmte on Public Expenditures: submitted papers in relation to a report of that cmte made at the last session of Congress, in relation to the conduct of Capt S H Webb, as a disbursing ofcr of the Gov't. 7-Select Cmte: to which was re-committed the bill for the relief of Henry M Shreve & to authorize the purchase of his patent for a snag boat, reported the same without amendment. 8-Resolved: that the Sec of the Navy be directed to report to this Hse any information in his Dept in relation to the improvement in gun carriages made by Lt G J Van Brunt, of the Navy. 9-Ptn of W Carothers, Saml Patten, & 88 other citizens of Hanover township, Beaver Co, praying Congress to adopt the plan to issue 200,000,000 of Gov't stock to be distributed among the States. Ptn of Henry Mellen & 37 other citizens of Champaign Co, Ohio, for the same. Ptn of Alvah James & 100 other citizens of Muskingum Co, Ohio, praying for the same. 10-Memorial of Geo Weaver & 107 other citizens of Mercer Co, Pa, praying Congress to adopt measures to prevent the desecration of the Sabbath, by abolishing the transportation of the mail on the Sabbath & opening & keeping open the post ofc on that day. Ptn of Truman C Stanford & 35 other citizens, ptn of Hugh Wallace & 35 other citizens, of Mercer Co, Pa, for the same-prevent desecration of the Sabbath.

FRI MAR 3, 1843
Hse/o Reps: 1-Cmte on Public Lands: referred the bill from the Senate for the relief of John R Williams, reported the same without amendment. 2-Cmte on Indian Affairs: to which was referred the claim of Garry Henart, made a report thereon, which was ordered to be laid on the table. 3-Cmte of Claims: was referred the bill from the Senate for the relief of Richd Patten, reported the same without amendment. 4-Cmte on Commerce: made an adverse report on the ptn of Wm Nixon. 5-Letter from the Sec of the Treas, transmitting, in obedience to an order of the Hse of the 23rd inst, the report of Wm Robinson, the agent sent by the Gov't to Europe to negotiate a loan for the use of the U S. 6-Memorial of Amos S Slaymaker & 104 other citizens of the city & county of Lancaster, Pa, praying Congress to pass an act for the issue of $200,000,000 of Gov't stock, to be divided among the States. Ptn of Nathl Kinzer & other citizens of Franklin Co, Pa: for the same.

Circuit Court of Wash Co, D C. Wm Tyler, a bankrupt; & Richd W Griffith, a bankrupt: have filed their ptns for their discharge & certificates: hearing for each on the first Mon in Jun next. –W Brent, clk

Circuit Court of Wash Co, D C. John W Dexter has filed his ptn for the benefit of the Bankrupt Law: hearing on the first Mon in Apr next. –Wm Brent, clk

Destructive fire at Cincinnati: on Sat, in the smoke-house of Messrs Pugh & Alvord, at the corner of Walnut st & the Canal, explosion was awfully terrific, & from 8 to

12 persons were immediately killed. Of those positively ascertained to be killed this morning, were:

Jos Bonsall

H S Edmands, Pork Packer

J S Chamberlain, Pattern Maker

John Ohe, a German laborer

Caleb Taylor, of the late firm of Woodnut & Co

Severely wounded:

H Thorpe, Inspector of Pork

T G Shaeffer, Printer

Mr Alvord, firm of Pugh & Alvord

Saml Schooley, a lad

Mr Finch, Carpenter

John Blakmore, Machinist

Geo Shillito, firm of Worthington, Shillito & Co

Senate: 1-Resolution of the Leg of N Y, in favor or the release of Amos Kendall. 2-Cmte on Naval Affairs: a bill for the relief of Saml Thompson. 3-Cmte on the Post Ofc & Post Roads: a joint resolution to authorize the Postmaster Gen to settle with J & P Voorhees. 4-Bill for the relief of Boyd Reilly was taken up.

Notice to Passengers going South. The Steamboat carrying the great Southern mail, connecting with the Richmond Railroad at Aquia Creek, leaves Bradley's Wharf every morning, until further notice. An Omnibus will call at Gadsby's & Brown's Hotel in the morning to convey passengers to the boat free of charge.
--F Black, agent

Mrd: on the 28th ult, by Rev S A Roszel, of Va, the Rev Geo W Israel, of the Balt Annual Conference, to Miss Sarah R, 2nd d/o Thos Woodward.

Crmnl Crt-Mar 1, 1843. 1-Martin Lauxman was indicted for stealing, on Jan 15, 1843, a cow & calf, value of $25, the property of the Hon C A Wickliffe. Jury found a verdict of not guilty. 2-Thos Plumsell, a county constable, was indicted for refusing to assist in arresting Jas Barnes, a peace-breaker, when called on by Saml Scott, a constable, in the discharge of his duty. The Jury found him not guilty. 3-Geo Lipscomb, indicted for selling liquor without a license near a negro camp meeting in Wash Co: found guilty. 4-Robt Scott, indicted for assault & battery upon Peter W Jordinson, & was found guilty.

J Smith Dodge, Dental Surgeon, having been sick & unable to attend to his engagements, will remain in Washington until Mar 4, Ofc #3, Pa ave, between the Railroad Depot & Capitol.

Creditors of John Purdon are to meet at the ofc of Walter Lenox, Atty at Law, on Mar 4, at 11 a m.

SAT MAR 4, 1843
A stray buffalo cow has been about my stable all winter. The owner may have her by applying to me at the War Dept, paying for this ad, & remunerating me for the expense of taking care of her. –Wm Markward

Monroe Academy, on H st between 8th & 9th sts: course of study is such as is pursued in the best academies in the country. References: A Kendall; Jos S Wilson-principal clerk of private land claims; Rev J Davis; Jas Darden, of the Post Ofc Dept. –John E Norris

Hse/o Reps: 1-The bill for the relief of Benj Ogle Tayloe, which had been returned from the Senate with an amendment, coming up by general consent: laid on the table.

Jas Williams, Cabinet & Chair Wareroom, Pa ave, near 4½ st. I have a good assortment of furniture, which I will sell low for cash. Old furniture taken in exchange for new. Old furniture & chairs repaired & repainted.

Orphan's Court of Wash Co, D C. Letters testamentary on the personal estate of Wm Magill, late of said county, dec'd. -Jos Fowler, exc

Circuit Court of Wash Co, D C. Thos Mitchell has filed his ptn for the benfit of the Bankrupt Law: hearing on the first Mon in Apr next. Same for Silas Reed; & Cranstoun Laurie. –Wm Brent, clk

To Printers. H Worrall & Co continues to manufacture, at their old established Iron Foundry, Printing Press & Saw Manufactory, #s 22, 24, 26, & 28 Elm st, N Y. –Henry Worrall, Noah Worrall

Murder & Suicide. We learn from a gentleman from Jamestown, that on Feb 22, Alvin Cornell murdered his wife, by cutting her throat with a razor. He then cut his own throat. Mr Cornell was formerly postmaster at Ashville, & during the last summer resided in this place, & assisted in teaching the village school. Since then he has been at Michigan, & returned only 10 days since. He had an interesting wife & family of children. It was generally supposed he was laboring under a species of derangement, to turns of which he has been subject for several years. –Mayville Sentinel

Died: on Mar 2, in Wash City, after a short illness, John Douglass Simms, for some years Chief Clerk in the Navy Dept. Mr Simms was a native of Va, & a s/o the late Col Chas Simms, of Alexandria, a distinguished ofcr of the Revolutionary war. Educated at Princeton College, N J, he has left that institution with a high literary reputation, & afterwards practiced law for several years. In his death his family mourn the loss of a beloved protector. His funeral is on Mar 5 at 2:30 o'clock, from his late dwlg, on Pa ave, near the West Market.

Died: on Wed, Frances Eliz, d/o Geo V & Mary Hall, in her 7th year.

Columbia Typographical Society meeting at Buckingham's Room, Sat, at 7:30 p m. --Jas Wimer, Rec Sec

MON MAR 6, 1843
The vessel **Emma Isadora** sailed from Boston on Wed for Smyrna, under the direction of the American Board of Com'rs for Foreign Missions. Passengers: The Rev Justin Perkins, lady, & child; Rev Edwin E Bliss & lady; Misses Catharine Myers & Fidelia Fisk, all destined to the Nestorian Christians in Persia; & the Rev David T Stoddard & lady, destined to the Independent Nestorians. Mar Yohannan, Bishop of the Nestorian Chr, was also a passenger in the same vessel. [Correction in Mar 7 newspaper: Rev Edwin E Bliss & lady are destined to the Independent Nestorians, & the Rev David T Stoddard, & all the other Missionaries, to the Nestorian Christians of Persia. --Advertiser]

Maj Antoine Dequindre died at Detroit, Mich, on Feb 24. In the last war with Great Britian, amidst the most trying scenes on the frontier, he distinguished himself as the commander of a company of independent volunteers, for which he was handsomely complimented by the Leg of his State within the last 2 years.

The Rev Jas T Johnson, Rector of St Paul's Chr in Alexandria, D C, has been elected Bishop of the Episcopal Church in Alabama.

Died: on Mar 3, at the residence of her brother, John L Brightwell, near Wash City, Mrs Martha Pickrell, in her 67th year.

Died: on Feb 12, at Charlestown, Mass, Mrs Sarah E L Taylor, w/o the Rev Fitch W Taylor, Chaplin in the U S Navy.

Died: on Mar 5, Sarah Wilson, infant d/o Geo & Mary Ballinger, aged 7 months & 26 days.

For sale: a farm in Fairfax Co, 12 miles from Wash, containing about 200 acs. It is in the occupancy of Mr Wm Swink, who will show the premises. For further particulars inqure at the Law Ofc of Messrs Swann & Swann, near the City Hall.

Patrick & Barnard Flanagan, the 2 brothers under sentence of death in Cambria Co, Pa, for murder in the first degree, & who were to be executed on Fri last, have been respited by the Govn'r until Apr 21. New testimony has been discovered, which may give a different aspect to the question of their guilt or innocence. The Flanagans were convicted of the murder of an old lady named Holder, whose money was supposed to have tempted their cupidity.

Wash Corp: 1-Act for the relief of Wm Thomas: fine imposed by judgment of J D Clark, for a violation of the law in relation to hawkers & pedlars, is remitted, provided Thomas pay the costs of prosecution. 2-Act for the relief of Louis Galabrun: fine imposed on Galabrun by judgement of J D Clark for a violation of an act of this Corp in relation to the erection of wooden bldgs, is remitted: provided Galabrun pay the costs of prosecution. 3-Act for the relief of Benj F Wright, by judment of John D Clark, for a violation relative to the sweeping of chimneys, is remitted: provided that Wright pay the cost of prosecution.

For rent: farm in Alexandria Co, called **Preston**, about 4 miles from Washington. Also, another country residence in the same neighborhood, called **Oakville**. The dwlg & other bldgs on the premises are complete. Also, in the same neighborhood, another farm near the Columbian Factory containing 270 acs. Information at the Law Ofcs of Messrs Swann & Swann, near the City Hall, or my residence, on I st, between 17th & 18th sts west. Also, several Servants to hire. –Francis Swann

TUE MAR 7, 1843
Lists of Acts passed at the 3rd Session of the 27th Congress:
Act for the relief of:

Richd Snead	John Javins	Jonathan Britton
S & M Riche	Wm Allen	Boyd Reilly
John Hodgkin	Benj J Totten	Robt G Ford
Saml E Jennings	Allen Rogers	Chas Waldron
John Skirving	Wm Gale	Geo C Johnston
Jacob White	Solomon Emerson	Jas Gray
Saml Weller	Lyman N Cook	Eliz Powers
John Wolfenden	John F Wiley	Geo A Winslow
John Core	John Hicks	Jeremiah Kimball
John Wharry	Geo Waddle	John E Hunt & others
Wm G Sanders	Saml Lord	Jos Hover & Abelard
Nancy Poleresky	Richd Rush	Guthrie
Richd Patten	John Drysdale	Peters, Moore & Co
John R Williams	Garret Vleit	Nancy Wilson
J R Vienne	Horace Wetherell	Andrew Fisher
Eliz Munroe	Benj Thruston	Gamaliel E Smith
Saml Dicy	Danl Penhallow	Jas Sweetman
Asahel Brainard	Saml M Asberry	Saml Lord
Robt B Lewis	Jos Ellery	Wm Gale
Jos Nimblett	Jas S Calhoun	Wm Fabre
Jas Pepper & others	Johnson Patrick	Wm W Street
Chas B Hall, of Cincinnati	John Skinner	Snow Y Sears
	Thos D Gilson	Ferdinand Leibert
Robt Ramsay	Jos R Chandler	Burr & Smith

Isaac & Thos S Winslow	Peter Lionberger	Ruth Mathiot
Joshua Drew	Adms of John Jackson	Robt Layton's children
Barent Stryker	Saml Hambleton	Lgl reps of Robt T Spence
Jas M Morgan	Mary Crawford	
John R Delany	Caspar W Wever	
	Wm Allen	

Lgl reps of Lt Wm S Eveleth
Lgl reps of Robt A Kelly
Lgl reps of John Peters, dec'd
Hugh Riddle, of the State of N Y
Cornelius Wilson & Jas Canter
Eliz Gresham, wid/o Geo Gresham
John P Skinner & the legal reps of Isaac Green
Richd Coke, jr, Robt Anderson, & Geo W Southall
Mary McGee & Susan Pierce, heirs at law of Geo Neilson
Nancy Hambright, wid/o Capt John Hambright, dec'd
Lgl reps of Capt Saml Shannon, dec'd
Mary Williams, wid/o Jacob Williams, dec'd
Jas B Sullivan, of the county of Rapides, in Louisiana
Hannah Jenkins, wid/o Jas Jenkins, dec'd
John McGinnis, a sldr in the late war
Mary W Thompson, wid/o the late Lt Col Thompson, of the U S Army
Wm De Buys, postmaster at New Orleans
Heirs of Madame De Sisser & their legal reps
Lgl reps of Danl Brent, late Consul of the U S at Paris
Edwin Bartlett, late Consul of the U S at Lima, Peru
Chas Gordon, owner of the schnr **Two Sons**, & legal reps of the crew of said vessel
Act to revive an act entitiled: "An act for the relief of John Davlin"
Stockbridge tribe of Indians in the Territory of Wisconsin
Knott Martin, 3rd, & Arnold Martin, owners of the fishing schnr **Only Son**, & others
Hugh Riddle, of the State of N Y
Asahel Lee, Harvey Lee, & Lemuel Lee
Heirs, or the assignees of the heirs, of Isaac Todd & Jas McGill
Geo Randall, John C Haskell, & Elisha H Holmes
John Randolph Clay, late Sec of Leg of the U S at the Crt of Vienna
Heirs of Philander Smith & Jas Young
Chldrn of Mary Rhinevault, dec'd
Gorham A North, one of the sureties of Saml Edmonds, dec'd
Elisha Moreland, Wm M Kennedy, Robt J Kennedy, & Mason E Lewis
Thos Weaver & Jacog Heyberger, sureties of the Norrisstown & Valley Railroad Co
Act to amend an act entitled "An act for the relief of Geo Mayfield," approved Jul 27, 1842
Reps of Alex'r Macomb, Robt Jennings, & the heirs & legal reps of Jas Roddy, dec'd, sureties of Saml Champlain, late a paymaster in the army of the U S

Pension to: Israel Thomas; Danl Welch; Nancy Williams, wid/o David Williams, who was one of the captors of Maj Andre.
Joint Resolutions:
Authorizing the Postmaster Gen to settle with J & P Voorhies
Explanatory of an act for the relief of Thos King
Presenting thanks of Congress to Saml T Washington, for the service-sword of Gen Washington & the staff of Benj Franklin, presented by him to Congress

Saml T Bicknell, Atty & Counsellor at law, Maryville, Blount Co, East Tenn. He will attend to the collection of claims in any part of the Eastern Division of Tennessee.

Circuit Court of Wash Co, D C. John M Cutts, a bankrupt; Benj R Smith, a bankrupt; Edw Smith, a bankrupt; each filed his ptn for his discharge & certificate: hearing for each on the first Mon of Jun next. –W Brent, clk

We learn that the Pres of the U S has revoked the sentence of the Naval Court Martial under which Cmdor Ballard was suspended from command for the period of 12 months. –Balt Amer

A son of Mr Rathburn, of Auburn, & a student in Geneva college, was accidentally drowned a few days since by breaking through the ice on Seneca lake.

Mrd: on Dec 29 last, at Hydropolis, parish of Avoyeles, Lousiana, by Rev Abbe Francais, Dr Benj Dulany to Miss Josephine De Generes, d/o J De Generes, late of Fairfax Co, Va.

Mrd: on Jan 10 last, by Rt Rev Antoine Blanc, L Florval De Generes to Miss Josephine Abat, both of New Orleans.

Died: Mar 5, in Wash City, after a painful illness, Eliz C, only child of Richd B & Mary Ann Nally, aged 18 months & 8 days. Her funeral will take place this morning, at 10 a m, from the corner of H & 9th sts.

Died: on Mar 5, Mrs Jane Van Riswick, aged 54 years. Her funeral is this afternoon at 2 p m.

Died: on Sun last, Eliz P Smith, eldest d/o John A & Sally Smith. Her funeral will be from the residence of her parents, near the city of Washington, this day, at 11 a m.

Circuit Court of Wash Co, D C. Bankrupts: Lambert S Beck; Nelson R Robertson; John Espey; Jas Thomas; Geo W Robinson' Douglass Vass; Isaac S Lauck; & Jas Nokes: each filed his ptn for his discharge & certificate: hearing for each on the first Mon in June next. –Wm Brent, clk

Delinquent lands in Alleghany Co: unless the taxes, with costs of advertising, due on the lands in the following list, shall be paid to the Collector of the Tax for said county, or to Chas Farquharson, agent, residing in Balt City, on or before Jun 1 next, the said lands will be sold at public auction. –Patrick Hammill, Collector of the County Tax in Alleghany Co for 1842.

John Bugh's heirs/*Chance*-378 acs: 1841-$4.33; 1842-$1.40
J Buffington/*Part of Western Connexion*-1,108 acs:1841-$5.52; 1842-$4.24
J Brengle/lots-250 acs: 1842-$1.52
Robt H Beaty & John W Ott & others/lots-300 acs: 1842-$1.85
Wm Cook/*Stony Ridge, Deer Park*; 2,388 acs: 1842-$11.13
Wm Campbell's heirs/*Pink of Alleghany*-1,384 acs: 1842-$20.95
Walter Chandler/lots-250 acs: 1842-$2.08
Nicholas Callen/lot-50 acs: 1842-.95
Jas Cunningham's heirs/*Meadow Mountain*-645 acs; *Latent Worth*-4,624 acs: 1842-$75.68
Thos Chester/lot-50 acs: 1842-$1.40
Henry Coulter/lots-150 acs: 1842-$1.52
Marmaduke W Conner/lot-50 acs: 1841-$3.74; 1842-$1.40
John Davis/lots-150 acs: 1841-$4.25; 1842-$1.52
Thos Ellicott & Meredith/lots-300 acs: 1841-$6.00; 1842-$5.05
Henry Everly/lots-150 acs: 1842-$1.52
Geo Fitzhugh/lots-150 acs: 1841-$4.01; 1842-$1.85
Thos Galloway/*Part of Rights of Man*-189 acs: 1842-$3.06
Wm & John Johnson/*Part of Paley, add to to Mount Airy*-621 acs: 1842-$6.11
Reverdy Johnson/*Eden's Paradise Regained*-1,000 acs: 1842-$7.75
Lillias A P Jones/*Republican Bonum*-200 acs: 1841-$4.96; 1842-$1.85
Anthony Kennedy/lots-300 acs: 1842-$1.85
Sheperd C Leakin/lot-50 acs: 1841-$3.21; 1842-.73
Thos Turner/lots-200 acs: 1842-$1.40
Wm Vandiver's heirs/*William's Discovery*-400 acs: 1842-$1.85
Henry W Webb/lot-50 acs: 1842-.73
Saml Young/lot-50 acs: 1842-.73
District #2:
John Brice/Huron 200 acs, *Grove* 200 acs, *Ington* 200 acs: 1842-$5.73
Philip Clayton/lot-50 acs: 1842-.95
Geo Felger/lot-50 acs: 1841-$3.22; 1842-.84
Benedict Hall/lots-200 acs: 1842-$1.40
Wm Meley's heirs/lots-200 acs: 1841-$7.22; 1842-$1.85
Wm Magruder/lot-50 acs: 1842-.84
Capt Marberry/*Squirrel Range*-187 acs: 1842-$2.19
District #3:
Levin H Adams/lots-250 acs: 1842-$2.35
Chas Croxall/lots-200 acs: 1842-$1.40

Matthew St Clair Clarke/lots-200 acs: 1842-$1.90
Matthew St Clair Clarke & Geo Templeman/lots-250 acs: 1842-$4.57
Benj Davis/lot & *Gensang*-70 acs; *Fair Hill*-194 acs: 1841-$5.95; 1842-$2.22
Allen T Edmonds/lots-250 acs: 1841-$5.15; 1842-$2.35
Jas Parker/lots-200 acs: 1841-$5.21; 1842-$1.90
Henry C Gaither/lots-200 acs: 1842-$2.80
John Gwynn's heirs/*Hunter's Art*-325 acs: 1842-$4.89
David Hopkins/lots-200 acs: 1842-$2.35
Benj Garrett/lots-200 acs: 1842-$2.80
Geo Gaither/*Montgomery*-130½ acs: 1841-$3.60; 1842-$1.68
John Gunby/lots-200 acs: 1842-$2.35
Robt Halkerson/lots-200 acs: 1841-$5.21; 1842-$2.35
Wm Grindage & R W Templeman/*Political Emancipation*-1,068½ acs: 1842-$3.41
Henry Hawkins/lots-200 acs: 1841-$4.23; 1842-$2.80
Wm Jewitt/*Jewelry*-702 acs: 1842-$2.59
Thos Kennedy's heirs/11 lots, 50 acs each: 1841-$11.47; 1842-$1.40
Saml D King/lots-200 acs: 1841-$5.21; 1842-$1.90
Nicholas Manger's heirs/ lots-200 acs: 1841-$5.21; 1842-$2.35
Thos Mason's heirs/lots-250 acs: 1841-$5.21; 1842-$2.35
Jas Morris/lot-50 acs: 1841-$3.37; 1842-.96
Chas Morgan & Wm Bower/*Improvements*-1,000 acs: 1841-$6.24; 1842-$4.38
Wm Murdock's heirs/lots-200 acs: 1842-$2.35
Chas J Nourse/lots-250 acs: 1842-$3.54
Henry Northup/lots-200 acs: 1841-$6.21; 1842-$2.13
Nathl Ramsey's heirs/lots-200 acs: 1842-$1.90
Thos Reese/lots-200 acs: 1841-$5.21; 1841-$1.90
Richd Ridgely's heirs/lots-200 acs: 1842-$1.90
Thos S Theabold/*War of Independence*-255 acs: 1841-$6.59; 1842-$2.20
Geo Templeman/lots-600 acs: 1842-$6.42
G W Templeman & Z W Denham/lots-600 acs: 1842-$4.03
G E Templeman & Wm Grindage/*Java Resurveyed*-1,131 acs: 1842-#.05
Jerard Wood's heirs/lots-200 acs: 1841-$4.96; 1842-$1.90
Chas S Willett/lots-100 acs: 1841-$3.99; 1842-$1.90
District #4:
Jarret Burk/lots-200 acs: 1841-$4.96; 1842-$1.90
Benj Fowler/*Fowler's Lot*-1,298 acs: 1842-$4.88
Duff Green/*Brant's Mills St*-100 acs; *Limestone*-60 acs; lots-300 acs; *Leatherwood Bottom*-29½ acs; *Pretty Prospect*, etc-430¼ acs: 1842-$52.79
John Hoye & John A Smith/*Part Flowery Meads*-121½ acs; *Part Moore's Farm*-192½ acs; *Minerals in anticipation*-122½ acs: 1842-$5.93
John E Howard, jr/1-9th *Beatty's Plains*-900 acs: 1842-$13.15
Union Company/*Coal & Iron Banks*-5,631 acs/ Gen Duff Green's iron & ore lands-5,126 acs; *Hoye's coal*, iron, & lime discovery-2,752 acs: 1842-$136.42
District #5:

Thos Hammond/*Mills*-111½ acs; *Hammond's corner*-169½ acs: 1842-$4.72
District #6:
Jas Beatty/*The Request*-156¾ acs; *Lost Glove*-56¾ acs: 1841-$6.87; 1842-$3.88
Peter Conner's heirs/ 2 lots in Cresaptown: 1841-$1.40
Jas P M'Crackin/Hse & lot in Cresaptown: 1841-$3.21; 1842-$1.40
Virgil Maxcy & others/*Quanto*-125 acs; *Rabbit's Walk*-116 acs; *Trio*-100 acs: 1841-$7.78; 1842-$6.63
Wm Potts/*Friendship*-15½ acs: 1842-$1.91
John G W Waters & Chas F Mayer/*Attempt*-200 acs: 1842-$3.20
Cumberland Town:
Wm Brent/lots: 1841-$4.59; 1842-$2.35
M St Clair Clarke/*Commercial Mart*-30 acs: 1842-$1.41
Edw Parnell/lot #105: 1842-$1.40
Jas R Wallace/lot #58: 1842-$1.40
District #7:
Chas F Hettick/*Miller's Chance*-20½ acs; *Wilson's Risk*-57¼ acs: 1841-$3.98; 1842-$1,88
District #8:
Nicholas Brewer/*Heath's Neglect*-191 acs: 1842-$2.29
John Evans' heirs/*Evans' Purchase*-150 acs: 1841-$4.77; 1842-$2.35
Saml Goodrich/*Dry Hill*-22 acs; *Fox Chase*-29 acs; *What you please*-73 acs: 1841-$5.24; 1842-$2.98
Jas Hook/*Piney Plains*-987 acs: 1841-$13.34; 1842-$14.34
Richd J Orme/*Lovely*-119 acs: 1841-$4.46; 1842-$1.58
Caroline & Chas Johnson/*Covent Garden*-1,840 acs: 1841-$9.87; 1842-$5.14
David Kelley/*Part Elder Spring*-200 acs: 1841-$4.00; 1842-$1.90
John King/lots-850 acs: 1842-$8.95
Jacob Koontz/lots-200 acs: 1842-$2.69
Jas M Mason, agent of Bank of Columbia/lots-280 acs: 1842-$3.25
Marietta McLaughlin/lots-500 acs: 1842-$4.70
Robt Nelson & Richd H Beatty/lots-150 acs: 1842-$2.02
John Ogleby's heirs/lots-200 acs: 1841-$3.75; 1842-$1.90
Chas Oliver/*Thomas & Ann*-2,000 acs; *Hinch's Discovery*-1,001 acs; *Land Flowing with milk & honey*-2,745 acs: 1842-$272.00
John P Paca/*Buck's Bones*-500 acs: 1841-$5.50; 1842-$2.70
John T Ritchie/lots-400 acs: 1842-$2.90
Geo Templeman/*Cingefield*-294 acs; *Reimbursement*-200 acs: [no amount]
Jas W McCulloh/*Mecklenburg*-864 acs; *Sweet Pink*-26½ acs; *Fairfax*-1,059 acs; *Eutew*-200 acs: 1842-$24.23
Geo H Whetter/lots-100 acs: 1841-$3.37; 1842-$1.90
John Welsh/lots-100 acs: 1842-$1.90
Marcus S Waring/lots-100 acs: 1842-$1.90
-John M Carleton, Clk to the Com'rs of Alleghany County, Md

Household furniture at auction: on Mar 10, at the residence of Mr Vincent King, on the south side of Pa ave, between 10th & 11th sts: a very excellent lot of furniture: Hair seat sofa, cane seat & other chairs; mahg sideboards, extension dining & other tables; window curtains, Venetian blinds; parlor, chamber, hall & step carpets high & French post bedsteads, feather beds, mattresses, bedding; bureaus, wardrobes, washstands, toilet sets. –R W Dyer & Co, aucts

Groceries at auction: on Mar 9, at the store of Geo Lipscomb, on 7th st, near Pa ave: all the groceries now in the store. –Robt W Dyer & Co, aucts

For rent: a 2 story brick dwlg on Capitol Hill. The key may be obtained at Mr Houston's, East Capitol st, adjoining the premises. Rent $150 per annum.

WED MAR 8, 1843
Caddo [Red river] Gaz of Feb 8 states that on the 7th a wretched looking man was arrested in the streets of that place by 3 Texians, who charged him with having commited a diabolical murder on his son-in-law. His name is Saunders. It seems that a few day since, Randolph married his dght, contrary to the father's wishes, who sent for his son-in-law, & on his arrival, shot him dead. The deed was done near Marshall, Harrison Co, Texas.

Nathl Chipman, L L D Prof of Law in Middlebury College, & known as the author of several valuable law books, died at Tinmouth, Vt, on the 15th, in his 91st year.

Powhatan Mansion was recently destroyed by fire, together with its contents. It is about a mile from Richmond, Va. There was an insurance of $7,000 on the mansion, & $3,000 on the furniture.

On Wed, as the Rev W Bathurst was delivering his customary lecture at St Giles' Chr, Oxford, England, his bands by some means managed to get caught in the flame of the candle lighted at the side of the pulpit. Immediately his face was enveloped in flames. Many rose to offer their assistance, at seeing the peril in which the reverence was placed. Although the burns are not of a very serious nature, they will produce inconvienience for some time to come. Several of the congregation fainted, & shrieks were heard in all parts of the church. –Globe [Latest news from London received in this ofc.]

Mr Joel Evans, of Phil, died on Sat last of apoplexy. His wife had died suddenly 2 days previous, & was to be buried on the day Mr Evans expired. He was in the yard giving directions relative to the funeral of his wife when attacked.

Valuable farm for sale: my land, about 13 miles from Gtwn, & 5 miles west of Cmdor Jones' farm, on the Gtwn & Leesburg turnpike road. Improvements are 2 good log dwlgs & other out-houses. Farm contains 350 acs. Apply to the subscriber,

2 miles above the Great Falls, on the premises, or to Mr Geo St Clair, Bradley's Wharf, Washington. –Saml Jackson

Appointments by the Pres:
John C Spencer, of N Y, to be Sec of the Treas, vice Walter Forward, resigned.
Edw Everett, of Mass, now Minister of the U S at London, to be Com'r to China.
Wm W Irwin, of Pa, to be Charge d'Affaires to Denmark, vice J R Jackson, dec'd.
Geo Brown, of Mass, to be Com'r to the Sandwich Islands.
Albert Smith, of Maine, to be Com'r in conformity to the 6th article of the treaty between the U S & Great Britain, concluded on Aug 9, 1842.

Consuls:
N Berry, for Lyons, vice S Allinson, resigned.
John Hartman, for Barracoa, vice F H McCready, resigned.
Wm H Vesey, of N Y, for Lisbon, vice Israel P Hutchinson, resigned.
Morgan L Smith, of N Y, for Velasco, vice A M Green, resigned.
Chas Thompson, jr, of Mass, for Merida & Sisal, in Yucatan.
Henry Mahler, of N Y, for Zurich.
Franklin Gage, of Maine, for Cardenas.
Jas B Higginson, of Mass, for Calcutta.
John Black, for the city of Mexico, vice W B Jones, resigned.
Geo W Pell, of N Y, for Westphalia & the Prussian provinces of the Rhine.
Fred'k List, of Phil, for the Kingdon of Wurtemburg.

Marshals:
Edw Harden, to be Marshal of the U S for Georgia, vice Wm J Davis, whose commission has expired.

Custom House Officials:
Collectors:
Wm Littlefield, reappointed at Newport, R I.
Calvin Blythe, Phil, Pa, vice Thos S Smith.
Peter S Bowdoin, Cherrystone, Va, vice Geo Holt, dec'd.
Surveyor:
Dennis Dawley, Norfolk, Va, vice N W Parker, whose commission has expired.
Land Ofcrs:
Registers:
Abraham Edwards, reappointed at Kalamazoo, Mich.
Jas H Birch, Plattsburg, Missouri.
Receivers:
A Dorsey, New Orleans, La, vice A S Lewis, dec'd.
Edw M Samuel, Plattsburg, Missouri.
Edw Randolph, reappointed at Columbus, Miss.
Geo W Womack, Greensburg, La, vice Thos Womack, dec'd.

Justices of the Peace:
John D McPherson, A T Smith, Wm Waters & Richd Key Watts for Wash Co, D C.

Supreme Crt of the U S: Mar 7, 1843. Jas M Porter, of Pa, was admitted atty & counsellor of this Court. #29: Jas C C Bell et al, vs, Matthias Bruen. In error to the Circuit Court of the U S for N Y. Mr Justice Catron delivered the opinion of this Court, reversing the judgment of the said Circuit Court in this cause, with costs, & remanding the same for a venier facias de novo.

Heavy verdict: $8,000 in damages has been rendered by a Jury of Tompkins Co Crct [N Y] for a breach of promise of marriage. The parties to the suit were Mary Conrad & Josiah B Williams, both of the village of Ithaca.

Died: on Mar 4, at Balt, Thos Baltzell, of the house of Thomas & Philip Baltzell, one of the most extensive dry goods firms in the city. Mr Baltzell died after a short illness, in his 63rd year. He has been for more than 40 years engaged in business. He was one of the bravest of the defenders of the city at the battle of North Point, & in the official report of Gen Stricker honorable mention is made of his name, for the courage & intrepidity which he evinced on that occasion, as adjutant of the 39th regt.

For rent & possession Apr 1, a commodious frame dwlg hse, with back bldgs, on 6th st, between H & I sts, occupied at present by Mr A Baldwin. Apply to A Rothwell.

Miss E Wake has commenced the Millinery & Mantus making, in all its various branches at the corner of 10th & E sts, opposite the Medical College.

Circuit Court of Wash Co, D C. Bankrupts: Saml Ball; Jacob Staub; Jas W Brown; Thos Lumpkin' John I Wilkins; & Hanson Barnes, have each filed a ptn for his discharge & certificate: hearing on the first Mon in Jun next. –W Brent, clk

Blazing Chimneys: yesterday there were 2 alarms of fire in quick seccession & the firemen rendered assistance. The chimney in the house of John Waters, police constable, was blazing; the second in the dwlg of Mr Mitchell, shoemaker. Both were speedily extinguished without much injury to the bldgs.

For sale: sloop **City**, about 3 years old, about 9 tons burden, Balt built, in good condition, & is a very fast sailer. Application to be made to the Capt on board the sloop, lying at Lambell's Wharf. –Hudson Short

Died: John Dowling, from Galena, Ill, arrived at Brown's Hotel on Feb 28. The next morning he said, at the bar, that he had lost a check for $500 on the Metropolis Bank. He locked his room, & went out with the key in his pocket; & as he did not return, the proprietors of the Hotel became fearful some accident had befallen him. On Mon they heard that an old man had died a day before at the Asylum, [or Poor-house.] Mr Morse, the bar-keeper, had the coffin opened, & found that it was Mr Dowling. He learned that the day he left the Hotel, he was found in the evening near the Navy

Yard, & some person there kept him all night, & the next day sent him to the Poorhouse. He was evidently of deranged mind. When his room was broken open, his baggage & papers were found there, & among his papers the $500 check which he supposed he had lost. He gave not evidence of being deranged when he left the Hotel. He was interred on Mon in the Catholic burial ground attached to St Patrick's Church.

Mrs Ann H Scott, Pa ave, south side, between 3½ & 4½ sts, is now prepared to receive Boarders, both citizens & strangers.

Orphan's Court of Wash Co, D C. Letters testamentary on the personal estate of Edmund Hanly, late of said county, dec'd. –Jane Hanly, John C Harkness, Saml Redfern, excs

Copartnership notice: I have this day associated with me my brother, Robt W Smoot; the business will therefore in future be conducted in the names of Smoot & Brother. We will receive from the Northern Auctions a genr'l assortment of Spring Goods. –John H Smoot, south side of Bridge st, near High st, Gtwn

THU MAR 9, 1843
Capt John H Aulick appointed Commandant of the Navy Yard at Washington, to succeed Capt Kennon, who has been appointed to the head of the Bureuaof Construction, Equipment, & Repair, in the Navy Dept.

Jas Madison Porter, of Pa, appointed by the Pres Sec for the Dept of War, in place of Mr Spencer, & yesterday entered on the discharge of his duties.

Sale of valuable real estate on Mar 24, on the premises: a tract of land in PG Co, of which the late Alfred Tolson, of said county, died seized & in possession, known by the name of *Milford*, about 6 miles from D C, containing about 230 acs. This land adjoins the estates of Henry Tolson & Reese A Gantts. Its improvements are good. The real estate is subject to an annuity of $66.66 2/3 during the life of Mrs M B Tolson. She has also a life estate in the dlwg house & the appurtenances thereto. –Henry Tolson, agent

Circuit Court of Wash Co, D C. Chas K King, a bankrupt, has filed his ptn for his discharge & certificate: hearing on the first Mon in Jun next. –Wm Brent, clk

Notice. I forewarn all persons from purchasing, receiving, or otherwise trading for a due bill dated Feb 27, 1843, drawn by me in favor of John M Hilleary for $170, as I have not received value therefore, & will not therefore pay it. –Thos S Ferral, Bladensburg, Mar 4, 1843

Trustees sale of valuable real estate: on Mar 30, on the premises: all that tract of land & real estate, lying & being in PG Co, Md, of which John T Dodson, late of said county, died seized & in possession, known as ***Chilton Castle Manor Resurveyed***, containing 329¼ acs: land adjoins D C: is 4 miles from the Capitol.
-H Tolson, trustee P S-The above land will be sold in whole or divided, to suit purchasers.

For rent, the house at present occupied by Capt Aulick, of the U S Navy, in Franklin Row. Apply at the premises, or to Richd France.

Circuit Court of Wash Co, D C. Henry B Foster, a bankrupt, has filed his ptn for his discharge & certificate: hearing on the first Mon in Jun next. --Wm Brent, clk

Circuit Court of Wash Co, D C. John C Burche has filed his ptn for the benefit of the Bankrupt Law: hearing on the first Mon in Apr next.

<u>Promotions of the Army: General Orders #19: Adj Gen Ofc, Wash, Mar 6, 1843.</u>
Promotions:
<u>6th Ret of Infty:</u>
Brvt 2nd Lt Rudolph F Ernst, to be 2nd Lt, Feb 9, 1843, vice Emory, resigned.
<u>Brevets:</u>
Capt D D Tompkins, 1st Regt of Artl, to be Maj by Brevet, for gallant & meritorious conduct in the war against the Florida Indians, to date from Sep 11, 1836.
Capt Harvey Brown, 4th Regt of Artl, to be Maj by Brvt, for gallant conduct on several occasions, & general efficiency in the war against the Florida Indians, to date from Nov 21, 1836.
Maj John Harris, of the Marine Corps, to be Maj by Brvt, for gallantry & good conduct in the war against the Florida Indians, particularly in the affair of Hatches Lustee, to date from Jan 27, 1837.
Capt B L Beall, of the 2nd Regt of Dragoons, to be Maj by Brvt, for gallantry & successful services in the war against the Florida Indians, to date from Mar 15, 1837.
Capt Geo W Allen, 4th Regt of Infty, to be Maj by Brvt, for gallant conduct on several occasions, & general efficiency in the war against the Florida Indians, to date from Dec 25, 1837.
Capt John Munroe, 4th Regt of Artl, to be Maj by Brvt, for conduct uniformly meritorious & efficient during 3 campaigns against the Florida Indians, to date from Feb 15, 1838.
Capt Saml Ringgold, 3rd Regt of Artl, to be Maj by Brvt, for meritorious conduct, in activity & efficiency in the war against the Florida Indians, to date from Feb 15, 1838.
Capt Washington Seawell, 7th Regt of Infty, to be Maj by Brvt, for meritorious & successful services in the war against the Florida Indians, to date from Jul 18, 1841.
Capt R D A Wade, 3rd Regt of Artl, to be Maj by Brvt, for gallantry & successful services in the war against the Florida Indians, to date from Nov 6, 1841.

Capt Geo Wright, 8th Regt of Infty, to be Maj by Brvt, for meritorious conduct, in zeal, energy, & perserverance, in the war against the Florida Indians, to date from Mar 15, 1842.

Capt R H K Whitely, of the Ordnance Dept, [late 1st Lt in the 2nd Regt of Artl,] to be Capt by Brvt, for gallant conduct in the war against the Florida Indians, to date from Jul 19, 1836.

Capt T B Linnard, of the corps of Topographical Engineers, [late 1st Lt in the 2nd Regt of Artl,] to be Capt by Brvt, for gallant conduct, activity, & enterprise in the war against the Florida Indians, to date from Sep 30, 1836.

1st Lt J W Anderson, 2nd Regt of Infty, to be Capt by Brvt, for gallant & successful conduct in the war against the Florida Indians, to date from Aug 23, 1841.

Brvt Capt W G Freeman, 1st Lt in the 4th Regt of Artl, Jul 7, 1838, & Brvt Capt in the Staff, Dec 2, 1841, to be 1st Lt by Brvt, for gallantry on several occasions, & uniform good conduct in the war against the Florida Indians, to date from Nov 21, 1836.

1st Lt Geo Taylor, 3rd Regt of Artl, to be Capt by Brvt, for gallantry & meritorious services in the war against the Florida Indians, to date from Mar 1, 1842.

1st Lt John T Sprague, 8th Regt of Infty, to be Capt by Brvt, for meritorious & successful conduct in the war against the Florida Indians, to date from Mar 15, 1842.

1st Lt P N Barbour, 3rd Regt of Infty, to be Capt by Brvt, for active & highly meritorious services in the war against the Florida Indians, to date from Apr 15, 1842.

1st Lt Ripley A Arnold, 2nd Regt of Dragoons, to be Capt by Brvt, for gallant conduct in the war against the Florida Indians, to date from Apr 19, 1842.

1st Lt Geo H Talcott, of the Ordnance Dept, [late of the 3rd Regt of Artl,] 1st Lt, Sep 15, 1836, to be 1st Lt by Brvt, for gallant conduct on several occasions in the war against the Florida Indians, to date from Dec 31, 1835.

1st Lt Horace Brooks, 2nd Regt of Artl, [1st Lt, Feb 8, 1837,] to be 1st Lt by Brvt, for gallantry & good conduct in the war against the Florida Indians, to date from Dec 31, 1835.

1st Lt Wm H Fowler, 1st Regt of Artl, [1st Lt May 1, 1839,] to be 1st Lt by Brvt, for gallantry & good conduct in the war against the Florida Indians, to date from Jan 15, 1838.

2nd Lt Geo H Thomas, 3rd Regt of Artl, to be 1st Lt by Brvt, for gallantry & good conduct in the war against the Florida Indians, to date from Nov 6, 1841.

2nd Lt F D Callender, of the Ordnance Dept, to be 1st Lt by Brvt, for active & highly meritorious services in the war against the Florida Indians, to date from May 1, 1842.

Appointments
Military Storekeeper attached to the Ordnance Dept:
J M Galt, of Va, Dec 28, 1842.

Transfers:
Brvt 2nd Lts G T Mason & T C Hammond, of the late 2nd Dragoons-the first to Co K, the 2nd to Co G, which they will join without delay. The Supernumerary 2nd Lts will take precedence in the Regt according to their Academic rank.

Resignation:
2nd Lt J R Emory, 6th Infty, Feb 3, 1843.
By command of Maj Gen Scott: -R Jones, Adj Gen

Died: on Mar 7, in Balt, of consumption, Mr John Keith, in his 38th year. His funeral will be from the house of his brother-in-law, in this city, on H between 6th & 7th sts, this afternoon, at 3 p m.

Died: on Feb 25, in Wash City, Miss Mary Jones, aged 28 years, d/o the late Saml Jones.

FRI MAR 10, 1843
The Albany Evening Journal announces the death of Robt Hunter, Pres of the Canal Bank, one of the most useful & respected citizens of that city. The Canal Bank has lost 3 Presidents within the last 4 years.

A Sporting Country. Fort Snelling is a military post of the U S in the Territory of Iowa, at the foot of the Falls of St Anthony, on the majestic Mississippi, just where it receives the tribute of the River St Peters.

Letter from a physician in Yucatan, dated at Carmen Laguna de Terminos on the 9th ult, announces the death of Chas Russell, the American Consul at that port, who died on the preceding day. Mr Russell was a native of Phil, & had resided in Mexico about 12 years.

Sir Wm Drummond, a wealthy Scotch baronet, is at New Orleans preparing for a pleasure party to the Rocky Mountains during the coming season.

Supreme Crt of the U S: Mar 9, 1843. #34-Sarah J Jewell et al vs, Benj Jewell et al. In error to the Circuit Court of the U S for S Carolina. Mr Chief Justice Taney delivered the opinion of this Court, reversing the judgment of the said Circuit Court in this cause with costs, & remanding the same for a venire facias de novo. #37- Bernard McKenna vs, Chas B Fisk. In error to the Circuit Court of the U S for Wash, D C. Opinion of this Court: reversing the judgment of the said Circuit Court in this cause with costs, & remanding the same for a venire facias de nova.

Distressing fire at the house of Mr Richd McDowell, about 7 miles from New Brunswick, N J, on Mar 1. The agonized parents were unable to save a son in an upper room. Fire destroyed all the contents.

For rent, one of the 3 brick dwlgs on 8th st, in the first square north of the Patent Ofc. The house is in good repair. Inquire of the subscriber, 11th & G sts. –Mgt Stewart

Crmnl Crt-Wash: Mar 6, 1843. 1-Jas Vevans, alias Bevan, pleaded guilty to stealing a silver spoon, the property of the Hon Chas A Wickliffe, in Wash City. Fined $1 & to be imprisoned 2 months in jail. 2-Matthew Stark, free negro found guilty of stealing, on Jan 6, a pair of boots of the value of $3, the property of A Coyle & Son. Fined $3 & to be imprisoned 3 months in jail. 3-Mgt Hopkins, free negress, found guilty of stealing a quilt of the value of $2, the property of Wm Thomas. Fined $2 & to be imprisoned for 2 months. Mar 7: Erastus Stimpson found guilty of stealing at Fuller's Hotel, on Jan 7, articles, the property of John D Brown, a boarder in that hotel. To be imprisoned 2 years in the penitentiary. Mar 8: Chas Erb found guilty of keeping a disorderly house on Capitol Hill. Sentence: fined $30, & to give security in $200 for his good behavior, & to keep the peace for the space of 12 months, & stand committed till the security was given. Security was immediately given by the dfndnt. Mar 9: 1-Wm Spicer indicted for keeping a gaming table in Wash City. The dfndnt said his name is Wm Zimmerman, not Wm Spicer. Verdict for the dfndnt. 2-Jas Digges, an old convict, found guilty for stealing a gun, the property of Benj Herbert. To be imprisoned 3 years in the penitentiary. 3-Geo Lipscomb, convicted of selling liquors without a license at a negro camp meeting: fined $16 & costs. 4-John O'Neale, convicted of an assault: fined $16 & costs.

Died: yesterday, in Wash City, of consumption, Mrs Mary Wilson, w/o Mr Noah S Wilson, & d/o Mr Bernard & Letitia Gilpin, of Sandy Spring, Montg Co, Md, in her 31st year. A husband, 2 infant children, & her parents, brothers, & sisters, will have the lasting sympathy of every one who knew the departed.

The Exchange Hotel, Balt, Md, has been refitted & furnished in the most elegant manner, & will be open on Mar 13. –Erastus Coleman

Circuit Court of Wash Co, D C. In the cause of the ptn of Wm H Hoburg & others, for the division of the west half of lot #150 of Beall's Addition to Gtwn, with the appurtenances, comprising the real estate of Harriet, otherwise Henrietta Hoburg, dec'd, among the heirs at law of the dec'd, consisting of Wm H Hoburg, Mary Ann Roberts w/o Wm D Roberts, Lucinda J A Hoburg, Amelia A Gallant w/o Peter Gallant, Edw C Hoburg, Sophia Sutherland w/o Geo W Sutherland, the undersigned com'rs notify that they will proceed on Mar 21 next, on the above premises, to execute the commission directed to them by the Court in the above cause. –John Mountz, Jenkin Thomas, John Myers

St Patrick's Day cmte of arrangements for the celebration of the anniversary of St Patrick, on Mar 17. Dinner to be on the table, at the Assembly Rooms, on La ave, at 4 p m. Tickets: $1.50. Nett proceeds to be appropriated for the benefit of St Vincent's Orphan Asylum. –Philip Ennis, John Devlin, Wm Dowling

SAT MAR 11, 1843
Treasury notes lost near 11th st & Pa ave: one of $500, bearing interest, dated Feb 12, 1842, endorsed y T L Jones, in favor of Messrs Gales & Seaton, & one of $50, dated May 20, 1842, bearing interest. A handsome reward will be given for the above information. –R Farnham, Bookseller, 11th & Pa ave

A family of counterfeiters: Mary Shepherd, about 60 years old, had been found guilty by the Court of Sessions on Mon, & was sentenced to the State Prison for 7 years & 1 month. She is the mother of a numerous family, the greater of whom, & also both their parents, are now in different State Prisons, or sentenced to be sent there. The mother was sentenced, her son, Jas Shepherd, was; her dght was sentenced & her husband is in the State Prison of Ohio, one of her sons is in the State Prison of N J, another in the State Prison at Sing Sing, & a 3rd will leave this city for the same place, accompanied by his mother, in a day or two. All have been convicted of similar offences-counterfeiting. Jour Com

David Holman, jr, of Millville, Mass, s/o Rev D Holman, of East Douglas, was so severely injured by being suddenly thrown between the wheel & flume of his mill on Sat last, that he died a few hours after.

Orphan's Court of Wash Co, D C. Letters of administration on the personal estate of John D Semmes, late of said county, dec'd. –Eleanor C Semmes, admx

Circuit Court of Wash Co, D C. Anthony Holmead has filed his ptn for the benefit of the Bankrupt Law: hearing on the first Mon in Apr next. –Wm Brent, clk

Naval Intelligence: The frig **Macedonian**, Capt Mayo, at Norfolk, has been designated as the flag-ship of the African squadron, under Cmdor M C Perry.

Appointments & Promotions in the Navy of the U S.
Capt Beverly Kennon, to be Chief of the Bureau of Construction, Equipment, & Repairs, in place of Capt David Conner, resigned.
Cmder Andrew Fitzhugh, to be Capt from Feb 14, 1843, to fill the vacancy occasioned by the death of Capt Isaac Hull.
Lt Geo A Magruder, to be Cmder from same date.
Passed Midshipman John Contee, to be a Lt from same date.
Wm G Jackson, to be a Chaplain from Oct 19, 1842, to fill the vacancy occasioned by the resignation of Jared L Elliott.

Promotions in the Marine Corps:
Col Archibald Henderson, on Mar 4, 1843, to be a Brig Gen by brevet, to take rank from jan 27, 1837, for gallant & meritorious services while in command of the marines in Alabama, Florida, & Tennessee, during the campaign against the hostile Indians.

Maj John Harris to be a Maj by brevet, for gallantry & good conduct in the war against the Florida Indians, particularly in the affair of Hatchee Lustee, to date from Jan 27, 1837.

Capt Wm Dulany, on Mar 4, 1843, to be a Maj by brevet, to take rank from Mar 3, 1843, for meritorious conduct. –P G Howle, Adj & Inspec. Headqrtrs of the Marine Corps, Adj & Inspec ofc, Wash City, Mar 10, 1843.

Mrd: on Mar 9, at Sharon, the residence of Cmdor Thos Ap C Jones, by Rev Dr E Dorsey, the Rev Thos C Hayes, of the Balt Annual Conference, to Miss Juliana Wainright Gordon, d/o the late Wm Gordon, formerly of Northumberland Co, Va.

Died: on Thu last, in Gtwn, in her 28th year, Mrs Mary Magruder, consort of Dr H Magruder, & d/o the late H H Chapman. Her funeral will be from the residence of her mother, on Dunbarton st, on Sun, at 3 p m.

MON MAR 13, 1843

Temperance Benefit. At the suggestion of many of his friends, Philip Boteler has consented to hold a Temperance Meeting, to enable him to pay for the repair of his Hack, which was broke by his horses taking fright & running away, this winter. Messrs Raymond & Whipple will address the audience, & Mr Boteler will give his extraordinary Experience in his career of Intemperance. Singing by Messrs Dulany, Thompson, & others. Tickets 12½ cents at Apollo Hall, on Mar 14; & at the usual places.

For sale: 2 story frame house, with the lot on which it stands, on lot 24 in sq 485, being on 5th st west, between G & H sts north. On the back alley is a good stable. Inquire on the premises of Thos Clements.

Gen H A S Dearborn, Adj Gen of Massachusetts, has been removed from that ofc by Govn'r Morton on application of the Locofocos of the Legislature, on the express ground that when the constituted authorities of Rhode Island were threatened with mob violence he loaned them some of the State arms of Massachusetts. His virtues, & not any fault of his, procured him the honor of this proscription. He is a gentleman whose abilities & acquirements would adorn any station in life.

Died: on Mar 11, in Wash City, Mrs Caroline M Dunscomb, w/o Danl E Dunscomb, & d/o the late John P Mumford, of N Y C. Her funeral will be on E st, 4 doors east of 14th st, on Mon at 4 p m.

The Bridgeton [N J] Chronicle says that Mrs Sarah Smith, who died in that place on Feb 28, was a lineal descendant of the Royal family of Sweden. Her great grandmother, Eliz, was compelled to flee from her native country when she was 16 years old. She was concealed in a hogshead on board of a ship at Stockholm for some time before the vessel sailed for America. She brought many valuables with her across the waer, concealed on the ship; but after the vessel had sailed over the Atlantic she was wrecked on the Jersey shore. This lady, with a few of the crew, barely saved their lives. In her destitute condition, on the shore of a vast wilderness, as N J then was, she fell in with a hunter by the name of Garrison. They married & by him she had 10 children. Her youngest son, Wm, was born when she was in her 55th year. She died in her 95th year. She has now a grandson living in Bridgeton, who was brought up by her until he was 9 years of age, to whom she related this narrative. This gentleman computes his grandmother's descendants in the country at more than a 1,000 souls.

Balt, Mar 10. The elegant mansion house of Henry Tiffany, near the corner of Madison & Hoffman sts, was destroyed by fire last evening. The house had recently undergone a thorough repair & was unoccupied. Some furniture was saved. Mr Tiffany has a policy for $7,500. –Patriot

Local News-Wash: fire broke out last Sat in the frame bldg occupied by Mr Thos Hyde as a snuff & tobacco store, on Pa ave, near 11th st. It was quickly consumed. The adjoining bldgs, occupied by David Miller, silver plater, Mr Stear, butcher, Messrs Hamilton & Kidd, carpenters, were also speedily consumed. The bldgs belonged to Wm H Stewart & Wm Orme. There was no insurance on the property. Fire was purely accidental. [Mar 15 newspaper: Mr Hyde's loss is about $250; Mr Stear, has suffered more than we supposed. As both are young beginners in business, with limited means, the loss must be severely felt.]

Appointments by the Pres: 1-Geo Brent, Collector of the Customs at Alexandria, D C, vice Jos Eaches. 2-Greenberry Dorsey, Receiver of Public Moneys for the district of lands subject to sale at New Orleans, La.

Supreme Crt of the U S: Mar 10, 1843. #38-The U S, plntf, vs Henry Eckford's excs, on a certificate of division in opinion from the U S Circuit Court for N Y. Regarding: payments made by Saml Swartwout subsequent to Mar 28, 1834, should be appropriated in discharge of his indebtment on that day.
#72-Wm Taylor et al, appellants vs Geo M Savage, exc. Mr Chief Justice Taney delivered the opinion of the Court, dismissing the ptn of V M Benham for leave to perfect & docket a cross appeal. #52-Jas Todd, appellant, vs Otis Daniell, on appeal from the Circuit Court of the U S for Maine. The decree of the said Circuit Court was affirmed with costs & 6% damages.

TUE MAR 14, 1843
Furnished house or rooms to let, or house will be rented without furniture to a good tenant. Located opposite Fuller's Hotel. Immediate possession. –Mary G Handy

Elections in Mass: Stephen P Webb, the Whig candidate, was on Tue last elected Mayor of Salem, Mass, by a vote of 774, while B F Brown, the Locofoco candidate, received 287. Nathl Wright, the Whig candidate, was on the same day elected Mayor of Lowell, receiving 1,903 out of 2,102 votes.

Died: on Mar 11, in Wash City, Mrs Eliz Rose, w/o Mr Robt Rose, in her 70th year. Her funeral will be from her late residence near the Navy Yard, on Wed, at 2 p m.

Circuit Court of Wash Co, D C. Jas France, a bankrupt, has filed his ptn for his discharge & certificate: hearing on the first Mon in Jun next. –Wm Brent, clk

Circuit Court of Wash Co, D C. Fred'k Reinhart has filed his ptn for the benefit of the Bankrupt Law: hearing on the first Mon in Apr next. –Wm Brent, clk

WED MAR 15, 1843
Delaware College & Academy's summer term will commence on May 10th, & continue for 10 weeks. These institutions are on the great Balt & Phil railroad, which renders access convenient from both the North & South. For particulars apply to the Rev John C Smith or Jacob Gideon, Washington, or to Wm S Graham, Principal of the Academy, or to E W Gilbert, Pres of the College.

The New Mirror, every number embellished with an original & exquisite design on steel. Edited by Geo P Morris, illustrated by J G Chapman. Terms: $3 per annum; single numbers 6½ cents. [Periodical] -Geo P Morris, Editor & Proprietor, #4 Ann st, near Broadway

Michl Hare, of Union township, Erie Co, Pa, a soldier of the Revolution, died on Mar 4 at the advanced age of about 116 years. He was the oldest pensioner on the roll-had been a resident of Erie Co about 43 years-walked twice a year 5 miles to Waterford for his pension & retained his natural faculties to the last. He was honest, brave, & patriotic Funeral honors were paid to his remains at St Peter's Chr, Waterford. Peace to his ashes! -Erie Gaz

The schnr **Robin Hood**, to & from St John, [N B] for Boston, was wrecked at Duxbury beach in the severe blow of Tue last, & the owner, Mr Donavoe, of St John, his son, a resident of Boston, & John Ford, a passenger, were lost. The first two perished with the cold & the last was drowned. Their bodies were taken to Plymouth for interment.

Crmnl Crt-Wash: Mar 13, 1843. 1-David Jenkins, free negro, found guilty of stealing a quilt, a pillow, & other articles, on Jan 18, 1843, the property of Ignatius Fugitt. 2-Chas H Williams, free negro, found not guilty for stealing on Jan 10th $10.50 in silver, the property of Wm Baltimore. 3-John Fowler, a white lad, found guilty for an assault & battery on the public highway on the person of Jerry, the slave of Horatio Bell. Sentenced to pay a fine of $10, & give security in $100 to keep the peace & be of good behavior for 1 year. Mar 14: negro Saml Gassaway, a slave, was put on trial this morning, under an indictment charging him with breaking into the storehouse of Jas & Henry Thecker, at Gtwn, & stealing 3 pairs of boots & a quarter box of cigars. The prisoner being indicted for a capital offence, great exertion was made by Mr Hoban in conducting the defence. The jury found the prisoner guilty, & recommended him to the mercy of the Court.

Danl H Lombard, of East Boston, while crossing the ice between Chelsea Point & East Boston, near Breed's Island, Thu, fell through & drowned. He was formerly a resident of Readfield, Maine, & about 40 years of age, & has for a time past, been engaged in teaching a school at Chelsea Point.

Died: on Mar 9, suddenly, Mrs Eleanora Clements, consort of F H Clements, of PG Co, Md, in her 22nd year. She has left to mourn her loss a disconsolate husband & 4 small children.

Died: on Thu last, in Wash City, of chronic rheumatism, Wm Rawlings Thompson, aged 14 years, after a long & painful illness.

Good situation for a woman. My family wishes to engage the services of a white woman who is accustomed to the care of small children. She should also know how to do plain sewing. Testimonials as to disposition, character, & capacity will be required. –G C Grammer, near the City Hall

Died: on Mar 2, at Nashville, Tenn, Lipscomb Norvell, sr, an ofcr in the American Army of the Revolution, aged 87 years. He was a native of Hanover Co, Va; entered the army in 1776, at the age of 20, & after serving in the Northern campaign under Washington-participating in the battles of Brandywine, Trenton, & Monmouth-was transferred to the Southern service, & as a lt of infty, was taken prisoner at Charleston, where he remained on parole till the close of the war. He subsequently [in 1787] removed to Ky, &, as an early pioneer to the West, encountered the dangers & endured the hardships of the then Indian frontier. After rearing a large family in Ky, he removed to Nashville, a widower, in 1827, to spend his declining years with a portion of his children, who had preceded him to Tenn. He was for more than half a century a member of the Baptist Chr, & has left to his posterity a name for worth & integrity spotless through life.

Mrs Jane Taylor can accommodate a lady & gentleman with genteel board & lodging. Her house is situated between 9th & 10th sts, 4 doors from Dr Gunton's, over Mrs J Visser's Fancy Store, Pa ave.

Mrs Tilley can accommodate 3 or 4 gentlemen with board & rooms, either with or without families. Residence is on C st, between 9th & 10th sts.

Mr R Buchhofer, who has just arrived from Switzerland, has brought with him a lot of first rate Gruyere Cheese, & a quantity of Milchzucker, [Milk Sugar,] a medicine for homoeopathic physicians, which the subscriber offers for sale at his confectioner store, Pa ave, near the War Dept. –Benedict Jost

Notice: was committed to the jail of Fred'k Co, on Feb 23 last, as a runaway, a bright mulatto boy, who calls himself Levi E Stevenson. He is about 11 years of age. He says he is free and that his father lives near Clarksburg, Montg Co, Md. The owner, if any, is requested to come & have him released; he will otherwise be discharged according to law. –Geo Rice, Sheriff of Fred'k Co

THU MAR 16, 1843
Notice: In consequence of the demise of Edmund Hanly, the copartnership heretofore existing under the firm of Shepherd & Hanly, of Wash City, is dissolved. Alex'r Shepherd will close the business & settle accounts. –Saml Redfern, & John C Harkness, Acting excs -A Shepherd

Sale of hsehold & ofc furniture, & valuable house & lot: on Mar 23, at the late residence of the Hon W D Merrick, on 5th st: [furniture similar as above with: excellent refrigerator, passage oilcloth; large writing table, painted bookcase & desk; mahg bookcase & hat-rack.] The lot is on 5th st, & the dwlg is an excellent & well built 2 story brick house, with a brick ofc with 2 rooms next adjoining. The title is unquestionable. -R W Dyer & Co, aucts

Richd Pollard has resumed the practice of the Law. He will attend the Courts of Albemarle, Buckingham, Nelson, & Amherst, Va. He will go to Washington whenever his charge may require him to do so.

Household furniture at public auction, by order of Orphan's Court of Wash Co, D C: on Mar 18, at the late residence of J D Simms, dec'd, Six Bldgs, all his household & kitchen furniture: mahg hair-seat lounge & rocker; mahg pier table, French plate pier glasses; maple cane-seat chairs, moreen curtains; mahg celerette, marble top; mahg dining & breakfast tables, mantel lamps; dinner & tea sets; silver soup ladle, creampot & bowl; cut glass decanters, tumblers, & wines; silver table, dessert, & tea spoons, plated candlesticks; good ingrain carpets; hall lamps, high & low post bedsteads; best feather beds, mattresses, & bedding; wardrobes, bureaus, washstands, basins, & ewers; chamber carpets, curtains, chairs -R W Dyer & Co-aucts

Circuit Court of Wash Co, D C. Jacob Colclazer, a bankrupt, has filed his ptn for his discharge & certificate: hearing on the first Mon in Jun next. –W Brent, clk

Morgantown [Va] Journal: on Mar 3 Warick Breakiron, s/o Mr Jacob Breakiron, aged about 15 years, went into the wheelhouse of the rolling mill for the purpose of letting down the gate, & is supposed to have been caught by the wheel & thrown under. His head was completely severed from his body. His body passed under the wheel through a space of not more than an inch, & was completely crushed.

FRI MAR 17, 1843
Passed at the 3rd Session of the 27th Congress: Annuities & grants: to Josiah H Webb, $50. To Rachel Dohrman, $300. To Eliz C Perry, $400.

Mr & Mrs Archer's Academy for Young Ladies, Lexington st, 5 doors east of Chas, Balt, Md: board & English tuition per annum-$250. Refer to the following gentlemen, who, for the most part, have children or wards in the school:

Maj Gen Winfield Scott, U S Army	Capt H A Thompson
Chas Davies, L L D	Dr R W Hall
Rev D Wyatt, Balt	Dr J R Dunbar
Rev J G Hamner, Balt	F J Dallam
J H Bernard, Caroline Co, Va	Thos Finley
Hon Stevenson Archer	Wm Reynolds, Balt
Hon R B Magruder	
Rev E W Gilbert, D D Pres of Oakland College, Miss	

Orphan's Court of Wash Co, D C. Ordered, on application, that letters of administration on the personal estate of John Keith, late of said county dec'd, be granted to John Tretler, unless cause be shown to the contrary.
-Ed N Roach, Reg/o wills

A late number of the Houston [Texas] Telegraph furnishes the following list of the names of the Texians who were killed & wounded at the battle of Mier:
Killed:

Dr Towers	H Jackson	Bapet
John White	Jones	One name not known
Jas Austin	Haumer	
Jos Berry	Dickson	

Wounded:

A McKinnell	Lynn Robo	N N Maton
W H Kuykendall	H H Catts	Jas J Barber
David Allen	John Hughes	Jas C Kid
Edw Keeve	Wm Y Scott	R Beale
J B Hill	D H Gattias	Lewis Hays
Geo B Piland	Henry D Vaks	Theodore Malby
Wm Ripley	Stanley Lockerman	Jas H Wey
Malcolm McCady	Wm McLeges	

Crmnl Crt-Wash: Mar 13, 1843. 1-Wm Noland, found guilty of striking Wm Trader & knocking him down in the street & robbing him of sundry pieces of silver coin of the value of $9.20. Noland is said to be an old offender. 2-Benj A Thorn, John

Langdon, Saml Black, & Mark Ferris, found guilty for a riot on Dec 16, 1842, in the house of Wesley Ferrall, not far from 12th st canal bridge. Thorn to pay a fine of $50 & to give security in $250 for his good behavior for 1 year, & to stand imprisoned until the fine was paid & the security given. Langdon was fined $25; Black fined $10; Ferris fined $5. Crmnl Crt-Wash: Mar 14, 1843: The murder case: Chas Williams, free negro, was tried on the heinous charge of murdering his wife, Deliah Williams, near Gtwn, on Jun 24, 1842. Mr Carlisle was engaged in making an able address to the jury at 3 p m, when we left the court-room. [Mar 18 newspaper: Verdict-guilty. The prisoner appeared to be much affected.]

Notice: by viture of an order of distress from John H King, trustee for Jas Williams' heirs, & to me directed, I shall offer at public sale, for cash, on Mar 20, on the premises, now occupied by Alfred Taylor, on 5th st, between H & I sts, all the household & kitchen furniture of the said A Taylor, to satisfy house rent.
–Lambert S Beck, bailiff

Gadsby's Hotel, Wash City, Mar 17, 1843. In consequence of the great scarcity of money, the charge for board at this hotel will be $1.50 per day. Liquors & wines of all sorts reduced to one half the former rates. –Wm Gadsby, Proprietor

SAT MAR 18, 1843
Oil paintings at auction on Mar 20, at my store. –Wm Marshall, auct

The N Y Spirit of the Times of last week comes to us with an admirable engraved portrait of Col Wm R Johnson, the Nestor of the turf. It is by Dick, after a painting by Inman, & one of the best things of the kind ever issued in the U S. Does it intend to enter the Colonel for the Presidential plate, that it brings him forward in such excellent style? -Pennsylvanian

A great excitement at New Brunswick, N J, by the removal from ofc of Saml C Cook, Postmaster for that city-a gentleman against whom there is no just ground of complaint, political or other-& appointing in his place John Simpson, of whom we know but nothing besides being an ultra politician of the Locofoco school, who did, during the cavass of 1840, denounce not only Gen Harrison, but Tyler too, as a traitor to Jacksonism.

Orin Porter Rockwell, the Mormon who has been accused of attempting to assassinate ex-Govn'r Boggs, of Missouri, last summer, was apprehended at St Louis on Mar 6 & committed to jail. He will now have to stand trial.

Wm Dandridge, age 15 years, s/o Capt Wm Dandridge, of Dinwiddie Co, Va, on Mon, while hunting alone, came to his death by an accidental discharge of his shot gun. Late in the evening his gun was found on one side of a fence & his gun on the other. He had been shot in his right eye; supposed it was instant death.

Treas Dept, Wash, Mar 18, 1843. Sealed proposals will be received at this Dept until Apr 17 next for bldg the hulls of one, two, or three Iron Steamers, to be used as Revenue Cutters on the sea coast. –J G Spencer, Sec of the Treas

For sale: lot #20 in square 373–on south side of N Y ave, between 9th & 10th sts. For terms inquire of Jos Bryan, at his carpenter's shop, on I st, between 9th & 10th sts.

We understand that the steam frig **Missouri**, Capt J T Newton, has been ordered to the Washington Navy Yard, to undergo some slight alterations in her machinery. The new brig **Perry**, will shortly be launched from the navy yard at Gosport, Va. –Army & Navy Chronicle, Mar 16, 1843

Army & Navy Intelligence.
7th Infty: Maj Nelson died at Tampa Bay on Feb 27. Capt Jacob Brown, of the 6th, being the senior Capt of Infty, becomes Major of the 7th, & has been ordered to Baton Rouge as commandant of that post.
6th Infty: the transfer of Capt Brown to the 7th as Major, gives promotion to the following ofcrs:
1st Lt Saml Woods to be Capt.
2nd Lt Jas Belger, [Adj,] to be 1st Lt.
Brvt 2nd Lt R W Kirkham, of the 2nd Infty, to be 2nd Lt.
A Naval Genr'l Court Martial, for the trial of Cmder Wm Ramsay, Lt Chas H Poor, & others, have been ordered to convene on board the U S ship **Pennsylvania**, in the harbor of Norfolk, on Mar 25. The Court will be composed of: Cmdor E Pendleton Kennedy, Pres
Members:
Cmdor W Branford Shubrick
Capt Chas W Skinner
Capt David Geisinger
Capt John Paul Zantzinger
Capt Thos T Webb
Capt Bladen Dulany
John L Upshur, of Va-Judge Advocate

Capt Jos Smoot
Cmder Wm H Gardner
Cmder David G Farragut
Cmder Robt B Cunningham
Lt Wm Green
Lt Sidney Smith Lee

Died: on Feb 24, in Carroll, Mr John Owens, aged 107 years. He was born at Salisbury, in Conn, served in the old French war, & was a sldr & pensioner of the Revolution. He removed to Warren, Pa, in 1807; settled in Chautauque Co in 1812, where he has since resided. His habits were remarkably active, & at the aged of 94 would mount a spirited horse from the ground.

Mobile Adv & Chron, of Mar 8, contains the following: Pleasant H May, once the editor of the "Flag of the Union," at Tuscaloosa, & some 3 years since atty at law in this city, fell overboard from the steamboat **New Albany** at the wharf, the evening before last, & was drowned. His body was found yesterday, & duly interred.

Died: Feb 27, at Tampa Bay, Fla, Maj Jos S Nelson, of the 7th Regt Infty, U S Army.

MON MAR 20, 1843
Sale of fashionable & good household furniture: on Mar 24, at the residence of the Hon Walter Forward, corner of 3rd & C sts, all his very excellent furniture.
–R W Dyer & Co

For rent, a store & dwlg, corner of Md ave & 12th st, sq 299, at present occupied by Mr J C R Wimsatt, whose time will expire on Mar 31, 1843. Inquire of Mr Wimsatt, occupant of said house, or to Edw Mattingly, near the Navy Yard, Wash.

Sunshades just receiver, with plain & ivory handles; 1 case Parasols; 1 case Cambric Umbrellas. Seasonable new goods. –Wm M Perry, 2nd door west of 7th st, & opposite the Centre Market.

Laws of the U S passed at the 3rd Session of the 27th Congress.
1-Act for the relief of Asahel Brainard: that the Sec of War be, & he is hereby, required to pay, out of any moneys in the Treas, at the rate of $20 a month, to A Brainard, in lieu of the pension now received by him, commencing from & after the passage of this act. Approved, Feb 24, 1843.
2-Act for the relief of Saml D Rose, of Pa, & John Baker, of Ohio, & Judah Case, of Pa, each, his prorata proportion of the $230 now in the hands of the Post Ofc Dept, which is a part of the money received from Wm Martin, of Pa, who was convicted of robbing the U S mail in Pa, in 1835, & who confessed that he took from Rose $110, from Baker $115, & from Case $470; on each said persons giving bonds, with surety to the satisfaction of the Postmaster Gen, to repay said money, if it shall hereafter be shown to belong to any other person or persons.
3-Act for the relief of Nancy Hambright, wid/o Capt John Hambright, dec'd: that the Sec of War be directed to pay to her a pension, under the act of Jul 7, 1838, for 18 months' service of her husband, John Hambright, as a capt of a volunteer company of light-horse, raised during the Revolutionary war, in the service of the U S.
4-Act for the relief of Thos King, of Tenn: Com'r of Pensions to place his name on the pension roll of invalid pensioners, & to pay to said King the sum of $8 per month during his natural life, to commence on Mar 4, 1842.
5-Act for the relief of Wm Fabre: to be paid $120.42, being for prize money due to him when a sailor on board the vessel **Saratoga**, on Lake Champlain.
6-Act for the relief of Robt G Ford: Sec of the Treas cause to be audited, settled, & paid, to Ford the amount of the accounts in his favor, & in favor of Robt Williams, for provender furnished Gen Nelson's brig of mounted volunteer militia in the service of the U S in 1837.

7-Act for the relief of Mary Williams, wid/o Jacob Williams, dec'd: that Mary Williams, of East Hartford, Conn, wid/o Jacob Williams, a Revolutionary sldr, dec'd, be placed on the pension roll, under the act of Jul 4, 1836; & that she be paid a sum equal to the pay of a sldr, under such annual pension while she remains a widow as her said husband would have been entitled to had he been living on Jun 7, 1832.

8-Act for the relief of Geo Mayfield: that he select & enter 640 acs of land, granted to him by the provisions of an act of Jul 27, 1842, be, & the same is hereby, extended one year; & the said Mayfield shall be permitted to enter said land in one entire section, or in qrtr sections, subject to private entry, & not in the occupancy of any actual settler, as he, in his discretion, may determine.

9-Act for the relief of Jacob White: to place his name on the Revolutionary pension roll; & that he be allowed & paid annually, during his natural life, a pension under the act of Jun 7, 1832, for 22 months' service as a capt, & 6 months' service as a private, to commence on Mar 4, 1832: Provided, that the full amount of pension already received by the said Jacob White be deducted from the pension granted him by the provisions of this act.

10-Act for the relief of Benj J Totten, of the U S Navy: to be paid the difference of compensation between a sailingmaster & a lt in the navy, for the period during which said Totten acted as lt on board of the U S schnr **Dolphin**, in 1833, by the temporary appointment of J C Long cmder; said Totten furnishing to the Navy Dept satisfactory evidence of the fact.

11-Act for the relief of Geo Randall, John C Haskell, & Elisha H Holmes: or their legal reps, to be paid the sum of $3,471.57, being the amount of labor bestowed & expenses incurred by them as contractors for removing the bar at Saybrock, in Conn, over & above the amount appropriated by the 24th Congress for that purpose.

12-Act for the relief of John Wharry: that the judgment recovered in the district court of the U S for the district of Ohio, against John Wharry & his sureties, as postmaster at Greenville, Ohio, be, & the same is hereby, discharged, & that the penalty of $98.51, included in said judgment, be repaid to said John Wharry together with interest thereon, from Jun 22, 1838.

13-Act for the relief of Jos Hover, Abelard Guthrie, & Edmund Ogden: their heirs or legal reps, patents to be issued for the lands by them entered at the land ofc at Lima, Ohio, in Jul, 1841, agreeably to the entries-the patents to said lands having been withheld on account of informality in the entries: Provided, said lands shall not have been sold to other purchasers by the U S before the date of this act-Mar 1, 1843.

14-Act for the relief of Mary Crawford; wid/o David Ross Crawford, late of the U S Navy, be placed on the roll of pensioners, & that there be paid to her such sum, as an annual pension, as she would have been entitled to receive had her late husband been a lt in the service at the time of his death.

15-Act for the relief of Wm Allen, of Portland, Maine: be placed on the roll of invalid pensioners, at the rate of $5 per month, to commence on Jan 1, 1839, & to be continued so long as said Allen's disability shall continue to be total.

16-Act for the relief of John R Williams, of Mich, be granted the tract of land [so described,] in Detroit, Mich, containing 640 acs; this grant being in satisfaction [so far as said Williams is concerned] of the claim confirmed to John R Williams & Jas May by the com'rs.

17-Act for the relief of Richd Patten: to be paid $50, that being the price of one telescope for observing coincidences, & 2 large spirit levels, & 2 bubbles, delivered by him to the naval storekeeper at N Y, for the use of the navy.

18-Act for the relief of Solomon Emerson, of Mass, that his name be placed on the invalid pension roll, & to pay him at the rate of $4 per month, from & after Feb 5, 1842.

19-Act for the relief of John Core: to pay him the sum of $80, for a horse which was killed while in the public service.

20-Act granting to Jas Lowe $1,000 & a section of land: to pay to Capt Jas Lowe, of Westmoreland Co, Va: that the one section of land is to be located on any of the public land subject to private entry; the same being granted as a testimonial to him of the consideration in which Congress hold his gallantry & peril in the rescue of an American brig, her crew, & passengers from the hands of pirates.

21-Act for the relief of the heirs of Madame De Lusser & their legal reps: that the land described in the special report of the register & receiver of the land ofc for the district of St Stephens, Ala, dated Jul 3, 1834, be confirmed to the heirs of Madame De Lusser, to whom they were originally granted by the French Gov't in 1763, & to their legal assignees or their heirs: Provided, however, that this act shall be so construed as to operate as a relinquishment of the title of the U S only.

22-Act for the relief of John E Hunt & others: that the Com'r of Indian Affairs to pay to Forsyth & Hull $1,455.38; to R A Forsyth, $2,529; to Elisha Mack, $84.57; to Isaac Hull, $195; to Jas H Forsyth, $935.48; to R F Hollister, $50; to Jas Wilkeson, $35; to John E Hunt, $2,018.35, out of any moneys due, or that may hereafter become due, from the U S to the Ottowa tribe of Indians, by existing treaties, on account of an order drawn by 19 chiefs, headmen, & warriors of said tribe, dated Ottowa Indian Reserve, Osage river, Sep 2, 1839, requesting the payment of said several sums of money, as herein directed: Provided, that each individual to whom payment is herein directed to be made shall only receive such proportion of his respective claim, out of any sum that may be due to said tribe, less than the whole amount of said claims, as his claim bears to the whole amount of said claim.

23-Act for the relief of Thos D Gilson, late sheriff of Clinton Co, N Y: to be paid $151.85, in full for his official services in assisting to preserve our neutral relations on the Champlain frontier.

24-Act for the relief of Wm G Sanders: to be paid $900, being the amount allowed for a store-house, a dwlg house, & one other house, owned by him, & destroyed Jan 21, 1836, by order of Capt F S Belton, 2nd artl, U S army, he being then cmder at Fort Brooke, Fla, to destroy the cover of the enemy in approaching the fort, as well as to prevent the said 3 bldgs being occupied & burned by the hostile Indians in the vicinity of the fort, with a view of setting on fire the block-houses & other defences.

Letter to the Boston Atlas, dated Exeter, N H, Mar 14, announces the death on that day of the Hon Tristam Shaw, late a member of Congress from N H. He arrived here on the 8th & was soon after attacked with a fever, which terminated his life a few hours since. Mr Shaw's age was 57.

Eliz Gough, late of said county, dec'd. –Edw Plater, administrator of E Gough

Crmnl Crt-Wash: Mar 17. 1-Negro Arnold, found not guilty of attempting to set fire to the dwlg-house of Isaac H Wailes, in Wash City, on Feb 6, 1843. 2-Negro W Howard found not guilty of an assault upon Chas Kiernan. 3-Negro Henry Fletcher found guilty of assault with intent to kill his wife Eliz Fletcher, on Dec 19, 1842. 4-Negro Danl Smallwood found guilty for stealing, on Mar 1, 1843, $1.50, the property of W H Morgan. Mar 18. 5-John Keller found guilty of attempting to break jail on Dec 13, 1842. 6-Fred'k Rothfritz pleaded guilty to 4 indictments charging him with stealing, viz-a shawl the value of $1.00, the property of Adam Friedenberger. One pair of boots of the value of $6, 2 pairs of boots of the value of $8, 2 pairs of shoes of the value of $5, & one cap of the value of $1.00, the property of Wm Ortereger. One watch of the value of $9, the property of Geo Augerman. One watch the value of $8, the property of Henry Boothe.

A duel took place on Mar 10 at New Orleans between Judge Waggaman, a member of the Senate of Louisiana, & formerly of the U S Senate, & Mr Denis Prieur, lately Mayor of New Orleans, in which the former was severely wounded, though not deemed to be in a dangerous situation. The cause of the quarrel has been of long standing.

Orphans Crt of St Mary's Co, Md. Letters of administration on the personal estate of Eliz Gough, late of said county, dec'd. –Edw Plater, administrator of E Gough

New Orleans, Mar 9-a rencontre took place on board the steamboat **President**, between Capt Cyprian Rhodes, pilot of that boat, & Mr Warden P Stevenson, pilot of the steamboat **Swan**, in which the former was shot through the breast with a pistol, & died in a few minutes-not, however, until he had inflicted several wounds upon Stevenson with a knife, which are believed mortal. Stevenson was a young man, who felt aggrieved about some expressions Capt R had made respecting him to a young lady. -Bulletin

Wm Campbell & Thos Campbell, brothers, sons of the late Mr Loudon Campbell, of Alexandria, were in a boat down the river, engaged in shooting wild fowl, when the snow storm of Thu last occurred. They lost their way due to the sleet & darkness, & were exposed for the whole day & night to the storm. The youngest of the brothers, Thos Campbell, benumbed by the cold, died. Wm Campbell survived, but had his limbs dreadfull frostbitten. He reached the residence of Dr Henry P Dangerfield, in PG Co, Md, where assistance was rendered, & where he now remains under the medical care of the Dr. –Alexandria Gaz

TUE MAR 21, 1843
The undersigned continues to purchase Books, new & second-hand, at private sale. His customers include scholars of every class, Books of every class, & in various languages. –Jas Riordan, Pa ave

Circuit Court of Wash Co, D C. Paul Stevens, a bankrupt, has filed his ptn for his discharge & certificate: hearing on the first Mon in Jun next. –Wm Brent, clk

Gen Tom Thumb, jr, the Wonderful Dwarf, will be exhibited at Washington, on the Mar 21st, 22nd, & 23rd, at Elliot's bldgs, Pa ave, between 3rd & 4th sts. The smallest specimen of a man ever before heard of, is 11 years old, 25 inches height & weights but 15 pounds, being precisely his weight when but 6 months old. Admission 25 cents; children under 12 years of age, half price.

For sale: 100 acs of land in Wash Co, nearly opposite the Navy Yard. Also, for rent, adjoining the above land, a dwlg hse, with 6 rooms, in complete repair, besides the kitchen & room over it, with out-bldgs, & a well of fine water in the yard. –Griffith Coombe, Eastern Branch, Wash City

Geauga Republican: the dwlg house of Mr Cyrus Millard, in the northern part of Russell township, in this county, near Judson's mill, was entirely consumed by fire on Mar 7, in the absence of Mr & Mrs Millard; & their 4 youngest children & a relative, a lad of 14, were burnt in the bldg. Northing saved.

Valuable real estate for sale: the farm on which I now reside, on the Potomac river, in Loudon Co, Va, about 5 miles from Leesburg, containing 757 acs. The improvements are a large 2 story brick dwlg house, nearly new, with a well of fine water within a few feet of the door, with all necessary our-houses, such as a smoke house, ice house, corn house, barns, & stables. I will sell the whole farm, or 200 to 300 acs, as the purchaser may desire. –Wm T T Mason

For rent or sale, the dwlg house & premises on the corner of 14th & N Y ave, at present in the occupancy of Capt Page of the Navy. It has a stable & carriage-house, wood-house, & milk-house. –Jas Larned, 13th st

Circuit Court of Wash Co, D C. John Hall has applied to be discharged from imprisonment under the act for the relief of Insolvent Debtors: hearing on the first Mon in Apr next. –Wm Brent, clk

Circuit Court of Wash Co, D C. Jas Robertson, Jas H Bayard, Jas N Newbold, Herman Cope, & Thos S Taylor, vs. Clara F Forsyth, Alfred Iverson & Julia his wife, Mary A Shaaf, Murray Mason & Clara his wife, John Forsyth, Virginia Forsyth, Rosa Forsyth, Anna Forsyth, Robt Forsyth, Robt Bowie, & Robt S Chew. Cmplnt's bill charges that they are joint creditors of John Forsyth, dec'd, in the principal sum of $3,200, besides interest & costs, on 2 notes of the dfndnt, John Forsyth, endorsed successively by the dfndnt, Alfred Iverson, & the dec'd, & duly protested; that the dec'd died intestate, leaving a widow, the dfndnt, Clara F Forsyth, & the dfndnts Julia, Mary, Clara, John, Virginia, Rosa, Anna, & Robt Forsyth, his only children & heirs at law; & seised in fee simple of lots 5, 8, 9, & 10, in sq 27, in Wash City, which lots have descended to, & are held by, said children, subject to the widow's right of dower & certain incumbrances for purchase money to said Robt Bowie, & for other debts; that the dfndnt, Chew, is administrator of the dec'd, & the personal estate in his hands is wholly inadequate to satisfy the remaining debts of the dec'd; that the dfndnts John Forsyth & Alfred Iverson reside & are beyond the Dist of Col, & have no property therein except their interests, by reason of the premises, in said lots of ground. Objects of the bill are, an account & distribution of the personal estate & a sale of the said lots, with the appurtenances, to satisfy the debts & costs of cmplnts, & such other creditors of the dec'd as may be made parties to this suit, insofar as the personal estate shall not be sufficient therefore; & the widow of the dec'd is made a party dfndnt, that she may make her election whether to reserve her right of dower, or let the premises be sold discharged thereof, & receive in lieu an equivalent allowance by the Court out of the purchase money. All the dfndnts, excepting Robt S Chew, reside & are out of D C. Next Court date is Mar 20, 1843. –W Cranch -W Brent, clk

Sale of very handsome furniture, on Mar 23, at the residence of the Hon Mr Roosevelt, corner of 16th & H sts, [Mrs Madison's house,] part of his very excellent household furniture. –Robt W Dyer & Co, aucts

The U S sloop of war **Concord** was lost on the rocks in the Mozambique channel about Oct 2; on Nov 2, Capt Boerum, Purser Hart, & one of the crew were drowned by the upsetting of a boat in crossing the bar of the Zangola river. The U S sloop of war **John Adams** was at the Cape to take the ofcrs & crew. She was hourly expected at St Helena. [This information is by the arrival at Boston of the ship **Maria Theresa**, from Manilla.] [Mar 22 newspaper: Loss of the U S ship **Concord**, & the death of Capt Boerum, her Cmder, are confirmed. Capt Boerum was a native of the State of N Y; entered the naval service on Sep 1, 1811, & was in service during the whole of the war of 1812. His commission as Commander bore date on Feb 9, 1837.]

Died: on Tue last, in Queen Anne's Co, Md, Thos C Earl, aged 72 years, Reg/o Wills for that county.

Died: on Mar 19, Alida Van Renesselaer, infant d/o Lt Col T Cross, U S A.

Died: on Thu, at Phil, the Hon Geo Turner, aged 93. He was a native of England, but joined the American army on the breaking out of the Revolutionary war. He was a capt in the service, & commanded in S C, & distinguished himself in several severe engagements, especially in the affair generally known, from the fatal effects of the courage & perserverance on both sides as the "Slaughter Pens." He was the personal friend of Washington, & received from him a commission as Judge in the Terr of the U S Northwest to the river Ohio, dated Sep 12, 1789. Major Turner continued to reside in the West until about 10 years since, when he came to visit a part of his family in Phil, & postponed from time to time his return until he was called to a better home. –Phil Inq

Died: on Mar 14, at Woodbury, near Leonardtown, St Mary's Co, Md, Mrs Sophia Leeds Leigh, consort of Geo S Leigh, & eldest d/o the Hon John Leeds Kerr. An afflicted husband & numerous children are left to mourn.

Died: on Mar 6, at Frostburg, Md, in her 73rd year, Mrs Hannah Skinner, w/o the Rev J L Skinner, formerly of this Wash City, but for several years past a resident of Frostburg. From early youth Mrs Skinner was a member of the church of Christ.

WED MAR 22, 1843
Laws of the U S passed at the 3rd Session of the 27th Congress.
1-Act for the relief of Geo A Winslow: to be paid the sum of $144, it being the amount due him for premium money in enlisting recruits during the last war with Great Britain.
2-Act for the relief of the heirs of Philander Smith & Jas Young: that they are hereby, confirmed in their claim [according to the portions by them respectively owned] to a tract of land containing 1,500 arpens, about 6 miles from Baton Rouge, La, originally granted to Armand Duplantier, by Baron de Carondelet, on Oct 25, 1796.
3-Act for the relief of Eliz Gresham, wid/o Geo Gresham, late a Revolutionary pensioner: Elis Gresham to be allowed a pension for 5 years, at the rate of $600 a year, to commence on Jul 7, 1838, & to be paid as other pensioners are paid under the act of Jul, 1833.
4-Act for the relief of John Skirving: to be paid $3,287.25, for building furnaces for warming the Treas Dept.
5-Act for the relief of Benj Truslow, of Stafford Co, Va: to be placed on the roll of Revolutionary pensioners of the U S, & allow him $80 a year during his life, deducting therefrom whatever amount of pension which may have been allowed & paid to Truslow prior to the passage of the act of Congress passed Jun 7, 1832.
6-Act for the relief of S & M Riche: That so much of a judgment which was obtained ty the U S, in the district court of the U S for the district of Ky, for the sum of $108.53, besides damages & costs, against John F Moore; late postmaster at Gaines' Cross Roads, in Ky,& the said S & M Riche, his securities, as is in the nature of penalty, be, & the same is hereby released, as against said S & M Riche: Provided, that the balance of said judgment, if not already paid, shall be paid within 60 days from the passage of this act.

7-Act for the relief of Saml Lord, of Charleston, S C: he is discharged from all further liability upon a judgment obtained & now outstanding against him as surety on a custom house bond given to the U S by How & Fitch, in 1818, upon said Lord first paying, or securing to be paid, to the U S the sum of $1,000; & that the Sec of Treas be, & he is hereby, authorized & directed to execute a release to said Lord, for said judgment, upon his paying, or securing to be paid, in a satisfactory manner, the said sum of $1,000.

8-Act for the relief of Knott Martin, 3rd, & Arnold Martin, owners of the fishing schnr **Only Son**, & others: that the collector of Massachusetts, is authorized to pay to them, late owners of the fishing schnr lost at sea, called the **Only Son**, burden 68 tons & 57 9/5^{ths}, & to the legal reps of the persons composing her late crew, such allowance, to be distributed according to law, as they would have been entitled to receive had the schnr completed her fishing term, & returned into port.

9-Act for the relief of Jonathan Britton, of Otisfield, Cumberland, Maine: name to be placed on the pension roll, & pay him a pension, at the rate of $80 per annum, from Mar 4, 1831, during his natural life.

10-Act for the relief of Horace Wetherall, an invalid pensioner, be paid, at the rate of $8 per month from Aug 1, 1839, to Oct 30, 1840.

11-Act for the relief of Chas Waldron: or his legal reps, to be paid the sum of $1,179.61, it being for bldgs & other property destroyed at Micanoopy, Fla, in 1836, by order of the ofcr than in command at that post, to prevent them from falling into the possession of the enemy.

12-Act for the relief of Andrew Fisher: or his legal reps, to be paid the sum of $79, being the amount of expenses incurred by him in repairing the damages done to the light-house keeper's house at Gibraltar, on the Detroit river, while in the possession, by impressments, of the U S troops under the command of Gen Brady, in 1838.

13-Act for the relief of Gamaliel E Smith: to be paid $350 for work done & materials furnished for the erection of a dwlg house & light-house on Mount Desert rock, in Maine, in 1829.

14-Act for the relief of Jas Gray, of Wash Co, Pa: to be paid at the rate of $8 per month, from & after Jan 1, 1843.

15-Act for the relief of Chas B Hall, of Cincinnati: to be paid the amount of a certain judgment recovered by him in the Circuit Court of the U S for the district of Ohio, at Dec term, in 1840, against John B Warren, late surveyor of the port of Cincinnati, Ohio, for damages occasioned by the unlawful seizure & detention of certain goods, under orders from the Treas Dept.

16-Act for the relief of Richd Rush: to pay him the sum of $3,815.73, for extra services in converting the Smithsonian funds received by him, as agent of the U S, into gold coin, & for his aid & supervision in transporting the same from London to the mint at Phil.

17-Act for the relief of the legal reps of Lt Wm S Eyeleth: cause a credit of $846.82 to be passed to the account of Lt Wm S Eyeleth, as of the date of his death, to be ascertained by the order announcing his death at the Engineer Dept; & that the Sec of

Treas cause to be paid to his legal reps, such sum of money as is due for his services & emoluments at the time of his death, to be ascertained as aforesaid.

18-Act for the relief of John Drysdale: to be paid agreeable, to his rank as assistant adj gen of the 2nd brig of Florida militia, ordered into the service of the U S by Gen Jos Hernandez, in 1835, on the principles adopted by him in paying the ofcrs & non-commissioned ofcrs of the 2nd regt of said brig, under the act for their relief, approved Mar 3, 1839, provided the time of service to be paid for shall not exceed 5 months & 11 days.

19-Act for the relief of Richd Sneed: Solicitor of the Treas authorized to suspend, for a reasonable time, the collection of a judgment against Richd Sneed, in the Circuit Court of the U S for the district of N C, in favor of the U S, rendered at May term, 1842; Provided, that Richd Sneed shall execute & deliver to the Solicitor of the Treas a bond for $1,239.44, with such security as the said Solicitor shall approve; & Provided, further, that Richd Sneed shall use all proper dispatch, under the directions of the Solicitor of the Treas, to enforce the collection of certain refunding bonds taken by him & the other execs of Stephen Sneed, dec'd; as also of a certain decree had in the U S Circuit Court for the district of N C, in favor of the U S, against Nathl M Sneed & Albert Sneed; to be applied, when collected, to the credit of the judgment aforesaid: Provided, that there shall be no suspension of proceedings upon said judgment, or any delay or indulgence given upon it, which would work the discharge, release, or forfeiture of any right of the U S; it being the only object of this act to give a reasonable time to said Richd Sneed to subject to the payment of the said judgment of all the estate of his testator, Stephen Sneed, dec'd, which the original judgment against him bound, for the convenience & benefit of the said Richd Sneed, without prejudice to the U S.

20-Act for the relief of Jos R Chandler: that the clk of the district crt of the U S for the eastern district of Pa be required to credit the dfndnts in the judgment in favor of the U S against Wm C Graham, Geo H Hart, Jos R Chandler, & John Connell, obtained before said court, with the following payments, to wit: Sep 9, 1829, $100; Oct 28, 1829, $100; Jan 5, 1830, $100; Feb 26, 1830, $200; Jun 26, 1830, $200; & that the said court be authorized to allow to said dfndnts such other credits on said judgment as to said court may appear just & equitable, not exceeding $300.

21-Act for the relief of Eliz Powers, wid/o Timothy Powers, dec'd: name be put on the roll of Revolutionary pensioners, & that she be paid, during her natural life, at the rate of $80 per annum, commencing on Mar 4, 1831.

22-Act to allow a pension to Nancy Williams, wid/o David Williams, one of the captors of Maj Andre. Sec of War to place her name on the roll of Revolutionary pensioners, & pay to her $200 annually, during her life, to commence on Aug 2, 1831, at which date the said David Williams departed this life; the same to be paid as other pensioners are paid.

23-Act for the relief of John Hicks: name to be placed on the invalid pension roll, & that he be entitled to receive at the rate of $8 per month during his natural life, commencing Apr 1, 1840.

24-Act for the relief of Edwin Bartlett, late Consul of the U S at Lima, Peru: to be paid the sum of $9,062.50, in full of all demands for the services of a diplomatic character rendered by the said Edwin Bartlett, in the interval between the death of Mr Thornton, late charge d'affaires to Peru, on Jan 25, 1838, & the recognition of his successor [Mr Pickett] on Jan 30, 1840.

25-Act for the relief of Wm Gale, of N Y C: to repeal all acts passed Jul 4, 1836, as prohibits the extension of a patent after the expiration of the term for which it was originally issued, & the same is suspended, as far as shall be necessary to authorize the renewal of a patent to Wm Gale, of N Y C, for his invention of what is denominated in his former letters patent, "a new & useful improvement in the manufacture of silver spoons & forks," subject, however, to all other restrictions & conditions in said act contained.

26-Act for the relief of Asahel Lee, Harvey Lee, & Lemuel Lee: Sec of the Treas to audit & settle the account due to the above, on the contract entered into by them on Aug 10, 1837, with Capt C A Ogden, acting on behalf of the U S, by which they agreed to erect a bridge across the Kaskaskia river, & to construct a certain part of the Cumberland road in Illinois; & that he pay said amount, when ascertained.

27-Act for the relief of Chas Gordon, owner of the schnr **Two Sons**, & the legal reps of the crew of said vessel. The collector of the port of Belfast, Maine, to pay such sum as would have been entitled to as bounty had she completed her voyage, said vessel having been lost after having been employed in the fishing season upwards of 3 months; which sum shall be distributed, according to law, among the heirs & legal reps of the persons composing the crew of said vessel, in such proportions as said crew would have been entitled to if they had survived.

28-Act for the relief of Richd Coke, jr, Robt Anderson, & Geo W Southall, sureties of Peyton A Southall, in his official bond to the U S as a purser in the navy, be released from their liabilities on said bond, & from any suits brought or judgments obtained thereon against them, or any of them, provided they shall first pay to the U S Treas, the sum of $1,958.62, with interest thereon from May 30, 1836, & also all the costs of any suit against them on the trial aforesaid.

29-Act for the relief of John Randolph Clay, late Sec of Leg of the U S at the Court of Vienna: To be paid the sum of $3,750, in full of all demands for services of a diplomatic character rendered by the said John Randolph Clay in the interval between Sep 18, 1840, the day of the recall of Mr Muhlenburg, late Minister Pleni to Austria, & the recognition of the successor [Mr Jenifer] on Mar 18, 1842.

30-Act for the relief of John Wolfenden: to be paid a sum of money, annually, equal to the amount paid at the naval asylum at Phil, for the support of a seaman in the U S service, but not exceeding $108; said payment to be made semi-yearly, & to continue during the life of said Wolfenden.

31-Act for the relief of Johnson Patrick: or to his legal reps, the sum of $1,351.76 for boarding certain Pottawatomie chiefs while holding a council at Prairie road, in Kalamazoo Co, Mich, in the summer of 1832.

Whe whaling ship **Gen Williams**, Capt Bailey, during the gale of Thu night, being bound for New London, Conn, with 4,000 barrels oil, came to anchor off Black Point, in L I Sound, but immediately dragged & it was necessary to cut away her masts to prevent her going ashore. . Capt Bailey, with 5 men, left the ship in the boat to procure assistance, but in gong through the surf the boat swamped, & all on board of her perished.

Died: yesterday, at the residence of his mother, on N Y ave, Mr Jos McPherson, of the firm of Adams & McPherson, in his 28th year. His funeral is this day at 2 p m.

Died: on Mar 21, after a lingering illness, Mrs Miriam Ball, in her 75th year. Her funeral will be on Mar 23, at half past 3 o'clock, from her late residence.

Died: on Mar 21, in Wash City, of a lingering illness, Miss Mary Gallaher, d/o Thos & Sarah Gallaher, aged 21 years. The "Female Sodality of St Matthew's Church" are respectfully invited to attend the funeral service at St Patrick's Church this evening at 4 p m precisely.

The schnr **Thomas**, Capt Sproul, from Belfast, Me, for Boston, was driven ashore on Lynn Beach on Fri. Capt Sproul & a young man named Rufus Chapman were saved. Wm Russell, Wilford Chapman, Robt Harvey, Danl Wheeler, & Henry Ford [boy] drowned. Had they remained on board a few minutes longer, the life-boat, which was on her way, would have saved them all; but they left in their own boat, which swamped almost immediately.

Mrd: on Mar 18, by Rev J P Moore, D A Wilds to Lucy E Miller.

On Sat, Mr John Mitchel, sexton of Trinity Chr in Catharine st, Phil, between 2nd & 3rd sts, was found dead in the ash-hole of the furnace of the church. It appears he fell head foremost into the ashes in passing down a few steps. There was a contusion on the side of his head. He was about 55 years of age.

Charleston, Mar 18. We have to record the death of John Julius Pringle, an eminent & virtuous citizen of Charleston, who died in his 90th year. He was Speaker of the Hse/o Reps: of this State from 1787 to 1789, & filled the ofc of Atty Gen from 1792 to 1810, having largely assisted in the formation of our State Constitution. –Patriot [No date-current item.]

David W Holman, aged 30, s/o the Rev David Holman, of Douglass, Mass, died from an accident in the factory in Millville, when he slipped down between the buckets & bulkhead. He lived about 6 hours & retained his reason to the last, bidding his wife & child an affectionate farewell.

Fire last Mon in the frame bldg occupied by Mr John B Morgan as a grocery store, on the north side of Pa ave, near the Capitol, spread rapidly to the adjoining frame bldge occupied by Mr Patrick Moran, & known by the name of the Railroad Hotel. Mr Moran's hotel, owned by Mr Gregory Ennis, was uninsured: damage about $500.

Mysterious disappearance: the Fred'k Citizen, Mar 17. Rev John L Pitts left his home on foot on Mon last & without giving his family any intimation as to where he was going or when he intended to return, has not been heard of or seen since. On Wed the country was scoured for miles around by a large body of citizens, & the Monocacy river was dragged for miles, but no clue as to his whereabout. [Since the above extract was in type, we learn he is probably somewhere in the neighborhood.]

Crmnl Crt-Wash. 1-Wm. Noland, convicted of grand larceny, to be imprisoned in the pen for 4 years. 2-Washington Causine, an old offender, convicted of grand larceny, to be imprisoned in the pen for 2 years. 3-Fred'k Rothfritz, convicted of grand larceny in 3 cases, to be imprisoned in the pen for 3 years. 4-Fred'k Rothfritz, convicted of petit larceny, to pay a fine of $1 & be imprisoned 1 week in jail. 5-Dominic Borg, convicted of grand larceny, to be imprisoned in the pen 2 years. 6-Wm Gibbs, free negro, convicted of theft, econd offence,] to be imprisoned in the pen for 3 years. 7-Jas Shorter, free negro, convicted of grand larceny, to be imprisoned in the pen 3 years; to take effect one day after the rising of the next term of the Circuit Court. 8-David Jenkins, free negro, convicted of theft, [second offence,] to be imprisoned 3 years in the pen. 9-Betsy Brown, convicted of grand larceny, to be imprisoned in the pen 2 years. 10-Eliz White, convicted of petit larceny, to be fined $2, & imprisoned one month in jail. 11-John Keller, convicted of breaking jail, to pay a fine of $5 & costs, & be imprisoned one month in jail. 12-In the case of negro Chas Williams, convicted of murder, the prisoner's counsel deferred the argument on motion for a new trial until the June Term.

THU MAR 23, 1843
We feel the deepest sorrow in stating the death of a most amiable & accomplished young lady in the town of Petersburg, Va, Miss Mary Louisa May, the 4th d/o Judge May, in her 20th year. She breathed her last on Monday. Peace be unto her. –Richmond Enquirer

Revolutionary Pensioners: Widows of ofcrs & sldrs of the Revolution who were pensioned under the act of Congress of Jul 7, 1838. By an act of Congress, passed Mar 3, 1843, those widows who received, or are entitled to receive, pensions, under the above act, are entitled to one year's additional pension, from Mar 4, or for such portion of that period as they may survive. As it will be necessary for applications, the undersigned offers his services in prosecuting their claims before the Dept. The whole fee in the case of the widow of a sldr, will be $5; for widow of ofcrs in the line or staff, $10; to be forwarded on application. –Alex'r Ray, Agency Ofc, next door to the Pension Ofc, Wash.

The ship **Columbia** arrived at Boston on Mon, making her passage from Liverpool in 15½ days. She brought 54 passengers from Liverpool, 9 of these for Halifax. Among the passengers are Sir Chas Metcalfe, Govn'r Gen of the British Provinces in North America, & his suite. Sir Chas is to succeed Sir Chas Bagot, who returns to England as soon as his health permits. Capt Spencer, late in command of the U S ship **Columbia** in the Mediterranean, & brother of the Sec of the Treas, is also a passenger.

Appointments by the Pres. Land Ofcrs:-Receivers:
Saml J Bayard, Fairfield, Iowa, vice Jos C Hawkins.
Richd B Servant, Kaskaskia, Ill, vice Saml Crawford.
Robt H Booth, Tallahassee, Fla, vice R B Semple, resigned.
Custom-House Ofcr: John Bryan, Appraiser at Charleston, S C, vice Jeremiah A Yates.

Letter from Cmder Conover, of the U S ship **John Adams**, dated Table Bay, Cape of Good Hope, Dec 26, 1842. The Portuguese brig **Union** arrived here a few days since with the surviving ofcrs & crew of the U S ship **Concord**-the ofcrs & men under charge of the 1st Lt Mr Gardner, who has officially communicated to me the loss of the **Concord**. Capt Boerum, Purser Hart, & Jas Davis, ordinary seaman, were drowned on Nov 2, while crossing the bar at the mouth of Lorango river in the gig. I have taken 5 midshipmen & 60 men on board the **John Adams**. The remaining ofcrs & crew will proceed to Rio de Janeiro in the Portuguese brig which conveyed them to this place. The **Concord** is injured, but not a complete wreck.

Died: Dr Jenison, a native of one of the New England States, but for many years past a resident of Chihuahua, Mexico, where he was connected with extensive mining work. –N O Picayune [No date-current item.]

Mrd: on Mar 21, by Rev J C Smith, Mr John U Moulder to Miss Emily J Longdon, both of Wash City.

Died: on Mar 9, in Wash City, Miss Eleanor, d/o Mr Thos Cisil, of Montg Co, Md, in her 18th year.

Post Ofc Business: the undersigned continues to transact business for mail contractors, pensioners, claimants generally, at the Seat of Gov't.
–Jesse E Dow, Wash, 8th st, near the Gen Post Ofc.

Notice. We forewarn all persons from purchasing, receiving, or otherwise trading for a note or instrument of writing given to Mr J P Gannon, on or about Dec 29 last, purporting a reward to be given for the arrest & committal of 2 runaway negromen, the property of Mrs Sarah Marshall, of Chas Co, Md, as we are determined not to pay unless compelled by law. –Wm M Maddox, for self & John A Cox

FRIDAY MAR 24, 1843
$100 reward for runaway negro man Joe Hamersly: carpenter by trade, about 28 years old. –Wm Hamilton, near Port Tobacco, Chas Co, Md

Benj D White, recently convicted at Le Roy, Genesee Co, N Y, of the murder of his father, has been sentenced to be hung on Apr 29 next. His father was a pious man, possessed of some property, & universally esteemed. The son had conceived a strong hatred of him for supposed ill treatment, & especially because he was a Christian. Several quarrels had occurred between them.

Jos Tricott was on Mar 9 sentenced to be hung in New Orleans for setting fire to & robbing the ofc of Messrs Hollander & Brown.

Circuit Court of Wash Co, D C. John S Hutchins applied to the Hon Wm Cranch, Chief Judge, to be discharged from imprisonment under the act for the relief of Insolvent Debtors within D C: hearing on the first Mon in Apr next. –Wm Brent, clk

Wash Corp: 1-Ptn of Simeon Bassett & others, praying the removal of a nuisance near the junction of A st north & 2nd st east: referred to the Cmte on Improvements. 2-Act authorizing A H Young to erect a frame bldg on lot 13 in sq 374: rejected at its 3rd reading. 3-Cmte of Claims: on the ptn of Danl Paulien, reported the prayer ought not to be granted. Same cmte asked to be discharged from its further consideration of the ptn of Eliz Purrell. 4-Ptn of Robt Farnham: referred to the Cmte of Claims. 5-Cmte of Claims: bill for the relief of Thos Goddard-passed.

P Barton Key, Atty at Law: will attend the Courts of the Dist of Col & the adjoining counties.

Died: Mar 22, in Wash City, after a few days sickness, Mrs Caroline Beall, w/o Mr Benj Beall, aged 26 years. She leaves a fond husband & 2 small children [one an infant] & numerous anxious friends to mourn her irreparable loss, the more so because it was not expected but a very short time before her death. Her funeral will be from the residence of her husband, near 6th & F sts, on Mar 24, at 3 p m.

SAT MAR 25, 1843
Geo Luff, of Gibraltar, a passenger on board the ship **Orient**, which arrived at New Orleans a few days since, fell overboard on Mar 13, & was drowned. He was a friend of Francisco Rodella, who shot himself near the Fireman's Cemetery on the Sunday preceding, & came out with Gibraltar in the same ship. They were both recommended by their friends to the care & good ofcs of Mr Wm Massar, who has

now the melancholy duty of communicating to the mother of each the intelligence of their untimely end. -Bulletin

During the year 1842 have died [says the Courrier Francaise] the last of the Absesses of France, [Madame the Countess de la Marche;] the last of the Chanoinesses of Remiremont, [the Countess of Arma de Monspey;] the last of the Prelate Abbes of Flanders, [the Abbe Delvigne;] the last of the Augustinian Monks of France, [the Abbe Mollard;] the last of the Hermits of Switzerland, [the Hermit Kauffman,] found frozen in the forest of Dufikon; the last of the Councillors of the Parliament of Navarre, [M du Parage;] & the last of the companions of the famous Paul Jones; & the last of the companions of Cook. This is an entire age, which has disappeared.

Military Cap Manufactory in 3rd st, #101, a few doors below Race st, east side, Phil, where he still continues to manufacture Military & Sportsmen's Articles of every description. –Wm Cressman

On Sunday evening last the Rev Jos Dickey, minister of the 3rd Presbyterian congregation of Rathfriland, while concluding his sermon, was shot & killed by someone unknown, firing through the window. Rev Dickey is universally beloved, & to what cause an attempt on his life is to be attributed it is impossible to conceive. -Belfast paper

Chas Seaton, Atty at Law, Richmond, Va. Having been appointed by the Govn'r Com'r of the State of Ky for the State of Va, will take acknowledgments of all deeds & other instruments of writing to be used or recorded in Ky.

Wash City lots for sale: lots #10 thru 16 in sq 36. Lots 15 & 19 in sq 102; lot 1 in sq 122; lots 31 & 33 in sq 24; & 76½ feet front on N W side of sq 952, Also, the strip of land on the hill side, adjoining the residence of C Schwartz, above Gtwn. Apply to W Chandler, corner of West & Congress sts, Gtwn

Boarding: house on D, between 6th & 7th sts. –Eliz Larcomb

Mr Jos Von Hohensteg, late of the Austrian marine corps, is informed, by order of the authority of the city of Budwers, in Bohemia, that the late Mr Francis Chas Helfert having left by his last will half of his property to the said Jos Von Hohensteg, he is requested to take possession of what was left to him; the more so as in virtue of another clause of the last will of Mr Helfert, that the same property, with interest, if not claimed by Mr Jos Von Hensteg before the end of 6 years after the publication of the decree of the court, is to be employed for the benefit of the hospital of the poor in the city of Budwers. –Schmid, Burgemerster -Budwers, Oct 11, 1842

Laws of the U S passed at the 3rd Session of the 27th Congress.

1-Act for the relief of Jas S Calhoun: to be paid $15,900, in full for the claims of Jas S Calhoun, against the U S, for the use & detention by an ofcr of the Gov't of the U S of the steamboat **Anna Calhoun**, & the barges **Mary Eliza & Antoinette**, & that the same be paid out of any money in the Treas not otherwise appropriated.

2-Act for the relief of John Javins, of Pa: to be put on the roll of invalid pensioners, & be paid at $8 per month during his natural life; to commence on Dec 1, 1841.

3-Act for the relief of John F Wiley: to be placed on the roll of invalid pensioners, & that he receive $4 per month from Mar 1, 1834.

4-Act for the relief of Jas Sweetman, of N Y: to be placed on the pension roll, & to pay him at the rate of $8 per month, from & after Feb 21, 1842.

5-Act for the relief of Jos Nimblett, of Vt: to be placed on the roll of invalid pensioners, & to be paid at the rate of $8 per month, from Jul 12, 1839, being the time when the taking of the testimony was completed.

6-Act for the relief of Gorham A Worth, one of the sureties of Saml Edmonds, dec'd: Mr Worth is hereby, acquitted, released, & discharged from all liability whatever to pay, or cause to be paid, a certain bond, executed by him to the U S in 1813, conditioned in the penal sum of $20,000, for the faithful discharge of the duties of Saml Edmonds, as principal paymaster of the militia of the State of N Y.

7-Act for the relief of the legal reps of John Peters, dec'd: Sec of War to issue a duplicate of warrant #1,922, for 100 acs of land, bearing date Mar 6, 1833, issued in favor of John Peters & Sarah Farnum, as heirs at law of the said John Peters; & the same, when issued, shall, in every respect, have the same force & effect as the original warrant, which original warrant is hereby declared to be null & void.

8-Act for the relief of John Skirving: to be paid the sum of $600, for services performed by him upon the public bldgs, in 1839, 1840, & 1841.

9-Act for the relief of Saml K Jennings: Com'r of Patents to renew, for the period of 14 years, the letters patent granted to Saml K Jennings, of Balt City, in 1814, for an apparatus for the speedy generation, & convenient, prompt, & agreeable application of heat to the human system; & that he embrace in said renewal of letters patent the improvement subsequently made by said Jennings in its mode of application; subject, however, to the rules & usages of the Patent Ofc, & all the provisions, except as aforesaid, of the act entitled "An act to promote the progress of the useful arts," & all acts in addition & amendatory therein.

10-Act for the relief of Nancy Wilson: wid/o the late Capt Wm Wilson: her name to be placed on the pension roll, & pay to her 5 years' full pay of a capt, in the manner provided by the act of Jul 7, 1838, allowing pensions to certain widows: Provided, that all moneys heretofore received by the said Nancy Wilson, on account of the Revolutionary services of her husband, be deducted from the above pension.

11-Act for the relief of John Hodgkin: to be paid the sum of $3,515.50, being the balance of his account for painting & bronzing done on the N Y customhouse, under the direction of the com'rs appointed by the Pres of the U S to superintend said work.

12-Act for the relief of Thos Weaver & Jacob Heyberger, sureties of the Norristown & Valley Railroad Co: That the time for actually & permanently laying upon any railroad the railroad iron imported into the port of Phil by the Norristown & Valley R R Co during 1839, to entitle the same to a drawback of duties, is hereby extended one year; & the Sec of the Treas is authorized to cause all proceedings upon the judgments obtained against the sureties on bonds given for the duties upon the importation of said iron, to stay for & during the said term of one year; & if, at or before the expiration of the said one year, it shall be proved to this satisfaction that the whole or any part of the said r r iron has been actually & permanently laid upon any railroads in the U S, then to order the whole, or a proportionate part, of the said judgments to be marked satisfied, upon the dfndnt paying the costs.

13-Act for the relief of the legal reps of Robt T Spence: to be allowed the credit of $425.10, with interest on $245.10 thereof from the time that the U S calculated & recovered interest in the judgment obtained by them against the said reps, on account of the liability of her intestate as security of G K Spence, on a balance appearing upon the books of the Treas Dept to be due from the said G K Spence of Treas notes by him received in 1815, & like interest on $175 thereof from the same time, provided that time be not anterior to Nov 9, 1819; & if it be, then from Nov 9, 1819, upon a judgment in favor of the U S, & against the said rep, in a suit upon a bond executed by her intestate as the security of the said G K Spence.

14-Act for the relief of Hannah Jenkins, wid/o Jas Jenkins, dec'd: her name is to be placed on the pension roll, & to be paid a pension for 11 months' service of her husband in the Revolutionary war, under the act of Jul 7, 1838. [Amount of pension was not included.]

15-Act for the relief of Jos Ellery, of the State of N Y: name to be placed on the roll of invalid pensioners; & shall be entitled to receive a pension at the rate of $6 a month, from Jul 2, 1842, & to continue during his natural life.

16-Act for the relief of Peters, Moore & Co: to be paid the sum of $2,166.66, in full payment & satisfaction for services rendered by them in transporting the U S mails on the turnpike from Phil to Lancaster, from Jan 2, 1836, to Feb 1, 1837.

17-Act for the relief of the heirs, or the assignees of the heirs of Isaac Todd & Jas McGill: That all the right, title, interest, claim, & demand of the U S in, over, & to the following described tract or parcel of land, in the State of Mich, known as claim #270, entered on the records of the land board at Detroit, under the act of Mar 26, 1804, be, & the same is hereby, relinquished to Jas McGill, his heirs & legal reps, & to those legally holding under him or them; & all the right, title, interest, claim & demand of the U S in, over, & to the following described tracts or parcels of land, in the State of Michigan; that is tracts #267 & #268, as entered on the records aforesaid, under the act aforesaid, & the same is hereby, relinquished to Isaac Todd, his heirs & legal reps, & to those legally holding under him or them: Provided, that the said relinquishment on the part of the U S shall not take effect until the said McGill & Todd, their heirs, or those holding & claiming the said land through them, for a consideration to be fixed by the valuation, upon oath, of 3 disinterested men, to be selected by the Sec of War, & paid by the U S out of the sum of $50,000 appropriated by the act of Sep 9, 1841, entitled "An act making appropriations for various fortifications for ordnance, & for preventing & suppressing Indian hostilities," shall execute to the U S in such form & with such covenants as shall be prescribed by the Sec of War, a good & sufficient deed to the following described part of said tracts: that is to say, a tract adjoining on the s w side the land lately purchased by the U S from B B Kirchivell, [boundaries given,] containing 40 acs more or less, which is hereby reserved to the U S for militarypurposes.

18-Act for the relief of the legal reps of Danl Brent, dec'd, late Consul of the U S at Paris: to be paid the sum of $4,084.20, deducting therefrom the sum which he may have received during the same period as the consul of the U S, in full discharge of all demands for the diplomatic services of the said Danl Brent during the suspension of the regular diplomatic intercourse between the Gov't of France & the Gov't of the U S, in 1835 & 1836.

By order of distress from John H King, trustee for Jas Williams' heirs, I shall offer at public sale on Mar 28, on the premises, now occupied by Alfred Taylor, on 5th st, between H & I sts, all the household & kitchen furniture of the said A Taylor, to satisfy house rent. –Lambert S Beck

The residence of John Hill Carter, in Pr Wm Co, Va, was, we regret to say, entirely destroyed by fire on Sat last. None of the furniture in the house was saved.

Died: on Mar 23, in Wash City, after a protracted illness, Mary Eliz Deeble, in her 19th year. She was a member of the Fourth Presby Church, Rev Mr Smith's. Her funeral will take place on Sabbath, Mar 26, at 2½ p m. from the house of her father, Mr Edw Deeble, on 9th st, between H & I sts.

Died: on Mar 15, at the residence of her son-in-law, Mr Saml B Sands, in Clark Co, Ohio, after a long & painful illness, Mrs Rachel Phillips, aged 67. She was a resident of Wash City for a long period, but for the last 12 years had been living in Ohio.

Died: on Mar 23, after a long & painfull illness, Mr Randolph Low, aged 44 years. His funeral will be in St Peter's Chr, on Mar 26, at half past 2 o'clock.

Died: on Mar 21, Mrs Ann Eliza Empie, consort of the Rev Adam Empie, Rector of St James' Church in Richmond.

Geo Robertson, Chief Justice of the Supreme Court of Ky, has resigned the ofc which he has held so long with such benefit to the State & credit to himself. He was elected to this post in 1830. He returns to the practice of the law.

Lt Gilliss, U S Navy, has returned by the steamer **Columbia** from his mission to visit the observatories of Europe. He has purchased for the depot of Charts & Instruments at Wash a complete set of astronomical instruments, which will not be surpassed by those of any observatory extant, except the Imperial Russian Observatory at Pulkova. --U S Gas

MON MAR 27, 1843
Jas Houston, a native of Saco, Maine, was killed on the Eastern Railroad, 2 miles from the Kennebunk depot, on Sun last. A man named Livingston was at the same time severely wounded. They had been engaged in clearing snow from the track, & foolishly attempted to get on the train while in motion, although repeatedly cautioned against it.

The Grand Jury of Gloucester Co, N J, have found a true bill against young Mercer for the murder of Heberton. Trial is to commence tomorrow.

St Patrick's Day celebration in Wash City. Mr John Boyle presided, assisted by Edw Stubbs. Among the invited guests who were present were Mr Geo P Custis, Mr Seaton, Mayor of the city, & Mr Robt Tyler, & Mr Hoban. [Mar 29 newspaper: Mr B B French, says he is a native of the "Granite State-N H," & this was the nearest he could come to the honor of being Irish. He speaks of his being totally unprepared to speak.]
Volunteers toassistants by:

Jas Maher	Owen Connolly	John Griffin
Thos Jordan	John McLeod	John Foote
Ambrose Lynch	Geo Savage	Wm Hill
Wm Dowling	Patrick Sullivan	John O'Connor
Gregory Ennis	P Finegan	Terence Lubin
Edw Stubbs	John Ously	Geo Hill
Jas Lawrenson	John McDermott	T Jordan
W P Faherty	Thos Moore	T Jordan, jr
Martin Reneham	E McCubbin	Thos Gordon
John Fleming	John J Byrne	J T Towers
Jas Maguire	R P Dowden	John Boyle
Barney Kelly	Michl O'Brien	T Donoho
Michl McDermott	John Foy	Thos Kernan
John Skirving	Jas Fitzgerald	Philip Enni
Jeremiah Sullivan	A R Locke	Chas P McCarty
Edw Maher	J Caton	Jas Handley
Michl Dooley	P H Caton	

A lad, between 14 & 15 years of age, by name Jas Dawson Cox, familiary called by his associates "Fat Cox," disappeared from the residence of his mother, on C st, in Wash City, Tue last. He is easily indentifie by a lisp & want of the forefinger of the left hand. Any information of his whereabouts tending to relieve the anxiety of his family will be thankfully received. [Alex Gaz]

John J Audubon, the distinguished Naturalist, arrived in Cincinnati on Sat week, & left shortly after for the Rocky Mountains, to procure materials for his great work on American Quadrupeds.

On Fri last Mr John Perry, of Charlestown, Va, committed suicide by shooting himself with a rifle. He was an industrious hard working mechanic, & an honest man in all his dealings; but had been much depressed in spirits for a day or two previous to the commission of the fatal act. –Virginia Advocate

Circuit Court of Wash Co, D C. John T Bishop, a bankrupt, has filed his pen for his discharge & certificate: hearing on the first Mon in June next. Same for John Starret. –Wm Brent, clk

Bailiff's sale: on Apr 1, on the sq opposite the Centre Market, Wash City: goods & chattels, namely: a couch body, 2 feed boxes, 2 thorough braces, a lot of old iron, a stove, a barrel, a hogshead, a lot of old lumber, a single harness, a lot of old harness, 2 buckets, seized & taken by distress, as the property of Fred'k Golding, sen, to satisfy Jas Woodruff, for rent due to the said Jane Woodruff on Mar 1. The above goods will be sold to the highest bidder for cash. –Hezekiah S Woodruff, bailiff

A man named Vermillion was brought before Justice Goddard last Sat, under the charge of kidnapping a negro belonging to Mr Robt Jackson, of Fairfax Co, Va, & was hired to a Mr Thos Heaton, residing in the upper part of Loudoun Co, Va. The magistrate considered it his duty to require Vermillion to give bail, in default of which he was committed.

Laws of the U S passed at the 3rd Session of the 27th Congress:
1-Act for the relief of Robt Ramsay: name to be placed on the roll of navy pensioners, & to be paid a pension at the rate of $5 per month; to commence & be computed from Dec 30, 1837.
2-Act for the relief of Geo C Johnston: to pay to him the amount due & to become due to the Shawnee Indians, under the act of Congress, approved Jul 14, 1832, on account of a debt due from said Indians to said Johnston, & which the said Indians have ordered to be paid out of the annuity granted by said act; provided the sum paid pursuant to this act shall not exceed the sum due to Johnston by said Indians, exclusive of interest, to wit, $18,510.
3-Act for the relief of John Davlin: that the act for his relief, approved on Mar 2, 1839, be revived in his favor, or his legal reps, & shall continue in force 12 months from & after the passage of this act.
4-Act for the relief of Danl Penhallow: to place his name on the roll of invalid pensioners, & cause to be paid to him at the rate of $4 per month, from & after Mar 4, 1842.

5-Act authorizing the Sec of the Treas to refund to David Watkinson & Co a part of the duties imposed on a certain quantity of tin & iron imported by them into the port of N Y: between Jul 18, 1831, & Nov 20, 1832, which had been shipped by the same to importers in the city of Hartford, in their original packages, where importers reside, & where it was intended to use the said goods, the sum of $906.50: Provided, that due proof be given, to the satisfaction of the Sec of the Treas, of the compliance, in good faith, on the part of the importers, with all the requisites of the law, as they would have applied if the goods had been placed under the custody of the proper ofcr of the customs at N Y.

6-Act for the relief of Robt Layton's children: to pay to his widow, if any widow there be, or, if no widow, to Richd Layton, Eliz Gordon, John Layton & Chas Layton, the surviving children of Capt Robt Layton, dec'd, late a pensioner of the U S, the sum of $1,124, it being the amount of pension, improperly suspended, which fell due to said Capt Robt Layton between Mar 4, 1835, and Mar 8, 1838, the day of the said Capt Robt Layton's death.

7-Act for the relief of Mary McGee & Susan Pierce, heirs at law of Geo Neilson, dec'd, a sldr of the late war, are hereby authorized to enter, free of cost, one qrtr section of 160 acs of any public lands subject to sale at private entry, & that a patent issue to them for the same; which qrtr section shall be taken for & in full consideration of the land bounty to which the said Geo Neilson would be entitled to if living.

8-Act for the relief of the legal reps of Robt A Kelly: the Sec of Treas is authorized to cause the claim for the services of the said Kelly as register of the land ofc at Opelousas, La, in making a report to the Sec of the Treas, in 1840, in obedience to an order of the com'r of the Genr'l Land Ofc, & in conformity to "An act for the final adjustment of claims to lands in the State of Louisiana," approved Feb 6, 1835, & for money paid by the said Kelly for translating instruments of writing filed among the papers of claimants under said law, to be audited, settled, & paid out of any money in the Treas not otherwise appropriated: Provided, That the sum so paid to the reps of said Kelly shall not exceed $500 for his services, & $100 for money paid for translations.

8-Act for the relief of Hugh Riddle, of the State of N Y: Sec of War cause to be issued to Hugh Riddle, a warrant for 160 acs of military bounty land, according to the provisions of an act entitled "An act for completing the existing military establishment," passed Dec 24, 1811.

9-Act for the relief of Garret Vleit: Com'r of the Genr'l Land Ofc be directed to audit the account of Garret Vleit, for surveying done in laying out certain towns in the Territory of Wisconsin, mentioned in an act passed on Jul 2, 1836, & an act passed on Mar 3, 1837, in relation to surveying said towns; & that he allow said Vleit such portion of the price agreed on for the whole work, as the work performed by him, accepted, used, & approved by the proper dept, bears to the whole work, to complete said surveys, as fixed in the contract signed by R T Lytle, surveyor general, & the said Vleit, on Mar 16, 1837. Sec 2-And be it further enacted, that said Com'r, in settling said account, deduct the amount already paid to said Vleit.

10-Act for the relief of Geo Waddle, of Ky, to be placed on the roll of invalid pensioners, & pay him $4 per month, to commence on Mar 4, 1840.
11-Act for the relief of Lyman N Cook, of N Y, to be placed on the roll of invalid pensioners, & to pay him at the rate of $11.25 per month during his natural life, commencing on Jul 1, 1840.
12-Act for the relief of Boyd Reilly: Sec of War & Sec of the Navy be, & they are instructed to receive from Boyd Reilly his patent right for the use of the different forms of apparatus invented by him, for the application of gas or vapor of any description to the human system, which are at present in use, or may at any time hereafter be introduced into the hospitals of the army, the navy, & the penitentiary of the U S, & on board of the national shipping; & also to settle the amount of compensation due to him on principles of equity; the sum awarded to be charged in equal proportions to the contingent expenses of the army & navy, or to hospital expenditures of such service: Provided, the same shall not exceed the sum of $5,000.
13-Act for the relief of Allen Rogers, of Maine: Sec of the Treas to pay to Rogers, or to his assigns, owner of the brig **L'Orient** the sum of $282.05, in full for provisions furnished certain invalid seamen returning from Rio Janeiro in said brig, & that said sum be paid out of any money in the Treas not otherwise appropriated.
14-Act for the relief of Saml M Asberry: to be allowed a pension by an act approved on Jun 28, 1836, & the same is hereby, increased to the sum of $6.40 per month, in lieu of the sum heretofore allowed; & that he be paid at the rate of $6.40 per month from Jan 31, 1837, deducting therefrom $4 per month, that being the sum he has heretofore received.
15-Act for the relief of Jeremiah Kimball, of Watertown, N Y, to have his name restored to the roll of invalid pensioners, & to pay him, during his natural life, a pension of $5.33 1/3 per month, commencing on Aug 2, 1839.
16-Act for the relief of Nancy Polerecsky: name to be placed on the roll of pensioners, under the act of Jun 7, 1838, & allow & pay her a pension at the rate of $20 per month for the term of 5 years, agreeably to the terms of said act of Jul 7, 1838.
8-Act for the relief of Jas B Sullivan, of Rapides Co, La: he is hereby authorized & permitted to complete his purchase of lot 16, [or part of it, containing 143 acs & a 60th part of an acre,] being lot 16, in township #5 north of the 31st degree of north latitude, of range #3 west of the basis meridian, in the s w district of La, in the parish of Rapides, La, & containing according to the register's certificate, 153 acs & the 60th part of an acre, in virtue of his right of pre-emption, according to the act of Congress of Jun 19, 1834, any law to the contrary notwithstanding; which said land is hereby declared to be no part of section 16, reserved for the use of schools in the congressional township in which the same is situated.
17-Act for the relief of Mary W Thompson, wid/o the late Lt Col Thompson, of the U S Army: that the sum of $750 be paid to Mrs Mary W Thompson, in further & final satisfaction of all claims for agencies & services rendered by the said Colonel Thompson, out of the line of his military duties: Provided, That nothing herein

contained shall interfere with the acts heretofore passed for the relief of the said Mrs Thompson.
18-Act for the relief of John McGinnis, a sldr in the late war: to be issued a land warrant for military bounty land for his services during the late war.
19-Act for the relief of Ruth Mathiot, wid/o Geo Mathiot, a sldr of the Revolution: to place her name on the pension roll, & to pay her the sum of $71 per annum, from Apr 4, 1840, during her natural life.
20-Act for the relief of Robt B Lewis: to refund & pay to him the sum of $15, being the amount of money paid by him into the Treas of the U S, as fees, on the surrender by him of a patent, granted Jun 26, 1836, for the purpose of correction & reissue; his application for a reissue having been denied at the Patent Ofc, & he thereby having been deprived of the benfit of his said patent for the residue of the term remaining unexpired.
21-Act granting a pension to David Welch, an Oneida Indian, of Madison Co, N Y, to be placed on the invalid roll of the Albany agency of N Y, & that he be allowed, during his natural life, a pension of $6 per month, commencing on Jan 1, 1840.
22-Joint resolution explanatory of "An act for the relief of Thos King." That it shall be the duty of the Sec of War, instead of the Com'r of Pensions, to carry into execution the act of the present session of Congress entitled "An act for the relief of Thos King," approved Feb 24, 1843.
23-Joint resolution to authorize the Postmaster Genr'l to settle with J & P Voorhies, contractors for carrying the mail on route 2,246, between Dayton, Ohio, & Indianapolis, Indiana, from Mar 7, 1841, to Feb, 1843, one trip a week, if in his opinion, under the circumstances of the case, in justice & equity they are entitled to such allowance.

TUE MAR 28, 1843
The Albany Argus announces the appointment of Jas D Wasson to be Postmaster for the city of Albany, in place of Gen Solomon Van Rensselaer.

Hse/o Reps: 1-Resolved, that the letter of the Sec of the Treas, in relation to the removal of Jonathan Roberts from the ofc of Collector of the port of Phil, be referred to a Select Cmte. To the cmte was also referred a letter of the Sec of the Treas in relation to the removal of Calvin Blythe as collector of the port of Phil. Resolved, that the cmte be discharged from the further consideration of the subjects referred to them.

The Balt Annual Conference of the Meth Episc Chr has been in session since Mar 15 & adjourned finally on Sat last. The following are the appointments by the Conf for the Potomac District:

T B Sargent, Pres Elder	L F Morgan , Gtwn
A Griffith, Alexandria	S A Roezel, Gtwn
J Lannahan, Alexandria	F Macartney, Leesburg
W B Edwards, Wesley Chapel	Jas Watts, Fairbax

B F Brooke, Fairfax
E P Phelps, Loudoun
S Kepler, Loudoun
C E Brown, Warrenton
J White, Stafford
D Ball, Stafford
W Evans, Fredericksburg
R T Nixon, Westmoreland
[& one to be supplied,] Westmoreland
T Wheeler, Lancaster
G W Israel, Lancaster
P Doll, Rock Creek
W H Coffin, Bladensburg
G D Cummings, Bladensburg

John Davis, [Wesley Rohr, to labor among the colored people,] & J Hanson, [sup] Foundry

The subscriber wishes to get a Country Mill on rent or shares. He has no other family than a wife. Good references can be given. Please address me, through the post ofc at Owingsville, Howard District, Anne Arundel Co, Md. –Thos Jones

Mrd: on Mar 14, at Lancaster City, Pa, by Rev John McNair, Mr Jas A Sterrit, of Springfield, Ohio, to Miss Eliz S Bryan, d/o the late Geo Bryan, of said city.

Died: on Mar 20, at Exeter, near Leesburg, Loudoun Co, Va, after a short illness, Wilson Cary Selden, in his 45th year; a gentleman highly esteemed & respected by all who knew him.

Died: on Feb 17 last, in Smyth Co, Va, about 30 miles from Abingdon, Mr Richd Roberts, formerly of or near Alexandria, D C.

Littleton Hunt, an old sldr of the Revolution, who served 5 years, & who was in the battles of Guilford & Eutaw Springs, was drowned on the night of Mar 12. He lived in Gwinnett Co, Ga, & was found dead in the Apalache river. It was supposed the horse on which he rode got into deep water & occasioned the accident. Mr Hunt was about 107 years old.

On Mar 15, Mr Hiram Hastings, aged about 20, was found buried beneath the snow, about 2 miles from Windsor, Vt, near the foot of the Ascutney mountain. On the preceding evening he went to the house of a sick neighbor, to see whether any thing was necessary for their comfort; &, in returning home, not by a path that had been at all used, it seems that the mass of snow on the brow of the hill was started by him from its place, & carried him several rods down, overwhelming him to the depth of several feet, whereby he perished.

The town of Wakefield, N H, has elected to the Legislature John Burns, an old Revolutionary sldr, who fought at Bunker Hill, & who also served during the last war. He will be 88 years old next August.

Capt Ellicott, of the British frig **Spartan**, which ship visited Boston last summer, was recently tried by court martial on board the ship **Imaun 74**, in Port Royal

Harbor, West Indies. He was charged with causing Midshipman Delacy M Gieig to be flogged by the boatswain of the ship. The charge was fully proved; but it being also proved that the conduct of the Midshipman afforded very gross provocation, the Capt was merely sentenced to be reprimanded. Com Byng presided at the court martial.

WED MAR 29, 1843
Appointments by the Pres: John G Deshler, to be Atty of the U S for the Terr of Iowa. Isaac Leffler, to be Marshal of the U S for said Territory.

Crmnl Crt-Wash: Mon last. Admitted as Attys to practice in this court: Chas S Wallace, Chas F Frary, & John D Turner.

Reply of John T McLaughlin, Lt U S Navy, late Cmder of the U S squadron on the coast of Florida, in a communication addressed to the Hse/o Reps: on Feb 28, 1843, by Wm P C Barton. /Barton was tried on Feb 11, 1818, for falsehood in his intercourse with the Navy Dept, by which he procured the removal of Surgeon Thos Harris from the Naval Hospital at Phil, & himself to be ordered there in his place. Barton stands convicted before 2 courts of his peers. /A long service of peril & hardship, worked out in canoes in the swamps of Florida, brought me into more intimate communion with the ofcrs of that squad than usually falls to the lot of a commander, & with honest pride I can say never was commander more ably sustained, nor had the honor of commanding more true & noble spirits; every one of whom would have spurned the crime imputed to the whole by Wm P C Barton, with a loathing & disgust as deep as they will all entertain for the iniquitous suspicions of which they have been made the subjects. –John T McLaughlin, Wash, Mar 23, 1843. [Coverage was 2½ columns. McLaughlin was accused of improperly, carelessly, or wantonly expending the medical supplies, etc. Barton induced the Hse/o Reps to believe that a gross fraud upon the Gov't had been detected.]

Charleston Mercury: announces the death of Dr Edw W North, who for a long time was Mayor of Charleston. He presided at the late Calhoun district meeting, apparently in his usual health on Tue, & died that night. He complained of indisposition on retiring to bed, was seized with a fit of coughing, called for assistance, & died of the rupture of a blood vessel in the throat.

Army & Navy Chronicle: Cmder W H Gardner & Cmder R B Cunningham have been relieved from serving as members of the naval general court-martial ordered to convene at Norfolk on Mar 25th, & Cmder W Jameson & Cmder C Lowndes have been detailed in their stead.

Salem [N J] Standard states that on Mar 16, Mr Clement A Hinchman, of Mannington township, while in a mill at Sharpstown, was caught by his apron in a part of the machinery, & so much injured as to die in about 10 minutes after his release. He was a young man of excellent character, recently married.

Wash Corp: Mar 27, 1843. 1-Ptn of W E Paterson, praying remission of a fine: referred to the Cmte of Claims. 2-Ptn of Wm H Burdine, praying remission of a fine: referred to the Cmte of Claims. 3-Cmte of Claims: asked to be discharged from the further consideration of the ptn of Jos Milburn, praying remission of a fine. 4-Cmte on Improvements: ptn of Wm Doughty & others, for the curb-stone to be set & footway paved on the north side of sq 402: passed. Same for the ptn of Danl Gold & others, for the same. 5-Cmte of Claims: adverse to the ptn of Danl Paullen: recommitted to the cmte.

Died: on Mon last, in Wash City, Mrs E M Janney, formerly of Alexandria. Her funeral is this morning at 9 a m.

Died: on Tue, Henrietta E Fitzhugh, d/o Saml Fitzhugh. Her funeral will be at the house of her father, corner of 6th & H sts, this afternoon at 3 p m.

The valuable merchant mill of Fielding Williams, 6 miles north of Clarksville, Tenn, was burned down on Mar 15. Loss was about $16,000, & no insurance.

Comr's sale of valuableland: decree of the County Crt of Fairfax, in the case of Jas W Coakely & wife, against Mary Allison, wid/o John Allison & others: sale on the premises on Apr 15, that valuable farm, recently owned by the said John Allison, containing about 158 acs. This land lies about 4 miles south of Alexandria-the road to Mount Vernon dividing the same. Improvements are a good dwlg, stables, good well of water in the yard, fine young orchard. This is one of the best farms in Fairfax. Possession given forthwith, & Mr Jones, now living on the premises will show the same. –Saml Catts, R I T Wisson, Geo Padgett, Jno R Dale, com'rs

Mathew McLeod announces to the inhavitants of Wash that, on Apr 3 next, he will open an academy in the Northern Liberties' engine house. References who examined the scholars Sat last: Jas Hagan, M D; Philip Smith, M D; J H Wheat; & H King, M D.

Vessels wanted: I want 2 good vessels to load for N Y, with despatch, flour & grain. –W S Compton, Water st, Gtwn

THU MAR 30, 1843
Whigs of Va: the following have been appointed by the Pres of the late Whig State Convention of Va to compose the Central Whig Cmte of Va:

R T Daniel	Dr A L Warner	Fleming James
Jas Lyons	Dr L W Chamberlayne	Jas W Dibrell
Jas W Pegram	Arch Pleasants	Robt H Jenkins

Peter W Grubbs	Jas M Wickham	Henry Clarke
Saml F Adie	Dr Geo Watson	Jas Winston
Hugh W Fry	Dr Micajah Clarke	Robt C Stanard
H L Brooke	John Wight	Alex'r Moseley

The report of the shooting of 5 seamen on board the U S ship **John Adams** cannot be true. Another report also in circulation of Capt Voorhees, of the Navy, having shot Lt Boyle is certainly false.

Furnished house for rent: the subscriber being under the necessity of declining housekeeping: located near the corner of 6th & F sts, & at a low rent. –Benj Beall, at the store of Middleton & Beall, Pa ave.

Died: on Mar 21, at his residence, in Hanover Co, Va, after a lingering illness of several months, Capt John Woodson, aged 81 years; leaving many children & relations, & numerous friends to lament their loss, though his gain.

Trenton State Gaz: the Old True American Inn, kept by Henry Katzenback, on Mill Hill, in Trenton, was burned on Tue. Two of the boarders, Germans, were burned to death, as was also an 8 year old d/o Mr Katzenback. One of the boarders who died was Anthony Heiden, who was employed in a porttery near the Eagle tavern. The tavern was very old: is known in the history of the country as the head-qrtrs of Gen Washington on Jan 2, 1777, being the place where the council of war was held which decided the march upon Princeton.

Jas Fitzgerald, a young Irishman, was killed yesterday by the train to Nashua passing over him near the covered bridge over Pawtucket Canal, about a mile from Lowell [Mass] depot. The dec'd was deaf & dumb & did not hear the train. He was carried home to his father's house, where he died in half an hour. –Lowell Cour

FRI MAR 31, 1843
Chas Willmer's American Newsletter & European Intelligencer was established in Jul, 1842, & published at Liverpool. Orders to the publisher, Chas Willmer, Transatlantic Newspaper Ofc, 6 South John st, Liverpool.

Supreme Court of the U S, Jan Term, 1843. Arthur Bronson, cmplnt, vs John H Kinzie & Juliette his wife, Edmund K Bossing & John S Bossing, the Pres, Dirs, & Company of the State Bank of Ill, Jay Hathway, Mary Ann Wolcott, Danl S Griswold, Caroline Dunham, & Alonzo Huntington. Case: on Jul 13, 1838, John H Kinzie executed a bond to Arthur Bronson conditioned for the payment of $4,000 on Jul 1, 1842, with interest, to be paid semi-annually; & to secure the payment of the money & interest, Kinzie & wife on the same day conveyed to Bronson in fee simple, by way of a mortgage, one undivided half part of certain houses & lots in the town of Chicago, with the usual proviso that the deed should be null & void if the principal & interest were only paid; & Kinzie, among other things, covenanted that if default should be made in these payments, that it should be lawful for Bronson or his reps to enter upon & sell the mortgaged premises at public auction, & as atty of Kinzie & wife, to convey the same to the purchaser, & out of the moneys arising from such sale to retain the amount that might then be due him on the aforesaid bond, with the costs & charges of sale, rendering the overplus, if any, to Kinzie. The interest not having been paid, Bronson, on Mar 27, 1841, filed his bill to foreclose the mortgage. The questions presented by the Circuit Court we therefore answer: 1st- That the decree should direct the premises to be sold at public auction without regard to the law of Feb 19, 1841. 2nd-The decree should direct the sale of the mortgaged premises without being first valued by 3 householders. We shall direct these answers to be certified to the Circuit Court. Test: Wm Thos Carroll, Clk Supreme Crt U S

The barque **Margaret Hugg**, from Rio de Janeiro, arrived in Hampton Roads on Tue last, having on board 182 ofcrs & men, of the crew of the late sloop of war **Concord**, they having arrived at Rio on Feb 4, a portion in the U S ship **John Adams**, & the remainder in the Portuguese brig. List of the ofcrs:

Z Holland, Lt	G A De Russey, Acting Purser
John C Spencer, Surgeon	N T H Moore, Assist Surgeon
C J Van Alstine, Acting Master	H A Clemson, Passed Midshipman

Midshipmen-6:

W H Jameson	J Myers	J E Hart
B A Marr	J J Pringle	
Chas Fales, Acting Gunner		E Kemp, Acting Boatswain
J Whitney, Acting Sailmaker		L Smith, Acting Carpenter

Mrd: on Mar 28, by Rev J Raub, Mr Geo T Langley to Miss Mary Ann Edwards, all of Wash City.

Henry Clay, associated with his son, J B Clay, is again a practitioner at the bar of the courts in Ky.

Silks & French Chintzes for sale: Wm M Perry, west of 7th st, opposite Centre Mkt.

Bishop, who murdered his wife at Chesterfield last fall, was executed at Elizabethtown, Vt, agreeably to sentence, on Fri. He made a full confession upon the gallows, & assigned as the reason for his desperate deed that 3 of his neighbors were in the habit of visiting his wife in his absence. The rope having swollen by the storm the knot did not render, & the poor wretch suffered a world of agony- struggling with convulsive effort for more than 5 minutes. Our informant says "Sleeping or waking, I am haunted with it, & would give all I possess could I shake off the horrid recollection." -Burlington [Vt] Free Press.

Beef! Beef! Beef! Better yet than ever: grazed & fed by Mr Robt L Wright, of Loudoun Co, Va. For sale on Sat in his stalls, in the new Centre Market house of Washington. –Henry Weaver

Died: on Mar 24, at Honeywood, Berkeley Co, Va, Mrs Eliz Colston, relict of Rawleigh Colston, in her 85th year. This lady was the eldest sister of the late Chief Justice Marshall, whom she strongly resembled in many respects.

Died: on Mar 26, in Wash City, after a short illness, Mr Fred'k Golding, sen, aged about 55 years. He has left a disconsolate family of children to mourn his loss. He was a kind & affectionate father & a benevolent neighbor.

Died: on the 27th ult, Mr Chas Higdon, of Westmoreland Co, Va, in his 85th year, a sldr of the Revolution.

Died: Mar 21, at Rappahannock Academy, the Rev Chas C Taliaferro, aged 36 years.

Died: on Mar 15, at his residence in Culpeper, after a lingering & painful illness, Peter Hansbrough, of Coles Hill, in his 74th year.

Wash Library Co meeting at the Library Rooms 11th st, Apr 3. Judges of Election: Messrs S W Denham, Robt Farnham, & John Sessford, jr. –Jas F Haliday, sec

SAT APR 1, 1843
The Natchez Courier of Mar 14 says: "Judge Bosworth, Parish Judge of Carroll Parish, La, was yesterday shot by a young man on the plantation of Mr Behler, about 30 miles above this city, on the river. The Judge was shot in the right arm with a double-barrelled shot-gun so badly that amputation was deemed necessary, & was performed. The cause of the difficulty we have not learned."

On Tue a physician, Jas G Thorn, residing at 420 Peal st, N Y, suddenly lost his senses & became a raving manian: tearing the clothes from his body, rushed into the street nearly naked. He was brought to the prison & locked up. –N Y Courier

Army & Navy Chronicle of Mar 30. 1-The Sec of the Navy has appointed Capt Lawrence Rousseau, Cmder Henry A Adams, & Lt Stephen Johnston to make an examination & survey of the harbor of Memphis, Tenn, for ascertaining the practibility of establishing at that place a naval depot & yard for bldg & repairing steamships & other vessels of war. These ofcrs will meet at Memphis on Apr 20. 2-On May 1 next the following changes, by transfer, in the stations of these ofcrs, will be made: S M Pook from Portsmouth, N H, to Boston; Josiah Barker from Boston to Portsmouth, N H; Foster Rhodes from N Y to Norfolk; Francis Grice from Norfolk to N Y.

Mary Richey, about 17 years of age, employed in the family of Mr Wm Gormley, in Alleghany City, Pa, was burned to death on Sat last. She fell asleep & her clothes took fire from a candle. She died in about 2 hours.

Mrd: last evening, in Wash City, at Gadsby's Hotel, by Rev Mr Stringfellow, Dr R E Robinson to Miss Virginia E, y/d/o J E Stainback, all of Petersburg, Va.

Died: on Mar 31, in Wash City, Miss Geraldine R Orme, d/o Rezin Orme, in her 17th year. Her funeral is at Mr G H W Randall's, on Sunday morning, at 9½ o'clock.

Norfolk Herald contains particulars of a lamentable tragedy which occurred there on Wed last, which resulted in the death of Mr Melzar Gardner, Editor of the Portsmouth "Chronicle & Old Dominion," in a rencontre with Mordecai Cooke, jr, of Norfolk. Mr Gardner drew a pistol from his pocket & a scuffle took place with Gardner taking the charge in the pistol through his body. The ball had struck the heart, & in less than 15 minutes life was extinct. Mr Gardner was a native of Mass, & has left a wife & 2 children. It was a family quarrel, politically speaking; but its fatal termination is sincerely to be deplored.

MON APR 3, 1843

Street smoking in Boston is severely punished. On Sat week some constable caught Geo Penniman with a cigar in his mouth, & as Geo had been twice warned to desist, the official determined a fine should be the consequence. He was fine $2 & costs for each offence, amounting to about $10.

Susanna Shaw, a native of Ireland, aged about 30 years, who had been unwell for several years, on Sat went to the Medical Institute in Broadway, where Dr Revere prescribed to her pills of strychnine, ordering 16 pills, of which 8 pills taken at once are sufficient to cause death. Dr Frey, the apothecary, put them up, & Dr Wainwright carried them to her himself, giving both oral & written directions for her to take only one each night. Finding no relief, she took 10 pills. Her mother became alarmed, but the woman died before 3 o'clock.

New Orleans Bee of Mar 24: The Hon Geo A Waggaman expired yesterday, following a duel. For the last 3 days it was quite certain he was dying, as mortification had begun its work of death. The femoral artery had been completely severed. The dec'd was made aware of his approaching dissolution several days ago. He breathed his last surrounded by his wife, children, & a number of friends. His funeral will take place today from the Senate Chamber at the State House.

The Hon Saml McRoberts, Senator of the U S from Ill, died in Cincinnati on the 27th ult, aged about 40 years, after a short illness, resulting from a cold taken in crossing the mountains on his way home from the session of Congress which has recently closed.

Rear Admr Vansittart, of the British Navy, died a few days since at his seat of Eastwood, near Woodstock, U C. He was in his 65th year.

Appointments by the Pres: 1-Murphy V Jones, Collector of the Customs at Wilmington, N C, vice Wm C Lord. 2-Abelard Guthrie, Register of the Land Ofc at Lima, Ohio, vice Jas Watson Riley. 3-Chas Murray, Purser in the U S Navy, vice Thos Gadsden, resigned.

Died: yesterday, after a tedious illness, Mr Michl Coleman, in his 47th year. His funeral will be from his late residence, near St Peter's Church, Capitol Hill, at 4 p m today.

The Courier & Enquirer mention the death of Hoxie Barter, late of N Y, a qrtr-gunner on board the U S brig **Boxer**. He was lost overboard during a tremendous gale from the north, on the night of the 27th or 28th ult. He was a most valuable seaman, & his loss deeply deplored by all on board.

Sec of State for the Commonwealth of Pa give notice there are now remaining in his ofc, uncalled for, 6 silver medals, which were voted by the Leg of Pa at its session of 1813-14 to those citizens of Pa who nobly & gallantly volunteered on board the American squadron on Lake Erie, in 1813, in compliment of their patriotism & bravery in that naval action. These medals bear the names of & belong to John Cook, Josiah Goodrich, Isaac B Seal, Jacob Levenselter, Lyman Griswelt, & Jos Woods, & those interested are invited to make application for them at the Sec's ofc.

P W Browning, Merchant Tailor, Pa ave, between 3rd & 4th sts, Wash. [Local Ad]

The old jail is being converted into a hospital for indigent lunatics. Work is under the direction of Mr David A Gardner. The Pres has been pleased to appoint Drs Miller, Lindsly, & Thomas, physicians.

Total Abstinence Society of the Executive Depts: meeting on Thu last: addresses delivered by Hon Walter Forward, Rev Mr Rich, Dr Sewall, & Jas Bradford, of Ohio. Ofcrs elected for the ensuing year are:
Pres-Hon John Williamson
V Pres-Hon Henry L Ellsworth, Presley Simpson
Corr Sec-Francis C Goode
Rec Sec-Sylvanus Holmes
Exec Cmte: Maj J W Barker, Chas A Davis, John J Law, John F Sharretts, Jos Manahan, Josiah F Polk, A W Zevely. The following were appointed delegates to attend the Grand Temperance Convention, to be held in Balt on Apr 5, viz: Hon Walter Forward, H L Ellsworth, John Williamson, Presley Simpson, J B Rooker,

Chas B Davis, Geo M Phillips, F C Goode, John F Sharrets, Wm Anderson, Josiah Dent, B F Pleasants, & T B Hampton.

Copartnership has been formed under the firm of Murray, Randolph, & Semmes, in the wholesale & retail Grocery business in the new brick warehouse south side of Pa ave, near the corner of 4½ st. -John R Murray, Wm M Randolph, John H Semmes

Application will be made at the Mayor's ofc for the renewal of a certificate of Corp 6%, stock #192, dated Nov 21, 1837, for $1,000, issued in favor of R L Page, the original having been lost or mislaid. –R L Page, per W B Page, atty

Robberies last Sat in Wash City: the grocery store of Mr John A Donohoo, at the corner of D & 7th st; the other at the grocery store of Mr B H Reed, at the corner of F & 13th sts.

TUE APR 4, 1843
Peach Trees for sale: 20,000 prime inoculated trees for sale at my nursery, Haddonfield, N J, at the very reduced price of 5 cents each. These trees are from 5 to 6 feet in height, & of good thickness; are from 2 years old from stone, & 1 year's growth on inoculation; 20 varieties. Refer to Capt Wm A Weaver, of Wash. –David Roe

Jas Edgar Crown, Atty & Counsellor at Law, #14 Fayette st, Balt, Md. He refers to: Jos H Bradley & Jas Hoban, Wash. John Glenn & R J Brent, Balt, Md.

For rent, the brick house lately occupied by Mr M Delany, nearly opposite the City Hall. Apply at his store, corner of 4½ st & Pa ave, or at Mrs Smoot's, F st, between 13th & 14th sts.

Trustees sale: decree of St Mary's Co Crt, acting as a Crt of equity, in a case in which John J Allstan, assignee of Thos W Gardiner, & Robt H Gardiner are cmplnts, & Richd H Miles, administrator of C L Gardiner, & others are dfndnts, the trustee will sell on May 9 next, all that tract or parcel of land called *Brambly*, containing about 450 acs, being the real estate of which Dr Chas L Gardiner died seised & possessed. This land lies on the Wicomico river, about 6 miles below Chaptico, & has a good dwlg house & all necessary out-houses thereon, & all are in good repair. –Richd H Miles, trustee

Frankfort "Commonwealth" of Mar 28:
The Hon W W Southgate is announced as a candidate for Congress. The Hon L W Andrews; the Hon John White; & the Hon Jas C Sprigg; are candidates for re-election to Congress. The Hon P Triplett declines being a candidate for re-election to Congress. The Hon W O Butler has been nominated by a meeting of Locos at Louisville as a candidate for re-election to Congress. Geo W Barber is a candidate

for Congress in the first [Boyd's] district. W R Vance, of Jefferson, has been nominated for Congress by a meeting of Whigs in Carroll. The Hon Thos F Marshall, in a speech at Lexington on last Wed, declined being a candidate for re-election to Congress.

Trustee's sale of improved property in Wash City: deed of trust dated Feb 11, 1841, & of record in the Land Records for Wash Co, D C, in liber W B, #82, folios 501 to 505, from Mary J McCarty to me as trustee, all that piece or parcel of ground lot #10 in sq 290, fronting 17 feet on 12th st west, with an excellent 2 story brick house thereon, & opposite King's Gallery. It will be sold subject to the dower right of the widow of the late ____ Gardiner. –Edw Dyer, trustee -R W Dyer & Co, aucts

Furniture at auction on Apr 10, at the residence of Mr Beesely, south side of La ave, near 6th st, a very handsome assortment of furniture, as he is removing to the country. –Wm Marshall, auct

Boarding: Mrs E O Robinson, corner of B & 1st sts, Capitol Hill, can accommodate 2 or 3 gentlemen & their wives. She has no family to incommode in any way those who may be pleased to reside with her.

At Norfolk, on Fri, Mr Mordecai Cooke, jr, was examined before Alderman Leigh, in relation to the death of Mr M Gardner, late editor of the Portsmouth Dominion, &, after a laborious investigation, was discharged.

On Sat week, Conzaque Duplesses, aged 22 years, from Canada, was in the employ of John Hill & Co, Stoneham, Mass. He came in contact with a hay hook, which entered his abdomen. Medical aid was instantly called, but after lingering 36 hours, the unfortunate man expired.

For rent: 2 story frame dwlg house on I st, first east of 7th, containing, with back bldg & attic story, 8 rooms, with a good garden lot adjoining: rent $132 per year. Apply to J Fugitt & Co, Centre Mkt Sq.

Ranaway on Dec 27, 1842, Davy Thomas, aged about 22. As he went off without having received punishment, & was at the time on good terms with myself & overseer, the subscriber believes there is not the possibility of a doubt but that he was seduced away by some white man, either for the purpose of selling him or carrying him to a free-State. He is about 5 feet 4 inches, short & thick, bushy woolly hair, of black copper color. I will give $100 to any person bringing Davy home, or securing him in jail so that I get him again, & all reasonable charges. –Francis Neal, near Port Tobacco, Chas Co, Md.

Circuit Court of Wash Co, D C. John W Dexter, a bankrupt, has filed his ptn for his discharge & certificate: hearing on the first Mon in Jul next. –Wm Brent, clk

Dr Richd S Steuart, of Balt, has been elected Prof of the Theory & Practice of Medicine in the University of Maryland, in place of Prof Potter, dec'd.

Passed Assist Surgeon Richd W Leecock, of the U S brig **Somers**, committed suicide on Fri in the gun-room of his vessel lying at the Navy Yard, Brooklyn, by shooting himself through the head with a pistol. He has been attached to the **Somers** ever since she has been in commission, & enjoyed the highest respect & esteem of all with whom he was associated. He was 28 years of age & a native of Norfolk, Va. This occurrence which closed his life is attributed to a settled melancholy & partial derangement induced by a long & severe attack of the yellow fever, which he contracted on a former voyage to the coast of Africa in the U S schnr **Grampus**. -Tribune

New Orleans, Mar 25. Jos Tricotti, convicted of the crime of arson & burglary, suffered the penalty of the law when he was executed yesterday. Asked if he had anything to say, he answered, that on his soul he had never entered Mr Hollander's dwlg, or set fire to his house. His sufferings, when suspended, appeared to be brief. -Bee

WED APR 5, 1843
A N Girault intends to open a class early next week in the study of the French Language, either at his residence, Pa ave, 4th door above the War Dept, or at his school-room on 11th st, over the Wash Library.

Fatal affray took place in Augusta, Ga, on Mar 30, in which, says the Sentinel, Wm R Harding, clerk at the Arsenal, received a mortal wound from a pistol shot by Wm H Platt, in a street fight with pistols & a Bowie knife, the latter being the assailant.

Circuit Court of Wash Co, D C. Henry Miller, a bankrupt; & Jonathan Elliot, a bankrupt: have each filed a ptn for discharge & certificate: hearing on the first Mon in Jul next. --W Brent, clk

Wash Corp: 1-Mayor nominated John McGarr as additional police constable for the 5th Ward: same was considered & confirmed. 2-Cmte of Claims: bill for the relief of John Brady: passed. 3-Ptn from Wm P Elliot & others: referred to the Cmte on Improvements. 4-Ptn from John McDermott & others: referred to the Cmte on Improvements. 5-Resolved that W J Bronaugh have leave to withdraw his ptn & papers from the files of this Board. 6-Ptn of W A Guista, praying remission of a fine: referred to the Cmte of Claims. 7-Ptn of Wm H Gunnell & others, praying for the improvement of 4½ st: referred to the Cmte on Improvements. 8-Ptn of Wm Thomas, praying remission of a fine: referred to the Cmte of Claims. 9-Communication was received from Chas Murray, resigning his ofc of police magistrate of the 2nd Ward: read & adopted. 10-Cmte on Improvements: asking to be discharged from further consideration of the ptn of C A Wickliffe & others: taken up & agreed to. 11-Cmte of Claims: adverse on the ptn of Levi Stowell: taken up & agreed to. 12-Bill for the relief of Wm H Yates: read the 3rd time & passed. 13-Cmte of Claims: ptn of Eliz Purrell recommitted with instructions to report a bill for the relief of the petitioner. 14-Ptn of Ely Davis was taken up & agreed to

Local News: Wm Wilson, a young man, was arrected last Sun under the charge of breaking into the stores of Mr John A Donohoo & Mr W B Reed, of Wash City. The prisoner was committed for further examination.

THU APR 6, 1843
Appropriations made for the half calendar year ending Jun 30, 1843, & the fiscal year ending Jun 30, 1844, during the 3rd session of the 27th Congress of the U S A, commencing Dec 5, 1842, & ending Mar 3, 1848. 1-Payment to Jos Russ & Stephen J Roach, in full for labor bestowed & money expended in repairing or constructing a road leading from Pensacola to Tallahassee, Florida, under the act approved Feb 17, 1836: $2,000. 2-For taking down the 2 old furnaces in the crypt under the rotundo, & bldg 2 new ones, cutting out the necessary flues, according to a proposition of John Skirving, under date of Feb 1, 1843: $1,454. Similar work under the first story of the center of the Capitol, according to the proposition of John Skirving to the Chrman of the Cmte on Public Bldgs: $7.973. 3-Pay Jas Kelly for preparing & publishing charts, under supervision & direction of the Joint Cmte on the Library: $20,000. 4-For compensation of the Pres of the U S: $25,000. 5-For the payment of 3 drafts, drawn on the dept of Govn'r Doty, for goods, provisions, & presents, procured & delivered by him to the Sioux Indians, while holding the treaty with them in 1841, & which treaty was rejected by the Senate at its late session, for said half calendar year: $13,776.49. 6-For compensation to Saml C Davidson, for carrying mails of the Genr'l Land Ofc to & from the city post ofc, from May 19 to Sep 6, 1842: $45.61. 7-Annuities & grants to: Joshiah H Webb-$50; Rachel Dohrman-$300; Eliz C Perry-$400. 8-Payment to Isaac Babbitt, of Boston, in execution of a contract made with him by the Sec of the Navy for the purchase of Babbitt's "anti-attrition metal." Pursuant to the act of Congress of Aug 29, 1842: $20,000. 9-To satisfy contracts entered into in Aug, 1836, by Maj Gen Thos S Jesup, then commanding the army in Alabama, with the Creek tribe of Indians: $12,000. 10-
Private Claims:
Saml Hambleton: $970.84
Jas Lowe: $1,000.
Allen Rogers: $282.05
Wm G Sanders: $900.
Edwin Bartlett: $9,062.50
Peter Lionberger: $100.
Caspar W Wever: $1,500.
Richd Rush: $3,815.73
Jas M Morgan: $378.

David Watkinson & Co: $906.50
Joshua Drew: $240.
Peters, Moore & Co: $2,166.66
Snow Y Sears: $400.
Jas S Calhoun: $15,900
Johnson Patrick: $1,351.76
John Skirving: $600.
John Core: $80.
Thos D Gilson: $151.85

Geo Randall & others: $3,471.57
Chas Waldron: $1,179.61
John Randolph Clay: $3,750
Wm Fabre: $120.42
Geo A Winslow: $144.
Reps of Robt A Kelly: $600
Andrew Fisher: $79.
Gamaliel E Smith: $350
Wm W Street: $625.
John Hodgkin: $3,515.50
John Skirving: $3,287.25
Robt B Lewis: $15.
Richd Patten: $50.
Mary W Thompson: $750.

Owners of the fund received from the British Gov't as an indemnity for slaves lost from on board the ship **Comet** & the ship **Encomium** at Nassau: $7,965.28

Mrd: on Mar 23, at Christ Church, in Savannah, by Rev Edw Neufoille, Capt Ebenezer S Sibley, of the U S Army, to Maria Henrietta, y/d/o the late Judge Cuyler.

Died: on Apr 4, after a short but painful illness, Jas Forbes, eldest s/o Mr Robt Beale, in his 13th year. His funeral will be today at 12 o'clock.

The Eastern Mail brings news of the death, at his residence, in Lower Red Hook, Dutchess Co, N Y, on Apr 1, of Gen John Armstrong, in his 85th year. He was a sldr of the Revolution, Minister to France during the reign of Napoleon, & Sec of War during the period of the war of 1812, of which he wrote a history.

The steamboat **Union**, at the Long Bridge, will commence running again this day. My friends & customers may expect good accommodations. —G T Raub, Captain

FRI APR 7, 1843
The German National Gaz, a newpaper devoted to the Political, Social, & Literary interests of the day, will be published in Wash City, by Apr 20th, the first number of the weekly. —P A Sage & Co, Publishers, Wash, D C.

The Editor of the N Y Tribune speaks feelingly of his old friend & fellow-craftsman, Melzar Gardner, lately a resident of Hartford, Conn, who died in Norfolk. He was hardly more than 30 years old & has left a wife & 3 young children.

The venerable Bishop Roberts, of the Methodist Episc Church, died at his residence, near Lawrenceport, Indiana, on Mar 27th.

The U S ship of war **Vandalia**, Cmder McCluney, sailed from N Y on Sun for Norfolk.

Cattaraugue Republican reports the trial of Nathl A Lowry for forgery, at Warren, Pa. The jury came in with a verdict of not guilty, but that the dfndnt pay the costs.

The splendid bldg in Balt at the corner of Calvert & Balt sts, known as Cohen's banking house, has been purchased by Messrs Johnston & Lee for $18,000 cash.

There is a ground rent on the lot of $310 a year, which can be purchased out at 6%, making the whole property in fee stand $23,166 2/3. -Patriot

The Canton Register of Nov 15 mentions the death, at Kooloongsoo, of Mrs Boone, w/o an American missionary, & d/o Chancellor Desaussure, of S C. She died of the prevailing fever on Aug 30. Mr Boone & wife sailed for the East in 1836, & settled first at Batavia, whence they removed to Macao in 1840, & thence to Kooloongsoo after the cessation of hostilities.

A negro named Joseph, belonging to Mr Richd Wilder, of Chowan Co, N C, died on Sat week, aged 118 years. He was one of the witnesses of the Revolution, & was present at the burning of Norfolk. Jos' wife is yet living & is 116 years old. They had lived together 78 years.

John J Joyce has opened a Grocery Store at the corner of 13th & G sts, & has constantly on hand a superior assortment of every article in that line.

$50 reward for the recovery of the articles stolen from my house on Apr 4, by some thief or thieves who entered the house through the front window & took:
2 large soup Ladles, silver   1 silver Chalice
2 doz silver Table-spoons   1 silver Butter-knife
1 doz silver Dessert spoons   1 large silver-plated fruit basket.
2 doz German silver forks   -Edw Simmes

House for rent on 18th st, between south B & Va ave, near the residence of Maj Howie. Apply to the subscriber, at the carpenter's shop, corner of 12th & E sts. –John W Wise

To let or lease: commodious 2 story brick house on Pa ave & the corner of 2nd st east, only one square from the Capitol. –John S Devlin

Potatoes for sale at our Grocery Store, 7th st, between H & I sts. –Ailer & Thyson

Hardware: opposite Brown's Hotel: R M Waring & Co.

Patapsco Female Institute, is at Ellicott's Mills, near Balt, Md. Summer session commences May 10th & continues for 22 weeks. –Mrs Lincoln Phelps, Principal

Orphan's Court of Wash Co, D C. In the case of the exec of Richd Coxe, dec'd: Mar 25th has been selected for the settlement & distribution of the said estate.
–Ed N Roach, Reg/o wills

Orphan's Court of Wash Co, D C. Letters of adm on the personal estate of John Keith, late of said county, dec'd. -John Tretler, adm

Circuit Court of Wash Co, D C. Saml M Bootes, a bankrupt, has filed his ptn for his discharge & certificate: hearing on the first Mon in Jul next. –Wm Brent, clk

Jas Reddin has applied to the Hon Wm Cranch, Chief Judge of the Circuit Court of Wash Co, D C, to be discharged from imprisonment under the act for the relief of Insolvent Debtors within the Dist of Col: hearing on the 3rd Mon in Apr inst. –Wm Brent, clk

More burglaries: On last Tue the dwlg of Mr Edw Simms & Mr Geo Parker, both on C st, were robbed.

Wash Corp: 1-Act for the relief of Wm H Yates: the fine imposed for a violation of the act in relation to hackney carriages, is hereby remitted: provided the said Yates pay the costs of prosecution.

Died: Apr 5, Mrs Adela Wheeler, in her 35th year, after a painful & lingering illness. Her funeral is this Fri, at half past 3 o'clock, from the corner of G & 20th sts west.

SAT APR 8, 1843
The situation of Principal in the Upper Marlborough Academy is now vacant, & the trustees wish to employ a suitable person to take charge for one year from May 1 next. The salary is fixed at $700 per annum; & there is a house & garden attached to the Academy. –Jno B Brooke, Pres Trust U M A

Household furniture at auction: on Apr 11 in front of the Furniture Wareroom of Mr Thos M Haislip, Pa ave, between 11th & 12th sts. –Wm Marshall, auct

To the Public: I certify that Jas A Ratcliff, lately appointed constable by the Court of Wash Co, has given bond, which has been approved & has in other respects complied with the requisitions of the law in such cases. –Wm Brent, clk
+
The subscriber respectfully solicits the attention of his friends & the Public in general to the above appointment. He wishes to render himself popular in the capacity of an ofcr, all business entrusted to him will be attended to with promptness & punctuality, his mind being made up in all cases to fork over the money as soon as collected without delay. All persons having unsettled accounts, notes, or due bills can have the same settled with despatch by sending them for me to G L Giberson, Thos C Dunn, & John D Clark, Justices of the Peace, or to the stores of Middleton & Beall, Richd M Beall, John M Donn, & H Richey, Pa ave. –Jas A Ratcliff

On Sat, Mar 12, no less than 4 Revolutionary sldrs died in Alleghany township, Westmoreland Co, Pa: John Delap, aged 80; John Gallagher, aged 104; Robt Doods, aged 79; & John Johnson, aged 103.

Mr Wm R Harding, who was shot at Augusta, Ga, a few days since, in a street-fight with Wm H Platt, has since died of his wounds. Coroner's jury verdict: willful murder against Mr Platt, who was the assailant in the affray.

The Apalachicola papers announce the death of Hezekiah Hawley, U S Marshal of the Apalachicola district, & a highly respected & influential citizen of that place.

David Chandler, only 24 years of age, who has spent half his life in prison, has been sentenced to the State prison in N H for the 3rd time.

Serious affray in Marion, Ala, on Wed week, between Col Martin A Lea & N B Lockett, in which the former was so severely wounded by a pistol shot that he died on Sat morning. Col Lea formerly represented Perry Co in the Legislature, & subsequently was engaged in commercial pursuits in Mobile.

Marshal's sale: in virtue of 4 several writs of fieri facias issued from the Clk's ofc of the Circuit Court of Wash Co, D C: sale on May 5, the following real property, viz: lot 4 thru 8 in sq 287; lot 7 has a small 2 story brick tenement thereon; lot 8 has a shop & tan-vats. All are in Wash City, D C: seized on as the property of Geo Cover, & sold to satisfy judicials 90 thru 93 & 122, to Nov term 1842, in favor of the Union bank of Gtwn. -Alex'r Hunter, Marshall of D C

Circuit Court of Wash Co, D C. Wm W Street, a bankrupt, has filed his ptn for his discharge & certificate: hearing on the first Mon in Jul next. –Wm Brent, clk

The trial of Singleton Mercer for the murder of Hutchinson Heberton, which began at Woodbury, N J, on Tue, ended on Thu, when the jury returned a verdict of not guilty, & he was discharged from custody.

Monroe Edwards, the celebrated forger, jumped off the dock at Sing Sing on Wed, & has not been seen or heard of up to the time when a deputy-keeper was dispatched to N Y with the intelligence of his escape.

The late Gen John Armstrong: entered the army of the Revolution at age 18 years; was Aide-de-Camp to Gen Mercer, & with him at the battle of Princeton when his Gen fell. He continued in service throughout the war, & at its close was, with the rest of his unpaid companions, discharged. It is known to all familiar with our history that the discontents of the army, then lying at Newburg, at being turned adrift when their services were no longer needed, without any provision for the arrears due them, were both great & just. Armstrong deeply felt the wrong, & in the famous Newburg letters, anonymous indeed, but since known to be his, he endeavored to stir them up to the redress of their own grievances. Gen Armstrong was selected by Mr Jefferson as Minister to France & resided there during the 10 years of the brilliant career of Napoleon. At the breaking out of the war, he was called into service with the rank of Brig Gen: assigned to the command of the military dept which embraced N Y C & N Y State. In 1813, he was taken by Mr Madison into his Cabinet as Sec of War: the fall of the Capitol was laid at his door, & he soon retired to private life, from which he has never since emerged. –N Y American

Army & Navy Intelligence: Ofcrs & Troops stationed at Fort Washita:
Capt B L Beall, 2nd dragoons, I company, commanding company & post.
Capt T L Alexander, 6th Infty, commanding company C.
Capt G A H Blake, 2nd dragoons, commanding A troop.
Lt W J Newton, 2nd dragoons
Lt J Monroe, 6th Infty, A A Q M & A C S
Lt John H Hill, 2nd dragoons
Lt P W McDonald, 2nd dragoons, post adjutant.
T C Hammond, 2nd dragoons.
Medical Staff-Wm J Sloan, Assist Surgeon

Navy Orders:
Surgeon E Du Barry, appointed to the frig **Macedonian**, & as fleet surgeon of the African squadron.
Resignation: Purser Thos Gadsden.   Appointment: Arthur W Upshur, of Va, Purser

Jas Myers, of Mifflin township, Ohio, was recently found dead near the city of Columbus. It is supposed he came to his death by a fall from his horse. He was 30 years of age & a worthy citizen.

Circuit Court of the U S for the district of Alabama has decided that the marriage of a white man with an Indian woman, according to the forms & customs of the Choctaw nation, is void; that a civilized man is incapable of contracting marriage with a savage, & that their offspring is illegitimate & could not inherit.

Died: Apr 6, in Wash City, Josephine S, d/o the Hon John C Clark, of N Y, in her 15th year. Loneliness & sorrow overwhelm her bereaved parents. Her funeral is today at 12 o'clock, from Mrs Owner's, on Capitol Hill.

Died: on Mar 28, at his residence, near Dinwiddie Court-house, Va, John Hill Smith, in his 60th year, after a long illness. He was the s/o Larkin Smith, of King & Queen, for several years Speaker of the Hse of Delegates, & subsequently appointed by Mr Jefferson to the ofc of collector of the port of Norfolk. John Hill Smith entered the Hse of Delegates at an early age. He was subsequently a practitioner of law in Lynchburg, whence removing to Richmond, he was elected a member of the Exec Council of State, a post he filled for several years. -Whig

MON APR 10, 1843
Sale of valuable warehouse & wharf on Water or Causeway sts, Gtwn: deed of trust executed Dec 2, 1838, recorded in Liber W B, #66, folios 472 & 476, & at the request of all the persons concerned, the subscriber will offer for sale on the premises on Apr 20, the lot, south side, opposite to Jefferson street, fronting on said sts, extending back to the channel of the Potomac river, covering a space of about 38,000 sq ft. Improvements are a large brick warehouse, 2 stories high, & a dry wharf of about 60 feet in width to within about 30 feet of the channel. The subscriber, as trustee, will convey to the purchaser all the right & title given in the said deed of trust, which is believed to be indisputable. –Rd Smith, trust -Edw S Wright, auct

Valuable improved lands, on the turnpike leading from Gtwn to Rockville, Md, for sale at public auction. By virtue of a deed of trust executed by the late Jos Mourse, on Sep 30, 1825, duly recorded in liber W B, #14, folios 212 to 217: sale on Apr 27:
Part of a tract called *Friendship*, containing 8¾ acs;
Part of a tract called *Friendship*, containing 7¾ acs
Part of a tract called *Friendship*, containing 70½ acs
Part of a tract called *Pretty Prospect*, containing 82¾ acs
Part of a tract called *Mount Airy*, containing 45½ acs
Part of a tract called *Gizor*, containing 46 acs
Part of a tract called *Resurvey* or *Lucky Discovery*, containing 31 acs, 2 roods, & 21 perches
Part of a tract called *Pretty Prospect*, containing 3 acs
The improvements consist of a large 2 story stone dwlg house on one of the tracts with out bldgs; in the other a 2 story frame dwlg, also with the necessary out bldgs. -Rd Smith, trustee -Edw S Wright, auct

Circuit Court of Wash Co, D C. Alex'r Shaw, colored, has applied to be discharged from imprisonment: hearing on the 3rd Mon of Apr next, when his creditors are requested to attend. –Wm Brent, clk

The Bedford [Pa] Inquirer of Mar 24 records the death of John Thos Vowell, who visited that neighborhood a year or 2 ago, & employed himself in teaching school until Feb 21 last, when he was found dead in his bed by the family of Mr Conrad Ickes, at whose house he boarded. It is represented that his friends reside in the Dist of Col, for whose information this notice is published, that they may be advised of his decease.

Circuit Court of Wash Co, D C . Richd J Young has applied to be discharged from imprisonment: hearing on Apr 17th, when his creditors are requested to attend. –Wm Brent, clk

Capt Collins, of the steamboat **Cutter**, which recently burst her boiler in Pittsburg, has been arrested on the complaint of a man & his wife who were injured by the explosion, & held to bail in the sum of $5,000.

For rent, from May 1 next, the 3 story house on G st, at present occupied by Col Croghan. Inquire of Mr Jas Houston or the occupant.

Local News-Wash: Wm Wilson, who was arrested on suspicion of having robbed numerous places recently, was committed, in default of bail, to answer to the following charges: Robbing the Howard Institution on Mar 19: the property of Mary Joye. Robbing carpenter's shop of John W Shiles, at 12th & Canal sts, on Mar 28. Stealing from the grocery store of Wm Allen, on La ave, on Mar 31. Breaking into & robbing the grocery store of Bushrod W Reed, at 13th & F sts, on Apr 1st or 2nd, & stealing from there seventeen Fowler's one dollar notes, payable in Wash, on Apr 1st or 2nd. Breaking into & robbing the grocery store of JohnA Donohoo, at 7th & D sts, on Apr 1st or 2nd. The prisoner is about 25 years of age, & said he was from N Y C.

Health Report: 27 deaths have been reported for the month of Mar, 1843.
–Harvey Lindsly, Pres

TUE APR 11, 1843
Schedule of debts due from confederated Tribes of the Sac & Fox Indians to be paid by the U S under the provisions of a Treaty made & concluded at the Sac & Fox Agency, Terr of Iowa, Oct 11, 1842. This schedule is annexed as a part thereof:

Pierre Chouteau, jr-Co	St Louis, Mo-licensed traders	$112,109.47
W G & G W Erving	Indiana, do do	$6,371.83
J P Eddy & Co	Iowa, do do	$2,332.78
Thos Charlton	Van Buren Co, Iowa	$78.69
R B Willoughby	do do	$25.00
Francis Withington	Lincoln Co, Mo	$4,212.58
Jesse B Webber	Burlington, Iowa	$116.69
J C Wear	Jefferson Co, Iowa	$50.00
David Baily	Lincoln Co, Mo	$75.00
Thos W Bradley	Iowa	$20.00
John J Grimes	Lincoln Co, Mo	$625.00
Wm Settles	do do	$320.00
John S David	Burlington, Iowa	$20.00
F Hancock	Van Buren, do	$20.00
C G Pelton	Burlington, do	$34.00
J Tolman	Van Buren, do	$115.00
J L Burtiss	Lee Co, do	$715.00
Isaac A Lefevre	Van Buren, do	$348.00
Jeremiah Smith, jr	Burlington, do	$4,000.00

Wm & Sampson Smith	Jefferson Co, Mo $60.00	
John Koontz	[blank]	$6.50
Robt Moffet	New Lexington, Iowa	$129.63
Antoine Leclair	Davenport, do	$1,375.00
Mgt Price	Lee Co, do	$9.00
Jesse Sutton	Van Buren, do	$22.00
Jefferson Jordan	do	$175.00
Jeremiah Wayland	St Francisville, Mo	$15.00
Wm Rowland	Van Buren Co, Iowa	$460.32
Edw Kilbourne	Lee Co, do	$10,411.80
Perry & Best	do	$22.75
P Chouteau, jr & Co	St Louis, Mo	$26.00
Job Carter	Van Buren Co	$28.00
Francis Bosseron	St Louis, Mo	$26.00
Jas Jordon	Van Buren, Iowa	$1,775.00
Sampson Smith	do do	$54.00
Louis Laplant	Iowa	$122.00
Wm Phelps	Clark Co, Mo	$310.00
Wm B Street	Iowa	$300.00
Julia Ann Goodel	do	$855.00
Geo L Davenport	Davenport, Iowa	$320.00
G C R Mitchell	do do	$100.00
David Noggle	Van Buren, do	$20.00

Robt Brown, assignee of Cutting & Gordon, Van Buren Co, Iowa, $73.25
W C Cameron, assignee of A M Bissel, [bankrupt], Burlington, Iowa, $283.14
-John Chambers, Com'r on the part of the U S. Alfred Hebard, Arthur Bridgman, Com'rs appointed by the Commission of the part of the U S for examining & adjusting claims. Done at the city of Wash, Mar 23, 1843. John Tyler, by the Pres: Danl Webster, Sec of State

Meeting of 6 brothers recently took place at Eaton, Madison Co, N Y, whose ages averaged 70 years. Dr Silas Clark, of Herkimer Co, aged 75: his brothers Nathl 79, Jas 71, John 69, Saml 67, Josiah 64, all vigorous & healthy.

Every enlisted man of the garrison of Fort Ontario, Oswego, N Y, commanded by Capt E K Barnum, 2nd Regt of Infty, is a member of the Total Abstinence Society.

[Abstract from Art VIII: The Sacs & Foxes have caused the remains of their late distinguished chief, Wa-pil-lo, to be buried at their agency, near the grave of their late friend & agent Gen Jos M Street, & have put into the hands of their agent the sum of $100 to procure a tombstone to be erected over his grave, similar to that which is over the grave of Gen Street; & because they wish the graves of their friend & their chief to remain in the possession of the family of Gen Street, they wish to give to his widow, Mrs Eliza M Street, one section of land, to include the said graves & the agency house & enclosures around & near it; & as the agency house was built at the expense of the U S, the Sacs & Foxe agree to pay them, the sum of $1,000, the value of said bldg, assessed by gentlemen appointed by them, & Govn'r Chambers, Com'r on the part of the U S, to be deducted from the first annuity, payable to them under the provisions of this treaty, & the U S agree to grant ot the said Eliza M Street, by one or more patents, 640 acs of land, in such legal subdivisions as will include the said burial grounds, the agency house, & improvements around & near it, in good & convenient form, to be selected by the said E M Street, or her duly authorized agent.]

The treaty was signed in the presence of:

John Beach, U S Indian Agent & Sec	C F Ruff, Lt 1st U S Dragoons
Antoine Le Clare, U S Interpreter	Arthur Bridgman
Josiah Swart, U S Interpreter	Alfred Hebard
J Allen, Capt 1 st Dragoons	Jacob O Phister

-John Chambers, Com'r on the part of the U S, in the Terr of Iowa, Oct 11, 1842. [22 Sacs signed with their "X" mark. 22 Foxes signed with their "X" mark.]

Appointment by the Pres: Mordecai Myers, Collector of the Customs at Savannah, Ga, vice Jas Hunter.

Died: on Sun last, in her 21st year, Mary Jane McDonald, eldest d/o the late John G McDonald, of Wash City. Her funeral is today at 12 o'clock from her late residence, Capitol Hill.

Died: on the 16th instant, at his residence in Barnesville, Ohio, Hon Thos Shannon, aged 56, formerly a Rep in Congress from Ohio. [Note: this is Apr 11th paper. 16th instant is copied as written.]

Died: on the 23rd ult, at his residence, in Fred'k Co, Md, Mr Jacob B Miller, aged about 33 years. Mr Miller left his house about half an hour before sunset, apparently in good health, & went to his barn, at which place he was found dead about an hour afterwards.

Died: on Apr 3, at Janeville, Clarke Co, Va, Mrs Sarah Page, wid/o the late Robt Page.

Died: on Mar 26, Mrs Lavinia V M Patrick, the w/o Dr S Patrick, in her 38th year. She has left a family of 7 children, one of whom but a few weeks old-the loss of an affectionate, pious, judicious mother. [The Society of Charleston [Va] has been called to mourn her loss.]

Died: on Mar 26, at St Louis, Mo, Mrs Mary E, wi/o Mr John Addison, late of Wash City. She has left a husband & one child to mourn her loss.

The U S steamer **Cincinnati**, 6 days from Tampa Bay, via Cedar Keys, Port Leon, & Pensacola, arrived at New Orleans on Mar 30, bringing Capt Boneville, Lt Hopson, Lt Britton, Lt Grant, & Surgeon Holmes, with companies F & C, of the 7th Infty.

WED APR 12, 1843
To rent, on 7th st, between F & G sts, the Store & Dwlg house lately occupied by Mr Brooks. A good stand for a Patent Agency, or almost any business: opposite the Patent Ofc. Apply at the Factory of Bates & Bro, on G st, Wash.

Chancerty Sale of property on C st: Jonathan Seaver vs Chas S Fowler & others-in Chancery. Sale on Apr 25, lot #29 in reservation #10, fronting north on C st, with a 3 story brick dwlg, & all needed out-houses attached thereto. –D A Hall, trustee -R W Dyer & Co, aucts

For rent: the house occupied by the subscriber, & possession given on Jun 1. -M Ronckendorff. For sale, a Soda Fountain, with cooler, ticket-box, complete & in perfect order.

The Galveston Gaz says Gen Thompson has asked the release of Mr Jones, of Gonzales, & Mr Maverick, on the ground they are both his personal friends, & that the latter is a relative, & has promised that they shall accompany him on his visit to the U S in Apr. There is a prospect that Judge Hutchinson will also be released. There is no certainty in relation to the other prisoners.

Newport Standard: on Mar 21, at Petersburg, Perry Co, Pa, Isaiah Hatton, age 8 years, endeavoring to get a drink, was caught between 2 massive wheels of the Duncannon Rolling Mill, & killed.

Mr Jacob Stroube, an old & respectable citizen of Bracken Co, Ky, met a fearful death on the 23rd ult. His coat caught among the cogs of his mill & he was mangled shockingly. He survived only a few minutes after he was discovered by his sons.

Mrd: on Apr 10, at the residence of Dr Sewall, by Rev John Davis, Mr Joshua Follansbee to Miss Louisa Sewall, all of Wash City.

Mrd: on Apr 11, by Rev W B Edwards, Wm Anglis Batchelor, of N Y, late of London, England, to Miss Lucretia Ann Gibbs, of Wash City.

Died: yesterday, at the residence of her mother, on N Y ave, Miss Jane McPherson. Her funeral is today at 2 p m.

Died: on Mon, Roderick Hampton, jr, for many years an assistant messenger in the Gen Land Ofc. His funeral will be from his late residence, at the corner of 16th & L sts, this afternoon at 3½ o'clock.

At Apalachicola, Fla, on Mar 15, Mr Fell, mate of the British ship **Rothschild**, was drowned, with 4 apprentices, who were in the boat with him when it capsized in a squall. They were all English.

Wash Corp: 1-Ptn of Jas E Thumlert, praying remission of a fine: referred to the Cmte of Claims. 2-Ptn of Robt Cohen, for the remission of a fine: referred to the Cmte of Claims. 3-Ptn for the relief of R Farnham: referred to the Cmte of Claims.

Col Devoe, with a number of Indians, are in town from their great western wilds: Indian Chiefs, Warriors, & Braves. They will entertain with Singing, Dancing, Feasting, Apr 12, 1843, at the Nat'l Theatre, Wash. Among the distinguished Chief's & Braves are the following:
Nan-Neuce-Fush-E-To, or Buffalo King: Sac chief, age 60 years, covered with scars & honors of war. He has killed with his own hand 100 Osages, 2 Mohawks, 2 Kas, 2 Sioux, & 1 Pawnee. He speaks 9 Indian dialects, has visited nearly every tribe, & is one of the most noted chieftains living.
No Chee, or Man of Fire, a war chief, was distinguished in the last war.
Wa-Con-To-Kitch-Er, an Iowa Chief, one who communes with the Great Spirit-the Prophet.
Louis Te-Un-Ka, the Ribs, s/o the Buffalo King; Paconnee, brave in battle, quiet in peace an Iowa; & Cow Hick-ke, s/o the principal Chief of the Iowas; are 3 brave young war-chiefs. The latter is one of the noblest & handsomest chiefs ever seen. Mon-To-Gah, the White Bear, wears a medal from Pres Monroe. Cho-Tum-Pe, an Iowa Chief.

Circuit Court of Wash Co, D C. John Purdon, a bankrupt, has filed his ptn for his discharge & certificate: hearing on the first Mon in Jul next. –Wm Brent, clk

THU APR 13, 1843
For sale, lot 13, in sq 200, fronting on north I st. This lot is in the same sq with St John's Church. This & many other lots, belonging to St Vincent's Orphan Asylum, are for sale. –Thos Carbery

For sale: ***Fountain Inn***, long known to the traveling public: spacious hotel in Balt City on the east side of Light st, about 117 feet south of Balt st, being one of the most central locations in the city. It contains 75 rooms. The lease on the property will expire on Oct 1, 1846, & the rent is only $2,000 per annum, [except for the last year of the lease, the rent for that year being $2,500.] Apply to Wm B Norris, John Glenn, trustees, Balt, Md.

The U S frig **Columbia**, Capt Shubrick, & schnr **Enterprise**, Lt J P Wilson, were at Montevideo Feb 18.

Treaty made & concluded at La Pointe of Lake Superior, in the Terr of Wisc, between Robt Stuart, Com'r on the part of the U S, & the Chippewa Indians of the Mississippi & Lake Superior, on Oct 4, 1842. Signed by: Robt Stuart, Jno Hulbert 41 Indians with name & X mark; Henry Blatchford & Saml Ashmun, Interpreters. In presence of:

Justin Rice	Chas M Borup	Jas P Scott
Chas H Oakes	Z Platt	Cyrus Mendenhall
Wm A Aitken	C H Beaulieu	L M Warren
Wm Brewster	L T Jamison	

Claims allowed by Robt Stuart:

Edw F Ely: $50.80
Z Platt, atty for G Berkett: $484.67
Cleveland North Lake Co: $1,485.67
Abraham W Williams: $75.03
Geo Copway: $61.67
John Kahbege: $57.55
Alexis Carpentier: $28.58
John W Bell: 186.16
Antoine Picard: $6.46
Michl Brisette: $182.42
Francois Dejaddon: $301.48
Pierre C Duvernay: $1,101.00
Jean Bts Bazinet: $325.46
John Hotley: $69.00
Francois Charette: $234.92
Louis Ladebauche: $322.52
Peter Crebassa: $499.27
B T Kavanaugh: $510.82
*American Fur Co: $13,365.30
Z Platt, atty for Jos Gauthier: $614.30
Z Platt, atty for J B Uoulle: $64.78
Z Platt, atty for Wm Johnson: $390.27
Wm Brewster: $2,052.67
Chas W Borup, or order $122.90
Z Platt, atty for Francois Gauthier: $167.05
Z Platt, atty for Antoine Mace: $170.35
Z Platt, atty for Wm Morrison: $1,074.70
Z Platt, atty for Saml Ashmun: $1,771.63
Z Platt, atty for Thos Connor: $1,118.60
Z Platt, atty for Isaac Butterfield: $1,275.56
Z Platt, atty for estate of E Roussain: $959.13

Augustin Goslin: $169.06
Wm A Aitken: $935.67
Jas P Scott: $73.41
Augustin Bellanger: $192.36
Louis Corbin: $12.57
Alexis Corbin: $596.03
Geo Johnston: $35.24
Lyman M Warren: $1,566.65
Jos Dulau't: $144.32
Jean Bts Corbin: $531.50
John Hulbert: $209.18
Jean Bts Couveillion: $18.80
Nicholas Da Couteau, withdrawn
Pierre Cotti: $732.50
**John Jacob Astor: $27,994.98
Chas H Oakes: $4,309.20
J B Van Rensselaer: $62.00
Wm Bell: $17.62
Michl Cadotte: $205.60

Francois St Jean & Geo Bonga: $366.84
Z Platt, atty for estate of Danl Dingley: $1,991.62
Clement H Beaulieu, agent for the estate of Bazil Beaulieu, dec'd: $596.84
W H Brockway & Henry Holt, excs to the estate of John Holiday, dec'd: $3,157.10
This claim will be paid as follows, viz: Wm Brewster, or order: $1,929.77
Wm Brewsters & Jas W Abbott: $2,067.19. The parties to this claim request no payment be made to either without their joint consent, or until a decision of the case be had in a court of justice. Seal of the U S affixed in Wash City, Mar 23, 1843. – John Tyler -Danl Webster, Sec of State
[*American Fur Co to be paid as follows: American Fur Co-$12,565.10 Chas W Borup-$800.20]
[**John Jacob Astor to be paid as follows: Chas W Borup-$1,676.90 Z Platt-$2,621.80 John Jacob Astor-$23,696.28]

Mrd: on Apr 11, by Rev Mr French, Mr Chas F Lowrey, formerly of Charleston, S C, to Miss Anne Moriah Haliday, of Wash City.

Mrd: on Tue, in Gtwn, by Rev Mr Butler, Lt John Danl Kurtz, U S Corps of Engineers, to Jane, d/o the late Thos C Wright, all of that place.

Mrd: on Apr 6, Mr Edw T Bailey, of Wash, Del, to Miss Mgt Griffin, of Brandywine Hundred.

Died: on Mar 20, near Nottingham, PG Co, Md, after a short & severe attack of bilious pleurisy, Mrs Henrietta Priscilla Worthington, in her 42nd year, w/o Walter B C Worthington, d/o Mrs Eliz M Waring, & granddaughter of the late Govn'r Bowie, leaving to her bereaved & afflicting husband 5 interesting infant children as pledges of their union. Previous to her attack her health had been unusually good.

Died: on Mar 26, at Locust Grove, Chas Co, Md, after a short illness, Mary Jane, w/o Dr Edw Miles, in her 24th year. A young wife & mother was snatched by the relentless hand of death.

Mrs Timms can accommodate with board 2 or 3 gentlemen with their ladies, or several single gentlemen. Her house is pleasantly situated south side of Capitol sq.

Journeymen Bricklayers: meeting on Apr 13, at the Franklin House, [Mr Thos Baker's,] corner of 8th & D sts, Wash.

The Rt Rev Wm R Whittingham, Bishop of the diocese of Md, is to administer the rite of confirmation in St John's Church this morning & Christ Church, Navy Yard, this afternoon, at the usual hour for services.

FRI APR 14, 1843
The brig **Delaware**, which cleared from Phil on Mon last for Rio Grande, took out a handsome steamboat, the parts so nicely fitted as to enable the owner to have her put together on her arrival there. This steamboat is owned by Mr Chas W Diehl, of Porto Allagra, & is intended to navigate the upper streams of that country, & was built by Messrs J Byerly & Son, of Kensington. Her engine was built by J P Morris.

Capt E M Stevens, at Marion, in this State, died on Mar 31, from a wound from a pistol ball in the thigh, received accidentally during the encounter that occurred a few days previous at that place between Martin A Lea & Napoleon Lockett, in which the former was killed. Capt S was an industrious & respected mechanic, a native of Connecticut, but for the last 6 years has resided at Marion. –Mobil Advertiser

Orphan's Court of Wash Co, D C. Letters testamentary on the personal estate of John Wells, jr, late of said county, dec'd. -Hannah Wells, excx

Delaware Republican ofc: on Sat last Jacob Cannon, at Cannon's Ferry, Sussex Co, Delaware, one of the firm of the long established house of Isaac & Jacob Cannon, was shot with a gun loaded with shot by Owen O'Day, of that neighborhood. He survived from 1 p m of that day until Mon at 3 o'clock. The provocation was the alleged improper collection of a small debt of $18.

For rent: dwlg house over Mr B Schenck's Fancy Store, on Pa ave. Inquire of P H Borland, one door east of Beers' Temperance Hotel.

For rent: new 2 story brick house pleasantly located in the First Ward, on 18th st, corner house; water convenient. For terms inquire of Henry Walker.

For rent: large & commodious house & lot on G st, west of the War Dept, at present occupied by T Hartley Crawford. Apply to Mr Crawford or Jas L Edwards.

Died: on Apr 4, at his residence, in the borough of Butler, at qrtr past 5 o'clock, Tue morning, Gen Wm Ayres, in his 72nd year. [A nice legal question, & one of much importance, will arise from the circumstance of this gentleman's death taking place at the time it did. Gen Ayres was never married, but left an illegitimate son, who was to heir his estate; & neglecting to make any will, he applied to the Legislature to have this son legitimatized, & an act to that effect was passed & approved on Apr 4, at about 12 o'clock. The question naturally arises, is the son legitimate? The propery left is about $200,000. There are numerous collaterate heirs.
–Pittsburg American]

Mobile Advertiser: In the future Mr C C Langdon will be the sole editor & proprietor of the Advertiser. -Bee

Notice: Ran away from the subscriber on Apr 12, an indented apprentice to the cigar & tobacco business, named Chas Jardine, between 17 & 18 years of age. All persons are hereby cautioned from harboring or employing him, under the penalty of the law, & six cents reward will be given to whomever shall lodge him in jail or surrender him to me. –Jas Lawrence

SAT APR 15, 1843
New York, Apr 11. About 7 years ago Saml Rowe, of Rankin Co, Miss, obtained a mulatto boy, Wm Stewart, alias Jennings, from the Almshouse or Farms in this city, on the usual conditions, which were, not to remove him out of the county, & within about 4 months since made application & succeeded in obtaining a boy named John Collins, & 2 small girls, named Lucy Curry & Mary Ann Florida. He removed all to Mississippi & employed the children on his farm. The Mayor, being apprized of these facts, selected ofcr John Huthwaite to proceed there & arrest him. He succeeded in obtaining the children, & arrested Rowe who had abducted them. About 150 miles abot New Orleans, during the night, Rowe jumped from the steamboat & escaped. The children were brought here in safety & lodged in the Alms-house. -Herald

Buffalo Commercial of Tue. Cases of Seduction. Crct Court: Suit of Bridges vs Andrews was an action brought to recover damages for the seduction of his dght. Verdict, $300 for plntf. The parties reside in the adjoining town of Hamburg. Another suit was that of Enders vs Snearley, being an action for breach of marriage promise. Verdict, $1,000. The same parties were engaged in a 2nd suit, brought by the parent of the plntf to recover damages for the seduction of his dght. Verdict: $4,000 damages. The defendant made no defence, but submitted the case without remark. M Fillmore, who was retained as associate counsel with H K Smith, for the plntfs, addressed the jury at the closing up of the trial with great effect.

On Sunday, Ivory Dana about 40 years of age, residing in Canton village, about 12 miles from Boston, committed suicide by hanging himself. He has left a wife & several children. No reason has been assigned for this rash act.

A Louisville [Ky] paper says that Jas Robinson, a stage-driver between that city & Bardstown, has been driving on that road for the last 10 years & traveled 117,000 miles, & never upset his coach or met an accident by which a single person was hurt. Robinson is one of the best ships in America.

Maj Roswell Franklin, the last survivor of the massacre of Wyoming, died recently at Aurora, N Y. He was a native of Conn. His father emigrated to the valley of Wyoming, Pennsylvania-both engaged in the battle with the Indians & English of that place, which was so disastrous to the settlers. The mother & one sister were butchered before their eyes-another sister was taken prisoner, & retained by the

Indians 11 years at Niagara-the dec'd was also take prisoner & retained among them about 3 years, near Mount Morris, Livingston Co, N Y.

Teacher wanted: to conduct a small school of 10 pupils at the Hot Springs for the coming 6 or 7 months Communicate with Th Goode, Hot Springs.

Balt, Apr 13. Capt Elliott Ward, of the brig **Atlantic**, arrived recently at this port from Port Spain, Trinidad, & left in the cars yesterday for Phil, on his way to New Haven, Conn, to visit his family, who reside there. At Havre de Grace he was taken ill & suddenly expired. The body was brought back to Balt by the train of cars last evening, & met by Mrs Ward, who had come on in the boat yesterday afternoon, expecting to find her husband in Balt. -Patriot

Virginia: elections for Reps to Congress: following are Whig candidates, as far as we are informed:

Jas H Langhorne	John M Botts	Chas J Faulkner
Geo H Gilmer	Hill Carter	Alex H H Stuart
Richd H Toler	Willoughby Newton	Geo W Summers
Wm L Goggin	Saml Chilton	

Alexander H H Stuart declined being a candidate.

Two days from England. McNaughton, the man who deliberately shot Mr Drummond, the Sec of Sir Robt Peel, has been acquitted on the ground of insanity.

Mrd: on Thu last, by Rev J C Smith, Lt Chas N Hagner, of the U S Topographical Engineer Corps, to Laura Isabella Stansbury, d/o Arthur J Stansbury, of Wash City.

Died: on Apr 14, in her 37th year, Mrs Mary Ann Evens, w/o Benj Evens, of Wash City. Her funeral will be from her late residence on H st, near 7th, on Sun next, at half-past 2 p m without further notice.

Died: on Thu last, in her 25th year, after a protracted & painful illness, Mrs Mary Magdalen, consort of Michl R Shyne, of Wash City. The grief inflicted upon her bereaved husband & sorrowing relatives & friends by the loss of this truly estimable lady, is greatly mitigated by the beautiful example of resignation & Christian preparation with which she met the event so dreadful to the unprepared. Fastened upon by that fell destroyer, consumption, she was long aware of her approaching dissolution; &, with the most exemplary submission, she prepared herself to submit to her Savior's will. May she rest in peace! Her funeral will be from the residence of her husband, near Blagden's wharf, on Mar 15, at 2 p m.

Died: on Mar 28, at his residence, *Oak Grove*, in Chas Co, Md, after a short & painful illness, Geo R Spalding, in his 37th year. In this severe dispensation none can feel, except the devoted wife, the intensity & acutemess of the blow. Universally esteemed & beloved by a large & numerous circle of friends & acquaintances, he has thus suddenly been cut off in the midst of his usefulness.

Died: on Apr 13, after a long & painful sickness, Saml Bootes, aged 77 years. His funeral is this afternoon, at 4 p m, from his late residence, on Bridge st, Gtwn, opposite the Farmers' & Mechanics' Bank.

The splendid mansion of the late Chancellor Sanford, at Flushing, N Y, which cost we believe more than a hundred thousand dollars, has been sold at auction for $15,400. The purchaser is R Beatty.

MON APR 17, 1843

The New Mirror, every number embellished with an original & exquisite design on steel. Edited by Geo P Morris-Editor & Proprietor, illustrated by J G Chapman. Distinguished from every other periodical. –G P Morris, #4 Ann st, near Broadway.

Escape from drowning occurred on Sun last. Mr Abraham Zane, of Annapolis, Md, in attempting to cross the bay at Kent Island in a small sailboat, was overtaken, when about a mile & a half outside of Sandy Point, by a gale that upset the boat, & he was thrown into the water. She drifted 15 or 20 yards from him, but being an expert swimmer he reached her & secured her. After about 4 hours the boat drifted into shoal water near the residence of Mr Pascault, on the island, & he was thus relieved; but not before he had become unable to speak or move. A brief moment longer, & it would have been all over for him.

Mr Jas F Hopping, of Chatham, Morris Co, N J, committed suicide on Wed last by opening a vein in his arm. He was found in the barn, a corpse, with a letter stating that he believed he had committed the unpardonable sin, & was weary of life. He was a Justice of the Peace, & an intelligent & influential citizen. He has left a wife & family.

On Sun last a Silver Medal was presented to Cpl Philip Cahill, of U S Marines, attached to the frig **Brandywine**, by Cmdor Parker, in the name of the ofcrs of the frig **Constitution**, for his gallant & noble conduct in saving from drowning midshipman Weaver, who fell overboard from that ship while lying off the navy yard on Feb 3 last. Cmdor Parker complimented Cpl Cahill for his praiseworthy conduct, & concluded his remarks by announcing his promotion to the rank of Sergeant.

Mr Jas R Valient, of Balt, was drowned in Back river, below that city, on Wed last, by the upsetting of a small boat, in which he was attempting to cross for the purpose of gunning.

For sale, on accommodating terms, a superior German Rosewood Piano, new, of fine tone & finish; 6 octaves, Andre Stein, maker. Inquire of Robt Keyworth's store, on Pa ave.

Vicksburg Whig of the 1st inst: A gentleman from Jackson informs us that Col W H Shelton, former Pres of the Brandon Bank, drowned himself in Pearl river yesterday. It appears he was an important witness in the case of Graves, the absconding Treasurer, & had been a good deal concerned with him. Mr S was charged with having loaned Graves a large amount of money, & having borrowed the same from a Mr Crane. Mr Crane demanded the money of Mr S, & threatened to take some measures to recover it. Mr S, with Mr Coffee, left Brandon for Jackson early in the morning. Mr S wrote a letter to Mr Crane, declaring that Graves had taken off with the money. Mr S left his pencil, watch, hat & coat, & horse at a shanty, & then walked into the river. The body was felt with a pole, but had not been recovered when he left. [Apr 24 newspaper: Mrs Graves, the wife of the fled treasurer, sent word to Govn'r Tucker that the money belonging to the State was in her possession & requested him to call & receive it. She gave the gentlemen who were sent, a bag of gold & a bundle of U S Treas notes amounting to $95,365.20 to be delivered to the Govn'r. This reduced her husband's defalcation to $46,000. She has reflected honor for herself & her children, a passport which will confer respectability anywhere. –Tuscaloosa Monitor]

Work just issued by Godey & McMichael, of Phil, called "In Town & About, or Pencillings & Pennings." The designs are by that rising & gifted young artist, Felix O C Carley. The Illustrative descriptions are by our contemporary of the Pennsylvanian, Jos C Neal. We have sketches of the News Boys;Boys that Run with the Engine; & of Corner Loungers. –Phil Inq

Circuit Court of Wash Co, D C. John Hardison has applied to be discharged from imprisonment under the act of the relief of Insolvent Debtors: on Apr 29 creditors are requested to attend. –Wm Brent, clk

The residence of Mrs Maria Tilghman, at Bennett's Point, in Queen Anne's Co, Md, was destroyed by fire on Apr 7.

Died: on Fri last, Mrs Ann Evens, consort of Benj Evens, of the Land Ofc. After a long & protracted illness, borne without a murmur, she resigned her spirit to God who gave it amid praise & rejoicing.

Died: on Apr 15, at his residence on H st, Mr John Donn, aged 69 years. For the larger portion of his life he resided in Havre de Grace, Md. He died at peace with all mankind, & in full triumph of faith in Christ.

Died: on Apr 5, at Apalachicola, Fla, of a long & lingering illness, Mr Jas O McCauley, aged 35 years, a native of Wash. He has resided in Fla for the last 9 years, & has left a wife & 2 children to mourn his loss.

Died: on Mar 25, in Chesterfield Co, Va, Thos Gregory, in the 91st year of his age. He was a sldr of the Revolutionary war; an active, industrious, & temperate man. He was married twice, by which marriages he had 20 children. An aged companion & 10 of his children survive him, & nearly 100 grandchildren & great grandchildren.

F Y Naylor, Tinner & Coppersmith, Pa ave, between 3rd & 4½ sts, Wash. [Ad]

For rent, a 2 story brick dwlg with kitchen attached, on H between 18th & 19th sts, & within one square of the War & Navy Depts. Lately been occupied by A Thos Smith. For further particulars inquire of the subscriber adjoining. -David Hines

Gtwn Adv: On Wed last, the bakery of Mr Fred'k Pascoe, on Cecil st, was destroyed by fire, & some adjacent bldgs were injured. It is believed to be the act of an incendiary by a lad name Danl Steiner, who was in Mr Pascoe's employment. This lad has since been arrested & committed for further examination.

For sale: a likely negro girl, for a term of years. A country purchaser would be preferred. For terms apply at the Fancy Store of Jas P McKean, Pa ave.

TUE APR 18, 1843
Benton [Mo] Banner of Apr 1. Mr Chas Peale, formerly a citizen of this county, but more recently a resident of N Y, was thrown from his horse a few days since in Holmes Co, & instantly killed. This makes the 3rd brother out of a number of 6, who settled in Yazoo Co several years ago, who has come to his death by violent means. Henry Peale, the eldest of them, met his death in the summer of 1840, by being violently thrown from a vehicle. J M, a younger brother, was shot dead in a rencontre last fall, & now Chas, whose business in Mississippi was to adjust the affairs of his dec'd brother, Jas M, is by the hand of Providence, as suddenly ushered into eternity. Thus the hearth of a father is made desolate.

For sale: valuable property on F st, between 14th & 15th sts, adjoining the property of D Clagett. A 2 story brick house & a frame bldg, which rent for $200 per annum. Also, a 2 story brick house & lot near the War Ofc, opposite Major Andrew's. –J I Stull, Cashier Farmers & Mechanics Bank, or Chas J Nourse

Circuit Court of Wash Co, D C: in Chancery. B Henri Lubiez Klimkiewiez, vs, Kosciusko Armstrong, Hypolitus J A Estko, Catherine Estko, wid/o Thadeus Estko, dec'd, & Romanus, Martina, & Louisa Estko, children of said dec'd; Mr Bonnissant, sen, who, on Jun 4, 1816, was notary at Milet, dept of the Seine & Marne, in France; Thadea Emilie Wilhelmine Zeltner, Marie Charlotte Julie Marqueritte Zeltner, or the proper rep of each & every of those parties, et al, dfndnts. Bill charges that Gen Thadeus Kosciusko, on Mar 5, 1798, whilst on a visit to the U S, made a certain last will & test, the object of which was to dispose of certain personal property & assets that he held in the U S, & constituted Thos Jefferson the executor thereof, & as late as Sep 15, 1817, republished & renewed the same, & in the same yeaar, died without having revoked it; that, after his death, the said will was duly proved, & said Thos Jefferson having refused to execute the same, letters of administration with the will annexed were granted to the Orphan's Court of Wash Co, D C to Benj L Lear, who, dying before closing the administration, letters of adm de bonis non with the will annexed were granted by the same Orphan's Crt to Geo Bomford, one of the dfndnts to the present suit; that the particular dispositions of said property & effects expressed to be made in & by said last will & test have proved void & inoperative for uncertainty, & said property & effects are not covered by any other testamentary act of disposition left by said testator at his death, so that, as to said property & effects, he has died intestate. The bill further states that all debts of the dec'd & other charges upon said property & effects have been fully paid & satisfied, & there remains a large surplus in the hands of Geo Bomford, an administrator, for distribution; that the said dec'd, at the time of his death, had his domicil either in France of Switzerland, probably the former; that he never was married & left no issue, & that cmplnt is his next of kin, & so, by the law of his domicil, whether it be France or Switzeralnd, is the sole distributer of said surplus; that the dfndnts Mr Bouissant & the Misses Zeltner are said & believed to be legatees of said dec'd under a will designed to apply to other property, & to certain funds in France; they are made dfndnts, however, on the suggestion that by possibility the legacies might become a charge on said assets in the hands of Geo Bomford, as adm; this suggestion is not admitted by cmplnt, & he charges that the legacies have been fully satisfied out of the other funds of the dec'd primarily liable therefore; that the dfndnt, Kosciusko Armstrong, also claims to be a legatee of the dec'd, & that the legacy is a charge on said assets in the hands of Geo Bomford, which claim is denied by cmplnt; that the dfndnts of the name of Estko also make claims on said assets respectively as creditors & next of kin of the dec'd, both which pretensions are also denied by cmplnt; that nevertheless, by reason of said conflicting claims, the said adm refused to recognise the title of cmplnt & obliges him to litigate & establish the same by the present suit. The objects of the bill are to establish & quiet the title of cmplnt, & an account by the administrator of the assets in his hands, & payment & transfer of the same to the cmplnt as proper legal distributer thereof. It appears that the dfndnts, excepting Geo Bomford, reside & are out of D C. Dfndnts to appear in court on or before the first Mon of Sep next. -Wm Brent, clk -C Cox, solicitor for cmplnt.

Dr Grafton Tyler has removed his practice from Md to Gtwn, D C. Ofc & residence corner of Wash & Gay sts, opposite Miss English's Seminary. Professional business will be prompty attended to.

Miller is coming! and will be able to supply ice of a superior quality, having used extra exertions & means only to gather the most transparent & clean ice that Rock creek affords. –Michl Miller

F Pulvermacher announces that in consequence of the rainy weather, he will keep open his store a few days longer, & provides beautiful cheap laces, & ribands. Received a lot of new & pretty Nightcaps for ladies.

Obit-died: on Apr 6, Miss Josephine S Clark, d/o the Hon John C Clark, in her 15th year. She leaves an affectionate mother & doting father.

The body of Col Wm L Shelton, late Pres of the Brandon Bank of Miss, who committed suicide a short time since, by throwing himself into the Pearl river, has been found.

Georgia-Superior Court of Richmond Co: Bill in Equity for the sale of property. Thos T Maddux & others, cmplnts, vs, Martin Frederick & Nicholas Delarge, excs of Sacre P Turpin & others, dfndnts. It appearing to the Court that Amanda Turpin, Sarah C Turpin, & Henry W Turpin, 3 of the dfndnts in said bill, reside out of Ga, to wit, in the Dist of Col; it is ordered that they appear & answer said bill of cmplnt on the first Mon in Jun next, & that service of this order upon the said Amanda, Sarah C, & Henry W, by publication in one of the gazettes of D C once a week for 4 weeks preceding the next term. –Jas M Laws, clk.

Died: on Apr 16, Mrs Isabella R Compton, w/o Mr Wm T Compton, of Gtwn, D C. Her funeral is tomorrow at 3 p m, from the residence of Mr Compton, on 1st st.

Died: on Apr 16, with a long & painful illness, Mrs Mary Emeline Griner, consort of Mr Jos Griner, of the State of N Y, & only d/o Mr Nathl Plant, of Wash, in her 28th year.

Died: on Apr 16, in Wash City, Catesby Cocke, the infant son of Maj Jas D & Charlotte Graham.

Died: on Apr 3, of consumption, Lt Robt Q Butler, of the U S Corps of Engineers, aged 26. He was a native of Smithfield, Va, & graduated at the U S Military Acad in 1839: for the last 2 years filled the ofc of principal assistant Prof of Civil & Military Engineering at the Acad. A very severe & rapid pulmonary attack forced him to fly from the rigorous climate of West Point to seek the more genial atmosphere of the South, but he died on the passage. His remains were taken to Savannah & interred with military honors.

Died: on Apr 14, in Gtwn, Mary Emma, infant d/o Benj Reiss, aged 4 years & 7 months.

Died: Apr 16, in Gtwn, Henry H, infant s/o Dr H Magruder, aged 1 year & 13 days.

WED APR 19, 1843
Meeting of the N Y Historical Soc on Sat received the map which Mr Jay used in the arrangement of the Treaty of 1783, & on it the boundary line of the U S is represented by a red line, & in Mr Jay's own handwriting appears this memorandum near the line, "Mr Oswald's line." Mr O was the British Com'r to arrange the treaty. After Mr Gallatin concluded, Wm Beach Lawrence, a member of the Soc, conveyed to Mr Webster a request that he would address the audience on this subject. He said the treaty of 1783 granted nothing to the U S. It granted that Gov't no political rights whatever, & not an inch of terriroty. These were declared when her independence was declared; these were established when her existence as a free nation was established; these stood upon the declaration of 1776, they stand thereupon now, & thereupon they will ever stand. [Great spplause.]

The Sec of the Navy has appointed Prof Walter R Johnson, of Phil, Dr Thos P Jones, of Wash, & Mr Chas Reeder, of Balt, a Board of Examiners, to make experimental trials of inventions & plans designed to prevent the explosion of steam boilers & collapsing of flues. This Board is now in session at the Navy Yard in Wash City.

Wash Co, Md: Geo M Stewart was convicted at the recent term, on 2 indictments for burglary: the first for breaking & entering the house of Mr John Corby in Wmsport, the second for robbing the Wash Co Bank. He was sentenced to 15 years in the pen.

Mrd: on Apr 18, by Rev Jos P Moore, Mr Louis Muller, formerly of Balt, to Miss Eudocia Gelston Hills, formerly of Alexandria.

John Favro, a resident in Lowell, Mass, aged 28 years, was discovered on Tue near the new burying ground, dead. He was found in an upright posture, with a slipnoose around his neck, & the other end of the rope attached to the top of sapling bent down. He left his mother's house on Sun last. A bible & a Millerite hymn book was found about his person. He is said to have been living with a second advent believer in Boston during a few of the last weeks.

Messrs Geo Parkin & Co have disposed of the Pittsburg Advocate to the Hon Thos H Baird, who will conduct the editorial dept himself.

The Harrisburg papers give an account of a ruthless murder done in that neighborhood on the persons of Mr John Parthemore & his wife, residents of Susquehanna township. Their bodies were found by their son. Robbers are supposed to have committed the crime, as money was taken from the premises. A reward of $500 has been offered by the son for the apprehension of the murderer.

Orphan's Court of Wash Co, D C. Letters testamentary on the personal estate of Eliza Hodge, late of said county, dec'd. –Jas Marshall, exc

$50 reward for runaway, indented apprentice in the tailoring trade, Edw McNerhany, about 17 years of age. All persons are hereby forewarned from employing or harboring the said boy at the peril of the law. If he is delivered to me, or secured in jail, the above reward will be paid. –C Eckloff, Merchant tailor, Pa ave.

Shamrock Hill, for rent or sale: country residence about half a mile from Wash City, North Capitol st, leading directly towards its principal entrance. It contains upwards of 80 acs, & commands a fine prospect of the city, of the river Potomac, & surrounding scenery. The improvements are capacious. –John Boyle
Also, 1 or 2 dwlgs in Wash City for rent, & several lots for sale, lease, or to be exchanged for work & building materials.

A young man named Saml Owens, hack driver, met with a serious accident at the steamboat wharf yesterday. Owens very imprudently undertook to leap on board the steamboat **Osceola** as it was nearing the wharf, & the poor fellow was dreadfully crushed between the boat & the wharf. He is unable to speak & lies in a very precarious condition. [Corr of Apr 21: It was not the **Osceola**, but one of the Alexandria steamboats, that he was leaping on board, when he was so much injured. We learn that he was considered better by his medical attendants.]

Wash Corp: 1-Ptn from W B Laub: referred to the Cmte of Claims. 2-Ptn from Geo W Utermuhle & others: referred to the Cmte on Improvements. 3-Ptn of Henry Grieb, praying remission of a fine: referred to the Cmte of Claims. 4-Ptn of John P Stallings & others, for curb-stones & paving footway on sq 487: referred to the Cmte on Improvements. 5-Act for the relief of J A W Butler: passed.

THU APR 20, 1843
Fashionable Hats: J Maguire, 7th st, opposite the Patriotic Bank, Wash.

The undersigned having been appointed by the Circuit Court of Wash Co, D C a Notary Public, will attend to notarial business at his ofc, corner of 6th st & La ave, or at his residence on D st, 3rd door from 3rd st. –Wm Thompson

Circuit Court of Wash Co, D C. Thos Mitchell, a bankrupt, has filed his ptn for his discharge & certificate: hearing on the first Mon in Jul next. –Wm Brent, clk

The subscriber having arrived in Washington wishes to engage a Farm on shares or rent, & would have no objections to take charge of a farm, having been used to both slave & free labor. He may be seen at Wm B Lewis' variety store, near 11th st, on the Ave. Refer to J S Skinner, Gen P O. –Thos Bevan

For rent: 2 story brick house on N Y ave, between 9th & 10th sts. Possession given immediately. Apply to Mr Orsbourn, at the adjoining frame house, or to the subscriber. –Thos A Scott

Naval Court Martial was convened on Apr 10, on board the Texian sloop of war **Austin**, lying in the harbor of New Orleans, for the trial of 9 persons on a charge of mutiny on board the Texian schnr-of-war **San Antonio**, on Feb 11, 1842, whilst lying in the Mississippi river, opposite that city. Lt C F Fuller was killed, & Midshipmen Odell & Allen were wounded. The mutineers have been confined in the prisons of New Orleans until recently, when they were delivered to Com Moore, of the Texian navy, on the requisition of the Pres of that Republic. The chief witness against the prisoners is Jos D Sheppard, one of the parties implicated, who turned State's evidence upon a grant of free pardon by the Pres of Texas. Oswald, the sergeant of marines, was the principal instigator & leader. The plot was first broached at the Island of Mugeres, or Woman's Island, on the eastern shore of Yucatan, where the **San Antonio** & the ship **San Bernard** had gone to take in water. The attempt was to be made, by the crews of both vessels acting in conjunction, to capture both schnrs, take them to Vera cruz, & dispose of them to the Mexicans. When Capt Seeger & most of the ofcrs were on shore, the crew mutined. The fatal results are already known. It appears that a person who died in prison, named Benj Pumpelly, was the murderer of Lt Fuller, he having confessed the fact but a few hours previous to his death.

Hon John B Dawson, a Rep in Congress from the State of La, has been appointed by the Pres to the ofc of Postmaster of the city of New Orleans, in place of Gen Wm Debuys, resigned.

Richmond, Apr 18. Messrs Ellis & Ellet with told yesterday that their accountant, Mr Bernard Stegar, was drowned on Sun, in attempting to cross Bernard's creek, in Powhatan. He was in a buggy & ventured to cross the stream. Mr Stegar was a young man & had been married but a few months. He was on his way to bring his wife home, she being on a visit to her relatives in Buckingham. -Compiler

Shocking murder was perpetrated on the body of Mrs Malinda Horn, w/o Adam Horn, residing about 22 miles from Balt, on the Hanover turnpike road. Mrs Horn had mysteriously disappeared from her home about 4 weeks since, & no intelligence could be had of her. Her body was found in a coffee bag, in a ditch of a field fronting the house, with her head cut off, her legs & arms severed from the body. She was 18 years old & in a delicate situation. Her murder became a double murder. Mr Horn is said to have so ill-treated his wife as to cause her to leave him some time last fall, but she returned, & again was subject to frequent misusage. Neighbors are now looking for Adam Horn, who is a tailor by trade, about 45 years old, 5 feet & 6 inches high. –Balt Patriot

The suit of the U S against Jesse Hoyt, formerly collector of the port of N Y, & now charged with being a defaulter to the amount of $200,000, is before the Circuit Court sitting in N Y. [May 2 newspaper: heavy verdict against Jesse Hoyt of $220,837.85 damages & six cents costs. The Court stated that the claim for commission on receipts & disbursements made by Mr Hoyt was not contemplated by law, & could not be allowed. Mr Hoyt gave 6 sureties, on being appointed collector, who are bound in the sum of $200,000.]

N Y, Apr 18. Alderman Jeremiah Towle is just appointed by the Pres, Naval Ofcr for this port, in the place of Thos Lord removed, & Mr John S McKibbin, Appraiser, in the place of Edw Taylor, also removed. They will take possession this day.

FRI APR 21, 1843
Circuit Court of Wash Co, D C. Silas Read, a bankrupt; Anthony Holmead, a bankrupt; John R Dorsey, a bankrupt, & Fred'k Reinhart, a bankrupt: have each filed their ptn for his discharge & certificate: hearing for each on the first Mon in Jul next. –Wm Brent, clk

Gtwn College, Apr 18, 1843. Painful intelligence reached the Philodemic Soc of the death of Edw A Lynch, one of their first & most distinguished members He was a native of Va. He was sent at an early age to Gtwn College, D C: practiced law in Fred'k City, Md. As an orator, he forced the admiration of all who knew him. He was just entering on a political career in his adopted State, when the state of his malady urged him to seek a more genial climate. He visited the West Indies with his devoted & talented brother; & whilst they were on the Island of Santa Cruz, it pleased the Almighty to take them to another & a better region, in the flower of their age & the height of their usefulness. Resolved: condolences to his widow & afflicted family. Copy to be sent to the wid/o the dec'd, Mrs E A Lynch, & another to his valued brother, Lt Wm Lynch, U S Navy. –Geo Fenwick, Pres -Wm E Bird, Sec

The Vicksburg Sentinel announces the death of Mrs Shelton, whose husband committed suicide lately. Her physical organization sunk under the moral torture & she expired in spasms.

Mrd: on Apr 20, by Rev Wm Mathews, Mr John Anderson to Mrs Martha R Costigan.

Mrd: on Apr 13, by Rev Mr Davis, Mr Benj F Weeden to Miss Mary Causin, all of Wash City.

Mrd: on Tue, in Balt, by Rev Mr Coskery, Alex'r Young to Ann T Seekamp, d/o the late David Williamson, jr, of Balt Co.

Died: yesterday, after a short illness, Mrs Johanah Fitzgerald, w/o John Fitzgerald, in her 44th year, leaving a large family to deplore her loss. Her funeral will be from her late residence on H st, between 4½ & 5th sts, at half past 3 p m, this afternoon.

Died: on Apr 12, in Westport, Conn, of consumption, Mr Henry L Luff, printer, formerly of Wash City. He was a young man of kind feelings & affectionate disposition.

Died: on Apr 17, at the residence of his son, Prof Proudfit, in New Brunswick, N J, in the full possession of his faculties, the Rev Alex'r Proudfit, D D, in his 75th year.

SAT APR 22, 1843
Cmdor David Porter, who has for some years past been Charge d'Affaires at Constantinople, died at that place on Mar 3.

Mrs Beck & Miss Wake inform the ladies of Wash that they have just received from N Y, the latest fashions of Bonnets & Caps, with approved styles of Dress Patterns & Costumes. 8 or 10 young ladies who want to learn the above business can apply at the corner of 10th & E sts, opposite the Medical College.

Valuable property for sale in Page Co, Va: deeds of trust from Benj Blackford & Son: sale on Jun 22 of *Isabella Furnace*, near Luray, Page Co, 3 farms of limestone land on Hawksbill creek; one containing 344 acs; one containing 321 acs; one containing 480 acs. On the same day, Isabella Furnace & *Speedwell Forges*: will sell 1,000 acs of Woodland with the forges. Apply to A S Tidball, Winchester; Chauncy Brooks, Pres Western Bank, Balt; or the undersigned Luary, Page Co, Va. –N W Yager, A Kendrick, trusts

Miss Jane E Biscoe, south side of Pa ave, between 9th & 10th sts, has just received a fashionable supply of Spring Millinery.

Alexandria Brewery for sale or rent: located at Wolfe & Union sts, near the Potomac river, from which the water is drawn for brewing. My friend, Mr Jas Entwisle, has & is now managing the business for me, & will give more particular information to anyone interested. –Wm H Irwin

Circuit Court of Wash Co, D C. Wm Smitha has applied to be discharged from imprisonment under the act for the relief of Insolvent Debtors: hearing on Apr 29 next. –Wm brent, clk [Smith<u>a</u> as copied.]

Mrd: on Apr 18, by Rev Mr Matthews, Wm E Stubss to Catharine Anne, d/o John Boyle, all of Wash City. [Stub<u>ss</u> as copied.]

Died: on Apr 20, Mrs Mgt King, aged 34 years. Her funeral is this afternoon, at 3 p m, at her late residence on 6th st, between G & H sts. Members of the Female Sodality, of which she was a member, are requested to meet at St Matthew's church on Sunday, to say the Ofc of the Dead.

Died: at her residence, Morgantown, Va, Mrs Sarah, consort of Dr O'Kelly, of consumption, leaving a husband & 4 children, & a large family connexion to mourn her untimely loss. [No date-current item.]

Wm C Orme having made an assignment to the subscriber of all his stock in trade, book accounts, & other debts, for all his creditors equally, his stock of goods will be offered for sale at his store in a few days. Those indebted are to make payment to J B H Smith, an atty for the trustee. –John N Brown, trustee

Circuit Superior Court of Law & Chancery for Fauquier Co, Va. The Bank of the U S in Pennsylvania, vs, John B Steenberger & others. Cmplnt & dfndnt are notified that May 22 next, at the ofc of Saml D King, a J P in Wash City, on F st-on May 25, at the Union Bank of Md, Balt City-& on May 29, at the ofc of J Brice Smith, atty at law, Wall st, N Y, I shall take the depositions of sundry witnesses, to be offered in evidence on my behalf, as a petitioning creditor of said John B Steenberger, in said cause. –W W Corcoran -J M Mason, Counsel

Capt Leighton, of the brig **Abigail Richmond**, who arrived at Wilmington N C, on Apr 15, from St Thomas, informs that before he left there intelligence was received that Capt Cozzens, of the brig **Pilgrim**, of Balt, had been tried in Guadaloupe on the charge of robbing a house at Point Petre of $40,000 at the time of the earthquake there, convicted, & sentenced to 10 years' labor in the galleys in France, whither he was to be sent. The sentence would have been much severer, but that he had rendered good service to some of the inhabitants in their distress caused by the earthquake. Capt Cozzens belongs to the State of Maine.

Household & kitchen furniture at auction at the Navy Yard, this day, at 12 o'clock, at the residence of Mr M R Shyne, on L st. –R W Dyer & Co, aucts

MON APR 24, 1843
Circuit Court of Wash Co, D C. Louisa Ballard, a bankrupt, has filed her ptn for her discharge & certificate: hearing on the first Mon in Jul next. –W Brent, clk

The Friends of the American Colonization Society met on Apr 17 in Rev Mr Berry's Church, Gtwn.
Franklin Knight appointed agent in the plan to raise $20,000 by subscriptions to enable the Society to obtain entire authority over the whole line of the African coast, from Cape Mount to Cape Palmas; when Mr Gurley, the Sec of the Soc, explained the present condition, wants, & prospects. Cmte appointed:

Rev Mr Steel	Anthony Hyde	Thos Jewell
W G Ridgely	Edw Myers	Thos Brown

-Jas McVean, Chairman -J H Offley, Sec

Great fire in Newbern, N C, on Apr 18, which destroyed at least 100 bldgs. It originated in the saw-mill of Mr John Blackwell. No other particulars are given. [Apr 27th newspaper: Many lost all the property they possessed. Many were turned out of doors. All contributions to be directed to Wm G Bryan, Postmaster.]

The question of removing the seat of Gov't of Canada from Kingston to Montreal has been set to rest by Sir Chas Metcalfe, the new Govn'r, who states explicitly that he has no instructions to remove it.

Ruliff Voorrees, a wealthy farmer of North Branch, Somerset Co, N J, went out on Wed for the purpose of hunting game. He was found soon after a corpse, having shot himself. He was about 50 years of age, & has left a highly respectable family.

Mr A F Judlin, upholster, South Calvert st, recently received from Paris a letter conveying the intelligence that by the will of a relative lately dec'd there was now on deposite in the Bank of France, subject to his order, the snug sum of L25,000 sterling, or $100,000. Mr Judlin, we learn, has taken departure for France to assume possession of the cash. --Balt Sun

The brig **Statira** & the brig **Samson** arrived at New Orleans on Apr 12, from Port Leon, Fla, having on board companies A, B, G, H, & I, of the 3rd regt of U S Infty. Their destination is Jefferson Barracks. The following are the ofcrs: Maj Wm W Lear, in command; Capt Cotton & Capt Wheeler; Lts Gordon, Johns, Bowman, Dobbins, Richardson, Brooks, & Sikes. Non-commissioned ofcrs & privates, 258.

Nelsonian Reminiscences, by Lt G S Parsons, R N. Just published & for sale at Morrison's Bookstore.

On Thu an attempt was made to enter the sore of Mr John E Rigden, in Hanover st. The door into the basement story was bored with an augur in several places, so as to make a hold large enough for a man's arn; but, we presume, becoming alarmed, they made off without affecting an entrance into the store.

Fire on Thu night proceeded from a wooden stable belonging to Mr Emmert, the confectioner, whose house is on Bridge st. The bldg & its contents were destroyed.

Wash Corp: 1-Act for the relief of John Brady: That the fine imposed on John Brady by judgment of Jas Marshall, for a violation of the ordinance in relation to dogs, be, & the same is remitted; provided the said Brady pay the costs of prosecution.

On Apr 16, the body of a seaman, named Crocker, belonging to the Navy Yard, was found near Benning's bridge, in the Eastern Branch. He had been missing since Jan.

TUE APR 25, 1843
$100 reward for runaway my negro man Chas Brown, 33 years old, about 5 feet & 10 inches: rough carpenter by trade. He has a wife in Port Tobacco. –Edmund I Plowden, near Chaptico, St Mary's Co, Md.

Mr Atty Gen Legare is at present on a visit to his residence in Charleston, S C.

Wayne Co [N Y] Whig states that on Wed week Horace Riffort stabbed his brother in the abdomen & it caused his death on the Fri succeeding. Horace was beating his wife, when his brother interfered in her behalf; a scuffle ensued, which was terminated by the fatal stab. Rum was the prime cause.

R E Hornor, Postmaster of Princeton, [a suspected Clay Whig,] is superseded by the appointment of Dr A J Berry, [Tyler.] Dr B has not been a citizen of the place more than 2 years. –Newark Advertiser

Mrd: on Mar 22, by Rev Walker Timberlake, Wm Tompkins, [formerly Editor of the Charlottesville [Va] Advocate,] to Miss Eliz H, d/o Christopher Clarke, all of Flavanna Co, Va.

Mrd: on Apr 24, by Rev Mr Stringfellow, Wm Fuller, of Augusta Ga, to Miss Susan T, d/o Capt F Black, of Wash City.

Died: yesterday, after a long illness, at his residence in Gtwn, Leonard Mackall, of the Treas Dept, in his 76th year. Mr Mackall was one of the oldest & most esteemed citizens of Gtwn, illustrated in an emiment degree by his life the duties of a citizen & Christian. Funeral from his late residence at 4 p m today.

Sale of pews in St John's Church, Gtwn: rates ranging from $40 to $125. Cmte:
W G Ridgely   A H Marbury   P G Washington

For rent: 2 story brick house, one on the corner of I & 18th sts. Inquire of Robt Cruit, at his Butter Store, on F st, between 14th & 15th sts, where families can be supplied with good Butter at all times.

Proposing to employ a competent Female Teacher for the education of our younger dghts, we would receive into our family, if early application be made, 3 or 4 girls not exceeding 12 years of age. The terms will be moderate. –R Y Brent, Highlands, Montg Co, Md

For rent: a large 3 story house on Pa ave, between 3rd & 4½ sts, adjoining Polk's Boarding house. Inquire of John Sinon.

Chas Co Court, sitting as a Court of Equity. Mar Term, 1843. Ratify sale by Peter W Crain, trustee, for the sale of the real estate of Aladdin Campbell, dec'd. –C Dorsey -John Barnes, clk of Chas Co [Md] Court

Chas Co Court, sitting as a Court of Equity. Mar Term, 1843. Ratify sale by Peter W Crain & Geo W Matthew, trustees for the sale of the real estate of Benedict Jameson, dec'd. –Clem Dorsey -John Barnes, clk of Chas Co [Md] Court

Obit: Leonardtown, Md, Apr 21, 1843. About 2½ months ago we witnessed the interment of Miss Sally Leigh, the eldest d/o her parents, who had departed after a lingering illness of several months. About 6 weeks after we were summoned to the same spot to perform the last sad offices to the mortal remains of her mother, Mrs Sophia L Leigh, the d/o the Hon John Leeds Kerr, whose departure hence, it may be said, was a victory over the grave, for her life had plucked the sting from the arrow of death. The tears for the sister, mother, & father may be said to form a continued stream, for within one month from the departure of his beloved wife, Geo S Leigh has been called to join her. He died on Apr 15 after a protracted illness of several months. At various times within the last 20 years he has been the rep of his county in the Leg & the Electoral College.

Fire near Pittsburg on Mon destroyed a Bucket factory belonging to Mr Bugher; a Salaeratus factory, owned by Mr Isaiah Dickey, & a number of frame dwlgs. Loss is estimated at $8,000.

WED APR 26, 1843
A destructive fire occurred at Maysville, Ky, on Apr 18, in the livery stable of Otho H Davis, which spread to houses belonging to Messrs Henry & Peter Lee, & occupied by Messrs Cutter & Gray, grocers, Messrs Collins & Brown as a printing ofc of the Maysville Eagle, Jos Frank, tinner, & Richd H Lee, cotton store.

Lt J I Boyle, U S Navy, of whom it was reported that he had been shot by Commandant Voorhees, arrived at N Y on Sat, from Bremen, in excellent health. We are pleased to learn that no difficulty has ever existed between the 2 ofcrs named. –Balt Am

The List of the Caesars. We announce today the death of Mr Chas Augustus Caesar, of Cambridge, at age 80 years. He was the last male descendant from Sir Julius Caesar, Knight, who was Judge of the Admiralty, Master of the Rolls, Chancellor of the Exechequer, & a Privy Councillor in the reign of James & Charles I. The family was of Italian origin, & its ancestors, under the surname of Adelmare, had been long seated in the city of Treviso, 12 miles from Venice, in the rank of nobility, according to the usual meaning of that designation on the continent. Of these, Peter Maria Adelmare, of that city, a doctor of both laws, flourished towards the end of the 15th century. He mrd Paola, the dght & coheiress of John de Paola Caesarino. The 2nd s/o this marriage, Caesar Adelmare, came over to England in 1550, & eventually appointed physician to Queen Mary. Dr Adelmare mrd Mgt, d/o Martin Perin, or Perient, Treas in Ireland, & had by her 5 sons & 3 dghts, the eldest of the former being the Sir Julius Caesar, of whom we have already spoken, who was born at Tottenham in 1557, died Apr 18, 1636, & was buried at St Helen's, Bishopsgate st, London. –Cambridge Chron

Louisville Journal: the trial of Godfrey Pope, charged with the murder of Leonard Bliss, jr, has resulted in a verdict of not guilty.

Mr W A Smith, believed to be from Norfolk, Va, was lately found dead on the river bank near Augusta, Ga, under what circumstances the paper before us does not state. He was decently interred, & his trunk & other property placed in responsible hands.

A tavern kept by Mr Blanchard, in Lombard st, Balt, was destroyed by fire last Mon, under circumstances which leave little doubt that it was the work of incendiaries. Mr Blanchard & his wife had to escape through an upper window; the bar was robbed of about $40; 2 men taken in as lodgers the night before are missing. These men said they were from Washington.

The Oldest Man of Modern Times. It is stated in a foreign paper that the celebrated Thos Parr was born in the reign of Henry IV. He was taken to London by Lord Arundel, in 1645, & introduced to Charles II;   & he died the same year- contributed to his drinking wine, which his constitution was not accustomed to; he died at age 152. One of old Parr's sons died at age 109. A grandson died aged 113; & Robt Parr, great grandson to old Tom, died at Bridgnorth on Sep 21, 1757, aged 127. peculiar trait in the character of these 4 generations of Parrs was their temperate habits, amounting almost to total abstinence.

A rencoutre in Lincoln Co, Ky, a few days since, between Edmund Leach & B A McKenzie, in which the former was shot through the heart & expired immediately.

Dr T A Doniphan caught at one haul in the Potomac, a few days ago, 70 Bass Rock, weighing from 70 to 90 pounds each, in the whole, more than 5,000 pounds weight!

Mrd: on Apr 25, by Rev R T Berry, Capt Saml Purcell, of Loudoun Co, Va, to Miss Eliz Steptoe, d/o Col Nicholas Osburn, of Gtwn, D C.

Died: yesterday, after a brief illness, at her residence on the Heights of Gtwn, Mrs Mary Grayson. Her funeral is this afternoon, at 4 o'clock, from the residence of her brother-in-law, Col John Cox, Mayor of Gtwn.

To Brick-Masons & Carpenters. Those persons intending to put in proposals for the rebuilding of the National Livery Stables, on C st, will please do so by Apr 28, as on that day contracts will be closed. -Walker & Kimmell

THU APR 27, 1843
Cmte on Indian affairs, to whom was submitted a communication from the Sec of War, recommending that a pension be granted to Milly, an Indian woman of the Creek nation: the accompanying statement of Lt Col Hitchcock, as well as from the published history of the period, that, in 1818, during the Indian war in the South, Milly saved the life of an American citizen, who had been taken prisoner by several warriors of her tribe, & who was about to be put to death by them. [The act revives the recollection of the rescue of Capt Smith by the d/o Powhatan, the celebrated Pocahontas.] Milly is the d/o the Prophet Francis, a Creek chief, who acquired a melancholy celebrity from his execution by order of Gen Jackson during the Indian war of 1817, 1818. At the time of her action, she was under 16 years of age, her nation was at war with the U S, & her father a most decided enemy of the white people. The condition on which his life was finally spared was, that he would shave his head after the Indian fashion, & adopt their dress & manner of living. To this he assented. Some time afterwards the white man sought his benefactress in marriage, but she declined, & subsequently married one of her own people. Her husband is now dead. Her father was put to death in the war of 1817, 1818, & her mother & sister have since died. She has 3 children, a boy & 2 girls, all too young to provide for themselves. The Sec of War recommends that a pension of $8 per month be allowed her during the remainder of her life. The power of the Gov't to confer such bounties has been frequently exercised. In 1824, Congress passed an act granting to Gen Lafayette & his heirs $200,000 & a township of land. In 1834, an act was passed granting to 235 Polish exiles, transported to the U S by order of the Emperor of Austria, 36 sections of land, within the limits of the State of Ill or the Terr of Michigan. The cmte report a bill allowing her a pension of $96 per annum during her lifetime.
+
War Dept, Wash, Apr 16, 1842: letter from J C Spencer to the Hon Jas Cooper, Chrmn of the Cmte on Indian Affairs. I have the honor to transmit a report of Lt Col Hitchcock, in the case of Milly, etc. It may be an inducement to preserve the lives of those captured by hostile Indians, & be the means of mitigating, to a great degree, the barbarous cruelty of savage warfare. –J C Spencer
+
Washington, Apr 13, 1842. Letter from E A Hitchcock, Lt Col 3rd Infty, to the Hon J C Spencer, Sec of War. He spoke to Milly who is now about 40 years of age: she had 8 children, & 3 are living. A small pension, [$50 or $75 a year,] with a clear exposition of the grounds of its allowance, may have a salutary influence upon savage customs in future times. It is probable she will not be able to recover possession of some negro property, now held by the Seminoles, belonging to her.

The story of Milly Francis is recorded in a volume entitled Indian Wars, in which there is a picture representing the preparations for putting the white man to death, while the Indian girl is represented as pleading for his life to her father. –E A Hitchcock

A Coroner's inquest was held in N Y on the body of a 2 year old child, Bridget Greenan, who bit off the phosphorus on the end of matches & swallowed it. After severe vomiting she died on Sat.

Mr Rufus Welch, of the Olympic Circus, is about to sail from N Y for Leghorn.

Accidents: in Brooklyn, N Y, on Fri, Alex'r Williams, aged 5 years, while visitng the Governess of the Orphan Asylum, his aunt, went to the roof to play & fell through the skylight, injuring himself so badly that he died 14 hours later. On the same day, the 7 year old s/o Mr John Keese, while on board a steamboat at the South Ferry, fell into the river & drowned. Two children were burned to death at Sidney, Upper Canada, on Apr 4, by the destruction of their father's, Saml Bush, dwlg. Edw Taylor, from the Great Western Iron Works, was upset in a skiff & downed in the Alleghany river on Mon. Body not yet found.

Are you the man of the house, inquired a stranger of a citizen one day. No, but my wife is, was the subdued response.

The subscriber wishes to engage a Governess to teach the higher branches of an English education. The number of pupils will be 6 or 7. Apply to Robt Ghiselin, near Nottingham, PG Co, Md.

Appointment in the N Y State Gov't: Michl Hoffman, sometimes called the Admiral, formerly a leading member of the Van Buren party in Congress, to be Agent of the State Prison at Sing Sing–a really important appointment, we suppose, but it sounds oddly as a promotion.

Adam Horn, the man who is suspected of having murdered his wife, a short time since, in Balt Co, Md, has been arrested in Phil. It has come to light that Horn murdered a former wife in 1840, in Logan Co, Ohio, where he was known by the name of Andrew Hellman. [Nov 29 newspaper: trial at Balt was brought to a close on Mon: verdict against the prisoner of murder in the first degree.]

Mrs Polly Cornell, of Hanover, Chautauque Co, N Y, committed suicide a few days since by cutting her throat with a razor. She was about 25 years of age & for some time had been afflicted with a very depressing melancholy.

Very handsome & fashionable furniture at public auction: on May 2, at the residence of Capt J G Williams, on F st, between 12th & 13th sts: all his household furniture. –Robt W Dyer & Co, aucts

Mrd: at Petersburg, Va, by Rev Mr Baily, Mr Henry Hammett, formerly of Gtwn, D C, to Miss Mary A Robinson, of Greensville Co, Va. [No date-current item.]

Mrd: on Apr 25, by Rev Mr Edwards, Mr John Lang, of Gtwn, to Miss Anna E Vonsson, of the same place.

Died: on Apr 7, at Little Rock, Ark, after a painful illness, Wm Cummins, in his 43rd year. Mr Cummins was a native of Jefferson Co, Ky, & emigrated to Arkansas about 18 years ago, where he acquired a high character at the bar & in society.

Died: on Mar 29 last, at his residence in York Co, Va, Dr Fred'k B Power, in his 50th year, after a lingering & painful illness.

FRI APR 28, 1843

English papers brought by the steamer **Britania**: London Examiner of Mar 25: Robt Southey, poet & scholar, has been released from suffering, which for more than 2 years has been a matter of the deepest sympathy, anxiety, & sorrow. He died at Gretna House on Mar 22, in his 69th year. Few men have written so much & written so well. [This is followed by a poem "On the Death of Southey," by Walter Savage Lander.]

Abstract from a N Y Correspondent. Further note on Robt Southey: Caroline Bowles, a literary female toady in his family, the most sycophantic & injurious, married Southey after he had become imbecile, & it is not surprising that after a life of toadyism, she, should fancy that she had acquired, the better half of Southey's glory & position.

Chas Bates & Morris K Whitlock, 16 & 18 years of age, were drowned on Apr 17 in a small pond near the village of Ridgefield, Conn, while out on a gunning excursion.

Americans in Paris have been spoken of in the London paper: the Globe of Apr 7 says: "Madame Tudor, an American lady, is noted for the immense crowds that she assembles in her saloons. Her fetes, indeed, are called assemblages of the whole world, or the world condensed, for there is scarcely a nation in any of the four quarters of the globe that is not represented in the mansions of this wealthy lady."

Saml Tenney, Vice Pres of the Merchants' Ins Co of Boston, had both bones of his right leg broken below the knee, on Sat. He was hastily passing a truck which was unloading bales of compressed cotton, when one of the bales struck him in the leg, throwning him down, & thus causing the injury.

The new Gov't of Hayti has been established under Gen Herard, who made a triumphant entry into Port-au-Prince on the 21st, at the head of the revolutionary army, to the number of 15,000. Pres Boyer, Inginac, & the old ofcrs were all deposed by proclamation for treason. Col Touro, who commanded the arsenal, had threatened to blow it up before he would surrender. He kept the town in a state of alarm for 2 days, & more than half of the inhabitants deserted the town. On the second day, Touro seated himself in the magazine with powder strewed all around him & applied the match. He blew himself up because he could not brook the idea of giving himself up.

Circuit Court of Wash Co, D C. Wm B Guy has applied to be discharged from imprisonment under the act for the relief of Insolvent Debtors: hearing on the 3rd Mon in May next. –Wm Brent, clk

Col Jas R Cook was recently killed by a man named Adkins. Adkins is dangerously wounded. They had been drinking together when they came to blows respecting a horse. The disgraceful practice of wearing murderous weapons is universal in Texas. By standers did not try to arrest the quarrel.

Mrd: on Apr 25, by Rev W B Edwards, Mr A J Duvall to Miss Eliza Brown, d/o Mr John Brown, all of Wash City.

Mrd: on Apr 27, by Rev W B Edwards, of Wash City, Henry Ashton Garrett to Miss Mary Ann Boswell, both of Montg Co, Md.

Wash Corp: 1-Ptn of H Creutsfeldt, praying the remission of a fine: referred to the Cmte of Claims. 2-Ptn of Jacob Syfferly, John P Stallings, & others, to set curbstone & footway on south side of sq 487: passed.

SAT APR 29, 1843
Household furniture at auction on May 1 on Pa ave, between 9th & 10th sts, adjoining Mr McGrath's Tavern, a small but first-rate lot of furniture. –Wm Marshall, auct

It is with deep sorrow we have heard of the death of John M Garnett, of Essex, a most estimable man. The Commonwealth of Va contained within it limits no nobler spirit. He was an old school gentleman-a patriot of that day when selfishness did not enter into the composition of patriotism. –Richmond Whig of yesterday

A Nothern newspaper requests information of Thos Gross, who, in 1798 was a seaman on board the brig **Mary**, of N Y, & in 1809 commanded the ship **Iris**, of Balt. If he is now living, or if he has a widow or children now living, they may be put in a way of learning something of their advantage from England, by addressing a letter [postpaid] to Wm Hyde, bookseller, Portland, Maine, giving their place of residence, & their present condition & circumstances.

Mobile papers: Judge A Hutchinson, Wm E Jones, & Saml A Maverick, who were taken prisoners in San Antonio, Texas, in Nov last by the Mexicans, arrived at Mobile on Apr 20: released through our Minister at Mexico, Gen W Thompson, & were brought from Vera Cruz to Pensacola in the U S ship **Vincennes**. Information was also received that Geo Van Ness, C Peterson, L Colquhoun, John Bradley, & Jas Trueheart had also been released, at the instance of Gen Thompson & friends in this country.

Orphans Crt of Chas Co, Md: public sale on May 17 at the late residence of Alexius Boarman, late of said county, dec'd: 12 or 13 likely young negroes, among whom are 2 carpenters; 4 head of horses, 2 yoke of oxen, several cows, all the sheep & hogs belonging to the dec'd; also all his furniture. –Wm Queen, Wm Jameson, adms of Alexius Boarman

Judge Parke, a worthy old citizen of 72 years, who was recently removed from the Paterson [N J] Post Ofc without just cause, died at his residence in that place on Mon, after a brief illness, induced, it is believed, by the ruthless treatment of men from whom he had a right to expect better things. –Neward Daily Adver

The Goddard estate was recently sold at auction for $92,000, to a citizen of Boston who commenced business as a tailor, & for a long time kept what is called a "slop shop" in Ann st. –Boston Bulletin

Mrd: on Apr 27, by Rev Dr Hawley, Saml Phillips Lee, Lt U S N, to Eliz, d/o Francis P Blair, of Wash.

Died: on Apr 18, at her residence in Wash City, Mrs Mgt Aukward, relict of Henry Aukward, dec'd, aged 46 years.

Died: on Apr 27, Minor, infant s/o Jos H & Martha Waring, aged 8 months.

Died: on Apr 21, in the vicinity of Fayettsville, N C, Mr John Lumsden, aged about 85. He was a sldr of the glorious Revolutionn, & retained through his life those stanch Whig principles which prompted him to his country's standard in that day of trial. His services, his patriotism, & integrity obtained for him many years [until age & infirmity incapacitated him] the ofc of Principal Doorkeeper to the Leg of N C.

Rev Thos M Flint will hold Divine service in the Methodist Protestant Church, near the Navy Yard, every Sabbath.

Wash Jr Artillerists meeting on May 1 at 8 o'clock, in full summer uniform, for parade. By order of Capt F H Williams. —J E Buckingham, O S

Orphan's Court of Wash Co, D C. Letters of administration on the personal estate of Danl Brent, late of said county, dec'd. -J C Brent, exc

Circuit Court of Wash Co, D C. Cranstoun Laurie, a bankrupt, has filed his ptn for his discharge & certificate: hearing on the first Mon in Aug next. —W Brent, clk

The steamboat **Harry of the West**, on her way from New Orleans to St Louis, met with a sad disaster on Apr 19, about 3 miles above Commerce, when the boilers exploded. P B Sherwin, of N Y, was injured; A Fitzgerald, & the mate of the boat, was injured; Mr J Smith, of Yazoo, Miss, is among the missing. The steamer was a new boat, except her boilers, & one of the largest & most magnificent that ever left the Cincinnati ship yard.

MON MAY 1, 1843
Mr C Field, of the New Orleans Picayune, has joined the expedition which is about to leave St Louis for the Rocky Mountains under the auspices of Sir Wm Drummond Stewart & Mr Audubon.

J H Gibbs, Ornamental Hair & Fancy Store, Pa ave, between 8th 9th sts: assortment of Gimps, Fringe, & Buttons. Also, every variety of Fans & Sunshades. [Alex Gaz]

Circuit Court of Wash Co, D C. Chas F Buxenstein has applied to be discharged from imprisonment under the act for the relief of Insolvent Debtors: hearing on May 18 next. —Wm Brent, clk

Francis McClure, an old & respected citizen of Pa died at his residence in Mifflin township on Sunday last, at the advanced age of nearly 104 years. He was formerly for nearly 30 years an associate judge of the Court of Common Pleas for Alleghany County.

Middleton, Conn has elected a Whig Mayor, Chas R Alsop, in place of Noah A Phelps, the new Loco Sec of State.

The Court Martial at Governor's Island for the trial of Maj Payne, on charges preferred by Gen Wool, met again on Tue, but for want of a quorum, occasioned by a disagreement among some of the ofcrs, adjourned to meet again yesterday. In the mean time the difficulty has been referred to Pres Tyler for decision.

Govn'r Cleveland, of Conn, was upset while riding in a wagon on Tue, & fell so hard on a heap of stones as to break his knee-pan.

Col R M Johnson, ex-Vice Pres of the U S, reached New Orleans on Apr 20, on a visit to his friends there.

Mrd: on Apr 25, in Gtwn, by Rev R T Berry, Dr E Boyd Pendleton, of Martinsburg, Va, to Maria Lucinda, y/d/o the late Col Chas Pendleton Tutt.

A son of Henry S Richards, who resides about a mile north of Poughkeepsie, N Y, was drowned on Sat. He went in a small sailboat with an older brother, & it suddenly capsized by a flaw, while yet near the shore.

K J Rypma, Prof of the Piano, announces to the Ladies of Washington, that he is now prepared to give lessons on the Piano. He will attend to the tuning of Pianos as based upon the calculations of Chladni & Scheibler, being founded upon the mathematical principles of acoustics. Orders left at Mr Geo Savage's Store, Pa ave, or directed to the subscriber, at Mr R H Harrington's, Capitol Hill. –K J Rypma

Circuit Court of Wash Co, D C-in Chancery. Frances F Cook vs Caroline L Cook & others. Jas Owner, jr, trustee appt'd by the Court, has sold lots #1 & #44 in sq 732 with the bldgs thereon, & that Frances F Cook, the cmplnt, became the purchaser thereof, for the sum of $1,750: ordered that the same be ratified & confirmed by the Court. –W Brent, clk

Circuit Court of Wash Co, D C engaged for several days in the trial of Cassedy vs William. Outline: Mr Williams purchased on Oct 9, 1840, a negro boy of Mr Cassedy, of Leesburg, Va, for $550, & paid the amount in Millington money. In a few days the Millington Bank exploded, & its paper became utterly worthless. It was contended by the plntf's counsel that the institution originated in the grossest fraud, & that the dfndnt had good reason to know of the insolvency of the bank at the time of the payment of the money. It was contended by the dfndnt's counsel that the money circulated as current money for several days later than Oct 9; that the dfndnt was ignorant of the condition of the bank, & paid the money to the plntf in good faith. The jury found for the plntf.

TUE MAY 2, 1843
The Exchange Hotel, Balt, a beautiful house, having undergone a thorough renovation, was re-opened a few weeks ago by Mr Erastus Coleman, of Boston.

For rent, brick house which has been my residence more than 6 years past. It is on Washington st, at the foot of the heights of Gtwn, D C, near the residences of Col Carter & Col Washington, in an agreeable neighborhood. –W H S Taylor

For sale, a very handome Phaeton, intended for 1 or 2 horses, the property of a private gentleman. As good as new. It may be seen at McDermot's Carriage Repository, corner of 3rd & Pa ave.

For rent: large 3 story boarding house at present occupied by Mrs Adams, & formerly by Mr Jos Wimsatt, on Pa ave, between 3rd & 4½ st. Also, the house at present occupied by me, on Missouri ave, between 4½ & 6th sts. For further particulars inquire of the subscriber, at his Woodyard on 6th st. –Geo Mattingly

The London [Canada West] Inquirer: on Apr 16, the Rev Richd Flood, worthy clergyman of Delaware, & 17 other gentlemen of the congregation, were returning from divine service in crossing the river in a small scew, adjacent to the site where the bridge had been swept away, the temporary convenience was hurried down the stream until it came in contact with a jutting-out tree. The whole party clung to the tree & remained there 4 hours, until a canoe could be obtained from the village of Kilworth. Four of them were chilled through & perished in view of their companions & spectators on shore, who could render them no assistance. Those who perished were: Maj Somers, Jas Rawlings, Geo Robinson, & Wm Edmonds, all natives of England.

Whig Members of the Leg of N Y:

Andrew B Dickinson	Anson Bigelow	Jas W Porter
Abram Dixon	Wells Brooks	Elijah A Rice
Gideon Hard	Jas C Brown	Pelatiah Richards
Jas G Hopkins	Jedediah Dewey, jr	Saml Russell
Nehemiah Platt	Danl H Fitzhugh	Saml Shumway
Harvey Putnam	Thos T Flagler	John I Slingerland
Elijah Rhoades	Robt Flint	Robinson Smiley
Erastus Root	Jerome Fuller	Robt Smith
Saml Works	Robt Haight	Danl d Spencer
Sylvester Austin	Willis Hall	Enoch Strong
Geo R Babcock	Alonzo Hawley	John Sweeney
Elezazar Baldwin	Jos H Jackson	Aaron Van Schaack
Eldridge G Baldwin	Harry McGraw	Ira Wait
Odin Benedict	Milton McNeal	Emory F Warren
Truman Benedict	Adolphus F Morrison	Elisha Wright

Died: on Apr 30, at the residence of her grandfather, in Wash City, near the Navy Yard, after a long & painful illness, Miss Julia A V Blakeslee, aged 16 years, 5 months & 9 days.

Meeting of the Medical Dept of the Nat'l Institute at the Patent Ofc on May 2. –Marcus C Buck, sec

Valuable property for sale: lot #10 in sq 407, fronting 50 feet on E st. Located in the neighborhood of the Gen Post Ofc. Inquire of A Rothwell.

Improved Fairfax land for sale. Wishing to remove nearer to Washington, the subscriber offers for sale or exchange the highly desirable property on which he resides, & which has recently undergone extensive repairs & improvements. It is in Fairfax Co, Va: 244 acs: bldgs are extensive. –A B Fairfax

Orphan's Court of Wash Co, D C. Letters of adm, with the will annexed, on the personal estate of Wm Worthington, late of said county, dec'd.
–Harriet Worthington, excx W A

WED MAY 3, 1843
Assoc of American Geologists & Natural Historians: meeting at Albany: Prof Henry D Rogers as Pres & Benj Silliman, jr, appointed Sec. Men of science in attendance: Mon Nicollet, Prof Emmons, Prof Vanuxem, Prof Dana, Prof Beck, Dr Houghton Dr Owen, Mr Emerson, Mr Haldeman, & Mr Hall. On Thu, a number of new members were elected into the Association. List of those already in attendance:
Scientific Assoc: Convention at Albany, Apr 26, 1843.
Names of attending members & residence when at home:

Wm C Redfield, N Y C	J N Nicollet, Balt
John Gebbard, jr, Schoharie, N Y	MattheW H Webster, Albany
Lewis C Beck, Brunswick, N Y	Giles F Yates, Schenectady, N Y
Henry D Rogers, Phil	Jas Hall, Albany
Geo B Emerson, Boston	Ebenezer Emmons, Albany
Lardner Vanuxem, Bristol, Pa	Jas Eights, Albany
A Osborn, Herkimer Co, N Y	Jas P Espy, Wash, D C
Oliver Smith, N Y, of Mechanics'Ins	Franklin Everett, Canajoharie, N Y
Edw Lascelle, Williams College, Mass	E N Horsford, Albany, N Y
Simon Z Haven, Utica, N Y	Ebenezer Emmons, jr, Albany, N Y
J W Baily, West Point, N Y	Benj Silliman, jr, New Haven, Conn
D D Owen, New Harmony, Pa	Geo S Weaver, Cambridgeport, Vt
S S Haldeman, Columbia, Pa	John L Hayes, Portsmouth, N H
E S Carr, Castleton, Vt	Chas T Jackson, M D, Boston, Mass
John H Redfield, N Y C	Lyman Wilder, Hoosick Falls, Rens
Douglass Houghton, Detroit, Mich	Co, N Y

The Mr Shuster suspected of robbing the Balt Cathedral, is *not* the son-in-law of Mrs Pawley. Shuster, we are now told, is a single man.

A man named Whitmore drowned in the Potomac on Sun last. His dead body was found next morning.

Phil papers announce the death of the wealthiest inhabitant of that city. Mr Jacob Ridgway, who, since the decease of Stephen Girard, has been regarded as the wealthiest citizen of Phil, departed this life on Sun at his residence in Chestnut st, opposite Independence Hall, in his 75th year. He had been ill for some days, & was attended in his last hours by several of our most eminent physicians. Mr Ridgway was knocked down in the street a few weeks ago by a horse & vehicle, & was indisposed from the time of the accident. He was a self-made man, & died worth about $6,000,000 in property of various kinds. In early life he was a ship-carpenter; subsequently American Counsul at Antwerp, during the critical period of the last European war. His immediate heirs are a son, Mr John Ridgway, & 2 dghts, Mrs Dr Rush & Mrs Roatch. The latter is a widow, & neither of the dghts have children.

Great fire at Wilmington, N C on Apr 30: at least 200 bldgs, we think, of every kind, are destroyed: the old warehouse known as McKay's; the dwlgs of Mrs Robeson, Mr Anderson, & Mr Calder; all the Railroad Depot bldgs; & numerous other bldgs.

Died: on Mon, at his residence on the Heights of Gtwn, Henry J Grayson, aged about 30 years, only child of the late Mrs Mary Grayson, & grandson of the late John Threlkeld. Only 3 weeks since mother & son were in the enjoyment of high health, & gave every promise of a long life. A violent desease, originating in cold, first prostrated the son, & whilst he lingered under its attack, the fatigues & anxieties of his devoted mother hurried her to the grave a week ago, after an indisposition of only 2 or 3 days; & there is every reason to suppose that distress of mind at this loss has contributed to the end of the son. They will be widely recognized as much esteemed members of one of our most ancient & honorable families, & especially identified with the history of our town through their ancestor, [Mr Threlkeld,] who was one of its founders. His funeral will be from his late residence, at 4 o'clock this afternoon.

By virtue of a writ of fieri facias, issued by John D Clark, a J P in & for Wash Co, D C, at the suit of Peter Callan, against the goods & chattels, lands & tenements of Nicholas Harper, dec'd, which are [or were] in the possession of Patrick Tracy, exc of said Nicholas Harper, dec'd, to me directed, I have seized & taken in execution all the estate, right, title, interest, property, claim, & demand at law & in equity of the said Nicholas Harper, dec'd, & of the said exc, Patrick Tracy, in & to one chest & its contents; shall offer the same for sale to the highest bidder by public auction, for cash on May 9. –S Moore, constable

Dying Establishment, south side of Pa ave, between 4½ & 3rd st. -F Cudlipp

THU MAY 4, 1843
Appointments by the Pres: J F Cox, Henry Naylor, Joshua Pierce, Chas R Belt, Lewis Carbery, John Cox, & Robt White, to be members of the Levy Court for Wash Co, D C. Jesse E Dow & Chas R Belt to be Justices of the Peace for Wash Co, D C.

Furniture Warehouse, corner of B & 7th st. Leonard O Cook grateful for the patronage of his friends & public prior to the calamity [fire] which totally befell him at his old establishment on D st, between 8th & 9th sts. I have also 2 furniture cars for hire. Those in want can have their furniture hauled with cars, as I have 2 careful drivers. –Leonard O Cook

Sawing & Turning establishment on the corner of 7th & B sts, opposite Shepherd's Lumber Yard. -B J Tayman &Co

Alexandria Canal Co: Wm Fowle, Pres; Hugh Smith, Phineas Janney, Robt H Miller, Thos E Baird, Robt Jamieson, & G H Smoot, Dirs.

Mutiny on board a Texian sloop of war: sentence of death against 4 men. In the New Orleans papers of the 22nd the result of a Court Martial held on board the ship **Austin**. Landois, Hudgine, Allen, & Simpson undoubtedly expiated their offences yesterday noon at the yardarm of the ship Austin. These men were tried, & no doubt of their participation of the murder of Lt Fuller is entertained by those wwho heard the evidence presented to the Court. The example of their execution will exercise a most beneficial effect in preserving the discipline of the navy of Texas.
1-Fred'k Shepherd, not guilty
Antonio Landois, guilty of all charges & sentenced to suffer death
3-Jas Hudgins, same.
4-Wm Barrington, sentenced to receive 100 lashes on the bare back.
5-Isaac Allen, guilty of the 1st & 3rd charges, & sentenced to suffer death
6-John W Williams, guilty of the 3rd charge, & sentenced to receive 50 lashes, but recommended to mercy.
7-Edw Keenan, guilty of the 3rd charge, & sentenced to receive 100 lashes.
8-Wm Simpson, guilty, & sentenced to suffer death
The sentence of the Court in the case of Midshipman R H Clements will require the action of the Pres of Texas. We sail first for Galveston, when I will sail direct to attack the squadron off the coast of Yucatan.
Yours truly, E W Moore

Mrd: on Tue last, at the Second Presby Church, by Rev Mr Rich, Rev Alonzo Hayes, of Barnstable, Mass, to Miss Malvina A, d/o E Gilman, of Wash Co.

Mrd: May 2, by Rev Chas Rich, Henry Ingle to Rosina Cheshire, all of Wash City.

Mrd: Apr 26, by Rev Mr Brown, Mr Ebenezer Bray to Miss Eliz Powers, both late of PG Co, Md.

Died: on Apr 20, suddenly, at Marlboro, Mrs E Harrison Brookes, w/o Capt John Brookes, & d/o Mrs Sarah C Waring, of PG Co, Md.

Obit-died: on Apr 6, at his residence near New Madrid, Missouri, after a painful illness, Dr Robt W Dawson, in his 52nd year. He was born in Montg Co, Md, & emigrated to this county in 1812, when he engaged in the practice of his profession.

In 1815 he was elected to the Territorial Leg. In 1820 he was chosen a rep to the Convention assembled for the formation of the State Constitution. In 1822 he was elected to the State Senate, to which ofc he was successively elected until 1836. A kind husband, an indulgent father to his family, his loss is irreparable. As a physician, he was kind & attentive. –J K

Circuit Court of Wash Co, D C. David C Davis has applied to be discharged from imprisonment under the act for the relief of Insolvent Debtors: hearing on May 18 next. –Wm Brent, clk

FRI MAY 5, 1843
Excellent chamber furniture at auction on Mon next at the residence of Miss Briscoe, on Missouri st, between 4½ & 6th sts. Also, a very handsome new & superior toned Rosewood Piano Forte, made by Stein, & Piano stool. –R W Dyer & Co, aucts

Newark Daily Adv of May 3. A family of 4 persons, consisting of John Castner, wife, & infant child, & John B Parke, [a brother-in-law,] living at Change Water, near Port Colden, on the Morris Canal, was found barbarously murdered early on Tue, by a neighbor who was passing towards the port. Mr Parke's was an unmarried man of about 60 years of age. A hired boy, age about 15 or 16, was found stabbed in his bed, severely wounded, not knowing how he was hurt. Mr Parke is said to have drawn several thousand dollars from the Belvidere Bank, which was found undisturbed in his closet. Castner's desk was found opened & may have been robbed. Castner was a strong atheletic man about 34 or 40 years of age. [May 8 newspaper: supposed murderers arrested at Hackettstown, N J: tracks led to the house of Chas Coleman, in said town, who with an Englishman, Auble, were arrested. Mr Castner's dght left home the day before the murders on a visit, & being in haste, left her bed unmade, & it is supposed that the murderers seeing what appeared as if a person had just left, went away without searching further for the money.] [May 13th newspaper: Coleman, Auble, & the Englishman, have all been discharged from custody. The boy is recovering & knows the man who struck him. Due to his delicate condition the physicians forbid his being questioned.]

Punishment of death in Vermont. Trial of Eugene Clifford, recently convicted of the murder of his wife at St Albans. It is the judgment of this Court that for the offence you suffer death by hanging, to be executed upon you as soon as may be in due course of law, after the expiration of one year from this 21st day of Apr, 1843; & in the mean time, & until the punishment of death shall be inflicted upon you, you be forthwith committed to solitary confinement in the State prison in Windsor, in Windsor Co.

Rev Eugene Kincaid & lady, of the Baptist mission in Burmah, arrived in N Y on Sunday last, via England, in the ship **Samuel Hicks** from Liverpool. Mr Kincaid has been absent nearly 14 years, & has returned to his native land on account of his health. He has brought with him, besides his 3 children, 2 of the children of the Rev Mr Comstock, of the same mission, who will remain with their relatives in this country. –N Y Tribune

Dissolution of the partnership in the name of J Fugitt & Co, by mutual consent. –Thos Blagden, Jos Fugitt [The Lumber business will hereafter be conducted by Jos Fugitt on his own occount.]

To the press of the District, this week has been added a German Journal: "Deutsche National Zeitung," German National Journal. Edited by Mr Albert Shucking, a European by birth, but familiar by residence with the politics of this country. Mr P Augustus Sage is the publisher & proprietor.

Died: on May 3, at Balt, Mr Anthony Preston, of Wash City. His funeral is this afternoon, at 3 p m, from his late residence on 9th st, opposite the 4th Presby Church.

Died: on May 4, Chas McCarty, a native of the county of Galway, Ireland, in his 35th year. His funeral will be from his late residence on 13½ st, near the Long Bridge, at 4 p m today. The Wash Benevolent Soc are requested to meet at their hall to attend the funeral of their dec'd member.

Died: on May 3, at his residence in the 1st Ward of Wash City, Cary Pratt, in his 85th year, after being confined to his bed from Sep 4 last, the day he drew his pension, to the 3rd inst, [the day of his death;] which long confinement he bore with Christian feeling-scarcely a murmur escaped his lips. Peace be to his ashes.

Wash Benevolent Soc: Philip Ennis, Pres; Jas Handley, 1st V Pres, P H Caton, 2nd V Pres; Jas McCarthy, Sec; Wm Dowling, Treas. $100 donated to the Cholera Hospital & $100 donated to the Female Orphan Asylum, & some smaller donations to other objects.

A free negro, John Smith, was suddenly killed yesterday at Gtwn, while working under a bank in Green st, not far from the C & O Canal. A large body of earth fell upon him & he was almost instantly killed.

An 18 months old child named McClelland, whose parents are from Balt, was burnt to death last Mon at the Navy Yard during the absence of the mother, who had left the child in the care of another dght.

Wash Corp: 1-Ptn from Chauncey Bestor & others in behalf of the Baptist Church: referred. 2-Ptn of Chas Miller & others, remonstrating against the centre range of the new part of the Centre Market being used for the sale of vegetables: referred to the Cmte on Police. 3-Bill for the relief of Wm B Laub: indefinitely postponed. 4-Ptn of Wm E Patterson: read & adopted. 5-Ptn of Alfred Heltmiller: referred to the

Cmte of Claims. 6-Ptn of John C Rives: discharged. 7-Ptn from Henry Walker & others, praying that the vegetable stalls may be removed from the new part of the Centre Market-house to the wings thereof: referred. 8-Ptn of W H Stewart & others, respecting the graduation of K st north: referred to the Cmte on Improvements.

SAT MAY 6, 1843

London Morning Post of the 24th ult: "Notice to all concerned. I. Wm Camack, of Wash City, U S, do hereby, declare that no person in England ever heard me say I was a diplomatic person from the above. I have said, & declare, I am known by all those I have said to any or every man in the Kingdom, & I do say no man in London knows my business to this city; yet, every man may know, if he will read the papers printed in London before I leave: & I hold myself responsible for all I say or do, either to this Gov't or to individuals. –W C N B: All Anonymous letters burnt without reading."

Gideon Brooke has again taken charge of the Periodical Agency at Wash: ofc at the old stand, one door west of Beers' Temperance Hotel, Pa ave, between 3rd & 4½ sts.

U S Marine Corps orders:
Lt Col W H Freeman, on leave of absence, to await further orders at Boston.
2nd Lt J S Devlin ordered to marine barracks, N Y, & as disbursing ofcr for that station, in addition to his duties in the line.
2nd Lt W W Russell, joined at headquarters, & placed on drill.
Capt A N Brevoort, receiving-ship, Norfolk.
Lt Col S Miller, command of marine barracks at N Y, & to take charge of the recruiting service; to reside at Phil.
1st Lt H B Tyler, to the coast of Brazil, as commanding marine ofcr in that squadron.
Capt T A Linton, to command of marine barracks at Gosport, Va.
Capt J G Williams, to command of marine barracks at Pensacola.
–Army & Navy Chronicle

Stuart, the American painter, painted a whole length picture of Washington for the Marquis of Lansdowne. From this a copy was taken, & an engraving made from it by Jas Heath, engraver to the King, from which he realized $60,000, the largest amount probably ever made by one engraving. Mr Stuart did not receive one cent therefrom. –Phil Gaz

Florence [Ala] Gaz gives an account of a destructive fire in that town on Apr 17. The store houses of Chas Gookin, & Scruggs, Savage & Co, were destroyed. The bldgs belonged to Messrs Anderson & Hanna.

John C Kemble, formerly editor of the Troy Budget, & a member of the N Y State Senate, died in the Insane Asylum at Worcester, Mass, on the 14th ult, aged about 50. Mr K was ruined by a connexion with Barstow, defaulting & absconding cashier of the Commericial Bank of Albany. This compelled him to resign his seat in the Senate. He removed to Wisconsin, but his reputation followed him, & a sense of his downfall soon stung him to madness. He has been confined in the Asylum for the past 2 years. -Tribune

Died: on the 25th ult, in Balt, Dr Nathan T H Moore, Assist Surgeon U S Navy. [Dr Moore was on board the U S ship **Concord** at the time she was wrecked, & had but lately returned home.]

MON MAY 8, 1843
Passengers brought by the ship **Hibernia**, Capt Judkins, from Liverpool arrived at Boston on Thu: Col Holloway, Mrs Holloway & 5 children, governess, nurse, & male servant; Mrs Forsyth & dght, Miss Stewart, Miss Seney, Finch, Mr & Mrs Bennett, Miss Ornden, Mr & Mrs Wainwright, Lt Col Slade, Capt Robinson & servant, Mr Lumsden & servant, Lt Tipen & servant, Capt Broughton, Messrs Brand, Oliver, John Oliver Colt, Whiteford, Shaw, J Dilmore, Forsyth, W Colquhoon, John Smith, Allen, John Finch, Brockesby, Thos Curry, Whitehead, Alex'r Brand, John Stewart, Morgan, Chanunard, Bominger, Chas D Lery, N Gorid, McKinnon, Patterson, Frye, Glass, John Laurie, bearing dispatches; J H Van Allen, Greenchilds, Richardson, Hindman, Nimmo, J H M Bartlett, Alexander, Oaky, English, Poston, Koy, D Montrinat, Hilton & 6 sappers, Cam & Mrs Murray, & T Waddell. From Halifax to Boston: Dr Frazer, Miss M Coolidge, Mr Kidston, Miss Shannon, Mrs Cromebee & infant, Mr & Mrs Grasin & 6 children. [The **Hibernia** is larger than the other ships of the Cunard line & is probably more perfect in all her arrangements than any steamship which has yet crossed the Atlantic.]

Jacob Shipman, the absconding messenger, has been arrested at Carlinsville, Macoupin Co, Ill, without resistance. He said he had done nothing wrong & wished to return. He will start for N Y immediately.

Royal R Hinman has presented to the Historical Society of Connecticut a heavy silk Military Sash worn by Gen Richd Montgomery at the time when he unfortunately fell, fighting for American liberty in Canada, during the war of the Revolution.

Died: on May 7, of apoplexy, Mrs Anna H Adams, in her 63rd year. Her funeral will take place this afternoon, at 2 p m, from her late residence, corner of F & 12th sts.

Died: on May 6, Mary Eliza Carbery, aged 8 years, 8 months & 19 days. This amiable, affectionate, & interesting little girl was the last & only child of Capt Thos Carbery, of Wash City. Her funeral will take place this morning at 10 a m.

John S Cone, charged with stealing bank notes out of a letter while carrying the mail, about 6 years ago, & who broke jail some time since, was tried on Wed in the

District Court of the U S at Charleston, S C, was found guilty, & sentenced to 10 years imprisonment.

Public sale of land for Canal scrip: undersigned Trustees for the C & O Canal will offer the following lands in the State of Md, at the Court-house door in Hagerstown, on May 31, these lands being in Wash Co:
1-Island in the Potomac river, opposite *Millstone Point*: about 4 acs.
2-Land lying between the canal & the river, above Hancock, purchased of Geo Brent, about 40 acs.
At the Court-house door in the town of Cumberland, on Jun 2:
3-Land containing from 40 to 50 acs, about a mile & a half below Cumberland, purchased of Eliz Dick.
4-Land, about 18 acs, being part of the *Mine Bank farm*, lying between the canal & river at the *Point of Rocks*.
At the ofc of the Collector of Tolls, in Gtwn, D C, on Jun 8, the following in Montg Co, Md:
5-Island in the Potomac, called *Cupid's Bower*, opposite the 15th section of canal: about 12½ acs.
6-Land on the southern side of the canal, adjoining the 22nd section: about 25 acs.
7-Island in the Potomac, opposite to the 22nd section of the canal: about 16 acs.
8-Land on the south side of & adjoining to the 24th section of the canal: about 4 acs.
9-Island in the Potomac called *Bald Eagle Island*, near the 30th section of the canal: about 6 acs.
10-Island in the Potomac called *Short Island*, near the 23rd section of the canal: about 8 acs.
11-Part of a tract of land called *Long Acre*, & part of a tract called *Variation*, both containing about 67 acs, & lying on both sides of the canal, about 2 miles & a half below Seneca.
12-Part of a tract of land called *Mount Nebo*: about 18 acs: on the south side of the canal, 2 miles & a half below *Edwards' ferry*.
13-Part of a tract called *Accord*, principally on the south side of the canal, 3 miles about Edwards' ferry: about 37 acs.
14-Land lying on the south side of the canal, near *Conrad's ferry*: about 7 acs, purchased of Joshua Chilton.
After the sale at Hagerstown, the following pieces of land will be offered at public sale:
15-Land on the south side of the Canal, a little below *Mill-stone Point*, purchased of Geo Chambers: about 10 acs.
16-Land on the north side of the Canal, about a mile above *Mill-stone Point*, suitable for warehouses: about 1 ac.
17-Land on the north side of the Canal, near to Lock #53: about 3 acs.
18-A piece of land containing from 10 to 15 acs, lying between the Canal & the river, about 8 miles below Cumberland: called *Resurvey on Cillur's Discovery*.
After the sale at Frederick:

19-Land containing about 20 acs, lying on the south side of the Canal, immediately above Berlin, purchased of Emerentienne Corbaly.
-John Ingle, for Chesapeake & Ohio Canal Co

National Blues: resignation of Capt L J Middleton, in his inability, in consequence of a distant residence, to attend longer to the duties of his ofc. Resolved: that, in the opinion of this meeting, the loss of our captain, who, being connected with us from our organization, has shared with us alike in prosperity & adversity, maintaining throughtout a spirit of untiring energy & constant devotion to our best interests, is calculated to awaken in us feelings of profound regret & heartfelt sorrow. –Francis A Tucker, chairman -M P Mohum, Sec

TUE MAY 9, 1843
For sale: 2 story frame house & lot on south B st, between 10th & 11th sts west, fronting on the Mall. Inquire of the subscriber, Francis B Lord, G st, between 5th & 6th sts.

Re-married: in this village, [says the Glenn's Falls Clarion,] on Apr 22, by Rev J Wells, of the Baptist Chr, Mr Jos Francis, to his own faithful spouse, with whom he had lived in harmony for the last 21 years. The former marriage was solemnized according to the rites of the Roman church, &, at this late day, the wife began to have doubts about the scriptural legality of the ceremony, & refused to share the bed & board of her liege lord until the knot had been tied in language she could understand. The disconsolate swain, with his old sweetheart, started on foot for this village, a distance of 2 miles, where the ceremony was performed as above stated.

Yesterday Danl Webster resigned the ofc of Sec of State. Hugh S Legare, Atty Gen of the U S, is appointed to be Acting Sec of State for the present. Caleb Cushing, of Mass, is appointed Minister & Com'r to China, in place of Edw Everett, who declines the appointment.

Trustee's sale: decree of the High Court of Chancery of Md in the case in which Robt Sewall was cmplnt & Sylvester I Costigan & others were dfndnts: sale at auction on Jun 13, at the Court-house door, at Leonardtown, St Mary's Co, Md, the most valuable tract or tracts of land known as *Cedar Point Plantation*, containing in all 964 acs, more or less. Improvements consist of a commodious dwlg-house, granaries, corn-house, barns, ice-house, dairy, brick house for overseer, negro qrtrs, & stables lately erected. Present tenant, Mr T O Spencer for will show the same.
–Jas I Gough, trustee: Chaptico, Md

Died: on Sat, at N Y, Gen Jarrat Stillwell, in his 86th year. Gen Stillwell was a sldr in the Revolution, & took an active part in its great & glorious events.

Died: on May 5, at N Y, the Rev Thos C Levins, in his 54th year.

Died: on Apr 26, at his residence in Dighton, Mass, the Hon Hodijah Baylies, aged nearly 87 years.

Died: on Arp 29, at Cleveland, Ohio, Hon Joshua Mills, M D, aged 46.

Yesterday Danl Webster resigned the ofc of Sec of State. Hugh S Legare, Atty Gen of the U S, is appointed to be Acting Sec of State for the present. Caleb Cushing, of Mass, is appointed Minister & Com'r to China, in place of Edw Everett, who declines the appointment.

Furniture at auction on May 9, at the residence of Mrs Eddes, on Green st, between Dunbarton & West sts, Gtwn: her entire stock of household & kitchen furniture. --Edw S Wright, auct

WED MAY 10, 1843
Meeting of the Association of American Geologists on May 1. Prof H D Rodgers, Pres. Dr C T Jackson read a paper on the organic composition of soils & their characteristic salts & compounds. Dr Locke, of Cincinnati, was chosen the next Pres, & Dr David Dale Owen, of Indiana, Sec. In addition to the members in attendance upon the Convention, are the following:

E O Tuckerman, Schenectady, N Y
Saml B Buckley, N Y
T Romeyn Beck, Albany, N Y
Wm H Seward, Auburn, N Y
John Johnston, Middletown, Conn
Amos Binney, Boston, Mass
Jonathan Pierson, Schenectady, N Y
Prof Alonzo Porter, Schenectady, N Y
Silas Totten, Hartford, Conn
Chas H Olmsted

The Pres of the U S left this city yesterday in the steamboat **Oseola**, for his farm in Chas City, Va, where he contemplates a stay of 3 weeks. -Madisonian

The Govn'r of Md has refused to surrender Horn, arrested in Phil some time since for the murder of his wife, & now in prison at Balt, to the authorities of Ohio, by whom he was demanded to answer for a like offence committed in that State. The Govn'r says he must first be tried in Md, & if not convicted there, he will be handed over to Ohio.

Mrs Davis, Louisiana ave, between 6th & 7th sts, can accommodate some 8 or 10 gentlemen with good board, they finding lodging; also, 3 or 4 with board & lodging. Boarding only $2.50 per week; board & lodging $3.00 per week to those who pay punctually; some others can be accepted. All persons indebted to Jas Davis will please pay their bills immediately, so that he may be enabled to pay his bills.

Rev Thos C Levine. The death of this reverend gentleman deserves more than a passing notice. The late Rev Thos C Levine was in the 54th year of his age, &

formerly pastor of St Patrick's Cathedral in N Y C. He was a native of County Louth, Ire. He entered as a student in the Jesuit's College at Stony Hurst, in Lancashire; & due to his particular aptitude for math was sent to Edinburgh to attend the lectures of the celebrated Playfair & Leslie. Fully qualified to fill the chair of natural philosophy in the College of Clongows, near Dublin, & also in the Univ of Gtwn, D C -N Y Courier & Enquirer

For rent, the 3 story brick house on East Capitol st, Capitol Hill, lately occupied by Mr Houston. Inquire of Rebecca Burche, N J ave, near Coombs' wharf.

House for sale cheap: 2 story frame house on the west side of 4½ st, between Md ave & Va ave. Apply to Jos H Daniel, Merchant Tailor, 5 doors west of Brown's Hotel. Or at the store of G W Hinton, on the corner of 4½ st & Md ave.

Wash Corp: 1-Bill for the relief of Thos Goddard was taken up & indefinitely postponed. 2-Bill for the relief of Alfred Hutmuller: referred to the Cmte of Claims. 3-Ptn of Smith Thompson, jr: referred to the Cmte of Claims. 4-Bill for the relief of J A W Butler: passed. 5-Ptn of Geo W Kendrick, praying remission of a fine: referred to the Cmte of Claims.

Circuit Court of Wash Co, D C. John Henry Ford, [colored,] has applied to be discharged from imprisonment under the act of Insolvent Debtors: hearing on the 4th Mon in May next. –Wm Brent, clk

THU MAY 11, 1843
We learn from the Howard District Press that a personal altercation, attended with violence, occurred last Thu between the former Sheriff of Howard Dist, Anne Arundel Co, Md, & Richd Iglehart, jr, in which the latter was wounded by a pistol ball, passing threw his arm & entering his side. Dispute originated respecting the possession of some land near *Oakland Mills*, & the difficulties occurred on the spot.

On Thu week Mr Lossell, of Evans Mills, Jefferson Co, while grinding a shingle knife on stone propelled by water, was, by the violence of the same, caught & thrown forward into the gearing, & crushed to death. He was about 40 years of age, & has left a wife & 2 children in very indigent circumstances.

The Newport Herald states that the identical chair in which Govn'r B Arnold sat, 180 years ago, & received & displayed the charter of 1663, in presence of all the freemen of the Colony, was introduced into the Senate chamber on Tue, & was filled by Govn'r S W King.

A few days since, at Cincinnati, Judge Wood, while sentencing a man to death, named Andrew Walton, convicted of murdering one John Carroll, remarked that of the 60 capital cases which had come under his judicial notice, at least 50 had originated in drunkenness.

Valuable Rappahannock land for sale: the estate on which he resides, called *Gaymont*: 2,200 acs: about 45 valuable negroes: & bldgs of every description. Possession given when desired, & the premises shown, in my absence, by my manager Mr Jeter, or my neighbors, Philip Lightfoot or John Tayloe.
–John H Bernard, Port Royal, Caroline Co, Va.

Albert, a superb thorough-bred short horned Bull, will serve a limited number of cows at $5 each. Apply to the subscriber at the farm next above Mason's foundry on the road leading to the Falls bridge. –W W Burrouges

Died: yesterday, Miss Mary Kennedy, at age 35 years, after an affliction of several months, which she bore with Christian patience & resignation. Her funeral will be from her late residence on H st, near 21st west, today at 3 p m.

Died: on the 26th ult, at the home of Davis Richardson, in Fred'k, Md, after a severe & protracted illness, Mrs Columbia Sprigg, w/o Wm Motter, of Wheeling, Va, & d/o the late Otho H W Sprigg, of Fred'k Co, Md, aged 21 years. The dec'd has left a fond husband, a child of 3 years of age, & a large circle of relatives & friends to mourn her early departure.

Ramon F Santamarina, from Spain, is desirous of obtaining employment as a Confectioner: he has had experience. Address him throught the City Post Ofc.

FRI MAY 12, 1843
Wm P Briggs, a Whig, has been removed from the ofc of Collector at Burlington, Vt, & Mr Hyde, the late Van Buren Collector, appointed in his place. Mr Briggs was one of the delegates to the Harrisburg Convention.

Orphan's Court of Wash Co, D C. Letters of adm on the personal estate of Anthony Preston, late of said county, dec'd. –Mary Preston, Jacob Gideon, adms [The administrators have appointed Mr Sylvanus Holmes their agent, authorized to attend to the collecion of all accounts & debts due to the estate of the late Anthony Preston, request all persons indebted to be prepared to settle when called on, as it is intended to make a speedy settlement of said estate.]

The National Standard, a newspaper printed at the capital of Mexico, is excessively indignant because Mr Stephens obtained from Yucatan, & presented to the N Y Historical Society, a number of ancient & valuable manuscripts throwing light on the history of that country, & recommends that a law be passed prohibiting foreigners from carrying away any monuments of antiquity & manuscripts that may hereafter be found.

Curious fact appears in the Occident, translated for that work from a French publication: "The widowed mother of the wealthy bankers Rothschilds, while her sons inhabit palaces in London, Paris, Vienna, Naples, & Frankfort, still resides in the small house in the Jewish quarter of Frankfort, [on the Main,] in which her husband lived & died. Upon his death she declared that she would only leave for the tomb the modest dwlg that had served to cradle this name, this fortune, & these children. The house is so remarkable for neatness that it forces the attention of the strangers. It unfolds a trait of the Hebrews as old as affection & respect of the wives of the Patriarchs for their lords."

On Fri last, Michl Hawkins, the steward of the steamboat **Pulaski** was scalded on board the boat, & died at Pittsburg on Sat. Wm Coon, a deck-passenger, of Collins, Erie Co, NY, is not expected to recover.

A murder was committed at the 90 miles station of the Georgia central Railroad on May 2, on Mr Harbard. Mr H had some difficulty with Mr Goulding, & went to his house. Goulding was prepared with a double-barrelled gun, with which he deliberately shot Harbard as he approached his house. [Copied from another newspaper.]

Mr Isaac Cannon, [brother of Jacob Cannon who was a few weeks ago killed by Owen O'Day] died at his residence, Cannon's Ferry, on Sat last. Thus the hand of death in a few weeks has broken up the well-known & wealthy house of Isaac & Jacob Cannon. They were considered the wealthiest individuals in the county. Neither of them has left children; their only near relative is a widow sister residing in Balt. Isaac was the entire legatee of his brother, Jacob, with the exception of a small real estate in Balt, devised to his sister. –Wilmington [Del] Journal

Wash Corp: 1-Act for the relief of J A W Butler: fine imposed upon him by judgment of Saml Drury, for keeping a dog without a license, be, & the same is hereby remitted, upon the paying of the costs of prosecution by said Butler.

New Orleans, May 3. A planter by the name of Adams & his brother, residing about 8 miles from Covington, were killed by about a mob of 20 men who rode up to Adam's place on Tue last. Adams had been engaged in a lawsuit with some of his neighbors, which terminated in his favor. Both Adams & his brother were fired upon & killed. Adams' wife escaped with her son, aged about 12 or 15 years, & reached Covington in safety, after having been fired on. Another brother of Adams arrived in the city yesterday, with a letter from the D A requesting the Govn'r to furnish the necessary force to capture the assailants. Great excitement was produced by the outrage. -Bee

Cincinnati, May 7. A copper soda fountain at Mr Geo M Allen's drug store, corner of 6th & Main sts, burst with great force carrying away one end entirely. A young man, Mr Saml Langtree, was engaged in charging it. It was buried in Mr Langtree's forehead to the depth of a finger or more, & no hopes are entertained for him. He will not probably survive an hour. The negro helping him was not injured. -Chron

New Orleans Bee of May 4. We learn from an authentic source that the inhuman order of the Mexican Gov't to decimate the Texian prisoners, who rose upon their guard & attempted to escape at Salado, was carried into effect on Mar 25, & the following ofcrs & sldrs were shot to death:

Capt Wm M Eastland		Sgt J N McThompson	
Privates:			
J N Torrey	W H Cowan	K H Dunham	J L Ca_h
J L Shepperd	C H Roberts	K W Harris	J N Ogden
Henry	E E Etz	M C Winn	
Whaling	J Tombul	P Maher	

Private E D Cocke, formerly an editor at Houston, Texas
Private Thos L Jones, of Austin, more recently of Houston

SAT MAY 13, 1843
Pittsburg Sun: Mr Danl Howe, a Revolutionary sldr, who resided in East Deer Township, in that county, was killed by a bull, who knocked him down & gored him in a shocking manner. Mr Howe was a native of Md, & was 84 years of age at the time of his death. [No date-current item.]

American Tract Society held their 18th Anniversary at the Broadway Tabernacle, in N Y, on Wed: chair was taken by the Pres, Theodore Frelinghuysen. Addresses were made by the Rev Messrs Hoisington, Kincaid, Scudder, Nevin, & Beecher, to a crowded audience.

Hodijah Baylies, who died at Dighton, Mass on Apr 26, aged nearly 87 years, was the youngest of 6 brothers, one of whom died at the age of 93, one at 86, one at 83, one was over 70, & the other died young & unmarried. He was born at Uxbridge, Worcester Co, in Sep, 1756, & when very young came with his father to Taunton. His father, Nicholas Baylies, was a native of Coalbrook Dale, Shropshire, England; Eliz Park, his mother, was a native of Newton, near Boston. Thos Baylies, the grandfather of Judge Baylies, a native of the parish of Alve Church, in Worcestershire, Eng, emigrated about 115 years since with a part of his family. Judge Baylies graduated at Harvard in 1777, & was of the same class with Rufus King & the late Judge Dawes. He entered the Revolutionary army as Lt, & his first service, after recruiting, was on the Hudson, during which he was attacked with a near fatal fever. Gen Lincoln selected him as one of his aids-de-camp. When Gen Lincoln capitulated Maj Baylies became a prisoner of war; as soon as his exchange was affected he rejoined the army, & was called into the military family of

Washington as one of his aids-de-camp. After the surrender of Lord Cornwallis, Gen Lincoln was appointed the first Sec of War, & Maj [then Lt Col] Baylies remained in Washington's family until the termination of the war. In 1784 he returned to the North, & married the dght of Gen Lincoln. In 1810 he was appointed by Govn'r Gore, Judge of probate for Bristol Co. He was one of the handsomest men in the Revolutionary army; his bearing was martial, his deportment easy & graceful, & his manners polished & extremely engaging. Your son, said old Robt Treat Paine to his mother, has all the elegance of the British ofcrs without any of their vices. With the exception of Col John Trumbull, he is believed to have been the only surviving field-ofcr of the Revolutionary army. The members of Washington's military family, at the various periods of the Revolution:

Edmund Randolph	Cobb	Chas Cotesworth
Mifflin	Humphreys	Pickney
Read	Tilghma	Jackson
Hamilton	Jonathan Trumbull	-Taunton Whig
Laurens		

Raymond P Dowden, a clerk in the Treas Dept, was arrested on Thu last, charged with the embezzlement of certain cancelled Treas notes. He sent the notes to a female in Balt of the name of Mrs Augusta A Dorsey, residing in Lombard st, to pass away; but she failed in the attempt, except for one note which she sold to a broker. Dowden has been held to bail in the sum of $2,500 for his appearance at Court.

The Raleigh Register [N C,] states that a gold mine has been discovered on the waters of the Middle Creek, in that county, by Maj Wm F Collins, of Raleigh, which promises a rich yield of the precious metal.

New Establishment: Post Ofc Café, corner of 7th & E sts. Long experienced as a caterer. –P A De Saules

Army & Navy Chronicle. 1-A Thos Smith, Chief Clk of the Navy Dept, has been appointed Acting Sec of the Navy, during the absence of the head of the Dept. 2-The board for the examination of Midshipmen, to take place at the Naval asylum, Phil, on May 22:

Cmdor Geo C Read	Capt Benj Page
Capt Wm Compton Bolton	Capt John Gwinn
Capt John Percival	Prof Wm Chauvenet, Math Examiner

Obit-died: on Apr 6, at his residence near the town of New Madrid, Mo, Dr Robt D Dawson, in his 52nd year. He was long a resident of this county, during which period he filled many important trusts. He was the presiding ofcr of the New Madrid County Temperance Society since its organization. –C D Cook, chrmn;
-T D O Morrison, Sec

Army orders: Adj Gen's Dept:
Brvt Maj S Cooper, Assist Adj Gen, assigned to duty at the headqrtrs of the 3rd military dept, & to report to Maj Gen Gaines, at St Louis.
Brvt Capt J H Prentiss, Assist Adj Gen, assigned to duty at the headqrtrs of the 1st military dept, to report to Brig Gen Arbuckle, at New Orleans.

Engineer Corps:
Capt John Sanders, in charge of improvements on the Ohio river. Address, Pittsburg, Penn.

Topographical Engineers:
Capt C Graham, on survey of the communication from Albemarle sound to the Atlantic ocean. Address, Wilmington, N C.
Capt F W Hughes, on duty in the Bureau.
Capt T B Linnard, at Natchitoches, La, in charge of the improvements of Red river.
Lt w H Emory, attached to the Bureau.
Lt J E Blake, on duty in Florida under Gen Worth.
Lt L Sitgreaves, attached to the Bureau.
Every member of the corps is on duty.

1st Artl:
Brvt 2nd Lt Jos Stewart & C L Kilbourn, relieved from duty at Fort Adams, & assigned to companies in their regts, where their services will be most needed.

3rd Artl:
Brvt 2nd Lt R W Johnston, transferred to company A, & to duty at Fort Johnston, N C.

5th Infty:
2nd Lt Paul D Geisse, transferredf from the 7th, to take rank next below 2nd Lt Norvell, & assigned to company E.

7th Infty:
2nd Lt Henry Little, transferred from the 5th, to take rank next below 2nd Lt Henshaw, & assigned to company H.

Navy Orders:
May 3: Lt A A Harwood, ordnance duty
Lt S F Hazard, sloop **Decatur**, Norfolk
Passedmidshipman J A Doyle, receiving vessel, Balt.
Gunner Thos Dewey, ordinary, N Y
May 4: Lt C H McBlair, leave, 4 months
May 5: Lt J J Forbes, furlough renewed 3 months
Boatswain Wm Hart, ordinary, Boston
Carpenter Loman Smith, sloop **Vandalia**, vice John Cahill, relieved on account of unfitness for sea service, & ordered back to receiving ship at Norfolk.
May 6: Lt J J Boyle & Surgeon J F Brooke, leave 3 months each, having returned by permission from the Mediterranean.
May 8: Lt C C Barton, sloop **Levant**, Norfolk
Lt J H Adams, sloop **Decatur**, Norfolk

Lt W A Jones, receiving ship, N N.
Lt J H Sherburne, leave 3 months, having returned from coast of Brazil on a sick ticket.
Surgeon D Egbert, Balt station
Lts J C Walsh, C Steedman, J Humphreys, & A B Davis, coast survey under Cmder Gedney.
Passed Midshipman M Woodhull & D Ammen, coast survey under Lt Blake.
Passed Midshipman C Sinkler, receiving vessel, Phil.
Gunner Thos Lewis, sloop **Decatur**, Norfolk.
Carpenter J M Webb, ordinary, N Y
May 9: Lt G M Bache, Passed Midshipman F S Haggerty, R N Stembel, & A H Jenkins, coast survey, under Cmder Gedney.
Lts C H Davis, J B Dale, S P Lee, Passed Midhsipmen J N Maffitt & S Bent, coast survey, under Lt G S Blake.
Passed Midshipman J B Carter, depot of charts, etc.

John & David McDaniel, charged with the murder of Charvis, the Santa Fe trader, arrived at St Louis, Mo, on May 2. The marauding party consisted of 15, all of whom participated in the robbery; but 8 refused to take part in the murder, & separated from those who proposed Charvis' death. Names of the party:

John McDaniel	Christopher Searcy	2 Harris brothers
David McDaniel	Schuyler Oldham	John McCormick
Wm Mason	Thos Towson	Nathl H Morton
Jos Brown	Dr Jos de Prefontaine	Benj Tolbert
Gallatin Searcy	Saml O'Berry	

The first 7 named composed the party in favor of the murder, & the first 4 committed the deed.

Mrd: on May 11, by Rev Mr Bulfinch, Mr Wm Bates to Miss Mary Tonge, both of Wash City.

Mrd: on May 11, by Rev Chas Rich, H Milton Thompson, of Michigan, to Jane Owen Smith, of Wash City.

Mrd: on May 10, at Bladensburg, by Rev Mr Decker, Rev Henry V D Nevius, of Powhatan Co, Va, to Miss Mgt E Ross, of Bladensburg.

MON MAY 18, 1843
New publications: 1-History of the Hawaiian, or Sandwich Islands, by Jas J Jarves Traces of unknown discoverers, earlier than Cook; traditionary times down to the year 1841.
2-American Naval Biography, by John Frost, Phil, published by E H Butler. The first of a series of lives embraces those of Paul Jones; Cmdor Richd Dale, the lt of the ship **Bonhomme Richard**; & Cmdor Alex'r Murray.

3-Campbell's Foreign Monthly Magaxine for May, Phil, Jas M Campbell. Good portrait of Prof Wilson: biographical sketch of M Thiers, Dan O'Connell's History of Ireland.

Old Hundred. The music, in harmony of 4 parts, of this venerable popular church tune, was composed by Claude Goudimel about 1554. The composer, who was chapel master at Lyons, France, died in 1572, a victim of religious opinion. It is a popular musico-historical error that Martin Luther was the composer of this noble choral. –K J R

P W Snow, late American consul at Canton, died at Providence, R I, on Sun last, at the age of about 58 years. Mr Snow returned to the U S about 2 weeks since in the ship **Valparaiso**, arrived at N Y. He was greatly enfeebled by a disease from which he had long suffered.

Levi S Hollingsworth, Clk of the Common Council of the city of Phil, died suddenly on Wed, at the bath-house of R Harmer, in 3rd st, near Arch, while bathing. His death was caused by apoplexy. He had been Clerk for several years, & was highly respected.

Mr Wm Morgan, of Clark Co, Va, & 2 of his servant men, were drowned in the Shenandoah river, on May 6, by the upsetting of a boat, in which they were crossing with some farming utensils.

Mrs Wilson, at Portland, on Wed, was acquitted by the jury, of participating in the murder of her husband. She said she was in bed when Thorn committed the deed, & he had threatened to kill her if she made any alarm or resistance. Thorn had previously been convicted of the murder. –Boston Courier

Phil, May 11. Jacob Shipman was arrested with a considerable amount of money belonging to Brokers of this city, & Brokers & Banks in N Y. He was committed to prison.

The Govn'r of Md has refused to pardon Capt Jos Owens, who was convicted of murder in the 2nd degree, & sentenced to confinement in the pen for 7 years, at the Apr term of Anne Arundel Co Crt. –Md Republican

Managers of the Complimentary Ball to be given to the ofcrs of the Steam-frig **Missouri**, as a manifestation of the sense entertained of their polite attentions to the citizens of Wash who have so freely visited that splendid ship, during her former & present visit to Wash City:

W W Seaton	Maj W Trumbull	Robt Tyler
Gen G Gibson	Lt J T McLaughlin	W A Bradley
Gen A Hunter	P R Fendall	Dr R Miller

Wm B Scott	Maj A A Nicholson	Chas Lee Jones
Dr J M Thoams	Dr J F May	Lt O Carr
T H Blake	Lt G Thom	R S Hill

List of passengers per steamship **Great Western**, Capt Hoskin, from Liverpool: [Arrived in 12½ days on May 12th.]

Mr J B Bonsall, of Phil
Dr Bonson & lady, N Y
Master J Bonson, N Y
Mr E Bentley, ditto, & 2 sons
Mr E V Child & son, Phil
G C Crook, England
J S Daniell, Balt
J Day, England
Albert Day, Pa
Miss De Troy, Paris
Mr Jas Eddy, Boston
J Froste, England
Mr & Mrs Finn, Ireland
S W Forbes, Boston
P Falconer, Scotland
Mr & Mrs Featherstonhaugh, U S
J Gyngell, sr, & ladies, U S
J Gyngell, jr, U S
G B Hall & lady, Canada
P Holland, Liverpool
Mr W N Jackson, Sheffield
B H James, U S
A Krazen, Russia
Mr Leckie, Glasgow
M LeRoy, Paris
W W Moore, Ireland
A Millier, U S
E MacGregor, U S
J H Morgan, England
Thos Owen, Md
B Pattison & lady, Glasgow
Miss Pattison, Glasgow
W A Ritchie, Ohio
Mrs E Reynolds, Dublin
W H Ridgeway, England
J Rogers, Wolverhampton
Miss Smith, Boston
G Trenton, Cork
J Tanner, England
H Whittel, Ireland
Mr D S Walland, Monmouth
Mr Higginson, England, 4 children & servants
Mr & Mrs Bute & child, of England, & servant

Information received in Wash City from authorities in New Orleans to the Sec of the Treas, that John M Breedlove, Jos W Jewell, & Sawyer Reines, charged with stealing in New Orleans, large sums of money in Treas notes of the U S, viz, about $90,000 were in the Wash City. Warrant was issued to ofcrs Burr, Waters, & Dexter, by Justice Giberson on Fri, & the next day, Breedlove, Jewell, & Reines were arrested. Breedlove was arrested by Capt Goddard, attended by ofcr Burr & W H Howison, one of the Auxiliary Guard, at a well-known house of ill fame situated south of the Washington Canal, on 4½ st. Jewell & Reines are about 40 years of age. Breedlove is a gentle looking young man.

Died: on Apr 26, at Ottowa, the Hon John Robinson, one of the Judges of the Supreme Court of the State of Illinois. He was for 12 years a Senator of the U S from Ill, & was very generally respected.

TUE MAY 16, 1843
The Massaachusetts Historical Society is to celebrate the second Centennial Anniversary of the Confederation of the New England Colonies on May 29 instant, at Boston, when a discourse will be delivered by the Hon John Quincy Adams.

Circuit Court of N Y, last week, an action was brought by Mr Jas Germond against Augustus Flicher, for damages for the loss of his son's services, which he was derpived of for nearly 5 months in consequence of his having been bitten by dfndnt's dog, & also to recover the cost of doctors & nursing his son while he was ill. The jury returned a verdict of $135 for the plntf.

New Orleans Bee of May 8. Messrs David Morgan & David C Hatch, 2 of the San Antonio prisoners who had escaped from the Castle of Perote, arrived in this city yesterday.

Died: on May 4, at his seat of Smithfield, in Montg Co, in his 69th year, Col Jas P Preston, formerly Govn'r of Va, & who, for more than 40 years, has enjoyed an almost unbounded personal popularity. He was one of the few survivors of the purer generation which immediately preceded this; men who were cradled in the Revolution; too young to share its perils, but who imbibed its illustrious spirit. Such a race of men we shall never see again in this country. In the war of 1812 Col Preston was appointed by Pres Madison to command of a regt: which he led into action, & at Chrisler's field & received the wound in his thigh which compelled him to abandon the service, & maimed him for life. He returned to Va & was made Govn'r of the State; then, by Pres Monroe, postmaster of the city of Richmond, which he relinquished 5 or 6 years ago, & retired to his native mountains, in the bosom of his own household, in the presence of his wife & children.
–Richmond Whig

Died: May 11, at Bellevue, PG Co, Md, the residence of Lloyd M Lowe, his father, after a painful & protracted illness, Mr Jas R M Lowe, of Loudon Co, Va, in his 44th year, leaving a disconsolate widow & 6 small children to mourn his irreparable loss.

Mrd: on Thu last, by Rev O B Brown, Mr Sylvanus Washburn to Miss Mary Jane Bell, 8th d/o Mr Chas Bell, all of Wash City.

The St Louis Organ of May 3 says: Gen Gratiot's trial closed on Sat. The jury, under the instructions of the Court, gave a verdict in favor of the U S for about $30,000.

Jos Martin has established a Bookbindery on La ave, east of the Wash Bank.

Obit-died: on Sat last, at the residence of her son, L S Skinner, of PG Co, Sarah Skinner, d/o the late Fred'k Skinner, of Calvert Co, & relict of Levin Skinner. Death has in reality no sting for one whose life was so exemplary.

Fauquier White Sulphur Springs, 50 miles from Alexandria, will be opened for reception of visitors on Jun 1. Board for 4 months-$80; for 2 months-$60; for one month-$35; for 2 weeks-$18; for one week-$10; for one day-$2. Horses at 50 cents per day or $12 per month. –D Ward, agent

Great bargain in a farm: the premises on which Gen Washington once resided, within half a mile of the town of Fredericksburg, Va, now offered for sale. Tract about 950 acs; the whole is offerd at the trifling sum of $12,000; the river land is worth the money. Inquire of Sidney Teasdale, on the premises, or of the subscriber at his residence in New Haven, Conn. –Thos C Teasdale

Public sale: by order for distress: sale in Wash City on May 20th, of the goods & chattels seized & taken to satisfy house rent due in arrears by Susan Ann Stretch to John Gadsby. –Jos Smith, bailiff

WED MAY 17, 1843
N Y Commercial Advertiser. A few days since the ship **Montezuma** arrived at Liverpool & we published a complimentary card to Capt Lowber for his exertions in saving the crew of a French brig which was fallen in with in a sinking condition. A letter from A Williams, who was a passenger in the **Montezuma**, gives an account of the rescue. The wreck was first seen by Mrs Cipriant, the d/o the late John Wilson, of this city. The rescue occurred on Apr 2. Mrs Cipriant was the only lady on board. Dr Pattison & Rev Mr May were also passengers. Mrs Cipriant & the mate Moore spoke French, through which we learned that the brig had been dismasted & shattered, as we then saw her, 7 days previous, & all by one single sea.

The King of Prussia has presented to M Meyerbeer, the composer, the gold medal awarded in Prussia to eminent men in the arts & sciences.

Jas Watson Webb, editor of the Courier & Enquirer, was tried at Coopertown last week for a libel on J Fenimore Cooper. The jury could not agree on a verdict-5 for conviction, 7 for acquittal. –Tribune

Prince Augustus of Saxe Coburg is nephew of the reigning Duke of Saxe Coburg Gotha, of the King of the Belgians, of the Duchess of Kent, mother of the Queen of England, & of the Grand Duchess Anna Feodorouna, wid/o the Grand Duke Constantine, brother of the Emperor of Russia. He is also brother of the King of Portugal & the Duchess de Nemours, & cousin-german of Prince Albert, consort of Queen Victoria. He is in his 24th year, having been born on Jun 13, 1818, & is one year younger than his bride, who was born on Jun 3, 1817.

We understand that, at the last dates, our esteemed townsman, Robt Walsh was in London, with his lady, enjoying the hospitality, as he certainly does the respect, of the distinguished people of that metropolis. U S Gaz

Geo W Graham, a young man, who was arrested at Winchester, Va, some time since on a charge of purloining money from the mail while he was employed as an assistant in the Winchester post-ofc, has had his trial before the U S District Court, sitting at Staunton, & was acquitted.

Circuit Court of Wash Co, D C. Lewis Godfrey has applied to be discharged from imprisonment under the act for the relief of Insolvent Debtors: hearing on May 29, 1843. –Wm Brent, clk

Wash Corp: 1-Cmte of Claims, asked to be discharged from further consideration of the following ptns: ptn of Cleland K Denneale, of Owen McCue, of F C Labbe, of Wm A Scott, of Richd N Barry, & of Sidney Talbertt. 2-Bills for the relief of Wm Thomas; & of Jesse Leach: passed. 3-Elected Commissioners:

Robt W Bates	Stephen P Franklin	Wm Ashdown
Saml Stott	Jacob Gideon	Jas Owner, sen
Saml Drury	John P Ingle	W M Ellis
Nicholas Callan, jr	Danl Homans	Thos Thornly
Willard Drake	Jas Tims	Noble Young
John McClelland	John B Ferguson	

For rent: the 2nd house east of the Medical College on E st, known as Green's Bldg, lately occupied by Andrew Smith. The house is in good order. –A Coyle, trustee

Lives of Eminent British Lawyers, by Henry Roscoe, 2 vols price $1.25. –F Taylor

THU MAY 18, 1843
For rent: commodious 3 story brick bldg on E st, near the Globe ofc. Key may be found at the apothecary store of Mr James, corner of 14th st & Pa ave. Apply to Mr Balaam Birch, C st, west of 12th. Also, a 3 story brick house on 14th st at E. Apply as above.

The Mansion House, Phil, south 3rd st, is undergoing a thorough repair. It has been leased to Mr Jos Head, long & extensively known as the late occupant.

Teacher: Trustees of Primary School #1, in Marlborough District, PG Co, Md, will receive applications for a teacher: salary about $350 per annum. –W W W Bowie, Henry Jones, Wm Clarke, Trustees

Marshal's sale: in virtue of a writ of fieri facias, from Circuit Court of Wash Co, D C: sale on Jun 16, before the court house door: all that part of lot #20 in sq 254, of

Wash City, referred to in a deed from Sarah How & E P Pearson, executors of Robt How, to Wm Dowling, dated Jul 18, 1835, the said part of lot fronting 19 feet & 11½ inches on the south side of F st north, & running 155 feet to an alley, & being the premises now in the occupancy of said Dowling. Seized & levied upon as the property of Wm Dowling, & sold to satisfy judicials #192, to Mar Term, 1836, in favor of Wm Lee, use of Robt G Bickley. –Alex'r Hunter, Marshal Dist of Col

To Edw Watts & Eliz his wife, Cary Breckinridge, John Breckinridge, Robt Gamble & Levitia his wife, Henry W Bowyer & Matilda his wife, _____ Burch & Eliz his wife, & Jos [or Jas] Breckinridge, reps of Gen Jas Breckinridge, late of the State of Va, dec'd. Take notice, that the undersigned Comers appointed by the Circuit Court of Wash Co, D C, to divide between the heirs at law of the said dec'd the real estate, in said county, of which he was seised in fee simple at the time of his death, consisting of lots #13 thru 17, lots 20 thru 26, in sq #186, in Wash City, will proceed upon the premises on May 26, to execute the said commission. –A Rothwell, E J Middleton, Henry Naylor

Alexandria, D C, May 16. The new bell on the First Presby Chr in this place has been placed in the steeple & tried. It is one of the finest toned bells we have ever heard. It was cast at the foundry of Messrs T W & R C Smith, of this place, & does great credit to that excellent establishment. –Gaz

At the recent term of the Mass Supreme Court, Maria Clark recovered $1054.00 damages for an alleged breach of a marriage promise. There was no positive proof of an engagement: an express promise is inferred from circumstantial evidence.

The Naval Court Martial sitting at Norfolk arrived at a decision in the case of Cmder Ramsay on Mon last. Its nature cannot be known until it is officially promulgated.

Sarah Fix, a young girl of Reading, Pa, was strangled by a clothes line. She was sent into the garret to take down a clothes-line, & in climbing up to loosen it from a hook, was caught in the line by her neck, & instantly strangled. He mother heard the fall, & found her life had become extinct.

At Wilmington, Del, on Wed, a negro man was convited of assaulting Mr Jacob Stanhope with intent to kill. Sentence: 1 hour in the pilloy, 120 lashes on the bare back, 2 years & 6 months imprisonment, 37 years sold as a servant, & $12,000 fine.

Mr & Mrs Archer's Academy for Young Ladies, Lexington st, 5 doors east of Chas, Balt, Md. Refer to the following gentlemen, who, for the most part, have children or wards in the school:
Maj Gen Winfield Scott, U S Army
Chas Davies, L L D
Rev E W Gilbert, D D Pres of Newark College

David Hunt, Mississippi
Mr John P Watson, Mississippi
Rev J Chamberlain, D D Pres of Oakland College, Mississippi
Reb d Wyatt, Balt
Rev J G Hamner, Balt
J H Bernard, Caroline Co, Va
Hon Stevenson Archer; Hon R B Magruder; Capt H A Thompson; Dr R W Hall; Dr J R Dunbar; F J Dallam; Thos Finley; Wm Reynolds; Balt.

Mrd: on May 16, by Rev John C Smith, Wm H Lowry to Mgt Jane, eldest d/o Edw Deeble, all of Wash City.

Mrd: on May 16, near Rockville, Montg Co, Md, by Rev John M Jones, John W Ferguson, of Wash City, to Miss Sarah Ellen, d/o the late Wm Prather, of the former place.

Mrd: on Apr 25, in Gtwn, D C, by Rev R T Berry, Dr E Boyd Pendleton, of Martinsburg, Va, to Maria Lucinda, y d/o the late Chas Pendleton Tutt.

Died: on May 17, in Wash City, Miss Virginia J Cheshire, y/d/o the late Archibald Cheshire. Her funeral will be from the residence of her mother on 7th st, today at 4 p m.

Died: on Apr 23, at his residence in Prince Edw Co, Va, Wm Berkeley, long remembered by the citizens of said county as a valued friend & public spirited & useful member of society. For many years he was the Treas of the Commonwealth of Va. He was a Christian gentleman, of the highest style of man.

Wine store removed to Donohoo's new 4 story bldg, between 3rd & 4th sts, on Pa ave. –T F Semmes

FRI MAY 19, 1843
Mrd: on May 18, at St John's Church, by Rev Mr Hawley, Philip Lansdale Cox to Mary, d/o the late Jas H Roy, of Va.

Assignee's sale of real estate: in the matter of Thos A Hawks, a bankrupt, & by virtue of decree in bankruptcy, passed in this cause in 1842, by the Circuit Court of Wash Co, D C, vesting in me all the property & right of property of the said Thos A Hawks, I shall sell on Jun 2 next, at public auction, on the premises, lot #1 in sq 518, in Wash City, containing 35,200 sq feet of ground. This lot lies immediately north of the new jail, at the corner of G & 4th sts, having a front of 200 feet on 4th st, & 176 feet on G st. –D A Hall, assignee -R W Dyer & Co, aucts

Ofcrs attached to the U S sloop of war **Vandalia**, which sailed from Hampton Roads on Fri last for Chagres. Wm J McCluney, Cmder
Lts:
Wm S Young, Wm P McArthur, Henry H Lewis, Geo W Harrison

Purser: Robt S Moore		Assist Surgeon: Thos M Potter
Surgeon: Danl S Green		Acting Master: Jas C Williams
Midshipmen:		
Chas H	Chas P	Robt F R
Baldwin	McGary	Lewis
Edmund	Francis G	Edw E Stone
Shepherd	Clarke	J J Waddell
Acting Boatswain: Edw Lyons		Capts Clk: Wm D Cobb
Acting Carpenter: Loman Smith		Master's Mate: Wm F Smith

Passengers:
Cmdor A J Dallas, Cmder-in-Chief Pacific Squad
Geo Brown, Com'r to Sandwich islands
Seth Sweetzer, Consul at Guayaquil
Lt Neil M Howison, U S Navy
Lt C F Wooster, 4th Artl, U S Army
Mr Miller, Cmdor's Sec
Passed Midshipman Alex'r Murray, Acting Master
Morah Willis, Cmdor's Clk

Gen Wall, late of the U S Senate, was attacked with paralysis on Sun at his residence in Burlington & was in a very dangerous situation. He was seized with dizziness while in church in the morning, & on reaching home retired to bed. About 4 o'clock he was taken with paralysis, affecting his speech & right side. –Newark Adver

Died: on May 10, in Balt, after an illness of 4 months, Mr Arthur D Coad, of St Mary's Co, Md.

Ofcrs attached to the U S brig **Somers**, now at Norfolk, & bound on a cruise in the West Indies.

John W West, Lt Commanding	Geo W Clark, Midshipman
Wm J H Robertson, 1st Lt	J W A Nicholson, Midshipman
Jas F Armstrong, 2nd Lt	Wm H Hudson, Midshipman
J R W Mullany, Asting Master	Paul Loyall, Commandant's Clk
H M Hieskell, Purser	John Ritter, Master's Mate
Wm B Sinclair, Assist Surgeon	Edw T Storms, Purser's Steward

In Equity. Geo Bomford vs John L Smith & Christopher E, Jas, Thos, Philip, Fisher, Eliza, Alex'r, Octavins, & Christopher Gadsden, & P Gadsden Edwards, Jas F, John B, Catharine, & Rebecca Edwards, the heirs-at-law of Philip Gadsden. Cmplnt, Geo

Bomford, purchased, in 1827, lots 19 & 20 in sq 169, in Wash, D C, from John L Smith; that said Smith acted in this sale to cmplnt as the agent of Jas F Edwards, E H Edwards, John Gadsden, Ann M Gadsden, & R B Barksdale, who had conveyed these lots to said Smith for this purpose of sale; that the said J F Edwards, E H Edwards, John Gadsden, Ann M Gadsden, & R B Barksdale owned these lots as devisees of Jas Fisher, dec'd; that the same had been conveyed to Jas Fisher by Philip Gadsden, of S C, dec'd, for a valuable consideration, the sum of $1,600; that this last deed of conveyance was not executed in the form, & recorded within the time, required by law to pass the fee; & the bill expressly charges that it was the intention of said Philip Gadsden to convey the fee simple in these lots to said Jas Fisher; that the above named dfndnts, excepting J L Smith, are the heirs-at-law of Philip Gadsden; that they all reside at a great distance & out of D C; that cmplnt has never been able to obtain from the said heirs of P Gadsden a deed confirming & quieting his title to these lots, though entitled to the same; & the bill of complnt prays the Court to decree that the said heirs of P Gadsden convey & release to cmplnt all their title & estate in said lots as said heirs at law, & that they be forever debarred & enjoined from making any claim as said heirs against cmplnt, his heirs, or assigns for or on account of said lots; & for further relief in the premises. The dfndnts aforeside reside out of D C: the Court, ordered that the said absent dfndnts appear, in person or by solicitor, in Court & answer cmplnt's bill, & show cause, why he should not have relief as prayed, on or before the first Mon in Oct next, or else that the said bill be taken pro confesso against them. –Wm Brent, clk
-J B H Smith, Solicitor for cmplnt

Died: on May 15, at Alexandria, Alex'r Moore, after a lingering illness, in his 58th year. Mr Moore was appointed Register of Wills for Alexandria Co in 1807, & continued to fill that ofc until his death. He has left an interesting family & many friends who regret the loss they have sustained.

Died: on May 14, at Farmville, Va, Mrs S M Sydnor, w/o the Rev Thos W Sydnor, & d/o the Rev Dr Chapin, of College Hill, D C, aged 25.

Died: on May 17, in Wash City, Peter W Gallaudet, in his 88th year. All the excellance of the patriot, philanthropist, & Christian were in beautiful harmony in the chaacter of this venerable man. Early in life he took his stand for the rights of his country, & shared in the battle of Trenton & other distinguished actions of the Revolution. He was honored with the special confidence of Washington. He strived to establish the Washington Manual Labor School; & the Howard Institution of our city can bear witness how faithfull he devoted himself to the cause of charity. His funeral will take place from his late residence, on 12th st, near E, on Fri, at 4 p m.

Mr H W Hilliard, Charge d'Affaires of the U S to Belgium, sailed from N Y on Mon, in the packet ship **Stephen Whitney** for Liverpool, on his return to his mission, with his family. [One of the children of Mr Hilliard, a young lad of 6 years, had a strong disinclination to make the voyage & managed to escape from his family at the time of embarkation. The ship was detained, messengers were dispatched to the Mayor's ofc, & sent about the city. He was found in an hour's time in Courtland st, attentively examining some prints in a shop window. The little fugitive was immediately restored to his anxious family, & went to sea with them.]

Mediterranean Squadron: correspondence of the Balt Patriot. Genoa, Mar 26, 1843. Capt W C Nicholson, late of the sloop **Preble**, transferred to the command of the sloop **Fairfield**, vice Bigelow, transferred as captain of the ship **Columbus 74**, vice Spencer, returned home. Cmder Stephen B Wilson, of the **Columbus**, transferred to the command of the **Preble**. Lt T G Tilton promoted to acting cmder, & ordered as such to the **Columbus**, vice Wilson, to the **Preble**. Lt Melancthon Smith, from the **Fairfield** to the Preble. If not made to stop at too many ports on our way thither, will reach N Y about Jun 20.

SAT MAY 20, 1843
Public sale: virtue of the last will of Capt Joshua Hutchison, dec'd, late of Fairfax Co, Va: sale on Jun 19 next, at Fairfax Courthouse: one tract of about 180 acs lying on the Little River Turnpike Road & Cub run, adjoining the lands of Mrs Harriet Lee & Elijah Hutchison & others. One other tract, in the same county, adjoining the lands of Silas Hutchison, Wm S Daniels & others: about 180 acs. One other tract adjoining the last mentioned, on the confines of Loudoun & Fairfax, being about half in each county: contains about 132 acs, & has on it a comfortable dwlg house, kitchen, & out-houses. Mr Redding Hutchison or Mr Silas Hutchison, living near the lands, will show them. –Burr W Harrison, exc

Excellent chamber furniture at auction: on May 23: at the residence of Miss Briscoe, on Missouri st, between 4½ & 6th sts. Also, a very handsome new superior toned Rosewood Piano Forte, made by Stein, & piano stool. –R W Dyer & Co, aucts

The undersigned Com'rs, having been appointed by the County Court of St Mary's Co to appraise & divide the real estate of the late Saml Maddox, of said county, dec'd, give notice that they will meet on the premises on Jun 19 next, for the purpose of discharging the duties of said commission. –John H Key, H D Swann, M Shanks, Jos Shemwell, Wm Biscoe, Com'rs

Dissolution of Partnership between John Campbell White, Campbell P White, & the undersigned. Persons indebted will make payment only to the joint order of the partners. In a short period the undersigned will have completed his preparations for continuing the former business on his own account. –Jos White Balt, May 18, 1843

Departures for Europe: the steamer **Hibernia** left Boston for Halifax & Liverpool on Tue, with mails containing 14,000 letters & 70 bushels of newspapers, & with the following passengers: Messrs Henry Oxnard, Lorenzo Papanti, Mrs Papanti &

servant, Miss S E Pratt, Mr Geo Pratt, Mrs Mary Mayers, Rev A Urquhart, Mrs Urquhart, nurse & child, J G Ward, Rev R H Neale, Jacob Hittinger, Rev Robt Turnbull, Joshua Leavitt, Jona D Steele; John Parrott, U S Consul at Mazatlan; Mrs T S Perry, Providence, R I; Dan A Calderon de la Barca, late Spanish Minister at Wash & in Mexico, Mad Calderon de la Barca, Miss McLeod, John Bottomley, Wm Lattimer, Lewis Atterbury, B B Atterbury, Mr Munkittuck, Mrs Munkittuck, Jno C Martin, C W Sampson, Mrs Sampson, Chauncey Ives; Thos Cook, C W Thomas, Leonard I Wyeth, J H Wilson, Stephen Crocker, F A Huntington, Wm A Ryan, of N Y; J R Willmer, Phil; Meredith Calhoun, La; Eugene Rayseau, John Arrowsmith, of New Orleans; Henry Eyre, London; Wm O English, Hull, England; Wm Crawford, Glasgow, Scotland; F A Campbell, Royal Artillery; H W Barlow, Royal Engineer; Chas L Roberts.

In the packet ship **Silvie de Grasse**, from N Y for Havre: Dr Heap, U S Consul at Constantinople; Mr Francois Gallay & wife, of Belize, Honduras; Mr B Fourquet, of Mexico; Hon Wm H Dangerfield, of Texas; Rev J B Chaupes, Mrs Theodore Cecily, & Mrs Mary Cecily, of Vincennes, Ind; Mr Francois Rapp, Mr A Emanuel, Mr M Levy, & Mr S Brentano, of New Orleans; Mr A B Williman, of Charleston, S C; Dr Reilly, of Ohio; Henry Seldon, of Phil; Mr B U Schneider, of Beardstown; Mr Chas Irminger, & Mr W H Coles, of N Y.

Mr L M Parsons states, in the Lorain Republican, that he has in his door yard a block of white limestone as near the form of a bust as could be expected from the hand of nature. It was found in 1838 by Alfred Lamb, in Brighton, Lorain Co, Ohio, covered with a thick coat of moss. In 3 places upon it, 1533; & when found there was a draught on the stone of a 3 masted ship in full sail.

For rent: a 2 story brick house, with stable, carriage-house, & lot, within 6 minutes walk of the Centre Market. Inquire of Mr J F Caldwell.

Accident at Marshalton, near Westchester, Pa, on Tue of last week. A boy, 13 or 14 years, s/o Milton Clayton, was leading a horse to water, & had the chain or strap attached to the head halter wrapped around his arm. The horse, taking fright, ran off, jumped over a fence, dragging the boy after him, by which he was so much lacerated as to cause his death.

Chas A Clinton, for many years clerk of the Supreme Court of N Y, has been summarily removed, & Jesse Oakley, a brother of Judge Oakley, appointed in his place.

Fire was discovered in a stalbe occupied by the Hon Mr Wickliffe, Postmaster Gen, in the rear of 7th st. The fire extended to an adoining bldg in the occupany of Dr T P Jones, which was partly burnt, & much of his valuable chemical apparatus considerably damaged. The carriage horses were saved. The bookbindery of Mr Sullivan was saved.

A Diving Bell, for the purpose of raising the wreck of the ship **Erie**, is constructing at the furnace at Fredonia, by Messrs McClure & Chapin. The weight of the bell is about 3 tons & is capable of being used to the dept of about 80 feet. It will be ready in about 2 weeks. –Buffalo Courier

Military & Naval Intelligence.
1-Board for the examining of the Assist Surgeons, will convene at N Y C, on Jul 1. Board will consist of: Surgeons Thos G Mower, Henry A Stinnecke, Chas S Tripler, & Assist Surgeon J J B Wright as Supernumerary & Recorder.
2-A Board of Naval Constructors will meet on May 25, for consideration of subjects connected with the bldg of vessels of war. The Board will consist of: Col S Humphreys, Chief Naval Constructor, Messrs F Grice, J Lenthall, F Rhodes, & C D Brodie.
3-3rd Infty: Captains L N Morris, O Wheeler, J Vanhorne; 1st Lts: J M Smith, S D Dobbins; 2nd Lts: R R Johnson, O L Shepherd, J B Richardson, W T A Brooks, C T Baker; Assist Surgeon W Levely; & 323 privates, arrived at Jefferson Barracks on Apr 21, in the steamer **Meteor**, from New Orleans.
4-Lt Col E A Hitchcock, Maj W W Lear, Capts H Bainbridge & J W Cotton, Adj P N Barbour; 1st Lts W S Henry, L S Graig, & W H Gordon; 2nd Lts W B Johns, D S Irwin, T Jordan, D C Buell, A W Bowman, & G Sykes; Assist Surgeon A W Kennedy; & 312 privates, arrived at Jefferson Barracks, shortly after the **Meteor**, in the steamer **Ben Franklin** from New Orleans. –Army & Navy Chronicle

Houses & lots at auction: improved property on North Capitol st, immediately opposite the splendid mansion of Capt Wilkes. Sale on May 25, on the premises, lot #7 in sq 685, with two 2 story frame houses. These houses are nearly new. Title unquestionable. –Wm Marshall, auct

Trustee's sale of valuable property: by deed of trust from Jos Nourse to me, dated Apr 30, 1829, & duly recorded among the land records of Wash Co, D C: sale on Jun 17 next, of lot 8 in square 168; lots 6 & 7 in square 141; & lot 10 in square 347. On payment of the purchase money, I will convey all the right, title, & estate that was in said Jos Nourse, which is believed to be indisputable. –J I Stull, trustee
-R W Dyer & Co, aucts

Died: on May 13, at Cincinnati, Mr Henry Driver, aged 33 years, formerly of Caroline Co, Md.

Saml Olden, of Princeton, N J, lately dec'd, bequeathed the interest of $8,000 for the support of a missionary of the Episc Church, to be employed in N J; the interest of $6,000 in aid of the domestic missions in N J; to Trinity Church, in Princeton, $500 for the erection of a parsonage; the interest of $400 in aid of the Parish School, & $100 for books for the Sunday School attached to Trinity Church.

MON MAY 22, 1843
The Hon Caleb Cushing, Com'r to China, arrived at Norfolk on May 19 from Balt, & visited, about meridian, the U S ship **Brandywine** & the ship **St Louis**, now lying at anchorage off the Naval Hospital, & destined for the Chinese seas, where he was received with the usual honors & salutes. Mr Cushing does not go out in the **Brandywine**, but some of his effects will be taken out in her. –Beacon

Confectionary: The subscriber informs the public that he is prepared to execute all orders for Confectionary for weddings, balls, with neatness & punctuality, at reduced prices, & of the best materials, at his store, Pa ave, between 12th & 13th sts. –J Beardsley

From the Western Frontier: 1-Sir Wm Drummond Stewart's party reached Madame Chouteau's Landing, below Westport, in good health, where they encamped, to await the arrival of another party from St Louis. In the mean time, they were making all necessary preparations for their long march. 2-Some of the goods of Charvis have been recovered, but his body has not been found. Six more of the persons who were concerned in his robbery & murder have been arrested & brought to St Louis, where they were committed to jail to await their trial. Their names are: Wm Mason, Thos Towsan, Dr Prefontaine, Wm Harris, S S Berry, & N H Morton.

W W W Bowie lost a new & commodious tobacco-house by fire last week, together with most of his improved plantation implements & some tobacco. His loss is at least $1,400. The fire is thought to have been the work of an incendiary. –Marlboro [PG Co, Md] Gaz

Mrd: on May 18, by Rev Henry King-ford, Albert G Newton to Harriet Louisa, y/d/o Wm Pratt, all of Alexandria.

Died: on May 20, Mrs Anne Belt, w/o Thos J Belt. Her funeral will be at her late residence, on 7th st, this day at 2 p m.

For rent: commodious brick dwgl on 10th st, south of Pa ave. Inquire of J J Dermott, or the subscriber, Alexandria. –Jno F M Lowe

Valuable PG, Md land for sale. The subscriber having determined to go to the West, offers for sale one of the most desirable plantations in this section of the country. This land is near the stage road from Wash City to Port Tobacco, about 4 miles from Washington: contains 400 acs: with large well finished frame dwlg, & necessary out houses. Also, a valuable grist mill, the toll from which is sufficient to pay a miller. –C A Gantt

$10 reward will be paid to any one who will restore to the owner a small white poodle dog, which was lost last evening in the neighborhood of the Patent Ofc in Wash City, or give such information as will lead to his recovery. Inquire at Mrs McGunnigle's boarding house, 10th st.

Wash Corp: 1-Act for the relief of Jesse Leach: fine imposed by judgment of Jas Marshall, for a violation of an ordinance of this Corp relative to the burning of chimneys, be & the same is remitted: Provided, that the said Leach pay the costs of prosecution. 2-Act for the relief of Wm Thomas: fines imposed by 2 judgments of John D Clark, relative to the keeping of dogs, be & the same are hereby remitted: Provided, the said Thomas pay the costs of prosecution.

The inventor of the Spiral Carriage Springs, Mr John S Tough, of Balt, made a visit to Wash City last Thu in a handsome family carriage hung on spiral springs. The invention has been favorably noticed in the Balt papers, & appears to be of great public utility.

A narrow escape from instant death occurred last Tue, when a little boy named J Chauncey was dangerously wounded by a kick from a horse, while playing on the sidewalks. The would laid open the forehead of the child, however, we understand he is now placed out of danger. He will be disfigured for life. –Local News

TUE MAY 23, 1843
Pope Gregory XIV has presented to the church of Petits Peres, at Paris, the entire body of the Roman martyr St Aurelia, taken from the catacombs of St Priscilla, at Rome, in May last. Depositing this holy relic on the altar will take place today. [French paper]

Capt John Ferguson, a veteran of the Revolution, now living in Bedford, N H, when in the prime of life, cut a willow walking stick from a tree in Haverhill, Mass, & upon his arrival at Pelham, N H, where he then resided, he placed his cane in the ground about 6 rods north of the old meeting house in that town. The cane may be seen in the shape of a tree, measuring 15½ feet in circumference at the smallest place below the branches, which are of corresponding proportions with the trunk.

The Paris Moniteur announces that King Louis Philippe would go into mourning for 11 days for the Duke of Sussex.

The Maison Rouge Property is the estate unsuccessfully claimed by Maj Gen Gaines. The present claimant is Mgt Maison Rouge, as dght & heiress to the late Marquis, & as yet the preliminary portion of the case has only been reached by the Court. The question determined by the Court at this time is not the right of the plntf to the property, but clearly establishes her right to be considered as the legitimate dght &

heiress at law of the dec'd, leaving for future investigation all the various questions of title to particular estates, whether by purchase, inheritance, or prescription.

The husband of Taulioni, Count Gilbert de Voisins, died a few days ago at Paris.

Richd Arkwright, the richest commoner in Europe, died in the latter part of April, at his seat in Derbyshire. He is supposed to have held more, in every description of funds, than any other British subject.

Circuit Court of Wash Co, D C. Jas A Beveridge; Thos Thorne; Danl J Dowling; & Geo Parker [colored] have each applied to be discharged from imprisonment under the act for the relief of Insolvent Debtors: hearing on May 31. –Wm Brent, clk

Mrd: on Sabbath evening, by Rev John C Smith, Mr Jos M Caho to Miss Martha Virginia Thomas.

Mrd: on May 18, in Gtwn, by Rev Mr Butler, John Hedges to Mary A, eldest d/o R H L Villard, all of that place.

Mrd: on Dec 13, 1842, at the head of Bay Prairie, Texas, by Rev Mr Huff, Henry P Cayce, of Cedar Grove, Texas, to Miss Mary Francis Slade, late of Wash City.

Mrd: on Feb 27, at the head of Bay Prairie, Texas, by Rev J Palmer, Henry F Hanson to Miss Charlotte W Slade, both late of Wash City.

Mrd: on May 11, at Cincinnati, Hon John McLean, one of the Justices of the Supreme Court of the U S, to Mrs Sarah Bella Garrard.

Died: on Sun last, at the residence of Col Braxton Davenport, [his son-in-law,] in Jefferson Co, Va, Maj Henry Bedinger, of Berkeley, aged 89 years. Maj Bedinger was one of the few sldrs of the Revolution who had lived to see the experiment of free government tested for more than half a century. His remains were attended to Sheperdstown by Capt Rowan's artillery, & buried with the usual military honors.

Died: on May 22, Thomas, infant s/o R J & Ellen Pollard, aged 2 years, 4 months & 4 days. His funeral is today at 4 p m, from his father's residence, on C st, between 6th & 7th sts.

Died: on May 9, at Clarens, Fairfax Co, Va, in his 28th year, Mr Luke Oeconomos, a native of Greece. He came to this country about 7 years ago, to acquire a more liberal education than his own land could give him. He graduated from the College of N J in 1840 & was at the time of his death a teacher of the Greek language in the Fairfax Institute. His disease was consumption, which gave indication of its existence only in the present year. He continued to fulfill his duties until a few days before he died.

Died: on Apr 13, Franklin Adamson, s/o John & Rebecca Adamson, in his 16th year. On May 3, Mrs Rebecca Adamson, w/o John Adamson, in her 48th year. [From information of the relatives & friends in Md, from which State they emigrated some 4 or 5 years since.]

Valuable land for sale at reduced price: a portion of the estate known as *Long Meadows*. This farm consists of 198 acs, & was formerly owned by Cmdor Decatur, Cmdor Rogers, & Col Bomford, & was then estimated to be worth $100 per ac. The road from the Turnpike gate to Mrs Benning's bridge forms the southern boundary of this property. For terms apply to Bradley & Thruston, Genr'l Agents, 6th st, Gadsby's Hortl; or to Mr Young on the premises.

Trustee's sale: deed of trust from Geo Bomford, trustee, et al to me, dated May 23, 1836: sale on Jun 4 next, of lot 14 in the subdivision of sq 462 of Wash City, with a 2 story brick dwlg. –Clement Cox, trustee -R W Dyer & Co, aucts

Marshal's sale: in virtue of a writ of fieri facias on condemnation, issued for the Circuit Court of Wash Co, D C: sale on Jun 19, of the following real property, viz: lots 11, 12, & 13, in sq 728, & lot 20 in sq 729, in Wash City, seized, taken, & condemned as the property of John Lynch, & sold to satisfy judicials #27 to Mar term 1840, in favor of Raphael Semmes & Stanislaus Murray. –Alex'r Hunter, Marshal D Col

WED MAY 24, 1843
Death by lightning. A s/o Mr Ostrander, at Fultonville, Montg Co, N Y, was killed by lightning on May 15, while in the field plowing.

H B Stacy, appointed by Pres Tyler himself Postmaster at Burlington, was dismissed last Sat week. Dana Winslow, whose sole recommendation consisted in having edited for a year or two one of the puniest & least reputable Locofoco sheets in New England, has been appointed his successor. –N Y Tribune

The St Louis Republican of May 13 says that among the passengers on the ship **Missouri**, from New Orleans, we find the names of: Maj Thomas, U S A; Hon W D Merrick, of Md; Rev J Twitchell, Col F Stean, Baron Israel Wagner, from Saxony; Col Bostwick, & Col Arthur.

The Maysville [Ky] Eagle announces the death of Jos B Reid, the Mayor of that city, on May 13. About 3 days previous the thumb of his right hand was broken by a fall, which finally resulted in lockjaw, & terminated his existence.

F M Peeple of Perry Co, Ala, who recently received $20 for assisting a gentleman in some business, gambled & lost it all, together with $60 he borrowed in his father's name. He was so depressed that he procured a gun & shot himself.

Mr Edw Dewey, a young man of high respectability, recently a clk in the store of Mr Isaac Clark, of Northampton, Mass, was seriously injured on Mon of last week, in N Y C. He was preparing alcohol over a fire for making opodeldoc, when the vessel exploded & he was enveloped in flames. He is sadly burnt.

Chas Newmeyer, Miniatur Painter: south side of Pa ave, between 9th & 10th sts.

Very excellent & nearly new household furniture at Public Auction: on May 29, at the residence of Mrs Mary Ronckendorff, on Pa ave: a part of her excellent furniture. --Robt W Dyer & Co, aucts

Wash Corp: 1-Ptn from Jas A Lenman & others: referred to the Cmte on Improvements. Same for the ptn of Chas Lyons & others. 2-Bill for the relief of J E Fowler & Co was referred to the Cmte of Claims. 3-Letter received from Jas Carbery, tendering his resignation as a member of this Board. 4-That Wm J McCormick, Danl Homans, & Jas Tims be appointed com'rs to hold an election in the 4th Ward to fill the vacancy occasioned by the resignation of Jas Carbery. 5-The reports of the Cmte on Improvements, asking to be discharged from the further consideration of the ptns of A Rothwell & of Henry Smith, were taken up & agreed to. 6-Cmte of Claims adverse to the ptns of Geo Hercas, Wm Benedic, Thos J Fletcher, Jos Milburn, Henry Grub, P H Brown, & of Thos Dooley, were severally taken up & agreed to. 7-Report of the Cmte of Ways & Means asked to be discharged from the further consideration of the ptn of C Coltman, was taken up & agreed to. 8-Bill for the relief of Henry Thomas was laid on the table till Mon next.

Died: yesterday, after a 6 weeks illness, of consumption, Mr Geo W Campbell, in his 23rd year. He was a kind & affectionate son & brother, & his loss will long be felt by his widowed mother & only surviving brother, as well as by all his friends. He was generally known in the central part of the city as having been for the last 8 or 9 years attached to the Globe ofc. His funeral is today at 3 p m, from the residence of his mother, on La ave, near 7th st, over Squire Morsell's [magistrate's] ofc.

Rev Dr Milnor, of N Y, to preach in Trinity Church this evening at 8 p m.

Died: on May 19, at Washington, Guernsey Co, Ohio, of pulmonary comsumption, in her 58th year, Mrs Ann McCreary, relict of Jas A McCreary, dec'd, formerly of Balt, & mother of the senior editor of the Wheeling Gaz.

THU MAY 25, 1843
Franklin Ins Co of Wash will hold a meeting on Jun 5 for the election of 12 Directors for the company. Ofc next door to the Patriotic Bank. –G C Grammer, Pres

Edmund I Lee has associated with him in the practice of law his son Chas H Lee. One of them will attend the courts of Fairfax & Loudoun Cos, Va. Ofc on Royal st, over the new Market-house, Alexandria.

For sale or exchange: farm near Gtwn, on the turnpike leading from Gtwn to Rockville, on which I now reside. The tract contains about 180 acs: comfortable improvements. Apply to me on the farm, or to John H King, Gtwn. –Wm McNeer

Circuit Court of Wash Co, D C. John Hodgkins; & Wm B Guy; have applied to be discharged from imprisonment under the act of Insolvent Debtors: hearing on May 31. –Wm Brent, clk

Alabama: the Whig nominees for Congress, thus far, are: Jas Dillet, of Monroe; J W A Pettit, of Barbour; J S Hunter, of Lowndes; Elisha Young, of Greene.

Mrd: on May 23, in Wash City, by Rev J C Smith, David S Todd, of Phil, to Miss Lydia Catherine, d/o the late Wm Hunt, of Wash City.

Mrd: on Tue, by Rev John C Smith, Mr Wm H Nalley to Miss Ellen H Knowles, d/o H Knowles, all of Wash City.

Mrd: on May 18, at Cincinnati, Ohio, by Rev John T Brooke, Rufus King to Mgt, d/o Dr Landon C Rives.

Died: on Feb 23 last, at his residence in Goochland Co, Va, Mr Robt Pleasants, aged 100 years, 11 months & 8 days. He was a man of industrious & domestic habits. –Richmond Whig

Died: Apr 6, at sea, on board the U S ship **Columbus**, on his way from Genoa to Port Mahon, in his 24th year, Saml Todd, eldest s/o Purser John N Todd, U S Navy.

We hear that the American Institute has appointed John R Peters, jr, as its agent to proceed to China, under the auspices of the Ameircan embassy, which shortly goes out. –N Y Evening Post

Rt Rev Dr Loras, Bishop of Dubuque, Iowa, will celebrate Holy Mass & preach at St Matthew's Church tomorrow, Ascension Day, at 10:30 a m. –J P Donelan, Pastor

The Cement Mill above Hancock, belonging to Mr Geo Shaffer, was destroyed by fire on Fri last. Loss estimated at $8,000. It was supposed to be the work of an incendiary. –Hagerstown Pledge, May 23.

Capt I P Baker, of the barque **Anita**, which cleared from Boston on Saturday for Puerto Cabello, is now on his 50th voyage to the above place. –Boston Journal

On Fri last, Spencer, who was convicted of the murder of his son in Hardin Co, Ky, was taken to the church in Elizabeth to hear his own funeral sermon! On Sat he was driven to the gallows, where he met his doom. –Louisville Kentuckian

Isaac Leavitt, of Scituate, Mass, arraigned before the Supreme Judicial Court at Plymouth, on Tue, for the murder of Mary Knapp, replied he supposed he was guilty.

Q C Yelvert was recently murdered in Dale Co, Ala, by a father & 2 sons, named Boles, over a quarrel about land. A reward of $1,000 is offered for the murderers. –Balt Pat

Mr Chas T Pavey, residing near Leesburg, Ohio, was killed on May 17 by falling from a horse which he was engaged in breaking. He was a good citizen.

FRI MAY 26, 1843
The U S steam ship **Union** arrived in Boston harbor on Sat from Norfolk, & it is the intention of the Cmder, Lt Hunter, under the direction of the Gov't, to visit the various ports on our seaboard. She is 1,040 tons burden, & is rigged as a 3 masted schnr, with a square foresail. She is propelled by 2 engines of 140 horse power each, which work horizontally, turning vertical shafts, which enter the paddle wheels in the center of a sort of hub, & give them a rotary & horizontal motion. Lt Hunter is the inventer. Engines were constructed by Mr Wm M Ellis, of the Wash Navy Yard. Vessel was built by Mr Francis Grice, naval constructor at Norfolk, all under the superintendence of Lt Hunter.

Another Millionair Gone. Peter Lorillard, in his 80th year, died May 24 at his residence in Westchester. He has ranked for many years amongst the wealthiest of our citizens. –N Y Com Adv

Sir Chas Bagot, the late Govn'r Gen of Canada, died at Kingston on May 19. His long illness had prepared his friends for this afflictive event. His remains are to be conveyed to England in the frig **Warspite**, now lying in N Y, in which vessel Mrs Bagot & family will also return to England. [May 27 newspaper: He died at Alwington house, surrounded by his family: Lady Mary Bagot & family will also return to England. Sir Bagot arrived in Canada in Jan, 1842.]

The U S schnr **Grampus**, Lt Com Downes, bound on a cruise to the southward, went to sea from Hampton Roads about 60 days since, & except once, it is believed that she had not since been heard of. Great fears are entertained that she has been lost. Her ofcrs: Albert E Downes, Lt Commanding; Lts: Geo M McCreery, Wm J Swann, Hunn Gansevoort; Jas S Thatcher, Purser; T S K You, Master; E C Conway, Assist Surgeon; Midshipmen, A J Lewis, E N Beadel, Geo L McKenney, Capt's clk.

The monument ordered by the Legislature of R I to be erected over the remains of the late Com Oliver H Perry has just been completed, after a delay of 16 years. It is on the n w corner of the new Burial Ground in Newburyport, rising in a square of 50 feet, enclosed with an ornamental iron fence.

Seventy-five persons of the Mormon faith passed through Albany up the Erie canal on Sat last, destined for the city of Nauvoo, Ill. They were principally from N H.

Naval: the U S ship **Brandywine** & the ship **St Louis**, destined for the East Indies, dropped down from Norfolk to Hampton Roads on Mon. They were expected to go to sea on Tue. Ofcrs attached to the **Brandywine**: F A Parker, commanding East India squadron
Lts: Chas W Chauncey, T H Hunt, W W Bleecker, Wm T Muse, J B Marchand, R B Pegraw, A Ludlow Chase
Master: Thoms M Crossan
Purser: D M F Thornton
Fleet Surgeon: Geo Balcknall
Chaplain: Geo Jones
Cmdor's Sec: A R Bogardus
Assist Surgeons: Richd W Jeffrey, A F Loyal
Capt's Clk: Leroy Parker
Purser's Clk: Pollard Webb
Passed Midshipmen: Andrew Wier, W E Boudinot
Midshipmen: John S Maury, D C Hugunin, Jas H Somerville, E D Denny, Wm L Powell, Jas Heron, Wm H Weaver, John P Jones, Allen McLane, Thos Young, Augustus McLaughlin, Wm Lee Koren, Copeland P Jones, Chas M Mitchell, Wm H Murdaugh.
Attaches to the Chinese Mission: Dr Kane, Messrs West, Herness, O'Connell, & Robt McIntosh.
Ofcrs attached to the ship **St Louis**: Harrison H Cocke, Cmder
Lts: Lewis G Keith, John R Tucker, Benj M Love, Montgomery Hunt
Surgeon: Saml C Laurason
Purser: Jas C Douglass
Master: Geo H Preble
Assist Surgeon: J C Bishop

Midshipmen: John Laurens, Marshall J Smith, Cyrus H Oakley, Stephen D Spence, Fred'k P Wheelock, Nathl S West, Tenant McClanahan, Washington Hammon, Jas L Johnston
Cmdor's Clk: Henry R Weightman
Gunner: J B Benthall
Sailmaker: Chas H Harvey
Passengers to Rio Janeiro: Cmdor Danl Turner, to command Brazilian squadron; Peter Turner, Flag Lt; Cmdor's sec & Cmdor's clk.
The U S storeship **Lexington**, bound to the Mediterranean, went to sea from N Y on Mon. Ofcrs:
Wm M Glendy, Lt Commanding
Lts: Theodore P Green, Andrew F V Gray, Wm May
Acting Master: Edw C Anderson
Purser: Wm Speiden
Passed Assist Surgeon: John J Abernethy
Midshipmen: Wm A Webb, Wm W Roberts, Dawson Phenix
Capt's Clk: Jos Hoban
Master's Mate: Colston Gale
Purser's Clk: Theodore Quastoff
Passengers: Com Saml Downing, to take command of sloop **Fairfield**, in the Mediterranean; Thos Hale, clk to Cmder Downing.

SAT MAY 27, 1843

O Davis, Whig Postmaster at Newburgh, appointed by Pres Tyler, has been removed by him, & Jas Belknap, a Van Buren Locofoco, [partner in the lumber business of Hon J G Clinton, M C] appointed in his stead. Ransom Birdsall has in like manner been removed at Elmira, Chemung Co, & Levi J Cooley appointed. -Tribune

Mr E W Trimble, first engineer of the steamboat **Belle**, of Pittsburg, lately lost his life near Cape Girardeau, on the Mississippi river, by being thrown overboard at night by a deck hand named Peter Chaullier, in revenge for a reproof which he had received from the Capt in consequence of a complaint from Mr Trimble. The offender was secured, & is now held to answer for is cime.

Circuit Court of Wash Co, D C. Wm S Nicholls, a bankrupt, has filed his ptn for his discharge & certificate: hearing on the first Mon in Aug next. –Wm Brent, clk

We understand that the Pres has appointed Bernard Hooe, Reg o/Wills for Alexandria Co, vice Alex'r Moore, dec'd. –Alexandria Gaz

May 24 is the birthday of Queen Victoria. The frig **Warspite** was decorated with flags. The U S ship **Caroline** hoisted the British flag, as well as her own.

At a recent term of the Common Pleas in Harrison Co, Ohio, Esther Anne Davis procured a verdict of $2,000 against J Holmes for a breach of promise of marriage.

At Reading, England, Apr 11th, an American actor, Mr Harrington, was performing the part of Long Tom Coffin in the Pilot. At the end of the second Act, in drawing a pistol it became intangled in the girdle & it went off, & Mr Harrington was so wounded as to cause his death.

The Hon S Breese, U S Senator from Ill, came very near being shot by his brother-in-law in Bellville on Sunday last. The difficulty grew out of ill treatment of Breese's wife's sister by her husband. -St Louis Republican, May 12

Mrd: Thu last, by Rev Septimus Tuston, Mr John Truscott to Miss Mgt Grafley, both of Wash City.

Died: on May 19, at Brooklyn, L I, Francis Harman Ellison, Master in the U S Navy, in the 82nd year of his age, & father of Lt F B Ellison.

Died: on May 24, in Balt, after a long & protracted illness, Bushrod W Craufurd, of Greenwood, PG Co, Md.

For rent: handsome 2 story brick house on south side of N Y ave, between 9th & 10th sts. Apply to Mr Osbourn, at the adjoining frame house, or to the subscriber. –Thos A Scott

MON MAY 29, 1843

The Military Academy: War Dept, May 24, 1843. The following ofcrs of the Army will compose a Board for the inspection of that institution for the present year:

Maj Gen Winfield Scott	Capt H Brewerton, Corps of Engineers
Brvt brig Gen G M Brooke, Infty	Capt L J Beall, Rifle Regt
Col Jas Bankhead, Artl	Capt J C C Asey, Subsistence Dept
Capt A Mordecai, Ordnance Dept	Brvt Catp W G Freeman, Adj Gen Dept
Capt W H Swift, Topog Engineers	

The Board will assemble at West Point on Jun 5. –J M Porter, Sec of War
By order: R Jones, Adj Gen Adj Gen Ofc, May 24, 1843.

Correction: M Calderon de la Barca sailed for Europe in the steam packet **Hibernia**. Not from the U S for Mexico.

Army Intelligence: Wash, May 21, 1843. When the number of privates in any company of dragoons, artl, infty, or riflemen falls below the number fixed by law, 50 for dragoons & riflemen, 42 artl & infty, the captains, under the directions of their respective colonels, will, when practicable, fill the vacancies as they may happen, by enlisting [or re-enlisting] such good men as may be obtained at or in the vicinity of their stations. No extra expense for recruiting parties or the hire of rendezvous will be incurred. By commnand of Maj Gen Scott: R Jones, Adj Gen

Transfer: May 24: Brvt 2nd Lt J W Abert, 5th Infty transferred to the Corps of Topographical Engineers, & ordered to report to the Colonel.
--Army & Navy Chronicle

The principal men attached to the large caravan of Santa Fe Traders lately arrived at Independence, Mo, reached St Louis on May 17, having with them 16 bales & 12 boxes of silver, & a quantity of furs, belonging to Jose Gutierrer, John Pravis, Jas Floris, P Arando, J Olaro, M Sandrue, J C Armigo, R Armigo, W Glasgow, & N W Greene. It is said the specie amounts to $300,000.

Mr Louis Bourdon, [son-in-law of Maj Papineau, well known in Canada,] who was one of the Canadian patriots of 1839 sent into exile in New South Wales, made his escape from that place, & arrived in N Y on Wed.

Sgt Watson was killed at Fortress Monroe, on Wed last, by the bursting of a gun. He had been for some time attached to the U S service, & was much esteemed both by ofcrs & men. --Norfolk Beacon

The Arkansas Intelligencer contains an account of the murder of Mr Cox, his wife & small child. An Indian & a negro, supposed to be the murderers, were brought back to the civil authorities of Scott Co. They confessed to the murders & of robbing the house of something like $1,000. The populace became so much enraged that they went to the jail, took the negro out, tied him to a stake, & burned him to death.

La Senora Maria de la Cruz Carvallo was born at San Rafael de las Gandas, Canton of Guanare, province of Barinas, in Venezuela. She was born in 1699, never been married, nor never had a child, her hair turned entirely gray, & at age 133 returned to its original color, black. She lost her sight entirely at age 118, but recovered it naturally at age 139; she is at present a little deaf. Her principal occupation is spinning & sewing. Up to Jan 31, 1843, she was still alive.
--El Venezolano, Caracas, Apr 26, 1843.

A man named Valnier, a native of St Domingo, died at Merida [Yucatan,] on Apr 5, at the age of 117. Until he was 105 years of age he retained his sight, & his intellectual faculties were unimpaired up to his last moments.

Lost, on May 23, from the hack driven by a black man, Frank Nokes, between the railroad depot in Washington & the Woodyard, in PG Co, Md, a carpet bag containing sundry articles: a portable desk, its cover marked out as a chess board, containing several pieces of jewelry & writing materials. I did not know it to be lost until my arrival at Mr Mullikin's on Charles' branch. I will give $5 for the bag & its contents; or for information that may enable me to recover it. –M Oden, Bellefield, near Upper Marlboro, PG Co, Md

Election will be held on Jun 5 next for one member of the Board of Aldermen, to serve for 2 years, & 3 members of the Board of Common Council, to serve for 1 year. Com'rs:

John McClelland	S P Franklin	John B Ferguson
Wm Drake	J C McKeldon	Jas Owner, sen
Nicholas Callan, jr	J Gideon	Wm Ashdown
Wm J McCormich	R W Bates	Wm M Ellis
Jas Tims	Saml Stott	N Young
Danl Homans	Saml Drury	Thos Thornley

Cigars: new brand of Plantation & Lavultabayer: also Cheroots, the largest in market. –W H Winter, #6, east of Gadsby's, sign of Jim Crow

$50 reward for the apprehension of Wm Wilson alias Watson, the burglar, who escaped from the Wash Co prison. Alex'r Hunter, Marshall for the Dist of Col

The English Lutheran Church has been presented with a valuable lot of land for the erection of a place of worship. They had been meeting in the City Hall. The gentleman who gave this land is our fellow citizen, Gen John P Van Ness. The formation of this Society was made by Rev A A Muller, D D, who is now its pastor. A Lutheran Church has existed among us for some years, in which the services are conducted in the German language.

TUE MAY 30, 1843
Mr Jos B Chadwick arrived at N Y on his way from Zanesville, Ohio, to Boston, at which place he stated his friends reside. He retired to bed, but died during the night, laboring under consumption.

Died: on May 27, Rudolph, infant son of E R & Susan Ward, aged 2 years, 3 months & 14 days.

Died: on May 13, in Weybirdge, Addison Co, Vt, Silas Wright, after an entire confinement of more than 5 years from extensive paralysis. Mr Wright was in his 84th year, & was the father of the Hon Silas Wright, jr [now Senator of the U S.]

Andrew Jackson Campbell, who was a clerk in the Louisville post-ofc while his brother was postmaster, & who established himself as a lawyer at Van Buren, Ark, was recently murdered in returning to that place from his circuit. His body was said to be horribly mangled. These are all the particulars that have come to our knowledge. –Louisville Journal [May 31st newspaper: Campbell was formerly of the law firm of Paschall & Campbell: waylaid & killed within 10 miles of home; many citizens scouring the country in search of the assassins. –Gaz]

Copy of an inscription on a tombstone in Litchfield, Conn: "Mary, wife of Deacon John Buel, died Nov 4, 1768, aged 90. She was the mother of 13 children, 101 grandchildren, 274 great grandchildren, 22 great great grandchildren. Total, 410, of whom 336 survived her."

For sale: house occupied by the subscriber, in Wash City, being the middle tenement in Franklin Row, K st, between 12th & 13th sts. –Robt Greenhow

Potatoes for sale: .50 per bushel, at the store of David P Shoemaker. –Hubbard Scranton, Gtwn

WED MAY 31, 1843
Lady Bagot & family, 5 servants, Capt Bagot, & Capt Cholmondet, from Canada, arrived on Sat at the City Hotel, N Y, to take passage, with the remains of her dec'd husband, on board the British frig **Warspite** for England.

The Dirs of the Shannondale Co have engaged Capt Jos F Abell to superintend that elegant establishment the coming season. He has made himself favorably known to the public during his residence in Charleston.

Hon Garret D Wall, of N J, has so far recovered from his paralysis as to be able to attend to public business.

Pittsburg Gaz of May 25: In the U S Circuit Court, Judge Baldwin presiding, on yesterday, the jury rendered a verdict of $6,776.04 against David Lynch, late postmaster in this city, & in favor of the U S. The claim consisted of various sums of money received by the dfndnt from other postmasters & other persons under instructions from Amos Kendall, Postmaster Gen.

Orphan's Court of Wash Co, D C. Letters of adm, with the will annexed, on the personal estate of Eliz Brown, late of said county, dec'd. –H H Dent, adm

Circuit Court of Wash Co, D C. Wm O'Brien; Lewis W Thomas [colored;] have each applied to be discharged from imprisonment under the act for the relief of Insolvent Debtors: hearing on the 2nd Mon in Jun next. –Wm Brent, clk

Cmdor Moore, of the Texas sloop of war **Austin**, in a letter to the Editors of the New Orleans Tropic, dated "Off Lerma, May 5," says: On Apr 21, I commenced carrying out the sentence of the court martial, released Fred'k Shepard, & pardoned John W Williams, who was sentenced to receive 50 lashes with the cats, but strongly recommended to mercy; 22nd carried into effect the sentence in the case of W

Barrington-100 lashes with cats; 25th, carried into effect the sentence of Edw Keenan-100 lashes with cats; & informed the prisoners Antoine Landois, Jas Hudgins, Isaac Allen, & Wm Simpson that the court had sentenced them to death, & that they would be hung at the foreyard on the following day, at meridian, which was carried into effect on the 26th, at the time appointed, in latitude 23 deg 31 min north, & longitude 88 deg 19 min 22 sec west. I shall not attempt to describe to you the preparation or my feelings on the occasion. I have never seen a man executed. They hung for an hour, [during which time the crew got their dinner,] when they were lowered on deck & given to their messes, for the purpose of preparing them for interment. At 2:30 the bodies were committed to the deep, each one separately; the funeral service was read by Thos P Anderson, surgeon.

Mr Matthew Johnson, the chief engineer on board the steamboat **Rainbow**, was drowned at Wilmington, Dela, on Fri night, while attempting to board, by walking over the foot plank. He is represented as having been an amiable young man, married, & the father of 2 children.

Explosion of fire damp, or carburetted hydrogen, first in the Wyoming region, took place at the coal mine of G M Hollenback, at Mill Creek, on Tue & 3 miners, John Wallace, Jonathan Simnard, & Henry Powell, were badly burned. Wallace is not expected to recover; Simnard burned very severely; & Powell was injured in the face, hands, & arms. –Wilkesbarre Farmer

Sweet Springs, Monroe Co, Va: this property, which for the last 8 or 10 years has been in the possession of Dr John B Lewis, was rented out in Mar last, & is at present in the possession of Messrs Archibald Gibson & Jas H McCartney, who inform the public that they will open as usual during the present season, for the accommodation of visiters. –Archibald Gibson, Jas H McCartney

Farm at public auction: sale on Jun 20; farm contains 93 acs; about 3 miles from Wash City, lying between lands owned by Messrs Worthington, Redin, & Tayloe. Mr Levi Osbourn, living on the place, will show it. –Wm B Osbourn for himself & the other heirs of Archibald Osbourn, dec'd.

Warren [N C] *Sulphur Springs* will open for visiters on Jun 16: located within 11 miles of Warrenton. -Wm D Jones

Red Sulphur Springs, Va: will open for visiters on Jun 1st. –Jas A Dunlap

Circuit Court of Wash Co, D C. Case of the ptn of Cary Breckenridge et al for a division of the real estate of Gen Jas Breckenridge, dec'd, lying in Wash City, D C, between his heirs at law. The com'rs value the real estate consisting of the following lots in sq 186, of Wash City, as follows: #13 at $305; #14 at $675; #15 at $232; #s 16 & 20 at $353; #17 at $350; #19 at $346; #s21 thru 25, at $289 each, & #26 at $288.

The real estate will admit of a fair & equal distribution without loss & injuy. They allot in fee simple in severalty to Letitia Gamble lots 13 & 16; to Eliz Watts lots 20 & 21; to Matilda Bowyer lot 14; to Cary Breckenridge lots 24, 25, & 26; to John Breckenridge lots 15, 22, & 23; to Eliz Burch lot 17; & to Jas or Jos Breckenridge lot 19; &, for equality of partition, they charge said share of Cary Breckenridge with the payment to Letitia Gamble of $66.50, & to Eliz Watts of $75, & charge said share of John Breckenridge with the payment to Eliz Watts of $7.50, to Matilda Bowyer of $49.50, to Eliz Burch of $12.25, & to Jas or Jos Breckenridge of $16.25. Ratify same. –Wm Brent, clk

Died: on May 26, in Wash City, Cary Selden, in his 61st year. He has for a long time been a resident of Wash, & for the last 17 years filled the ofc of Naval Storekeeper at this place. He left a large family & a numerous circle of friends & relatives. Mr Selden was a native of Va, one of the 3 sons of Col Miles Selden, of *Tree Hill*, & possessed in an eminent degree the characeristic traits of his family, of strict honor, a generous & hospitable spirit, & an urbanity, which won universal esteem.

Died: on the 17th ult, at his residence near Denton, Caroline Co, Md, in his 57th year, Thos Culbreth, who for 13 years had filled the ofc of Clk of the late Exec Council of Md with marked ability. Previous to this he served one year, 1813, in the Leg of his State, & 4 years, from 1816 to 1820, in the U S Congress. He was an indulgent parent & an affectionate husband, & has left a widow & 4 children.

Circuit Court of Wash Co, D C: Mar Term, 1843, in Equity. John McPherson Brien vs Luke T Brien & others. Ratify sale by trustee of lots 2 & 3 in subdivision of lot 12, in Gtwn, to Jacob G Smoot, for the sum of $1,705.32; lot 9 in the same subdivision, to Jas Fullalove, for $936; lot 10 in the same subdivision, to Wm Fischer, for $1,104; & lot 1 in the subdivision of lot 18, in Gtwn, to John Pickrell, for $1,880, being all the real estate which, by the said decree, he was authorized to sell. –Wm Brent, clk

THU JUN 1, 1843
Thos Jones was struck by lightning & instantly killed on Fri, when the storm was over Adams' Valley, near Richmond Va. He resided with his aged mother & 2 sisters, who were dependent on him for support.

Mrd: on May 18, at Milton, Pa, by Rev Geo Hildt, Mr John Porter, Editor of the Milton Ledger, to Miss Eliz Pilling, formerly of Wash City.

Jos King, confined in the jail at Richmond, Va, escaped on Sat. He tried to liberate a fellow prisoner named Heath, sentenced to be hung for murder & granted a new trial. In this he failed, for want of time. King has made several escapes, & is denominated a second "Jack Shepherd."

Died: in New Haven, on Sun, Noah Webster, L L D, in his 85th year. Dr Webster has been a long time before the public as a prominent individual in the various depts. of society. He was born in West Hartford, Conn, Oct 16, 1758. He was a descendant of John Webster, one of the first settlers of Hartford, who was a member of the colonial council from its first formation, & subsequently Govn'r of Conn. Noah Webster entered Yale College in 1774. In his jr year, in the time of Burgoyne's expedition from Canada, he volunteered his services under the command of his father, who was captain in the alarm list. In that campaign all the males of the family, 4 in number, were in the army at the same time. Mr Webster graduated with high reputation in 1778. During the summer of 1779 he resided in the family of Mr, afterwards Chief Justice, Ellsworth at Hartford. He was admitted to the bar in 1781; published in 1783, at Hartford, his first part of a Grammatical Institute of the English Grammar. He enjoyed vigorous health till within a few days of is death. On Mon of last week he was slightly unwell, but no alarm was felt by his family. His disorder soon took the form of pleurisy, & he gradually sank under the attack. –New Haven Daily Herald

Mrs Dr Yates, better known as Miss Emma W Willard, formerly of the Troy Seminary, has obtained a divorce, through the Legislature of Conn, & allowed to assume her maiden name.

Died: on Mon, at N Y, in his 83rd year, Wm Bell, whose retired habits of late years have secluded him from the acquaintance of the present generation, but who was well known & truly loved, & honored by a few friends, no longer young. Sixty years ago he went out to China as supercargo of the ship **Empress**, of N Y, owned by Robt Morris, Wm Constable, & other eminent men of that day, & he made several voyages in that capacity. Mr Bell was a Scotsman by birth, & lived in N Y, with the exception of occasional absence, every since 1783. -American

Died: on the 30th ult, after a short illness, Mrs Agnes M Havenner, consort of Thos H Havenner, of Wash City, & d/o John Paterson, sen, of Petersburg, Va.

New Orleans. On May 23 the towboat **Phenix**, Capt Annable, having in tow the ship **Flavius**, from Liverpool, burst 3 of her boilers, below Carrollton. On the **Phenix**, Chas Davis, an Irishman, John, a Portuguese, & Geo, an American, were knocked overboard & drowned. John Clarke, the pilot of the **Phenix**, severely scalded, is not expected to live. Jas Skinner, 2nd engineer, is dangerously scalded, with but little hope of recovery. Capt Annable escaped unhurt. -Tropic

Died: on May 12, at Waynesville, Ill, from injuries received in being thrown from a horse on the morning of that day, Mr Saml M Richardson, aged 25, s/o the late Chief Justice Richardson, of N H, & only brother of Mrs B B French, of Wash City.

FRI JUN 2, 1843
Virginia Gaz of 1771 gives an account of a great freshet which occurred in May of that year. Inscription: The foundation of this Pillar was laid in the calamitous year 1771, When all the great rivers of this country were swept by inundations never before expiernced, Which changed the face of Nature, & left traces of their violence That will remain For ages. It stands not far from *Malvern Hills*. There are inscriptions on it in memory of the first Richd & Jane Randolph, of Curles, & of Elizabeth Randolph. –C C: Petersburg, Va, May 24, 1843.

A fatal duel was fought at Clinton, La, on Sat week between A C Hawsey & Rufus Brooks, in which the former was killed.

Servant wanted. The subscriber wishes to hire a colored woman for house-work; a slave would be preferred from the country. Apply to Christopher O'Neale, at the 6th Ward Hotel, Navy Yard.

House & lots in square 104 for sale at Public Auction: on Jun 14: deed of trust executed by Jos Forrest, on Feb 2, 1838. Sale of the following lots & parts of lots in square 104 in Wash City, with improvements, consisting of a 2 story brick dwlg-house & other out-houses, viz: lot 13; part of lots 10 & 11, fronting on F st; part of lot 1, fronting on 10th st. –Richd Smith, trustee -R W Dyer & Co, aucts

We learn from the Louisville Kentuckian that Moses Dawson, of Cincinnati, a gentleman who has been prominent in political life as an editor & writer, died on the 24th ult. [Jun 3 newspaper: it appears that the announcement of the death of Moses Dawson is not true.]

The Indians are said to tame horses by breathing smartly into their nostrils. It was tried on a Durham calf who after the second attempt, followed us to the barn like a dog. –Gloucester Telegraph

Mrd: on Jun 1, by Rev J W French, Mr A Hamilton Derrick to Miss Emma Lyons, all of Wash City.

Died: at Balt, after a very short illness, Jas Cheston, Pres of the Farmers' & Planters' Bank. He was a sldr of the last war-one of the gallant defenders of the city in 1814 at North Point, & was an ofcr on that occasion. [No date-current item.]

SAT JUN 3, 1843
N Y Tribune. Locofoco Postmasters appointed in place of Whigs removed:
Almerin Gallup, Schoharie, N Y, vice Jabez W Throop.
Fred'k A Hoyt, Goshen, N Y, vice J W Gott.
Henry I Chadeyne, Canterbury, vice Titus Adams.
Reuben Van Alen, Salisbury Mills, vice Peter Cannon.

Tos J Morrin, Saratoga Springs, vice J Ellsworth.
Danl Ground, Marine Town, Ill, vice Geo B Judd.

Mr Hervy, of the Lexington Intelligencer, has disposed of that paper to D C Wickliffe, of the Observer & Reporter, by whom the 2 papers will be united & conducted hereafter under the name of the Observer & Reporter. –Louisville Journal

Orange Island, or **Miller's Island**, is at present owned by Mr John F Miller: part of it is cultivated as a cotton plantation; it is in the parish of St Martin, about 9 miles of Iberia, & contains 4,000 acs of land, & 100 acs of woodland. When Mr Miller purchased the land in 1832 there were on it 150 orange trees, which are now 30 years old. He has since planted about 900 trees. –Franklin [Attakapas] Banner

N Y Tribune: The Deserted Wife. $5 reward. Left my bed & board, without any just cause or provocation, my husband, Alex'r Thompson, to whom I was lawfully married by Squire McKendree. The said Thompson left this city a few days since for parts unknown to his loving & devoted wife. My husband is about 24 or 25 years old, but has not yet arrived at years of discretion. He is about 5 feet 6 inches in height, dark complexion, blue, jealous-looking eye, & is usuallysuspicious & distrustful of those he takes an interest in. Anyone who will give information of the above parsonage to me, at Columbus, will receive the above rewrd, & the thanks of a most chaste, virtuous, & disconsolate wife. –Eliz G Thompson [Editors who feel disposed to aid the cause of injured innocence will please publish the above.]

A German immigrant, Chas Hart, on his way to Ohio, was crushed to death on board the canal boat **Little Western**, while pasing under a bridge, near Pittsford, last evening. One of the eastern packets was passing at the time & the swell raised the boat up against the bridge. The dec'd was instantly killed. Two other persons were severely injured at the same time. –Rochester Democrat

The Govn'r of Md has commuted the punishment of Fred'k Fritz, convicted of the murder of Mrs Eleanor Davis at the Point of Rocks, & sentenced to be hung, to confinement in the penitentiary for life. Doubts are entertained as to the sanity of Fritz at the time of the commission of the murder.

Marshal's 'sale: by authority of a writ of fieri facias, #55 judicials for Wash Co, Oct term, 1821, issued from the Clerk's ofc of the said county & to me directed, Wm A Bradley, use of Elias B Caldwell, against Saml Eliot, jr, I shall expose to public sale on Jun 22, the following lands in Wash City, viz:

Lots 9 thru 16 in sq 299	Lots 25 thru 33 in sq 388
All of sq 354	Whole of sq 436
Lots 1 & 2 in sq 385	Whole of sq 473
Lots 1 thru 18, lots 59 thru 76, in sq 387;	Lots 20 thru 26 in sq 502
	Lots 27 thru 68 in sq 502

All of square 545
All of sq east of square 546
All of sq 547
All sq 549
All sq 596
All sq east of sq 596
All sq 597
All sq east of sq 547
All sq 549
All sq 596

All sq east of sq 596
All sq 597
Lot 9 in sq 54
Lot 1 in sq 463
Lot 1 in sq n w of sq 492
South part of sq 542
North part of said sw 542
All sq 563
All of square 546, except the n w corner thereof

Lots 4 thru 6, lots 11, 12, 17, 18, & 19, & part of 20, in sq 503
Seized & taken in execustion as the lands of Saml Eliot, jr, & will be sold to satisfy the above named writ of fieri facias. Sale before the County Court-house door. –Tench Ringgold, Late Marshal of D C

Mrd: on Thu last, in Edenton, N C, by Rev Mr Johnson, Hon Wm B Shepard to Miss Ann Collins, of Edenton.

Mrd: on Thu, by Rev John C Smith, Mr Dennis O Hare to Miss Mary M Hammack, all of Wash City.

Died: on Tue last, at Alexandria, D C, Edmund I Lee, aged 71 years & 10 days. He was one of the oldest & most respectable citizens of Alexandria; educated for the bar; appointed Clerk of the U S Circuit Court for this county, which ofc he filled for many years. He was several times Major of Alexandria. –Alex Gaz

Died: on May 28, after a long & painful illness, Miss Charlotte Campbell, aged 16 years.

Died: on May 29, Mrs Mgt Freeman, relict of the late Col Freeman. Her funeral will be from her residence, Seven Bldgs, on Sat, at 3 p m.

R M Waring & Co: Dealers in Hardware & Cutlery. Opposite Brown's Hotel, 2 doors west of 6th st.

MON JUN 5, 1843
Tradesmen & mechanics are invited to the extensive Sawing & Turning establishment on the corner of 7th & B sts, opposite Shepherd's Lumber Yard. We hope by strict attention to business to merit a share of public patronage.
–B J Tayman & Co

New & Seasonable Goods: striped lawns; Maurselines; Balzareens; silk, Gentlemen's, boys', & servants' wear. –G W Adams, at the old store of Adams & McPherson, Pa ave, between 8th & 9th.

Cheap Dry Goods & Bonnets: at the Cheap Cash Store, Corner of 8th st & Pa ave. –H Carter & Co

Shoes! Fresh supply of those new splendid new Slips at $1. Misses' fancy Gaiters, very cheap. -J S Clagett, at Clarke's Dry Goods store, 2 doors east of 8th st.

Death of Lord Fitzgerald. This nobleman, the Pres of the Board of Control, died on Thu at his residence, Belgrave sq, London; the eldest s/o the late Baroness Fitzgerald, by the Rt Hon Jas Fitzgerald, & succeeded to the Irish barony in Jan, 1832, on the death of his mother.

Wm Crump, of Powhatan Co, Va, has been appointed Naval Storekeeper for the Washington Navy Yard, vice Cary Selden, dec'd.

During the absence of the Sec of War, who left here on Fri, the Pres appointed Saml Humes Porter, to be Acting Sec of the Dept of War. –Madisonian

Capt Isaac McKeever assumed the command of the U S razee **Independence**, at N Y, on Fri, in the place of Capt Stringham, who is relieved from that command at his own request.

A fine boy, named Tascoe, was drowned last Thu, near Lenox's wharf, not far from the Long Bridge. It appeared he was alone in a skiff, & it is presumed he had been tempted to get into it [finding the skiff unlocked to the wharf as it ought not to have been] for the purpose of amusing himself with a ride on the water.

Gen Wm S Murphy, of Ohio, U S Charge d'Affaires to Texas, arrived in New Orleans on the 24th ult. He was to leave for Texas on the 29th ult.

Indiana Election:

District	Locofocos	
Whigs		
1	John W Payne	Robt D Owen
2	Jos L White	Thos J Henley
3	John B Matson	Thos Smith
4	Caleb B Smith	No nomination
5	David Wallace	Wm J Brown
6	Geo G Dunn	John W Davis
7	E W McGaughey	Jos A Wright
8	Danl Mace	John Pettit
9	Saml C Sample	E M Chamberlain
10	David Kilgore	Andrew Kennedy

The attractions at the Military Encampment, to commence at Fred'k today, will be increased by the presence of the fine company of U S Light Artl, stationed at Fort McHenry, under command of Maj Ringgold.

Died: on May 20, at Louisville, Ky, very suddenly, Maj Asher Phillips, formerly a paymaster in the Army, aged 48 years.

Died: Mar 25 last, at Genoa, Lady Erskine, w/o Lord Erskine, her Majesty's Envoy Extra & Minister Pleni at the Court of Munich, & d/o Gen Cadwallader, of Phil, U S.

Orphan's Court of Wash Co, D C. Letters of adm, with the will annexed, on the personal estate of Peter W Gallaudet, late of said county, dec'd. Claims to be settled on or before Jun 5; they may otherwise by law be excluded from all benefit of said estate. –E Gallaudet, adm w a

Wash Corp: ordinances: 1-Act for the relief of J E Fowler & Co: fine imposed by judgment of John D Clark, for a violation of an ordinance relative to the sale of hats, boots, & shoes, be remitted: Provided, Fowler & Co pay the costs of prosecution. 2- Act for the relief of Alfred Hutmuller: by judgment of J D Clark, for a violation of the ordinance in relation to the enclosure of streets, is hereby remitted, provided Hutmuller pay the cost of the prosecution; & provided that Hutmuller, within 10 days after the passage of this act, remove his fence so as to conform to the existing law of the Corp in relation to the enclosure of streets.

TUE JUN 6, 1843
Mr Wm Abbott, the comedian, whose illness in N Y was mentioned, experienced another severe attack of apoplexy on Thu, & died that day. He was one of the old school of actors, & had a long time held a high rank in his profession in England. He came to this country some 3 or 4 years ago.

Fire at Taunton, Mass: 10 bldgs on Main st were consumed by fire last Wed night. They were principally occupied as stores & the occupants were J O Bart/Burt, Solomon Woodman, Geo Townsend, Chas Babbitt & Son, E M Perkins, E C Crane, Chas Godfrey, J & W Reed, E G Baker, C R Pierce, Stearns & Stanley, Mrs Leonard, & J Lufkin.

Caleb Gammage Eastman, Editor of the "Spirit of the Age," one of the most virulent Locofoco papers of Vt, has been appointed Postmaster at Woodstock, Windsor Co, in the place of Joel Eaton, "reformed." Mr Eaton received his appointment 2 years ago from the same Tyler administration which has now displaced him. He had discharged his ofc with eminent fidelity. –Albany Journal

Chas W Roberts, who was appointed Postmaster at Salem, N J, seeing the general course of Mr Tyler, sent in his resignation recently. On Wed 2 commissions were

received in town; one for Solomon H Merrit, the former postmaster under Mr Van Buren, & the other for Wm Mulford, one of the vice presidents of the late Tyler convention at Trenton! Mr Merritt's was dated one day later than the other, & of course confers upon him the appointment. So that the Tyler man is jilted.
-Newark Adv

Henry Cornell, about 17, was instantly killed at N Y, last week, when he ran into a black man going in the opposite direction. The shock of the collision was so violent that Cornell instantly fell backwards upon the pavement, & was taken up dead. Physicians were unable to help him. –N Y Tribune

A laborer, Peter Spelman, residing in Darkesville, Berkeley Co, Va, was shot on May 28, by a young woman named Susan Waggoner, who it seems did the deed in self defence. Miss Waggoner has been imprisoned for investigation.

Fatal re-encounter took place in the court room during the session of the Court at Canton, Miss, on May 20, between Mr Jeremiah Ellington & T C Tupper. Mr Tupper was addressing the jury upon the trial of a criminal case, in which Ellington was prosecutor, & was commenting legitimately upon the evidence, when Ellington came up behind him, & struck him over the head with a huge stick. Mr Tupper seized a sword cane that lay near him, & stabbed Elligton under the left arm. Mr Elligton died a few minutes afterwards. Judge Rollins adjourned the Court for a short time.

Geo R Wall, about 22 years of age, residing with his mother at 94 North Howard st, Balt, destroyed his own life on Fri by taking laudanum. It is supposed he committed the act through partial mental alienation.

Mr Wm Cook, s/o Mr Geo Cook, of Augusta Co, Va, while employed one day last week in bathing the leg of a colt for some disease, received a kick from the animal in the stomach, which caused his death in about 10 minutes. Mr Cook was not quite 21 years of age, & a promising young man.

Result of the Annual Election, held yesterday, for members of the Board of Aldermen, to serve 2 years, & members of the Common Council, to serve 1 year.
Alderman:
*John D Barclay   *Jos W Beck
*John Wilson   *Nathl Brady
*John W Maury   *Edw W Clarke
Common Council:
*Wm Wilson   Alex'r McIntire   Lewis Johnson
*Richd M Harrison   *Jas F Haliday   John W Maury
*Chas A Davis   *Ignatius Mudd   Geo Crandell
Geo Lowry   *Nicholas Callan, jr   *Saml Bacon

*John T Towers	N C Towle	Marmaduke Dove
John F Callan	*Jos W Beck	*Geo H Fulmer
John Y Bryant	John Fitzpatrick	*Jas Crandell
Jonathan T Walker	*John McCauley	*Jas Cull
Jas Douglass	*Wm Dixon	R H Harrington
Jas H Birch	*John E Neale	Thos Kelley
Geo Watterton	Wm P Ferguson	Benedict Milburn
*Simeon Bassett	John L Maddox	Francis Riley
*John Lynch	T A Doniphan	

To fill a vacancy in the Board of Aldermen, occasioned by the recent resignation of Jas Carbery.
Jas Adams-90; Jos W Beck-9; Geo Watterston-2
*Those marked with an asterisk [*] are elected.
The following were elected last year & their term of service has not expired:

Wm B Magruder	John H Goddard	Saml Byington
Wm Orme	Jas Adams	Jas Marshall

Criminal Court: Grand Jury: Wash City

Thos Carbery, Foreman	Roger C Weightman	Francis Dodge, sen
	Richd Cutts	John McCobb
Geo Thomas	John Carter	Josh Smoot
Benj O Tayloe	John Cox	Chas R Belt
Chas A Burnett	Thos Fenwick	Edw M Linthicum
Robt White	John Mason, jr	Jacob Gideon
Jos Forrest	Joshua Pierce	Lewis Johnson
John Boyle	John W Maury	
Wm A Bradley	Levi Sheriff	

Valuable land for sale: part of **Delecarlia**, formerly owned by the late Clement Smith, containing about 150 acs. Another tract, about 769 acs of land in Stafford Co, Va, late the property of Mrs Bronaugh. –Bradley & Thruston, Gen Agents, 6th st, Gadsbys Hotel

Trustee's sale: decree of the Circuit Court of Wash Co, D C, as a Court of Chancery, made in the cause of Jas Townley et al vs Nicholas L Sutton et al: sale in front of the premises, on Jun 16, the Lot of Ground in Gtwn at the s w corner of Bridge & Washington sts, together with the improvements, consisting of several frame tenements. –Clement Cox, trustee -Edw S Wright, auct

Trustee's sale: decree of the Circuit Court of Wash Co, D C, as a Court of Chancery, made in the cause of Jas Townley et al vs John Mountz et al: sale in front of the premises, on Jun 16, a portion of the real estate of Henry Knowles, jr, dec'd, viz: a valuable Lot of Ground on the west side of Washington st: with a commodious 2 story brick dwlg & other extensive bldgs. Also, an undivided moiety of a Lot lying south of the above property & improved by a comfortable brick dwlg: fronts on Washington st. Also, a divided third part of the Lots #188 & 189 of Beall's Addition to Gtwn. –Clement Cox, trustee -Edw S Wright, auct

Police Intelligence-Wash. 1-Yesterday committed to jail by Justice Morsell, negro Aaron Coakley, charged, on the oath of Jilson Dove, Jas B Phillips, & Benj Marlow, with attempting to set on fire a frame shop, the property of the said Jas B Phillips, in Wash City. 2-Also committed to jail, by Justice Goddard, Jas Simonds, charged on the oath of Geo Hoblitzell & Anthony Cobell with having, on Jun 4, 1843, stolen wheat flour, the property of said Hoblitzell, out of his boat in Gtwn. 3-On Sun last, a free Negro, Richd Stewart, was committed to jail, charged upon the oath of Benj Kirk with having stabbed Jos Lacy, free negro, in the market-house at Gtwn, during a fight. We understand that Lacy is very severely wounded.

WED JUN 7, 1843
Capon Springs, 22 miles west of Winchester, Va, will be open for visiters on Jun 15. Board per week, $7; per day, $1; children & servants, half price. –J C Waddle

For sale: on Jun 27, at Port Tobacco, Chas Co, Md, the estate called ***Charleston***, formerly the property of Col John Campbell, lying in the lower part of said county, containing 805 acs of prime land. Improvements: excellent dwlg-house, corn houses, stables, barns, & granaries, all in good repair. Apply to Peter W Crain, Milton Hill, Chas Co, Md.

Orphan's Court of Wash Co, D C. In the case of Leonard Harbaugh, administrator of John Laughan, dec'd: Dec 5 next appointed for the settlement of the estate. –Ed N Roach, Reg of Wills

Mrd: on Jun 6, by Rev M P Gallagher, John P Waring, of Norway, Montg Co, Md, to Miss Eveline G, 3rd d/o Maj Manning, of D C.

Died: on May 30, at the residence of a kind friend & neighbor, Robt Beverley, of Blandfield, Essex Co, Va, in his 75th year.

Died: on Apr 12 last, at Cairo, in Egypt, where he had gone for the benefit of his health, Fairfax Catlett, s/o Chas J Catlett, of Va.

Excellent furniture & piano forte, at Public Auction near the Navy Yard, on Jun 13, at the residence of Capt Jas Edelin, on G st south, between 7th & 8th sts, near the Marine Garrison, all his household & kitchen furniture. –Robt W Dyer & Co, aucts

Mr J D Ansley, of Iowa Co, Wisconsin, publishes in the Mineral Point Free Press that he has received from the U S Gov't a permit to locate 27 sections of copper lands in the copper region bordering Lake Superior. He intends to proceed within a few weeks to Lake Superior to work the mines, & offers to adventurers & miners who are disposed to accompany him grants of land in his mining district on liberal terms.

THU JUN 8, 1843

W H Storms, a naval apprentice on board the U S ship **Independence**, lying at N Y, fell from a spar on Sat & was killed. At Phil, on Sun, a similar accident happened to Wm Williams, of the ship **Herald**, who was instantly killed by falling from the foretopsail yard.

Philip Null & John Poole, young men, residents of East Huntingdon township, Westmoreland Co, Pa, were accidentally drowned in a mill pond on May 25. The former lost his life in a generous endeavor to save that of his companion.

Columbus, Ga: Jury in the case of John Langdon Lewis, charged as an accessory after the fact in the late robbery of the Trust Co at that place, returned into Court with a verdict of not guilty. Thos C McKeen, charged as a principal in the same robbery, has had his case continued to the next term of the Court, on the ground of absent testimony.

Died: on Mon last, in Perth Amboy, N J, Mr Andrew Bell, a venerable citizen of that State, aged 86 years-the day of his death being the anniversary of his birth. He was one of the Board of Proprietors of N J, & for many years held the ofc of Surveyor General.

Died: a few days ago, in Charlotte, Va, Col Jos Wyatt, at the advanced age of 92 or 93. He was 44 years successively a member of the Housef of Delegates from Charlotte, or a Senator from the district to which that county is attached.

NOTICE: I have taken John Foy's old stand, corner of 10th & D sts, where I invite my old customers & others to call. A good house to let on Louisian ave, between 6th & 7th sts south. Apply to F Mohun, opposite, or to: -Jas Davis.

$5 reward for a Breast Pin, with a Guard Chain & a small pearl attached, lost between Balt & Wash City, this morning. The reward will be paid by leaving the same at this ofc. –Wm Rushworth, South Water st, Phil, Pa

Sale of furniture: order of the Orphan's Court of Wash Co, D C: sale on Jun 10: the household furniture & other personal effects of the late John Keith, dec'd; consisting of, in part: chairs, tables, carpets, crockery & glassware, bedsteads, beds, bedding, bureaus. Also, about 50 prime hams. Terms cash. -Robt W Dyer & Co, aucts

Sale of household furniture at auction by order of the Orphan's Court of Wash Co, D C: sale on Jun 15, at the residence of the late Wm Hayman, nearly opposite the Brewery. Furniture in good order:
Cane seat & other chairs, mahogany hair seat sofa
Rocker, mahogany dining & card tables
Mahogany sideboard, piano forte & stool
Dinner & tea sets, cutglass tumblers, wines, decanters
Handsome Brussels & ingrain parlor, hall, stair, & chamber carpets
Stair rods, engravings, plated candlesticks
Snuffers & trays, fire-irons, bookcases
High & French-post bedsteads
Best feather beds, mattresses & bedding
Mahogany bureaus, mahogany & other wardrobe
Washstand, toilet sets, lot of books
Radiator, [stove,] & chamber stoves. General assortment of kitchen utensils, refrigerator. –Robt W Dyer & Co, aucts

Sale by order of the Orphan's Court of Wash Co, D C: sale on Jun 22, at our auction store, a part of the personal effects of the late Miss Eliz Brown, dec'd. 112 shares Bank of Washington stock
$9,700 Corporation 6% stock of the City of Washington
Also, a lot of books, trunks, brass wire, an excellent guitar & case, & lot of music. -Robt W Dyer & Co, aucts

House & Lot on C st at auction: in Chancery-Jonathan Seaver vs Chas S Fowler & others. Circuit Court of Wash Co, D C: sale on Jun 21, of the west half of lot #29 in Reservation #10, fronting 27 feet on C st, with bldgs thereon-3 story brick house, well finished, brick milk-house, & stable, & a garden stocked with much valuable fruit. –D A Hall, trustee -Robt W Dyer & Co, aucts

Last sale of plants at auction at the greenhouse & flower garden of Mr Buist. Ladies are requested to attend the sale. Seats will be provided & an awning raised for their convenience. -Robt W Dyer & Co, aucts

Wm B Stone & Walter Mitchell, execs of Alex'r Greer, vs the heirs & reps of Wm Prout, dec'd. Ordered by the Court that the papers in this cause be referred to the Auditor of this Court, to ascertain & report the amount of the personal estate, & to state an account of the administration thereof according to law; also to take an account of the debts due by said intestate, Wm Prout, at the time of his death, & an account of his real estate. –Jos Forrest, auditor

FRI JUN 9, 1843
Everhart, who murdered his wife at St Marks, Fla, in the most inhuman & barbarous manner, was brought to trial on May 22 in the Superior Court for Wakulla Co. The

jury retired & were not absent more than 15 minutes, when they returned with a verdict of guilty. The Judge then pronounced the sentence of the law, that he [the prisoner] should be hanged on Fri, Jun 16 next.

Mrs S Masi, corner of 4½ st & Pa ave, has several large & desirable rooms, with which she would be happy to accommodate those wishing to board.

The Boston papers mention that among those to be present at the celebration of the completion of the Bunker Hill Monument, on Jun 17, is Gen Gideon Foster, a resident of Danvers, not 95 years old. He commanded the Danvers minute men who fought in the battle of Lexington, & has survived all those who served under him. He is in the enjoyment of excellent health.

The deed of bargain & sale of a house purchased by Shakspeare in Blackfriars, dated Mar 10, 1612, with the signature of the poet attached to it, which deed was sold in May, 1841, was again brought to the hammer, by Mr Evans, on Wed last, & sold for L145. In 1838 the British Museum gave L130 for the copy of "Florio's Essays of Montague, 1608, with the name "William Shakespeare" written on the fly-leaf. It was doubtless an authentic signature of the poet. On the former occasion when this autograph was sold it brought L160. It was publicly announced that it was bought by Mr Lambert Jones for the library of the city of London. During the life of Shakspeare, the lord mayor & aldermen successfully resisted the performance of a single play by Shakspeare within their walls, & now they give L145 for his signature.

At Columbus, Ga, on May 27, the young son of Mrs Eaton Bass, was drowned while bathing in the river. On the same day, Mr Simpler, who was trying to escape from the sheriff of Russell Co, Ala, was also drowned. His body had not been recovered up to May 31.

The Pittsburg papers state that Mr Chas H Eaton, the tragedian, had died of injuries received from falling off the porch of his lodgings.

Byron Padgett, a young man, of Louisville, Ky, was recently shot near Middletown. He & several others [all somewhat intoxicated] were shooting at a mark, when a quarrel ensued between him & Padget Hall, formerly of Va, who leveled his rifle at Padget, & shot him dead on the spot. Hall has been imprisoned for trial

Mrd: on May 31, by Rev Mr Massie, Hon Geo W Hopkins, M C of Abingdon, Va, to Miss Martha, y/d/o Dr Abner Crump, of Powhatan Co.

$50 reward for runaway negro man Jim Hawkins, aged 30 years. His parents live with Mr Alex'r McKee, living near the Horsehead in PG Co, Md, & has many acquaintances in Benedict & Calvert Co. –Nicholas V Miles

SAT JUN 10, 1843
On Fri last, 3 lads, John M Besse, Nathan Besse, & Wm Hooker, ventured out on a fishing excursion a few miles down Wareham harbor, Mass, & the wind blowing, the boat upset & all drowned. The oldest, J M Besse, must have got into the boat after she righted, as he was found dead in the boat the next morning. The two Besses were the sons of a poor widow, who was depending in a great measure on their industry for her support. –New Bedford Mercury

Magistrates' Court at Providence, Fairfax Court House, Va, on Jun 6, to try a free mulatto girl named Lucinda, who willfully & intentionally set fire to the barn & stables at Laurel Grove, in said county, belonging to Mr Jas Atkinson, which, with their contents, provender, farming utensils, were entirely destroyed on Apr 29. She was found guilty & sentenced to 5 years imprisonment in the State pen.

Jabez W Throop, Postmaster at Schoharie Court-house, N Y, has been removed for the following reason: You are charged with being a strong opponent to the administration of Pres Tyler; that you bestow your official patronage upon the "Schoharie Patriot," a newspaper published in said village, which is in the constant habit of denouncing John Tyler & his measures in the most coarse & approbrious manner. It is futher alleged that your age & consequent infirmity obliges you to perform the duties of your ofc by deputies, who are also violent opposers to Pres Tyler. An immediate explanation is required. –John A Bryan, 2nd Assist Postmaster Gen

Messrs A & R Buchanan's large warehouse in Louisville, Ky, was destroyed by fire last Sat.

Mrd: on Jun 6, near Piscataway, Md, by Rev Wm H Laney, Mr Presely N Athey to Miss Mary E Massey, both of PG Co, Md.

Died: on the 12th inst, in Montg Co, N C, in his 93rd year, Capt Edwin Ingram, a sldr of the Revolution. At an early period of the struggle he voluntarily left a home blessed with every comfort that heart could desire, & tearing himself from the caresses of a most amiable & accomplished companion, went forth to brave the hardships of the "tented field." At first he enlisted as a common sldr, but soon rose to the rank of Capt. He was in the regular army but a short time. He served under Gen Marion, & was on his way with him to join Gates when they heard of that ofcr's defeat at Camden. After the celebrated Flora McDonald had been plundered of her property in the neighborhood of Fayetteville, she removed to Mountain creek, in Richmond Co. The subject of this notice gave her such aid as was in his power, furnished her with a horse, & assisted her to Charleston, whence she departed for Scotland. To the extermination of lawless depredators Mr Ingram devoted several years of his life. For this service the Legislature voted him a gratuity of 500 pounds, which, on account of the embarrassed condition of the State, he refused to accept.

Jas Watson, who was arrested a short time since at Independence, Mo, as a participator in stealing Treas notes from the custom house in New Orleans, & Orin P Rockwell, the Mormon, who had been committed as the person who some time since attempted to assassinate Gov Boggs, recently made their escape from the jail in Independence. They were overtaken a short distance from the jail.

Last evening Col Hastings was returning to the city of Balt on horseback, on the Falls road, his horse became frightened, threw the rider, & dragged him some distance, one foot remaining in the stirrup. He was considerably injured, & would most likely have been killed had not a colored man caught the horse while it was running at considerable speed, & dragging Mr Hastings by one leg. –Sun

Stray mare found near Benning's bridge on Wed last. The owner can have her by paying the expenses & calling on the subscriber, near Benning's bridge, where the mare now is. –Henry Miller, Wash Co

Sale of household furniture & groceries, at Public Auction: at the residence of Mr Jas Davis, on E st, between 10th & 11th sts: on Jun 12. A general lot of Groceries & Store Fixtures. -Robt W Dyer & Co, aucts

Orphan's Court of Wash Co, D C: sale on Jun 16, by order of the Court, at the brewery of the late Wm Hayman, part of the Brewery Fixtures, Cart, Horse, & 156 butts & puncheons, 148 pipes, 374 hogsheads, 235 barrels, 412 half barrels, 218 kegs, funnels, buckets, kegs, counting house deaks & tables, stove, chairs, shovel & tongs, thermometer, cordage, box tools, lot corks, sheet lead measures, cellar rope, scales & weights. Also, 40 cords pine wood, dray horse, cart, halters & chains. 140 barrels of ale. -Robt W Dyer & Co, aucts

Valuable Fairfax land for sale: 510 acs, near Leesburg & Gtwn turnpike, less than 8 miles from the latter. For terms apply to Thos S Love, Fairfax Court-house, Va, or to the subscriber. Mr Hirst, who resides near the premises [on Cmdor Jones' farm,] will show the land. –Roger Jones, Wash, D C

For sale, either 40, 60, or 100 acs of land within the Dist of Col. The subscriber, having more land than he can clear & cultivate, offers at private sale a part of the farm on which he lives, adjoining Messrs Butt, Sheppard, & Bowes, on the Wash & Rockville turnpike road, about 4 miles from the city. –Henry Ould

Land for sale: tract of 100 acs on Rock creek, about 5 or 6 miles from Washington; it adjoins the property of Capt Carbery & others who have purchased land in the same vicinity. Any one wishing to purchase may get a bargain, as I have no use for it & am desirous to sell. –D Clagett

Boarding School for Boys in Burlington, N J, established for nearly 20 years & conducted by one of the subscribers will be re-opened on Nov 1 next. Benj V Marsh will take part in the general instruction & charge of the students. Either of the subscribers may be addressed, at West Haverford, Dela Co, Pa, or after Sep 9, at Burlington, N J. –John Gummere -Saml J Gummere

Land for sale: about 96 acs lying in Alexandria Co, D C, 6 miles from Alexandria. This property adjoins the farms of Mrs Gardner, Tench Ringgold, & Wesley Carlin, & the farm on which I live. -Jas H Carlin

Assembly Rooms have been fitted up in a style of elegance as a resort for both gentlemen & ladies. The house will be opened on Mon next, the 12th inst. –C Lapon

MON JUN 12, 1843
Franklin Ins Co of Wash City. Meeting held on Jun 5 & the following were elected Directors to serve the ensuing year:

Jas McClery	J M Roberts	Jos H Bradley
Jas C Hall	Nicholas Callan	Walter Lenox
Wm J McDonald	John Boyle	G C Grammer
John P Ingle	Wm A Bradley	John F Callan

St Louis Republican of the 30th ult, says: a s/o Danl Hubler, of this county, about 12 years old, was killed by lightning on Sun. Three or four others, among them Mr Hibler, who were standing near by, were severely injured.

Dr Jas Perrine has been removed from the ofc of Collector of the port of Mobile, Ala, & Collier H Minge appointed in his stead. Perrine, appt'd by Mr Tyler, was removed because he was suspected of "being at heart in favor of Mr Clay."
-Mobile Adv of 3rd inst

Mr Wm A Woodal, pump maker, while engaged in fixing a pump near Upper Marlboro, PG Co, Md, on Wed last, slipped into the well, & was instanteously killed.

On May 30, at Franklinville, Long Island, a fine youth named B G Fanning was thrown from a horse he was riding, under a harrow, in such a manner as caused him to receive a violent blow on the head from one of the teeth, which caused his death.

Mrd: on Thu last, by Rev John C Smith, Mr Wm Harrott to Miss Mary McPeak, all of Wash City.

Mrd: on Jun 1, in N Y, Dr Wm Maffitt, Assist Surgeon U S A, to Julia, d/o P Chouteau, jr, of St Louis, Mo.

Columbian Horticultural Society: election of ofcrs on Thu last: Wm Rich, Pres
V Presidents-5:

Geo Watterston	R S Coxe	D A Hall
Wm W Seaton	Geo Shoemaker	
A Suter, Treas	J M Cutts, Rec Sec	John F Callan, Librarian
J S Skinner, Corr Sec		
Council:		
John A Smith	Wm Buist	Wm Thompson
Dr W B Magruder	W Cammack	Chas Stott
Dr Gunnell	C H Wiltberger	Col Kearney
Dr Alex McWilliams	Robt Dick	John F Callan
Joshua Pierce	W D Breckenridge	
John Douglas	Gen Weightman	

Application has been made at the Treas Dept for the renewal of Treas Note #32,862, dated May 20, 1842, in favor of Richd Smith, for $50, the same having been accidentally destroyed. –John C Reommele, corner of 18th & K sts

Sale of very handsome & good furniture: on Jun 14, at the late residence of the late Mrs Col Freeman, in one of the Seven Bldgs, by order of the Orphan's Court of Wash Co, D C. -Robt W Dyer & Co, aucts

TUE JUN 13, 1843
Desirable private residence for sale: the western division of square 352 in Wash City, fronting 111 feet on Md ave: dwlg is covered with slate, & built in the most substantial manner of the best materials. $3,000 will be required in hand, the balance properly secured with interest will be made payable in 3 equal instalments.
–L H Machen

Mr C S Lobdell, the failthful & efficient Postmaster at Johnstown, N Y, has been removed, & H B Matthews, a Locofoco of the first water, appointed in his place.

Buffalo papers announce the death, on May 21, of Mrs Maria Wait, in her 31st year. She was the w/o Benj Wait, one of the Canadian political convicts. Her exertions in behalf of her husband & his fellow prisoners who were under sentence of death for political offences committed during the winter of 1837 & 1838 seemed almost superhuman. After procuring a commutation of the death sentence, she went directly to London, where she continued 10 months her unwearied exertions for their final release. She was most kindly received by the Queen. Through her exertions, the freedom of the island was extended to them & all the liberty they could enjoy in the land of their exile, & but for their escape, she soon would have procured their final pardon.

1-High Court of Appeals of the Commonwealth of Va, held at the Capitol in the city of Richmond on Feb 20, 1843, in the case of Private Geo Cottingham, a sldr of the U S Army, who some time since sued for his discharge on the plea of alienage. The public service has been put to great inconvenience in consequence of the vexatious & numerous writs of habeas corpus issued against the ofcrs, & on this false pretence nearly 400 men have effected their discharge, after a summary trial, in most cases by inferior tribunals, notwithstanding their voluntary enlistment & deliberate & solemn contract with the Gov't. –R Jones
2-The U S, plntf, against Geo Cottingham, dfndnt. Court is of the opinion that the dfndnt is not illegally detained in custody. It is therefore ordered that he be remanded into the service of the U S, according to the terms of his enlistment. –J Allen, C C
3-Supreme Court of the State of N Y. In the matter of Richd Wingall, a sldr of the U S Army.
In the matter of Peter Doyle, a sldr of the U S Army. The First Judge of Oswego Co, had upon habeas corpus, discharged the sldr on the ground that, being an alien, his contract of enlistment was void. These proceedings were removed by writs of certiorari into the Supreme Court of this State, & the cases were at the last Jan term argued by J A Spencer, U S Atty in behalf of the Gov't, & by Saml Stevens, in behalf of the sldrs. At the recent May term of that Court judgments of reversal have been given, thereby deciding that an alien enlisting into the U S service is bound by his contract, & cannot be legally discharged on habeas corpus. –Utica Gaz

Camp Frederick [at Frederick City, Md] was broken up last Sat. On Thu the troops were reviewed by Gen Geo H Steuart, of Balt, & on Fri by Gen Williams, of Hagerstown.

Nathan Hale, editor of the Boston Daily Advertiser, has been re-elected pres of the Boston & Worcester Railroad Co.

The whale ship **Lucy**, which arrived at New Bedford on Jun 9th, on Feb 10 had 2 boats stove by a whale, drowning 3 men, John W H Thompson, of Phil, cooper, aged 35; Philander P Booth, of Middleborough, aged 20; & Ephraim Shockley, of Middleborough, aged 16.

Mr Harvey D Durkee, a young man residing at Fort Edward, N J, was accidentally shot on May 29 by a boy who was in the act of crowding down a cap upon the tube of a rifle, which igniting was discharged, & the contents lodged in the thigh of Mr Durkee, which caused his death in a few days.

Swindler: who called himself Wm S Wright, was last week arrested at Balt upon the oath of Edw Dyer, Sgt-at-Arms of the U S Senate, charged with obtaining from him $250 under false pretences, inducing Mr Dyer to endorse a note for him upon the representation that he was a brother to the Hon Silas Wright, & temporarily destitute of funds. Wright, his wife Hannah H Wright, & their baggage, were examined, & a large bundle of letters were found in his possession, professing to be introductory from men of fame. Wright & his wife were committed to jail. –Balt Sun

Capt Zephin Lankford, of the schnr **Francis Jane**, of Somerset Co, Md, with a negro boy, a hand on board, was accidentally lost overboard from his vessel, during the heavy blow, Sat night. The only person left on board the schnr after the accident was a colored man, who at the time had the helm. It was utterly impossible for him to do anything to save the drowning men. This deprives a wife & 3 children of a protector.

Coroner Greenfield held an inquest on Sat last over the body of John Bromwell, age 13 years, who was drowned under painful circumstances in Carroll's Falls, near the Alms-house, Balt. He left his father's residence, in Pine st, with some other boys, to go bathing. While in the water he was seized by fits, to which he had been accustomed, & he perished.

A young lawyer discovers that an emigrant from the Emerald Isle was heir to an immense fortune, estimated to be worth $1,700,000 as a reward for his services, is Chas Grandison Thomas, who graduated at Harvard Univ in 1838. –Boston Bulletin

On Jun 3 Mr Evinger, of Floyd Co, Indiana, was in a stable with another man, when a horse near them was killed by lightning & Mr E's companion severely shocked. Mr E carried him into the house, where he found his wife had been killed. There was no damage done either to the house of the stable, & the 2 bldgs were some 40 or 50 yards distant from each other. This is most singular, since both deaths must have been caused by the same explosion.

Died: on Jun 2, at his residence in Orange Co, N C, Mr John Strayhorn, sen, in his 90th year. Mr Strayhorn was a sldr of the Revolution, & was a pensioner at the time of his death.

Correspondence of "The News." Fort King, May 28, 1843. We were much surprised last evening by the arrival at Silver Springs of the Rev Mr Halliday, who had ascended the Ocklawaha in a four-oared boat from its mouth. His reports having met with but few difficulties in his way. Mr Prevost, the U S surveyor, arrived her also last night with his party, having nearly completed his surveys. I was called upon to act as foreman of a jury of inquest, &, on arriving at the spot, recognised in the dec'd the person of Saml Garey, a young man formerly from Black Creek, & who had entered a tract of land about 2½ miles from here. He had put an end to his existence by blowing his brains out. He was no doubt immediately killed, for he placed the muzzle of the gun in his mouth, & there was no sign of any struggle.

Stop the Rascal! Richd N Avery [25] left Andover on May 29th taking with him $800 belonging to a boarding association of students at the Theological Seminary; & he also took with him the 16 year old son of a respectable gentleman of Boston. $100 reward for his return to Boston or Andover, or give such information as will tend to his detection. –Boston Mercantile Journal

$5 reward: strayed from my residence on C st, between 4½ & 6th sts, a dark brown Milch Cow. I will give the above reward to any person who will deliver said cow to me. –Stan's Murray

To let, a 2 story frame house on D st, between 6th & 7th sts. Inquire next door above, or at Jas P McKean's Confectionary Store, late Mrs Ronckendorff's, Pa ave, between 4½ & 6th sts.

For sale, a superior fine-toned Piano Forte, N Y make, 6 octaves. –J F Kahl, Piano Forte Maker, Pa ave, between 12th & 13th sts.

Wash Corp: election of ofcrs yesterday: Jas Adams, Pres of the Board; John D Barclay, V P; Erasmus J Middleton, Sec; Jacob Kleiber, Messenger.

WED JUN 14, 1843
The brig **Pecounic**, Capt Robt A Wilbur, arrived last evening from New Orleans, having on board the Capt, Geo G Smith, & crew of the schnr **Frances Kennedy**, foundered at sea. The F K was bound from St Thomas to Charleston, in ballast, having about $2,500 in specie on board. On Jun 3rd, in heavy weather, during the night, she sprung a plank, which let in the water & all efforts to free her were in vain. The brig **Pecounic** hove in sight just in time to take off the Capt & crew, saving them from a watery grave.

The Pres of the U S left Phil on Sat for Princeton, N J, where he remained during Sunday as the guest of Capt R F Stockton, of the U S Navy.

R M Miller was convicted last week at Grand Rapids, Kent Co, Mich, for the murder of an Indian woman. The Jury returned a verdict of guilty of murder in the first degree, & a recommendation for Executive clemency. This is the first conviction for a capital offence ever had in this State. The sentence was suspended until the next Nov term.

The Pottsville [Pa} Emporium of Sat states that on Thu last, as the Rev Mr Hassinger of that borough was driving into town, near the York Store, his horse became frightened & started a full run-when himself & little dght either jumped or were thrown from the wagon & seriously injured, the latter so much so that she died on the following morning.

A locomotive attached to a freight train from Cumberland ran off the track on Mon near the Point of Rocks. The fireman, a worthy young man named Jesse Aler, was thrown off & died soon after.

The extensive bagging factory of Saml Redd, at Lexington, Ky, was consumed by fire on Jun 6th. Loss very great-no insurance.

Public sale of negroes on Aug 30 next at the residence of the late John Carter, dec'd, near Upperville, Fauquier Co, Va, 50 or 60 valuable slaves, consisting of men, women, boys, & girls. They are sold for not fault. –Josiah Tidball, John A Carter, excs of J Carter, dec'd. At the same time & place: sale of a large number of horses & colts; farm stock, 60 head of fat cattle, a large quantity of wheat, corn, etc. –John B Carter, Robt Carter

Orphan's Court of Wash Co, D C. Letters of adm, with the will annexed, on the personal estate of Mgt Freeman, late of said county, dec'd. Claims to be exhibited on or before Jun 2 next. –Saml Agnew, Seven Bldgs, residence of the late Mrs Freeman.

Wm Hess, a German, died in Lafayette, La, of hydrophobia, a frightful disease, on May 30th. Four weeks ago he was bitten by a young dog, which at the time had the distemper, but was not supposed to be mad. The dog died in a few days after inflicting the bite. All medical aid proved unavailing.

Alexandria Canal Ofc: proposals will be received for bldg 4 locks, as the outlet of the Alexandria Canal to the river. –M C Ewing, Engineer in Charge

I O O F-The Grand Lodge of D C-meeting this evening at half past 7 o'clock. –Urias Hurst, sec

Horses: at the Franklin Stable, on 6th st. –N Rowles, Proprietor

NOTICE: I have removed my Law Ofc to my dwlg-house on Duke st, west of Washington st, in the town of Alexandria, D C. –Thos Semmes

For the National Intelligencer. ***The Maison Rouge*** property is the estate unsuccessfully claimed by Maj Gen Gaines, is a mistake. The suit of E P Gaines et ux vs Richd Relf, Beverly Chew, Chas Patterson, et al, in which the heirship of Mrs M C Gaines to the estate of her father, the late Danl Clark was tried, was decided in favor of the plntfs in the court below, from which an appeal was taken by the dfndnts to the U S Supreme Court, where the case lies already agued & ready to be decided at the next regular term. Mrs G's heirship once established, & her right to the whole of the Clark estate follows. The *Maison Rouge* property, known as the *Maison Rouge grant*, was part of that estate at the time of Mr Clark's death. So far from this being the estate unsuccessfully claimed by Maj Gen Gaines, it is but a portion of the estate thus far successfully claimed by him. X

To let: 3 story brick house, corner of 10th st & Pa ave: contains 12 rooms, 11 of which have fireplaces. Inquire at the store adjoining. –Michl Sardo, proprietor

Montevideo paper says: Govn'r Rosas has expelled the clergy of the order of Jesuits from Buenos Ayres in consequence of their having refused to hang up his portrait for public adoration over the altar of their church, as has been done by all the other friars of that city. The Buenos Ayres British Packet confirms the fact of their expulsion, but does not assign the same cause for it.

Mrd: on May 31, at Holly Hill, Caroline Co, Va, by Rev Jas Henshall, Lt Gabriel G Williamson, U S Navy, to Miss Gabriella, eldest d/o Pichegru Woolfolk.

Mrd: on Jun 1, at Mulberry Place, Caroline Co, Va, by Rev E L Magoon, Wm W Roper, M D, to Miss Betty Carr, eldest d/o Jourdan Woolfolk.

Died: on Jan 11, of inflammation of the brain, John W, infant s/o Arundel Smith, of PG Co, Md.

THU JUN 15, 1843
Mr Mason Cheesebrough, druggists, of Rome, N Y, on Sat was charging a soda fountain in his store when it exploded & a piece struck him in the head, the effects of which he died in a few hours. He was a young man, 25 or 26, more than commonly esteemed by the citizens of Rome & others.

Mr W E Robinson, a native of Ireland, a recent graduate at Yale College, will deliver a lecture on Mon next in the Apollo Hall, embracing a historical sketch of the connexion between Ireland & England.

Died: in Wash City, on Jun 2, John Cary, in his 114th year. This is the same "Old John," of whom some notice was taken in the Intelligencer last winter, when a joint resolution was pending before Congress to grant him a pension. He was born of African parents, in Westmoreland Co, Va, in Aug, 1729, 2½ years before the birth of Gen Washington, & in the same county. Had he lived 2 months longer he would have reached the full age of 114 years. He was with Gen Washington as his personal servant in the old French war, & in the battlefield on the Monongahela, in Jul, 1755, where Gen Braddock was defeated & slain, & where Washington covered the retreat & saved the remnant of the British army, & laid the foundation of his military fame. In the war of the Revolution, John followed to the camp & field his old cmder.

When retiring, Gen Washington presented him with a military coat, the same which the Gen had won at the siege of Yorktown. In old age reduced to extreme poverty, no money could ever tempt him to part with this coat. He wore it as a dress coat till within the last 15 years of his life. After the Revolution, John resided in Westmoreland Co for several years, where he became a devout member of the Baptist Church. He removed to this place & for the last 28 years of his life was a mbmer of the First Baptist Church in Wash City.

Among the actresses was Miss Butler, & Mrs Hun, the mother of Geo Canning. Her maiden name was Costello, occasioned by her marriage with the father of Mr Canning a breach between that gentleman & his relatives which was never healed. He died & her second husband was Mr Reddish, of Convent Garden Theatre; her third, Mr Hun, by whome she had 2 dghts. Munden was godfather to one of the dghts. Mrs Hun is dead; Mr Canning's letters to his mother are probably in existence. –Bentley's Miscellany

For rent: 2 story brick house with a basement, on south side of F st, between 13th & 14th sts. Inquire of Jos Abbott, on G, between 13th & 14th sts.

Mrd: on May 25, by Rev R D Herndon, Mr Jas H Maddox to Miss Jane F, eldest d/o Geo L Cochrane, all of Fauquier Co, Va.

Died: on Jun 13, in her 40th year, Mrs Charlotte Meade Graham, w/o Maj Jas D Graham, U S Topographical Engineers, & d/o the late Rich W Meade, of Phil. Her funeral is at 5 p m on Jun 15.

Died: on Jun 15, of consumption, Mary Eleanor Bruce, in her 17th year.

Died: on Jun 4, at Boston, Passed Midshipman John Brooke, U S Navy, aged 23 years, s/o the late Col A S Brooke, U S Army.

Wanted to hire: a middle aged colored woman, to nurse a child. She must be a good washer. For such a one liberal wages will be given. Inquire at Gadsby's Hotel. –Thompson Tyler

U S schnr **Grampus**. Charleston, Jun 3, 1843. Hon Abel P Upshur, Sec of the Navy: Sir: On the 11th March last my son, Passed Midshipman, Stockton Keith You, was permitted to pay us a short visit of 2 days from on board the U S schnr **Grampus**, which was at that time cruising off our bar. My son left us on Mon night, the 13th, in a pilot boat, & returned on board the **Grampus**. He told us when he left us that we might expect to hear from him from Norfolk about the 10th of Apr, but we have not been favored with a letter from him since he left Charleston. Reports are in circulation that great fears are entertained for the safety of said vessel. It will be a

great relief to myself & family if we could learn any thing about her destination. I am, with great respect, Jno C You.
REPLY: Navy Dept, Jun 6, 1843. Sir: Your letter of the 3rd instant contains the latest authentic information that has reached the dept from the U S schnr **Grampus**. No letter has been received from Lt Downes since he sailed from the Chesapeake in Feb. I am, respectfully, your obedient servant, a Tho Smith, Acting Sec of the Navy. [To John C You, Charleston, S C.]

FRI JUN 16, 1843
To the Great Falls of the Potomac: the Independent Grays have resolved to visit this romantic spot on Jun 20th: 2 large & well arranged boats will leave Congress st bridge at 7 a m arriving at the Falls about 10 o'clock, returning to town about 8 p m. Refreshments of every kind will be found on board the boats. Tickets $1, admitting one gentleman & 2 ladies. Tickets to be had in Gtwn at Messrs J L Kidwell's & Geo M Sothoron's drug stores; in Wash at Farquhar & Morgan's, First Ward, at Patterson's, corner of Pa ave & 9th st, & at McKean's, Pa ave, near 4½ st, & at Riley's, near the Navy Yard. Cmte of Arrangements:

Capt Smith	Lt Kidwell	Pioneer	Sergeant
Lt Hill	Lt Lutz	Bronaugh	Garret
			Wm A Waugh

Circuit Court: the Jury rendered a verdict in the case of the U S vs W P Zantzinger in favor of the plntfs for $8,253.21 with interest from May 31, 1843. We understand the claim of the U S against the dfndnt was for the sum of $8,881.72, & the dfndnt claimed as a set-off sum of $16,879.19, of which the jury allowed about $600. The dfndnt, by his counsel, had taken exception to the items disallowed by the Court, & will take the case to the Supreme Court.

Investigation yesterday before Justice Morsel, on a complaint by a young lady named Kremer against 3 females, Mary Ann, Catharine, & Tiny Hall, for a violent assault & battery upon Kremer in the streets of Wash City on Wed evening. Mary Ann Hall, one of the dfndnts, being held to bail for her personal appearance at the Criminal Court now in session. The other 2 were not arrested.

The price of Public Baths reduced to 25 cents per bath. Baths are open every day at 5 a m, & until 10 p m. House between 6th & 4½ sts. –P Aiken

Sale of handsome furniture: sale on Jun 22, at the residence of Mrs Prout, on C st, who declines housekeeping, all her furniture. -Robt W Dyer & Co, aucts

Assignee's sale of improved property. In the matter of John Purdon, a bankrupt. Circuit Court of Wash Co, D C: sale of all property & rights of property of the said John Purdon: sale of part of lot 7 in sq 319, which was bought by Purdon from Philip Otterbach on Jun 4, 1840, having a front of about 29 feet on the east side of 12th st, together with the improvements thereon, consisting of a 2 story frame house, which is under rent for $250 per annum. –D A Hall, Assignee -Henry Naylor, trustee -Robt W Dyer & Co, aucts

SAT JUN 17, 1843
The Hon Barker Burnell, M C, of Mass, died at his lodgings in Wash City, night before last, at the age of 45 years, a victim of the painful & wasting disease of consumption; which first declared itself at the close of the late session of Congress. Mr Burnell was a native & an inhabitant all his life in the hardy island, Nantucket. At 22 he was already a member of the Hse/o Reps in his native Commonwealth. A few years later he passed into the Senatorial body. He died as one must die who had slighted no duty & felt every affection-with regrets of a husband, a father, & a friend; but with the courage of a man & the confidence of a Christian. His funeral is on Sun at 4 p m, from Mrs McDaniels, near the corner of 4½ st & Pa ave. FUNERAL: Burial in the Congressional Burial Ground: procession-Physicians who attended the dec'd; pallbearers-Hon John P Van Ness, Hon Elisha Whittlesey, Gen Geo Gibson, Hon Thos H Blake, Hon Albion K Parris, Hon Thos H Crawford, Com Lewis Warrington, Hon Selah R Hobbie. The family & friends of the dec'd. Sgt-at-Arms of the Hse/o Reps:. Member of Congress who may be in the city. Ofcrs of the Hse/o Reps:. Ofcrs of the Senate. [The Pres of the U S absent from the city.] Heads of Depts. Diplomatic Corps. Judges of the Circuit Court of Wash Co, D C, with the Marshal & all other Judicial Ofcrs. Comptrollers, Auditors, & Civil Ofcrs of the Gov't. Ofcrs of the Army & Navy at the seat of Gov't. The Mayor, Members, & Ofcrs of the Wash Corp. Freemen's Vigilant Total Abstinence Society of Washington, of which the dec'd was a distinguished member. Citizens & strangers. Friday, Jun 16, 1843. [Jun 20th newspaper: Rev Mr Bulfinch, to whose church the dec'd was attached, & by whom he was assiduously attended during his last illness, at the request of Rev Mr Tuston, took part in the exercises. The widow & son of the dec'd suffered a great loss.]

Col Jas L McCaughan, of Smith Co, Miss, & formerly a rep in the State Leg, committed suicide by hanging on the 15th ult. Pecuniary difficulties, against which he had struggled for a year or two, led to the act. He left a wife & 5 or 6 children.

Capt Pierce, of the ship **Lowell**, from Canton, reports that the British barque **Diana**, Capt May, was blown up at St Helena by the explosion of her magazine. She had sailed for London. When opposite Ascension Capt May blew his brains out with a pistol, after which she returned to St Helena, & while at anchor she blew up, killing 2 & wounding 6 of the crew. It was supposed the second mate set fire to the magazine.

Army & Navy Intelligence: 1-Col Thayer, of the U S Corps of Engineers, is about proceeding to Europe on leave of absence for the benefit of his health. He will be accompanied by the son of Gen Parker, of the War Dept. 2-Floyd Waggaman appointed storekeeper for the African squadron to reside at Port Praya, Cape de

Verds; & Thos W Waldron for the East India squadron, to reside, probably, at Hong Kong. 3-A Marine General Court Martial to convene at Middletown, Conn, on Jul 10, for the trial of Brvt Lt Col Wm H Freeman, of said corps.

Nathl Harding, age 10 years, s/o Gen Wm G Harding, was instantly killed at Nashville on Jun 5 by being thrown from a horse.

Bloody affray on Jun 13 at Lexington Court house, S C, between Col H I Caughman & Dr Benjamin. Col Caughman attempted to cane Benjamin, who drew a knife & stabbed him in 9 places. Caughman is not expected to live.

Mrd: on Jun 6, at Brookville, by Rev Wm Pinckney, Mr Augustus P Webb, of Balt Co, to Miss Catharine E Pleasants, of Montg Co, Md.

Mrd: on Jun 1, at St Julien, Spotsylvania Co, Va, by Rev Wm Friend, Robt Hamilton, of Richmond, to Miss Helen, d/o the Hon Francis T Brooke, of the Court of Appeals.

Mrd: on Jun 14, at Alexandria, by Rev J N Danforth, Rev Rufus Wheelwright Clark, of Portsmouth, N H, to Eliza, y/d/o the late Rev Wm C Walton.

Mrd: on Jun 8, at Fairfield, Fauquier Co, Va, by Rev Geo Lemmon, Dr Richd Cary Ambler, of Richmond, to Miss Susan Marshall, d/o Jas M Marshall, sen.

Mrd: on Jun 8, in Fauquier Co, Va, by Rev Philip Slaughter, Jos Travis Rosser, of Petersburg, Va, to Miss Mary Walker Armistead, d/o Gen Armistead, U S Army.

Died: on Tue, at Alexandria, suddenly, Mrs Mary Minor, w/o Mr Danl Minor, in her 59th year.

Died: on Jun 7, at Raleigh, N C, of which place she ahd been a resident more than 40 years, Eliz Geddy, after a lingering illness, in her 73rd year. She was as extensively known, perhaps, as any lady in N C. Her whole life was a continuous career of kindness, charity, & love. –Raleigh Register

Died: on Jun 8, at York, Pa, Jacob Spangler, aged 75 years, formerly a Rep in Congress from York Co, & Surveyor General of Pa under Govn'r Findley & Wolf.

Died: on Jun 11, at Bristol, Pa, the Baroness Louisa D'Hauteville, w/o the French Consul at Phil, & d/o M de la Forest, Consul General of France at N Y.

Horse strayed from the premises of the subscriber, on 14th st west, between P & Q sts. He has lost a shoe from his right foot behind. $5 reward. –Julius Knop

Notice: the public are cautioned against purchasing lots 4, 5, & 6, in square 503, advertised to be sold by Tench Ringgold, late Marshal of D C, on Jun 22; the said lots having been sold for taxes, & purchased by me on Aug 15, 1837, & which lots were not redeemed, as provided by law. -Wm A Weaver

Warrenton Female Seminary, N C. Mr & Mrs Graves return their thanks for the favor with which they have been pleased to regard this institution during the few years it had been in operaton. Mr T H Vendenberg, an accomplished mucician, has charge of the musical dept. –N Z Graves, Principal

MON JUN 19, 1843
A shocking murder was this Thu committed in the Massachusetts State Prison at Charlestown. One of the prisoners, named Abner Rogers, suddenly rushed upon the warden, Mr Chas Lincoln, and with a sharp knife inflicted a wound to the jugular vein which produced instant death. Mr Lincoln was a humane & efficient ofcr, & had filled the post of warden for 11 years. He was 47 years of age, & has left a wife & 11 children. The murderer was put in irons to await the punishment due to the enormity of his crime. [Jul 1 newspaper: Boston Post says that insanity is to be plead in the defence of the prisoner Rogers, who recently murdered Mr Lincoln, the warden of the prison. The same plea was urged by the counsel of Glover, who pleaded guilty to the charge of assaulting Miss Austin, in mitigation of punishment. The papers are very indignant at the mildness of his sentence, 18 months in the House of Correction, for one of the most brutal & outrageous assaults ever committed. –Tribune]

Mr Nicholas Paul, who fell through the joists of the Western Tobacco Warehouse at Gtwn, to the floor below, on Thu last, died that evening of his injuries. The dec'd was a very aged man, & a respectable citizen of Gtwn.

Mrd: on Jun 14, by Rev Edwards, Mr J A Dixon to Miss Rebecca A Murphy, all of Wash City.

Died: on Jun 18, Gaetano Carusi, in his 81st year. His funeral will be from the residence of his son, on Pa ave, corner of 10th st.

Died: on Jun 18, Edw Michl, infant s/o Patrick & Martha McKenna, aged 2 years & 6 months. His funeral is today at 4 p m, corner of C & 13th sts.

New Orleans Courier of Jun 10th: death by violence of Dr Jas Hagan, for some time past Editor of the Vicksburg Sentinel, & formerly a resident of this city, where he yet has many personal friends. An affray took place at Vicksburg on Jun 7 between Dr Jas Hagan & G W Adams, s/o Judge Geo Adams, of Jackson, Miss. Adams walked up behind Dr Hagan as he was walking from his boarding house to his ofc, at 3 o'clock in the afternoon. A scuffle ensued, both falling to the ground, Hagan uppermost. Adams drew a pistol while down, & placed it to the back of Hagan's head; the ball entering the spine, caused instant death. Dr Hagan was unarmed, & no person near to render assistance. Adams was immediately arrested, & was admitted to bail in the sum of $6,000.

PUBLIC NOTICE; All persons interested are required to take notice that the letters of atty given by Isaac Bickley, of Bucks Co, Pa, to Jas I Dickins, of Wash City, D C, are revoked, & that all authorities & powers thereby granted have effectually & entirely ceased. –Lloyd Wharton Bickley, Phil. Atty in fact for Isaac Bickley.

The subscriber, an applicant for a pension, is desirous of having the testimony of one Peter Albright toward establishing his right to the pension claimed. The said Peter Albright resides at or near Phil; he is by profession a printer, at which trade he worked at this place previous to his removing to Phil. Should this notice catch the eye of anyone acquainted with said Albright, they would confer a favor on an old sldr by addressing him at the U S arsenal in this city. –Elemuel Robinett

Jas L Gibbs respectfully informs the public that he has established himself as a collector of debts, due bills, etc, in Washington & adjoining cities. Persons having accounts for collection will please leave them or their names at J H Gibbs' dressing rooms, Gadsby's Hotel, where they will meet with punctual attention.

John N Crockwell, of Winchester, Va, offers his services to the citizens of D C as a Collector. Letters addressed to the above in Winchester, Va, post paid, will meet with prompt attention.

TUE JUN 20, 1843
Newark Adv, Jun 15. The Grand Jury of Warren returned into Court this evening, bringing indictments against Jos Carter, jr, for the late murders at Changewater. [No other information.]

Dr Edw Jarvis, of Dorchester, had his leg badly fractured last evening by the upsetting of a chaise in Roxbury. The horse was frightened by some boys, who were firing Chinese crackers in the street. –Boston Journal

Seneca Falls Courier of last week states that Needham Maynard, of that village, a sldr of the Revolution, who fought at Bunker Hill, was there on his way to Boston, to join his countrymen in commemorating that battle, in which 68 years ago, at his country's call, he periled his life. Mr Maynard is 87 years old, he is the f/o the member of Congress, the Hon John Maynard, & was formerly a judge of Oneida County. He was of the Massachusetts line of infty, & one of the special aids, appointed on the day of the battle, to Gen Warren, & served in that capacity during the engagement. He had a brother killed in the battle.

Last evening a fire was discovered in one of the sleeping apartments of Mr D Harvey's hotel at Cambridgeport, & the body of a man was found on the bed. His name is Osman Wright, a resident of Fitchburg, Mass, where he has left a wife & family. –Boston Bee

John Slater, the distinguished manufacturer, lately died at Slaterville, R I. He was from England originally, & among the earliest of the pioneers in introducing the manufacture of domestic goods in this country. He was also the inventor of several important improvements in machinery.

Wm H Jones, of Perry Co, Ala, was recently sentenced to the penitentiary for 10 years, for whipping one of his negroes so cruelly as to cause his death.

Alex'r Swanston, of De Soto Co, Miss, lately drowned himself in the Mississippi river; about 12 miles below Randolph. Verdict of inquest: drowned in a fit of *mania a potu*.

The heirs of Jas Watson, late of the town of Alexandria, dec'd, by addressing the subscriber, postage paid, or calling on him at his ofc in Alexandria, will probably hear of something much to their advantage. –Lawrence B Taylor, Atty at law

B Schenck thanks the members of the Fire Companies, his neighbors & fellow citizens, for the prompt & efficient aid rendered in extinguishing the fire in his store on Jun 14.

Died: on Jun 17, in Wash City, Mrs Rachel coumbe, wid/o the late Wm Coumbe.

Died: on Jun 13, Sarah Virginia, eldest d/o John A & Eliz R Davis, aged 3 years, 6 months & 15 days.

Circuit Court of Wash Co, D C. Job P McIntosh; Lewis H France; & John J Roane: applied to be discharged from imprisonment under the act for the relief of Insolvent Debtors. Hearing for McIntosh on the first Mon in Jul next; hearing for France on the 2nd Mon in Jul next; hearing for Roane on Jun 26th. –Wm Brent, clk

Horses just arrived from Greenbrer County, Va, for sale. Also, one very fine mule. To be seen at Walker & Kimmel's Nathional Stable, Wash. –Stuart McClung

WED JUN 21, 1843
Norfolk, Jun 19. The U S brig of war **Truxton**, Lt Com't Geo P Upshur, bound to Constantinople to being home the remains of the late Cmdor Porter, went to sea from Hampton Roads on Fri.

Orphan's Court of Wash Co, D C. Letters testamentary on the personal estate of Ann Waring, late of said county, dec'd. −S Thomas, exc

Circuit Court of Wash Co, D C. Chas Marvell has applied to be discharged from imprisonment under the act of Insolvent Debtors: hearing on the first Mon in Jul next. −Wm Brent, clk

Circuit Court of Wash Co, D C. Francis A Dunn has applied to be discharged from imprisonment under the act of Insolvent Debtors: hearing on Jun 26 next.
−Wm Brent, clk

A son of Mr Bentley, the celebrated publisher of Burlington st, London, was killed a few days ago by falling from the banister at the top of the house. He was in the habit of climbing on the outside & then sliding down them.

Mr John H Sadler, of Holbeck, in Leeds, has invented a loom for weaving each sail of a ship, even of the largest class, in one entire piece, thus greatly increasing the strength & diminishing the weight.

Mrs Catharine A Ware, w/o Mr Chas Ware, died on Wed week, at Paris, where she had passed the winter. She was preparing to return to Liverpool with her family, when she was seized with apoplexy, to which she fell a victim. She was an elegant writer & a lady of most refined taste. In her native city, Boston, U S, she held a high rank for her great literary talent. She wrote from time to time in the columns of the Liverpool Chronicle.

The Rev Mr Galland, a Wesleyan preacher, & superintendent of the Hull East Crct, was seized with paralysis on Sunday, in the pulpit, & expired soon after.

A Brother & sister, children of Mr Campbell Adair, fell into a vat at Hillsborough distillery last week, & were scalded to death.

The Duke of Wellington purchased, on the day of the private view, Sir Wm Allen's fine picture of the Battle of Waterloo, which is now to be seen in the exhibition of the Royal Academy. The price was 600 guineas.

Marble Yard. Marble Mantels from the steam establishment of Mr Levi Taylor, Balt, can be seen at my warerooms opposite the Treas bldg, on 15th st.
−Jeremiah Sullivan

I contemplate closing out the stock of Dry Goods formerly belonging to Wm C Orme by Jun 5th or Jul 10th, with great bargains: in order to close the doors. −S T Wall, agent On Pa ave, between 8th & 9th sts, opposite the Centre Market.

Teacher wanted to take charge of Primary School District #2, PG Co, Md. Address either of the undersigned, near Good Luck post ofc: Wm C Anderson, Nathan Waters of Hy, Franklin Waters, trustees

Mrd: on Jun 7, at Llangollen, Loudoun Co, Va, by Rev Philip Slaughter, Wellington Gordon to Frances, d/o the Hon Cuthbert Powell.

Died: on Jun 10, in Westport, Essex Co, N Y, Mr Saml Pangborn, aged 86 years. By the demise of Mr Pangborn another patriot & hero of the Revolution has gone. He took a noble stand for the liberty of his country. He was at the battle of Brandywine, at the siege of Yorktown, & at several other engagements.

NOTICE: I, R C Clarke, do herby forewarn all persons from interfering in any way or manner with Wm H Hall, as the publication was caused by rumors which I have found to be false; he having never left my dwelling. –Robt Campbell Clarke, Barber

For rent: brick house in Phenix Row, recently occupied by Henry J Brent, fronting on N J Ave. Inquire of Wm P Elliot, N J ave, or at the Surveyor's ofc, City Hall.

THU JUN 22, 1843
To the Public: Tench Ringgold, late Marshal of D C, having advertised for sale on Jun 22, 1843, at the Wash Co court-house door, in virtue of a fieri facias issued in the case of Wm A Bradley, use of Elias B Caldwell, against Saml Elliott, jr, the following lots: 17 thru 19 in sq 503, in Wash City, D C, I give this notice to all whom it may concern, that I am the lawful owner of said lots, in my own right, as the wid/o the late Wm Whitmore, of said city, & as claiming the same for his children & heirs, he having purchased & paid for the same during his lifetime from the Bank of Wash, as will be seen by the deed made by the Pres & Dirs of said Bank to my dec'd husband, upon the 12th Jan, 1843, & recorded among the land records of Wash Co, D C. I further forbid the said Tench Ringgold, to offer said lots for sale, & I forewarn every & all persons from purchasing the same. –Ann M Whitmore, for herself & for the heirs of her dec'd husband, Wm Whitmore.

New-Family Groceries: on 7th st, a few doors below the Nat'l Intell. –S Holmes

On Jun 9, Lucretia Hall, aged 19, the beloved object of her parents, left her home near Westport, Essex Co, N Y, to visit her sister, about a mile distant, & in crossing a brook which was much swollen by a previous night's rain, she was precipitated into the rapid current & drowned. She was not missed until her body was found on the banks of the stream.

FRI JUN 23, 1843
The undersigned has purchased the stock in trade of Mr J P McKean, successor of L Johnson, dealer in Cigars, Tobacco, Snuff, Fancy Articles, Pa ave, between 4½ & 6th

sts, where he intends keeping on hand an extensive assortment of the articles above mentioned. -J M Dorsett [The dwlg attached to the store will be let to a good tenant if applied for soon. –J P McKean]

Lee & Espey, Cabinet-makers & Undertakers, south side of Pa ave, between 4½ & 3rd sts. Should our services be required as Undertakers in other than business hours we may be found at our residence on Md ave, south side, near 6th.

Wilson Scott, of Towanda, Pa, suddenly died at a party in Athens, when he became seriously ill, losing his senses, & died in a space of 2 hours. He leaves a destitute aged mother & her large family, who were dependent on him. He was a young & talented member of the legal profession. [No date-current item.]

Boston Mercantile Journal of Tue: Hugh S Legare, of S C, the eminent scholar, the orator, the accomplished statesman, is no more. He died Jun 20th, at the mansion of Geo Ticknor, in Park st. He had complained of indisposition soon after his arrival & was unable to participate in the celebration of Jun 17. The immediate cause of his death is said to have been inflammation of the bowels. He was attended by Dr Bigelow. [Jun 24 newspaper: A post mortem examination ascertained that death was occasioned by an internal strangulation, arising from the twisting of the intestine upon itself at the sigmoid flexure. Mr Legare was buried at Boston on Wed, at Mount Auburn, &, by particular request, no parade was made.]

Land for sale: 2 beautiful lots near the Race Course, not more than 2 miles from Wash City. #1 lot contains 30 acs. #2 lot contains about 12 acs. A plat of the land may be seen at Mr W T Dove's Grocery Store, near the National Theatre. –Wm Holmead

Crmnl Crt-Wash. 1-Geo Hall indicted & tried for a riot in the house of Mary A Hall, on Mar 8, 1841: verdict-guilty. 2-Chas Fearson, Jos B B Wilson, Geo Pomeroy, & John Hurdle found not guilty for a riot on Nov 2, 1842, at Gtwn. 3-Henry Fletcher, free negro, found guilty of assault only, for his assault on Eliz Fletcher, on Dec 19, 1842. He was found guilty of assault upon the said Eliz Fletcher with intent to kill her, by discharging a pistol at her on Dec 19, 1842.

Boston Daily Adv: announces the death of Wm Simmons, Senior Justice of the Police Court of Boston. He died on Sat after a protracted illness, at the age of 61.

SAT JUN 24, 1843
Boston papers. Capt Geo W Seaver has been removed from the ofc of Collector, & Lawson Nash from the ofc of Surveyor, of the port of Gloucester, & two Locofocos have been appointed in their places.

A young woman named Christina Cochran, alias *Gilman, who is accused of having murdered her husband in Jan last near Paisley, Scotland, by administering arsenic, arrived at N Y on Wed in the brig **Excel**, from Liverpool, & was arrested under the provisions of the late treaty, she having been demanded by the British Gov't through an agent sent to this country in the ship **Arcadia**. –Tribune
[Jun 28th newspaper: Case of Mrs *Gilmore. This young woman, recently arrived from Scotland, & charged with murder, had a hearing in N Y on Sat when her counsel, Thos Warner, said there were good reasons for believing her to be insane. He moved for an adjournment so that medical men may examine her. NOTE: *Gilman: Gilmore. No other articles between this date & Jun 28 fit the details of the article.] [Jul 24th newspaper: in the case of Christina Gilmour: fugitive from justice; charged with having murdered her husband in Paisley, Scotland: Com'r Rapalye has rendered his decision, affirming her commitment to trial.] [Jul 29th newspaper: on Wed she was remanded to prison to await the decision of the Pres of the U S.] [Aug 15th newspaper: in the matter of Christiana Cochran, otherwise Gilmour, an application for the allowance of a writ of habeas corpus by the British authorities. I accordingly refuse to allow the habeas corpus prayed for in this case. –Saml R Betts, U S Judge: N Y, Aug 12, 1843.]

A party of 800 children attached to the St Augustine Catholic Sunday School in Phil, having gone on an excursion on Tue last some distance out of the city, 5 of the boys strayed off & went into the water to bathe, when one of them, s/o Mr Andrew McCalla, of Phil, was unfortunately drowned.

Mrd: on Jun 22, in Gtwn, D C, by Rev John G Wilson, Mr Jas King to Miss Charlotte M, d/o Jos Libbey, all of that place.

Mrd: on Jun 14, at Kinloch, by Rev Mr Toles, Robt Beverley to Jane Eliza, d/o John Hill Carter, jun.

Mrd: Jun 22, by Rev Mr Trapnell, Maj W H Tuck to Mgt, only d/o Philemon Chew, all of PG Co, Md.

Died: on May 16, at the house of her grandfather, the Hon Wm Davidson, of Charlotte, N C, Miss Sarah Eliz Blake, d/o Jas H Blake, in her 16th year.

Died: on Jun 16, at Meadow Grove, Fauquier Co, Va, Edw Carter, in his 57th year. He leaves an almost heart-broken wife & a numerous family of children & relatives who surrounded the death-bed of this good man.

Army Intelligence.
1st Military Dept: Brig Gen Arbuckle having obtained leave of absence, the command of this dept has been assigned to Col Twiggs.

Fort Washita: Co D, of Dragoons, from Fort Gibson, & Co G, of riflemen, from Fort Towson, have been ordered to garrison this post, the command of which is assigned to Col Harney. On the arrival of G Co, of riflemen, Capt Alexander's Co C, 6th Infty, will rejoin the garrison at Fort Towson.

Dragoons: Companies C, F, & K, 160 strong, under command of Capt P St G Cooke, left Fort Leavenworth on May 27, to give escort to traders on the Santa Fe route. The escort was joined at Council Grove by a detachment of Co A, [25 men,] under Capt Terrett.

7th Infty: Headquarters have been removed, by order of Gen Arbuckle, from New Orleans barracks to Baton Rouge. The regt is under command of Lt Col Whistler. The garrison at New Orleans barracks, excepting a guard, will spend the sickly months at Pass Christian. –Army & Navy Chronicle

MON JUN 26, 1843
Died in Derry, N H, on Jun 8, Maj Geo Burnham, in his 94th year. He served in the Continental army through the entire Revolutionary struggle without a single furlough, even to visit his friends, & was engaged in most of the battles of the Revolution. He possessed an intellect of a high order, which he retained in an extraordinary manner to the latest period of his life.

Umbrella Repairing Establishment: being about to retire, to anyone desirous of entering into a light & easy business, I will dispose of my tools, patterns, together with the stock on hand, on the most reasonable terms. I will also give such instructions as will enable any one to conduct the business. –John M Farrar

Valuable bldg lot at Public Auction: on Jun 28, in front of the premises, a part of lot 18 in square 75, fronting on Pa ave: near the ofc of Esquire Drury, south side of Pa ave. -Robt W Dyer & Co, aucts

For sale or rent: the desirable private residence of the late Maj Cary Selden, on the corner of C & 3rd sts. The house is 4 stories high, built of the best materials, & finished in the best manner. -Robt W Dyer & Co, aucts

Official: Hon Abel P Upsur, the present Sec of the Navy, has been appointed to act as Sec of State ad interim. The ofc of Atty Gen, vacated by the death of Mr Legare, is yet vacant.

The New Haven Herald, under its obituary head, notices the death of Mr Justus Williams, a respectable citizen of Essex [Deep River] & an exemplary & worthy man, by lockjaw, occasioned by the applications of a Corn Doctor.

An admirable likeness of the Hon C A Wickliffe, Postmaster Gen, has just been shown to us. It is from a painting lately taken by Mr Geo C Burgham, of Missouri,

& mezzotintoed by J Sartain, of Phil. In this portrait the skill of the painter & the engraver are clearly manifested.

Crmnl Crt-Wash, Jun 23, 1843. 1-Thos McLaughlin, indicted for an assault & battery on Jos Johnson, carpenter, was found guilty. *Fined $5. 2-Edw Rhodes submitted, through Mr Woodward his counsel, to a presentment for selling liquors without license. *Edw Rhodes & Wm D Byan, both convicted of selling liquors without license, each to pay a fine of $16. 3-One prisoner, John R Pearce, convicted last Wed of a riot at the circus, escaped from the court-house immediately after the rendition of the verdict. He is still a fugitive & not yet retaken. [*Jul 14th newspaper: John R Pearce has been found.]

St Vincent's Orphan Asylum: Managers chosen on Jun 5th, for the ensuing year:
Mrs Newman   Mrs Chas Hill   Mrs Hughes
Mrs Talbot   Mrs Susan Graham   Mrs Dr Blake
Mrs Ann Hill   Mrs Stubbs   Mrs Riggs

TUE JUN 27, 1843
Chas F C Macolla, a Barrister of Nova Scotia, was the gentleman who jumped overboard from the steamer **North America**, a few days since, on her passage from St Johns to Boston, & was drowned.

Mrd: on Jun 22, at Wheeling, Va, by Rev Henry R Weed, Dr S W McElhenny, of Lewisburg, Va, to Miss Martha M, d/o Z Jacob, of Wheeling.

Circuit Court of Wash Co, D C. Harvey Dennison has applied to be discharged from imprisonment under the act for the relief of Insolvent Debtors. –Wm Brent, clk

Household furniture at auction: on Jun 30, at the late residence of Mrs Rachael Coombe, by order of the Orphan's Court of Wash Co, D C:
Mahogany dining & card tables
Lights, chairs, mantel glass, 2 clocks
Pianoforte, waiters, carpets, curtains, candlesticks
Bedsteads, beds, bedding
Washstands, bureaus, crockery & glassware
Knives & forks & a lot of kitchen furniture
2 sows & pigs, 2 shoats, cow, hens, & chickens.
-Robt W Dyer & Co, aucts

Very handsome new furniture at auction at the Cabinet Warehouse of Mr Wm McL Cripps, on 11th st, near Pa ave, a large assortment of household articles of his own manufacture; amongst which are the following articles: Mahogany hair seat & cane seat chairs
Hairseat sofas & sofa bedsteads

Mahogany dining, breakfast, card, & work table
Walnut & other French post bedsteads, cherry cribs
Mahogany & painted wardrobes
Marble top & plain mahogany & other washstands
Mahogany dressing, French, & plain bureaus
Handsome dressing tables, light stands, lyre pattern, round & square tops
-Robt W Dyer & Co, aucts

Excellent furniture at Public Sale: on Jun 29, at the residence of Mr Thos L Thruston, on C st, back of Gadsby's hotel, his household & kitchen furniture. -Robt W Dyer & Co, aucts

Army General Order: #39, War Dept, Adj Gen Ofc: Wash, Jun 24, 1843. The Pres of the U S directs that, as a mark of respect to the memory of the Hon Hugh Swinton Legare, Atty Gen, & Sec of State ad interim of the U S, who died at Boston, Mass, on Jun 20th, appropriate military honors be paid throughout the army. –Saml Humes Porter, Acting Sec of War [The Funeral honors will be paid to the memory of the dec'd at the military posts of the army. Guns will be fire every half hour, & the national flag displayed at half staff, from sunrise to sunset, on the next day after the receipt of this order. The usual badge of mourning will be worn on the left arm & on the hilt of the sword for 6 months. –R Jones, Adj Gen.]

WED JUN 28, 1843
Thos M T McKennan, the useful, & justly popular Rep in Congress from Wash Co district in Pa, has declined being a candidate for re-election.

Wm D Delany was, on Jun 24, elected Mayor of the Borough of Norfolk, Va.

Tavern stand on High st: Trustee's sale of real estate in Gtwn, D C: decree of Circuit Court of Wash Co, D C: sale on Jul 20th next: large 3 story brick Tavern, with stables, yard, & ground appurtenant, at the corner of High & Beall sts, fronting about 45 feet on High st & 138 feet on Beall st, now occupied by Wm Cunningham, formerly by Jacob Holtzman, dec'd. Also, the ground on the north side of Beall st, & the brick stable thereon, lying west of the large stable belonging to the tavern premises of the late Geo Holtzman, dec'd. The lot fronts about 65 feet on Beall st, & runs back to the brick wall north of the said st, & is situated for a public livery stable. –John Marbury, trustee -Edw S Wright, auct

Election for Reps in Congress from Louisiana will take place in the first week in Jul. The candidates are:

Whigs	Locos
Geo K Rogers	John Slidell
Edw D White	Alcee Labranche
Jas Belam	John B Dawson

John Moore   Gen P E Bossier

Mr John Scott, of Albany, N Y, solicits information from all who may be able to give it, of his son Solomon, a lunatic, who wandered away from his father's house in Jan. He is 24 years of age.

At the Whig Convention in the 4th Congressional district of Ill, T L Dickey was appointed a delegate from that District to the Whig Nat'l Convention which is to meet at Balt, in May, 1844.

The District Convention of the Whigs of the 3rd Congressional district of Vt, holden at Burlington on Jun 8, John Peck was unanimously elected a delegate to the Nat'l Convention to be holden in May, 1844, & Saml W Keyes as substitute. Both these gentlemen are said to be warmly in favor of the election of Henry Clay.

At the trial of Wm H Platt, in Augusta, Ga, for the murder of Mr Harding, 353 persons were "sounded" before a jury could be obtained. More than 50 witnesses were subpoenaed. The examination of 7 of them consumed 2 days. On Jun 22, the jury after an absence of about 45 minutes returned a verdict of Not Guilty. "Thus," says the Augusta Chronicle, "is settled, so far as the verdict of this jury can settle it, that in Richmond Co, in the city of Augusta, a man may, at midday, in the principal street of the city, shoot down another without provocation, or without such provocation as the laws of the land recognize, & be turned loose upon the country, with his hands imbrued with the blood of his victim, unwhipt of justice. If such a verdict met any other then the execration of the great mass of our population it would indeed be a deep disgrace."

The late Receiver at Chicago, Ill, Mr Prescott, has recently been tried before the U S Circuit Court at Springfield. He was charged with having embezzled between $10,000 & $12,000 of public moneys. The trial commenced on the 15th, & the following afternoon Judge McLean charged the jury, & the jury decided the prisoner not guilty without leaving their seats. –Balt Patriot

The Cheraw [S C] Farmers' Gaz says that a few days since the summer residence of Lawrence Prince, in the Sand Hills, near that place, was destroyed by fire, supposed to be the act of an incendiary. On Mon following Mr Prince, intending to move his family out on the next day, sent some servants to prepare the house for their reception, when they found it a heap of smouldering ruins.

Saml Somer, principal carpenter to the Tremont Theatre, in Boston, died on Thu from the effects of poison administered to him, through mistake, by his wife. The error was discovered, & a physician sent for, but medical aid proved of no avail. Mr Somers died in about 2 hours after taking the draught. He left a wife & 2 children to mourn his untimely end.

John O'Donnell & Adam Baker, lads, drowned in the Monongahela river, near Pittsburg, on Thu last, while bathing.

The body of Mr Jas Parker, of the firm of J & J Parker, distillers, at Pittsburg, was foun in the Alleghany river on Thu last. He had been missing for weveraal days.

John Grelaud, a high respectable citizen of Phil, was thrown from his horse on Wed, & injured so severely that he expired within a few minutes.

Recent deaths in N Y: we notice the obituary record of the death of Mr John Morrison, formerly one of our most active dry goods merchants. For a great number of years he was one of the firm of Kelly & Morrison. He retired some 15 years since, & had since devoted his time to religious & benevolent pursuits. He was a native of Ireland. In the death of Christian Bergh, at age 81, on Fri, our city has lost their oldest shipbuilder, & one that had built more ships probably than any man now living. He was an upright, honorable, & respected citizen. –N Y Express, Jun 26

The Hon Jas Madison Porter, Sec of War, returned to Washington this morning. The Hon C A Wickliffe, Postmaster Gen, has returned to the seat of Gov't.

Treas Dept: coupons attached to the certificates of stock issued by the U S for interest becoming due on Jul 1 next, will be paid on presentation at the Bank of the Metropolis, Wash City. They may be remitted through any of the depositories of the Gov't. –John C Spencer, Sec of the Treas

Circuit Court of Wash Co, D C. Wm Kehoe, a bankrupt, has filed his ptn for his discharge & certificate: hearing on the first Mon in Oct next. –W Brent, clk

Potomac land in market: A great bargain offered. I offer for sale my land in Prince Wm Co, Va, near Dumfries: contains 1,050 acs. The improvements are very superior; the dwlg, which is of modern construction, contains 10 or 12 spacious rooms, a large saloon, passages, & closets. It is built of brick, & cost some years since eight or ten thousand dollars; it is in good repair. It is about 25 miles from D C, immediately on the road leading from Fredericksburg to Alexandria. Mr Thos Golden, who lives near the place, will show it. –John A Parker, Tappahannock, Essex Co, Va

Stolen, on Jun 26, 2 pairs of sewed boots, a pair of morocco boots, pegged bottoms, made for E B Bray; a pair of calfskin boots, sewed bottoms, made for Jas Miller, the names written in each pair & John Goldin, maker. I will give $5 to any one who will bring the boots to me in their new state, as the thief has been taken & lodged in jail. –John Goldin

Mrd: on Jun 25, in Wash City, by Rev S B Southerland, Mr Geo M Millen to Miss Sarah B Smith, both of Fairfax Co, Va.

Mrd: on Jun 22, by Rev Mr Curtis, Jos B Ficklen, of Falmouth, Va, to Miss Ellen E, d/o Thos McGehee, of Woodburn, N C.

Mrd: on Jun 15, at St Augustine, by Rev Alex McClure, Capt John T Sprague, U S Army, A D C to Miss Mary, d/o Gen W J Worth, U S Army.

Died: at Newport, R I, Capt Edw S Johnson, of the U S Navy, in his 48th year. [No death date given-current item.]

Died: on Jun 23, at Pittsburg, Pa, Jas Findlay, in his 42nd year.

The laying of the corner-stone of a church edifice for the Third Baptist Church will take place on E st, near 6th, today at 4:30 pm. Rev J L Burrows, of Phil, to deliver an address: &, Rev Mr Muller will deliver an address. A Collection will be taken to aid in the bldg.

For sale on credit or lease on ground rent: lot on C st east of & adjoining the premises of G C Grammer. Inquire of H B Sweeny, at the Bank of Wash, or of the subscriber, at his ofc, in City Hall. -D A Hall

THU JUN 29, 1843

Macon [Ga] Messenger: Mr Ashbel L Stocking was accidentally drowned in the Ocmulgee river, below Macon, on Jun 19. When swimming with his clothes on, with a fishing party of 20 gentlemen, he became exhausted. He was about 22 years of age, a native of Chathan, Conn, where he has parents residing.

Mr Geo H Bohrer, of Brown Co, Ohio, was deliberately & in cold blood shot down while at work in his field. This horrible deed was perpetrated close by the side of one of Bohrer's little girls. Who the murderers are is not known, other than they were a clan of cut-throats, 3 of whom fired rifles from the skirt of the woods.

John Patullo, age 34 years, committed suicide on Sat at 27 Moore st, N Y C, by shooting himself in his bed room, with a double barreled gun. He was a native of Scotland, & a wholesale dealer in wines & liquors at 121 Mulberry st.

House & lot at private sale: on Va ave & 10th st, in square 383, fronting on 10th st west, with a new 2 story frame house, containing 5 rooms with a passage, completely finished. The owner is about to leave the city. Apply at the Confectionary of Mr J P McKean, on Pa ave; or at John P Stallings' shop, on the corner of 12th & E sts. Also, part of lot 11 in square D, fronting on Md ave, south side. -John W Wise

Wash Corp: communication from the Mayor asking the following nominations:
*Chas H Wiltberger, for the ofc of Register
Jos Radcliff, for the ofc of First Clk
Wm E Howard, for the ofc of Second Clk
Jos H Bradley, for the ofc of Atty
Wm P Elliot, for the ofc of Surveyor
Henry H Lowe, for the ofc of Inspec of Tobacco
Wm M McCauley, for the ofc of Sealer of Weights & Measures
Jacob Kleiber, for the ofc of Inspector of Flour & Saled Provisions.
Richd Butt, for the ofc of Intendant of the Asylum
*Peter M Pearson, for the ofc of Com'r of Canal
Caleb Buckingham, for the ofc of Inspector of Fire Apparatus

City Com'rs:
Saml Drury	*Wm Cooper, jr	John Magar-acting
John Sessford	*Thos J Barrett-acting	Saml Scott-acting

Police Constables:
Fielder B Poston	*Wm Wallis	*John Magar
John Waters	*Silas Moore	Saml Scott
R R Burr	*Thos J Barrett	

Com'rs of the Centre Market:
John H Goddard	Walter Clarke	Wm Orme

Clerks of the Markets:
Wm Serrin	H B Robertson, Assist	Peter Little
John Waters	clk	

Inspectors & Measurers of Lumber:
David A Gardiner	Benj Bean	John G Robinson
Wm G Deale	Wm Douglass	John W Ferguson

Wood Corders & Coal Measurers:
Jas Gaither	John Hilton	Nathl Plant
Saml Kilman	John W Ferguson	Richd Wimsatt

Gaugers & Inspectors:
Nicholas Callan	Florian Hitz

Measurers of Grain, Bran, Shorts, & Ship Stuffs:
Jas Gaither	John B Ferguson

Com'rs of the West Burial Ground:
Saml Drury	Jacob A Bender
Lewis Johnson	John Douglass, Sexton

Com'rs of the East Burial Ground:
Jas Marshall	Thos J Barrett, Sexton	John P Ingle

Scavengers:
Thos Riggles	Wm Johnson	*John Cox
Luke Richardson	Jos Fugitt	*Osburn Turner
Jas Hollidge	Jas Hollidge	

Assessors for the present year:
Saml Drury Wm Cooper, jr John C Fitzpatrick
For the Board of Health:
Dr Wm B Magruder Dr Harvey Lindsly Dr Jas G Combe
John D Barclay G C Grammer John B Ferguson
Dr H J F Condict Dr John F May Dr Noble Young
Jas Larned John P Ingle Marmaduke Dove

[Which nominations were considered & confirmed, except those marked with *].

Board of Aldermen:
The Chair announced the appointment of the standing cmtes, as follows:
Cmtes of this Board:
On Claims: Messrs Barclay, Beck, & Marshall
On Unfinished Business: Messrs Clark & Brady
On Improvements: Messrs Magruder, Orme, & Goddard
Joint Cmtes:
On the Canal: Messrs Marshall & Orme
On Enrolled Bills: Mr Maury
On the Money Transactions of the Corp: Mr Wilson
On the Accounts of the Register: Mr Maury
On the Asylum: Mr Goddard
Board of Common Council:
The Chair announced the appointment of the following standing & joint cmtes:
Ways & Means-Messrs Bacon, Fulmer, Harrison, Callan, Bassett, & Dixon
Improvements: Messrs Wilson, Mudd, Crandell, Neale, Bassett, & Towers
Claims: Messrs Fulmer, Harrison, Neale
Unfinished business: Messrs Towers & Davis
Elections: Messrs Lenox, Davis, & Cull
Police: Messrs Lynch, Lenox, McCauley, Cull, Haliday, & Harrison
Public Schools: Messrs Haliday, Davis, Fulmer, Towers, Neale, & Lynch
On Canals: Messrs Mudd, Wilson, Bacon, Bassett, Dixon, & Cull
Joint Cmtes:
On the Canal: Messrs McCauley, Mudd, Marshall, & Orme
On Enrolled Bills: Messrs Crandell & Maury
To Examine the Money Transastions of the Corp: Messrs Lenox & Wilson
On the Asylum: Messrs Bacon & Goddard
On the Erection of Wharves: Messrs Dixon & Wilson
To Examine the Accounts of the Register: Messrs Callan & Maury
To count & destroy defaced Due-bills: Messrs Lenox & Maury
Various petitions were presented by:
D Saunders Wm Dalton-remission of a fine
Wm Lord & others Ulysses Ward-remission of a fine
Robt Cruit & others Z Hazell-remission of a fine
John Mitchell-remission of a fine

The late Atty Gen of the U S, Hugh Swinton Legare, was sprung from that honorable stock which has given South Carolina so many eminent names-her Huguenot population; whom attachment to religious freedom led to seek refuge from French oppression. The early loss of his father, [who perished while he was a child] left him with a sister who died last year, & another whom his own death leaves completely desolate, the last of her immediate race-to the widowed care of that excellent mother who breathed her last in his arms here, a few months since. His riper boyhood was committed to the instruction of his teacher, Rev Mr Waddell, then [we believe] of Abbeville, & subsequently the Pres of Oglethorpe Univ of Ga, the master of Geo McDuffie, of Jas Pettigru, of Wm Harper, & of many distinguished pupils in that region. He passed into the college of his own State, then governed by Dr Maxcy, the able predecessor of Dr Thos Cooper. The brilliancy of his academic performances there won him, at age 18, not only the highest final honors of the collegiate course, but a reputation which already, before he had graduated, had fixed the eyes of his State upon him, as one of whom the very highest hopes might safely be entertained.

Board of health will meet at City Hall this day at 5 p m. --Jas Larner, Sec

FRI JUN 30, 1843
N Y Tribune. 1-Excellent place of resort [not a groggery] has been opened by Mr K H Van Rensselaer, on Bloomingdale rd, entitled "The Abbey." 2-The Catskill Mountains would attract more visiters from our city if they were further off & more difficult of access. Being but 10 hours from our city, & to be reached for a dollar or so, people think they cannot be worth much. Yet the scenery is delightful, the coolness is assured, & the view southward is magnificent.

Boston: destructive fire broke out last Sat in the bldg on the corner of Lancaster & Causeway sts, occupied by J & T Washburn, as a steam sawing & planning mill, & by Curtis & Littlefield, picture frame manufacturers. Destroyed the grocery store of Mr Pearson & carpenter shop of Benj Remick. The bldgs were owned by Messrs Hilton, Thos Brigham, & E Smith, jr. On the east side it consumed the blacksmith shop of Staples & Wilbur, Bryant & Welch, E T Underwood's stable, the shops of E W Pike, carpenter, J A Southworth, stairbuilder, & the stables of Fisher & Ames & B T Gould.

Rev Fr Mulledy, a priest of the order of Jesuits, formerly Pres of Gtwn [D C] College, & who recently returned from a visit to Rome, is Pres of the new Roman Catholic College at Worcester, Mass.

Bay State Democrat of Mon: announces the death on Sun of Rev David Damon, pastor of the Unitarian Society at West Cambridge, Mass. He was engaged at Reading on Fri last in preaching a funeral sermon, when he was attacked with a fit of apoplexy, which proved fatal.

Mrd: on Jun 28, by Rev Mr Hawley, Wm Gadsby to Mary Augusta Bruff, all of Wash City.

Commissioned ofcrs attached to the Mechanical Riflemen:
John McClelland, Capt   J W Gaither, 2nd Lt
Jos H Daniel, 1st Lt   F A Klopfer, 3rd Lt

Criminal Court-Wash: on Tue-
1-Nathan Gray, not guilty of stealing a horse, the property of the C & O Canal Co.
2-Geo Butler, negro, a servant in the house of Mrs Smoot: guilty of stealing 23 gold sovereigns of the value of $93, the property of Wm M King, a boarder. *Guilty, to be imprisoned in the pen for 2 years, to take effect on Jul 20.
3-Richd Brooks: guilty of resisting S Scott, constable, while in discharge of his duty.
4-Chas Taylor: not guilty of stealing carpenter's tools, the property of J A Somers.
5-John R Pierce: convicted during the present term of rioting at the circus, & who made a sudden disappearance from the court-room on the rendition of the verdict, surrendered himself, & was taken into custody to await the sentence of the Court.
*Fined $20 in the first case; fined $5 & 5 days in jail in the other 2 cases.
6-John Gary: indicted for a violent assault upon his wife, found guilty. Sentence: the prisoner who had been confined in jail about 6 months, to pay a fine of $5.
7-Wm Williams: found guilty of rioting at the circus on 3 successive nights, in company with Paradise & Pearce. Dfndnt recommended to the mercy of the Court.
*To be imprisoned 5 days & pay a fine of $20.
8-John Paradise: convicted of the same: sentenced to a fine of $10 in the first case, & $5 in each of the other two cases. The dfndnt was represented by Mr Jas Kelly, the employer of Paradise, that during the last year he had conducted himself in an orderly manner, & properly in every respect.
9-Thu: Trial of Ellen Davis, a slave, who was indicted for a capital offence, in attempting to take the life of Mrs Mary Shields, in Wash City, on Mar 26, by mixing nitrate of potash [saltpetre] with certain medical powders, prescribed for Mrs Shields by her medical attendant, Dr Hall. Strenuous effort was made by the prisoner's counsel, Mr Carlisle & Mr C S Wallach, who took exceptions to the law of the case as laid down by the Court, & argued to prove the prisoner's insanity, introducing several witnesses who testified in proof of it. Jury had not returned with a verdict by 6 p m. [Jul 1 newspaper: Verdict of guilty. Two of the jurors said if they had thought they were allowed to consider the plea of insanity, they would not have rendered a verdict of guilty. Motion for a new trial was granted.]

Lost between Bladensburg & Wash, a small Morocco Pocket-book, much worn, containing $10, one $5 note on one of the Banks of Phil, & $5 in one & $2 dollar bills; also, a check given by Chas H Carter, in favor of Henry L Carlton, for & 73.35, & by him endorsed, the payment of which has been stopped. The finder will be liberally rewarded by leaving the same at this ofc. –Geo W Taylor, Bladensburg, Md

SAT JUL 1, 1843
Midshipmen who passed their examination before the Board recently convened at Phil, in the following order of merit:

1-Archibald McRae	21-John D Read
2-Robt H Wyman	22-Courtlandt Benham
3-Edw A Barnett	23-Wm A Henry
4-Nathl C Bryant	24-Wm F de Jongh
5-Geo B Balch	25-C S Throckmorton
6-Jona M Wainwright	26-Wm H Thompson
7-Geo W Hammersley	27-John F Abbott
8-Foxhall A Parker	29-Geo H Cooper
9-Isaac G Strais	29-Bayse N Westcott
10-Egbert Thompson	30-Wm W Polk
11-Robt Townsend	31-John F Stenson
12-Joel S Kennard	32-Andrew Bryson
13-John Wilkinson	33-John Downes, jr
14-John Guest	34-Chas M Morris
15-Wm H Montgomery	35-Andrew J Drake
16-Donald McN Fairfax	36-Jas H Spotts
17-Robt H Getty	37-Jas M Duncan
18-Isaac N Briceland	38-Lardner Gibbon
19-Henry Rodgers	39-Robt A Knapp
20-John M B Clitz	

Naval Intelligence: 1-The U S frig **Macedonian**, commanded by Com Mayo, dropped down the Norfolk Navy Yard to the naval aanchorage on Tue. 2-The U S sloop of war **Marion**, Lt Cmndng Brent, arrived at Boston from Norfolk on Mon last. 3-The U S sloop of war **Boston**, Capt Long, before reported at Oahu, arrived Feb 13 from China, via Sidney, [N S W,] & Tahiti. She remained in port Mar 11, to sail first wind for Boston, via Valparaiso. 4-The U S ship **John Adams** was at Montevideo on Apr 29.

Miss Mary Ann Webb has this day associated herself with Mrs Bihler in her store. Miss Webb has been the principal assistant for the past 5 years. Fancy Store, Millinery, & Ladies hair Dressing Business, on Pa ave, between 9th & 10th sts. All persons indebted to Mrs Bihler will please come forward & settle their accounts.

Building Cmte of the Third Baptist Church return their tanks to the Rev Clergy, the Independent Order of Odd Fellows, & the citizens for their attendance at the laying of the corner-stone of their new bldg on Wed last, & regret the exercises were interrupted by the severe storm which dispersed the congregation. Cmte will receive any amounts which may be left with either of the following:

Wm H Upperman, Pa ave near 3rd st	Jas B Clarke, Market Space
Andrew Rothwell, at the City Hall	Chauncey Bestor, at the Patriotic Bank

Geo M Kendall, at the Post Ofc Dept   Edmund F Brown, at the Globe Ofc
A F Wilcox, at the War Dept
[Jul 3 newspaper: a large glass vase was placed in the cavity of the corner-stone & set in its proper position by workmen under the direction of Mr Wm Mann, the architect. The inscription was read by Mr J B Clarke. Abstract from the same: This corner-stone of a church edifice for the Third Baptist Church of the city of Washington, was laid on Wed, Jun 28, anno Domini 1843, with a discourse by Rev J L Burrows, of Phil. The Pastor elect of the church is Geo W Samson; the deacons, Robt P Anderson & Wm Mann. The first temporary minister was Kendall Brooks. Jacob Knapp preached 2 months. The bldg cmte are Andrew Rothwell, Robt P Anderson, Wm Mann, J E Fowler, Chauncey Bestor, Geo Wood, Harrison Taylor, Jas B Clarke, & Wm H Upperman. John Tyler, of Va, Pres of the U S; Wm W Seaton, Mayor of the City of Washington; population of the U S, 17,000,000; population of the City of Washington, 26,000; number of churches in the city of Washington-Presbyterian, 5, including 1 colored; Protestant Episcopal 4; Friends or Quakers 1; Baptist 5, including 1 colored; Methodist Episcopal 5, including 2 colored; Methodist Protestant 2; German Lutheran 1; English Lutheran 1; Unitarian 1; Roman Catholic 3. In the vase are deposited 1 copy of the Holy Bible; 1 copy of Watts & Rippon's Hymus; copies of the city newspapers of the day; the Baptist Record, Phil; the 11th Annual Report of the American Baptist Home Mission Society; the Baptist Memorial for Jun, 1843; the Baptist Missionary Magazine for Jun, 1843; the 5th & 6th Annual Reports of the American & Foreign Bible Society; the Triennial Baptist Register; the 16th Annual Report of the Baptist General Tract Society; the 2nd & 3rd Annual Reports of the American Baptist, Publication Society; the Almanac & Baptist Register for 1841, 1842, & 1843; the Baptist Advocate, N Y, Jun 22, 1843; the Religious Herald, Richmond, Va, Jun 22, 1843; the Christian Watchman, Boston, Mass, Jun 23, 1843; a roll of the records of the Independent Order of Odd Fellows.]

For rent: 2 story brick house next door to Rev Dr Laurie's, on Pa ave, lately occupied by Col H Northup. The neighborhood is a delightful one. –L Shepperd, Gtwn

The Boston Bee states that the Hon Abbott Lawrence & family have taken passage in the ship **Columbia**, to sail on Jul 1 for Liverpool

Mrd: Jun 21, by Rev T W Simpson, Edw Long to Miss Aurelia Anne Roach, all of Somerset Co, Md.

Military & Naval Convention for the promotion of the moral & religious interest of the public armed service assembled on Wed in St Bartholomew's Church, N Y C, & united in singing the *Te Deum* in appropriate collects by the Rev Mr Balch, the rector of the church. Present: Col Bankhead & Maj Davies, U S Army; Capt Hudson & Capt Sands, U S Navy; Rev Mr Gallagher, Rev Professor McVikar, & Rev Mr Parkes, U S Army; Rev Mr Stewart, U S Navy; Rev Mr Balch & Lt Harwood,

U S Marine Corps; Lt Foote, Bishop McIlwaine, Bishop Lee, & Surgeon Mower, U S Army; Professor Weir & Rev Mr Carder, U S Army; Professor Kinsley, Rev Mr Harris, & others. The Gen-in-Chief was prevented by a sudden call to Washington from being present. Letters were received from Professor Mahan, Bishop Polb, Bishop McCoskry, Rev Mr Wayland, & Capt English. Col Bankhead, of the Army was called to the chair. Cmte appointed to act in the interior:

Maj Davies, U S Army
Capt Hudson, U S Navy
Capt English, U S marine Corps
Lt Hinger, Revenue Service
Surgeon Mower, U S Army
Rev Mr Gallagher, late U S Army
Rev Mr Stewart, U S Navy
Rev Mr Carder, U S Army

Rev Mr Parkes, U S Army, & Sec of the Convention
Rev N Sayre Harris, 281 Broadway, permanent sec to this cmte.

Thos Swords, surviving partner of the ancient firm of T & J Swords, printers & booksellers, the senior of the existing firm of Swords, Stanford & Co, died at N Y on Wed at age 80 years. We know the brothers, Thos & Jas, came to this city from Shelburne, Noval Scotia, more than 50 years ago. We have a volume bearing their imprint, the works of Ann Maria Bleecker, published by subscription, we believe, in 1794, 49 years ago. The Messrs Swords & Co have for many long years been the publishing house of the Portestant Episcopal Church. The dec'd was an excellent man, who, living or dying, had not an enemy. –N Y Com Adv

New Bedford Mercury: letter describing a mutiny & murder on board the ship **Sharon**, of Fairhaven. It appears that 3 natives of Ascension Islands were taken on board to replace some of the crew who had left, & while the boats were away capturing whales, the natives massacred Capt Norris, who, with a boy, was the only person on board besides the natives. The boy escaped by climbing aloft & hoisting a signal of distress. The boats returned to the ship, & after a severe contest, & killing 2 of the natives, succeeded in boarding the ship & getting possession. The other was put in irons & conveyed to Sidney, where the **Sharon** arrived in Jan last.

The schnr **Cordelia**, Capt Ebenezer Cook, of Provincetown, a few days since, when 20 hours out on a whaling curise, Nantucket bearing W by N 35 miles, captured a very large right whale, & after saving 120 barrels of oil & $100 worth of bone, cut adrift & sailed for home, accomplishing a very short but profitable voyage, having been absent but 4 days. The whale is the largest that has ever been caught from Provincetown, & is supposed to be the largest ever seen upon our coast. –Boston Adv

Teachers: the Trustees of Easton Academy will elect a Principal for this Institution on Sep 28 next. In addition to a comfortable house & garden & the proceeds of tuition, of which the amount can scarcely be less than $700, the incumbent of the ofc receives a salary of $750; he is expected to employ at his own expense, an usher or assistant teacher. The Academy, founded in 1799, is now in a flourishing condition, the income for the current year exceeding $1,500.00, & the ofc lately vacated by the resignation of Dr Arnold is deemed worthy of notice. –John Bozman Kerr, Easton, Talbot Co, Md.

Fountain Inn, Light st, Balt, Md, [late Beltzhoover's] has been leased by the subscribers, who have completely refitted & renovated it throughout. –W W Dix, Arthur L Fogg, Proprietors

Address of the Central Cmte to the Whigs of Md, was signed by-

Jas Harwood	Geo M Gill	Chas H Pitts
Geo R Richardson	Thos Kelso	John L Carey
Wm H Gatchell	John P Kennedy	A W Bradford
Wm Reynolds	Jas L Ridgely	Jas O Law

Valuable bldg lot at auction on Jul 7: lot 1 in square 346, fronting on F st: immediately east of the residence of Thos H Gilliss, & opposite the newly erected residence of Mr Clagett. If desired, the lot will be divided into two lots. -Robt W Dyer & Co, aucts

Died: on Jun 23, at his residence, in Geneva, N Y, Dr Edw Cutbush, for many years chief surgeon in the U S navy, during a considerable portion of which time he resided in Washington, where his high personal & professional qualities commanded warm respect.

Died: on Jun 10, at his residence, in Pensacola, at the U S Navy Yard, after a protracted & painful illness, Nahum Warren, master of the yard, in his 59th year. He had been 28 years in the service of his country, in which he had sustained the unblemished character of a faithful & efficient ofcr.

Died: on Jun 29, in Wash City, Mgt Walsh, infant d/o Wm W & Bridget Ann Cox, aged 15 months.

Died: on Jun 30, Richd Headley, aged 25, of consumption. His funeral will be from the residence of his mother, on 13th st, near F, this evening, at 4 p m.

Died: on Thu last, Mrs Mary Simpson, in her 86th year, a native of England, but for many years a resident of Montg Co, Md, & relict of Thos Simpson. Funeral from her late residence, Simpsonville, Montg Co, Md, this evening, at 3 p m.

Union Guards, Attention! You are hereby ordered to meet for parade on Jul 3 at 4 p m, at the Armory, completely uniformed, armed, & equipped, as an escort to the Mechanical Riflemen, who leave this city on a visit to Richmond, Va.
–G W Harkness, Capt

Union Fire Co: meet at their engine house at 3 p m today, wearing fire hats, for the purpose of attending the funeral of Richd Headley, a late member of the company. –Chas Calvert, Sec

MON JUL 3, 1843
On Tue next being the 4th of Jul, our Ofc will be closed. Persons having notes due are requested to pay them on Mon, Jul 3. –Corcoran & Riggs

$50 reward for runaway negro man John Smith, between 30 & 35 years of age. Also, at the same time, Charlotte, wife of John, about 33 years of age, who has relations both in Newport & Port Tobacco neighborhoods. She has a sister living in Calvert Co, belonging to Mr Jas C Sedwick.
-Louisa Smith, near Brayantown, Md

Phebe Ann Hickelthorn, residing in Troy, Miami Co, Ohio, was drowned in the river at that place a short time since. It appears that she was a somnambulist.

Robt Stewart, the gentleman to whom his brother Alexander left the whole of his immense estate, & who was extremely wealthy, in his own right, before, died at N Y on Mon, in his 83rd year. He was uncle to Mrs Webb & Mrs Stewart, & held, previous to his death, the estate left by Alice Lispenard, which recently caused so much attention on account of the ejectment suits brought against it. Mr Stewart is supposed to have received the estates of Alexander in trust [covered by will] for the benefit of the children of the latter. Mr Stewart was married at a late period of his life, but did not reside long with his wife, who is still living. N Y Express

Wm Mullhall, a native of Ireland, aged 36, a waiter at the City Hotel, in N Y, drowned on Sun while at the Battery bath with some of his family. He was carried by the tide under a sloop & was drowned.

Lt H H Bell has been placed in command of the U S steamship **Union**, now at Norfolk, Lt Hunter having been detached on other duties.

The Chester [Pa] Republican announces the death of the Hon John Edwards, late member of Congress from that district. He expired at his residence in Thornbury, Chester Co, on Mon. He was a good citizen, husband, & father; in his death his family & the community have lost a valuable member.

Brvt Brig Gen Abraham Eustis, commander of the 6th military division of the U S army, died at his headqrtrs in Portland, Maine, on Tue last. His disease was congestion of the brain, & was of but short duration. Appropriate funeral honors were paid to his remains the day after his death, having been accompanied to the cars by a civic & military procession, & transported to Boston for interment.

The Locofocos of Maine held a State Convention at Bangor on Thu week, & Hugh J Anderson was nominated as their candidate for the ofc of Govn'r of the State at the next election. The vote stood-for Hugh J Anderson 162, Edw Kavanagh 124, scattering 13. The Convention recommends Mr Van Buren as the candidate of their party for next President.

Naval: the Prince de Joinville, who, with his bride, sailed from Rio de Janeiro, in the frig **Belle Poule**, for France, on May 13, while at Rio paid a visit to the U S frig **Columbia**, & was evidently well pleased with the unlimited hospitality & gentlemanly conduct of Cmdor Shubrick & his ofcrs during the marriage festivities. Balls & dinner were given on board the French line of battle ship **Marseilles** & the frig **Belle Poule**, when all the American ofcrs on the Brazil squadron were invited by the Prince.

Mr Henry Rankin, a contractor on the Schuylkill Navigation Company's works, met his death on Fri. Whilst witnessing the blasting of rocks near Manayunk, near Phil, a stone of great weight struck him over the right eye, &, fracturing the skull, caused instant death.

Mr J C Chapman, the freight agent of the Western Railroad Co, was killed at East Chatham on Tue, while removing a barn near the station. A beam fell upon him, fracturing his skull, breaking his back, & crushing him in an awful manner. He died almost immediately.

Died: on Jul 1, of apoplexy, after a short but painful illness, Capt Jos Johnson, aged 83 years. The dec'd was formerly a native of St Mary's Co, Md, but for the last 50 years a resident of Wash City. He has left a numerous family to mourn his irreparable loss. His perfect honesty, pure, upright, & steady priciples, endeared him to an extensive acquaintance. His funeral will take place at his late residence, near the eastern Branch, on Mon, at 3 p m.

Mr Wm A Stokes, Pres of the Repeal Association of the city & county of Phil, has resigned his ofc.

The Albany Daily Adv says it is not the intention of Mr Papineau, [now in France] to return at present to Canada. There is no truth that the Gov't authorized him to draw for arrears of salary, due to him.

Died: on Jul 2, Mrs Catharine Rousha, aged 70. Her funeral will be tomorrow at 9 a m, from the residence of her son, J Kane, on 10th st, 3rd door from E st.

Fire in E st on Sat broke out among some shavings in the yard adjoining the carpenter's shop of Messrs Barron & Turton, at the corner of 10th st, & destroyed it. The flames reached a frame bldg, belonging to Mr W H Stewart & occupied by Mr

John Mills, & was considerably injured. Soon after the fire, a small colored boy, named Black, was arrested on suspicion of setting fire to the shavings. He was committed to jail by Justice Goddard.

Another incendiary attempt on last Fri; fire was started in the large wood pile near the bakery of Mr John McKelden, on 7th st. Fortunately some of the neighbors saw the fire & extinguished it.

Criminal Court-Wash: on motion of P R Fendall, District Atty, on Jun 27, R M Harrison was admitted as an atty & counsellor of the Crmnl Crt. 1-Case of stabbing at Gtwn on Fri last: Richd Stewart, free negro, indicted for an assault & battery upon Jos Lacy, free negro, by severely stabbing him in the market-house at Gtwn, was found guilty. 2-M Buck, inducted for an assault & battery upon S Stettinius at the Railroad Depot, found guilty. The same dfndnt was also found guilty of an assault & battery upon Saml Stettinius while in the discharge of his duty as a justice of the peace. 3-John Johnson, free negro, guilty of an assault & battery on Geo Bean, a small white boy. Johnson threw a stone at the little fellow, which wounded him severely on the head. 4-Danl Stiner, a white boy, was indicted for setting fire to the stable of Fred'k Pascoe, in Gtwn, last Apr. He was found not guilty.

Headqrtrs Nat'l Blues, Jul 1, 1843. You are hereby ordered to parade in full summer uniform, with knapsacks, at 4 a m on Jul 4, for the purpose of visiting Rockville, Md. By order of Capt F A Tucker: W J Gary, 2nd Sergeant.

TUE JUL 4, 1843
The large & splendid steamboat **Columbia**, Capt Guyther, will make a pleasure trip down the Potomac on Jul 4th, leaving Riley's wharf at 9:30 a m, Navy Yard at 10, & Alexandria at 11. Will stop at Fort Washington, giving sufficient time for passengers to view the fortifications & the beautiful grounds & scenery. She will pass Mount Vernon, & proceed as far as Potomac Creek. She boat will return to the city about 10 o'clock the same evening. The properitor has made arrangements for the steamboat **Union** to leave Smoot's wharf at 8:30 a m to convey passengers to the **Columbia** & back again on her return free of charge. Dinner will be provided on board at a moderate price. Confectionaries, Ice Cream, & all other refreshments will be on board. The Marine Bank will accompany the party with Military & Cotillion Music. Tickets 50 cents each, to be obtained at all the principal Hotels in Wash, Gtwn, Navy Yard, & at Alexandria, & at the boat on the day of departure.

Sons of Temperance: Timothy Division #1, of Wash, will meet at the house of Brother Mantz, near the Treasury bldg, on Jul 4, to join in the Temperance Celebration of the day. By order of W P: Geo Cochran, Act R S

A Card: to the firemen & citizens generally! I return to you my sincere thanks for your kindness in your efforts to save my furniture at the late fire on E st, on Sat last, when my house was on fire. -John Mills [As my loss had been to me considerable, all those who are indebted to me will confer a favor by settling the same. Though small, it is of great importance to me at this time.]

Virginia-At a Superior Court of Chancery, for the Richmond Crct, held at the Capitol, in Richmond, on Apr 1, 1843: Sidney S Baxter, Atty Gen of the Commonwealth of Va, & the Pres & Dirs of the Literary Fund, Plntfs, against: Donald McNichol, Archibald McNichol, Peggy McNichol, John McLaughlin & Mary his wife, John Crow & Jean his wife, Alex'r McNichol, John McNichol, Francis McNichol, Geo Machine & Isabella his wife, Ellen McNichol, Elijah Cannon & Mgt his wife, Jas Bennett & Catharine his wife, Mary McNichol, & Nicholas Nelson & Jane his wife, dfndnts. The demurrer of the dfndnts to the bill of the plntfs being argued, it is the opinion of the Court that the said demurrer is insufficient: Therefore it is decreed that the said demurrer be overruled, & thereupon the dfndnts filed their answer to the bill, to which answer the plntfs by counsel replied generally, & the cause coming on this day to be heard by consent of the Atty Gen, & of the dfndnts by their counsel, on the bill, answer, & replication, was argued by counsel. On consideration whereof, the Court orders that publication be made for 3 months successively in the Richmond Enquirer, Richmond Whig, & Nat'l Intell, published in Wash City, requiring all persons claiming an interest in the estate of Dr John McNichol, a surgeon in the Navy of the State of Va, in the Revolutionary war, to appear here on the first day of the next Jan Term & make themselves parties dfndnts to this suit. –Wm G Sands, C C

Tapley H Stewart, one of the Caldwell gang of thieves & counterfeiters who lately had his trial at Little Rock, Ark, & convicted on 3 several indictments, has been sentenced to the State pen for 31 years. Amour Hunt, also convicted on 3 indictments, sentenced for 21½ years. All the gang, except one, have been tried & sentenced.

On Fri last Capt Josiah Cleaveland, of Owego, Tioga Co, N Y, who traveled 450 miles to be present at the Bunker Hill celebration on the 17th, died at Charlestown, Mass, in his 90th year: attacked with influenza immediately after the celebration, & fell victim to that disease. He was a native of Connecticut, was present at the battle of Bunker Hill, & in active service during the whole Revolutionary war, participating in many of its battles. At its close he held the commission of capt.

Lady Elgin, w/o Lord Elgin, the Govn'r of Jamaica, died at Kingston on Jun 7, in her 22nd year.

News-England. 1-Mr John Murdock, of the firm of Murdock & Venables, Wood st, London, a gentleman of considerable property, committed suicide last week, laboring under the delusion & apprehension that he would come to poverty. 2-His Grace the

Archbishop of York, who has this week consecrated the new churches at Elsecar & Kimberworth, is in the 87th year of his age, & has been Archbishop since 1807.

Army General Order #41: Jun 30, 1843. Announce the death of a distinguished brother ofcr, Brvt Brig Gen Abraham Eustis, who died at Portland, Maine, on Jun 27. The dec'd entered the Army a captain of light artl in 1808, in the expectation of the war that was not declared till 4 years later. In a career of 35 years he uniformly exhibited vigor in command, combined with high intelligence & impartiality, & in all relations, public & private, the sternest & most spotless integrity. –R Jones

Carrollton Advocate of the 17th ult states that the family of Mr B F Massey, of Jersey Co, Ill, were poisoned by eating the rhubarb or pie plant, which had been cooked in a common brass kettle. It is supposed that the acid of the plant extracted the poisonous material from the kettle. Two children of the family had died, & the wife of Mr Massey & a child were expected not to survive.

Death from Kreosote. Dr Wm R Boardman, of Hartford, Conn, lost his life on the 25th ult from taking this dangerous nostrum for the tooth-ache. A particle of it got into his throat, & caused such inflammation as to stop the breathing passage.

Mrd: on Jun 29, by Rev Mr Young, John T Baggott, of Fredericksburg, Va, to Annie Virginia, eldest d/o Capt Jos Nevitt, of Alexandria.

Died: on Jun 28, Mr John McRea Allison, formerly of Alexandria, D C, & for many years a classical instructor in the Alexandria Academy.

Accidents in N Y. 1-Jas White fell on Wed from a 2nd story window of the house 59 Anthony st, to be pavement below, & died before he arrived at the hospital. 2-Mr Wm Madden was engaged on Wed in the 3rd story of the job printing ofc 122 Fulton st, & by some sccident fell through the hatchway to the ground. He was taken to the hospital & is doing well & likely to recover. 3-John Closey, on Wed, fell downstairs at 51 Washington st, & broke his collar-bone. He was taken to the hospital & is doing well. 4-Thos Lynch, on Wed, while in a porter-house at the corner of Centre & Anthony sts, a friend stepped up to him as he was sitting on a table & in a playful manner pushed to the ground. Falling on his head he dislocated the vertebrae of his neck. He was at one taken to the City Hospital & died the next morning.

THU JUL 6, 1843
Those engaged in raising the wreck of the ship **Erie**, sunk in Lake Erie, are successfully employed with their diving bell in getting up the machinery. On the first letting down of the bell it struck upon the boat. Capt Chapin, its inventor, thinks he will be able to discover the iron safe which was on the boat. –Fredonia Censor

We learn from the Leonardtown Herald that on Jun 27 the mansion of H G S Key, in that vicinity, was struck by lightning, which demolished a portion of one of the chimneys. No one received any bodily hurt by the shock of the falling of the chimney.

The Batavia N Y Times states that Mrs Trace Avery, from Devonshire, Eng, died on board the cars just as the train entered that village on Sat last. She had braved the elements, & traveled 3,000 miles to enjoy the gratification of once more meeting her children, one of whom lived in that village & another in Stafford.

A young man named Thos Ayler was killed on the 25th ult at Ruthsburg, near Centreville, Md, by falling from a cherry tree. The tree stood near a fence, & he fell on the sharp end of a stake that projected from the fence, which entered his thigh running upwards some 5 inches. Medical aid was called, but it proved unavailing. He died in 28 hours after the fall.

Died: on Jun 30, in N Y, Chas McEvers, in his 43rd year.

Bank of the Metropolis: election of the Directors was made on Jul 3:

John P Van Ness	Thos Carbery	Nathl P Causin
Jas Thompson	Lewis Johnson	Geo W Graham
John Boyle	John W Maury	Geo Parker

On Jul 4th, according to law, John P Van Ness was re-elected Pres, & Chas Hill re-elected Dir to fill the vacancy in the board caused by the election of the Pres.

House & furniture for sale: the subscriber offers his 2 story brick house, on south side of C, between 3rd & 4½ sts, being one of the most pleasant locations in the city. -Chas Rich on the premises.

To let, neatly finished house, with back bldgs, 3 stories high, on C st, between 9th & 10th sts, near Pa ave. Apply to Robt Keyworth.

Orphan's Court of Wash Co, D C. Letters testamentary on the personal estate of Rachael Coumbe, late of Wash Co, dec'd. -Thos Carbery, Wm Jones, excs

Orphan's Court of Wash Co, D C. Letters of adm, de bonis non, on the personal estate of Wm Coumbe, late of Wash Co, dec'd. -Thos Carbery, Wm Jones, Adms D B N

Wash Corp: 1-Bill for the relief of John Mitchell: referred to the Cmte of Claims. 2-Ptn from H Johnson: referred to the Cmte of Claims.

Crmnl Crt-Wash: Jul 3. 1-Jas W Bingham was arrested in Wash City by ofcr Burr, under the charge of robbing his employer at Albany, N Y, to between $300 & $400.

The prisoner had been lodged in jail under a commitment for further examination. 2- Nelson Simms & Wm Stark, free negroes, were committed by Justice Donn for trial, charged on the oath of John Goldin with stealing 2 pairs of boots, the property of said Goldin. The prisoners were arrested by J A Ratcliff, constable.

Inquest was held on the body of a free mulatto named Jim Davis, who was found yesterday in the woods not far from the Columbian College. There was no evidence to satisfy in what manner the dec'd came to his death, & a verdict was rendered in conformity with that fact.

FRI JUL 7, 1843
Among the passengers in the steamship **Great Western**, on her late voyage to N Y, was Harmanus Bleecker, late Minister of the U S to the Netherlands, & his Lady; who will receive a hearty welcome back to his country from his numerous friends.

The Hon N P Tallmadge, U S Senator from N Y, arrived in Buffalo, N Y, on Jun 29, on his way to visit the Territory of Wisconsin.

The late Gen Abraham Eustis, Cmder of the 6th Div of the U S Army, died at Portland, on Jun 27, at age 58. He was born in Va, his father being an elder brother of Govn'r Eustis, of Mass, & his mother the sister of the late Chief Justice Parker. His father was a merchant in Va, & died when the Gen was quite young. He was an 1804 grad at Cambridge: studied law under his uncle, Chief Justice Parker, & admitted to practice in 1807, & opened an ofc in Boston. In 1808, Govn'r Eustis being then Sec of War, he was appointed a captain in the U S army, & when Congress organized the corps of Light Artl, one of the first companies of that corps was placed under his command. He distinguished himself at the capture of York, U C, when Gen Pike, the Cmder-in Chief, fell. He served in Fla in the late campaign, & was at the time of his death in command of the eastern line of the U S. For a long time he was in command of the Practical Military School at Fortress Monroe. He had left a very numerous family, having had 10 sons by his first marriage to Miss Sprague, of Dedham; & four of his sons have graduated at Cambridge. His widow was the sister of Gen Izard, of S C. –Salem Gaz

An affray took place on Jun 10 in Bloomfield, Stoddard Co, Mo, between Dr Chapman & Mr Danl Stanford, of that place, in which Chapman was killed. The weapons were knives or dirks.

Concord [Mass] Freeman of Sat: Miss Matilda Proctor, [9 years of age] d/o Isaac Proctor, of this place, died last evening. In endeavoring to enter the school room through one of the windows, the window came down upon her neck. She was found hanging from the window about 9 p m. It seems she had left something in the school house, the Primary School in the East District.

Jas M Layton murdered his wife upwards of 2 years in a most brutal manner in Perry Co, Mo. He was tried last month at Farmington, St Francis Co, & sentenced to be hung on Jun 17. His counsel took exceptions to something in the trial, & petitioned the Govn'r of Mo to extend the time of execution. It was suspended until Sep 1. On the 17th, however, thousands of citizens, not having heard of the suspension of the execution, suspecting foul play, broke open the jail, dragged forth their victim, & hung him with their own hands. Thus they murdered a murderer.

Rev Geo Beecher, Pastor of the Second Presby Chr in Scioto, accidently killed himself on Sat last. He had fired one barrel of a double barreled gun, & attempted to blow in the other when it went off, discharging its whole contents into his mouth & head, & killing him instantly.

Albany, N Y, Jonathan Wakeman was drowned in the canal on Jul 1. He appeared to be nearly 50 years of age. He had a large trunk on board the boat on which he had taken passage for Little Falls. The trunk contains articles of value. It appears from papers found on his person that he resided in Greenfield, Fairfield, Co, Conn.

Died: on Jun 26, in St Albans, Vt, Joshua Montefiore, aged 81 years, a native of London, author of "the Commercial Dictionary," Commercial & Notarial Precedents," Treatise on the Bankrupt Laws."

Died: on Jun 15, at *Pleasant Hills*, Benj Welsh, in his 58th year. He was a kid brother, an indulgent master, & a stout & unflinching friend. "Here lieth an honest man." -K

SAT JUL 8, 1843
Election of the Dirs for the Patriotic Bank of Wash, Jul 3, 1843:

*Wm A Bradley	J F Caldwell
Phineas Bradley	E Lindsley
G C Grammer	Wm Stettinius
Thos Blagden	Wm J McDonald
Wm H Gunnell	

*Re-elected Pres on Jul 4th.

For rent, a dwlg house & store [frame,] on 12th st, between G & H sts, recently occupied by Mr Quincy. For sale, the east half of lot 4 in sq 286, on N Y ave, between 12th & 13th sts. –N P Causin, jr

$10 reward for a bay mare that strayed from a stable on F st, on Jun 27. Reward be given if the mare is left at the residence of A Dickins, Wash City, or at Ossian Hall, Fairfax Co, Va.

For rent, the house now occupied by Moses Poor, on 6th st, between E & F sts.

Naval Intell: Passed Midshipmen to be Lts: Wm A Parker, from Jan 16, 1843; Jas D Johnston, from Jun 24, 1843; Thos R Ware, of Md, to be a Purser

Mrd: on Jun 21, by Rev Alex'r Jones, G H J Beckwith to Anne Lloyd, d/o Dr Saml Scollay, all of Jefferson Co, Va.

Died: yesterday, in her 30th year, Ann, consort of J L Peabody, & d/o Wm Ward. Her funeral is this evening at 4 p m from her late residence, Pa ave.

Died: on Jul 7, in Wash City, Geo Philips Lynch, s/o Jas & Jane Lynch, aged 14 months & 3 days. His funeral is this evening at 4 p m.

In the Circuit Superior Court of Law & Chancery for Fauquier Co: In Chancery. The Bank of the U S in Pa vs John B Steinberger & others. Cmplnt & dfndnts are notified that on Jul 31, 1843, at the ofc of Saml D King, a J P for Wash City, on F st, Aug 3, at the Union Bank of Md, in Balt; & on Aug 7, at the ofc of J Brice Smith, atty at law, Wall st, N Y, I shall take the depositions of sundry witnesses, to be offered in evidence on my behalf, as a petitioning creditor of the said John B Steinberger in said cause. –W W Corcoran

For rent: neat & comfortable brick dwlg house, 10 rooms, fronting on N Y ave, between 9th & 10th sts. Apply to John C Harkness, 2 doors west of said house.

Trustee's sale: decree of the Circuit Court of Wash Co, D C, made in the cause of Smith & Cissel complnts, against the heirs at law of Wm Hayman, dec'd, & others, dfndnts: sale in front of the premises, on Jul 25, of the lot of ground #15 in square 5, of Wash City, & all that part of lot #15 in square 5, lying east of the residence of Jos Smoot, with the improvements, embracing a valuable 3 story brick dwlg, with outbldgs. –Clement Cox, trustee -Robt W Dyer & Co, aucts

Obit-died: on Jul 3, in his 90th year, at his late residence on Prospect Hill, near Piscataway, PG Co, Md, Mr Richd Coe, another from among the few bleached & time-worn sldrs of the Revolution. Throughout 4 years of the long & bloody struggle he fought & suffered in Washington's own division of the patriot army, & at the end of that period he received his full & honorable discharge. For 60 years thereafter, he continued in an industrious civic life, rearing up his family in the love of his owned cherished virtues. -H

My engagement with the Shannondale Co during the spring season will in nowise interfere with the management of my Hotel in Charlestown. The utmost exertion will be made to minister to wants & needs by Mr Hughes, who has been engaged with me since the opening. –Jos F Abell

The Trustees of the Rappahannock Academy wish to engage the services of a well qualified English & Classical scholar as Principal tutor for the ensuing scholastic year. The Academy is in Caroline Co, Va. An unmarried man would be preferred. Apply, post paid, to the subscriber, at Fredericksburg, Va. –Wm P Taylor, Pres of Board of Trustees

MON JUL 10, 1843
Official: Cabinet arrangements completed:

Hon Abel P Upshur, Sec of State
Hon J C Spencer, Sec of the Treas
Hon J M Porter, Sec of War
Hon David Henshaw, Sec of the Navy
Hon C A Wickliffe, Postmaster Gen
Hon John Nelson, Atty General

Some of the decisions of the late Court Martial held on board the ship **Pennsylvania** at Norfolk:
Cmder Wm Ramsey, sentence not confirmed; reported to be 5 years suspension
Lt Edw M Vail, dismissed, Jul 3, 1843
Lt Chas H Poor, acquitted
Passed Midshipman Matthias C Marin, suspended for 2 years
Midshipman Chas T Crocker, suspended until Dec 30, 1843, without pay
Midshipman Albert G Enos, suspended until Jun 30, 1844, without pay
Midshipman Sam A Miller, dismissed Jun 30.

Coincidences:

Born:	President:	Retired:
1735	John Adams	1801
1743	Thos Jefferson	1809
1751	Jas Madison	1817
1759	Jas Monroe	1825
1767	J Quincy Adams	1829

Now it will be seen by this that Jefferson was born just 8 years after his predecessor Adams; Madison 8 years after his predecessor Jefferson; Monroe 8 years after Madison; & John Quincy Adams 8 years after Monroe. Another courious fact is that Adams was just 66 years old when he retired; Jefferson was 66; Madison was 66; Monroe was 66; & John Quincy Adams, had he been elected to a second term, would have been 66. Adams, Jefferson, & Monroe all died on the 4th of Jul. –N Y Evening Post

W Bartlett, barrister-at-law, died at Bideford last week, aged 73. He possessed a large fortune, & his estates in the neighborhood of Exeter are immense. –Herald

Orphan's Court of Wash Co, D C. Letters of adm, with the will annexed, on the personal estate of Jos Johnson, late of said county, dec'd. –Jas Johnson, Henry D Gunnell, Adm W A

On Jun 30, Isabella, d/o Mr S Jennison, of Langdon, N H, was playing with Danl Lakeman, aged 12 or 14 years, when the latter took up a gun in sport, not knowing it was loaded, & fired into her breast, killing her instantly. The innocent little victim was only 3 years old.

Circular to fellow citizens, near & remote, both in town & country, undersigned are a Cmte in behalf of the People of Fall River, Mass, make this their appeal for help amid the appalling calamity which has overtaken us. Fire on Jul 2 burnt nearly 200 bldgs; nearly 200 families are houseless & many of them are penniless. Send us what you can-food, clothing, money-send it addressed to either of us, & it shall be carefully distributed to the needy.

Jervis Shove	Wm Brown	Richd Borden
John Eddy	Orin Fowler	Jos F Lindsey
Enoch French	Jefferson Borden	
Asa Bronson	David Anthony	

Cmte: Fall River, Mass, Jul 4, 1843

Died: on Jul 8, Wm Reddall, s/o John Y & Cordelia V Laue, aged 3 months & 3 days. His funeral will be from the residence of Mrs Randall, corner of 13th & H sts at 4 p m today.

Died: on Jul 7, at Gosport, Va, where he had gone in consquence of his health, Saml Hutchins, of Wash City, aged 35 years.

Mr Robt Stewart, recently dec'd, turns out to have left quite a small property, instead of the immense estate which he was said to have left. –N Y Express

$5 reward for the return of a strayed black & white cow. Reward will be given if returned to the subscriber on C st, between 6th & 7th sts. -R J Pollard

TUE JUL 11, 1843
Letters have been received from Mr Perkins, the American Missionary in Persia, to the 16th May, at which time he had reached Trebisond, a city of 50,000 people on the Black sea, with his family & Mar Yohannan. The labors of the American Missionaries in the East are beginning to be highly appreciated.

Mr Chas Norman, sailmaker, a highly respected inhabitant of Bridgeport, Conn, was drowned in the harbor of that city on Jul 4. He was with another individual, out on a sailing excursion in a small boat, which was capsized by a sudden gust of wind. The other person, by clinging to the boat, was enabled to save himself until assistance came; but Mr Norman, having on a heavy overcoat which fitted so closely that he was unable to get it off, very soon sank. He has left a wife & 2 children.

Wm E Mayhew has been elected Pres of the Farmers' & Planters' Bank of Balt, to succeed the lamented Pres of that institution, Jas Cheston.

Mr Lemuel Austin, the man noticed by us last week as having disappeared suddenly from this village, was found in the town of Castile one day last week, in the woods. His mind was perfectly unstrung on the subject of Millerism that he had heard preached in the city. –Western New Yorker

Mr Gustavus Drew, of Skowhegan village, Maine, arrested some time since for sundry petit larcenies committed by him in the village: jury found a bill against him in the Jun term of Court. He was a hatter, had a wife, & 4 small children. On Thu in the criminal's box, becoming sick, it was found he had swallowed a large portion of kreosote, the most deadly of all drugs. He died about midnight, having his senses to the last. A portion of his letter to the Judge is as follows: "My object in writing is to say, I have a poor & feeble wife, 4 little children; they have none to help them. I have given way to a wrong propensity, & I have fallen. I now give my life as the forfeit; I hope that is enough. Spare my family any further trouble." [Abstract from the letter.]

The Fourth at Richmond. A dinner was provided for the Washington Mechanical Riflemen who visited for the occasion. On the 3rd the Blues, the Scarlet Guard, & the Grenadiers assembled at the Depot to receive the Wash Co, under the command of Capt McClelland. The Riflemen marched to Church Hill for their encampment. On the 4th the line was formed by the Military, consisting of:

Chesterfield Light Dragoons, Capt Weisiger
Henrico Dragoons, Capt McRae
Richmond Dragoons, Capt Gregory
Richmond Fayette Artl, Capt Ellis
Blues, Capt G W Munford
Scarlet Guard, Capt Jno D Munford
Grenadiers, Lt Com't A Richards

Reader of the Declaration of Independence: Capt Thos H Ellis
Orator of the Day: Mr John S Caskie
Prayer by Rev E L Magoon, Pastor of the Church

<u>Volunteer toasts at the dinner at Buchanan's Spring:</u>

Thos Ritchie
Col John Rutherford
Jas Cowardin
Lt E N Allen, Blues
Col G M Carrington
Maj Chas H Hyde, 4th Regt of Artl
Lt Bargamin, Grenadiers
Capt John D Munford
Capt Thos H Ellis
Lt Seaton, Scarlet Guard
Lt Com Richards
Cpl Boyd, of the Mechanicals
Orderly Sergeant Fordham, of the Artl
Lt Talbot, of the Artl
M B Poiteaux, jr, of the Blues
W Christian, Scarlet Guard
Lt Redwood, Scarlet Guard

Wash Corp yesterday: Jesse E Dow, elected a Police Magistrate in the place of Chas Murray, resigned. The nomination of Silas Moore & Wm Wallis, as Police Constables were confirmed.

Fire broke out last Sun in a brick stable belonging to Danl Carroll, in the rear of the family mansion not far from the Capitol. It is feared that some disorderly lads may have thrown fire into the stable.
[Mr D Carroll, of Duddington, tenders his sincere thanks to the Fire Companies of Washington & citizens generally for their prompt assistance in rescuing his stable from the fire on Sun last.]

Crmnl Crt-Wash. 1-Wm Richardson, free negro, the prisoner charged on the oath of Mrs Mitchell with these offences, was found guilty on the indictment for an assault, but acquitted him on the indictment of arson. 2-The trial of R P Dowden is fixed to commence on Thu next.

I am authorized to give a reward of $10 for the recovery of 6 brass screws or caps, taken from the fire-plugs on Pa ave, or $1 for each one delivered at my shop. –C Buckingham, Superintending Water pipes

NOTICE: The undersigned being about to leave Washington for his residence in N C, believes he has fully settled with all who had claims against him in this city; if he has omitted any one, he requests that the claims be left with Judge Bryan, at his rooms on 10th st, near Pa ave. –Gideon F Morris, Cherokee Co, N C.

WED JUL 12, 1843
The Hon Jas A Bayard is about to move from Delaware to N Y, to continue the practice of the law.

The Elkton Democrat states that on the 4th, at Chestertown, Md, a s/o Mr Vanhorn, aged about 18 months, having been carried by its nurse too near the muzzle of the cannon at the time of its firing, was struck with the wad & so much injured that it died in about 24 hours after the accident.

Mr Jas Irvine died at Balt on Sun, at his residence in Commerce st, from the effects of the painful disease, lock jaw. He had run a rusty nail through his foot some 10 days since when preparing the foundation of a new engine house about to be built for the Union Fire Co. –Patriot

Meeting of the ofcrs of the 4th Regt of Artl, convened at Carroll Hall, Fort Monroe, Va, on Jul 2, on intelligence of the death of Brig Gen Abraham Eustis, Colonel 1st Regt of Artl, there were present:

Col J B Walbach	Capt & Brvt Maj W W Morris
Capt P H Galt	Capt W P Bainbridge

1ˢᵗ Lt & Adj J H Miller	Capt J B Scott
1ˢᵗ Lt J W Phelps	1ˢᵗ Lt R C Snead
1ˢᵗ Lt T Williams	1ˢᵗ Lt J P J O'Brien
2ⁿᵈ Lt J P McCown	1ˢᵗ Lt T L Brent
2ⁿᵈ Lt S S Fahnestock	1ˢᵗ Lt E Bradford
2ⁿᵈ Lt H M Whiting	2ⁿᵈ Lt G W Getty
Maj F S Belton	2ⁿᵈ Lt C Benjamin
Capt & Brvt Maj H Brown	2ⁿᵈ Lt G W Rains

Lt Cutting, of the U S ship **Columbia**, died suddenly at Rio Janeiro about May 20.

Mr Hield, for some time a manager of the Nat'l Theatre in Wash City, died lately in Fla, where he had been performing with a dramatic corps. [Jul 17 newspaper: Mr Hield, we are happy to say, is alive & in good case. Long may he continue to be so! -N Y Express]

Fatal accident on Fri last at Bloomingdale road & 54ᵗʰ st, N Y. Mr Jas McGuire, a native of Ireland, aged about 48 years, with others, were blasting a rock in 86ᵗʰ st when they took shelter: a fragment of rock, about 100 pounds, fell with great force upon the roof, crushing it in & falling on the head of the dec'd, causing his death in 15 or 20 minutes.

On Sat week, a child of Saml B James, of the village of Ogendsburg, N Y, aged about 7 years, drowned from off the wharf near the Oswegatchie bridge. He inadvertently stepped backward into the water.

Columbia College, having received a legacy of $20,000 for that purpose from the estate of the late Fred'k Gebhard, of N Y, has established a German Professorship, & made the German language an indispensable portion of the collegiate course. We learn by the American that John Louis Tellkampf, a native of Hanover, s/o an eminent judicial functionary of that Kingdom, has been appointed to the Professorship. He has been in this country some 5 years, part of the time connected with Union College.

Jas M Reynolds, clk of the county com'rs court of St Clair Co, Mo, shot himself dead in his ofc at Belleville, on Jun 29. He was a nephew of Govn'r Reynolds. The cause which urged him to commit the fatal deed is unknown.

The s/o Peter Springstead, in Frankfort, N Y, aged about 10 years, suffocated in a bin of wheat on Jul 5. He was playing in the bin at Williams' warehouse, when the gate was opened & he was thrown under the wheat & smothered. His mother did not know of his death until she saw his dead body.

The creditors of Geo Marbury under the insolvent law are notified to produce their claims to me, duly authenticated, on or before Aug 15, in order that a dividend of the assest of the said Marbury may be made, which will be paid to the said creditors. –H Naylor, Trustee of geo Marbury

Circuit Court of Wash Co, D C. Chas Longdon; Jas J Martin; have each applied to be discharged from imprisonment under the act for the relief of Insolvent Debtors: hearing on Jul 18. –Wm Brent, clk

$100 reward for runaway negro Henry Holiday, about 35 years old; has a wife at Mr Hugh Perrie's, near Magruder's ferry, in PG Co, Md, & belongs to the heir of the late John R Gibbons, of whom the subscriber is guardian. My post ofc is at *Gallant Green*, Chas Co, Md. –Geo Gardiner, Guardian for John S Gibbons

Died: on Jun 23, in Geneva, N Y, Edw Cutbush, M D, formerly a highly respected resident of Wash City. He was born in Phil in 1772; was the pupil of Dr Benj Rush, & was a physician for 7 years in the Pennsylvania Hospital. In 1794 he was Surgeon Gen in Washington's expedition against the insurgents of Pa. In 1799 he entered the navy as surgeon, &, under Cmdor Barry in the frig **United States**, was chief surgeon of the fleet in the Mediterranean. In 1829 he was suddenly ordered by the then Sec of the Navy to sea service on board a schnr. The Dr, deeming this order very derogatory to his pretensions, resigned his commission after 30 years of faithful service. He retired to Geneva, N Y, where he was placed in the chemical chair of the college of that place & became Dean of the Medical Faculty therein. He died regretted & respected by all who knew him. –I G S

Mrd: on Jul 3, by Rev John Davis, Mr John Edw Moran to Miss Charlotte H P Dorsey, all of Wash City.

Died: on Sun last, in Alexandria, Mrs Ann Cazenove, consort of Anthony C Cazenove, of that place, beloved by her family, respected by her friends, & regretted by all who knew her.

Died: on Jul 6, at Montpelier, Wash Co, Md, the residence of the late J T Mason, John D Dutton, in his 70th year. The dec'd was a native of Scotland, but for the last 28 years had been an inmate of the house in which he died. The undivided confidence & esteem of the community in which he lived was his life, & their unfeigned sorrow followed him to his grave.

Died: on Jul 2, in Wash City, Mr Jas M Sinnott, in his 62nd year-a native of Wexford, Ireland, & for the last 25 years a resident of this District.

THU JUL 13, 1843
Boston Atlas of Mon: announce the loss of the British Mail steamer **Columbia**, Capt Shannon, which sailed from this port on the 1st instant. She was wrecked upon Black Ledge, near Seal Island, N S, on her passage to Halifax. All her passengers, among whom as the Hon Abbott Lawrence, of this city, with his wife & dght, were saved. We have by S Abbott Lawrence, a letter from the Hon Abbott Lawrence to his family in this city, giving the full particulars of the occurrence. Also another letter from Lt Parsons, the Mail Agent of the **Columbia**, to Geo W Gordon, Postmaster of this city. News of this event were forwarded to this city by S R Lyman, Postmaster at Portland, by special express. The ship **Margaret** will be dispatched from Halifax to Liverpool, taking the mails, & such passengers as may prefer to go forward in her in preference to awaiting the sailing of the ship **Hibernia**. The above is followed by a letter dated Seal Island, Jul 3, 1843 from Abbott Lawrence to his son, Jas Lawrence.
+
Yesterday the **Columbia** struck on the Black Ledge; fired our cannon; answered by a musket; the fog lifted & we saw a fishing schnr, Hitchings capt, who had with him a small boat in tow. It was prudent to take the ladies on board-14 in number, & 5 or 6 children. The passengers, 50 in number, are now all on shore. The mails are all here. Opinion is that the ship will be lost. Your mother & sister are quite well. – Abbott Lawrence This was followed by a letter from G S Parsons, Lt R N, British Mail Agent attached to the **Columbia**, to Geo Wm Gordon, Postmaster of this city. Seal Island, Jul 4, 1843: Mr Hitchens, the master of the light, for his great kindness to us cannot be too highly estimated. Help was provided by Capt Stairs, & the cool seaman like conduct of Capt Shannon, his ofcrs & crew, who labored with much zeal. –G S Parsons, Lt R N

Cmdor Jesse Wilkinson ordered to Boston as Port Captain. Capt S H Stringham appointed Cmdnt of the Navy Yard at Brooklyn.

The Hon John Holmes died at Portland, Maine, on Fri last, after an illness of several months. He had formerly been U S Senator from Maine, being the first elected after its separation from Mass, & had several years as a Rep to Congress. He was a member of the Convention which formed a Constitution for Maine, & chairman of the cmte which draughted it. At the time of his death he was the U S Dist Atty, & was appointed by Gen Harrison. He was a native of Massachusetts.

Detroit [Mich] Advertiser of Jul 6: Geo S Meredith, late of this city, was drowned in Saginaw Bay a few days ago while bathing. He was the s/o Jonathan Meredith, of Balt.

Mrd: on Tue, by Rev John C Smith, John S Kirkpatrick to Miss Mgt Weaver, all of Wash City.

Boston Daily Advertiser of Mon: Washington Allston, the distinguished artist, died suddenly, at his residence in Cambridge, on Sat night. He had suffered somewhat from ill health for 2 or 3 years, but his death was sudden & unexpected by his family & friends. He was in his 64th year. [Jul 17 newspaper: He was a native of S C, & entered Harvard College in 1796; embarked for London in 1801 with a brother artist, & spent 3 years as a student of the Royal Academy, of which West was then Pres. In 1804 he went with Vanderlyn to Paris, & thence to Italy, remaining 4 years. He returned to America in 1809, & married at Boston a sister of the late Dr Channing, & in 1811 sailed again for England. His picture "Dead Man raised by Elisha's Bones" gained from the British Institution, the prize of 200 guineas; the picture was afterwards sold to the Pennsylvania Academy of Fine Arts for $3,500. In 1813, after his own recovery from a severe illness, the sudden death of his wife cast him into the deepest depression. In 1817 he accompanied Leslie to Paris, & in 1818 returned to his native land & took up residence at Cambridgeport. He afterwards married a sister of Mr R H Dana, who has survived him.]

The schnr **Edward Burley**, Burke, arrived at Beverly, Mass, on Sat last from Cape Mount, west coast of Africa, May 18, having lost her mate & the cook, who were killed by the natives on the coast. On the 2nd of May Capt Burke fell in with the U S brig **Porpoise**, & communicated the circumstances to her cmder, who promised to look into the matter. The affair happened near where the ship **Mary Carver**, of Plymouth, was cut off, & her crew massacred, 2 or 3 years since. The natives are said to be fierce, cannibal-like race, & well fitted for treachery of this kind.
–Salem Register

The Westminster Carroltonian mentions the manufacture of a barrel of soap by Mrs Moul, of that town, without the aid of fire. The process is effected by the heat of the sun, without any trouble. Use an old barrel as a ley hopper, & draw off every now & than a bucket of ley, which is poured upon the grease, that should be placed in another barrel & set in a position where it is exposed to the rays of the sun, but to be covered over in rainy weather. In this manner, with the aid of occasional stirring, the soap will be fit for use in a few weeks. One barrel of ashes & 4 pounds of rendered fat will make a barrel of soap. It is not necessary to rend up the fat, as it may be thrown into the barrel in any state, & will be consumed by the ley. –Eds Nat Intell

Capt John Percival left Boston on Sat for N Y, to take charge of the ship of the line **Franklin** & take her to Boston, where she is to go into the dry dock for repairs. U S brig **Porpoise**, Cmder Stellwagen, of the African squadron, for Cape Palmas Jun 15, was left at Porto Praya, Cape de Verds, 12th, by the Rienzi, arrived at Boston. Lt A Lewis, late commanding, returned home in the ship**Rienzi**, invalided. Also, Passed Midshipman, Richd Allison, in charge of 6 U S seamen.

Fire at Lansingburgh, N Y on Sun in the stables attached to the large hotel there, known as Rensselaer House: flames extended to the main bldg & brewery belonging to Mr Parmelee, to the printing ofc of the Lansingburgh Gaz; consumed the Rensselaer House, a fine brick hotel; destroyed about 35 bldgs. About $45,000 in property destroyed or injured by the fire-insured to about $15,000. –Albany Journal

Piney Point & St Mary's: about 100 miles from Washington, we approached by steamboat from Balt, Norfolk, & Wash: at present it is kept by Col Gordon Forbes, a gentleman from the opposite shore of Va, whose manners make him popular with his guests. Here at the point there is no fatigue, no physical exertion, no bodily tax. I visited the site of the old town of St Mary's, I engaged the schnr **Louisa**, attached to the establishment, & with my friend steered for the venerable scene of Md's earliest existence. We rounded St George's point; entered the mouth of St Mary's river; passed St Inigoes. We saw the ruin of the State-house, old brick & pebbly mortar, not one stone standing upon another, the work of desecration had done its worst; we visited the Govnr's house, the bricks have tumbled into the cellar, & the cellar will soon be level with the wheat field. Some simple negroes were driving their yokes of oxen. Another church is built out of the very bricks that kept until that fatal day the old State-house above the ground, & the visiter has nothing of record save a solitary tombstone which has braved the storms of upwards of 2 centuries. There is no spot in American soil that can compare with St Mary's in interest; & it is singular that until only within 2 years it has come to be appreciated. -B

Allen Menter, 9 years, s/o Mr Phineas Menter, of Londonderry, N H, was instantly killed a few days since in a brick-yard, by becoming entangled in the machinery used for grinding clay. His head was so dreadfully mangled that it caused instant death.

Died: yesterday, at the residence of his mother, Albert Holcomb, the y/c/o the late Geo E Dyson, of Wash City, in his 6th year. His funeral is this afternoon at 4 p m.

Died: on Jul 2, in Andover, Mass, John Abbott, formerly of Brunswick, aged 84 years. He will be remembered for his long & useful services as an ofcr of Bowdoin College: was the first Professor of Language in that Institution, which ofc he held until 1816. Afterwards he was the Treas of the College until 1829, when he resigned that ofc, & has since resided mostly in Massachusetts.

Mr Thos J Shepherd, a member of the Fourth Presbyterian Chr, 9th st, will preach his trial sermon, after which he will be licensed, by the Presbytery to preach the Gospel of our Lord Jesus Christ.

For rent: 2 story brick house on 18th st, between H & I sts. Apply next door to Richd Joyce.

Local News: 1-Mr Pepper offers a reward of $50 for the recovery of his pocket-book, which was stolen from him last Mon. 2-The dwlg of Mrs Moulder, on Pa ave, was last Sun night attempted to be robbed; but the burglars, becoming alarmed, suddenly decamped without any spoils.

Crmnl Crt-Tue. 1-U S vs Wm S Wright, charged with obtaining $20 from Gen John P Van Ness under false pretences: guilty. The prisoner represented himself to be the brother of the Hon Silas Wright, who, in a letter submitted to the Court & Jury denied the honor of the relationship. The Rev Mr Hawley proved that some 6 or 8 years ago, the prisoner obtained $10 from him under the representation that he [the prisoner] was the s/o the Collector of the port of Nova Scotia. Mr Madison Cutts also testified that the prisoner attempted some years ago to defraud him, & the prisoner had assumed the name of Scott. He also obtained money from Edw Dyer under false pretences. 2-Jas O'Neal found guilty of an assault & battery upon Mary Naylor. 3-Robt Black, a free negro boy, about 12 years old, found guilty of setting fire to the carpenter's shop of Messrs Barron & Tuston.

FRI JUL 14, 1843
Trustee's sale of Ground rents & other property in Gtwn & Wash: decree of the Circuit Court of Wash Co, D C, passed in a cause wherein Julianna Williamson & others are cmplnts, & Geo W Williamson, Adolphus Williamson, Jos M Williamson, Garret V H de Witt & Julianna, his wife, Thos P Scott, & Chas A Williamson are dfndnts, the subscriber will expose to sale at public auction, on Sep 18, in front of the premises the following property in Gtwn, D C, to wit:
1-A rent of $79.50 per annum secured upon 53 feet front, part of lot 22 on High st. The improvements on the lot are a 2 story brick house, owned by Mr John Waters & occupied by Mr Richd T Queen.
2-Rent of $30 secured upon 30 feet front or thereabouts, part of lot 13. Improvements, 2 story frame houses belonging to Mr Ludeke.
3-Rent $27.50 secured upon 25 feet front, part of lots 127 & 128. Improvements, a 2 story house & store, partly brick & partly frame, occupied by Mr Kidwell.
4-Rent of $22 secured upon 22 feet front, other part of same lots. Improvements, a 2 story brick house belonging to D Craig's heirs.
5-Rent of $40.50 secured upon 36 feet 9 inches front or thereabouts, part of the same lots. Improvements, a new 2 story frame house belonging to Mr Kengla.
6-Rent of $51.70 secured upon 47 feet front, part of lot 157. Improvements two 3 story brick houses & stores belonging to Mr Geo A Bohrer.
7-Rent of $19.80 secured upon 18 feet front, other part of the last named lot. Improvements, a 2 story brick house occupied by Mrs Stone.
8-Also other part of lot 157, fronting 46 feet, with the frame tenements thereon, occupied Mr Mrs Crown.
9-Also part of lot 19, fronting 25 feet.
All the lots are upon High st & in Beatty & Hawkins' Addition. The rents are payable annually on May 1. All under authority of the same decree, the subscriber will expose for sale at public auction, on the same day, the following real estate in Wash City, namely: lots 6 & 7 in sq 291, with the brick houses thereon, now

occupied by Wm Thomas as a tavern near the new Theatre. If the terms of the sale are not completed within one week from the day of sale, the property will be resold on one week's notice at the purchaser's risk. –Ch A Williamson, trustee For further information apply at the ofc of the subscriber in Gtwn. –W Redin

Early in Mar, 1843, the passengers of the lost steamship **President** arrived, & related the circumstances connected with the loss of the vessel. Mr Tyrone Power gave a description of it. My name is Tyrone Power. My profession while on earth was that of comedian. I am a native of Ireland, & was at the time of this disaster on my return to my native country from the U S, having been eminently successful with my business. I had with me a large sum of money, & was anticipating the joy I should experience in rejoining my family. After being out a few days, a tremendous hurricane arose; after we had passed out of sight of the George's Bank, & we were driven against an iceberg with tremendous force, & the vessel immediately went to pieces. It was in the night, & awful was the scene that ensued. I believe I was one of the last that went down, having seized part of the vessel, to which I clumg as long as possible. I commended my soul to God toward whom I then became sensible I had been too much a stranger. After performing this duty I felt an inward pleasure, which assured me that his mercy had not been invoked in vain. I heard the voice of my dear friend Cookman, [a clergyman,] engaged in an earnest appeal to God, invoking his mercy upon all. In a few moments I sank beneath the waters, which closed over me; & that is about all the information I can impart in relation to the dreadful occurrence.

For rent: the new & elegant residence of the late Capt E Hanly, corner of G & 20th sts. Apply to Saml Redfern, near the Seven Bldgs.

Crmnl Crt-Wash. 1-Geo Hall guilty of conspiring to cheat Walter Reeves: fined $30 & 10 days in the county jail. Swindling Walter Reeves at cards: fined $5. Riot at the tavern of J H Clarvoe: fined $20. Assaulting the same: fined $5. Assaulting Wm Warren: fined $5. Riot at the house of Mary Ann Hall: fined $25. 2-Robt Jenifer, free negro, guilty of an assault on Cornelia Ann Lewis, colored woman: fined $20. 3-Wm Williams, guilty of a riot at the circus: fined $20 & 5 days in jail. 4-Henry Burke, guilty of assault & battery on Wm Simonds: fined $5 & give security of $50 for his good behavior. 5-John Gary, convicted of an assault upon his wife: fined $5. 6-Richd Stewart guilty of an assault & battery on Jos Lacy by stabbing him at Gtwn: fined $20 & 1 month in jail 7-John Johnson, negro, convicted of an assault on a white boy named John Bene: fined $10. 8-Danl Dakes, Wm Rollins, & Benj Angel, guilty of a riot in the street: fined $5 each. 9-Chas Bowles, negro, guilty of an assault on Sarah Bell, negress: fined $5.

Fatal accident at the Asylum for the Blind, in Columbus, Ohio, on Jul 7. A blind pupil, Geo Brown, aged 15 years, whose parents reside in Knox Co, had attempted to walk across the roof & fell to the pavement below. He fell on his head & face & expired in about 10 minutes. Chldrn had gone to the roof without the knowledge of the superintendent. –State Journal

Died: on Jul 12, in his 42nd year, J H Ritter, formerly of N Y, but for the last several years a resident of Wash City. His funeral will be at his late dwlg, on Pa ave, between 9th & 10th sts, at 10 a m this Fri.

A pardon was on Wed received by the Marshal of D C, from the Pres, in favor of John B Henderson, who was convicted about 5 years ago of counterfeiting Treas Notes & sentenced to 10 years in the pen. Henderson has not been confined quite 5 years; & during that period, as we learn from the late & present Wardens of the pen, his conduct had been very correct & becoming his unfortunate situation.

SAT JUL 15, 1843
The Hon J Q Adams arrived at Albany on Jul 11, on his way to Saratoga Springs, being the first time that he had ever in his life been at Albany.

Hon Wm W Southgate appointed Atty for the Commonwealth in the 2nd judicial district of Ky, in place of Wm K Wall, resigned.

Boston Mercantile Journal gives the following statistics of the town of ***Marblehead***, Mass: at the close of the Revolution, when the population was much less than at present, a statement made to the Gen Court of the sufferers by that war exhibited the following result:
Widows: 458   Fatherless boys: 364   Fatherless girls: 502
During the last war Marblehead furnished 1,400 men for the public service; no ship of war, privateer, fleet, of flotilla, prison ship or depot, was without a goodly number of reps from this patriotic town. All were not confined to the sea service; they composed one entire company of the 40th regt of regular troops; almost another of the flying artl, & many scattering recruits for other services were raised. At the close of the war, Dartmouth, the English prison-house, unfolded her gloomy gates upon 500 gallant fellows who hailed from this obscure fishing town.

While the Phil train of cars were passing up Fleet st, Balt, on Wed last, a s/o Mr Jonathan Hall, residing on Fell's Point, aged about 5 years, while attempting to get on the cars, was accidentally knocked down, & one of the wheels ran over his leg, mangling the flesh in dreadful manner. Dr Monkur was called to his relief. This is the 2nd accident that has befallen the family of Mr Hall in the same way; about 3 years ago he lost a child by having both his legs severed off by the wheels of a car.
-Clipper

Army Gen Order: #42, Headqrtrs of the Army, Adj Gen Ofc, Wash, Jul 7, 1843.
Promotions & Appointments in the U S Army, since publication of Gen Orders #19, of Mar 6, 1843.
Promotions: Corps of Engineers:
Brvt 2nd Lt W S Rosencrans, to 2nd Lt, Apr 3, 1843, vice Butler, dec'd-[brvt Jul 1, 1842.]
1st Regt of Artl:
Lt Col I B Crane, of the 4th Artl, to be Col, Jun 27, 1843, vice Eustis, dec'd.
2nd Regt of Artl:
Brvt Maj W L McClintock, Capt of the 3rd Artl, to be Maj, Jun 27, 1843, vice Payne, promoted.
3rd Regt of Artl:
1st Lt Wm Wall, to be Capt, Jun 27, 1843, vice McClintock, promoted.
2nd Lt W H Churchill, to 1st Lt, Jun 27, 1843, vice Wall, promoted.
Brvt 2nd Lt Jos Stewart, 1st Artl, to be 2nd Lt, Jun 27, 1843, vice Churchill, promoted.
4th Regt of Artl:
Maj M M Payne, of the 2nd Artl, to be Lt Col, Jun 27, 1843, vice Crane, promoted.
6th Regt of Infty:
1st Lt Saml Woods, to be Capt, Feb 27, 1843, vice Brown, promoted.
2nd Lt Jas Belger, to be 1st Lt, Feb 27, 1843, vice Woods, promoted.
Brvt 2nd Lt R W Kirkham, of the 2nd Infty, to be 2nd Lt, Feb 27, 1843, vice Belger, promoted-[brvt Jul 1, 1842]
7th Regt of Infty:
Capt Jacob Crown, of the 6th Infty, to be Maj, Feb 27, 1843, vice Nelson, dec'd.
8th Regt of Infty:
Brvt 2nd Lt Cyrus Hall, of the 1st Infty, to be 2nd Lt, Jul 1, 1842, vice McCalmont, resigned-[brvt Jul 1, 1842]
The following named Cadets, graduates of the Military Academy, are attached to the Army as supernumerary ofcrs, with the brevet of 2nd Lt, in conformity with the law, & the direction of the Pres, to rank from Jul 1, 1843.
Brvt 2nd Lts attached to the Corps of Topographical Engineers
Rank:
1-Cadet Wm B Franklin, of Pa
2-Cadet Geo Deshon, of Conn
Brvt 2nd Lts, attached to the Artl Arm
3-Cadet Thos J Brereton: Co A 4th Artl
4-Cadet John H Grelaud, of Pa: Co H 1st Artl
6-Cadet Isaac F Quinby, of N J: Co D 2nd Artl
7-Cadet Roswell S Ripley, of N Y: Co C 3rd Artl
8-Cadet John J Peck, of N Y: Co G 2nd Artl
9-Cadet John P Johnstone, of Va: Co C 4th Artl
10-Cadet Jos J Reynolds, of Indiana: Co I 4th Artl
11-Cadet Jas A Hardie: Co B 1st Artl

12-Cadet Henry F Clarke, of Pa: Co E 2nd Artl
14-Cadet Saml G French, of N J: Co F 3rd Artl
Brvt 2nd Lts attached to the Infty Arm
5-Cadet Wm F Raynolds, of Ohio: Co E 5th Infty
13-Cadet Jacob J Booker, of Indiana: Co A 1st Infty
15-Cadet Theodore L Chadbourne: Co A 2nd Infty
16-Cadet Christopher C Augar, of Mich: Co G 2nd Infty
17-Cadet Franklin Gardner, of Iowa: Co E 7th Infty
19-Cadet Edmund B Halloway, of Ky: Co C 4th Infty
21-Cadet Ulysses S Grant, of Ohio: Co I 4th Infty
22-Cadet Jos H Potter, of N H: Co F 1st Infty
23-Cadet Robt Hazlitt, of Ohio: Co G 4th Infty
24-Cadet Edwin Howe: Co B 5th Infty
25-Cadet Lafayette B Wood, of Va: Co C 8th Infty
26-Cadet Chas S Hamilton, of N Y: Co K 2nd Infty
27-Cadet Wm K Van Bokkelen, of N Y: Co B 7th Infty
28-Cadet Alfred Crozet: Co C 7th Infty
29-Cadet Chas E Jarvis, of Maine: Co G 3rd Infty
30-Cadet Fred'k Steele, of N Y: Co C 2nd Infty
31-Cadet Henry R Selden, of Vt: Co H 1st Infty
33-Cadet Fred'k T Dent, of Missouri: Co B 6th Infty
34-Cadet John C McFerran, of Ky: Co K 3rd Infty
35-Cadet Henry M Judah, of N Y: Co D 8th Infty
36-Cadet Norman Elting, of N Y: Co I 6th Infty
38-Cadet Chas G Merchant: Co B 8th Infty
39-Cadet Geo C McClelland, of Pa: Co E 3rd Infty
Brvt 2nd Lts attached to the Regt of Riflemen
18-Cadet Geo Stevens, of Vt: Co A
20-Cadet Lewis Neill, of Va: Co I
32-Cadet Rufus Ingalls, of Maine: Co B
37-Cadet Cave J Couts, of Tenn: Co C
The foregoing assignment to the Regts & Companies will be regarded as a temporary arrangement, necessary for the convenience of the service. Vacancies will be filled according to seniority in the particular arm, in conformity with the established rule.
Casualties:
Resignations:
2nd Lt J S McCalmont, 8th Infty, Jul 1, 1843
Deaths-3:
Brvt Brig Gen Abraham Eustis, Col 1st Artl, Portland, Maine, Jun 27, 1843
Maj J S Nelson, 7th Infty, at Tampa Bay, Florida, Feb 27, 1843
2nd Lt R Q Butler, Corps of Engineers, at sea, Apr 3, 1843
The ofcrs promoted & appointed will join their proper stations & companies without delay; those on detached service or acting under special instructions will report by letter to the commanding ofcrs of their respective regts.

The usual leave of absence allowed by the Regulations is hereby granted to the several graduates; at the expiration of which [Sep 30th] they will join their proper stations & regts.

Acceptances or non-acceptances of appointments will be reported to the Adj Gen of the Army; & in case of acceptance the ofcr will immediately subscribe to the Rules & Regulations enjoined by the 1st Article of War. He will also report his birthplace, & the state from which appointed.

The Headqrtrs of the 6th Military Dept are changed from Portland, Maine, to Portsmouth, N H.

On the mutual application of the parties, Col & Brvt Brig Gen Z Taylor, of the 1st, is transferred to the 6th Infty, & Col W Davenport, of the 6th, is transferred to the 1st Infty. They will be reported accordingly. By Command of Maj Gen Scott: L Thomas, Assist Adj Gen

Memoranda: Transfers:

2nd Lt G W Rains, of the Corps of Engineers, to the 4th Artl, to take effect on the happening of the first vacancy in that Regt.

2nd Lt Henry Little, of the 5th Infty, to the 7th Infty, to take place on the Army Register next below Lt Henshaw.

Brvt 2nd Lt J W Abert, of the 5th Infty, to the Corps of Topographical Engineers.

2nd Lt P D Geisse, of the 7th Infty, to the 5th Infty, to take place on the Army Register next below Lt Norvell.

Charlottesville Advocate: Mr Magruder retires from the editorial dept & is succeeded by Wm J Shelton, lately of Lynchburg, a young gentleman of fine abilities, & an ardent Whig. -Richmond Whig

The Bowling-Green Fountain, N Y. There exists an egg shaped plot of grass enclosed by an iron railing, no doubt bears the name from our Dutch ancestors applied to the use of which its name indicates, & enlivened by the sports & dances of Van Twillers & the Stuyvesants. In later time it was graced by a leaden statue of one of the Georges. At the commencement of the Revolution his leaden majesty was dethroned from his brick-built pedestal & converted into musket balls, used against his own, by the provincial troops. **Bowling-Green** is now ornamented by the most beautiful fountain in the city. It is surrounded by the residences of our wealthy citizens, or by hotels. The design of the fountain is by Mr Jas Renwick, jr. He has been most ably seconded by assistant alderman Pettigrew & Mr Aaron O Price, who took the contract for the building. –Commercial Advertiser

There are in Massachusetts 79 newspapers published weekly or oftener, 12 of them daily, 2 semi weekly. The oldest paper is the Massachusetts Spy, at Worcester, established in 1771.

The old charter of Connecticut is carefully preserved at Hartford. Mrs Ann S Stephens speaks of it in a letter to the Brother Jonathan: It is written in old English letter, & in one place the parchment is stained through by the sap or other moisture gathered in the trees which contained it. It was granted by Chas II, in 1662, & when Edmond Andross assumed the gov't, & threatened to remove the charter, it was concealed 18 months in the old oak to which its name is given. Though 181 years old, every word is distinct, & the whole fabric remains as firm as if manufactured yesterday.

Trial concluded in N Y on Tue: indictment against Jas L Winfree & Geo Cummings for a conspiracy to extort money from Wm R Gracie. The principal witness against the dfndnts was Gracie himself, who was shown to be a monomaniac, in that he was under the impression that there were people leagued together to take his life. He supposed his wife to be involved & refused to live with her. The point against Winfree & Cummings was, that by encouraging the notion of a conspiracy to take Gracie's life, got from him at various times money, which was to be used in ferreting out the conpirators & bringing them to justice.

U S Circuit Court, at Newport, R I, Judge Pitnam presiding: case in which the parties were Miss Abby Breck, plntf, & C Dalrympl, dfndnt, both of Providence, the damages laid at $10,000. Verdict for the plntf-$5,000.

Valuable James River land for sale: decree of the Circuit Superior Court of Law & Chancery for Albemarle Co, in a cause pending pronounced on May 18, 1843: sale on Aug 18 next, a tract of land in Buckingham Co, Va, called *Snowdon*: about 1,200 acs. Improvements: overseer's house, large & commodious tobacco houses, corn-houses, stables, & barns. On the James River opposite the flourishing town of Scottsville. This tract will be sold subject to the life estate of Mrs Sarah C Harris in about two-thirds of it, which had been allotted to her as tenant in dower; but we are authorized by her to state that she will sell her life interest to the purchaser of the residue, on the day of sale, on terms which cannot fail to be satisfactory, & which will be known before the sale, so the purchaser can obtain a fee simple at once in the whole tract. We will also sell, on the premises, a house & lot in Scottsville, on Main st, well suited for a dwlg-house & store. Also, on Aug 20, a lot in Warrenton, mentioned in said decree. –Edw H Moore, John H Colemen, Benj H Magruder, Com'rs

Sale of very excellent furniture on Jul 17, at the residence of the Rev Chas Rich, on C st, between 3rd & 4½ sts: all his household & kitchen furniture. -Robt W Dyer & Co, aucts

Died: on Jul 14, Jas Haligan, in his 40th year. His funeral will be at his late residence on East Capitol st, tomorrow, at 3 p m precisely.

Died: on Jul 9, Miss Sarah M Drayton, a native of S C, but latterly a resident of the city of Phil.

Died: on Jul 8, at his residence in Charleston, S C, the Hon Thos Lowndes, in his 78th year. Mr Lowndes was in the year 1800 chosen from his Congressional district a Rep in Congress, where he distinguished himself by his attention to business & eloquence in debate. He was the eldest s/o Rawlins Lowndes, the Pres of S C from 1778-1780; whose name, though celebrated among his contemporaries, & connected with the most stirring periods of our history, has been in a manner forgotten in the fame of his distinguished sons-the subject of this notice & the late Wm Lowndes.

Died: on Jun 18, at Port Gibson, Miss, Israel Irving, in his 75th year. The dec'd was a native of Sudbury, Mass, from whence he removed in 1789 to Marietta, Ohio, then a frontier post in the wilderness, where for some time he acted as commissary in the army under the command of Gen Wayne. In 1803 he removed to Mississippi, & erected the first frame dwlg in Port Gibson, where he has resided, & by industry & energy acquired a large estate.

Rev J G Wilson, Pastor of the Methodist Protestant Church, Gtwn, will preach in Mr Hardy's school-house, next Sabbath, at 4 p m.

Reward for gray horse that strayed away on Jul 4. I will give $5 if brought to me, one square from the Sugar-house, Navy Yard. –Wm Grinder

For rent: a 3 story brick dwlg on F st, lately occupied by Mr J Michard. Apply to W W Corcoran.

Notice: by virtue of a writ of distraint, to me directed, I shall expose to public sale, on Jul 20, one hack & harness, seized & taken as the property of Saml Adams, to satisfy stable rent due & in arrears to Mrs Ann Foy. –S Moore, bailiff

MON JUL 17, 1843
All persons having claims against Geo Lipscomb, late a resident of Wash City, will please present them to the subscribers, properly vouched according to law, on or before Jul 26, so that distribution of assets may be made as soon thereafter as practicable. -Robt W Dyer & Co, aucts

On Thu a small boat capsized in the Narrows, N Y Bay, by a sudden gust of wind, precipitating overboard Mr Chas Goodrich, a printer, of Fluton st, his wife & their son, about 4 years old; the child was washed from the arms of its mother 4 times, but the 5th time she was unable to recover it & it was unfortunately drowned. They were finally seen by Mr Augustus Noye, a resident of Staten Island, who shoved off alone in a skiff & took off the agonized parents.

Local News: the Lunatic Hospital & Infirmary is completed. The undersigned mechanics were engaged in its erection & completion:

Mr D A Gardiner, carpenter, contractor
Messrs Plant & Lewis, bricklayers, sub-contractors
Messrs Truscott & Birch, plasterers of inside work
Mr G W Harkness, plasterer of outside work
Mr W Lowndes, painter
Mr Nicholas Queen was superintendant of the work.
Credit of much of the interior of the Hospital goes to Dr T Miller. Drs Miller, Lindsly, & Thomas have been appointed by the President physicians to take charge of the Hospital.

Fatal accident: on Jul 10, as Mr Fred'k Gaither, whose residence is near Unity, in Montg Co, was returning home from Balt, where he had been to dispose of some cattle, & while he was riding in a sulkey with his son, a youth of 13, the horse attached to the vehicle became suddenly affrighted by the falling of Mr G's hat, & galloped off at full speed, overturning the sulkey, & throwing both Mr G & his son. The former being struck on the head & face with the iron part of the vehicle, had his skull so severly fractured & his face & cheek so terribly mutilated that he died on the spot; the latter, though rendered insensible by the fall, recovered in a short time, & beheld his father a mangled corpse. An elder s/o Mr G, who was traveling with him from Balt on horseback, witnessed the death of his father. Mr G left a widow & a numerous family to mourn his unexpected & melancholy end. He was in his 74th year. The accident took place on the Balt & Fred'k turnpike, near the 17th mile stone. His remains were conveyed to his residence, in Montg Co, for interment. It is a remarkable fact, that after the horse had run a mile with the broken vehicle dragging after him, he returned of his own accord & stood still close to the spot where the dead body lay.

Cmder Alex'r J Dallas, [late Browne,] a cmder in the U S Navy, died in Troy, N Y, on Wed last, [as we learn from the Whig.] He arrived in Troy in May, with his dght, on his way to Saratoga for the benefit of his health; but, on account of the coolness of the weather at the time, preferred remaining in the city. His health gradually declined until the day of his death. Mr Dallas was a native of Connecticut, & a nephew of the late Alex'r Jas Dallas, Sec of the Treas under Mr Madison. He entered the navy about 25 years ago, & has seen much service.

Engraving of Thos Wildey, the Founder of Odd Fellowship. We recommend to the patronage of this respectable brotherhood an exact likeness of their esteemed founder, which has lately been engraved by Sartain, from a handsone portrait of Mr Wildey, taken by Miss Sarah Peale, an artist of great celebrity, now on a professional visit in this metropolis.

Died: near Rockville, Montg Co, Md, Wm Thos, aged 19 months & 3 days, infant s/o Mr Singleton Prather & the late Mrs Charlotte Prather. [No date-current item.]

Marshal's sale: in vitue of four several writs of fieri facias, issued from the Clk's ofc of the Circuit Court of Wash Co, D C & to me directed: public sale, for cash, on Jul 27, at the premises of the late Maj Cary Selden, corner of C & 3rd sts, the following property, viz: mahogany clothes press & drawers, medicine chest, with furniture, forte piano, mahg sideboard, bookcase & books, 2 hair seat sofas, 2 doz parlor chairs, English clock, & 1 gray horse. Also kitchen utensils, etc, seized & levied as the property of Cary Selden, late of said county, & sold to satisfy Judicials 21, to Mar term, 1843, in favor of the Bank of Wash, use of Wm A Bradley; Judicials 131, to Nov term, 1839, in favor of Thos R Gedney; Judicials 4, to Nov term, 1843, in favor of Richd R Burr, use of John Purdy; & Judicials 12, to Nov term, 1843, in favor of John F Webb. –Alex'r Hunter, Marshal of D C

The strange & uncouth wooden fabric now going up in the eastern portion of the Capitol square, for the purpose of accommodating Mr Greenough's Statue of Washington, seems to strike every spectator with disgust. It is out of keeping with the bldgs & grounds around it. While on this subject, what has become of the statues Mr Perrico was employed some years ago to execute, for the purpose of decorating the blocks on either side of the steps of the portico? -An Old Citizen

Wash Corp: 1-Ptn of Geo McCauley: referred to the Cmte of Claims. 2-The nominations of Wm Wallace & Silas Moore as police constables were unanimously confirmed. 3-Ptn of B B Curran, asking remission of a fine: referred to the Cmte of Claims. 4-Ptn of Jas McGuire & others: referred to the Cmte on Improvements. 5-Ptn of Eliza Lowe, asking remission of a fine: referred to the Cmte of Claims. 6-Ptn of J F Callan & others: referred to the Cmte on Improvements. 7-Cmte of Claims: unfavorable reports on the ptns of Wm Dalton & Zachariah Hazle.

The partnership heretofore existing between the subscribers, under the firm of Walter Clarke & Sons, is this day dissolved by mutual consent. –Walter Clarke, Walter M Clarke, Geo B Clarke The business will be conducted for the future by Walter Clarke & Walter M Clarke, under the firm of Walter Clarke & Son. –Walter Clarke, Walter M Clarke

Information Wanted. Eliz Ridgeway, living near Bladensburg, PG Co, Md, would be pleased to receive any information that might be given of her son, Bennit R Ridgeway, who left PG Co, Md, on Jul 1, 1835, to go to some of the Western States. His friends received a letter from him dated Jul 7, 1835, post-marked Fredericktown, Md, & he has not been heard of since. [The Editors of the Western papers will be doing a humane & benevolent act by giving an insertion of the above notice, to appease the feelings of a distressed widowed mother.]

TUE JUL 18, 1843
The American Citizen is a another new weekly paper from N Y, to be published every Sat by John J R De Puy.

The Marquis Villalba, of Spain, family, & suite, arrived at N Y on Thu in the packet ship **Iowa**.

Mr St Vrain, a trader, of the firm of Bent & St Vrain, arrived at St Louis on Jul 5. When he reached Arkansas he found Snively & 180 Texians waiting the coming of the Santa Fe Traders, whom they intended to rob. They were well armed, & determined to accomplish their object if possible. The traders were under the escort of U S dragoons, Capt Cook, who being apprized of the position of Snively & his companions, proceeded up the Arkansas, that river being the boundary line, & give them protection as far as Bent's fort. We learn that Col Warfield was with Col Snively.

Among the passengers for England in the steamship **Great Western** are the names of Horatio Greenough, the sculptor, & his family. They are returning to Italy.

At Phil, last week, 2 boys named Theodore Miller & Jos Forbes, were held to bail in $150 each by the Mayor for firing a house on Jul 4th in Pa. A rocket was sent up by them which set the roof on fire.

On Sat on the Lehigh Railroad, the w/o Mr Theodore Titus, was killed. Mr & Mrs Titus, and their 14 year old son, had, simply with the aid of a common brake, came down the Tunnel plane and the first plane of Solomon's Gap. Mr Titus did not put on the shoes of the car & lost control of it, throwing Mrs Titus & their son some 30 to 50 feet. Mrs Titus was killed and Mr Titus & son were badly injured, though both are still alive.

A Miser. Died, on Sat, at his residence in Castle st, in his 81st year, Mr John Tolkenton, who carried on the business of hairdresser a few doors from Berner's st, managing to accumulate upwards of 60,000 pounds. –London Paper

Died: on Sun last, at the residence of his uncle, S J Potts, in Wash City, Thos Semmes, of Alexandria, D C. His funeral will be from his late residence in Alexandria this evening at 3 p m.

Died: on Jul 12, at Oswego, at the residence of Jas Platt, Mrs Alida Woolsey, wid/o Gen Melancthon Lloyd Woolsey, formerly of Cumberland Head, near Plattsburg, mother of the late M T Woolsey, U S Navy, aged 85 years, 1 month & 14 days.

Mr Michl Rice, who died at Congress Hall a night or two ago, came to this country a poor boy from Ireland, & has left a fortune of $80,000. He has no relations in this country, but is believed to have a poor sister in Ireland. –Phil Inq

Stolen from the dwlg of the subscriber, a black cloth coat, half worn, in which in the pockets were a silver snuff box, gilt inside, & a pair of brass frame spectacles. Suitable reward for the recovery of these & conviction of the thief. –John MacLeod, corner of D & 7th st

Outrageous Assault. On Sun last as a colored man belonging to Mr Mathew Wright, at the Navy Yard, was bringing apples & cherries from his master's farm, he was attacked by 5 lads, on the road leading from Good Hope to the Navy Yard, & most of the fruit was taken from him. Three of the lawless gang were apprehended & committed to jail; the other 2 found security for their appearance at the Criminal Court.

WED JUL 19, 1843
Constable's sale: on Jul 22, the furniture & goods, seized & taken as the property of Warren C Choate, & sold to satisfy four fieri facias in favor of John D Boteler, & one fi fa favor of Chas W Boteler & Son, issued by Thos C Donn, a J P for Wash Co. –Jas A Radcliffe, Constable

Just received, a small lot of choice quality country cured Bacon Hams, at the reduced price of .06¼
per pound. For sale by B L Jackson & Brother.

For rent: 2 story brick dwlg at the corner of I & 7th sts, adjoining the residence of Andrew Rothwell, containing 8 well finished rooms. For terms apply to Messrs R W Dyer & Co, Aucts, or to the subscriber. –John F Boone

Orphan's Court of Chas Co, Md. Letters testamentary on the personal estate of Jas B Pye, late of said county, dec'd.
-Ellen C Pye, excx; Edw A Pye, exc

$100 reward for runaway negro boy Henson Johnson, aged about 17. –Wm J Berry, living near Upper Marlborough, PG Co, Md.

$200 reward for runaway man Henry, bright copper color, about 25 years of age. He has a brother on the Navy Yard hill, Wash, named John Hall, with whom, or thereabouts, he may be concealed. -John Palmer, near Piscataway, PG Co, Md

The Mobile Register has a report of a coroner's jury upon the death of Mrs Ann Land, a poor widow in bad health, who died for want of food. She was found in an old mill with her sickly child aged about 5 or 6 years.

$100 reward for runaways, a mulatto woman named Margery, about 30 years of age, quite a likely servant, & rather stout; she uses a good deal of snuff, & talks rather through her nose. Also, her son Isaac, about 16 years of age, a very likely boy. They have relations living at *Seat Pleasant*, Mr Thos Berry's farm, also at Govn'r Sprigg's, either about 7 miles from Bladensburg. –Jos K Roberts, near Bladensburg

John Daly, cook at the Washington Hall in Tallahassee at the time of the fire at that place on May 25 last, committed to jail on Jul 5, charged with having confessed on different occasions that he set fire to the town.

Mr John H Duvall, of the house of Duvall, Keighler & Co, had his hand much injured by the accidental discharge of his fowling piece on Sat. The wounds are not deemed of a very serious character. –Balt American

Zetto Smith, about 15 years of age, s/o John A Smith, of Delphi, Onondaga Co, N Y, was killed there on Jul 4, by the bursting of a small cannon, which he was engaged in firing during the day. -Cazenovia Eagle

Accidents at Phil: on Sat Alex'r Warnock, aged about 26 years, a sailor in the U S service, was killed by falling from the roof of the Hope Engine-house into the yard. On the same day a fatal accident occurred on the Delaware, near the Navy Yard, by which Mr Thos Clifton, a tavern keeper, of 2nd st, Southwark, lost his life. He & a companion were in a small boat fishing, when they were run over by a steamboat.

A gang of notorious countereiters, Joel Nason, Geo Whitehouse & wife, & Jas Sherman, were arrested last week at their house on Bloomingdale road, N Y, where the ofcrs found every implement of the trade. The principal party concerned was a man named Nason, a black & whitesmith, from Boston, said to be worth $50,000 ot $60,000.

Mrd: on Jul 13, by Rev Mr Gannett, Henry W Longfellow, of Cambridge, Professor of Modern Languages in Harvard Univ, to Fanny Eliz, d/o the Hon Nathan Appleton.

Died: yesterday, Mrs Georgianna Force, w/o Wm Q Force, Editor of the Army &Navy Chronicle, & d/o Chas Lyons, of Wash City, aged 23 years. She had left a husband, an infant about 3 weeks old, & parents, to whom the loss is irreparable, but she lived & died a Christian. She had been about 4 years a member of the First Baptist Church. Her funeral will be from the residence of her father-in-law, Col Peter Force, on 10th st, near Pa ave, this morning, at 10 a m.

Died: on Jul 11, at Boston, Nathl Emmons, aged 84 years.

Died: at Casco, Maine, Mrs Sarah Whitney, aged 100 years, 8 months & 20 days, a member of the Society of Friends. [No date-current item.]

THU JUL 20, 1843
The Louisville papers announce the death of the Hon John Rowan in that city, on Jul 13, after a short illness. Judge Rowan, [as he has been long familiarly termed] must have been not far from 70 years of age, having been known to us in public life for more than 35 years. He first took his seat in Congress as a Rep from Ky, along with Col R M Johnson & the late Govn'r Desha, on Oct 26, 1807. On Mar 4, 1825, he became a Senator of the U S, & served until after the election of Gen Jackson to the Presidency.

Breach of Promise of marriage case decided in the Circuit Court at N Y on Mon last, on an action brought by Serena Purnell vs Wm Lamberson; plntf a young woman of excellent character; the dfndnt is a shipmaster. He has paid attention to plntf [who is an orphan, but has a brother & sister] for nearly 4 years, & promised her marriage, proof of which was shown in various letters to her & by his attention to her when in port. About a year ago he married a widow lady at the South. The plntf [who is of rather superior appearance] was shown to have been much attached to him & greatly affected at his desertion of her. The jury gave a verdict in favor of the plntf for $5,000.

Mrd: on Jun 20, at Grosse Isle, Mich, by Rt Rev Saml A McCoskry, D D, Rev Chas Fox to Anna Maria, d/o John A Rucker, of the former place. [See notice below.]
+
Mrd: at the same time & place, by the same, Lt J A Whitall, 5th Infty U S A, to Catharine E, d/o John A Rucker.

Died: on Jul 19, Wm Francis, 2nd s/o Wm W & Bridget Ann Cox, aged 3 years & 7 months. Thus within the space of 19 days two interesting children have been taken away from their afflicted parents. His funeral will be from the residence of W W Cox, on I, between 9th & 10th sts, this morning, at half past 8 a m.

Valuable residence at auction: on Jul 28, the east half of lot 268 of Bealle's addition to Gtwn, on the S W corner of Green & Stoddart sts, with a valuable 2 story dwlg, with out-houses, & pump. –Clement Cox, agent for Adiel Sherwood.
-Edw S Wright, auct

FRI JUL 21, 1843
A young German woman named Cecilia Beuhler attempted to drown herself by jumping into the Schuylkill, near Fairmount, on Mon. She was prevented by a police ofcr who was present, & was taken to the alms-house.

The U S frig **Macedonian**, Capt Isaac Mayo, for the African station, got under way from Hampton roads on Tue last, & went to sea with a fresh southerly breeze.

Death of a Revolutionary slde. Mr Phineas Camp died at the village of Whitesborough, N Y, on Thu last, aged 99 years & 6 months. He did not take a potion of medicine till after 80 years of age, except one during the Revolution when the camp fever prevailed. His death was free from pain & anxiety, & he manifested intelligence until within 2 hours of his departure. –Oneida Whig

The Library of Congress will be closed on Jul 26, & will not be opened until Sep 7, in order to enable the workmen to carry into effect the law of Mar 3, 1843, directing the construction of 2 furnaces under each end of the first story of the centre of the Capitol, for warming the rooms & passages upon & above the said first story, including the Congress Library room, & for laying the floor of the principal Library room with hydraulic cement. –J E Meehan, Librarian

Marshal's sale: by authority of a writ of fieri facias, issued from the ofc of the Clk of the Circuit Court of Wash Co, D C, & to me directed, Danl Carroll, of Duddington, Nicholas Young, & Wm Brent, use of the U S, against Wm Dudley Digges: public sale on Aug 2 next, part of a tract of land called *Chillum Castle Manor*, lying within the said district & county: seized & taken in execution as the estate & lands of Wm Dudley Digges, & will be sold to satisfy balance of Marshal's fees due on the fi fa. The debt, interest, & costs have been paid to the U S. –Tench Ringgold, late Marshal of D C. [The notice below followed. NOTICE: All persons are cautioned against purchasing at the above sale, as the same had been enjoined & as the execution under which Mr Ringgold now pretends he has a right to sell was entered satisfied on Apr 2, 1833, by order of the Solicitor of the Treas. –Danl C Digges, for himself & Atty for the other heirs of N D Digges.]

SAT JUL 22, 1843
Edmund B Freeman appointed Clk of the Supreme Court of the State of N C, to fill the vacancy occasioned by the decease of John L Henderson, late clerk; an excellent appointment.

John Lloyd, the pilot of the steamer that ran down a fishing boat on the Delaware river on Sat last, a casualty by which Mr Thos Clifton, of Phil, lost his life-has been arrested, examined, & committed to jail to await his trial on a charge of felonious homicide. A warrant was also issued for the captain of the boat, but he could not be found.

Administrator's sale: By order of the administrator of Peter Brown, dec'd, on the premises: house & lot: sale on Jul 26: all that lot or parcel of ground in Wash City, lying in square 797, beginning on south I st: with improvements, which are a frame house. -Robt W Dyer & Co, aucts

Jas Williams: Cabinet & Chair Wareroom, Pa ave, west of 4½ st. New, old, & will repair furniture.

NOTICE: by writ of fieri facias, issued by R H Clements, a J P for Wash Co, D C, to me directed, I shall expose to public sale, for cash, at the Centre Market house, in Wash City, the following goods & chattels, to wit: 1 wardrobe, 4 tables, 1 chest of drawers, 1 sofa, 6 clothes racks: seized & taken as the property of Wm Starks, & will be sold to satisfy a judgement in favor of Geo Scroggins. –John Magar, constable

Orphan's Court of Wash Co, D C. Letters of adm on the personal estate of John H Ritter, late of said county, dec'd. –P Kinchey, adm

Orphan's Court of Wash Co, D C. Letters of adm, with the will annexed, on the personal estate of Peter Brown, late of said county, dec'd. –Chas Brown, adm w a

Army & Navy Intelligence.
Changes have recently been made in the commanding ofcrs of the Military Depts. We annex a corrected list of them:
1-Col Twiggs, headqrtrs Pass Christian, Miss, during the summer months, & New Orleans in the winter.
2-Brig Gen Z Taylor, headqrtrs Fort Smith, Ark.
3-Maj Gen Gaines, headqrtrs St Louis, Mo.
4-Brig Gen Brady, Detroit, Mich.
5-Brig Gen Wool, Troy, N Y.
6-Col J B Crane, Portsmouth, N H
7-Col J B Walbach, Fort Monroe, Va.
8-Brig Gen Armistead, Fort Moultrie, S C.
9-Brig Gen Worth, St Augustine, East Florida.
The New Sloops of War now on the stocks, have already been named. They are the:
Portsmouth, at Portsmouth, N H
Plymouth, at Boston, Mass
Albany, at N Y
Germantown, at Phil
St Mary's, at Washington
Jamestown, at Norfolk
The Hon Geo H Proffit, Minister to Brazil, will take passage to Rio Janeiro in the U S sloop of war **Levant**, Cmder H N Page.
Tunis Craven has been re-appointed Naval Storekeeper at the Navy Yard, Brooklyn, N Y. -Army & Navy Chronicle

Sale at Alexandria by Geo White: orange, lemon, & other hot-house trees & flowering plants at auction.

Isaac Kell, senior, has been appointed weigher of the port of Alexandria

List of ofcrs of the U S ship **Macedonian**, lately sailed for the coast of Africa:

Capt, Isaac Mayo
Lts: Thos T Craven, Chas H Poor, B W Hunter, J J Almy, Wm B Whiting, Jas McCormick; John Contee, Flag Lt.
Acting Master, Matthew C Perry
Fleet Surgeon, Edmund L Du Barry
Purser, Henry Etting
Passed Assist Surgeon, Edw J Rutter
Assist Surgeon, Joshua Huntington
Prof of Math, Martin Roche
Lt Commanding Marines, Jabez C Rich
Capt's Clk, Wm C Tuck
Purser's Clk, Aug D Ashton
Passed Midshipmen: Geo H Cooper, Wm H Thompson, Andrew Bryson, Joel S Kennard
Midshipmen: D R Lambert, Peter Wager, jr, Theodorick Lee, Aaron K Hughes, A Colden Rhind, Lyman R Law, Alex A Semmes, Wingate Pilsbury, Robt A Marr
Master's Mate, Cornelius C Williamson
Boatswain, Joshua Bryant
Gunner, John Clapham
Carpenter, Amos Chick
Sailmaker, Wm H Brayton
Purser's Steward, Wm Beers
Surgeon's Steward, E J Busvine
Passenger, Floyd Waggaman, storekeeper of the African squadron.
-Beacon

Mrd: on Jun 12, in Newport, Ky, by Rev Mr Moore, John White Stevenson, of Covington, Ky, [formerly of Richmond, Va, & s/o the Hon Andrew Stevenson,] to Miss Sibella, d/o Maj Saml Winston, of Newport.

Mrd: on Jul 20, by Rev Wm B Edwards, Mr Jas A Bowen to Miss Eliz Turner, all of Wash.

Died: on Jul 15, at her residence in King George's Co, Va, after a long & painful illness, Mrs Lucy M Taliaferro, relict of John B Taliaferro, dec'd, & d/o the late Gov Barbour, aged 46 years.

Died: on Jul 12, at his residence at Elm Grove, Ohio Co, Va, Gen Danl Cruger, of Bath, Steuben Co, N Y, aged 64 years.

Died: on Jul 4, Mrs Eliz Armstrong, w/o the Hon Wm Armstrong, of Romney, Va, aged 57 years, leaving several children & grand-children to mourn her loss.

Trustee's sale of Confectionary & Fancy Store: on Sat, at the store of Mr D McInerny, north side of Pa ave, west of 4½ st, a general assortment: baskets, brushes, combs, boxes, raisins, preserves, candies, boxes of cigars, tobacco, peanuts, almonds. Also, the fixtures of the store: counters, glass cases, sliding sashes, fruit stands, scales & weights, marble slab: baking apparatus; furniture, tables, chairs, carpets, bureaus, wardrobes, settees, beds, washstands, kitchen furniture; coal stove, wood stove, refrigerator, meat safe. The store is for rent. –Michl Talty, trustee -W Marshall, auct

MON JUL 24, 1843
Mr Henry Daggett, a venerable citizen of New Haven, Conn, died at that place on Wed last, at the advanced age of 86 years. He was a s/o that sterling patriot, Naphtali Daggett, Pres of Yale College during the Revolutionary war; was an ofcr in the Revolutionary army & a pensioner; the oldest graduate of Yale College; a devoted Christian, & a prominent member of the Congrational Church. His wife survives him, with whom he lived in conjugal felicity nearly 60 years.

Col Craven, the late Naval Storekeeper at Brooklyn, who was displaced last fall, to make room for Paul R George, has been restored to his ofc by Sec Upshur.
–N Y Courier

The Wyandotts, the last tribe of Indians in the State of Ohio, have departed for their new home West of the Mississippi. Jacquis is the head Chief.

St Louis Era of Jul 13. We have seen a letter from the U S blacksmith at Willow creek, [Pawnee country,] to his friend in this city, giving an account of the murders committed by the Sioux Indians upon the Pawnees, & upon the wife of the blacksmith. His wife was shot on Jun 27. The husband had endeavord to save her by shutting her up in the shop, but she had not the time to bolt the door. They killed her & fell to whipping the blacksmith, without doing serious injury to him. The Indians also killed Lashapel, the U S interpreter, who had been in the country for 25 years; Capt Blue, first chief of the Pawnees; Tappagnes, the father-in-law of the interpreter; a son-in-law of the old chief Monlin, & several other chiefs & braves, young men, women, & children. Out of 41 lodges 21 were burnt. The horses were stolen or killed on the spot.

Chas Cole, jr, was arrested in Boston on Tue, charged with attempting to cheat & defraud the Massachusetts Bank of several sums of money, by forging the names of respectable merchants as signers or endorsers of notes, which notes were offered by Cole & discounted at the Bank. The forgeries amounted to over $2,500. Cole has hitherto borne a respectable character.

Promotions in the Navy: Cmder W K Latimer to be Capt; Lt Chas Wilkes to be Cmder; Lt Elisha Peck to be Cmder

Passed Midshipmen to be Lt:

John N Maffit
Washington Gwathmey
Wm Ronckendorff
Wm Beverly

John Hall
Francis Lawry
Wm E Le Roy
Maxwell Woodhull

The late fire at **Boucherville**. The village of Boucherville, near Montreal, dates from 1667, & was therefore, when destroyed by fire, 176 years old. 343 people out of a population of 651 have been thrown upon the world by this disaster.

Jos Jefferson, the comedian, who died in 1832, at Harrisburg, now lies interred in the Episcopal burying ground on the banks of the Susquehanna. The inscriptions says: "He was a member of the Chesnut Street Theatre, at Philadelphis, in its most high and palmy days, and a compeer of Cooper, Wood, Warren, Francis, and a host of worthies, who, like himself, are remembered with admiration and praise. He died at this place in 1832."

Wharton Jones, of Ky, has recovered $1,200 damages of John Van Zandt in the U S Circuit Court of Ohio, Judge McLean presiding, for harboring & concealing 9 slaves.

Mr Saml G Chase, of Hopkinton, N H, has invented a new railroad track, considered a very material improvement upon the one now in use.

Some inquiries were made a few days since, by Saml Kellogg, of Hartford, at the request of the British Consul, for the whereabouts of Edw Benson. The person sought for turns out to be an old tar, living in Wethersfield, Conn, who, on hearing the anxiety respecting him, made a visit to Hartford, to ascertain why he, an old sailor, poor & unknown, should be inquired for through the public press. The Times informs that he was entitled to a pension from the British Gov't of 19 guineas a year since 1823, & 6 guineas a year extra for extra wounds; making upwards of $2,400 now due him, with an income for life of 25 guineas a year. Benson was very poor & has 10 children. He was pressed into British service from an American whale ship, & served under Lord Nelson; was in several battles-at Trafalgar, among others, & in different actions, received 4 or 5 severe wounds. He is now 74 years of age, hale & hearty. –New Haven Register

Jacob Betsinger, of Lenox, Madison Co, N Y, committed suicide on Jul 8, by hanging himself. He did it in consequence of a difficulty with his father, who turned him out of doors on account of his having married a young lady in opposition to his wishes.

Annual Distribution of Premiums at the Balt Academy of the Visitation: Jul 19, 1843. Premiums awared to the following young ladies:

Mary Eliz Hooper, of Balt
Caroline Mann, of Balt
Josephine A Flemming, of Phil
Jane E Kernan, of Wash, D C
Francis Gosnell, of Balt
Mary Ann Wade, of Balt
Sarah Horton, of Balt
Louisa Smith, of Balt
Eliz M Combs, St Mary's Co, Md
Mary E Coad, St Mary's Co, Md
Leonora Judik, of Balt
Alice Gloninger, of Balt
Ellen Ann Manning, of St Mary's Co, Md
Mary E McHenry, of Balt
Mary Wm Anna Roper, of Phil
Catherine Schmuck, of Balt
Polymnia Ducatel, of Balt
Virginia Bunting, of Balt
Eliza Green, of Chas Co, Md
Mary Durkee, of Balt
Betsey Hillen Jenkins, of Balt
Anna Combs, of St Mary's Co, Md
Mary Helen Scott, of Balt
Eugenia Clark, of Balt
Mary Edmonia Pye, of Chas Co, Md
Ann Louisa White, of Balt
Eliz McDonald, of Balt
Priscilla Morgan, of St Mary's Co, Md
Teresa Lafitte, of Balt
Ann Ellen Jenkins, of Balt
Anna Combs, of St Mary's Co, Md
Anna Paca, of Balt
Ann Louisa Gittings, of Balt Co
Caroline Wynn, of Balt
Rosa Millard, of St Mary's Co, Md
Mgt C Baker, of Franklin, La
Virginia Coad, of St Mary's Co, Md
Anastasia Byrne, of Pikesville, Md
Anna Lennig, of Phil
Jane Mary Dugan, of Balt
Mary Eliz Wilcox, of Ivy Mills, Pa
Rebecca Hart, of Balt
Sarah Clark, of Balt
Ellen Ann Neale, of Balt
Emma Lennig, of Phil
Mar Letitia Judik, of Balt
Eliz Gosnell, of Balt
Adele Lafitte, of Balt
Eliz E Boarman, of Balt
Mary Eliz Cahill, of Norfolk, Va
Zeline Billups, of Balt
Valeria Bizourd, of Balt
Ambrosia Jenkins, of Balt
Eliza Ducatel, of Balt
Adeline Chassaing, of Balt
Mary Jarboe, of St Mary's Co, Md
Ann Tubman, of Eastern Shore, Md
Emma McDonald, of Balt
Isabel McLasky, of Mobile, Ala
Ann Clautice, of Balt
Missouri Morgan, St Mary's Co, Md
Henrietta Clark, of Balt
Mary Elder, of Balt
Victorine McLocky, of Mobile, Ala
Mary Ann Kraft, of Balt
Mary Ann Boyle, of Balt
Maria Louisa Eichelberger, of Balt
Anna Eichelberger, of Balt
Mary Clare Pye, of Chas Co, Md
Maria Josephine Campbell, Ellicott's Mills, Md

Fire on Fri broke out in a workshop in the rear of Mr Hicks' cabinet warehouse & dwlg, on High st, Gtwn: bldgs were destroyed: value of property about $1,400. About 18 months ago Mr Hicks had the misfortune to have his establishment destroyed by fire, & now it is burnt down again. Incendiary is suspected. On the same day the stable occupied by Mr E D Richards, not a square from Mr Hick's shop, was attempted to be set on fire. Fire on Sat found in a brick stable at the corner of 13th st & Md ave, belonging to Mr Wheeler, occupied by Mr Gunnell. A stable, a new carriage, & a quantity of hay were quickly consumed.

Last Wed in Gtwn, 2 brothers, Wm O'Brien & Jas O'Brien, attempted to take the life of their stepfather, Bernard Brien, by shooting him in his own house, situated on Bridge st, near the market house. The pistol went off suddenly, while Wm O'Brien was drawing it out of his picket; its contents lodged in the door-sill, & W O'Brien was sounded. W O'Brien was arrested by H Reaver, but afterwards made his escape to Balt. Jas O'Brien was arrested by ofcr Barnaclo, & put in the watch-house for safe keeping on Wed night. He was committed the next day, for want of bail, to the county prison to await his trial at the Criminal Court. There was a dispute about property formerly belonging to the own father of Jas & Wm O'Brien.

TUE JUL 25, 1843
The last Havana papers state that Jose Antonio Barranco, the cmndr of a company in a infty regt, was tried & condemned by Court Martial on Jun 26, for having wounded maliciously a sergeant in his company, which resulted in his death; & on the 28th, in virtue of his sentence, he was shot.

Leonardtown [Md] Herald: on Jul 13 an intemperate wretch, John Williams, residing in the neighborhood of Charlotte Hall, deliberately murdered his wife, after which he removed her lifeless body into the yard fronting the house, & then fled. He has not yet been arrested. His son, age 8 years, who saw his mother expire under the blows inflicted by her inhuman husband, seated himself close by the remains of his murdered parent, which he continued to watch over during the night, & did not leave until the neighbors assembled the following morning.

At N Y, on Fri, Francis Pier, aged 24, a native of Germany, foreman to Mr Fred'k Dunn, builder, of 93 Essex st, was at work on a scaffolding of the 3rd story of the new bldg at #11 on 12th st, when he accidentally slipped & fell on the scaffolding of the 2nd story, carrying it with him into the cellar, & was so severely injured that he died almost immediately.

Died: on Jul 20, at Balt, John Hutchings, formerly Cashier of the Md Savings Institution.

Died: on Jun 17, in Havana, where he had gone for his health, Maj Danl W Smith, late Consul of the U S at Matamoras.

Died: on Jul 10, at Little Rock, Ark, Israel McNulty, late of Balt, aged about 43 years.

Died: on Jul 20, at the Patapso Hotel, Ellicott's Mills, Md, Mr John L Dardenne, of Plaquemine, La, in his 50th year. He had but recently left home to witness the graduation of his son at the late commencement of St Mary's College in Balt. A severe attack of influenza arrested him upon his journey, & was followed by pleurisy, which terminated his life after a short illness. The presence of his son, & of several friends & neighbors who accompanied him to the North, alleviated happily, in some degree, the sadness of separation from his family. Mr Dardenne was a planter of high standing, an affectionate husband, friend, & father, & a most worthy & estimable gentleman.

Died: on Sun last, at the residence of her dght, in Charlestown, Va, Mrs Deborah Hite, w/o the late Capt Geo Hite, of Jefferson Co, at the advanced aged of 84 years & 4 months.

Died: on Jul 10, in Warren Co, Ky, Mr John Cosay, aged about 106 years.

Died: on Jul 22, Emma Le Roy, aged 13 months & 8 days, the only child of Hellen & Chas Mitteregger.

Died: on Jul 21, in Wash City, Thos, only s/o M L & M E Gittings, aged 1 year, 6 months & 2 days.

Barney Manly was arrested last Sun by Capt Goddard to answer to the charge of an unmanly assault of certain females, committed by him some time ago in Wash City. The prisoner was lodged in jail.

$5 reward for a strayed or was stolen from the commons south of the canal, Wash, D C, a buffalo or muly cow. –John H Clarvoe, opposite the Centre Market.

WED JUL 26, 1843
Lt Col Gates has been ordered to the command of Oglethorpe barracks at Savannah, Geo.
Lt Col Payne has assumed command of Fort McHenry, Balt.

Military Academy: the following named ofcrs have been detailed for duty at the Military Academy, to take effect on Sep 1:

Ofcrs ordered:	Ofcrs relieved
2nd Lt J Gorcas, ordnance	1st Lt W B Blair, 2nd artl
2nd Lt H A Allen, 2nd artl	Brvt Capt G Taylor, 2nd artl
2nd Lt A P Stewart, 3rd artl	1st Lt E J Steptoe, 3rd artl
2nd Lt A P Howe, 4th artl	1st Lt A E Shiras, 4th artl

Gtwn College, D C. Annual Commencement of Gtwn College was held on Jul 25, 1843. The degree of A M was conferred on Lt J Melville Gilliss, U S N & Geo W Watterston, of La.

Degree of A B was conferred on the following students:

Walter S Cox, of D C
Wm Marbury, of D C
Florence J O'Sullivan, of Pa
Walter Smith, of D C
John L Kirkpatrick, of Ga

Awarded silver medals or premiums:

Edw C Donnelly, of N Y
Eugene Cummiskey, of Pa
Francis H Dykers, of N Y
Wm E Bird, of Ga
Wm P Brooke, of Md
Geo Marshall, of Tenn
Jos L Brent, of D C
Nicholas S Knighton, of Md
Peter C Howle, of D C
Waldemar de Bodisco, of Russia
Jas A Iglehart, of Md
John W Archer, of Va
Virginius B Bilisoly, of Va
Richd Rochford, of Ireland
John Nevins, of D C
Jas E Fulton, of D C
Patrick F Drain, of D C
Felix Metoyer, of La
Eliel S Wilson, of Md
Henry Castellanos, of La
John H Denby, of Va
Chas L Denby, of Va
Richd H Clarke, of D C
Morgan Carr, of Pa
Thos A Carrico, of Md
Edmund H Cummin, of D C
Jos Cassin, of D C
Henry D Power, of D C
Isaac F C Littell, of La
Junius A Clifton, of Md
Robt E Doyle, of N Y
Jas R Fulton, of D C
John B Brooke, of Md
Wm H Williamson, of Ga
Victor Forstall, of La
Henry A Lilly, of Pa
Phidias Methot, of Canada
John Nevius, of D C
Jas Masicot, of La
Isaac F C Littell, of La
Wm D Vance, of La
Francis H Hill, of D C
Polycarp Fortier, of La
Jas O'Donoghue, of D C
Theodore Boucher, of D C
Denis Gainnis, of La
Bernard O'Reilly, of D C
John H Botts, of Poland
Henry D Power, of D C
Thos Burke, of Ireland
Jos R Gross, of D C
John L Jenkins, of Pa
Chas H Pendergast, of Md
Henry M des Rivieres, of Canada
Geo Roch Rolland, of Canada
John G Coldwell, of Ga
Wenceslas Tasche, of Canada
Chas Lecroix, of Canada
Edw V Edelin, of Md
Francis Porche, of La
C Eugene Panet, of Canada
Severin F Porche, of La
Henry Castellanos, of La
Sosthene Armand, of La
Chas De Blanc, of La
John L Jenkins, of Pa
Chas V Brent, of D C
John D Payne, of Ala
Robt W Keyworth, of D C
Danl C O'Driscoll, of D C
Andrew J Pageot, of France
Jas L Beattie, of Md

Chas W Beattie, of Md
Emilio Muruaga, of Spain
Roderick Masson, of Canada
Isaac Winston, of Ala
Ignatius C Roach, of Md
Augustus Pattrick, of N J

Class of Second Humanities:
Master Thos Burke was promoted to this class during the year
Class of Third Humanities:
Masters Henry D Power, Denis Gainnie, & Belgrade Lacoste were, during the year, promoted to this class from Rudiments.
Second Class of Mathematics:
Masters Jos L Brent, Wm E Bird, & John T Semmes were promoted to this class during the year.

Both for the rich & the poor, Florida is an easy country to live in; but how comfortably or how long to live, is another question. [Note following this: Mr Hambaugh, suttler, died of congestive fever at Cedar Keys; surgeon Elwes, of congestive fever, at Pilatka. Also died of this fever: Maj Wilson at Pilatka; Capt Garner, 3rd artl, at Picolata, on the St Johns; Maj Brown, at St Augustine; others might be named.]

Valuable property for sale: on Sep 4, the farm adjoining the Patuxent river, in Montg Co, Md, on which Jos Bond resides, containing about 175 acs: with a good 2 story dwlg house. Farm is about 19 miles from Wash City. –Caleb Stabler, Trustee: Sandy Spring, Md

In addition to my former stock of Window-glass, I have just received 132 boxes of various brands & sizes. Also, 100 kegs pure white lead, Wetherill's; varnishes: family groceries, nails, hinges, & screws. –Bushrod W Reed, corner of 13th & F sts

Sale of household furniture & dentist's instruments by order of the Orphan's Court of Wash Co, D C: sale at his late residence on Pa ave, between 9th & 10th sts, the personal effects of the late Dr John H Ritter, dec'd. -Robt W Dyer & Co, aucts

Norfolk Beacon: Com Alex B Pinkham, of the U S Navy, died at his residence on Sun, near the Navy Yard, Gosport, leaving a wife & 3 children. He was a native of Mass, & was distinguished for noble qualities & great professional skill & accomplishments.

Norfolk, Jul 24. The U S ship **Vandalia**, Capt McCluney, from Chagres in 13 days, arrived at Kingston, Jamaica, on Jun 19, having on board Lt Little of her Britannic Majesty's ship **Vindictive**, [Capt Nicholas,] with dispatches from England respecting Tahiti. Ofcrs & crew all well. -Beacon

Deacon Nathan Beers, of New Haven, Conn, has just been allowed arrears of pension as a sldr of the Revolution amounting to $3,360. He is 90 years old, & his first wife lives to share his good fortune.

The Trustees of the Washington Academy, in Princess Anne, Somerset Co, Md, wish to engage a Principal & an Assist Instructor to take charge on the first Mon in Oct next. Salary of the Principal will be $600; & if he has a family, a dwlg free of rent will be furnished him, or, in lieu thereof, an additional sum of $100 will be paid him, at the option of the Board of Trustees. The salary for the Assistant is $375, he furnishing his own board, etc. –W W Handy, S W Jones, I D Jones, Cmte on behalf of the Board of Trustees of the Washington Academy

Died: on Sun last, in Alexandria, Dr John Richards, long a useful citizen & a highly respected practicing Physician of that town, as well as for some years a greatly esteemed member of the First Presbyterian Church. Dr Richards was a native of Ireland; but, amid the throes & convulsions of that long-distressed & agitated land, in company with many others like minded with himself, he sought a refuge & a home in the then but sparsely peopled solitudes of our Western forests. Having settled himself at length in the town of Alexandria, it became thenceforward the place of his continued residence to the end of life, which happened in the 76th year of his age. –Gaz

Died: on Jun 27, at the residence of her brother, Launcelot Minor, of Louisa, Va, Mrs Diana Maury, wid/o the late Richd Maury, aged 74 years. This venerable pair had but recently come from the Far West to spend the evening of life with their son, Lt Maury, of the U S Navy, & among their kindred in Va. Mr Maury died, respected & lamented, in Jan, at his son's in Washington, & his widow, in Christian hope, on Jun 27. –Arena

Died: on Jul 20, at the residence of her parents, in PG Co, Md, Flavilla, eldest d/o Chas & Flavilla Duvall, in her 16th year.

Died: on Jul 24, Frank, s/o Capt Alfred Modecai, U S Army, aged 20 months.

THU JUL 27, 1843
Rittenhouse Academy: examination of the pupils will be held on Wed thru Fri of this week. The attendance of parents, friends, & all interested is respectfully invited. -C H & J E Nourse

Examination & exhibition: the subscriber informs that the 5th annual examination of his School will commence at 10 a m this morning, at the school house, & resume on Fri. –S G Bulfinch

For sale: a Farm of 411 acs in Montg Co, Md, on the main road from Gtwn, D C, to Fred'k City: several springs of water, two of them near the dwlg. The property will be shown by Dr Thos Patterson, living on the premises. –Bradley & Thruston, Genr'l Agents

The following are the names of the passengers of the ship **Columbia** who remained at Halifax to go out in the steamer **Hibernia**, in preference to sailing in the ship **Margaret**: Hon A Lawrence & Lady & Miss Lawrence, of Boston; Mr John Torrence & Lady, of Montreal; Mr E V Child, E L Child, & Mrs Child; Messrs Coskey, Coone, Hutchenson, Emerson, & Liney.

Mr T Eltonhead, a watchmaker & a silversmith, of Balt, died very suddenly on Sat, from a disease of the heart. He had been subject to the complaint for several years.

At Albany, on Sun, a young man named Skinner, a clerk in the store of Mr Pemberton, while bathing in the river, was seized with a cramp, & though a good swimmer, drowned. He was about 20.

On Sat a young man named Whitehead was drowned at Phil while swimming; & on the previous afternoon, at Phil, Bernard Hunt, 17, struck his head against something in the bed of the river, injuring him so that he died the next day.

St Louis New Era of Jul 11: Judge Engle admitted Wm J Harris, one of the men charged with the robbery & murder of Charvis, to bail in the sum of $6,000.

One of the crew of the ship **Glasgow**, a foreigner named Patrick Conway, came to his death on Sat last. During the day a smoke was raised in the hold of the ship to smoke out rats; at night the ship was closed up full of smoke. The dec'd went on board at night, not knowing of this, & was found dead in his berth the next morning. Verdict: death from suffocation. –Bath [Me] Telegraph

Buffalo Courier of Tue: a young man, Luther Hedge, 18, who was a hand in the oakum establishment at Black Rock Dam, was instantly killed while oiling the machinery. He was mangled terribly.

The brig **Ohio** arrived at Balt on Mon in 21 days from Guadaloupe: sailed from there on the 20th for St Thomas. On the same day Mr Atwood, 2nd mate, was taken ill & died on the 8th; her cmder, Capt Berls was attacked soon after, & died on the 10th; the chief mate, brother to the capt, also died on the 8th; & after the capt's death there were but 3 souls left on board all ignorant of navigation. The eldest seaman, Mr Watts, took charge of the vessel with the hope of reaching a port in the U S; & providentially, on the 18th, 100 miles from land, fell in with a Balt pilot boat, & she was thus brought safely into port.

The annual examination of old Gtwn College took place on Tue. The following pieces of original composition were delivered in a masterly manner, highly creditable to their alma mater, & giving high hopes of future promise:

Fall of Epaminondas	Wm E Bird
On Poetry	John L Kirkpatrick
Arnold	Eugene Picot
Canada	Eugene Panet
Erin's Son to America	Robt E Doyle
A los vencederos de Bunker Hill	Henry Castellanos
Fall of Jerusalem	Francis H Dykers
On Public Opinion	Florence J Sullivan
Bonaparte crossing the Alps	Edw C Donnelly
Le Mort de Jeanne d'Arc	Emilio Muruaga
Battle of Lake Erie	Eugene Cummiskey
Osceola	Peter C Howle
Dialogue on Greek	Virginius Bilisoly & Jas Lewis
The death of Bourbon	Geo Marshall
Genuine Liberty	Walter S Cox

Address of the Philodemic Society was delivered by John M Caussin, of Leonardtown, Md, & was unusually able & eloquent. The valedictory of John L Kirkpatrick was creditable to both his head & heart. Speeches were made during the afternoon by the Rev Mr Mullady, Geo Watterston, Gen Van Ness, Geo W P Custis, Geo C Washington, Richd Crawford, & Walter S Coxe. Pres Ryder caused a social & genuine feeling of enjoyment to pervade the company at the sumptious dinner in the hall.

The partnership, in the milling business, existing between the subscribers under the firm of Davis & Dodge, expired on Jul 11, by its own limitation. –Thos I Davis, Fra's Dodge. The business will be carried on by Thos I Davis.

For rent: comfortable 2 story brick house on south side of La ave, between 6th & 7th sts. Possession given immediately. Inquire of the subscriber at his carpenter shop on 6th st. –Francis Mohun

Venetian Blind Factory: south side of Pa ave, between 12th & 13th sts. –Wm Noell

$5 reward for return of strayed brown mare. –G W Kendrick, near the steamboat wharf.

Mr & Mrs Hellen have so far recovered from the effects of the poison which was infused into their tea about 5 weeks ago: the prisoner, Rose Dairy, brought from the jail, was fully committed for trial.

FRI JUL 28, 1843

Richmond Whig of Wed. Fatal rencontre: at Fauquier Court House last Mon between Robt E Lee & a young Mr Moore. The report is, that Lee had said he would horsewhip the father of Moore on sight. Moore accosted him to know whether he had said so. Lee responded that he had. Pistols were drawn & discharged. Moore's took effect just above the hip-although each fired twice afterwards. Lee was in the act of firing when he fell & expired. The difficulty grew out of the painful controversy connected with Judge Scott. Mr Lee, who was known to us as a gentleman of great worth & intelligence, was the son-in-law of Judge Scott. Mr Moore was the son, we presume, of one of the gentlemen who was summoned here last winter to give testimony in the case, which testimony was adverse to the Judge. [Robt E Lee was the s/o Chas Lee, dec'd [formerly Atty Gen of the U S.]

Boston: on Jul 23, two gentlemen of this city, Jas D Coffin & Geo D Dana, drowned when their sailboat upset. Coffin, was a dealer in fancy goods, 67 Wash st, & Dana, s/o Mr Geo Dana, was a merchant, 13 Long wharf. Both were highly respectable young men, & belonged to the company of New England Guards. -Adv

Breach of Promise: Miss Mary Long sued out a capias ad respondendum against the faithless swain Francis Gerrity, [both parties being natives of the Emerald Isle,] in the sum of $10,000, for refusing to complete an arrangement which had been made when on board ship, when crossing. Sheriff Stryker served a writ for $20,000 on Gerrity. Gerrity asked the sheriff to accompany him to Mary's residence: he did: Mary was a fine buxom looking girl: after some conversation, the sheriff & parties proceeded to the residence of the priest, & merged the suit in the abyss of matrimony. --Brooklyn News

Died: on Jul 6, in Sutton, Mass, Ann Lilly, aged 100 years. After she was 90 years old she would ply the spinning wheel & knitting needles as diligently as any spinster of 30. She was followed to the grave by a numerous processof her descendants-children, grand-children, great grand-children, & great great grand-children.

Died: on Sat last, at Boundbrook, Somerset Co, N J, Jacob De Groot, in his 95th year. The dec'd performed service in the war of the Revolution, for which he received a pension, & in later years was an acting judge & justice of the county. In this paper last week we recorded the death of his aged wife. They lived together nearly 70 years, &, after that long interval, have been separated in life but 13 days. - Messenger

Mr Isaac M Denson, warden of the alms-house in Balt Co, cut on Sat from the farm of the institution, a quantity of wheat, which he threshed, fanned, ground, bolted & baked into bread, ready for eating in 23 minutes from the time of cutting commenced. This was certainly quick work. --Patriot

The Editor of the Daily advertiser, published at Detroit, Mich, asks for information of Alonzo Cole, who enlisted on Oct 16, 1840, at N Y C, in the 3rd Regt of Artl, which was ordered to Florida the Nov following. If he be still alive, & will make known his present residence, the Advertiser says he will hear of something greatly to his advantage.

Sealed proposals will be received until Aug 7 for grading & gravelling 9th st west, from N Y ave to M st north. –Wm Cooper, jr, Com'r 3rd Ward; Danl Gould, John A Brightwell, Assist Com'r s [Other proposals followed for similar work in Washington, signed: Michl Hoover, R J Falconer, Jos Harbaugh, J C McKelden- Assist Com'rs.]

Firemen's Vigilant Total Abstinence Society meeting on Fri at Apollo Hall.
–E Brooke, sec

Messrs Editors: I have read with much regret an article in your paper, published as an advertisement, signed C Eckloff. It is false in facts. I have sort a home in this land of the free, endeavoring to pursue the even tenor of my way. Mr Ludwigh, the gentleman who comes in for large a share of Mr Eckloff's abuse, is a German scholar, of the Unitarian faith. I should not have noticed the miserable attack on Mr Ludwigh & myself had not several of my friends deemed it necessary; & have only now to say that while I condemn the ignorance of Mr Eckloff, I freely forgive the insults he has so gratuitously offered. –W Creutzfeldt [Abstracts from 3 paragraphs.]

Information wanted: Saml Bender left his home on Jul 13, with another boy to pick blackberries, & was seen the day following on the Leesburg road, since which no correct tidings have been obtained. He is about 12 years of age, dark hair, & large dark eyes, fair skin, & somewhat freckled. Any information will be most thankfully received by his parents in Washington. –Jacob A Bender

$10 reward for recovery of a package of money, lost in a small house attached to the Centre Market. The finder will receive the above reward by leaving the money with Mr Gideon's printing ofc, 9th st. -E M Heiste

For sale at a low price the house & lot in the Seven Buildings occupied by the Hon M Van Buren during his Vice Presidential term, & from the expiration of that term until recently by the Hon R J Walker. The house is next east of that owned & occupied by Capt Forrest, U S Navy. –H H Dent,
4½ st, near City Hall

An examination of the pupils of my school will take place this Fri in the school-room, being the Hall of the Franklin Engine-house, to commence at 9 a m.
–John Neely

SAT JUL 29, 1843
Navy Orders: Capt J Wilkinson to command Norfolk yard. Cmder J M Dale detached to rendezvous at Phil, waiting orders. Cmder R Ritchie to rendezvous at Phil. Capt J Downes to be Port Captain at Boston.

Family horse & carriage for sale. –Walker & Kimmell, Nat'l Livery Stable

Orphans Crt of Chas Co, Md: notice is given to the reps of Eliz Reeves, dec'd, that her executors will be prepared to pass a final account on the estate of said dec'd on the 3rd Tue in Aug next. –John Hughes, Geo Gardiner, excs of E Reeves, dec'd.

Marshal's sale: virtue of fieri facias issued from the Clk's ofc of the Circuit Court of Wash Co, D C: sale on the premises of Jas Gettys, formerly occupied by Mr Wm Hayman, & opposite Hayman's Brewery, in Wash City, the following property to wit: One negro woman named Elsey, about 33 or 34 year, a negro boy named Allen, the child of Elsey, about 15 or 16 years, 1 mahg sideboard, mahg dining table, mahg Northumberland tables, numerous articles of good furniture, candlesticks, glass ware, Japan waiters, China tea set, & many mscl articles. –Seized & taken as the property of Jas Gettys, & sold to satisfy judicials #1, to Mar Term, 1840, in favor of Archibald McIntyre, survivor of John B Yates. –Alex'r Hunter, Marshal of D C

Providence, R I, Jul 26. Four men, John Carpenter, 50, Henry Hawkins, about 24, Richd B Knight, & Geo Himes, left Baker's Folly on Mon for Newport in a two-masted sail boat, & when struck by a heavy squall the boat swamped & Messrs Carpenter & Hawkins were drowned. The two others clung to the boat until rescued about an hour later. Mr Carpenter left a wife & 5 children. -Journal

N Y Jul 27. Yesterday 3 men, Dennis Conroy, Patrick Kevan, & Andrew Mullady, were at work on a scaffold raised to the 2nd story of a new bldg in N Y, on 2nd st, when it gave way & they all were precipitated to the ground. Kevan died soon after reaching the hospital. Conroy had both legs broken, & his spine was much hurt. Mullady's injuries are internal, & his recovery is doubtful. -Courier & Enquirer

Academy of the Visitation, Gtwn, D C. Distribution of Premiums took place on Jul 24: assembly was honored by the presence of his Excellency the Pres of the U S, who presented the premiums & honorary certificates to the following young ladies:

America Semmes, of Gtwn, D C	Ann Howle, of Wash
Ellen Hamtramck, of Shepherdstown	Emily Noyes, of Gtwn
Mary Fulmer, of Wash, D C	Mary Catharine White, of Wash
Indiana Fletcher, of Lynchburg, Va	Mgt Rainey, of Gtwn
Mary Jane Cox, of Gtwn, D C	Sophronia Pickrell, of Gtwn
Loretta Pickrell, of Gtwn, D C	Ellen Spenser, of Phil
Virginia Dodge, of Gtwn	Eliz Hobbie, of Wash D C

Amanda Pierce, of Houlton, Maine
Corneila Matthews, of Lynchburg, Va
Mgt Brady, of Wash, D C
Sarah Gardner, of Wash, D C
Catharine Masi, of Wash D C
Eliza Bogue, of Gtwn
Mary Jane Russell, of Phil
Eliz Cox, of Gtwn
Mary Ann O'Connor, of Phil
Emily Mudd, of Wash
Genevieve King, of Gtwn
Catharine Conley, of Wash
Amelia Egan, of Alexandria, D C
Mary King, of Gtwn
Rosa Coddington, of Wash
Mary Ritchie, of Gtwn
Asa Wynn, of Petersburg, Va
Mary Jane Ready, of Charleston, S C
Mary Nevins, of Gtwn
Anne Templeman, of Gtwn
Mary C Hardy, of Chas Co, Md
Catharine Bates, of Wash
Eliz Fletcher, of Lynchburg, Va
Catharine Durham, of Wash
Matilda Semmes, of PG Co, Md
Mgt Leonard, of Gtwn
Catharine Masi, of Wash
Mary Huntt, of Wash
Mary Ann McLaughlin, Harrisbrg, Pa
Maria C Goldsborough, of Gtwn
Juliana Jenkins, of Balt, Md
Mary Ellen Hinton, of Delaware, Ohio
Caroline Arny, of Gtwn
Fanny Hobbie, of Wash, D C
Mary Young, of PG Co, Md
Mary Green, of Gtwn
Fanny Huntt, of Wash
Eliz Roach, of St Mary's Co
Felicity Lancaster, of Chas Co, Md
Caroline Dent, of Belair, Ga
Attaway Lewis, of King Geo Co
Anne Cummings, of Wash, D C
Mary Binda, of Sumter, S C
Augusta Scott, of Wash, D C
Emily Matthews, of Lynchburg, Va
Catharine Templeman, of Gtwn
Mary Ann Matthews, Lynchburg, Va
Maria Bohrer, of Gtwn
Amelia Brady, of Phil
Maria L Poor, of Balt
Sally Urquhart, of Teamsville, Va
Henrietta Keller, of Wash, D C
Caroline Keyworth, of Wash
Martha May, of Gtwn
Sarah Donoghoe, of Gtwn
Teresa Donelan, of Wash, D C
Virginia Mix, of Gtwn
Julia Young, of PG Co, Md
Eugenia Wynn, of Petersburg, Va
Ellen Cox, of Gtwn
Catharine May, of Gtwn
Sabina Semmes, of Gtwn
Mary Payne, of Gainsville, Ala
Augusta Bohrer, of Gtwn
Ellen Schultz, of Mexico
Camilla Lancaster, of Chas Co, Md
Theodosia Coalburn, of Twn
Dora Hernandez, St Augustine, E Fla
Sarah Pettit, of Gtwn
Clara Semmes, of Gtwn, D C
Catharine Blackstone, of Phil
Rosa French, of Wash, D C
Mary Coddington, of Wash, D C
Mary Wynn, of Petersburg, Va
Mary Fulmer, of Wash, D C
Indiana Fletcher, of Lynchburg, Va
Eliz Hobbie, of Wash D C
Mary E Howle, of Wash
Mary Jane Reedy, of Charleston, S C
Mary C White, of Wash
Mary Ann O'Connor, of Phil
Virginia Cassin, of Twn
Mary Poor, of Balt
Mary King, of Gtwn
Mary Nevins, of Gtwn
Cecilia Plowden, Chaptico, St Mary's Co

Died: on Sat last, Jas Theodore, s/o Mr Sylvester Barker, about 4 years old, from eating some of the poison hemlock which grows so abundantly in the burying ground adjacent to the Baptist Church in 3rd st. –Troy Budget

Bristol, R I. Mr Nathl Munro, an aged & very respectable citizen of Bristol, R I, drowned in our harbor on Jul 24, during the heavy squall. Mr Munro was in his boat fishing alone. He was about 70 years of age.

Died: on Jul 27, in Wash City, after a short but severe illness, Mrs Malinda Rhodes, in her 79th year. She died as she had lived a pious Christian. Her funeral is this morning at half past 9 o'clock, from the residence of her son, Jas Rhodes, near the Navy Yard, to St Peter's Church, when the funeral obsequies will be performed.

Died: on Jul 28, Wm, infant s/o Nathan & Rebecca Edmonston, aged 8 months & 9 days. His funeral is this moring at 8 a m, from their residence on L, between 8th & 9th sts.

Died: yesterday, in Gtwn, aged 65 years, Mrs Judith Wright, relict of the late Thos C Wright. Her funeral will be from her late residence on High st today at 5 o'clock.

MON JUL 31, 1843
Nat'l Institute Papers: by Lt M F Maury, U S Navy, read at the last meeting of the institution: resolutions passed appointing a cmte of 3 members consisting of Lt Maury, as Chrmn, Capt John S Chauncey & Lt J T McLaughlin, of the Navy. If every vessel in the navy, & as many as would in the merchant service, were each furnished with a blank chart, having only parallels & meridians drawn upon it to show latitudes & longitudes; if their cmders were requested to lay off the tracks of their vessels upon it everyday, with remarks showing the time of day, direction of the winds, the force & set of currents, & embracing generally all subjects that tend to illustrate the navigation of the seas through which they sail, I have greatly mistaken the character of American navigators if they would not gladly lend the Society a willing hand in an undertaking so praiseworthy & useful.

Annual examination of the pupils of the Institution for the Deaf & Dumb in N Y was held on Fri & Sat of last week. Board of dirs: Messrs Henry E Davies, Prosper M Wetmore, & Benj R Winthrop. Dr Milnor-President. A volume of poems was presented as a gift to Mr Harvey P Peet, teacher, signed: from his affectionate pupils:
Sarah Guile	Mariana Laubacher	Susan Swift
Virginia Butler	Frances Arnold	Julia A Hoffman
Eliz R Budd	Mary Ann Parker	

Circuit Court of Wash Co, D C. Geo Ford [colored] has applied to be discharged from imprisonment under the act for the relief of Insolvent Debtors. –Wm Brent, clk

Mr Horace B Dickinson, the capt of the diving bell boats employed over the wreck of the steamer **J M White**, about 80 miles below St Louis, was accidentally drowned on Fri night week by being upset in a small boat. He was from Hampshire Co, Mass, & about 40 years of age.

The body of Mr Peter Bier was found dead in the woods, a few miles from Louisville, Ky, on Fri week. Death was occasioned by bullet wounds, but whether his own act or that of an assassin is not known. He had been a resident of Louisville for many years, & was highly respected.

A rencontre with pistols took place at a hotel in Nashville, Tenn, on Wed night week, between Jesse J Bryan, of Clarksville, & Gideon C Matlock, of Carthage, which resulted in the death of Bryan. Matlock fled, & at the latest date had not been apprehended.

The packet ship **Memphis**, Capt Allen, 16 days from New Orleans, bound to N Y, was wrecked on Chickamicomico Island, 25 miles north of Cape Hatteras, on Jul 22. Passengers & crew saved; vessel & cargo lost.

The N Y papers announce the completion of Mr Weir's great national picture, representing the embarkation of the Pilgrims at Holland, which is designed to fill one of the panels in the Rotundo of the Capitol in Wash City.

Prof Downes, of the High School Observatory at Phil, gives notice through the papers of that city that he had seen the comet discovered early in May last by M Mauvais, Assist at the Paris Observatory.

The Halifax papers give an account of the wreck of the barque **Alert**, on Goose Island, about 30 leagues east of Halifax. She had recently been launched, & was under contract by the Messrs Cunard to convey the 64th Regt to Ireland. She sailed on Mon with the troops & 90 women & children, & in less than 24 hours, she was run on shore, where she went to pieces. During the perils & distresses of the shipwreck 5 infants were born. The lives of all on board were saved, but every article belonging to them, except what they stood in, were lost, & they are left in a deplorably wretched condition.

The Rev Squire Chase, the Superintendent of the Liberia mission under the care of the Missionary Society of the Meth Episc Church, died on Wed at Syracuse, N Y, whither he had gone to attend a Conference.

Died: yesterday, Mrs Sarah B Waring, consort of B H Waring, of the War Dept, in her 33rd year, leaving many friends to mourn her loss. Her funeral will be from her late residence on F st, between 19th & 20th sts, this afternoon, at 5 p m.

Died: on Tue last, after a long & painful illness, at the residence of her father, Capt Ambrose Cock, Fairfax Co, Va, Mrs Frances Elmira Burch, w/o Mr Wm S Burch, of Wash City, in her 20th year.

The Trustees of the Bladensburg Academy inform that the Rev John Decker, assisted by Mr Thos Granger, is in charge of the institution. –Benj O Lowndes, sec

Mount St Mary's College, Emmittsburg, Md: session of studies commences on Aug 16. –Rev John McCaffrey, Pres

Wash, D C. We are glad to perceive that the old "Central Academy," formerly the property of Mr McLeod, at the corner of 10th & G sts, is now being fitted up & put in complete order for a Male Orphan Asylum. It will be opened on Sep 1 next under the care & direction of the "Sisters of Charity."

TUE AUG 1, 1843
Accident at La Grange, Oldham Co, Ken, a day of two since, resulted in the death of Mr Nichols, the jailor of the county. He was fixing a timber at his steam saw mill, & as he stooped to arrange a cross piece, it flew up & struck him in the face with such force as to disfigure him very much & kill him instantly.

Sheriff Brayton, while on his way to Auburn, N Y, having in custody 5 prisoners sentenced to the State prison, joined company at Syracuse with a Sheriff who also had prisoners. Two of the prisoners from the 2 counties instantly recognized each other as old friends & associates. They were both classmates at Dartmouth College; one, Delancy, was expelled-the other Nichols, absconded. Each attempted to prey on the community, & each entered the State prison at one & the same time to expiate his crimes.

Seasonable Articles: Glenn's Roman Kalydor, a remedy for various affections of the skin, as pimples, freckles, blotches, morphew, or moth, tan, sunburn, tetter, ringworm, or almost any other obstinate disease of the skin, giving a clearness & beauty to the complexion. –Jas Clephane, Pa ave & 12th sts.

Mrd: on Jul 30, by Rev John Davis, Mr John W Easby to Miss Rozina M Lowry, all of Wash City.

Died: on Fri last, in Wash City, suddenly, in his 41st year, Mr Jas Douglas. He has deprived a fond wife of an affectionate husband, 5 children of a devoted father, & a large number of relatives of a tender relation. He was esteemed by those who knew him, & his loss will be sincerely felt by all.

Died: on Jul 28, at Phil, after a long & painful illness, Rebecca H Peters, in her 28th year, wid/o the late Dr Jos Harbaugh, of Wash City.

Patent Agency, Ofc n e corner of 7th & E sts. –F Benne & R J Young Refer to Hon H L Ellsworth, Com'r of Patents; Hon E Whittlesey, Auditor of the Post Ofc, Wash.

Household furniture at auction: on Aug 3, over the dry goods store of Mr R C Washington, the furniture of that establishment, which is in good order: Cane & wood chairs, mahg lounge, mahg dining & card tables, mahg sideboard, mantel glass, crockery, glass ware, carpet, toilet sets, washstands, kitchen requisites.
-Robt W Dyer & Co, aucts

Episcopal High School of Virginia: within 3 miles of Alexandria, D C, & adjoining the Episcopal Theological Seminary of Virginia, & on a healthy, commanding & beautiful eminence nearly 300 feet above the Potomac. The age of admission is in general over 14; a limited number received between 10 & 14. Charges are for each separate pupil per annum: $175. –Rev W N Pendleton, Rector

Yesterday a horse attached to a cab having a gentleman in it started at full speed from the Patriotic Bank towards the Centre Market. It struck a large stone & was overturned. The driver, Henry Fisher, employed by Messrs Walker & Kimmell was severely bruised, escaped without breaking his bones.

WED AUG 2, 1843
The Winchester Republican announces the sudden death, by paralysis, of Col Augustus C Smith, s/o the late Gen John Smith, for several years a member of the State Senate, & a much esteemed citizen. [No date-current item.]

Glymont for sale: beautiful farm, a part of the estate of Jas B Pye, late of Chas Co, dec'd, will be advertised by com'rs of the Court at its Aug session for sale. It will then be divided & sold without the dower portion. The whole is 664 acs: situated on the south bank of the Potomac, about 20 miles from D C. Letters addressed to his signature at Pomonkey post ofc will receive prompt attention.
-Edw A Pye

Following is a list of the ofcrs of the steam frig **Missouri**, bound to Alexandria, in Egypt.

John Thos Newton, Capt	Rodman M Price, Purser
S B Bissell, Lt	Wm F McClenahan, Surgeon
Geo R Gray, Lt	Francis Alexander, acting Master
John A Winslow, Lt	A S Taylor, Lt of Marines
Thos T Hunter, Lt	A J Bowie, Assist Surgeon
S F Blunt, Lt	John Farron, Chief Engineer

Passed Midshipmen:
- John M Wainwright
- C S Throckmorton
- D McA Fairfax

Midshipmen:
- J J Pringle
- J S Bohrer
- G M Newton, Capt's Clk
- A C Wakeman, Purser's Clk
- Robt Dixon, Boatswain
- Wm Burton, Gunner
- J D Freeman, Sailmaker
- Christopher Gordon, Carpenter
- H Sanford, 1st Assist Engineer
- H Hunt, 1st Assist Engineer
- Wm Scott, 1st Assist Engineer
- H Davidson
- Jos Fry
- J H March
- N Davis, 2nd Assist Engineer
- A S Palmer, 2nd Assist Engineer
- Theo Zeller, 3rd Assist Engineer
- Saml Archibold, 3rd Assist Engineer
- A W Parsons, Master's Mate
- J J Newton, Master's Mate
- C C Hinton, Purser's Steward
- D C Hanson, Surgeon's Steward

Wm Howitt's Rural & Domestic Life of Germany. Hernhut, the original settlement of the Moravians, is a neat modern-looking town of about 1,100 inhabitants. It is built with streets crossing at right angles & of white houses. The Single Brethren's House, & other bldgs, belong to the community. The same for the Single Sisters' House which stands nearby. Many private families live in their own separate houses. Chldrn like John Wesley, are probably taught to fear the rod & cry softly. They are not allowed to play in the street; you hear very little of them. Music is much cultivated among them. The women were distinguished by the ribands which tied their caps being the young girls had deep red; the unmarried women pink; the married women blue; the widows white or gray. They may contract marriage by mutual agreement, under the approbation of the elders; nothing is more common than for a missionary to send home, requesting them to choose him a wife, who is thus selected. Scarcely an instance has been known in which these marriages have not been completely happy ones.

From Florida: Billy Bowlegs is now the dominant Chief, being a nephew of Old Micanopy. What few Indians remain in the Territory trade freely with the whites, & have passed some severe laws among themselves against stealing cattle, hogs, or otherwise interfering with the rights of the citizens. -Savannah Republican

The subscriber offers for sale the farm on which he now lives, in Montg Co, Md, about 8 miles from the Washington market: about 105 acs, with a comfortable frame dwlg with 5 rooms in good order: a fine school within half a mile of the house. Apply to B L Bogan, Treasury Dept, Wash, or to the subscriber on the premises. –C W Lansdale

For rent: a neat 2 story brick house on H st, near the Washington City Orphan Asylum, in a genteel neighborhood. For terms apply to Geo Savage.

Mrd: on Sep 2 last, in Balt, by Rev Mr Henshaw, Lewis Walker to Susannah Virginia Miller, both of Washington.

Mrd: on Jul 27, by Rev Mr Coffin, Mr Reuben Middleton, of Missouri, to Miss Mary Ellen, d/o C C Hyatt, of Bladensburg, PG Co, Md.

Mrd: on Tue last, in Wash City, by Rev Mr Davis, Mr John G Lester, formerly of Balt, to Miss Mary Ann, d/o Jas H Bennett, of Fauquier Co, Va.

Died: on Jul 29, in Wash City, suddenly, Mrs Agatha Sardo, consort of Mr Michl Sardo, in her 59th year, in full triumph of the Christian faith, leaving a disconsolate husband, children, grand-children, & great grand-children to mourn her loss. She was born in the city of Catania, in the island of Sicily, emigrated with her family to this country about 38 years ago, & for the whole of the above period has resided in Washington. May she rest in peace! -B

Died: on Jun 27 last, at Rushville, Schuyler Co, Ill, Mrs Catherine S Hall, in her 43rd year, formerly of Alexandria, D C, & d/o the late Edw Ramsay, of Edinburgh, Scotland. A large circle of friends sympathize with the family of the dec'd under the bereavement they have sustained.

Died: on Jul 30, at Balt, Mrs Frances Hazlehurst, in the 62nd year of her age.

Vegetable Stalls for sale: in the West Markethouse. –Wm Serrin, clerk of the West Market

THU AUG 3, 1843
Extract of a letter from the junior editor of the N Y Express-E Brooks, who is now traveling in Europe. London looks like a great smoke-house, & men's mouths seem almost to vie with the chimneys in smoking the city: the universal Yankee nation-a country of tobacco growers. Spitting is the greater offence at home, but a specimen of English manners & English smoking gives me the borishmess & rudeness of home to the politeness of the land I have just left behind me. Among the Belgians & Dutchmen I could endure this as one of the customs of the country, but not in England.

Fatal Railroad collision on Tue near Reading, on the Pottsville railroad, between a train of cars with coal destined for Phil, & an empty train returning to the mines. Three men attached to the trains were killed instantly: Goe Heckman & Danl Fernwaldt, the other, name unknown. Gottfried Fernwaldt, father of Danl Fernwaldt, had his leg broken. Saml Shultz had several ribs broken, & Conrad Fegur, jr, was badly injured.

Mrd: on Aug 1, by Rev Mr Gassaway, Jas B Kirk, of St Mary's Co, Md, to Emily W, d/o W Redin.

Died: on Jul 25, at Upper Marlborough, Md, of cholera infantum, John Marshall, infant s/o Caleb C & Mary S Magruder, aged 2 months.

Boston Atlas of Sat: Coroner Mace Smith held an inquest yesterday on the body of Winthrop Smart, found in the water between the tracks of the Worcester railroad, near the Tremont road, lying on his face, his feet sticking in the mud. He experienced a great deal of pressure by his creditors for some debts of his sons, for which he became responsible. It seems his wife is possessed, in her own right, of an estate in Castle st, & an old creditor, for a debt not his own, sued Mr Smart a few days since. This led to his death. Mr Smart was ever an exemplary, temperate man, & a faithful husband, hardworking, conscientious, & always ready to pay his own debt. He has left a large family, is 65 year of age, formerly lived in Epping, N H. Verdict of jury: committed suicide by drowning.

FRI AUG 4, 1843
The schnr **Sarah Lavinia**, Dearborn, of Alexandria, was found abandoned near Martha's Vineyard on Sun last: scuttled, the capt's trunk rifled, & other indications of mischief. Piracy is suspected. The **Lavina** sailed from Alexandria Jul 1 for Antigua. She was towed into New Bedford & put in charge of the U S Marshal.
[Aug 5th newspaper: two of the pirates, Mathews & Babe, an Englishman, were arrested in N Y at the boarding house of Mr Knowles, #7 Washington st, N Y. The third is yet to be caught.]

The Journal of Commerce says that Oliver M Lownds, with the young Hayes, will go out in the steamer from Boston to co-operate on behalf of Messrs Jacob Little & Co with the English authorities in the prosecution of Clinton, whose true name is John Reed, an old offender. The new Treas notes which Reed has sent out to this country through an English bank, on each of which he committed a forgery, will be taken by Mr Lownds. Reed will probably be tried in England for the forgeries committed there, & if convicted, there will be no necessity for demanding him on the part of the U S Gov't. A Treas clerk will also accompany Mr Lownds.

Mr G R Leffler, iron worker, Pratt st, Balt, receiving a note to meet 2 persons at the foundry for an order for 10 tons of castings, met them at the appointed time. He was the victim of an assault & robbed of $1,275 in cash, which he had on his person, having just returned from Washington, where he had received the money. The thieves have eluded the police.

John Hays was found in the Basin, near the mouth of Jones' Falls, Balt, on Tue. Inquest was held by J D Hare, coroner, & verdict was rendered of accidental drowning. Mr Hays was a man of industrious habits, & has left a wife & 3 children to lament his untimely end.

Fire at Fort Deposite, Md, on Sat, consumed the dwlg house & carpenter's shop of Mr Elijah Reynolds, the Methodist parsonage house, & the dwlg house of Mr Alonzo Snow. Nearly all the furniture in each house was destroyed.

Died: on Aug 2, Ann Maria, d/o John W Ferguson, of Wash City, in her 4th year.

SAT AUG 5, 1843
Literature: Biography & Poetical Remains of the Late Margaret Miller Davidson, by Washington Irving. A new edition, revised. Phil: Lea & Blanchard. 248 pp-price 50 cents, in paper.

Young Ladies Seminary for Boarding & Day Pupils, Washington. M A Tyson & Sisters who have conducted a Seminary of some note for several years past in the city of Balt, intend resuming their Institution in this city on Sep 4 next. References:

Balt	P E Thomas	Moses Sheppard
Benj Hallowell	Jos King	Jesse Fahnestock
Hon Z Collins Lee	Hon A Nesbit	A B Murray
Gen Wm McDonald	John D Early	Danl W Hall
A Alexander, M D	John Feast	
Wm W Handy, M D	Saml Riggs	
H G Jameson, M D	Lewin Wethered	

<u>Washington:</u>   McClintock Young   Hon Judge Redgate
Jas H Caustin   Thos H Gillis

<u>Balt Co:</u>   Col N M Bosley   Henry Carroll

Public sale of the steamer **Chesapeake**; coppered & coppered fastened; length 136 feet, 24 feet 4 inch beam; dept of hold 7 feet 8 inches; burden about 240 tons; engine built by Watchman & Bratt, Balt.
-F Black, Agent: Washington

Horses for sale: just arrived a lot of 16 fine Western Horses, & 16 mules, part of them well broke, which will be sold low for cash by applying at the Franklin Stable, 8th & D sts. --N Rowles & Co, proprietors

Balt City Court-Special Session. Present, his Honor Judge Brice, Aug 3, 1843, 5 p m. State vs John McLean Gardner to inquire as to the sanity of the prisoner at the period of his assault on Hon C A Wickliffe. Jury:

Beale H Richardson	Henry Wilkins	Wm Colvin
John N Brown	Jas Harris, jr	Marcus Denison
John Hurst	Wm Schroeder	Alex'r Smith
Chas Gwynn	Wm F Murdock	

David Hoffman opened the case: ptn made in the name of Ann Eliza Gardner, mother of the prisoner, as next friend to him, & represented that he had been some time past in a deranged or unsettled state of mind. Mr Turner sworn: resides in Gtwn; is a clerk in the Land ofc; became acquainted with Mr Gardner on Sat last; was on board with him; entered into conversation with Gardner about his brothers; they laid down with their clothes on, 5 or 6 others in the room, woke up & went on deck. Mrs Gardner testified: since early youth John had been addicted to books; she wrote his father who is in N C in relation to his alienation of mind; since the departure of Col Gardner he has become worse. Court adjourned until tomorrow morning. [Aug 5th newspaper: Jurors do find the said John McLean Gardner was lunatic or insane on Aug 1, at the time of committing the offence charged against him, & is still so at the time of taking this inquisition.] [On the boat after the assault Gardner writes a letter to Wickliffe: On inquiry you will find that no human being instigated me by the remotest hint to commit what I have done to your person; therefore, sir, you being a man in high ofc, cannot be so ungenerous as to show any vindictiveness towards my family or connexions, whom I have always had too little regard for in pursuing their advice.]

Arbitration case was disposed of last week in the Grand Jury room, under a rule of Court, of Mrs Frances Swann against the Alexandria Canal Co, for damages on account of running their improvement through her farm [**Preston**] in Alexandria Co, D C. The estate had been in the family, from which Mrs Swann is descended, upwards of 170 years. An award of $7,000 was made in her favor. Gen Jones & Messrs Swann & Swann were present as counsel for Mrs Swann, & R S Coxe appeared as counsel for the Canal Co.

The Whigs of Anne Arundel Co, Md, have nominated Dr Stevens Gambrill, John Johnson, Nicholas B Worthington, Reuben Warfield, & Robt Garner, as their candidates for the next House of Delegates.

Messrs Rolph, Duncomb, & Montgomery received on Sat a free pardon from the Canadian Gov't. They have thus been restored to their rights & property, & will probably return to the homes from which they have been so long exiled. –Rochester Democrat

Trustee's sale of valuable real estate in the city of Annapolis: decree of the Court of Chancery of Md, the subscribers offer for sale all the real estate of Richd I Jones, being in said city, consisting:
1-Spacious dwlg house, with a large garden & lots attached. Persons disposed to purchase will examine it.
2-A lot on Duke of Gloster st.
3-House & lot on Market st, the lot about ½ an ac.
4-Lot 71, corner of west & Church Circle, upon which are 3 ofcs.
5-Lot & 2 houses on Northwest st.

6-Brick dwlg house, with a garden, on Prince Geo st, at present occupied by Gen Watkins, & a vacant lot immediately below, & 2 frame houses in the vicinity.
7-Lot near the dock, upon which is a brick building, fitted up for & used as a steam mill.
8-Two other frame houses on Prince Geo st, & a house on the wharf occupied by Mrs Birmingham.
9-Two lots on Cornhill st, on one of which there is a dwlg hnow occupied by Mr Hohns.
10-Brick house & lot on Green st, occupied by Jack Quynn.
Immediately after the sale the personal estate of Jones will be sold, consisting of a great variety of household & kitchen furniture, & slaves for terms of years. –J Johnson, T S Alexander, Trustees

$100 reward for runaway negro man Wm Smith, about 25 years of age: ranaway from the Mathew Bryan & Co's Iron Works, Rockbridge Co, Va, in Jun last. –John McCoull, near Spotsylvania Court-house, Va

Sale at public auction, in Port Tobacco, Md, on the 3rd Mon in Aug, 1843, all the thorough-bred stock of horses of the estate of the late Ed J Hamilton. –Ann L Hamilton, Geo W Matthews, excs

Female teacher wanted: services of a Governess qualified to teach English, Music, French, & Drawing. She will board in the family, & the number of pupils not to exceed 6. Apply to Thos C Kennard, near Chestertown, Kent Co, Md

Circuit Court of Wash Co, D C. Hugh M Boyd has applied to be discharged from imprisonment under the act for the relief of Insolvent Debtors: hearing on Aug 12. –Wm Brent, clk

Mr Jas Newell, an old sldr of the Revolution, who fought at the battles of Lexington & Yorktown, & at the taking of Ticonderoga, died in Boston on Sat last. He did not join the festivities of the completion of the Bunker Hill Monument on Jun 17th on account of illness.

Died: yesterday, of consumption, in her 37th year, Mrs Jane Waters, w/o Mr John Nelson Waters, leaving a husband & 6 children. She was for several years a member of the Presbyterian Church on F st. She was a native of Phil, & the y/d/o Mrs Mary Owen, formerly of Sunderland, Eng, who died in Wash City in 1832. Her funeral will be from her husband's residence on L st, near 18th, this morning at 10 o'clock. Her friends & acquaintances & those of her brother-in-law, Edmund F Brown, are invited.

Died: on Jul 25, in Upper Marlborough, of cholera infantum, John Marshall, aged 2 months, & at the same place, on Jul 30, of the same complaint, Mary Rebecca, aged 2 month & 5 days, infant children of Caleb C & Mary S Magruder.

MON AUG 7, 1843

By virtue of an order from Richd C Washington to distrain, & to me directed, I shall offer at public sale on the premises, lately occupied by Albert McDaniel, near Pa ave, in Wash City, on Aug 10, the following property, to wit: one pair of mahg card tables, one sofa, 18 Windsor chairs, 3 Venetian blinds, one pair of mahg dining tables, one mahg sideboard, one large sized mahg dining table, a looking glass, a rocking chair, 3 washstands, & one lot of carpeting; seized & taken as the property of the said Albert McDaniel, & will be sold to satisfy house rent due in arrears to Richd C Washington. –H R Maryman, bailiff

The Boston Atlas of Thu announces the death of Rev Francis Wm Pitt Greenwood, Pastor of King's Chapel, in that city. Mr Greenwood was much beloved & respected.

Army & Navy Chronicle: Thos Grosvenor King has been appointed Military Storekeeper attached to the Qrtrmaster's Dept, to be stationed at New Orleans, vice Capt J W Kingsbury, resigned.

John Crosby, a sldr of the Revolution died at his residence, in Barren Co, Ky, on Jul 10, aged about 106 years. He was at the surrender of Lord Cornwallis at Yorktown. About 30 years ago he removed from Va to his last residence. For the last few years of his life he drew a pension. He was an excellent citizen.

Richd Key Watts, Magistrate & Conveyancer, Pa ave & 10th st, Wash City. [Local ad]

The Capitol Hill Seminary for Young Ladies will open on Sep 1 under the superintendence of Mr & Mrs Richards. Communication can be made to the principals, at their residence, 2nd st, north side of the Catholic Church.

Cumberland Civilian: Mr Philip Chrony, a carpenter, whilst engaged at the railroad bridge across the South Branch, on Wed, accidentally fell off the timbers into the river & drowned. He leaves a wife & 2 children.

The Wheeling Gaz announces the death of Mrs Eliz House, at the age of 110 years lacking a few months. She was born near Annapolis, Md, where she resided until 1788, when she removed to Jefferson Co, Va, where she remained until the spring of 1801. She then, with her son-in-law, Mr Lansford, removed to Ky, & in the fall of the same year came to Ohio Co, Va, where she had resided ever since until the day of her death. Mrs House was left a widow during the Revolutionary war with 5 small children, whom she supported by her own industry. During the whole of her long life she enjoyed almost uninterrupted good health. She never was bled, nor did she ever even take a dose of calomel. She could read the finest print up to the time of her decease.

Mrd: on Jul 5, at Fort Washita, by Rev Mr Kingsbury, Lt John D Bacon, U S Army, to Miss Virginia L Beall, d/o Maj Benj L Beall, U S Army.

Died: on Jul 17, in Wash City, John M Rutter, a native of Cornwall, England, & for the several years past a resident of Fauquier Co, Va, aged 62 years.

Died: Jul 26, in Newport, R I, Ann C Shaw, y/d/o J C Shaw, aged 29 years. Her death was caused by lockjaw, occasioned by a fall from a chaise on Wed of last week. The injury was not considered dangerous until early this week; & even on the morning of the day preceding her death, her physicians had hopes; but in the course of the day all hope rapidly declined, & she herself expressed in writing, for she could not speak, her feeling that she must die, & at half past 11 she calmly breathed her last. –Newport [R I] Spirit of the Times, Jul 27]

Died: on Aug 3, at St Joseph's Roman Catholic Asylum, Phil, Sister Petronilla, Superior to that Asylum for many years past.

Died: at his farm, near Wheeling, Saml Sprigg, an eminent citizen & counsellor at law, aged 59 years. [No date-current item.]

Died: on Aug 2, at the residence of Mrs Beeler, in Wash City, of cholera infantum, Geo Washington, infant s/o Geo W & Susan V Phillips, aged 9 months.

Wash Light Infty to meet at the Armory on Mon at 7 p m. By order: Jos B Tate, sec.

Orphan's Court of Wash Co, D C. Letters of adm on the personal estate of Mary Laurence, late of St Mary's Co, Md, dec'd. –Thos Greeves, adm

TUE AUG 8, 1843
Tow sons of Mr John McDonnell, a worthy & industrious citizen, residing in Cleveland center, were both drowned in the Cuyahoga on Sat week. The boys were aged about 5 & 9 years. The elder brother made an effort to rescue the youngest one who got on a log which precipitated him out into deep water. –Cleveland Herald

Capt Wm W Hunter, of the U S Navy, the inventor of the "propeller" which bears his name, is at present on a visit to Pittsburg in regard to the construction of a steam vessel now building at that place, which is to be adapted to the engine of his invention.

Boston, Aug 3. On Tue last, the 12 year old s/o Thos H Perkins, jr, of this city, Francis C, came to his death when the gun he had accidentally discharged, & the whole charge entered his body causing instant death. He was out with his gun, attempting to get into a boat at Swan Island, in Kennebec river, the country residence of Mr Perkins, when it went off. -Atlas

Rev Dr Jas Richards, professor of Theology in the Theological Seminary at Auburn, N Y, departed this life on Aug 2, in his 77th year.

Dr Hahnemann, the founder of the homoeopathic system of medicine, died at Paris, where he had long resided, on Jul 2, at age 88 years. He was born in 1755 at Meissen, of poor parents, & was received doctor in physic at Heidelberg in 1781, & discovered the new system in 1790.

Died: on Jul 27, at Peru, Ill, after a few hours illness, Frederic Hall, M D, L L D, of this city, aged 64. He has been known as one of our most eminent chemists, mineralogists, & geologists. He was born in Vermont, graduated in 1803 at Dartmouth College; subsequently Prof of Natural Philosophy in Middlebury College, afterwards Pres of Mount Hope College, near Balt, & at the time of his death was Prof of Chemistry in the Medical dept of the Columbia College in this city.

Died: on Aug 3, Frances Lucretia, infant d/o John H & Frances E Gibbs, aged 7 months & 11 days.

Fatal accident in Groton, Mass on Sat week is recorded in the Boston Post. Mr John H Rice, of Ashby, lost his life in circumstances similar to those which recently caused the death of the Rev Mr Beecher, in Ohio. He had discharged one barrel of a double-barreled gun, & while blowing out the smoke, the other was accidentally discharged, & its contents lodged in his head, causing instant death.

Temperance Boarding House: Mrs Jane Cunningham has fitted up the house on 7th st, opposite the Patriotic Bank. She is prepared to accommodate gentlemen with board on the most reasonable terms.

The U S ship **Boston** arrived at Boston Aug 4 after being out the last 11 months, of which 9 were at sea. The whole amount of her sailing is upwards of 50,000 miles. Ofcrs of the Boston:

J Collins Long, Cmder
J G Benham, Lt
Henry Walker, Lt
J F Mercer, Lt
J N Brown, Acting Lt

Reed Werden, Master
R J Dodd, Surgeon
J H Wright, Assist Surgeon
N G Rogers, Acting Purser

Midshipmen:
Reuben Harris
Stephen Quackenbush
R B Lowry
Elisha Whitton, Acting Gunner
J R Fox, Acting Boatswain

Chas Dyer
Francis Gregory

Geo J Lozier, Sailmaker
____ Page, Master's Mate

Passengers:
R M Walsh, Sec of Leg, Brazil   A N Smith, Midshipman, U S Navy

Ofcrs of the ship **Yorktown** arrived at N Y from the Pacific: J S Nicholas, Comder
Lts:
J P Drayton   C F McIntosh
C W Pickering
Acting Master, M K Washington   Purser, T B Nalle
Surgeon, Van Horn
Midshipmen:
H R Stevens   R Aulick
P Shirley   H G D Brown
H Waskey   S S Bassett
R Savage
Clerk, J T Page   Carpenter, J McDonnell
Boatswain, ____ Cavendy   Sailmaker, W Wand
Gunner, J Martin   Master's Mate, J Vanstanberg

Ofcrs of the U S ship **Decatur** bound for the coast of Africe: Joel Abbot, Cmder.
Benj J Totten, Lt   John Q Adams, Acting Master
Saml F Hazard, Lt   Lewis Warrenton, jr, Purser
John Jas Glasson, Lt   Lewis Wolffy, Surgeon
Edw C Ward, Lt   Chas Eversfield, Assist Surgeon
Passed Midshipmen:
John F Abbott   Jas M Duncan
Midshipmen:
John T McFarland   Saml B Rathbone
Saml Wallace   Jas E Jouett
Wm W Lowe   Jos S Dade
John P Abbott, Capt's Clerk   Robt C Rodman, Sailmaker
John Mills, Boatswain   Geo Hutchinson, Purser's Steward
Thos Lewis, Gunner   Peter Hanson, Yeoman
Jos G Thomas, Acting Carpenter   John Johnson, Surgeon's steward

WED AUG 9, 1843
On Oct 4, 1777, the battle of Germantown was fought. Gen Francis Nash, of N C, commanded the reserve guard, which covered the American retreat & resisted in the attack of Gen Grey. Gen Nash was mortally wounded, it is said, by the same shot which killed Maj Witherspoon, of N J brigade. Gen Nash was carried off the field to the neighborhood of the American camp, & in a few days, he died. Gen Washington, in his dispatches, mentions his death with expressions of deep regret. On Nov 4, 1777, Congress passed a resolution that his Excell Govn'r Caswell, of N C, erect a monument

of the value of $500, at the expense of the U S, in honor of the memory of Brig Gen Nash who fell bravely contending for the independence of his country. This has never been acted on. Gen Nash is buried in the burial ground attached to the Methodist meeting house, about half a mile above Kulpsville, in Towemensing township, Montg Co, where there are 4 headstones, 3 in good preservation, the largest is that of Gen Nash, the others are those of Maj White, of N J, an aid to Gen Sullivan, Col Boyd, & the other is unknown. They were all ofcrs of rank who died of wounds received at Germantown. The burial ground is secluded & about 24 miles from Phil. Note by the Editors: In a private letter to his brother, Gen Washington, speaking of the action at Germantown, observes our loss in killed & wounded was about 1,000 men. In a word it was a bloody day. Gen Sullivan in his letter to the President of N H, writes among the ofcrs lost, was the brave Gen Nash, & my 2 aids-de-camp, Majors Sherburne & White.

Masonic meeting: Federal Lodge #1, at the Hall, 12th & Pa ave, this evening at 8 p m. –Jas Lawrenson, sec

$5 reward for return of strayed or stolen gray Horse. The horse is well known as I have for the last 2 years worked him in my furniture wagon. –Leonard O Cook

Carriages for sale: the subscriber, having quit the Coach-making, & now engaged in the House-building & Carpenter's business, offers great bargains in a variety of carriages. –Jos Fraser, 1st ward

On Thu last a lad about 14 years, s/o Mr Thos McNeal, living 2 miles from Elkton, Md, fell from a load of hay, & was severely injured by the prongs of 2 pitchforks running into him. There is probability that he will not recover.

Luke Clarke, 19, & Anson U Hungerford, 17, apprentices to Messrs Rodman & Spear, cabinet makers, Rodman, Jefferson Co, N Y, were drowned while bathing on Jul 29. Clarke was an orphan, greatly esteemed; Hungerford's father resides in Michigan. They were carried by the current beyond their depth. The bodies were recovered.

The large steam flouring mill owned by Col Wm Book, in Newcastle, Mercer Co, Pa, & the carding mill & turning machine adjoining, were consumed by fire on Fri last. Loss estimated at $6,000.

We learn that the Hon W P Fessenden, a highly valued Rep in the last Congress from the State of Maine, declines being a candidate for re-election. He writes: "The situation of my private & domestic affairs at the present time renders such a determination imperative."

A convict named Green McDonald was recently pardoned by Gov Shannon, of Ohio. The Cincinnati Sun says a fraud was practiced to get him out of the pen. A ptn was circulated inviting Pres Tyler to that city, to which the names of distinguished citizens were attached. So soon as all the names were procured, the heading was taken off & a ptn to Gov Shannon for the pardon of McDonald put in its place.

Accident at Davidson College, N C, on Jul 26: at the festivities of commencement. While making arrangements to set off a fire-balloon, a pan of spirits of turpentine caught fire, & nearly the whole contents of the pan were thrown on Marshall Kennedy, a s/o the late M T C Kennedy, of Mecklenberg Co. He was so badly burned that he died the next day.

Eden Island for sale: about 25 miles from Wash & Gtwn, in Montg, Md: contains about 360 acs; commodious & moderately sized brick dwlg house, ice-house, barn, stables, & qrtrs, most of them new & in good condition. Apply to Mrs Mary B Selden, near Alexandria, D C, or to Lucius Cary Selden, Belmont P O, Loudoun Co, Va.

Meeting of the Faculty of the Medical Dept of the Columbian College, held Aug 8, on the sudden death of Dr Frederick Hall, Prof of Chemistry: resolved, that our sincere sympathy be tendered to his bereaved family. --W P Johnston, M D: Dean of the Faculty

The nuptials of John Milbanke, only s/o Sir Ralph Milbanke, Baronet, & Miss Emily Mansfield, d/o the late John Mansfield, & grand-dght of the late Gen S Smith, of Md, were solemnized on the 13th inst, in the presence of a numerous circle of noble friends, including Viscount Melbourne, Viscount & Viscountess Palmerston, the Earl & Countess Cowper. The happy pair have gone to pass the honeymoon at Diggeswell, Welwyn Herts, the seat of Mrs Mansfield. --London Court Journal, Jul 15

Mrd: on Jul 26, in the Presbyterian Church, Woodville, Miss, by Rev Jas Purviance, Rev Robt Livingston Stanton, Pastor of said church, to Mrs Anna Maria Blackford, of Wash, D C.

Died: on Jul 6, at the White Sulphur Springs, in Meriwether Co, Ga, in her 39th year, Mrs Eliza Alford, consort of the Hon Julius C Alford, of Troup Co.

Died: on Jul 26, at Jefferson Barracks, Missouri, at the residence of Dr De Camp, Mrs Mary Augusta, consort of Lt John De Camp, U S Navy, aged 26 years.

Died: on Aug 3, in PG Co, Md, of consumption, Mrs Louisa Coombs, of this city, in her 44th year. Mrs C suffered a long & lingering illness, which she bore with marked patience & resignation.

Died: on Aug 1, at Germantown, Phil Co, Pa, Geo Dannehower, sr, aged 91 years, a sldr of the Revolution. He was in the battles of Germantown, Princeton, Brandywine, & at the massacre of Paoli.

Died: on Jul 23, at Walnut Grove, Kanawha Co, Va, Mrs Ann Smith Summers, wid/o Geo Summers, in her 85th year.

Died: on Aug 7, Mary, infant d/o Sidney & Mary J De Camp, aged 6 months

Died: yesterday, in Wash City, Isabel Ridgway, infant d/o Enoch & Mary Ann Ridgway, aged 7 months & 10 days. Her funeral will be this afternoon, at 3 p m, from their residence at 11th & E sts.

Died: on Jul 14, at Nassau, New Providence, of fever, after an illness of 4 days, Purser Frederick Stevens, U S Navy, attached to the U S brig **Boxer**. The dec'd was a son of the late Cmdor Thos Holdup Stevens. [Aug 10 newspaper: Age 25 years; remains of Mr Stevens were interred in Potters' Field on Jul 14, with every honor: band of the 3rd West India Regt were in attendance, also a detachment of that corps under command of Capt Hairing, which fired 3 volleys after the service was concluded. His Excellency Sir F Cockburn, attended by this private sec; the ofcrs of H M ship **Thunder** & schnr **Lark**; a few American gentlemen in town, also followed the corse to the 'bourn from whence no traveler returns."]

The Vicksburg Sentinel announces the death of Dr Willis M Green, brother of Gen Duff Green, who was one of the founders of that paper in connexion with Dr Hagan. [No date-current item.]

Jas Bergen, Insurance broker, & J G Hamilton, a colored broker, of N Y, were arrested on Fri last, charged with a conspiracy to defraud the Atlantic Ins Co of $50,000. A shipmaster named Sutton was to be the principal instrument. [Aug 19th newspaper: Grand jury of the N Y Court of Gen Sessions have returned a true bill of indictment against Jas Bergen, Jeremiah G Hamilton, & Richd Sutton for conspiracy, in sum of $50,000.]

Danl Daily, aged 27 years, an Irishman by birth, engaged in digging a well in Bedford, Pa, was killed when carbonic acid gas overtook him when he descended the almost completed well.

It appears that the murderers of Capt Chas Dearborn & his mate did not know how to navigate the vessel, & were obliged to desert her. They did not get much money. Mr Conway, of Alexandria, now in N Y has recognized a gold watch that belonged to the mate, Mr Walter A Nicholl, who is represented as a respectable Virginia family, & a young man of property. His uncle is one of the firm of Wyckoff & Nicholl, in N Y, & he has a sister spending the summer at Newport, R I. The vessel belonged to Mr Thomas, of Alexandria.

THU AUG 10, 1843

Western Frontier: from the Missouri Reporter, Jul 31. Santa Fe traders: Capt Cooke, U S Army, made an official report to Gen Gaines, of this Military Div, in which it appears that he disarmed a company of Texians, under command of Col Snively, on Jun 30 last. The larger portion proceeded to Texas with Col Snively. Col Warfield was one of the band. McDaniel, one of the murderers of Charvis, held a capt's commission, given to him by Warfield. Warfield was the only one of the party who had a regular commission.

Letter from Gen Gaines to Brig Gen Z Taylor. Headqrtrs, St Louis, Missouri, Jul 27, 1843. I received the report of Capt St G Cooke, of the regt of dragoons, he had met with & very properly disarmed 100 men professing to be Texians, whose object was to attack & capture the Mexican caravans found on the Santa Fe road, yet some of the men are supposed to be hovering about ready to pounce upon the unoffending caravans. The escort authorized by the Dept of War will be ordered to assemble as soon after Aug 6 as practicable, at or near Independence. –Edmund P Gaines, Maj Gen U S Army commanding

Phil Ledger of Tue: great flood at Chester: the borough & its neighborhood present scenes of desolation: our shores are strewn with wrecks, our streets filled with ruins: the stream rose 6 feet in 5 minutes: the first chain-bridge built in the world, stands no more, erected 30 years ago. Messrs Eyers, Kitts, Brobston, & Paxton are severe sufferes. The factories of Mr Crozer, of Mr Dickson, & of Mr Riddle, have been swept away. The entire family of Mr Rhoads, consisting of himself, wife, & 2 small children, all perished. Mr Flower was saved: his devoted mulatto woman tried to save him & she was swept away. Not less than 20 persons have drowned.

Fletcher Webster, Sec to the Mission to China, went to sea from Boston on Sat last in the brig **Antelope**, for Canton.

Annual Commencement of Dartmouth College took place on Thu of last week. Among the Alumni present were: Gen Erastus Root, who had returned after an absence of 50 years; Hon Danl Webster; Gov Hubbard; Levi Woodbury; Messrs Newcomb, Morris, Choate, & others.

Hon Geo Plumer, of Westmoreland Co, Pa, father of Hon Arnold Plumer, M C, & one of the pioneers of the West, died on Jul 8.

While gentlemen were shooting at a mark in Brown Co, Ohio, opposite Maysville, on Wed last, Mr J Lawwell, a highly respectable citizen of that county, a bystander, was accidentally shot by one of the sportsmen. He lingered until Thu when he expired. He has left a wife & numerous friends. -Eagle

Destructive fire in Balt on Jul 26: Losses to Messrs Elmes & Seaver, of their large hat establishment. Others who lost property: Messrs Parker & Winchester.

Henry Martin Magie, aged 15, s/o Rev O V Magie, of Elizabethtown, N J, was drowned at Perth Amboy, while bathing, on Fri last.

On Sat last Mrs Lovejoy committed suicide at her residence in Newark, N J, by taking opium. She appears to have been of intemperate habits, as is also her husband.

Died: on Aug 2, at Guilford, Conn, Theodore Lay, aged 21 years.

Died: on Jul 29, in Macon, Ga, in her 16th year, Miss Rebecca Ann Lamar, dght & only child of Gen Mirabeau B Lamar, late Pres of the Republic of Texas.

A young man named Buexestine was on last Tue committed for trial on the oath of Mr De Saules, under the charge of stealing money from the bar-drawer in his refectory, while Mr De Saules was in the cellar drawing beer for his customers.

$20 reward for dark bay Horse, strayed or stolen: is shod all round; & is pigeon toed. –Thos M Fuggitt, residence near the Navy Yard.

Orphan's Court of Wash Co, D C. Aug 8, this day, the will of Louisa Coomb, late of said county, dec'd, was presented to said Court for probate by the excs, & none of the heirs being present, notice is given the probate to said will will be on Tue next. –Ed N Roach, reg/o wills

FRI AUG 11, 1843
Boarding & Day School: Mrs C Breschard Burr at corner of E & 9th sts, Wash. School will re-open on Sep 11: board & tuition in English & French per annum-$200.

French & English Seminary for Young Ladies: corner of D & 4½ sts, opposite City Hall. Misses Reed & Cheshire will open on Sep 4. References:

Rev H Stringfellow	Dr P Bradley	Philip R Fendall
Rev Chas Rich	Rev John C Smith	Amos Kendall
Gen Jesup	Dr B Washington	John A Smith
Henry M Morfit	W W Seaton	Rev R R Gurley
Capt Howie	Jos S Wilson	

Late English papers. Fatal colliery accident on Mon at one of the pits belonging to the Fenton Park Co, an explosion of fire-damp occurred in which 9 lives were lost: sufferers were: Wm Baker 22, a sgl man; Jas Dawson 34, left a wife & 4 children; Peter Borston, left 3 children, Jacob Tipton 12 years old; Moses Heath 14; Jas Smith 38, left a wife near her confinemant & 3 children; John Shone 28, sgl; Saml Thornton 39, left 7 children; &

Alfred Tomkinson 20, sgl. The last 2 died in their humane attempt to rescue their fellow sufferers.

Dover [N H] Inquirer: states that Mr Benning Hanscom, a worthy & respectable citizen of Great Falls, was killed instantly on Jul 21, while at work with a circular saw. He had split a small piece of timber, leaving one part on the bench by the saw, when the former was driven through his heart, causing instant death.

Ofcrs attached to the U S ship **Columbus**, bearing the broad pennant of Cmdor Chas W Morgan, Jun, 1843.

B Cooper, Capt		E G Tilton, Cmder	
Lts:			
J M Watson	J R Goldsborough	T J Page	H N Harrison
F Chatard	A H Kelty	B F Sands	
		D B Ridgely	

L Maynard, 1st Master	P G Clark, Chaplain
Henry Cadwalder, 2nd Master	F Schley, Com'rs Sec
B F Bache, Surgeon	J McDuffie, Prof of Math
J N Todd, Purser	V L Godon, Passed Assist Surg
E L West, Lt Marines	J Hastings, Assist Surgeon

Passed Midshipmen:

F K Murray	J H Brown	E Beale	J C Howell

Midshipmen:

L McDougall	G D Chenowith	G S King	J L Fergeson
J M Bradford	W H Parker	G T Sims	W W Wiklinson
C S Bell	D Coleman	E T Andrews	
C K Graham	E Barret	E C Grafton	
E Johnston	G Harrison	S Phelps	

St C F Sutherland, Cmder's Clk	Chas Cobb, Gunner
J Tilton, Capt's Clk	Patrick Dee, Carpenter
H Spaulding, Purser's Clk	J Bruce, Sailmaker
Jas Simpson, Boatswain	Thos Shanton, Master's Mate

All are in fine health, not having lost a man by sickness.

Mrd: Tue, by Rev John C Smith, Mr John B Heno, of New Orleans, to Miss Eleanor Rollins, of Wash City.

Massachusetts Gazetter, an old publication: "In 1763, Shubael Thompson found a land turtle marked on the shell I W 1746, [supposed to be John Williams, who lived in the neighborhood at the time.] It had lost one foot. It was again found by Elijah Clapp in 1773, by Wm Shaw in 1775, by Jonathan Soule in 1784, by Jonathan Soule in 1790, Zenas Smith in 1791, & by Elijah Soule in 1810. Jonathan Soule found him again about 15 years ago, & again by him the present year, Jul, 1843. All the persons by whom it was marked formerly lived in the neighborhood where it was always found. –Thos Bennett

SAT AUG 12, 1843
High Court of Errors & Appeals of the State of Mississippi, pronounced by Chief Justice Sharkey, on Mar 29, 1843, in the case of John S Brien against John B Williamson, on the question of the validity of contracts for the sale of slaves introduced into the State, as merchandise, since May 1, 1833. The Constitution was adopted in 1832: "The introduction of slaves into this State as merchandise, or for sale, shall be prohibited from & after the first day of May, 1833: Provided, that the actual settler or settlers shall not be prohibited from purchasing slaves in any State in this Union & bringing them into this State for their own individual use, until the year 1845." The contract in violation of law or against public policy cannot be enforced: Judgment affirmed. Mar 29, 1843. [Published at the request of the Members of the Bar from different parts of the State in attendance at Jackson.]

I wish to rent a farm, in a healthy part of the country, large enough to employ from 6 to 16 hands. Apply to me personally or by letter postpaid, stating particulars. –C Hogan, Oxford, N C

C B Thornton has taken over the store recently occupied by Mr W C Orme, a Dry Goods store, on Pa ave.

Committed to the jail of Fred'k Co, Md, on Aug 3, as a runaway, a black boy, who calls himself Bill Hopkins, about 16 years of age. He says he belongs to Alex'r Todd, Ridgeville, Fred'k or Carroll Counties, Md. The owner is requested to come & have him released. He will be discharged according to law. -Geo Rice, Sheriff of Fred'k Co.

Annual Commencement at St John's College, N Y: distribution of premiums: Aug 12, 1843.

John Carroll, of N Y
John Turner, Brooklyn
Thos Doran, N Y
John O'Hara, Brooklyn, N Y
Thos Carroll, N Y
Hugh Fitzsimmons, Troy
Robt Kenny, Petersburg, Va
Wm D Morange, Albany
Theo Hatfield, N Y
Andrew J Smith, N Y

Thos Coghlin, N Y
Alex A Allemong, Charleston, S C
Gustavus Coutan, N Y
John O'Reilly, N Y
Henry Doyer, N Y
Philip Kerrigan, N Y
Thos Nowlan, Yorkville
Thos Kelly, N Y
Robt Sheehan, N Y
Robt Hogan, N Y

Jas Reynolds, N Y
Jas Brenah, Charleston
Dennis McCarty McGowan, Petersburg, Va
Van Livingston, N Y
Julien Livingston, N Y
Oscar Temegnio, N Y
Vincent Boisaubin, Madison, N J
Jos Del Campo, Tabasco, S A
Pancho Flores
John Quinn

John Devereux, Phil
Edw Mullen, N Y
Edw Petit, Bloomingdale
Edw Murray, N Y
Robt Sheehan, N Y

Wm D Morange
Wm Dutch
Lorenzo Meduna
Geo H Winship

Paul Berges, though not long enough in the Institution to obtain premiums, deserves particular mention for his application, great success, & gentlemanly deportment. Premium for the extraordinary diligence & success John Carroll. Premium for good conduct Thos Doran. Improvement on the flute Thos Nowlan; first premium for the piano Theo Hatfield; 2nd premium Oscar Temegulo; accesserunt Pancha Flores & Edw Burke; premium for the violin Andrew J Smith.

Was found, some time ago, a Gold Chain, which owner can have by coming forward, proving property, & paying for this advertisement. Inquire of Benj Spelman, at Brown's Hotel.

PG Plantation for sale: decree of the Crt of Chancery of Md, passed Jul 11 last, in a cause wherein Arundel Smith & Henry G S Key are cmplnts, & Wm G Sanders & Caroline E Sanders his wife, & others are dfndnts. Public sale at the hotel in Beltsville, on Sep 2, all that part of a tract of land called "***Friendship Enlarged***," or by some other name, lying in the neighborhood of Beltsville, PG Co, allotted by a decree of the Court aforesaid to the said Caroline, in the partition of the real estate of her father, the late Richd Snowden, which was sold by her to one Richd Smith, & by him to Saml Fitzhugh, John B Beall, & others, dfndnts, who have been since in the possession thereof, consisting of about 351¼ acs of land, more or less. -John Johnson, A Randall, Trustees

Real Estate at Public Sale: on Sep 1 next, 2 valuable plantations in PG Co, Md, 3 miles north of Upper Marlborough, Md. The Mill tract-387 9/10th acs; adjoins the lands of Chas Hill, Thos W Clagett, & Wm M Bowie; improvements are 3 large barns & a new saw-mill, now in operation on one of the best streams in the neighborhood. The other plantation containing 269 1-5 acs, adjoins the land of Otho B Beall & Washington J Beall; improvements are a dwlg house, 2 large tobacco barns, stabling, & other out-houses. –Roderick McGregor

David Babe & Wm Matthews, the men charged with piracy & murder on board the schnr **Sarah Lavinia**, of Alexandria, underwent a judicial examination at N Y on Tue, & were fully committed on the charges preferred against them: trial next Nov. Webster, the other member of the crew who participated in this dreadful outrage, is believed to have been arrested at Buffalo.

The case of the Commonwealth of Mass against Wm Wyman, Pres of the Phoenix Bank in Charleston, Thos Brown, jr, the Cashier of the Bank, & W H Skinner, a Dir & borrower of the Bank, on an indictment of embezzling the funds of the bank, came on for trial on Mon last in the Court of Common Pleas for Middlesex Co, now sitting at Concord. Skinner being indicted as accessory before the fact, applied for & was granted a separate trial. The others pleaded not guilty. Messrs Danl Webster & Franklin Dexter appeared as counsel for Wyman, & Messrs Rufus Choate & Sidney Bartlett for Brown & Skinner. Mr Asabel Huntington, D S for the 2nd dist, appeared on the part for the Commonwealth, assisted by Mr Wells. [Aug 22 newspaper: The trials of Wyman & Brown, at Concord, Mass, for embezzling, have resulted in a non-agreement & discharge of the jury in the case of the former, & a verdict of acquittal in the case of the latter.]

Died: on Jul 19 last, at his residence, **Woodberry Forest**, Madison Co, Va, Gen Wm Madison, in his 82nd year. He was a sldr of both wars, & was for many years a member of the Virginia Leg. Gen M was the youngest brother of Pres Madison, &, having deserved well of his country by his own services, it was left to another of the family to illustrate & adore the highest honor in her gift.

Died: on Aug 9, in Wash City, after an illness of 15 days, Richd Tasker Jackson, in his 18th year, s/o Wm B Jackson, formerly of PG Co, Md.

MON AUG 14, 1843
Harrisburg Intelligencer says: Gen Thos M Jolly, of the 23rd dist, is the first delegate appointed in Pa to the Whig National Convention to be held in Balt in May next, & is instructed to support Henry Clay for Pres.

An engineer on board the steamer **Tennessee Valley** threw one of the firemen overboard whilst the steamer was on her last trip from New Orleans to this place. [No names given.]

Govn'r Thomas has offerd a reward of $200 for the arrest of Jas Williams, who murdered his wife in St Mary's Co, a short time since. [Aug 21 newspaper: Jas Williams arrested Aug 20 in Wash City by Mr Dennis Pumphrey, & by him handed over to ofcr Burr, who lodged the prisoner in jail for safe keeping. He wept when lodged in jail and desired that a priest might be sent for.]]

The traitor B H A Collins, of Eastham, has been appointed light-house keeper at Cape Cod. –Boston Atlas [This Mr Collins is the person who, in the last Leg of Mass, deserted to the Locofocos, after having been elected a Whig, & by his vote secured the election of Morton as Govn'r of the State.]

Fred'k C Adams, s/o John Adams, of this village, on Wed last, was at Athens, & a rifle was fired by some person directly towards him, & the ball struck him above the eye & he was senseless for a time. The wound is not dangerous. Will people never learn to be careful with fire-arms? -Catskill Mass

Drowned on Feb 1, at the Falls of Wallamette river, near the Methodist mission, in Oregon Co, Mr Cornelius Rogers, Mrs Rogers, her sister Aurelie Leslie, Squire Crocker, & 2 Clatsop Indians. While passing over the rapids above, the boat was accidentally carried over the falls. Mr Rogers had married a d/o the Rev Mr Leslie, of the Methodist mission on the Wallamette, & resided near that mission. -Boston Journal

Died in Paris in Apr last, a remarkable person, Count Ribbing Leven, one of the assassins of Gustavus III, King of Sweden. It was at a masked ball, given at the opera house at Stockholm on Mar 16, 1792, that Gustavus was shot & in 13 days died. Ankerstroem, leading member of the opposition, was arrested & confessed his guilt. Cout Ribbing, Count Horn, & other accomplices were tried & capitally convicted. Ankerstroem only was executed.

The Hon Eli Shortridge, judge of the 9th judicial circuit of Alabama, died on Jul 20 at his residence in Talladega. His age was about 55 years. –Tuscaloosa Monitor

Mrd: on Aug 3, at Jacksonville, [E F] by Rev Mr Aubrey, of St Augustine, Mr Geo Grouard, Editor of "the Tropical Plant," to Miss Mary A Ryan, eldest d/o L Ryan, formerly of Va.

In the Supreme Crt of Ohio a young lady, Maria F Swank, had recovered $4,000 in a suit of slander against John B Zimmerman, a wealthy citizen of Hocking Co.

Gtwn Vinegar Depot: formerly kept on the Little Falls Mills, has been removed to Gtwn, where by new arrangements the largest orders can be filled. –J Rother, corner of Green & Alley sts, immediately back of the Union Hotel

Local News: On Sat last the jury returned a verdict of Not Guilty in the trial of R P Dowden. The audience clapped their hands on the announcement of the verdict. [The prisoner had been charged with stealing Treas notes.]

Stray cow & calf came to me near Benning's Bridge: owner is to come forward, prove property, pay charges, & take her away. –Henry Miller

TUE AUG 15, 1843
Hiram S Gardner, a young man acting as a Clerk in the Post Ofc at Johnson's Creek, Niagara Co, N Y, has ran off after being detected in purloining $90 from a letter received at that place.

John B Lamar, one of the Reps elect to Congress from the State of Ga, has resigned.

Mrd: on Sun, by Rev John C Smith, Mr Wm Henning to Miss Eliz Rolls, all of Wash City.

Mrd: on Aug 11, at Dewbery, Hanover Co, Va, by Rev John Cooke, Callender St Geo Noland, U S Navy, to Miss Mary Edmonia, only d/o the late Thos Nelson Berkeley.

Died: on Aug 12, at his residence in PG Co, Md, Mr Nathan Summers, in his 84th year.

Wm G Knight, a member of the London bar, who absconded in Jan, 1841, & came to this country with a large amount of money, the proceeds of sundry forged bills of exchange which he sold in London, had been recently arrested in Iowa, by Jas Young, of the Phil police.

Criminal Court-Wash: Aug 14.
1-Henry Fletcher, free negro, convicted of an assault with intent to kill his wife: 2 years in the pen. Fined $5 & costs on the assault charge.
2-Wm S Wright, convicted of obtaining money under false pretences from Edw Dyer: 2 year in the pen.
3-Robt Black, a negro boy, convicted of arson: 2 years in the pen.
4-G L Giberson, convicted of falsely imprisoning Jacob Wechter: fined $50 & costs.
5-Jas V Patten, convicted of assault & illegal arrest of Jacob Wechter: fined $5 & costs.
6-Marcus C Buck, convicted of an assault on S Stittinius: fined $30 & costs.
7-Buckner Bayliss, convicted of resisting L S Beck, cnstbl, in the discharge of his duty: fined $20 & costs.
8-Jas O'Neale, convicted of an assault & battery: fined $5 & costs.
9-Wm Richardson, convicted of an assault & battery on Mrs Mitchell: fined $5 & costs, & stand imprisoned till the fine & costs were paid.

Texian land for sale: 2 tracts: one has 1,470 acs, the other 640 acs, located & Gov't title. I will sell cheap for cash & trade. –Saml Rose, Gtwn, D C

Public Sale: decree of the County Court of Orange, rendered Jul 24, the subscribers will sell at public auction on Aug 31, **Willis Grove**, the late residence of Wm C Willis, dec'd. This estate lies in Orange Co, on the Rapid-Ann river, contiguous to the manufacturing Mills of Robt T Willis, & contains 1,010 acs. This farm is about 2 miles from the turnpike which leads from Fredericksburg to Orange Court-house, within 15 miles of

Gordonsville Depot: improvements are extensive, consisting of a dwlg-house, a 2 story frame bldg adjacent, a factory, a kitchen, stables, & a large barn. The subscriber will also sell another tract of 560 acs lying in the *Piney Woods*, about 4 miles from Willis Grove. –Robt T Willis, Richd H Willis, excs of Wm C Willis

WED AUG 16, 1843
Josiah S Little, of Portland, has been nominated for Congress by the Whigs of the Cumberland Dist, Maine. Hon Wm Pitt Fessenden, the late member, having been first nominated & declined.

The Mercer Co, Pa, paper states that Mr Thos Williams, his son, aged 12 years, & another young man, name not given, drowned while bathing about a mile above Edenbury, on Sat week. Mr Williams has left a wife & family to mourn his loss.

Died: on Aug 10, suddenly, at *Beall's Pleasure*, his farm, near Bladensburg, in his 30th year, of congestive disease, Dr Lemuel Sheriff, s/o Levi Sheriff, of D C, leaving a widow & 3 children to mourn the irreparable bereavement of a kind & affectionate husband & father. –W

Died: yesterday, Sydney, infant d/o T L Thruston.

For rent: commodious 2 story brick house on Missouri st, between 4½ & 6th sts. –Geo Watterston

For sale, for a term of years, a likely negro woman & 2 children, a boy & a girl. The woman is a good house servant, washer & ironer, & plain cook. –H R Maryman, Capitol Hill

By Divine permission there will be a Camp Meeting held on Aug 16 by the Colored Society of Bethel Church upon the plantation of Mr Jacob Hoyle, who will be the chief manager to preserve order upon the occasion. Our friends & Christians of all denominations, are invited to participate with us. N B: Horse feed will be sold near the ground. No intoxicating liquors will be permitted on or near the ground, not even cider.

THU AUG 17, 1843
Wash Corp-Aug 14. 1-Ptn from Mary Ann Rogan: referred to the Cmte of Claims. 2-Ptn from David S Waters: referred. 3-Ptn of Thos Welsh: referred to the Cmte of Claims. 4-Ptn of E Brooke & others, for a gravel footway on B st south, between 12th & 14th sts: referred to the Cmte on Improvements. 5-Cmte of Claims: Act for the relief of Eliza Lowe, wid/o the late Randall Lowe: read twice. 6-Cmte of Claims: referred-ptn for the relief of Wm Cruitzfeldt: laid on the table. 7-Cmte of Claims: bill for the relief of Jas E Thumlert; relief of Geo W Kinduck; & for the relief of Thos Lewis: read twice. 8-Ptn of J F Callan & others was referred: act authorizing a reservoir at the corner of 7th & E sts.

School for Civil Engineers: Washington Academy, E st,: will re-open on the first Mon in Sept next. –J Fill, Principal

For rent: 2 story brick house on 12th st, occupied for many years by the late P W Gallaudet. Inquire of Wm Gunton.

Circuit Court of Wash Co, D C. Louis Baker has applied to be discharged from imprisonment under the act for the relief of Insolvent Debtors: hearing on Sep 4 next. –Wm Brent, clk

FRI AUG 18, 1843
East Florida correspondence from a physician: Mr Hamburg & 4 ofcrs actually died of congestive fever during the years 1840 thru 1842. Dr Elwes died of brain fever; Maj Wilcox died of consumption; Capt Garner & Maj Brown both died of yellow fever contracted in St Augustine, & which there is ample evidence to show had been imported from Charleston. –A Physician, St Augustine, E F, Aug 5, 1843

Mr & Mrs True's Female Seminary, Capitol Hill, Washington. Terms: $4 to $10 per qrtr, depending on studies pursued.

Trustee's sale of valuable real estate in Gtwn: virtue of a deed of trust from Walter Smith, principal agent of the late Importing & Exporting Co of Gtwn, to the subscriber, dated Jun 24, 1824: sale on Oct 2 next: that block of bldgs at the n e corner of Cherry st continued & Water st, Gtwn, formerly occupied by said Company, embracing 2 three story brick warehouses fronting on Water st, & another 3 story brick bldg on Cherry st continued; also, a lot next north of the above, extending north on Cherry st continued to the premises of P W Magruder, on which is a small frame dwlg; also, 4 brick warehouses on south side of Water st, opposite to the first named bldgs. A plat of the property will be exhibited at the time of the sale. -J I Stull, Trustee -E S Wright, auct

Circuit Court of Wash Co, D C. T D Jones; Robt Mills; each applied to be discharged from imprisonment under the act for relief of Insolvent Debtors. Jones' hearing on Aug 28; Mills hearing on Sep 4. –Wm Brent, clk

At the cloth factory of Mr Richd Evans, in Danbury, on Aug 2, Mr Geo Sykes, a workman, was killed in an accident when the fulling mill was in operation. He was 24 years of age & a native of Yorkshire, Eng. –Hartford Courant

Balt, Aug 16. Drowned yesterday, while bathing, at Spring Gardens, Jos Benson Reese, s/o Rev John L Reese. The body was recovered in about 25 minutes. –Sun

At the first exhibition of the Rutland [Vt] County Agricultural Society, held at Castleton in 1819, Henry Francisco was present, aged 137 years, & ploughed a furrow with the oxen that day exhibited.

The ceremony of laying the corner-stone of the Epiphany Episcopal Church, on G st, between 13th & 14th sts, took place last Mon. Ceremonies were opened by the Rev Messrs Harris & Bean. Rev Mr Butler, of Gtwn, delived an address. Rev Mr French closed the ceremonies.

Miss Charlotte Pruden, aged 14 years, d/o Deacon Pruden, of Orange, Conn, was burnt to death last Sun in that town. She was alone in the house with an invalid sister, when her clothes caught fire, & she was so badly burnt that she died next day.

The first Bank in America was established by the Legislature of South Carolina in 1712. It issued L48,000 in bills of trust, which were lent out at interest.

An auctioneer of Exeter, Eng, announces that he is instructed by the excs of the late Rev Edw Leigh, of Paddington, to offer for sale, by tender, the satin cap worn by King Charles I at his execution.

SAT AUG 19, 1843
Emigration to Texas. 200 Emigrants Wanted: to accompany Mr Jacob Eliot to Trinity colony, in Texas, between Aug 10 & 15th next: $8 per month in cash will be paid to such young men as wish to go on as emigrants & work for the company till Mar 1 next; at which time, it is presumed, most of them will wish to enter upon the cultivation of their own lands: each emigrant will be entitled to 100 acs of good farming land: to heads of families the same wages will be given & 200 acs of land. Call on the undersigned, agent of the company, at his ofc on 4th st, over W Lynn & Co's auction room, or by letter, post paid, which will be duly attended to. –E B Ely, agent: Louisville, Ky, Jun 24, 1843

Naval Gen Court Martial has been ordered to convene on board the U S ship **Pennsylvania**, at Norfolk, on Aug 23, for the trial of Lt Addison R Taliaferro, & such others as may be brought before it. The Court will consist of:

Cmdor Jas Biddle, Pres
Cmdor Stephen Cassin
Capt Thos T Webb
Capt John Percival
Capt Bladen Dulany
Capt Jos Smoot
Capt John Gwinn
Cmder Wm Jameson
Cmder Wm M Armstrong
Cmder Robt B Cunningham
Cmder John Rudd
Cmder Jas P Wilson
Lt Wm Green-Members
John L Upshur, Norfolk, Judge Advocate

Ofcrs ordered to the frig **Savannah**, at N Y
Capt, Andrew Fitzhugh
Lts, H K Hoff, Wm H Noland, R F Pinkney
Surgeon, Edw Gilchrist; Purser, Dangerfield Fauntleroy
Passed Midshipman, Jas S Ridgely
Midshipmen, John Rell, Geo E Morgan
Gunner, Jas M Cooper
Carpenter, Francis M Cecil
Sailmaker, Wm Ryan

The last rays of hope for the safety of the U S schnr **Grampus** being now extinguished, we perform the mournful duty of publishing a list of the names of her ofcrs & crew:
Lt Commanding, Albert E Downes
Lts, Geo M McCreery, Wm S Swann, Hunn Gansevoort
Assist Surgeon, E H Conway; Purser, Jas S Thatcher
Acting Master, I S K You
Midshipmen, Andrew J Lewis, Edw N Beadel, Geo Minshall
Capt's Clk, Geo L McKenney; Ship's Steward, Isaac Stevens
Boatswain's Mates, Robt Ray, John Cook
Gunner's Mate, Wm Gale; Carpenter's Mate, Theodore Myrick
Ofcrs' Steward, Jos R *Servier; Ofcrs' Cook, Jas Hopkins
Qrtrmasters, Thos Piner, Geo Benson, John Carr
Captains of Forecastle, John Ryan, Jas Smith
Qrtr Gunners, Henry Edwards, Jas Fritz, Jas Bowen
Ship's Cook, Lewis Whillow
Yeoman, Chas L Clapp

Seamen:

H P Rollins	Clans Jakelsen	Thos Walsh
Antonio Rodrigues	Peter Collins	Wm Penny
Wm Conolly	John Hughes	Wm Gould
Wm Toland	Wm Hammond	
Price Argyle	Saml Chase	

Ordinary Seamen:

Hiram Carter	Wm Johnston	Jos Jones
Geo McGordes	Geo Spencer	John Scott
Wm Allen	Danl B Waldron	Patrick Moran
John J Palmer	Geo Collars	John Cugir
Thos Johnson	John Brown	Chas Howell
Isaiah Cooper	Henry Lewis	

Landsmen:

Ebenezer Perry	Thos Fritz
Peter Schannal	John B Mitchell
Edw Upson	Alex'r L Huntington

Henry Carter	Wm L Newhull	
Boys:		
Jas Webb	Nicholas P Broughton	John P Primrose
Henry Gray	John Murphy	Benj F Batts
Edwin C Holmes	John A Leonard	John Williams
Geo Geinzler	Nathl Kennedy	Henry Greenfield

[*Possibly Servier-name has a blotch partially over it. S___ier.]

[Aug 26 newspaper: U S ship **Pennsylvania**, Norfolk, Va, Aug 21, 1843. Sir: in reading your paper, I saw an account of the ofcrs & crew reported lost in the U S schnr **Grampus**. One of them was Isaac Stevens, ships steward; but I am very happy to state that I am alive & well. Several others in the list that did not go out of this port in her: Chas L Clapp, seaman, Geo Benson, q m, & Jas Smith, capt of forecastle. –Isaac Stevens P S: I forgot to mention that I had been in her previous to her going to sea this last time, about 2 years & 4 months, but left her on account of being sick. I S]

Naval Orders: 1-Cmder T W Freelon, Navy Yard, N Y 2-Cmder J R Sands, command of sloop **Falmouth**, vice J M McIntosh, relieved at his own request. 3-Lt Col S Miller, of Marines, relieved from recruiting service, & ordered to assume command in person of the barracks at Brooklyn. 4-Capt & Brvt Maj W Dulany, Superintendent of recruiting service, headqrtrs at Balt.

Mrd: on Aug 17, by rev Mr Stringfellow, Mr Geo D Wise, s/o the late Geo S Wise, U S Navy, to Laura, y/d/o Dr Frederic May, of Wash City.

Died: on Jul 28, in Leesburg, Va, Miss Olivia Clagett, d/o the late Dr Henry Clagett; a most exemplary sister, friend, & Christian.

Died: on Aug 5, in Lancaster, Pa, in her 50th year, Mrs Lydia Moore Reynolds, w/o John Reynolds, of Cornwall, in the county of Lebanon, & d/o the late Capt Saml Moore, of the Pa Line in the Army of the Revolution. Retiring & unobtrusive in her disposition, & disregarding all the allurements of a fashionable life, she devoted herself entirely to the duties of a dght, wife, mother, & Christian.

The freight train of cars from Middletown ran off the track on Tue and one passenger in the car, Mr Fitzsimmons, a very respectable man, with a family residing at Goshen, survived the accident, in great agony, for 3 hours.

About 43 years ago a British brig of war, mounting 20 brass guns, & having a very large amount of specie on board, sunk, with all hands, off Cape Henlopen. We learn from the Phil Inquirer that Capt Meeker, of N Y, whose ingenuity in such enterprises is well known, is now at the place where the brig was lost, with apparatus for raising her, or at least recovering her guns, & if possible, her treasure.

$50 reward for runaway servant woman Ann Middleton, a mulatto, 35 years of age.
–Wm W Harper, Alexandria, D C

MON AUG 21, 1843
Salem, Mass, Aug 17. The Hon Benj Pickman died yeaterday, in consequence of the fatal accident of the upsetting of his carriage a few weeks since. He was descended from a long line of respectable ancestors of this place. He was educated at Cambridge & married the dght of that eminent merchant Elias Hasket Derby. He served as a member of the Hse/o Reps in the Congress from Mar 4, 1809 ending Mar 3, 1811.

NOTICE: I, Johns Hopkins, do hereby caution & forewarn all persons from receiving or negotiating a certain note of hand, given by me in consideration of articles purchased at the sale of Jas B Taggart, made in Gtwn, Aug 18, 1843. Note is for $168.00, 90 days after date, with interest, made payable to Jeremiah Orme, & by him endorsed. I caution all persons from negotiating or receiveing the said note, as I have claims against the said Jas B Taggart more than sufficient to offset the amount due on the said note. –John Hopkins [See below.]
NOTICE: I, Jeremiah Orme, do hereby caution & forewarn all persons from receiving or negotiating a certain not of hand given by me in consideration of the purchase of articles at the sale of Jas M Taggart, made in Gtwn, Aug 18, 1843. Note is for $234. 99, 90 days after date, made payable to John Hopkins, & by him endorsed. I caution all persons from negotiating or receiving the said note, as I have claims against the said Jas B Taggart more than sufficient to offset the amount due on said note. –Jeremiah Orme

Orphan's Court of Wash Co, D C. The administrator of Mathew Pope, dec'd, appt'd the 3rd Tue of Oct next, for the final settlement of the estate of said dec'd. –Ed N Roach, reg/o wills

Died: on Jul 30, at his residence in Mason Co, Ky, Thos Tolly Worthington, in his 72nd year, leaving a numerous & highly respectable posterity. He was the s/o the late Saml Worthington, of Balt Co, & emigrated to Ky in 1795.

Died: on Wed last, at Salem, N J, Mrs Jane Hall, in her 88th year. She was the consort of the late Wm Hall, one of the earliest printers of the city of Balt, & the partner of Benj Franklin in printing & publishing the first newspaper in Phil.

St Mary's College, Balt, will resume classes on the first Mon in Sept.
–Gilbert Raymond, D D, Pres

Aug 18, 1843: the Enosinian Society of Columbian College expresses the feelings of the Society with regard to the loss sustained by them in the death of their honorary member & professor, the late Fred'k Hall, M D-L L D. Sympathy extended to his family.
–Jos R Garlick, Pres -Luther R Smoot, Rec Sec

$150 reward for 3 persons who escaped from the county jail of PG Co, Md, on Aug 19, by the assistance of some villain or villains, or $50 for either. 1-Jacob Sheffer, there for kidnapping, is 40 or 45, very stout made, says he was raised near Mercersburg, Pa. 2-John Beach, there for burglary, is about 23 or 24, & very fierce when spoken to. 3-Negro Danl, there for the murder of Smith, is very black & stout, speaks short & crabbed. –E S Baldwin, Sheriff PG Co, Upper Marlboro, Md

For rent: 3 story house on Pa ave, near the Railroad. Apply to Edw Simmes.

TUE AUG 22, 1843
Election Returns: Congressional representation from Ky:

Whigs	Locofocos
Willis Green	Linn Boyd
Henry Grider	Geo A Caldwell
John White	Jas Stone
W B Thomasson	Richd French
Garrett Davis	John W Tibbatts

For rent, a 3 story brick house in Bryan's Row, between 9th & 10th sts, on N Y ave. This house is built in the best modern manner, was completed in Oct last, & has just been papered. For further information inquire of the present occupant, or of the owner, Jos Bryan, who resides in the same block.

From the Oregon: the Methodist Missionary Society received advices from their establishment of Apr 1. The Rev Mr Frost, one of the missionaries, with his family, had left for the U S, via the Sandwich Islands. Some time in Mar, Mr Olly, a member of the mission, a carpenter, was drowned in the Columbia. He was an Englishman by birth, but for some time previous to his entering the mission had resided at Troy. He was married the evening before he left N Y for Oregon, some 6 years since.

Simon Smith, one of the deck hands on board the steamboat **Cinderella**, on Wed, while the boat was lying at Elizabethport, N J, hung himself with a rope, attached between two railroad cars on the deck.

Loss of the steamer **Pegasus**, which plied between Leith & Hull for several years, left Leith on Aug 19, struck on a sunken rock inside the Fern Islands, near the Goldstone Rock: water rushed in & the vessel sunk. Mr Billie, a passenger, Hillyard, another passenger, were holding on by the mast. A paper of later date had the following list of cabin passengers booked at Leith:

Mrs Edgington, from Edinburgh	Miss Floors
Miss Hopetoun	Miss Briggs
Miss Barton	Mrs McLeod

Mr McLeod
Mr Torry, from Hull
Mr Baillie, attendant on Mr Torry, saved
Mr Elton, the actor
Mr Hodgson

Rev Mr J McKenzie, Glasgow
Mr Banks
Mr Elliot & son, bought from Dundee
Mr Moxham
Mr Milne

Mr Hodgson, is brother of Mr W B Hodgson, sec of the Liverpool Mechanics' Institution. Rev Mr McKenzie is the colleague of the Rev Dr Wardlaw in the Theological Academy, Glasgow. His wife & family are at present living in Portobello. Mr Torry was an English gentleman of weak mind, who had been in Scotland for the benefit of his health. Among the passengers were the only son & dght of the Rev Field Flowers, the clergyman at Tealby, near Market Rasen, Lincolnshire. We have also the names of Mr Jas Hunter, s/o Mr Hunter, ironmonger, 15 Howe st; D Whimpster, late with Messrs Ireland & Son, linen drapers, South Bridge; Mr Martin, of Great Russell st, London, but a native of Edinburgh, & son. Susan Allan, d/o a sldr in the 25th regt, who was intending to go out to her father in India along with the sldrs of the 56th regt who were on board.

WED AUG 23, 1843
To the Editors. Wash, Pa, Aug 14, 1843. I send you a copy of an autograph manuscript of a patriot & sldr of the Revolution, the late Maj C P Bennett, of Delaware, & some years Govn'r of that State. The manuscript was mislaid, but being recently found, it was transmitted to the Hon Thos M T McKennan, of Pa. Manuscript is 2 colums long & contains the names of: Col Saml Patterson, of Newcastle Co, Dela

Capt Thos Kean
Gen Hugh Mercer
Gen Sullivan
Gen Putnam
Gen Baron De Kalb
Gen Lincoln
Gen Lord Cornwallis
Maj Gen Gates
Gen Green
Gen Morgan
Maj Jas Hamilton, of Pa
Col John Lawrence, of S C

Col Tarleton
Capt Kirkwood, of Dela
Capt Queenault
Lt Hyatt
Gen Washington
Marquis Lafayette
Baron De Viomenil
Capt Peter Jaquett
Lt Jas Campbell
Lt Thos Anderson
Gen Guest, of Md
Wm Winder, of Md

The foregoing is a correct statement of facts from memory after a lapse of upwards of 50 years. I acted my part through the whole scene. –C P Bennett

August Elections: Alabama: Mobile Adv of Aug 15:
Locofoco
Jas E Belzer
Dixon H Lewis
Whig-Jas Dellet

Wm W Payne
Geo S Houston

Felix S McConnell
Saml C Daily

Cmder J D Knight has been detached from the ship **Dolphin** on her arrival at Norfolk, & Cmder Henry Bruce ordered to take command of her.

Md Whig nominations of Delegates to the Gen Assembly:
Anne Arundel Co:
John Johnson	Dr Stevens Gambrill	Robt Garner
Nicholas B Worthington	Reuben Warfield	

For Dorchester Co:
Dr Jos Nichols	J Bond Chaplain
Dr Francis P Phelps	Levin Richadrson

For Calvert Co:
Saml Turner	J J Dalrymple	Jas S Morsell

For Harford Co:
Wm J Polk	Coleman Yellott
Dr Thos C Hopkins	Dr Francis Butler

Mr W Weymouth, of Lyman, Maine, was instantly killed by a stroke of lightning on Fri week. A woman lying on a bed in the same room was injured. Mr Weymouth was about 22 years of age.

Phil, Aug 20-Miss Mary Miller, residing in the vicinity of 2nd & Coates sts, was knocked down by the horses attached to a pleasure car, & fell upon the road in such a manner that 2 of the wheels of the car passed directly over her neck, causing instant death. –U S Gaz

On Fri last Mr Geo H Perriman, farmer, near Havre-de-Grace, Md, formerly postmaster at Perrimansville, had his arm caught in the machinery of a threshing machine & died the following day. He has left a wife & family to lament his premature death.

Died: the Hon Wm Halsey, of N J, in his chamber, of apoplexy. Some years since he had an attack of paralysis, but had so far recovered as to be able to attend to his private affairs & enjoy his family & friends. Judge Halsey had been a member of the N J bar for near half a century, having been admitted in 1794. He was a native of this county, having been born at Short Hills in 1770, & was 73 years of age. Three of his seniors only survive: Judge Ford, Robt Campbell, & Gov Williamson. –Newark Daily Adv

Died: on Aug 11, at **Rosewell**, the seat of his uncle Thos B Booth, in Gloucester Co, Va, Midshipman Wm B Browne, aged 21 years. His disease was pulmonary & protracted.

Died: Aug 21, in Gtwn, Wm Magruder, infant s/o John L & Rebecca M Smith, aged 10 months & 21 days.

N Y Express of Mon: Ex Alderman Saml Cowdry died suddenly on Fri, in the street, at the lower part of Broadway, being near Bowling Green, from an affection of the heart.

From the same, we notice the death of Augustus Greele, at age 55. He came to this city about 25 years ago, like many of his brethren from New England. He acquired an ample fortune & with his family spent some time in Europe. [No date-current item.]

James River land for sale: I offer for sale the place of my late residence, in Surry Co, known as **Four Mile Tree**: about 1,000 acs, about 5 miles from Jamestown, & is one of the most ancient residences in Va. The farm houses are all new, having been rebuilt within the last 5 or 6 years. The dwlg house is spacious & elegant, situated on the south bank of the river: 8 rooms, 4 on a floor, closets, lockroom, ample cellars, green-house, & a tasteful Ionic portico on each front. The ofcs are new & complete, including kitchen, wash room, dairy, ice-house, meat-house, lumber-house, & servants' rooms. If not sold privately before Oct 25, it will be sold publicly on the premises on that day. On the same day, will be sold, the household & kitchen furniture, the crops of corn & oats, the stock of horses, cattle, sheep, & hogs, with the plantation implements, including a new wheat threshing machine. Some valuable women & children will be sold at the same time. The overseer on the place, or my friend Drury Stith, residing in the neighborhood will show the same. Address the subscriber, Jefferson post ofc, Powhatan Co, Va: Philp St Geo Cocke

Public Sale: by decree of Circuit Superior Court of Law & Chancery, for King Geo Co, dated Apr 22, 1843, in 2 suits pending therein, one between Sarah M Grayson, admx of Sarah A C Selden, dec'd, cmplnt & Geo T Riding, sheriff of King Geo Co, & adm d b n of Robt O Grayson, dec'd, & others dfndnts; the other between John Yates & others, cmplnts, & Geo T Riding, sheriff of King Geo Co, & others, dfndnts, the undersigned com'rs, or any 2 or more of them, were directed to make sale of the real estate descended from the said Robt O Grayson, dec'd, together with the dower interest of the said Sarah M Grayson therein, wither altogether or in such separate parcels as they make think most advantageous. Sale on Aug 4, at **Mount Stuart**, the late residence of the said Robt O Grayson, dec'd, that tract of land, lying on the Potomac river, called **Mount Stuart**, supposed to contain about 800 acs, which was purchased by the said Robt O Grayson from the late Col John G Stuart. –Geo W Lewis, Wiley R Mason, Geo Fitzhugh, Law B Berry, Com'rs [Sale postponed til Spe 8, 1843. There are comprehended in the tract of land called **Mount Stuart** 2 small parcels purchased by the late Dr Robt O Grayson, the one from L F Stuart & the other from N Burchel-making the whole tract to be sold to consist of about 910 acs. At the same time the undersigned will offer for sale 2 undivided third parts of a tract of between 60 & 70 acs of land, lying near **Mount Stuart**, purchased by the late Dr R O Grayson from Wesley Stuart.

THU AUG 24, 1843
Household furniture at auction, on Aug 29, at the residence of Mrs Culver, on La ave, between 3rd & 4 ½ sts, nearly new & excellent household & kitchen furniture amongst which we enumerate the following:
Mahg hair seat chairs, hair seat sofa

Mahg dining & card tables
Mahg sideboard, window curtains & ornaments
Mantel clock, dinner & tea China, glassware
Ingrain, parlor, hall, step, & chamber carpets
Hall lamp, mahg dressing & other bureaus
High & French-post bedsteads, beds, mattresses
Wardrobes, washstands, toilet sets, chamber chairs
With a variety of other furniture & a good assortment of kitchen utensils.
-Robt W Dyer & Co, aucts

Mrd: on Aug 22, by Rev Mr Davis, Mr Columbus Denham to Miss Mgt E Tabler, all of Wash City.

Died: on Aug 23, Mr John Wm Smoot, in his 25th year, only s/o Walter & Mary B Smoot, after a long & painful illness, leaving a disconsolate widow & 3 small children. His funeral is this afternoon, at 4 p m, from his late residence.

Died: on Sat, after a short illness, Mr Lewis Wernwag, of Virginius, near Harper's Ferry, aged about 73 years. He was a native of Germany, but for the greater portion of his life a citizen of this country, & for the last 20 years a resident of Jefferson. He was a man of unbounded benevolence, a public benefactor; eminent architect & bridge builder, & the evidence of his genius & skill are to be seen in many of the most important bridges in this region of Va, in Pa, & in Ohio. He has left his numerous family only the legacy of his virtues & good example. –Charlestown Free Press

Wash Corp, Aug 21, 1843. 1-Ptn from Davis S Waters: referred to the Cmte of Claims. 2-Relief of Barney B Curran was referred to the Cmte of Claims. 3-Ptn of Eliz Cross: referred to the Cmte of Claims. 4-Ptn of Saml Wroe & others for gravel footwalk on H st to Mass ave: referred to the Cmte on Improvements. 5-Ptn of John McDermott & others, for improvement of 5th st west: referred to the Cmte on Improvements. 6-Ptn of John Scrivener & others, for curbstones & paving on I st: referred to the Cmte on Improvements. 7-Act for the relief of Adam Lindsay: was read.

Gtwn, Classical, & Mathematical Academy will be resumed on Mon next, Aug 28th. –W E Abbott

Groceries at Auction: on Aug 28, at the Grocery Store of Mr D L Lazenby, on N Y ave, between 7th & 8th sts: the balance of his stock. -Robt W Dyer & Co, aucts

FRI AUG 25, 1843
Mademoiselle Le Normand died on Jun 25: snatched away from her pursuits of occult science. Her first essay in the art of divination was at the convent of the Benedictines,

where she began to learn her cathechism at a very young age. She can never be replaced; it is in vain that vulgar fortune-tellers aspire to supply the void her loss has made.

In a collection of autographs at Vienna, which was sold in 1838, was a letter of 6 pages addressed by Martin Luther to the Elector John, & dated Jul 9, 1530. This bijou was bought for 200 florins by the Grand Duke of Lucca. A letter from Swedenbourg, written with his blood in his prison at Dresden, was also purchased by the Grand Duke for 50 florins.

The Albany Argus of the 23rd: report the death of the Hon Lucas Elmemdorf, who expired at the Carlton House, in this city. He arrived in the day boat, & had walked with his usual vigor, to the Carlton House, with a friend. He was then seized with faintness, & almost immediately expired. [Mr Elemendorf served as a Rep in Congress from Mar 4, 1797 to Mar 3, 1803; his name appearing on the Journal on all the great questions of that period, in company with those of Baldwin, Eggleston, Findley, Fowler, Gallatin, Gillespie, Gregg, Walter Jones, Macon, John Nicholas, New, Sumter, Varnum,& Venable. –Nat Intell]

Navy Orders: Capt R F Stockton ordered to the command of the new steamer **Princeton**, now in progress of completion in Phil. The following ofcrs have also been ordered to the same vessel: Lts E R Thompson, Wm E Hunt, & Robt E Johnson, Purser Thos P McBlair, & Midshipman R T Renshaw.

Shooting on the second day of the election in Danville, between Maj Jeremiah T Boyle & Mr Greenwood, in which the latter was shot with a pistol by the former, & expired in 12 hours. Maj Boyle surrended himself to the civil authorities: act was perpetrated in self-defence. –Lexington Observer

Improvements in Balt: superb stores-2 warehouses, 177 & 177½ south side of Balt st, bldg by Mr S Hess, carpenter, & Mr Jas L Armstrong, bricklayer, for Mr Leonard Jarvis. One is occupied by Messrs Wilkins & Wonn, & the other to be occupied by Messrs Murdoch & Co, as dry goods establishments. Warehouses: Messrs Johns, Hopkins & Bros are now erecting 3 on Lombard st: Messrs Dushane & Thompson are the bricklayers, & Mr Valentine Dushane carpenter. -Patriot

For rent: dwlg house recently occupied by Mrs Preston, on 9th st. Also the handsome 2 story dwlg at present occupied by Wm H Lowry. –A Shepherd

Furnished rooms & boarding: Mrs J C English, having returned from her visit to the North, informs the public that she is now prepared to accommodate a mess of 6 or 8 Boarders. Her residence is on the west side of 7th st, a few doors above the ofc of the Nat'l Intelligencer.

SAT AUG 26, 1843
A private letter from Mr M W Davis, of N J, who has been some time engaged in the effort to raise the steamer **Lexington** in Long Island Sound, states that they have at last succeeded, & that the hull has been raised & is now afloat. It is not stated that anything valuable has been recovered.

Cherry Lawn Boarding School for Young Ladies, which was opened in May last at the residence of Priscilla Barker, near Govanstown, Md, will commence on Nov 1 next: under the superintendence of Miss McClean, an accomplished lady from Boston, who had for several years been known in Balt as an instructress, part of the time in the family of Gen B C Howard. Reference may be made to: John Ward, Wm S Winder, Wm G Howard, Henry C Turnbull, in the neighborhood of the School. For further particulars address: John Prentiss, Falls Turnpike; Hon Benj C Howard, Elkridge; Wm Geo Read, L L D, Balt; Richd Thomas, M D, Balt.

Mr Sully had just completed 3 paintings of the Niagara Falls from careful drawings made by him on the spot this summer. The largest is a general view of the Falls as seen from the American side; another on the American side, taken from below & looking up the river from a rocky projection near the foot of the Falls; another is taken from the Canadian side, near the foot of the Staircase, in which the "Table Rock" is introduced, hanging over a mass of perpendicular rocks. The above pictures have been purchased by a liberal friend of the fine arts, B C Wilson, of Phil. –North American

Valuable bldg lots at public auction at the Navy Yard on Aug 28, lots 20 & 21 in sq 882, nearly opposite the apothecary shop of Mr Edw Clarke, within 1 sq of the Navy Yard gate. -Robt W Dyer & Co, aucts

A child of Mr Jesse Everett, a resident of Cazenovia, Ill, was poisoned a few days since, by chewing percussion caps, which it took from a box containing them, & which had been given it to play with. Death ensued in a few hours.

Rev L B Minor, of the Protestant Episcopal Mission at Cape Palmas, Africa, died at that place on May 29.

Navy Dept, Aug 17, 1842. Letter to Lt John T McLaughlin, U S Navy, Wash, from A P Upshur. Sir: I have considered the several charges preferred against you by Lt Fansill, of Marines, together with the explanations & counterproofs offered by yourself. I see no reason to proceed with them any further, nor to bring your conduct into question. The charges are dismissed. –A P Upshur [This was followed by a letter from the Navy Dept, Aug 24, 1843: The charges against you are therefore dismissed. –David Henshaw.] The whole aim & end of these publications being to give an injurious notoriety to my name, I request, in justice to myself, that those editors who have aided in disseminating the report that I am to be tried, will give a place to this communication in their cols. – John T McLaughlin, Lt U S Navy, Wash, Aug 25, 1843

N Y Commercial Advertiser says the Hon John M Niles, Senator elect from the State of Connecticut, is now in the insane hospital at Utica.

House to let: 2 story brick house on Missouri ave, lately occupied by Miss Briscoe, is for rent. Apply to Eleazer Lindsley, or John P Ingle.

U S store ship **Lexington**, W M Glendy, Lt Commanding, arrived at N Y on Aug 22, having on board a few of the ofcrs of the Mediterranean squadron, & about 50 men; the latter, having served out their time, are sent home to be paid off & discharged. The U S sloop **Preble** left Mahon on Jul 12 for the U S, to touch at Barcelona & intermediate Spanish ports; the U S ship **Delaware** sailed Jul 17 for Toulon & coast of Italy; ships **Congress & Fairfield** on a cruise up the Mediterranean. Spoke Aug 3, U S frig **Macedonian**, to touch at the Western Islands; all well. The U S brig **Porpoise** sailed from Cape Mesurado Jun 2 for the leeward: all well. The U S brig **Bainbridge** sailed from Curacoa Jul 28, for Santa Martha, & on a cruise to the leeward.
Ofcrs of the **Lexington**:
Wm M Glendy, Lt Commanding; Theodore P Green, Andrew F V Gray, Wm May, Lts; Wm Speiden, Purser; John T Abernethy, Passed Assist Surgeon; Edw C Anderson, Acting Master; Jos Hoban, Capt's Clk; Wm A Webb, Wm W Roberts, Dawson Phenix, Midshipmen; Colson Gales, Acting Master's Mate; Theodore Quastoff, Purser's Clk. The following Ofcrs, also of the Mediterranean squadron: S W Kellog, Assist Surgeon; John D Simms, Lt Marines; Ed F Tattnall, Midshipman; John Shannon, Boatswain

The Fredericksburg Union Manufacturing Co, having determined to close up their operation, now offer for sale the Lot & Bldgs, Machinery, Tool, & Fixtures-all the castings on hand. The undersigned cmte appointed for this purpose: Wm A Jackson, John Crump, Edwin Carter, John Metcalfe, Chas C Wellford

Mrd: on Aug 22, by Rev Mr Davis, Mr Jas W Barker to Miss Sarah A R Hines, all of Wash City.

Mrd: on Aug 24, by the Rev John Davis, Mr E G Tucker to Miss Susannah, eldest d/o Mr Levi Pumphrey, of Wash City.

Died: on Aug 20, at sea, Saml White, carpenter U S Navy, formerly of the Navy Yard, Washington, & lately attached to the U S sloop **Fairfield**.

Died: on Jul 13, at his residence in Calvert Co, Md, Col Jos Blake, in his 84th year. The death of this venerable gentleman will be felt as a melancholy bereavement, not only by his family & his personal friends, but by the whole community of his native county, the greater part of whom have been taught from their infancy to look up to him as the time-honored representative of prudence, industry, & integrity.

MON AUG 28, 1843
Rittenhouse Academy will resume on Sep 1. –C H & J E Nourse

Henry Stickle, a young man from the neighborhood of Greencastle, Pa, was drowned in the Potomac river, at Honeywood mills, in Berkeley Co, on Sat week, while bathing. He ventured into too deep water.

Appointments by the Pres: Gorham Parks, Atty of the U S for Maine, in the place of John Holmes, dec'd. Wm H Rogers, Atty of the U S for Delaware, in the place of Jas A Bayard, resigned. Edw W Clark, Justice of the Peace for Wash Co, D C. -Madisonian

U S ship **Vandalia** arrived at Norfolk on Fri, in 24 days from Chagres. List of her ofcrs: Wm J McCluney, Cmder; Wm S Young, Wm P McArthur, Henry H Lewis, Geo W Harrison, Lts; Robt S Moore, Purser; Danl S Green, Surgeon; Thos M Potter, Assist Surgeon; Jas C Williamson, Acting Master; Chas H Baldwin, Edmund Shepherd, Jas J Waddell, Chas P McGary, Francis G Clarke, R F R Lewis, Edw E Stene, Midshipmen; Wm D Cobb, Capt's Clk; Loman Smith, Carpenter; Edw Lyons, Boatswain; Wm F Smith, Master's Mate.

The U S schnr **On-ka-kye**, Lt Bispham, sailed from Norfolk on Fri morning on an experimental cruise of a few days.

Fatal duel at New Orleans on Sat week, between Mr Labranche, lately elected a Rep from the State of La to the next Congress, & Mr Hueston, editor of the Baton Rouge Gaz, in which Hueston was mortally wounded, & expired about 5 hours after the meeting. Mr Hueston was not wounded until the 4th round.

Rev Matthew Gambrell, of Anderson district, S C, committed suicide by hanging himself on Fri. He was about 50 years of age, & had been for many years an able & exemplary minister of the gospel in the Baptist Church. –Greenville Mountaineer

Fatal accident in Wash City on Fri last, when Caroline Harryman, an interesting child, fell from the window in the 3rd story of Mrs Gassaway's boarding house, on Pa ave, & survived the fall a few minutes.

Mrd: on Aug 17, at Newton Corner, Massachusetts, by Rev Mr Bushnell, the Rev Geo Whitefield Samson, Pastor elect of the Third Baptist Church of this city, to Miss Eliz Smallwood, d/o Thos Smallwood, of the former place.

Died: on Aug 25, at Alexandria, after a long & protracted illness, Mr Geo W Carlin, in his 58th year, an old & respected inhabitant of that place.

Died: at Alexandria, after a protracted & painful illness, Mrs Harriet, w/o Saml Reese, in her 29th year.

Died: on Aug 11, at the residence of Geo S Taylor, in Botetourt Co, Va, Miss Ann Price, of Alexandria.

TUE AUG 29, 1843
Benj Hallowell, of Alexandria, has been appointed Prof of Chemistry in the Medical Dept of the Columbian College, vice Dr Hall, dec'd.

The trial of Dr McClenachan for a violent assault upon the Rev Mr Aaron, a Baptist minister, terminated at Norristown on Fri. It was proved that Mr Aaron had slandered the dfndnt in his temperance lectures & in the pulpit. Judge Burnside sentenced Dr McClenchan & his brother to a fine of $30 & for each to be imprisoned for 30 days. –Phil Gaz

The Providence Journal says that the venerable Capt Dennis, a Revolutionary sldr, & for 12 years sheriff of Newport Co, has been removed from the ofc of keeper of the lighthouse at Dutch island, to make room for a brother of the Dorrite candidate for Congress in the eastern district of R I. It appears that the elder Mr Dennis was not himself the keeper-he resigned some time ago, on account of his advanced age, & his son, in every respect qualified for the duties, was appointed in his stead. Mr Dennis lived with his son & was supported by him. The veteran is nearly 90 years of age; he served through the Revolutionary war, but, from some error in the proof, was unable to obtain the pension to which he was justly entitled.

In the late flood in Pa we mentioned the very praiseworthy conduct of Mr Crozer towards Mr Jas Dixon, a heavy sufferer by the flood. Mr Dixon was indebted to Jos Gibbons, of this county, upon a bond in the sum of $650, & when news reached Mr Gibbons that Mr Dixon had lost all the avails of his hard labor for several years past, he immediately cancelled the bond & Mr Dixon is now no more his debtor. –Delaware Co Republican

On Friday last at the bathing establishment of Mr Green, at Long Branch, N J, Mr Wm Montgomery, a book-keeper of N Y C, drowned when he, together with his sister-in-law & a gentleman of Phil, waded beyond their dept. Two of the party were rescued-the third perished.

On Aug 2 a young man belonging to Waterloo, Monroe Co, Ill, Constantine L Omelveny, accidently shot himself & was killed instantly. He had started from his father's on a gunning excursion when the accident occurred.

Ezekiel Henry, who was a Rep from Bibb Co in 1841, & a candidate for the same place at the late election, killed his cousin, Crocket G Davis, messenger to the House in 1841, by stabbing, on account of the opposition of Davis to the election of Henry. The tragedy occurred at Centreville, Aug 8. Henry fled, & from the latest intelligence had not been taken. -Alabama Monitor

Mr Thompson L Bailey, of Cole's Island, Miss, lost his life at Maysville, Ky, on Fri week, by falling from a steamboat into the river, whereby he was drowned. His body having been recovered, it was attended to the grave by a large procession of the citizens of Maysville, including the Mayor & city ofcrs.

Died: on Aug 14, at his residence in Clarke Co, Va, Capt Thos Jackson, in his 80th year. He was a highly respectable citizen, & a resident of Fred'k & Clarke Counties for 55 years.

Died: on Aug 26, at Gtwn, Geo Plater Forrest, in his 49th year.

Miss H McCormick has removed her School from Capitol Hill to 4½ st, next door to Mrs Arguelles' boarding house, & will recommence on Sep 4.

For rent: handsome cottage residence south of Todd's Ice-house, & adjoining L H Machen. Inquire on the premises of G Brooke.

WED AUG 30, 1843
Copied from the Madisonian of last evening: "The Pres of the U S left the city this morning, with his dght & grand child, the latter still unwell, for the Winchester [Va] Springs."

C T Taylor writes to the Louisville Whig that the Rev Mr Anderson, near Oak Grove, Ky, has discovered a method by which he can teach the deaf & dumb to read & speak. It is usual for mutes to make ejaculations indicative of fear, hope, pleasure, pain & surprise; & from this he is said to have discovered a language for the dumb.

Hill's N H Patriot announces the death of Jonathan Garnage, of Fryeburg, Maine, aged 90. He fought at the battle of Bunker Hill, & was present at the late Bunker Hill celebration, & lost his reason from excitement produced by the occasion, in which state he died without any other apparent disease.

Eliza Hill, 16, met her death by falling from the 3rd story window of a house on Front st, Phil, on Sunday.

A little son of Mrs Susan P Coffin, of Edgartown, Mass, was so injured when struck violently by the vanes of a windmill, that his recovery was considered doubtful.

The Exeter News Letter, speaking of John Wentworth, of Chicago, Locofoco member elect to Congress, says: "He is under 30 years of age, but over 6 feet & a half in height-so that, although young, there is a good deal of him."

The Elkton [Md] Whig of Sat: Mr Jas Wolf, conductor of the train of cars running between here & the camp meeting, at risk to his own life, saved that of a deaf man who was walking in the middle of the track. Mr Wolf sprang out of the car & pulled the man from the track by his arm beyond the reach of the wheels.

Extensive sale of household furniture on Aug 30 at the residence of Mr A R Dowson, fronting the Capitol Square, all the household & kitchen furniture. Embracing the whole of the furniture of that large & well known establishment, & which is good & in good repair. -Robt W Dyer & Co, aucts

Commencement at Harvard University took place at Cambridge on Wed. Degree of A B conferred on:

W H Adams	H Holmes	H B Sargeant
C F Adams	H J Hudson	F R Sears
J G Bacon	J W Kingham	H D Sedgwick
F W Bigelow	F B Knapp	J G Sewall
W C Binney	F N Knapp	W A Smith
E Birchard	A Kuhn	E C Sprague
J W Boyden	J G Ladd	E Stimson
W Clark	F L Lee	E F Stone
A Clark	J A Loring	H N Stone
M G Cobb	J Lowell	J W Stone
L Cox	F McIntire	L L Thaxter
W Cushing	H B Maglathlin	A W Thayer
S D Dexter	J H Means	W D Tracy
H P Farnnam	E Morrell	J H Trask
J C Flint	H Parker	W Very
O B Frothingham	L Parks	J Vila
A B Fuller	C C Perkins	J H Walker
E Gassett	R G Pike	H Ware
R Gordon	W B Rice	S Webb
T B Hall	W A Richardson	J Wheelwright
R B Hildreth	T H Russell	H O White
T Hill	J J Russel	F C Williams

Degree of D D was conferred on:
Rev Ezra S Gannett, of Boston   Rev Danl Sharp, of Boston

Rev Alonzo Potter, Union College, N Y
Degree of L L D conferred on:
Wm H Prescott Boston   Jared Sparks, Cambridge
Geo Bancroft, Boston   Wm Smyth, Cambridge Univ, Eng

Mrd: on Aug 24, by Rev G Wilson McPhail, Mr Richd M Bremmer to Miss Angelina Portch, all of Fredericksburg.

Died: on Aug 25, at Charleston, S C, the Hon Jacob Axson, Recorder of the City & Judge of the City Court of Charleston, in his 49th year, after a period of protracted suffering. He had long served for many years as an alderman of the city, & a member of the Leg; as City Atty; & finally as Recorder & Judge, to which ofc he was eleced in 1836.

Died: on Aug 26, after a long & distressing illness, Jas Hutton, of Phil, for the last 20 years a clerk in the Navy Dept. It is a great consolation to his family that his last moments were calm & tranquil, & his friends trust that he now rests in the bosom of that God he loved & served when in health & strength.

Tomorrow, Thu, at the Baptist Church on 10th st, the Rev G W Samson, Pastor elect of the Third Baptist Church, will be set apart by ordination to the work of the gospel ministry. The Rev Mr Nague, of Boston, is to preach on the occasion. Exercises to commence at half past 7 o'clock. Public is invited.

Notice: sale on Sep 19 next that valuable estate near Pickawaxen Church, [the residence of the late Minchin Lloyd,] called **Milton Hill**, containing 491 acs, more or less. Improvements are a good 2 story dwlg house & necessary outbldgs. This is esteemed one of the most valuable and desirable farms in the whole county. –Walter Mitchell, trustee, Port Tobacco, Md

THU AUG 31, 1843
Mathemathical teacher wanted to take charge of the Mathematical Dept of a private institution at some distance from the city. The salary is liberal. Address I P Scott, post paid, Norfolk, Va.

Adrian Van Sinderen, of Brooklyn, N Y, died on Sun, aged 70. He had long been afflicted by a painful disease. He was a successful merchant & withdrew from business many years since with an ample fortune.

The New Orleans papers bring us intelligence of the death of J C de St Romes, of that city, for nearly 30 years the proprietor & editor of the Louisiana Courier.

Passed Midshipman Ridgely, of Balt, lost one of his hands last Sun, while on his way to N Y, by being thrown from the railroad cars at the Princeton depot. He was stepping from one car to another, when the train suddenly started, throwing him off. He fortunately fell outside of the track, & thus saved his life. [Sep 5 newspaper: his name is Jas Stewart Ridgely, s/o Gen Chas S Ridgely, who resides near this city. Having been ordered to the U S brig **Savannah**, at N Y, he was on his way there. The left hand, the one injured, was amputated soon afterwards, immediately above the wrist. He is now doing as well as could be expected, & will return to Balt in a few days. –Balt Patriot.]

Jas Shields, of Bellville, appointed by the Govn'r of Ill Judge of the Supreme Court of Ill, to fill the vacancy occasioned by the resignation of Judge Semple, who has recently been appt'd a Senator of the U S.

Miss Jane Harring, an accomplished young lady, the d/o a wealthy man of Franklin Co, Ia, committed suicide by hanging herself on Jul 16th. She had been reproved by her father for engaging herself to a young man to whom she was attached.

Mrd: on Aug 29, in Gtwn, D C, by Rev W Gassaway, Mr Geo Young, of the State of Georgia, to Mary, d/o Saml Humphreys.

Mrd: on Aug 29, at ***Pleasant Hill***, near Washington, by Rev Isaac W K Handy, Mr Francis S Dunham, of Berlin, Md, to Miss Leah Ann W Handy, eldest d/o S W Handy.

Died: on Aug 30, after a short & painful illness, Mr Geo W Moffitt, in his 24th year. His funeral will be from the residence of Hall & King, Pa ave, this afternoon at 4 p m.

Died: on Aug 29, Eliz Ann, eldest d/o Danl & Mary Quigley, aged 3 years & 8 months. Her funeral will be from their residence near the Navy Yard, at half past 3 o'clock this afternoon.

Died: on Mon last, in Wash City, after a long & protracted illness, Mgt Forble, in her 56th year. The dec'd was a native of Fredericktown, Md, but for the last 35 years a resident of this city.

Capt Thos H Sumner, of Boston, late master of the ship **Cabot** of N Y, claims to have discovered an infallible method of finding the true latitude & longitude of a vessel on any ocean or sea, by very plain & simple calculation. A correspondent of the New Bedford Mercury states that it is highly recommended by Prof Peirce, of Harvard College, by a cmte of naval ofcrs, by the Boston Naval Library, & by that worthy & indefatigable son of the ocean, Josiah Sturgis, Cmder of the U S revenue cutter **Hamilton**.

Mrs Dyson's Seminary for Young Ladies, corner of G & 9th sts, will recommence on Sep 4, 1843.

Wash Corp: 1-Ptn from Edw Hawkins: referred to the Cmte of Claims. 2-Relie of Eliza Lowe, wid/o the late Randel Lowe: read the 3rd time & passed.

Education: the exercises of the subscriber's school, on First st at the foot of Capitol Hill, will be resumed on Sep 4. –S G Bulfinch

Washington High School for Boys: will be opened on Sep 4: school room over the Wash Library, in North 11th st. –D E Arnold, A N Girault

NOTICE: My son Chas having been seduced from my house, & without a reasonable cause, I hereby forewarn every person or persons from harboring or employing him, under any pretence whatever, as I am determined to resort to the law in such case. –Amelia Baltimore

For rent: the house on 2nd st, north of St Peter's Church, containing 12 rooms, with pantries, good water near the door brought from Mr Danl Carroll's spring, & a lot adjoining with fruit trees, brick stables, carriage house & smoke house. Inquire of Jas Owner, Va ave, near the Navy Yard.

Columbia Flour Mills for rent: located on Rock creek, near Wash City. Application may be made at my residence, on north G st, Nathl Frye, Atty for the properties.

Handsome furniture at auction: on Aug 31, at the residence of Mr Wm Stettinius, on 4½ st, between Mr Dent's & Masonic Hall, all his household & kitchen furniture. Also, the dwlg house is for rent. For terms apply to Jno Purdy. –Wm Marshall, auctioneer

FRI SEP 1, 1843
N Y papers of Tue last: Willis Hall, of Albany, late Atty Gen of N Y, a Member of the State Leg, has been struck with a paralysis, in the prime of life. From the Albany Evening Journal of Tue regarding Willis Hall-Drs Cogswell & Jas McNaughton have confident hopes of his speedy restoration.

Phil, Aug 28-Mr Edw R Evans, who resides in Pine st, near 2nd, much intoxicated, shot himself with a small pistol, producing instant death. His wife & another lady heard the shot. Mr Evans was 36 years of age in Jan last. His father, who is one of the most prominent merchants in this city, is now absent in Va. His mother was in the house at the time of his death. The dec'd has left a wife & 4 children. -Gaz

On Tue, Chas Axe, about 43, from Mercer Co, Pa, a passenger in the train of cars from Harrisburg, committed suicide on the railroad, by throwing himself under the train. He was accompanied by his son, age 14 years, to whom he had early in the morning expressed a disposition to kill himself.

Five Roman Catholice Missionaries [Frenchmen] have been rescued from a horrid death in Cochin China, through the interposition of Mr Ballestier, the American Consul at Singapore. Having heard that they had been arrested by the King of Cochin China for preaching, & were to be executed by awful mutilation, Mr B sent a special message to the King by the Mandarins of some of his ship at Singapore that the French Gov't would visit such cruelty with exemplary punishement; that the Christian nations would not permit such barbarity. The King was constrained to defer his purpose. Meantime the French corvette **Heroine**, Capt Sevegne, was sent to demand their release: having succeeded, they returned to Singaport, where the missionaries went in a body to tender thanks to the American Consul. They then sailed for Europe.

Circuit Court of Wash Co, D C. John D Boyd has applied to be discharged from imprisonment under the act for the relief of Insolvent Debtors: hearing on Sep 11 next. –Wm Brent, clk

Boston Latin School: the announcement of the death of that venerable Biblical scholar, the Rev Dr Homer, of Newton, Mass, has brought to mind that he is probably the last survivor of the class of body that entered the Boston Latin school in 1766. This class had many members who attained a great distinction in both the new & the old world.
Prominent members of this famous class of Boston boys must prove interesting:
Isaac Coffin, an admiral of the White in the British Navy, & also a member of the British Parliament.
Sir David Ochterlony, a Lt Gen in The British Army & Knight of the Bath. He died at an advanced age in the East Indies.
Hugh Mackay Gordon, Maj Gen in the British Army, also died in the East Indies.
Sir Scrope Bernard Moreland, a member of the British Parliament. He also received the degree of LL D from the University at Oxford, Eng.
Constant Freeman, a Col in the U S Artl.
Saml Bradford, a Col in the U S Army, afterwards U S Marshal, Sheriff of Suffolk Co, & a member of the Massachusetts Leg.
Thos Dawes, successively a Judge of Probate, of the Municipal, & of the Supreme Court of the State.
Thos Walcutt, the well known antiquarian, for a long period one of the engrossing clerks in the Massachusetts Hse/o Reps:.
Saml Cooper, Judge of the Inferior Court & Notary Public.
Jas Prince, U S Marshal & member of the State Leg.
Jas Freeman, D D, one of the founders of the Massachusetts Historical Soc, the patriarch of the Unitarian Churches at the East, who, but for a dissenting creed, might have added to his other titles that of a Bishop.
Jonathan Homer, D D, just dec'd, an eminent divine, a brother by marriage, & by an unbroken friendship of nearly 3 qrtrs of a century, to the Rev Dr Freeman, though of precisely opposite theological opinions.

Wm Greenleaf, M D, & Shirley Erving, M D, both eminent physicians.
Saml Newman, Capt U S Army, slain in the battle with the Indians at Gen St Clair's defeat, in Ohio.
Thos Temple Fenton, raised to a respectable & lucrative ofc in England, through the recommendatory influence of his Harvard College class-mate Rufus King, then Ambassador to the English Court.
Benj Bethune, Capt in the British Army.
Of the following, the remainder of the class, some died young, & others were distinguished merchants: Danl Johonnot, Chas Apthorp Wheelwright, Wm David, John Gill, Robt McNeill, Thos Fletcher, Jonathan D Robbins, Jacob Eustis, John Ewing, John Laughton, & last, though not least, Thos K Jones, who for about 40 years was the leading auctioneer in Boston. Mr T K Jones was at the head of his class in 1766. At his hospitable table, nearly 20 years since, his surviving classmates, about a dozen in number, met & were joyfully entertained on the occasion of the visit to Boston of their early associate, Admiral Coffin. Twenty of this class were living in 1816, 50 years after they entered the class, & 12 only in 1826, 10 years after.

Meeting of passengers on board the steamboat **Ohio**, on her passage from Phil to Balt, on Aug 29, called for the purpose of expressing their views of the conduct of Capt Davis, of said steamboat, towards a family which he left on the wharf at Phil. On the motion of Col M I Cohen, of Balt, Gen Columbus O'Donnell, of Balt, was called to the Chair, & Lloyd Williams, of Norfolk, Va, appointed Sec. Capt Davis left a family, consisting of a gentleman & lady & 5 or 6 young children, when on the wharf, & after all the baggage belonging to them had been taken on board, particularly as very many of the passengers urged the Capt to wait until said family could reach the boat; & when, too, it wound not have caused a delay of more than 2 or 3 minutes; but instead, he persisted in leaving them & taking their baggage with him to Balt. Resolved, request the proprietors of this steamboat line to discharge the said Davis from his command. We concur most fully in the above resolutions:

Moses Hardin, Balt
L Jewet, Wilmington, N C
J J Rawls, Fla
H W Carman, Salisbury, N C
H B Spelman, Ohio
Henry Olmstead, Phil
J M H Allison, Indiana
Thos Dillard, Phil
A P Edgerton, Ohio
Wm Johnson, Ohio
Joel C Reynolds, Alexandria, D C
R D Townsend, S C
Robt P Chilton, Balt, Md
Andrew Terry, Connecticut

W E Perkins, N Y
J H Strobia, Richmond, Va
J H Pritchett, Tenn
J Davenport, jr, Va
Danl Wall, Balt
M I Cohen, Balt
S Lloyd, jr, Pittsburg, Pa
A Hayman, Wheeling, Va
S H Fiske, Savannah, Ga
E Lindsley, Wash, D C
C Burns, Balt
S P Franklin, Wash, D C
Wm Millsten, Charleston, S C
G Baker, Balt

C W Bingley, S C Elisha Appelgate, Louisville, Ky
W V Boyle, Phil S Field, Phil
N B Thompson, Phil

Rewards of 500 pounds & of 100 pounds British Currency. Ireland, Carlow, Dublin. If the person who, about 1815 or 1816, married the d/o a shoemaker at Carlow named Mary Dun [who in 1810 removed to Dublin as the mistress of a Capt in the Queen's Co Militia, afterwards a Baronet, with whom she was in keeping for several years] will acknowledge his marriage with the said Mary Dun, a reward of L500, or of $2,250, will be paid to said person on such marriage being legally proved by him; the proving of which cannot occasion to him either personal discredit or loss. A further reward of L100, or of $450, will be paid to any other person who will discover or find out the aforesaid Mary Dun's aforesaid husband, who is said to have gone to America about 1817, & to have again emigrated there about 1828. These two sums will be paid within one month after the above mentioned marriage has been proved in Ireland through the above mentioned evidence. The marriage referred to will be equally binding, though it may have been performed by a lawful Protestant Clergyman or a Roman Catholic Clergyman, or even by a Couple-Beggar. For further particulars, inquire by letter of Messrs Goodhue, N Y

Mrd: on Aug 15, near Harper's Ferry, by Rev Thos D Hoover, Mr Jacob Everhart to Mary Jane Gallaway, all of Fred'k Co, Md.

Mrd: on Aug 29, by Rev Thos D Hoover, John Riely to Ann R Water, all of Loudoun Co, Va.

Died: on Aug 31, Isaac T Degges, aged 19 years. His funeral will be from the residence of his father, Mr Wm Degges, on 20th, between E & F sts, this afternoon, at 4 o'clock.

Died: on Wed last, at Alexandria, Capt Mark Butts, one of the oldest & most respectable citizens, & for many years a shipmaster & afterwards merchant of that place. He was born in London in 1768, & emigrated to this country early in life. After his retirement from business he was appointed habor master of the port of Alexandria, in which situation he continued till his death. He leaves a large circle of relations & friends to regret his loss. –Gaz

Died: on Jul 27, at Shannondale Springs, Va, Mary Anna, infant d/o Rev T D & Catharine N Hoover, aged 4 months & 19 days.

For rent: 2 excellent dwlg houses: one about to be vacated by Mr Zevala, the other recently occupied by the family of Dr Hasler, of the U S Navy-both fronting the Greenhouse of Mr Buist, 12th st. –Lewis Johnson

Having obtained the services of a competent instructress, who has resided in our family for the last 3 months, with the view of forming a class, we would receive 3 or 4 girls not exceeding 13 years old by the year. Board & tuition-$150 per year. $20 per year for washing & mending. –R Y Brent, Highlands, Montg Co, Md

SAT SEP 2, 1843
That splendid & valuable property of Wm Slater, known as "*Rose Hill*," located one mile north of Fred'k city, Md, was disposed of last week by that gentleman for $100 per ac. This sale is quoted by the Fred'k Examiner as an evidence of the undiminished value of lands in that vicinity.

A land terrapin of the old school was found near the village of Marlborough, Md, by Mr Fielder Suit, who describes it as having on its under shell this inscription: "R Hill [or P Hill] 1746." -Gaz

Verbal accounts reached Balt on Thu from Elkton that A T Forward, of that village-a Locofoco member of the Hse of Delegates last year-was shot dead in an affray with P C Ricketts, editor of the Cecil Whig.

Madame Caroline de Pickler, [nee Greiner,] one of the most popular novel writers of the age, died at Vienna last week, at the age of 74. Urgalya, one of her works, has been introduced into our literature.

Petersburg Intelligencer records: on Mon, Geo Walker, aged 17 years, while gunning at Spring Garden, near Petersburg, Va, was accidentlay killed by the discharge of a gun in the hands of a negro boy. The dec'd was the s/o the late Mr John Walker, & has left an affectionate mother, with a large family circle.

Mrd: on Sep 1, in Wash City, by Rev Wm McLain, Mr Alfred L Norton, of New Orleans, to Miss Mary Findly Brown, d/o the late Alex'r Brown, of Pa.

Died: on Sep 1, in Gtwn, Mr Brooke Williams, in his 53rd year. The dec'd was the eldest s/o Elisha O Williams, a gallant ofcr of the Revolution, & for upwards of 25 years has discharged the duties of Chief Clk in the Adj Gen's ofc. He was a good citizen, a kind husband, & most affectionate father, &, after a severe illness of some months, has departed this life deeply regretted by all who knew him. His funeral will be from his late residence on the Heights of Gtwn at 4 p m this evening.

Died: on the 22nd ult, at Bridgehampton, L I, Gen Abraham Rose, aged 77, a sldr of the Revolution. He was a substantial farmer, a respected citizen, & was several times a member of the State Leg, & in 1839 was one of the Electors of Pres & Vice Pres, & cast his vote for Gen Harrison.

The Rev J P Donelan, of St Matthew's, will preach in St Peter's Church, Capitol Hill, tomorrow at half past 5 o'clock.

Valuable real estate for sale: the subscriber will dispose of a farm consisting of portions of the lands lately purchased by him of Arthur P West & the late Geo Calvert, containing 426 & 3/8 acs. It adjoins the lands of J B Brooke, Arthur P West, & H C Scott, & the **Mount Airy** estate, the residence of Ed H Calvert. It lies on the main road from Wash to Nottingham. To view the premises, call at the residence of the subscriber, **Poplar Hill**, PG Co, Md, or upon Danl C Digges, Upper Marlboro, who is authorized to effect a sale. –Robt D Sewall

Valuable farm for sale: I wish to sell my farm, lying in St Mary's Co, Md, situated equidistant between Chaptico & Newport, & 4 miles from either. It contains 500 acs: a good frame dwlg-house, kitchen, dairy, meat-house, overseer's-house, negro qrtrs, carriage house, corn-house, stables & barn, all in good repair. An unencumbered titled will be given. –Ann H Turner

Orphans Crt of Chas Co, Md. Letters of adm on the personal estate of John Posey, late of said county, dec'd. –Peter W Crain, administrator of Jno Posey

Circuit Court of Wash Co, D C-in Chancery. Smith & Cissel vs Wm Hayman's reps & al. Ratifly sale of the premises mentioned in the proceeding in the cause consisting of lot 16 & part of lot 15 in sq 5, of Wash City, to Thos Cissel for $3,000. –Wm Brent, clk

MON SEP 4, 1843
Lt Wm Maury was reported last week among the ofcrs of the ship **Lexington**, by mistake, for Lt Wm May. -Army & Navy Chronicle

Mr Wm K Barnard, of Dorchester, fell overboard from the steamer **Splendid**, on Fri last, while on the passage from Boston to Bath, & was drowned.

The U S sloop of war **Preble** arrived at Boston on Thu from the Mediterranean. She sailed from Boston on Jan 12, 1841, & has been absent from the U S nearly 32 months. List of ofcrs: Stephen B Wilson, Cmder; John P Gillis, E Lloyd Handy, Melancton Smith, Jas Madison Frailey, Edmund Lanier, Lts; J Vaughan Smith, Surgeon; L Tazewell Waller, Purser; Melancton B Woolsey, Acting Master; John L Nelson, Thos G Corbin, Pierce Crosby, jr, Martin Duralde, Thos S Phelps, Edw C Stout, John Madigan, jr, Leonard Paulding, Midshipmen; J C P DeKraft, Acting Midshipman; S F Emmons, Acting Master's Mate; Benj P Todd, Clerk; J G Gallagher, Sailmaker; Wm Craig, Gunner; Jeremiah B Trippe, Acting Boatswain; Saml Simonds, Acting Carpenter.

Sing Sing Chronicle: on Fri last 2 men, Lewis Miller & Chas Connard, were drowned in the Croton Reservoir, in Westchester Co, about half way between the Dam & Pine's bridge.

Naval Orders: 1-Capt W M Hunter, command of receiving ship **Ohio**, at Boston. 2-Cmder E W Carpender, navy yard Norfolk, by Sep 1, vice Saunders, detached. 3-Cmdor J Wilkinson, command of navy yard Norfolk, on Oct 1, vice W B Shubrick, detached.

Mrd: on Aug 26, at Graceham, Fred'k Co, Md, by Rev Ambrose Rondthaler, John L Davis, of Fred'k, to Miss Rosa L Nelson, d/o Hon John Nelson, Atty Gen of the U S.

Mrd: on Aug 27, at St Augustine, Fla, by Rev Mr Aubrey, Lt Col Thos F Bunt, U S Army, to Miss Maria Hernandez, d/o Gen Jos M Hernandez, of the Florida militia.

Mrd: on Aug 31, by Rev Mr Young, Mr John B Carson to Mgt Ann Gunsolve, both of the District.

Died: on Sep 2, in Gtwn, Alex'r, 2nd s/o Alex'r & Harriet de Bodisco.

Died: on Aug 28, at the residence of Dr Bayne, Mr C B Clagett, in his 23rd year. He was engaged in the prosecution of the study of medicine.

Died: on Aug 11, at *Rosewell*, the seat of his uncle, Thos B Booth, in Gloucester Co, Va, Midshipman Wm B Browne, U S Navy, aged 21 years.

Died: on Aug 25, in N Y, Sally F Williamson, w/o Cmder J D Williamson, U S Navy.

Died: on Aug 29, at the residence of his mother, in Alexandria Co, D C, Chas A Sommers, in his 21st year, s/o the late John Sommers. This young man was the subject of a serious affliction for years.

Rencounter took place at Port Hudson, La, on Aug 19, between Jas C Jackson & Geo W Bradley, which resulted in the death of the latter. There had been a long standing difficulty between the two.

Strayed from the subscriber, Fri, a cow. Liberal reward for whoever returns her. –Wm Mann, 6th & F sts.

Circuit Court of Wash Co, D C. Wm H McLean, a bankrupt, has filed his petition for his discharge & certificate: hearing on the first Mon in Nov next. –Wm Brent, clk

TUE SEP 5, 1843

The trial of Jos Carter, jr, indicted for the murder of John Castner, Maria Castner, John B Parke, & Maria Matilda Castner, near the village of Washington, Warren Co, N J, on May 1 last, commenced at Belvidere on Wed week, & has been in progress ever since.

Henry Page, one of the most prominent of the citizens of Md, died a few days ago in Boston, whither he had gone on a visit. His disease was the bilious fever, & only 2 or 3 days' duration. We believe he was a native of Dorchester Co: a most influential gentleman in that county. –Balt Patriot

John G Sligworth, of Clarion Co, Pa, whose barn & contents were consumed by fire early this summer, rebuilt his barn after which it was struck by lightning & all burned to ashes.

Died: on Sep 2, after a short but severe illness, Mrs Isabella Spurr, w/o Jas H Spurr, aged 30 years, formerly of Boston.

Three fatal accidents in Springfield, Mass. 1-A little s/o Jas Cristy, of Cabotsville, named Chas, age about 5 years, was drowned in a small cistern in the garden of Mr Lucius Harthan, in that village, on Aug 14. 2-A s/o Mr Augustus Ball, of Deerfield, was drowned while bathing in Deerfield river on the same day. 3-Geo Edw Henderson, aged about 10 years, was run over by a train of burden cars near Broad & Callowhill sts, & instantly killed.

Col Thos B McElwee, formerly a rep of Bedford Co, in the Leg of Pa, died at Bedford on Aug 22.

During a thunder storm at Richmond on Fri last the house of Mrs Coghill, on Adams' hill, was struck by lightning, & herself & her widowed dght, Mrs Sarah Johnson, were killed. Mrs Coghill had a dght & son; the dght shared her fate; the son was present to witness the awful deaths of his mother & sister. Mrs Johnson left a dght some 11 years old. -Compiler

Two young men, John Jackson & Jacob Lowers, were killed last Sun when killed by a falling tree. -Parkersville [Va] Gaz

For rent, the beautiful house & lot fronting the mall, formerly the residence of E Porter. For terms apply at the Bank of Wash, or to N Tastett, in the adjoining house, or to the subscriber, Marcus C Buck.

Circuit Court of Wash Co, D C. John L Dorsey, a bankrupt, has filed his petition for his discharge & certificate: hearing on the first Mon in Nov next. –Wm Brent, clk

In Chancery: Jonathan Seaver vs C S Fowler & others. Ratify sale of lot 29 in reservation 10 in Wash City, with improvements thereon, to Wm McLain, for the sum of $7,435. –Wm Brent, clk

WED SEP 6, 1843
Judge Lewis Summers, of Kanawha, died late Sat week, at the White Sulphur Springs, after a short illness. He was distinguished for many high qualities both as a jurist & a man; & the Commonwealth of Va has cause to deplore the loss of one of its most valued citizens in his demise. -Whig

Boston Journal: Wm A Wellman, the Deputy Collector of this port, has been removed from ofc & Adams Bailey, the former Deputy Collector, appointed in his place.
Edwin Wilbur, an ultra radical, appt'd Collector at Newport, R I, in place of Wm A Littlefield, removed.
Geo M Weston, Locofoco editor of the Age, had been appointed postmaster at Augusta, Me, in place of Perkins, Whig, removed.
Mr Bradbury, Locofoco, appointed postmaster at Calais, Me, in place of Glover, Whig, removed.
Henry Reed, Locofoco, appointed postmaster at South Brookfield, Mass, in place of A Skinner, Whig, removed.
O Marrin, Locofoco, appointed postmaster at New Braintree, Mass, in place of T P Anderson, Whig, removed.
These worthies have all done the dirty work to which they were appointed, & verily they have their reward.
Pea Nut Leland, a Locofoco member of the Senate of this State, appointed Collector of the port of Fall River.
Geo Savary, another Locofoco Senator, appointed postmaster at Bradford.
Fred'k Robinson, another Locofoco Senator, appointed Warden of the State Prison.
Seth J Thomas, a leading Locofoco member of the Hse/o Reps:, who tried so hard to get himself elected Speaker of that body, has been appointed Naval Storekeeper at the Navy Yard, Charlestown.
Wm Sawyer, also a Locofoco Rep, has been appointed postmaster at Charlestown.
B H A Collins, has received the promised reward of his treason, by being appointed to that deeply desired ofc, the keeper of the Eastham lighthouse.

Solomon Hillen has resigned the ofc of Mayor of the city of Balt, urged to retire from all the anxious cares, & complete the restoration of his health.

Mr Lemon Davis, of Mount Pleasant township, Westmoreland Co, Pa, was suddenly killed on Aug 26, by a fall from his horse, when he untook to run a race.

About 3 months since Mr Thos C Nichols, discount clerk & runner of the Branck Bank at Easton, Md, was dismissed from the employment of the bank in consequence of the disappearance of a letter containing a sum of money, The Easton Gaz of Sat says: It now turns out that the letter containing the money was received at the post ofc in this town on Thu last, from the Gen Post Ofc, having been sent from Rockville to Washington as a DEAD LETTER.

The U S ship **Levant** sailed from Hampton Roads on Sat last, having on board Mr Proffit, [late Rep in Congress from Indiana,] Minister to Brazil, accompanied by Mr Hackett, his private sec. She is to land at Rio Janeiro, & then to proceed to the Pacific & round the world. List of her ofcrs: Cmder Hugh Nelson Page

Lts:
Robt G Robb	Robt Handy	Chas C Barton	Jos H Adams

Louis McLane, jr Acting Master
Purser, John B Rittenhouse
Surgeon, Wm M Wood
Assist Surgeon, Jos Wilson
Passed Midshipman
John D Read

Midshipmen:
David Ochiltree	Wm M Gamble	A R	Chas Wooley
Geo P Welsh	E Gordon	Abercrombie	
C H Wells	Geo W Young	E H Scovell	

Capt's Clk, Wm V Taylor
Boatswain, John Dunderdale
Gunner, John Beckwith
Carpenter, John Green
Sailmaker, Jas Bennett

The Norfolk beacon says: A party have received permission from the Navy Dept to take passage in the **Levant** for the purpose of exploring the interior of South America. It consists of Passed Midshipmen I G Strain, Edmund Christie, Dr J C Reinhart, Master's-mate, J W W Dyes, & Edw Donelly. Mr Strain, who originated the expedition, is distinguished for an active & adventurous disposition. We wish the party success in their enterprise.

The 6 year old d/o Hugh McGovern, in Morris' Addition, Pottsville, was killed when trying to climb between 2 laden cars of coal on Sat & fell, expiring a short time after.

At Stuyvesant Falls on Mon, a young man named John Seaman, aged 19 years, employed in the cotton milles of Messrs A Van Allen & Co, got entangled with the main shaft & was killed.

Died: on Sep 4, at Berkeley Springs, Va, where she had gone for the benefit of her health, Mrs Mgt Cary Warrington, consort of Cmdor Lewis Warrington, of the U S Navy. Her funeral wil be from the residence of Cmdor Warrington, on Sep 6, at 11 a m.

Died: yesterday, in Gtwn, at her residence, Mrs Rebecca Forrest, relict of the late Gen Uriah Forrest, in her 80th year. Her funeral will be from her late residence this evening, at 5 p m.

Died: at **Ben Lomond**, the residence of her son-in-law, Gen W K Armistead, U S A, Mrs Eliz Stanly, relict of Hon John Stanly, of N C, in her 63rd year. The dec'd, about 40 years ago, gave up a fashionable life, joined the Methodist Episcopal Church, & has lived a consistent Christian ever since. Indeed, the Bible was her only book. In Newbern, N C, where she resided in affluence, her charities, her faithful discharge of the duties of wife, parent, & mistress will be long remembered. On Aug 30, 1843, suddenly & most expectedly to her children, who were watching around her bed, she calmly fell asleep in Him who is the resurrection & the life. [The Newbern Spectator is requested to copy.]

Died: on Mon last, at the residence of Capt Abell, in Charlestown, Jefferson Co, Va, after a long & painful affliction, Wm Goode, formerly of Berkeley Co, aged about 66 years. The dec'd was some years ago a rep of Berkeley in the House of Delegates.

Died: on Aug 28, at Balt, after a brief illness of one week, Mrs Frances Weems, consort of the late Rev Mason L Weems, at an advanced age.

A few day since, Alex Hopkins, residing in East Pike Run township, Pa, came to his death in a rather mysterious manner. He was found sitting on a chest in a room in which his insane dght had long been confined. He was an aged & respectable gentleman. –Wash [Pa] Reporter

Circuit Court of Wash Co, D C. Geo A O'Brien has applied to be discharged from imprisonment under the act for the relief of Insolvent Debtors: hearing on Sep 25. Same for Patrick Hagan. –Wm Brent, clk

Public sale: at the late residence of Chas Lewis, dec'd, near the Gum Spring, Loudoun Co, Va, on Oct 3, the land of Chas Lewis, consisting of 3 tracts, one containing 500 acs, on which he resided, adjoining the Gum Spring; it has on it a good dwlg-house, barn, & other out-bldgs. Another tract called the **Broad Run tract**, containing about 300 acs, on which there is a comfortable dwlg-house, good stabling, & other out-bldgs. The third tract contains 300 acs, & is all nearly in good timber. All of this land is near the Gum Spring, in Loudoun Co, Va. Also a comfortable dwlg-house & lot, together with a distillery, in the village of Gum Spring. The tracts will be shown by Jonathan Lewis, who lives on the first tract. The excx & exc will dispose of it privately if desired before the day of sale. –Martha J Lewis, excs; F A Lewis, exc

Orphans Crt of Chas Co, Md. Letters of adm on the personal estate of Geo R Spalding, late of said county, dec'd. –John F Spalding, Geo Brent, adms of Geo R Spalding

THU SEP 7, 1843
Closed for improvement: the N Y Cheap Lace store, between 10th & 11th sts, Pa ave, will be closed to make larger the inside of the store. –Jas T King

For rent, the dwlg-house, store-home, & fixtures, on the corner of 7th & G sts, opposite the Patent Ofc square. Inquire of John H Goddard, next door, or of Thos MacGill, 7th st, between G & H sts.

We learn that Hill Carter, of *Shirley*, on the Jas river, Va, reaped from 160 acs 5,280 bushels of wheat, averaging 33 bushels per acre! At *Westover*, the seat of John N Selden, on the Jas river, 100 acs of wheat averaged 30 bushels per ac; also a noble product.

Died: on Aug 24, at Charlestown, Jefferson Co, Va, Mrs Ann A Beckham, w/o Fontaine Beckham, of Harper's Ferry, & the only remaining d/o the late Maj Jas Stephenson, aged 35 years.

Balt, Sep 6. Yesterday as Geo Moon & Jeremiah Hopkins were coming up the river in a sailboat, from a fishing excursion, a schnr passed then, when a jest from the small boat produced a reply from the hands of the schnr, which led to a mutually insulting altercation. Both parties landed together at the Iron-ore wharf, near Spring Gardens, when the quarrel renewed-Moon & Hopkins being on board the schnr. Words flew and Hopkins at length missing his companion, found him senseless on the floor of the cabin. He died soon afterwards. The body was brought into town & conveyed to the former residence of the dec'd in Bath st, near North. No arrests had been made, the schnr having left the wharf as soon as the body was removed. -Sun

Honeywood Mills for sale: in Berkeley Co, Va; at Dam #5, on the C & O Canal & the Potomac river: frame mill, saw mill, kiln, corn-houses; built most substantially; large brick house-13 rooms with necessary ofcs; 10 acs of land attached to the premises. Address W Woodville, Balt

Circuit Court of Wash Co, D C. Jas L Griffin has applied to be discharged from imprisonment under the act for the relief of Insolvent Debtors: hearing on the 4th Mon in Sep. Same for Wm Smith. –Wm Brent, clk

FRI SEP 8, 1843
The Rochester Democrat announces the death, at Mount Morris, on Sep 3, of the Hon Graham H Chapin, a lawyer in Rochester, & formerly a Van Buren member of Congress from the Wayne district.

The pretended robber at Frederick. Mr Edw Ing, jr, a broker of this city, was not robbed as he had said. Strong suspicions which existed that he himself was the robber & had not taken the money out of Balt were fully confirmed by his own disclosures and the recovery of all the money. We presume that he has left town, never to return again.

Mrd: on Aug 31, at Augusta, Maine, Lt Robt M A Wainwright, of the U S Army, [Ordnance Corps,] of Wash City, to Miss Ann Eliza Child, eldest d/o Jas L Child, of the former place.

Mrd: on Aug 22, in Boone Co, Ky, by Rev Mr Lynn, Johnson Chapman to Miss Eliz P Gaines, both of Chicot Co, Arkansas.

Died: on Sep 7, after a protracted illness, Mrs Eliz Williams, in her 85th year.

Died: on Sep 4, Geo, eldest s/o Wm H & Sarah Stewart, in his 22nd year.

Died: on Aug 18, at his residence in Wilson Co, Tenn, in his 86th year, Wm Gray, a Revolutionary sldr, & one of the worthy pioneers of that State.

For rent: the farm of the late L G Davidson, near Capt John Mills', Montg Co, Md. Apply to Mrs E G Davidson, at her residence in Gtwn, D C. –Rockville Journal

On Tue Mr Thos Baynes, residing near the Chemical Works, on Federal Hill, Balt, skinned a cow that had suddenly died, & on Mon his arms & hands were greatly swollen, supposed to have been caused by the inoculation of some poisonous substance, which had caused the cow's death. We have noticed several cases of this kind, one of which resulted fatally.

We learn from Newark that John Henry Wood, 10 years old, s/o Jos Wood of Manington, died on Thu when in climbing a fence he fell on an open knife that was in his hand, & stabbed himself in the breast.

Frederick White Sulphur: these springs [which are better known as Jordan's] are beginning to be appreciated. Among the visiters there at present we may name the Pres of the U S, Chief Justice Taney, & their families; Gen Roger Jones, of the army; Judge Nicholas, of Richmond; Judge Randall, of Fla; & the Hon Edw Davenagh, acting Govn'r of Maine. Mr Jordan's excellent table is unsurpassed in quality, fare, & the style of serving it up.

For rent: the very desirable dwlg-house on Third st, Gtwn, recently occupied by Mr Jas B Taggart. For particulars apply to M Adler, agent, Gtwn.

Wash Corp: 1-Ptn of W D Nutt & other: referred to the Cmte on Improvements. 2-Bill for relief of Eliz Cross: rejected. 3-Bill for the relief of Eliza Lowe: with a amendment- was agreed to. 4-Ptn of John H Shreves, claiming the reward offered for giving information which led to the apprehension of a certain incendiary: referred to the Cmte of Claims. 5-Act for the relief of Barney B Curran: that the fine imposed on him by judgement of Chas Murray, in relation to the projection of stove-pipes through bldgs, be & the same is hereby remitted, provided the said Curran pay the costs of prosecution.

We have before us a neat little volume entitled "The Washington Directory & Gov't Register for 1843," containing the names of all persons employed in the executive depts at Wash, or holding other appointments in D C; a full list of all the Ministers, Consuls, & Commercial Agents of the U S; the Judges & ofcrs of the Supreme Court, & ofcrs of the Senate & Hse/o Reps; a list of the ofcrs of the Army, Navy, & Marine Corps, & of the Revenue cutter sercice; the names of all householders in Wash City with their places of residence & occupation, etc. It is compiled by Mr Anthony Reintzel.

As Mrs Havener was returning home in her market-wagon from the city market on Tue morning, about a mile from the Eastern Branch, a bear, belonging to the proprietor of a tavern, rushed into the road, frightening the horses & causing them to run off, when Mrs H was thrown out & killed. Much indignation is expressed in the neighborhood at the tavern-keeper not keeping the bear chained. Mrs H has left a husband & 4 children to lament her sudden demise. It has been stated that a child was also very much hurt. [Sep 12 newspaper: it was a cart, not a carry-all; it was one horse, not horses; the bear was chained to an appletree in Mr Boiseau's yard, within a few feet of the road, & would frighten any horse coming along. The bear has been removed & taken to another place.]

A little girl, d/o Mr Birch, of Wash City, who resides on the Mall, not far from Md ave, was so severely burnt on Wed last that she died yesterday.

SAT SEP 9, 1843
St James Hall, near Hagerstown, Md: the diocesan School for boys, under the visitorial supervision of the Bishop of the Diocese & the Rev Dr Muhlenburg, of St Paul's College, N Y. Next session will open on Oct 2, to continue 10 months.

Navy Orders: Cmder S F Dupont, command of brig **Perry**, at Norfolk. Cmder Henry Henry, command of ship **Yorktown**. Cmder G J Pendergrast, command of ship **Boston**. Cmder J L Saunders, Navy Yard, Wash.

The U S steamship **Princeton** was launched from the Phil navy yard on Thu last. Ofcrs ordered to the **Princeton**: Capt Robt F Stockton, Cmder; Lts Wm E Hunt, Edw R Thompson, & Robt E Johnson; Passed Misdhipman Edw A Barnert; Acting Master, Madison Rush; Gunner, Robt S King.

The N Y Wash Monument Assoc was organized on Tue & is prepared to proceed to business. Col John Trumbull [formerly Aid to Gen Washington] was elected Pres, Hon Robt H Morris, [Mayor,] V P; Nicholas Dean, Sec, & Moses H Grinnel, Treas.

Mrd: on Sep 7, at the Navy Yard, Wash, by Rev Jas B Donelan, Jos Walsh, M D, to Miss Eliz Smith, of Wash City.

Mrd: on Sep 1, by Rev Robt T Nixon, Mr Wm B Ball, of Stafford Co, to Miss Frances E Rollins, of King Geo Co, Va.

Died: at Liverpool, Eng, after a painful illness, Elenora, consort of W A Spencer, U S N, & d/o the late Peter Lorillard, dec'd, of N Y. [No date-current item.]

Died: on Aug 17, at his residence near Jackson, Miss, Hon Jas C Mitchell. He was for a number of years a member of the Congress from Tenn, Judge of the Crct Court in the same State, & at the time of his death was a Rep in the State Leg of Miss.

Died: at Valparaiso, whither he had gone for his health, being troubled with pulmonary complaints, John Temple Bowdoin Winthrop, s/o the late Lt Govn'r Winthrop, of Boston, at age 47. Mr W, in various public capacities, has long been before the public eye in his native city. He was the elder brother of the present member of Congress from the Boston district. [No date-current item.]

Died: on Aug 23, in the parish of St John the Baptiste, La, after a brief illness, Dr Thos Norvell, late postmaster of that parish. Dr Norvell was a brother both of C C Norvell, the able editor of the Nashville Whig, & of John Norvell, ex-U S Senator from Michigan.

Died: Aug 30, of a short illness, Mrs Sally Mason, consort of Stevens T Mason, of Selma, Loudoun Co, Va.

Died: on Wed last, at Alexandria, Mrs Sally Moxley, an old & respectable inhabitant of that place, in her 78th year.

Died: yesterday, Amos Kendall Gold, aged 1 year & 8 months, s/o Danl Gold of Wash City. His funeral is today at 1 o'clock, from the residence of Mr Gold.

Died: on Sep 6, in Gtwn, Marian Frances, infant d/o Chas S & Eliz Rebecca Jones, aged 12 months.

Died: on May 29, 1843, at Cavalla, near Cape Palmas, West Africa, Lancelot B Minor, aged 29 years, s/o the late Gen Minor, of Fredericksburg, Va. He sailed for Africa in 1837, where he acted as missionary for nearly 6 years; the climate, together with exertion, had gradually wasted a constitution never strong, & prepared him to sink under an attack of African disease.

John Schnierle was on Tue last elected Mayor of the city of Charleston.

St Charles [Missouri] Adv states that by the will of the late Thoms Lindsay, sr, of said county, all his slaves, 12 or 15 in number, are to be liberated on condition that they emigrate to Liberia within a given time. The old servants have determined to remain in this country as slaves, while the younger ones have resolved to go to Liberia. Mr Lindsay also gave a portion of his estate to the missionairies of the Presbyterian Church to aid them to carry on their Christian labors.

Richmond Compiler of yesterday: On Wed last Fletcher Heath, [about 24] the murderer, escaped from the jail in Henrico Co by picking locks & cutting through walls. At the same time Thos Cocke, charged with kidnapping slaves, & John Sheridan, in for gambling, made their escape by the same means.

Two brothers, Nelson & John Doolittle, aged 15 & 17 years, were drowned on Sunday while bathing in the Seneca river, in the town of Clay, Onondaga Co, N Y.

Messrs Davis & Vigers are instructed to sell by auction, on Nov 14, [unless sold previously] a fine property, consisting of 12,700 acs, situated in Md, U S. The estate is 15 miles west of Hancock, 22 miles east of Cumberland, & distant only 17 days' journey from England. Ther is a very comfortable cottage residence now occupied by the family of the proprietor, in the midst of 200 acs of cleared land; post ofc is 2½ miles off. For further information apply to J J Speed, Balt, Md, Messrs J C & H Freshfield, 5 New Bank Bldgs, & Messrs Davis & Vigers, 3 Frederick's Place, Old Jewry, London.

NOTICE: committed to the jail of Fred'k Co, on Sep 4, as a runaway, a black man, who calls himself Wm Giles, about 22 years old; says he belongs to Mr Dick, of Gtwn, D C. The owner, if any, is to come & have him released; he will otherwise be discharged according to law. –Geo Rice, Sheriff of Fred'k Co, Md

MON SEP 11, 1843

Nock's Improved Patent Leaf Holder, or Temporary Binder, Jos Nock has obtained a patent for the above & is now prepared to manufacture the same for the market generally. Capitol Hill, Aug 3, 1843: Matthew St Clair Clarke, Clerk Hse/o Reps U S-only perfect invention for the purpose that I have seen. Recommendations also from Professor John H Hewitt-Prof of Music; F A Wagler, Nathl Carusi, & Benj Reiss. -Jos Noch, N Y ave, near the Glass House

The Govn'r of Ill has appointed Jesse B Thomas to be Judge of the State in the place of Stephen A Douglas, resigned.

Henry Saunders, the young man who committed various forgeries on different Banks in N Y was arrested last Wed in Boston, on board the ship **Loo-Choo**, in which vessel he had passage for New Orleans. [Sep 18 newspaper: Formal examination before one of the magistrates of N Y on Wed last: made a full confession: he implicates Ragge. The prisoner was committed in full, & his father, after being examined, was discharged.]

Joshua Gilchrist, in the employ of the Railroad Co, fell between two of a train of freight cars on their passage to Charleston, S C, on Tue, & died shortly after being conveyed to his place of residence.

A little girl, 5 years of age, d/o Mr Geo Bereman, who resides in Franklin st, Balt, fell on Tue last from the back balcony of the house, 2 stories to the ground. Every attention was paid her by Dr Theobald, but we are sorry to learn the hopes of her recovery are slight. –Sun

John Meekins was lost overboard from the schnr **Francis Thomas**, Capt Jacobs, on Thu, 20 miles north of Cape May. The vessel was from N Y, bound to Balt, & he accidentally fell over while sitting on the rail of the vessel during a calm. He belonged to the Eastern Shore of Md, where he has relatives residing.

Drownings: Mr Jacob Amsden, of Dana, Mass, was found drowned in a pond in New Salem, on Mon of last week. A man named Pemberton, of Bradford, was drowned on Tue while getting hay in the marshes.

Died: on Aug 25, Charlton Grosh, aged 13 years, one of the pages in the Hse/o Reps:. Contributing to the support of his widowed mother by his exertions, he was at the same time her assistant in the care of his younger brothers & sisters. Obedient to all placed over him, diligent & affectionate as a pupil.

Circuit Court of Wash Co, D C. John Simms, [colored] has applied to be discharged from imprisonment under the act for the relief of Insolvent Debtors: hearing on the 4th Mon in Sep. –Wm Brent, clk

Masonic: Federal Lodge #1 meeting this evening at 7 p m. –Jas Lawrenson, sec

Wash Light Infty: ordered to meet at the Armory tomorrow at 8 a m, with knapsacks, etc, for 2 days camp duty. By order of the Captain: John Brannan, Sergeant

Columbian Horticultural Society: exhibition was held on Thu at the City Hall: Pomegranate tree bearing ripe fruit was exhibited by Mr Jas Maher, the public gardener. Other exhibitors: Mr Wm Buist; Mr John Douglas; Messrs Wm Cammack & Geo Riggs; Mr J A Smith; Mr John Kedglie; Mr Cassady, gardener to Mr Riggs; Mr Arnold, gardener to Mr John A Smith; Miss E Gardner; Dr Gunnell; Mr Lemuel Wheat; Mr Geo Watterston; Mr Wm B Breckenridge; Mrs A Suter; Alex McIntire; J Lyons; & J S Skinner-Corr Sec. Wm Rich, Pres of the Soc. –Alexandria Gaz

NOTICE: All persons having money, papers, & business in my hands as Constable, will please to call at my house, & receive the same, as my health is at present such that I am not able to attend to out-door business; they will, at the same time, come prepared to pay all costs & charges that may be due on the respective cases. I am ready to pay over all moneys collected by me to the proper person or persons to whom the same may be due. –F W Jirdinston, Constable, square 20, 1st Ward

TUE SEP 12, 1843
Reprint of an old book: New York in 1695, by Andrew Miller, London: reprint in 1843. This book by Rev Miller is possessed of but little interest. It has but few statistics, & deals too much in generalities. To those who are given to the gathering of traditions, the possession of it will not come amiss. –N Y Com Adv

P A De Saules, of the Post Ofc Café, announces that he has procured a first-rate French Cook & is now prepared to furnish Mock Turtle soup of the most approved kind at 18¾ cents a dish.

On Fri Michl Calligan, a seaman on board the U S sloop of war **Preble**, was examined at Boston, & committed to jail to answer at the next term of the Dist Crt for manslaughter, in killing Thos Smith, also a U S seaman on board the **Preble**, on Jul 23. It appeared that the accused had challenged Smith to fight, but, finding himself mastered, drew a sheath knife & stabbed him, causing his death.

On Fri, at Gtwn, a man named Hamilton, a stevedore, recently from N Y, drowned while in the act of catching some drifting timber while in his boat. He has left a wife & family to mourn his loss.

The late Benj Pickman was born on Sep 30, 1763, & descended from a family who had for many generations been a leading one in Salem. He entered Harvard College in 1780; in 1784 he went abroad, passing a year in Dijon, France; also made himself familiar with the father-land in Eng. In the autumn of 1789 he was married to Anstiss, d/o the elder Elias Hasket Derby, & devoted himself to mercantile pursuits. In 1809 he entered Congress, declining to serve more than one term. In 1837 he removed to Boston, where he continued until the spring of the present year, when he returned to die at home. -Boston Courier

On Mon of last week, in Antrim, N H, Jesse Combs took his gun for the purpose of shooting pigeons, but the gun not firing, he took off the lock & the gun accidentally discharged & the contents lodged in the stomach of one of his sons, who soon expired. The dec'd was 8 years of age. –Lowell Courier

Died: on Sep 11, after a lingering illness, Mr J N Nicollet, the eminent mathematician & astronomer. He was a native of Savoy & a citizen of France, but had passed the last 10 years of his life in this country. Friends of the dec'd are invited to attend his funeral, from Galabrun's European Hotel, on Wed, at 12 a m. [Sep 15 newspaper: the solemn offices of the Catholic Church were perfomed by Rev Mr Donelan, after a few touching remarks. Mr Nicollet was born at or near Sallenches, in Savoy, between Geneva & Mont Blanc. By age 20 he proceeded to Paris & became a favorite pupil of Laplace.]

Died: on Sep 8, of consumptin, after a protracted illness, Mrs Ann Eliza Cross, w/o Saml S Cross.

Died: on Aug 26, at Washington, Pa, Mr Henry Arnold, in his 99th year. He was in the battles of Brandywine & Paoli; at which latter place, while serving as a drum-major, his drum was shivered to pieces by a cannon or musket ball while suspended over his back. Up till the time of his death he received a pension from the Govn't; & until that time, he regarded his right of suffrage as one of the most inestimable privileges of a freeman. - Reporter

Mrs R A Beck has removed her Mantua-making & Millinery establishment from E st to Pa ave.

WED SEP 13, 1843
Insurance against fire: Aetna Ins Co, of Hartford, Conn, insures bldgs of every description, goods, furniture, & other property on the most favorable terms. Applications made be made to the subscriber, the agent of the company, at his ofc, over the Hat store of Wm B Todd, on Pa ave, Wash. –D A Hall, Agent [The ad following the above one has D A Hall, Atty at Law, removing his ofc from that of City Hall to the room over W B Todd's Hat Store, on Pa ave.]

Circuit Court of Wash Co, D C. Richd Shaw has applied to be discharged from imprisonment under the act for the relief of Insolvent Debtors: hearing on the 4th Mon in Sep. –Wm Brent, clk

The Hon Elisha Whittlesey is said to have tendered his resignation of the ofc of 6th Auditor of the Treas.

Prof Richd S McCulloh, of Jefferson College, Canonsburg, Pa, is to deliver the Anniversary Address before the Franklin & Philo Literary Societies of that Institution on Sep 28, the day of commencement.

Antoine Geisler, a German, lately tried at Riverhead, L I, for the murder of Mr Smith & family, has been pronounced guilty by the jury. Sentence has been suspended till May.

Chas Co Court, sitting as a Court of Equity, Aug term, 1843. Jas Young jr & Jas Young, jr, as next friend of Sarah E Young, Jane Young & Francis Young, vs, Wm Young, a minor, Jos Haislep, & Jos B & Geo W Haislep, minors. Ratify sale made & reported by Henry May, heretofore appointed trustee for the sale of the property in the proceedings in this cause. Report states the amount of sales to be $800. –C Dorsey -Jno Barnes, clk

Obit-died: The author of this feeble tribute to the memory of an exemplary wife, mother, & friend, saw announced in on the death of Mrs Mgt Cary Warrington, at Berkeley Springs, whither she had gone for the benefit of her health. He knew her well, & cannot see her place vacant without an effort to record his humble opinion of her worth & virtue. Amiable, modest, & unobtrusive, few but those who were intimately associated with her could properly appreciate her character. –Mem

Md Whig nominations of Delegates to the Genr'l Assembly.
Montg Co:
Alex'r Kilgour   David Trundle
Saml D Waters   Lyde Griffith
Queen Anne's Co:
Matthias George   Jas Tilghman   Saml T Harrison
Caroline Co:
Tabdiel W Potter   Robt H McKnett   Wm M Hardcastle

Died: on Sep 10, at her residence in Gtwn, in her 90th year, Mrs Eleanor C Courts, relict of the late Dr Richd Hendly Courts, of the army of the Revolution.

Houses for rent: 2 story frame dwlg house, on E st, with garrets & back bldgs, 10 rooms. Also, a 2 story brick dwlg house on N J ave, on the square next south of the residence of the subscriber. –Thos Blagden

THU SEP 14, 1843
On the first day of the election in Calloway Co, Ky, a man by the name of Skaggs was killed by a Dr Crosswell. Skaggs, says the Mill's Point Hunter, had made a threat to kill Crosswell, & armed himself with a gun & approached him, as is supposed, for that purpose, when Crosswell drew a pistol & shot him down.

Columbus [Geo] Messenger narrates the following distressing story: Mrs Walker, consort of Wm Walker, a highly esteemed & wealthy citizen of Harris Co, was on Tue before last, precipitated in her carriage from the bridge over the Mulberry & drowned before it was possible to extricate her from the stream. Mr Walker & his brother were a short distance behind; before they reached the spot Mrs W was buried in the swollen creek. The mother & servant girl rose no more until they were drawn from the water cold in death. Mrs W's child was the only one who could be saved.

From the West Tenn Whig, published at Jackson, on Aug 29, an affray took place between Mr John H Rawlings, of Jackson, & Col Jos S Douglass, of Perry Co, in which the latter was badly wounded. Rawlings made his escape.

Capt Wm Dennis, late keeper of the Dutch Island lighthouse, near Newport, R I, died at that place on Tue last, at the advanced age of 93 years. He was a native of Newport, & s/o Capt John Dennis, a famous commander of privateers in the old French war. At an early age he commenced a seafaring life, & at the beginning of the American Revolution commanded a merchant ship from the port of London; but on the first news of the hostilities he left & returned home. During the contest he commanded no less than 6 privateers, which were fitted out from different ports. He was twice taken prisoner. After the peace he again entered the merchant service, in which he continued for several years. In 1801 he was appointed sheriff of Newport Co, & held the ofc for 12 successive years. About 1827 he was appointed keeper of the Dutch Island lighthouse, the duties of which he satisfactoryily performed, notwithstanding his advanced age, until within a few months of his death. –Rhode Islander

Col Thos F W Vinson, sheriff of Montg Co, Md, died at Rockville on Fri, aged 60 years, after a lingering & protracted illness, leaving a wife & 4 children to lament his death. Two sheriffs have died in this county within 2 years, & before the expiration of their terms of ofc. Danl H Candler succeeds Col Vinson, having received the highest number of votes at the last election.

Haverhill [N H] Gaz: on Thu a lad 6 years old, s/o Mr Stephen Harris, was run over by the morning train of cars at the depot. His right leg had to be amputated & he died during the night.

Prof Reese has resigned the chair he held in the Wash Univ of Balt, & returned to N Y, the city of his former residence.

The Montg Journal states that Mr Johnson Hardesty, a respectable farmer in said county, was attacked by a young man named Jones, & struck upon the head with a stone, so as to fracture his skull & endanger his life. He was alive at the last account. Jones made his escape to Va. This promising youth was in the employment of the man whom he attempted to kill, & is the s/o Jones who is now serving his term of punishment for murdering Bloyce in that county some 9 years since.

Wash Corp: 1-Ptn of Jacob & others regarding curbstone & footpath on G st, between 8th & 9th sts: passed. 2-Ptn of Rev Wm Mathews & others, asking the repair of the road leading from the upper end of 7th st to the Catholic Burial Ground: referred to the Cmte on Improvement. 3-Ptn of Edw Maynard & others for a gravel footway across 14th st, on a line with the south side of H st: referred to the Cmte on Improvement. 4-Ptn of John

West, praying the remission of a fine: referred to the Cmte of Claims. 5-Act for the relief of Henry Thomas: reported the same without amendment.

In Menard Co, Ill, on Aug 25, Mr Isaac Cogdale was injured so badly by the sudden explosion of a rock blast, which hung fire for a time, that it became necessary to amputate one of his arms. His face & left hand were dreadfully lacerated.

An elegant carriage or hack will be sold at less than half-price, as the owner has no use for it. It has been very lttle used & is in thorough repair. Apply to Dr A Spear, southeast room, 1st floor, in the State Dept, or, after ofc hours, at the Boarding house of Miss Chisholm, 4½ st, east side, 3rd door north of Pa ave.

Dedication of the Odd Fellow's Hall lately erected at the Navy Yard, belonging to Harmony Lodge #9 & Union Lodge #11, will be dedicated today: oration will be delivered at the Methodist Church, Navy Yard, on 4th st east, by Rev Dr Muller, pastor of the English Lutheran Church: aided in the service by Rev Mr Southerland, of the Methodist Protestant Church, & the Rev Mr Brown of the Meth Episc Church.

$200 reward for runaways from the subscriber, living near Queen Anne Post Ofc, PG Co, Md, negroes Robt Herbert & Bill Wells, the latter about 22 years of age. –Jas Mullikin

We, the undersigned, citizens of Wash, are anxious to take another excursion down the river as far as Indian Head, under Capt Duvall & his company. The day we leave to him & his company to select.

J Maher	P Ennis	John Lynch
H Knowles	Wm P Fatherty	Wm Dowling
G Ennis	G Conolly	J Hendley
D Little	M Renahan	P Moran
J Foy	J McGrath	Thos Galt
W Hill	M Dooley	J Sullivan
P Brady	T Baker	F Hill
T Lumpkin	John B Sullivan	Thos Walls
Edmund Stubbs	J Q Adams	F Donohoe

The above was read at the meeting of the Morgan Rifle Co, on Sep 8. Tickets admitting a gentleman & 2 ladies, $1. Cmte of Arrangements:

Capt R E Duvall	Lt J Goddard	Sergeant A R Locke
Surgeon G Sothoron	Ensign J Franck	

Lost, a pair of Gold Spectacles: suitable reward. Leave at the residence of T L Noyes, on H st, or at the State Dept. –J H Noyes

FRI SEP 15, 1843
A well on the beautiful grounds of Jas C Church, at Fort Hamilton Narrows, Long Island, sunk on Sun last. It had been built about 18 months, was 45 feet deep, well walled up with stone, & disappeared in a perpendicular line about 15 feet below the surface, carrying with it the well-house. A rumbling noise was heard by the inmates of the house a few minutes previous to its downward career. –N Y Courier

On Sat last, in this city, by the premature discharge of one of the small brass pieces, known as Harrison #2, belonging to a company of boys, 2 lads were seriously injured. One, s/o the widow of the late Simeon Hathaway, had both of his hands, with the exception of the thumb on the left hand, entirely blown off, & one eye badly burnt. The other boy injured was the s/o Mr John Slocum, who had charge of the gun, & received a severe wound in the side & was considerably burnt. -Hudson Gaz

A Benedictine monk, father Chas Berg, member of the celebrated Abbey of Benedictines, at Melk, in Lower Austria, recently put an end to his life by piercing his heart with a poinsoned stiletto. He is called by the Vienna correspondent of the French Journal des Debats, one of the most distinguished writers of Germany, & had acquired great fame as a critic. From letters written on the day of his death, it appears that he determined to commit suicide from his great weariness of the monastic life. He has twice made a journey to Rome with the single object of obtaining from the Pope a release from his vows. He was 49 years old.

Longevity. Old Sergeant Reid, who was in the ranks at the battle of Bunker's Hill, & an actor in many other deeds of arms, still survives, although in his 108th year. He is no longer able to sit at the door, basking himself in the sun, & crooning or lilting songs he learned in youth. A short time ago he was struck with paralysis, which deprived of the power of locomotion. When visited lately we found him fast asleep, his breathing unimpeded, his chest broad & deep, & his arms brawny & muscular as ever.

The late Railroad accident on Tue. In regard to the occurrence, the passage ticket has printed on it, as one of the regulations of the company, that "No person is permitted to stand upon the platform in front of the car." All those standing on the platform of the car when the axletree broke were more or less injured, while, of the 50 or 60 persons inside of each of the 3 cars which were almost shattered to pieces, only one person sustained a slight bruise. Of the persons injured all except 4 have been removed to their homes in Balt, & are doing well. Messrs Child, Pugh, Cooper, & McCabe still remain at the York hospital, the first in good spirits; the other 3 are doubtful, but not altogether in a hopeless condition.

Forgery discovered at N Y: the perpetrator of it is Jas C Whitmore, of New Haven, Conn, the inventor & patentee of the friction primers, which are used for exploding charges of artillery. The forgeries were committed by counterfeiting the signatures of

Col Craven & Capt Stringham to receipts for primers purporting to have been delivered at the Brooklyn navy yard, which forgeries were cashed by the City Bank of New Haven to the amount of $2,425. Whitmore is among the missing. $200 reward for his apprehension is offered by the Bank. [Sep 21 newspaper: Whitmore was committed to prison to be sent to Connecticut for trial. N Y, Sep 19, 1843.]

Gustavus Barbett arrested in New Orleans on an affidavit made by a female charging him with being a participator in the murderous attempts lately made on the life of young Mr Converse. Examination was appointed for Sep 7, when some of the mystery which hangs over this matter might be explained.

Young Corson, who was arrested & indicted at Bangor, Maine, for the robbery of the post ofc, by abstracting a letter containing a check for $500, has been arraigned before the U S District Court at Wiscasset, where he plead guilty, & was sentenced to 2 years imprisonment in the county jail.

Mrd: Aug 22, by Rev John Davis, Mr Wm W Edwards, of Balt, to Miss Ellen R Fisher, of Montg Co, Md.

Died: on Sep 14, John Dennison, infant s/o John C & Mary McKelden. His funeral is this Fri at 10 a m.

Died: on Sep 10, Wm Henry, y/s/o Richd & Harriet Palmer, aged 3 years & 27 days.

Balt, on Sep 12 an accident occurred during the firing of the salute by a detachment of the Junior Artillerists on Federal Hill, by which 2 engaged in this act were rather seriously injured. After several rounds were fired, & while reloading, a man from the Fort, named Myers, who was assisting, forgot to sponge the gun previously to the putting in of the charge, &, as is usual, some wadding of the previous load had remained in, & being on fire ignited the new charge & it went off. Lt Fred'k Henn, of the N Y Nat'l Grays, residing in Montgomery st, who was assisting, & Myers, the sldr from the fort, were before the muzzle of the piece, & received in their faces the force of the explosion. It is feared Mr Henn will lose one eye, it being rendered entirely blind for the time being. The entire side of the face is much injured. The face of Myers is still more burnt. He was taken to the fort utterly unable to see. -Sun

The Nat'l Jockey Club Races, Wash, D C, will commence Oct 10 & continue for 4 days. –Wm Holmead

I Mudd is the Chairman of the Bldg Cmte for the erection of a Temperance Hall. The plan may be seen at Mr Geo Savage's store, Pa ave.

For sale or rent: 3 story brick house on Missouri av, next to the corner of 4½ st. Also for rent, the dwlg over C B Thornton's store, a few doors west of Brown's Hotel. Apply to Wm Ward.

SAT SEP 16, 1843
Dec 9th the annexed list of property will be sold by public auction, at the City Hall, in Wash City, to satisfy the Corporation for taxes due thereon for the years stated, unless the said taxes be previously paid to the Collector, with such expenses & fees as may have accrued at the time of payment. –A Rothwell, Collector

Adams, Wm	1840-42	$90.73
Andrae, Cornel	1840-42	$22.98
Abbot, Jos	1840-42	$5.72
Allen, Jas [colored]	1840-42	$1.50
Bean, Benj	1840-42	$111.78
Butler, Jas	1838-42	$15.05
Boss, Jas H	1839-42	$118.78
Bottemly, John, heirs of	1838-42	$25.80
Brent, Eleanor & Robt Y	1838-42 $3.30	
Ball & Ford	1836-42	$182.89
Breckenridge, John	1840-42	$42.00
Bullus, John, heirs of	1840-42	$28.60
Bullus, Oscar & Alex'r	1840-42	$12.42
Bickley, Robt S	1840-42	$35.38
Burch, Thos	1840-42	$9.73
Boyle, John	1840-42	$7.62
Ball, John B, heirs of	1840-42	$13.95
Brooke, Nancy	1837-42	$10.84
Brady, Nathl	1836-42	$8.12
Broom, Robt [colored]	1840-42	$9.93
Berry, Rhoda L	1839-42	$25.35
Bingey, Thos S	1840-42	$14.31
Burch, Thos A	1839-42	$6.84
Buist, Wm	1840-42	$42.69
Bender, Jacob A	1836-42	$85.05
Coyle, Francis, heirs of	1840-42	$229.65
Crown, Hessy	1838-42	$34.77
Corcoran, Thos & Wm D Henley	1839-42	$29.96
Columbian College	1838-42	$125.75
Clagett, E L	1840-42	$120.40
Chapman, Mary	1840-42	$115.44
Colt, Rozwell L	1840-42	$106.41

Name	Year	Amount
Caldwell, Timothy & Jas Moore	1840	$79.99
Davidson, Henry	1840-42	$34.38
Davidson, Justina	1840-42	$26.83
Davidson, Lewis G, heirs of	1839-42	$58.24
Davidson, Sarah	1840-42	$23.64
Davidson, Wm	1841-42	$31.24
Dowson, Alfred R	1840-42	$127.72
Dermott, Ann R	1840-42	$584.27
Davidson, John, heirs of	1840-42	$19.22
Davidson, Saml C	1840-42	$25.92
Duley, Thos A	1839-42	$34.17
Eccleson, Saml	1840-42	$1.44
Etting, Solomon	1840-42	$18.45
Evans, French S	1840-42	$24.09
Elliot, Seth A	1839-42	$33.82
Eckloff & Wagler	1840-42	$63.33
Fuller, Azariah	1840-42	$31.68
Foulkes, John E & others	1840-42	$57.12
Fossett, Jas	1841-42	$37.76
Fletcher, Wm	1839-42	$7.56
Forrest, Richd, heirs of	1839-42	$239.73
Grigsly, Baylis	1839-42	$1.32
Givison, Wm	1838-42	$1.35
Greenleaf, Jas	1838-42	$41.92
Hall, David A	1839-42	$109.23
Horsey, Outerbridge	1838-42	$1.40
Halliday, Robt	1840-42	$2.40
Hunt, Saml, & John Patterson	1840-42	$12.42
Hibbs, Chas	1839-42	$90.32
Handy, Jas H, heirs of	1839 & 1842	$61.55
Hoover, John	1841-42	$55.80
Henshaw, J L	1838-42	.45
Hamilton, Matthew, heirs of	1839-42	$21.52
Handy, Edw G	1839-42	$52.00
Handy, Saml W	1839-42	$50.68
Hamilton, Saml, heirs of	1840-42	$7.83
Jones, Walter & Bank of Washington	1840-42	$103.68

Name	Years	Amount
Kurtz, Danl	1838-42	.82
Kirby, Francis	1840-42	$4.14
Keller, Jonas P	1838-42	.15
Kemp, Mary	1840-42	$6.21
Kerr, Henrietta	1840-42	$12.90
Kerr, M A	1840-42	$8.13
Kerr, R E	1840-42	$66.09
Lowe, Saml P, heirs of	1839-42	$44.64
Law, Thos, heirs of	1839-42	$136.56
Lee, Wm	1841-42	$18.78
Lutz, John	1840-42	$5.58
Longacre, J B	1839-42	$7.89
Leddy, Owen	1840-42	$53.26
Ludlow, Thos W	1840-42	$22.35
Middleton, Arthur	1840-42	$382.61
Macgill, Basil	1840-42	$10.53
Munro, David	1840-42	$285.92
Mullen, Dolly	1841-42	$29.46
McKean, J P	1840-42	$52.29
McGuire, J C	1839-42	$57.40
McDermott, Michl	1840-42	$91.42
Mackall, Benj F	1840-42	$3.99
Mountz, John, in trust for Miss Chateline	1841-42	$2.76
Morris, Thos	1840-42	$2.94
Maxey, Virgil	1836-42	$6.67
McKnew, Z W	1840-42	$79.09
Macgill, Thos	1840-42	$95.37
Morrow, Wm	1840-42	$65.13
Nailor, Allison	1838-42	$6.62
Neilson, Hall	1840-42	$6.06
Neale, Henry A	1837-42	$1.82
Nicholson, John	1840-42	$21.63
Nicholson, Jos H, heirs	1838-42	$1.58
Nicholls, Wm S	1839-42	$12.60
Nicholls, W S, in trust	1838-42	$39.69
Packard, Perez	1839-42	$375.52
Porter, Robertha N & John E	1839-42 $75.87	
Pennock & Ash	1839-42	$6.60
Parrott, Richd, heirs	1839-42	$1.08
Phillips, Wm	1839-42	$25.28
Queen, Nicholas L	1839-42	$16.08

Name	Years	Amount
Richardson, Davis	1839-42	$18.54
Ross, Davis	1836-42	$1.80
Rozier, Henry	1837-42	.82
Rench, Jacob, & Lodowick Young	1840-42	$14.49
Riddle, Jos	1839-42	$5.40
Riley, E O	1838-42	$5.58
Sharpe, Arthur, heirs of	1840-42	$10.28
Shaefe, Benj	1839-42	$4.20
Sands, Comfort	1840-42	$6.60
Smith, Paca	1840-42	$4.35
Sterrett, Saml	1838-42	$55.95
Sidebotham, Wm, heirs	1840-42	$5.52
Simmons, Wm	1839-42	$18.60
Seitz, Geo	1840-42	$31.32
Semmes, M A E	1840-42	$29.01
Semmes & Murray	1839-42	$33.40
Stretch, Susan A & E B Scott	1840-42	$91.25
Sewall, Thos, of Balt	1840-42	$77.58
Simpson, Tobias, heirs of	1840-42	$14.40
Shaw, John, & D G Day	1841-42	$45.00
Thomas, Hope	1840-42	$11.46
Thompson, Jos	1841-42	$44.95
Villard, Adam	1840-42	$39.33
Van Cortland, Philip	1840-42	$2.94
Van Coble, Aaron, & Co	1840-42	$52.14
Venable, Chas, heirs of	1840-42	$75.56
Van Ness, John P	1839-42	$31.50
Wright, Joel	1840-42	$20.82
Wallace, Jas	1836-42	$1.25
Whalen, Nicholas	1841-42	$59.06
Waddell, W C H	1840-42	$3.42
Willink, Wm & others	1839-42	$19.86
Walker, Corcas	1839-42	$65.76
Wood, Ferdinand F, heirs of	1840-42	$48.63
Walker, Henry	1839-42	$16.65
Walls, John, jr	1840-42	$26.84
Williamson, Jos	1841-42	$26.46
Ward, Ulysses, & impts Cassandra Ward	1938-42	$158.84

Young, Jas	1838-42	$44.50
Young, McClintock	1840-42	$26.43
Young, Abraham	1839-42	$1.60
Young, John	1838-42	$5.17
Young, Nicholas, heirs of	1839-42	$8.16
Young, Richd	1839-42	$3.36
Zellers, Jacob	1840-42	$6.21

Military Convention on Aug 16, at Norwich, Vt: the Pres, Jas Udall, being absent, Gen t B Ranson was elected Pres pro tem; W E Lewis & J Swett, jr, appointed secs. Capt Alden Partridge remarked on the original design of the convention. Cmtes formed included:

Col T J Nevins	Capt A Partridge	Col Herman H Cornings
Capt J A Hall	Gen T B Ranson	Hon Franklin Pierce
Col W E Lewis	Gen Artemas Cushman	Hon Edmund Burke

Balt College of Dental Surgery will commence on the first Mon of Nov next. Horace H Hayden, M D, Dental Physiology & Pathology. Capin A Harris, M D, Practical Dentistry. Thos E Bend, jr, M D, Special Pathology & Therapeutics. W R Handy, M D, Anatomy & Physiology. Tickets for the whole course-$105. -W R Handy, Dean

Excellent Chamber Furniture at Auction: on Sep 19, at the residence of Mr P W Browning, on Pa ave, between 3rd & 4½ sts,. -Robt W Dyer & Co, aucts

Marshal Bertrand, one of the warmest friends & most distinguished Marshals of the Emperor Napoleon, is now on a visit to New Orleans. He arrived there on Thu week from Havana, accompanied by his son, & is expected to remain but a few days.

The Northampton Courier announces the death of Gen Ebenezer Mattoon, of Amherst. He was a distinguished ofcr in the Revolutionary war, & was subsequently a State Senator, Sheriff of Hampshire, Adj Gen of the State, & Maj Gen of the 4th Div of the Massachusetts Militia. He was always an exemplary member of society, & died in his 89th year.

U S Sldrs. 150 U S troops, under the command of Col Pierce, passed through Boston on Tue on their way to Fort Adams, Newport, from Houlton, Maine. They are described as a fine hardy looking set of men.

Horse strayed from the subscriber. A reward of $2 will be given for the delivery of the above. –Andrew Rupert, on 9th st.

Lime, Lime! 250 barrels of superior Thomaston Lime. Persons wishing to purchase can be accommodated by called at Capt W Warder's or on G W Markness.

Died: on Sep 10, at Montpelier, Va, the seat of his aunt, Mrs Madison, after a lingering illness, Wm Temple Payne, s/o John C & Clara Payne, of Ky-a youth of high promise & principles, beloved & lamented by his family & friends.

Died: on Sep 15, Henry Francis, y/c/o Geo & Caroline Barny Harrington, aged 8 months & 7 days.

Died: on Sep 6, in Mobile, Ala, Mr Seth W Ligon, a native of Va, aged 55 years, but for the last 20 years a resident of Mobile. He was as much beloved for his amiable qualities in Va as he was in Alabama, where he was well known by the cognomen of honest Seth. The writer of this notice was a personal friend of the dec'd & knew that he deserved the great Poet's praise, that "an honest man is the noblest work of God." -A B T

Mr John Douglass Bemo, [so named in baptism,] son of Hus te-kul luk chee, formerly Principal Chief of the Seminoles, & nephew of Oseola, will give an account of his remarkable conversion, & urge the duty of Christian missions, tomorrow evening in the Presbyterian Church, 4½ st, at half past 7 o'clock.

For rent: the large 3 story brick house & store corner of 10th st & Pa ave. –Michl Sardo, 10th & H sts

MON SEP 18, 1843
Trustee's sale of valuable property: in Wash City, Oct 9, all the west half part of lot 5 in sq A, with the 2 story brick dwlg & other improvements thereon. –John Kurtz, trustee - Robt W Dyer & Co, aucts

The Minister of Russia, the Chevalier Alex'r de Bodisco, with his family, left this city last week, to embark at N Y for his own country; to which, on leave of his Gov't, he makes a visit after several years' absence. He arrived at N Y on Fri & probably by this time is on his way across the Atlantic. Speaking our language with the fluency of his own, he has mingled with ease & without ostentation with our citizens. The best wishes of our community attend him & his estimable & lovely lady.

Trustee's sale of houses & lots: deed of trust from John Foote, to me duly recorded: sale on the premises on Sep 25: the whole of lot 21 & the southern part of lot 22 in sq 564, fronting on 3rd st west, with the improvements, which are 2 new frame houses. –John F Pickrell, trustee -Robt W Dyer & Co, aucts

Orphan's Court of Wash Co, D C. Letters testamentary on the personal estate of Fred'k Hall, late of said county, dec'd. -Danl W Hall, David A Hall, excs

The U S Gov't having recently allowed Nathan Beers, of New Haven, Conn, the arrears of a pension due him, amounting to $3,360, the old veteran magnanimously distributed the amount among those who were his cresitors in 1820, when he failed in business.

Jacob Shipman, who was arraigned a few days ago before the Court of Gen Sessions at N Y, on a charge of felonious embezzlement in appropriating to his own use $15,000 in gold belonging to the Union Bank of that city, was acquitted by the Jury on Thu upon a technical point of law-they having returned a verdict that "the offence was not committed within the jurisdiction of the State," on the ground that the intention to appropriate the money to his own use was not conceived until after he had arrived in Phil. He will doubtless be arraigned & tried in the latter city.

Boston Transcript. On Tue at Taunton, 3 men, Jos Clark, Jos Pettes, & Square Davis, engaged in blasting rocks near the river, were frightfully injured when the powder ignited & exploded unexpectedly.

The downward steamboat train on the Eastern railroad when near Wells, Maine, ran off the track, killing the engineer, Horace Adams, almost instantly by the tender falling upon him. No harm occurred to the passengers, except that one lady was very slightly injured by the shock.

Sister Frederika, a Sister of Charity, died on Mon of the yellow fever. She had recently arrived from the North, & died after an illness of 6 days, a martyr to the noblest & most beautiful of the Christian virtues, to a profession requiring the loftiest courage & the purest distinterestedness & magnimity of which human nature is capable. –N O Bulletin

Local News. The great flood on Sat last caused extensive injuries to public & private property in Wash City & in Gtwn. Among the sufferers were: Messrs F & A H Dodge, Messrs Pickrell, Lowry, Davidson, Fearson, Brown, Dixon, Ratcliffe, McPherson, Smoot, & Miller & Duvall.

On Sep 15, a small boy, s/o Mr David Wilson, of **Greenleaf's Point**, accidentally fell from the Fish wharf, foot of 6th st, & was drowned. Up to this time, Sunday, his body has not been recovered. It is hoped by his bereaved parents that if any one finds it they will either return it to his father's residence, on Greenleaf's Point, or give information where it may be obtained.

Found, on Sat last, near the Railroad Depot, a small bag containing a wedge of gold & other things, which the owner can obtain by calling on the subscriber at the ofc of the Nat'l Intell. –Ed Deeble

TUE SEP 19, 1843
View of Hanover, Va: from a Pioneer's Sketch Book: Jan, 1837. On the South Anna branch I saw standing, in 1825, near Ground squirrel bridge, the old church built for & for many years occupied by the venerable Saml Davies, [late Pres of Princeton College, N J,] who preached in this region for 11 years; &, just after Braddock's defeat in 1755, in the following year, in haranguing troops to protect the frontiers from the invading savages, he pointed out the heroic youth Geo Washington [then Col] as reared up by Divine Providence to be the saviour of his country. There stands about 2 miles west of the Pomonkey river, the venerable old courthouse in which Patrick Henry made his first essay as a public speaker in the Parson's case; & there stands the same old tavern where Henry attended the bar, after his first marriage, for his father-in-law, & studied the statute laws of old Virginia. Near to, or in the slashes of Hanover, Patrick Henry, as well as Henry Clay, were born. East of the South Anna we may find a place, though nothing now more than an old farm, yet styled Scotchtown. Here resided the illustrious patriot & statesman at the breaking out of the American revolution. Here his family resided, whilst Henry had to encounter many mental & personal afflictions known only to his family physician. His soul was bowed down & bleeding under the heaviest sorrows & personal distress. His beloved companion had lost her reason, & could only be restrained from self-destruction by a strait-dress. On the North Anna river was a place called *Oakley*, the residence of Govn'r Nelson, who commanded the Va forces at the siege of Yorktown. We passed to *Merry Oaks*, where the ruins of an old farm can be seen. This is the birthplace of Henry Clay, now called Harry of the West.

Died: on Sun last, in Wash City, in her 92nd year, Madam Delia Tudor, wid/o the Hon Wm Tudor, of Revolutionary memory. Her funeral will take place from her late residence at 11 a m, today; at which the friends of the dec'd & those of her dght, Mrs Comm Stewart, are invited to attend.

Died: On Sep 9, in Balt, Mrs Eliz Mgt Gross, at the advanced age of 112 years. During her lifetime she enjoyed uninterrupted health, having never taken any medicine, or having any attendance from a physician, until 3 year since, when she had a fall & broke her arm, which she was enabled to use again in a few weeks.. She was followed to the grave by her descendants to the 5th generation.

Household furniture at auction: on Sep 26, by deed of trust, executed on Oct 18, 1842, by C H Van Patten, at the apts over C J Nourse's exchange ofc, West of Todd's hat store, Pa ave. –D A Hall, trustee -Robt W Dyer & Co, aucts

A young lawyer by the name of Emmett Quin, of Doylestown, Pa, left his ofc, books, & clothing on Aug 20 last, alone. He left a note to his brother; & fears are entertained for his safety. The Buck's Co Intell has an advertisement signed by his mother & father, imploringly beseeching the return of the wanderer.

For sale: the subscriber wishes to sell a very valuable lot of ground adjoining the residence of Mrs Bealle, about a mile north of the Capitol. It contains about 12 acs. Inquire of Mr David Moore, adjoining the land, or to the subscriber. Also, a small tract of land adjoining Judge Dorsey's, & 2 miles from the village of Bladensburg. This tract contains 50 acs: a small dwlg is on the land. Inquire of Mr Jno Anderson, in Bladensburg, or the subscriber in Wash, D C. –Jas Moore

$50 reward for runaway negro man Henson, about 24 years of age. I brought him from the neighborhood of Upper Marlborough from Mr Marien T Lamar's, where he was raised, Jan 1 last; he has some relations in that neighborhood; his father is living in Anne Arundel Co, on the farm of Mr Walter Smith. –Richd I Bowling. P S: Any communication respecting him will be addressed to me at Greenesville, PG Co, Md.

WED SEP 20, 1843
Wm & Mary College lectures will commence on the 2nd Mon in Oct. The price of Board, including washing, lights, & fuel, at other Boarding Houses in town, cannot exceed $150. The price of Board here put down at $130, is that paid to the College Steward. The Students boarding with him lodge in the College Bldg. Gentlemen preparing themselves for Medical Graduation at any Institution, can obtain the necessary preparation from Prof Millington, who gives a private course of Med Instruction: Fee $30.
–T R Dew, Prof

The Auditor of the Circuit Court of Wash Co, D C, will audit the accounts of the trustee appointed by said Court, on Oct 2, in the cause of Jas Townley & others, vs, the heirs & reps of Henry Knowles, jr & others. Those having claims or being interested in the distribution of said estate will make their claims known on that day. –Jos Forrest, Aud

Valuable estate for sale: on accommodating terms, his plantation, known as ***Bowieville***, & in PG Co, Md: contains 754 acs: the dwlg, built at great cost, & out of the best materials, stands on a commanding eminence, overlooking a beautiful country. This plantation lies in th centre of that delightful region of country known as the ***Forest of Prince George's***. –Robt Bowie, Good Luck P O, PG Co, Md
'
Died: on Sep 3, at the residence of his father, John P Erwin, near Nashville, Tenn, his only son & namesake, John P Erwin, jr, in his 26th year.

Died: Sep 16, in Wash City, Mrs Nancy Cranch, aged 71 years, w/o Judge Cranch; & on Sep 17, her brother, Jas Greenleaf, aged 78. [Sep 22 newspaper: obit of Mrs Cranch: for upwards of 40 years had Mrs Cranch been known to the inhabitants of this District as filling with exemplary attention the most important relations of social life. In the education of her children, her own singular equanimity & wisdom, with the high qualities of her husband, enabled them to avoid those difficulties which so often embarrass the parental relation. Mrs Cranch was a dght of Wm Greenleaf, formerly Sheriff of Suffolk Co, Mass. She was one of a numerous family of brothers & sisters, among whom the wid/o the late venerable Dr Webster & others survive her. One, Jas Greenleaf, well known as among the earliest settlers of this city, outlived his beloved sister but a few hours.]

Information wanted. The undersigned, some 12 or 13 years ago, while yet a boy, left his father's family, &, not having been settled as to a permanent residence since that time, neglected keeping up a correspondence with then, consequently knows nothing of their present whereabouts. When he left them they were living near Lachine, in Canada. The family consisted of his parents, Jas & Mary McClernin, & of his 3 sisters, Mgt, [or Peggy,] Biddy, & Mary. Any information concering them will be thankfully received by the son & the brother, who is anxious to return & once more take his place in that circle where is to be found the greatest share of worldly happiness. –Patrick McClernin, Milledgeville, Ga -Sep 15, 1843

The flags of the shipping at the port of Phil were at half-mast on Sun, in respect for the memory of Capt Jacob Wing, one of the oldest shipmasters in the city, who died very suddenly the day previous. On Sat morning he appeared to be in good health; but at noon, as he was entering his dwlg in Southwark, he suddenly fell dead across the threshold. During a long life, many years of which were devoted to the pursuit of his profession, he obtained & commanded a high respect for his integrity & moral worth.

Mr Richd Feddeman left the residence of the late Thos C Earle, [where his grandfather Judge Earle, now resides,] in a gig, to go to his home, which is at the adjoining farm known as the "**Silk Farm**.' Search was made for him, & he was found wandering about the field perfectly insensible & speechless. This is the 3rd time within 2 years that this young gentleman has met with accidents which were in each previous case near ending his life; first from the kick of a horse, second from shooting himself, & now in the manner above described. He is known as an amiable & exemplary young man. –Queen Ann's [Md] Telescope

The largest person ever known in Ireland, with perhaps the exception of Philip Macoule, the celebrated Irish giant, was Roger Byrne, who resided in Ossory, & was buried on May 13, 1787, in the churchyard of Rosennallis, in Queen's County. He weighed 100 pounds more than the noted Bright, of Maiden, in Eng, who weighed 460 pounds, & 160 pounds lighter than Danl Lambert, who died in 1809, & weighed 739 pounds. We believe that the heaviest man ever known in New England was Caleb Towle, an industrious, wealthy, & respectable citizen of Centre Harbor, N H, who died in 1822, from an extraordinary increase of flesh. Though short of 5 feet 10 inches high, he weighed 515 pounds. –Boston Journal

A Teacher of academic learning wishes to obtain a situation in some healthy village or country place in an academy, high school, select school, or some promising primary school. Inquire personally or by letters, postpaid, of the following gentlemen, of Balt, viz: Messrs Armstrong & Berry, 134 Balt st, & the Rev Dr F Waters at Franklin, or direct a letter to Wm S Dix, Princess Anne, Somerset Co, Md.

Postponed sale of valuable improved property near Pa ave, in Wash City. Sale on Sep 25. Decree of the Circuit Court of Wash Co, D C, passed in the case of Juliana Williamson & others, vs, Geo W Williamson & others, for the sale of the real estate of David Williamson, dec'd, for division among his devisees, that very valuable piece of property on 13th st west, now occupied by Capt Wm Thomas as a hotel, & known as lots 6 & 7 in sq 291, corner of 13th & E sts: upon which are 2 very good 2 story brick houses, with extensive back bldgs, stables, etc. –Ch A Williamson, Trustee -Robt W Dyer & Co, aucts

THU SEP 21, 1843
Phil, Jun 7, 1843: letter from the Phil Bar to the Hon Jas Kent inviting him to a dinner to express their feelings. Signed:

John Sergeant	Ferd W Hubbell	Josiah Randall
Chas Chauncey	Henry D Gilpin	Richd Vaux
Thos J Wharton	Wm W Meredith	

Reply from Chancellor Kent: dated N Y, Jun 12, 1843: declines the invitation: he is on the verge of 80 years of age & for some time past thought it proper to withdraw myself as much as possible from public duties & festivities.

Independent Order of Odd Fellows: Ofcrs installed on Tue last to serve for 2 years:
P G M Howell Hopkins, of Pa, M W G Sire
P G M Wm S Stewart, of Mo, R W D G Sire
P G M Jas L Ridgely, of Md, R W G Sec
P G M A E Warner, of Md, R W G Treas
P G M Rev Albert Case, of S C, R W G Chaplain
P G Richd Brant, of N J, W G Guradian
P G John E Chamberlain, of Md, W G Messenger

Paul Bertus, Recorder of the First Municipality of the city of New Orleans, put an end to his existence on Sep 10, by taking poison. As to pecuniary matters he was considered tolerably well off. Myster hangs over the causes which induced him to commit suicide. A large concourse of person attended his funeral & showed how greatly he was esteemed.

The Alton [Ill] Telegraph of Sep 9 says: there are 4 Roman Catholic churches in progress of erection or completion in this State at the present time, that we know of; one at Chicago, one in Alton, one at Edwardsville, in the same county, & one in Shawnestown.

Marshal Bertrand, after receiving every mark of distinction which it was in the power of the people of New Orleans to bestow, had taken his departure. The Louisiana Legion, the Wash Btln, & the Regt of Louisiana Volunteers made their appearance in full military costume. The military repaired to the residence of the Marshal, escorted him to the Place d'Armes, where they were reviewed by the distinguished guest, who had served under Napoleon. From thence he was escorted to the steamer **Admiral**, upon which he embarked for the Hermitage, amid the roar of cannon & the shouts of the multitude.

Died: yesterday, of complicated & lingering disease, Mary Eliz Meehan, aged 19 years & 9 months, d/o John S Meehan, Librarian of Congress. Her funeral will be from the house of her father, on North B st, Capitol Hill, near N J ave, tomorrow, at 10 a m.

Died: on Sep 14, in Martinsburg, Va, of dropsy, Mr Lewis Minchin, formerly a resident in Wash City, in his 34th year.

Died: on Sep 20, in his 40th year, Wm S Nicholls, [colored] after an illness of about 48 hours. His funeral is today at 3 p m.

Wash Corp: 1-Ptns of Francis Selden & of Nicholas Ferreton, praying the remission of fines: referred to the Cmte of Claims. 2-Ptn of Randall Pegg, praying for the remission of a fine: referred to the Cmte of Claims.

Dissolution of Partnership existing under the name of J H & C Goddard was dissolved on Sep 18 by mutual consent. The grocery business will be carried on by Calvin Goddard alone. –J H Goddard, C Goddard

Valuable farm & woodlands at private sale near Wash City: 2½ miles from the Centre Market, adjoining the lands of Dr Worthington & Messrs Holmead & Pearce: contains 300 acs: divided into the following portions; Lot 1-about 128 acs, with a dwlg-house, barn stable, manager's house, negro qrtrs, & other out-bldgs. Dwlg is cottage style, having piazzas on 3 sides, forming a square of 50 feet. Lot 2-50 acs, bounded on the south by the country road leading to *Pearce's Mill*. Lot 3-37 acs 3 roods & 23 perches, chiefly in wood. Lot 4-34 acs 3 roods & 23 perches, chiefly in wood. Lot 5-34 acs 3 roods & 16 perches, heavily timbered & rich. The title is perfect. Mr King, the manager, will show the boundaries, & for price & other particulars, apply to me, at Gtwn, D C. I am only induced to dispose of this property from a desire to locate myself in one of the States, with a view to the practice of my profession. –Richd W Redin

FRI SEP 22, 1843
Lumber caught adrift. The subscribe has caught a large lot of lumber in the Canal during the recent freshet, which the owner or owners can have be proving property & paying charges. –John A Rollings, on the wharf between 6th & &7th sts.

A pressed lead-pipe factory has been established in Cincinnati by Messrs S & G E Sellers, formerly of Phil.

The young lady so brutally murdered a few weeks since in the parish of Caldwell, was Harriet Cummins. Capt Goodrich, of the steamboat **Levi Welch**, informs that she came on board his boat at the mouth of Red river, [about 15 miles from where her body was found on Sep 23,] where she was landed on Jul 17th or 18th. She was accompanied to the boat by Mr White & another person, one of whom, Capt G does not remember which, paid her passage. She stated that she had property coming to her in the neighborhood of Tunica, from which she had as yet received nothing but her education, & was apprehensive of unfair dealing on the part of those having it in possession, & was then on her way to see an uncle residing within 10 miles of Columbia, to get him to settle her affairs. She is represented as a modest, intelligent, & interesting girl, & as having possessed a good education. We hope the perpetrators may be ferreted out.

N Y, Sep 19-a distressing accident at the arsenal in Centre st, in which Henry Storms, s/o Gen Storms, was the unintentional cause of inflicting a severe wound upon a young lad about 15 years of age, John Daley, who lives in Duane st. Storm was shooting at a large plank target & when he discovered the ball had gone through the fence and into the shoulder of Daly who was leaning against the fence. The ball was removed and the wound was not considered dangerous. –American

The Cincinnati Message says: on Thu in this city, J Kamalenoski, the s/o a wealthy citizen of Warsaw, who himself was a native of Poland, aged perhaps 30 years, committed suicide. Soon after his arrival in this country, he became acquainted with a girl near Norfolk, Va, & married her in 12 months from the time he arrived in the U S. He emigrated with his family, consisting of a wife & 5 children to this city during the past summer. Soon after their arrival here, a young man named Joyslin, formerly a neighbor to the wife of Kamalenoski, became very familiar about there house. Finally, about 3 weeks ago, the wife of Kamalenoski left her home & children & took up her residence with Joyslin, on Longworth st, where they lived as husband & wife until Wed last, when Joyslin told her he had a wife in Va, & that it was his determination to return to her on the following morning. Mrs Kamalenoski remonstrated with him, & he avowed his determination to leave the city. The vicious woman returned to her husband, he knowing of her conduct. The husband turned and unlocked his trunk, took a pistol therefrom & shot himself through the heart.

Mrd: on Sep 19, by Rev John P Donelan, Capt Geo T Raub to Miss Ann E Reily, both of Wash City.

Died: on Sep 1, after a short illness, in his 56th year, the Rev Stephen W Presstman, for the last 20 years the faithful & universally beloved Rector of Immanuel Church, Newcastle, Delaware.

Died: on Sep 14, in Phil, Chas Stewart Fry, aged 21 years, s/o Wm Fry. -Phil paper

Household furniture at auction: on Sat next, in front of our auction store, a variety of household furniture, part of the personal estate of Mrs Louisa Coombs, by order of the Orphan's Court of Wash Co, D C. -Robt W Dyer & Co, aucts

The Caddo [Lou] Gaz of Aug 23 gives the particulars of a murder in that region. John W Rice killed Wm Moran in self defence, & was immediately acquitted.

NOTICE-I forewarn all persons from trusting any person or persons on my account, as I will pay no debts of their contracting. –Jno H Clarvoe

Wash Corp: 1-The Mayor is authorized to accept the arrangement entered into by John Foote with his creditors, & upon the same conditions, as far as the said John Foote is indebted to the Corp of Wash, for a fine for selling liquor without a license.

SAT SEP 23, 1843
For rent: the house on K st near his excellency Mr Fox's residence & Gtwn. Apply to Messrs Geo Johnson or Jos Smoot of the neighborhood for information of the propreitor's residence.

The infant dght of the Queen of Portugal is to be baptized Donna Maria Anna Fernanda Leopoldina Michaela Ralaela Garbriella Carlota Antonia Julia Victoria Praxedes Gonzaga de Braganza e Bourbon Saxe Coburg e Gotha. -Sun

St Matthew's Church: most Rev Dr Eccleston, Archbishop of Balt, will impart the Papal Benediction at the high mass on Sep 24. The Rev Mr Ryder, Provincial of the Society of Jesus will preach on the occasion.

Circuit Court of Wash Co, D C. Page C Dunlop has applied to be discharged from imprisonment under the act for the relief of Insolvent Debtors: hearing on Sep 30. –Wm Brent, clk

A letter from Vienne [Isere] says: Archeological excavations principally directed to discover the mortal remains of Guy de Poisien, Archbishop of Vienne, have been going on in a part of a wide Roman st. Several tombs of great antiquity were opened & that of the reverend prelate was at last laid open. His bones were taken up & deposited near those of his brother Etienne, in the Church of Sant Maurice.

Madam Delia Tudor, whose decease, in this city, in her 92nd year, has been very recently announced. She was the Widow of the Hon Wm Tudor, who was, at age 24 years, appointed by Congress to be the first Judge Advocate Gen of the Army, in which he afterwards held the rank of Lt Col. She was the mother of the Hon Wm Tudor, whose name is endeared to his friends & to his country by his public services & by the literary works which he left. It was because of her son that she came to reside in Wash City, where after he died from the service of his country in a foreign land, she continued to reside from choice.

Dress-making: Mrs E W Randall has taken the house over the dyeing extablishment of Mr L Denham, Pa ave, between 9th & 10th sts.

For rent: a well finished house on N Y ave, between 9th & 10th sts. Apply to H J Wilde, on Indiana ave, or to Jos Bryan, on the premises.

Attention Antiquarians! The house & lot where Mary, the mother of Washington, lived & died, in Fredericksburg, Va, will be sold on the premises on Oct 21 next. Having removed to my present residence at Union Theological seminary, I have determined to sell, & will make the terms accommodating. -Saml B Wilson

Dissolution of Copartnership between the subscribers by mutual consent. Henry Bradley is authorized to liquidate & settle all accounts. –Henry Bradley, R Estep [See below.]
+
New Firm: R Estep, of the late firm of Bradley & Estep, & J T Catlett, of the former firm of Bradley & Catlett, having associated themselves under the firm of Estep & Catlett, have bought out their entire stock at a price below cost. We shall be in receipt of new goods of every style. –Estep & Catlett [Alexandria Gaz; Potomac Advocate; Marlborough Gaz]

Cumberland Civilian noticing the late flood says the rains caused the Potomac & Will's creek to rise beyond that of last spring. On Fri last the bridge across Will's creek, erected by Mr Geo Hoblitzell in the rear of his dwlg, was carried off, & with it a part of his back bldg. One negro girl, aged about 9 years, & another negro child in the cradle, were lost. Mrs Hoblitzell, & a negro woman, the mother of the young child, in their efforts to to save the children, were both severely injured by the falling timbers. Had it not been for the embankmanet recently made by Messrs Letson & Rutter along the mouth of Will's creek, the lower part of the town would again have been inundated.

MON SEP 25, 1843
Col Richd M Johnson arrived in Washington on Fri. Also arrived on the same day, the Hon David Henshaw, Sec of the Navy; the Hon Walter Forward, late Sec of the Treas.

A most brutal murder was committed near Knoxville, Tenn, on Sep 5, on the person of John Sutton, a sldr of the Revolution, aged 95 years, for the sake of obtaining $33, the pension money which the old man had drawn that day.

New Fall Goods just opened: Wm M Perry's, 2nd door west of 7th st, opposite Centre Market.

Among the passengers of the ship **Caledonia** is Mr Wm Macready, the celebrated tragedian. The Liverpool Times says he is justly celebrated as the first tragedian in England.

The Hartford [Conn] Daily Courant says that the carriage shop of Messrs L W & A Penfield, of Monroe, Conn, was consumed by fire on Sep 14th. No insurance-loss at about $8,000 to $9,000.

On Wed, in the Court at Salem, N J, Alex'r Novoscoski, alias Edw Bronowski, alias Edw Smith, was convicted of bigamy. It was proved that at present he had 4 wives living, & that the whole of them had been at the house of a relative of one of his wives in this city. This fellow was a few months back arrested here, on the charge of his last wife, whom he married in Salen, of cruel treatment. Sentence deferred.

Two of Dupont's Powder Mills, near Wilmington, Del, exploded on Thu, killing Michl Burl.

Peter G Chandler, tried in the Criminal Court at St Louis for throwing the engineer of the steamboat **Belle of Pittsburg** overboard , had been found guilty of murder in the 2nd degree, & sentenced to 50 years in the pen.

The large barn belonging to Mr Philip Nicodemus, near Westminster, Carroll Co, Md, with his entire crop of gran, hay, etc, was consumed by fire on Mon last. The fire was communicated by a candle which some of the family had been using after nightfall in the barn in getting out grain.

Mrd: on Sep 5, at Meadowville, Fauquier Co, Va, by Elder Traverse D Herndon, Mr Jas W Lungeford to Miss Harriet Bruin.

Mrd: on Sep 7, by Elder Traverse D Herndon, at Fruit Farm, Fauquier Co, Va, Mr Madison E Thomas, merchant of Jackson, Miss, to Miss Sarah C, 4th d/o Jas S Pickett.

Mrd: on Sep 13, at *Woodbourne*, the residence of Mrs Elvira A Bruce, in Halifax Co, Va, by Rev Mr Grammer, Jas M Morson, of the city of Richmond, to Miss Ellen C Bruce, d/o the late Mr Jas Bruce.

Died: yesterday, Mrs Sarah Ann Jones, w/o Dr Wm Jones, Postmaster of Wash City, & d/o the late Thos Corcoran, of Gtwn. Her funeral is this afternoon at 4 p m.

Died: on Sep 19, in Norfolk, Mrs Esther P B Upshur, w/o Arthur W Upshur, Purser of the U S Navy, in her 23rd year.

Died: on Sep 20, in Wash City, Mrs Mgt Hunt, of N Y, but late of Balt, aged 32 years.

Died: on Sep 15, at the residence of his brother, Robt Baylor, in Jefferson Co, Va, Col Richd G Baylor, sheriff of Norfolk Co, aged 32, leaving a wife & 6 children.

Died: on Sep 19, after a lingering illness, Cornelia Victoria, infant d/o Jas William & Mary Ann Davidson, aged 10 months & 27 days.

The City Post Ofc has been removed to 7th st west, north of the Gen Post Ofc. –Wm Jones, P M

PUBLIC NOTICE: This is to notify the public that from & after this date I will pay no debts whatever except such as may be contracted by myself in person or upon a written order from under my own hand. -John Hardiso [Hardiso could be Hardison. The last letter is partially missing.]

Fresh Family Groceries: store on 7th st, opposite the Patriotic Bank. –S Holmes

TUE SEP 26, 1843
An attempt was made last week, in the night, to blow up the house of John B Wood, of Manchester, N H. A keg of powder was placed under the house, & a slow match applied. It exploded injuring the house very much, but not destroying it. A reward has been offered for the apprehension of the perpetrators.

Mr Aymer, a well known American Circus performer, recently broke his neck at Batty's Circus, in the Isle of Jersey. A London paper says that Mr Batty is the proprietor of the Royal Amphitheatre & that Mr Aymer concluded his performance with a double somerset, & in throwing it the ill-fated artist, instead of alighting on his feet, fell on his neck, & death was the immediate result.

The Gloucester Telegraph of Sep 20 contains an account of the loss, in a gale on Aug 20, of the schnr **Byron**, Capt Geo Watson, of that place, with all on board, numbering 10 persons, 6 of whom have left families.

Mrd: on Jul 29, at Brighton, England, Rt Hon Lord Erskine, Envoy Extra & Minister Pleni to the Court of Munich, in Bavaria, Germany, to Ann Bond, d/o the late John Travis, of Phil.

Died: on Sep 5, at his residence, Spring Hill, near Augusta, after a protracted illness of 10 months, Gen Wm Watts Montgomery, in his 49th year, leaving a wife & 7 children to mourn their irreparable loss.

House to rent: for the term of 18 months, from Nov 2: located in F st, at the corner of 6th: rent $300 per annum. Apply to the subscriber on the premises, any day between the hours of 3 & 5. –E J Sylvester

House for rent: the entire dwlg over the store of Mr Allen on Pa ave, between 9th & 10th sts. The undersigned having removed to a smaller house, offers for sale the furniture of several rooms, with the carpets fitted complete, which are nearly as good as new. –John Allen

Disgraceful breach of the Sabbath & the Public peace. On Sun last Pearse & Turton, who had a previous quarrel in a brothel, undertook to have an affair of fisticuffs, & a pitched battle, which took place near the residence of Chas Hill, in 14th st. About 200 persons were present during this disgraceful scene.

The body of Henry Wilson, who fell into the Potomac on Sep 15, was found on the shore of Dr Danigerfield's farm, near Alexandria. The corpse has been restored to the poor boy's afflicted parents residing at **Greenleaf's Point**. On Sat last was also found in the same place the corpse of a pretty well dressed female, apparently a middle-aged woman, who has not been recognised.

WED SEP 27, 1843
Circuit Court of Wash Co, D C. Wm Casey has applied to be discharged from imprisonment under the act for the relief of Insolvent Debtors: hearing on Oct 2. –Wm Brent, clk

Copartnership of the firm of Bentley, Randall & Co, dissolved my mutual consent on Aug 10, 1843, the undersigned disposed of his entire interest in the business of the late firm, patent rights excepted, to his late partners, Dudley A Randall & Paris H Keach, doing business under the firm of Randall & Co. All persons indebted, & all having claims against the late firm, will call on Randall & Co. –C W Bentley

Orphan's Court of Wash Co, D C. Letters of adm on the personal estate of Saml White, late of said county, dec'd. –Mary A White, admx

The late Hon Lewis Summers, of Va, died on Aug 27, at the White Sulphur Springs, Va & was for more than 24 years past one of the Judges of the General Court of Va. Judge Summers was born on Nov 7, 1778, in Fairfax Co, Va, being the eldest s/o Geo & Ann S Summers. His father was several times a member of the Leg of Va as a delegate from Fairfax Co. His mother only preceded him to the grave about 5 weeks. Judge S entered upon the duites of active life during the Presidency of the elder Adams. In 1808 he removed to the West, settling for a short time in Gallipolis, Ohio; in 1814 he took up his residence in Kanawha Co, where he continued ever since to reside. Judge Summers was early imbued with pious feelings & with religious instructions by parental care, & by the pastoral nurture of the Rector of Christ Church, Alexandria. –Kanawha Gaz

For sale: the thorough bred horse Javelin which will be exhibited on the Race course at Wash during the 2 first days of the races. Javelin is 7 years old, was bred by the late Gen Irvine, was got by Daghee, who was bred in England by Comm Burne, & brought out to Canada by him. Javelin's dam was Grand Duchess, bred by the late John Randolph, of Roanoke, got by Gracchus, his grand dam Duchess, imported, bred by the Duke of Grafton. -Robt W Dyer & Co, aucts

Wood & Coal for sale. For further particulars inquire at his wood-year, on 11th st, near the Canal. -Peter Casanave

Golden Hill Seminary, Bridgeport, Conn: French & English School for Young Ladies, Mrs S A Burr, [a native of France] Principal. School will re-open on Nov 1. School is located on Long Island Sound, only 4 hours from N Y. All boarders will attend the Episcopal Church with the Principal, unless the parents or guardians desire that they sould attend other churches. References may be made to the following:

Rev G S Colt, Bridgeport, Conn
Hon Andrew T Judson, Hartford, Conn
Hon Saml Ingham, Essex, Conn
Rt Rev Benj T Onderdonk, D D, N Y
Rev Wm Berrien, D D, N Y
Rev Edw Y Higbee, N Y
Rev Antoine Verren, N Y
Rev Benj F Futler, N Y
C V S Kane, N Y
Rev T W Colt, D D, New Rochelle, N Y
Hon Milliard Fillmore, Buffalo, N Y
Edw Pittman, Balt
Col Garland, Detroit, Mich
Col Andrews, Charles, S C

Rev Wm Hawley, Wash
Ch W Goldsborough, Wash
Hon Amos Kendall, Wash
W W Seaton, Wash
M St Clair Clarke, Wash
Thos L Smith, Wash
Vinal Luce, Wash
Gen Jesup, Wash
Gen Towson, Wash
Col Cross, Wash
Wm Easton, Mibile, Ala
Hon Geo W Crabb, Mobile, Ala
Hon Levi Woodbury, U S Senate

Fall & Winter Fashions: Robb, Winebrener & Co: just opened their new fashions: all will be made up in a superior manner at their old establishment, 102 Chestnut st, Phil.

Teacher wanted to conduct a small school at the Hot Springs, to be composed of 6 females in the ordinary branches of English, & 5 or 6 young men in the Latin, Greek, & Mathematics. Salary of $300, with board, washing, etc, will be given to one who can funish satisfactory evidence as to character & qualifications. None others need apply.

Univ of Md annual course of lectures in the Medical Dept of the Univ will commence on the last Mon of Oct next, & to be continued till Mar 1 following. –Saml Chew, Principal

Glen Ross for sale: by authority given to me by the last will & test of Richd Ross, late of Montg Co, Md, dec'd: sale on Feb 5 next, the farm & plantation on which he resided at the time of his decease; about 470 acs; estate lies on the main road leading from Wash City to Brookville, & adjoins the lands of Thos Wilson & others, & is in the vicinity of the land recently purchased by Francis P Blair on the same road. The improvements are a large commodious dwlg-house, with a spacious stone kitchen adjoining; stone stables, with barns, & all necessary out-bldgs attached, & an ice house. At the same time will be sold a small tract of 7 or 8 acs adjacent to Glen Ross, with 2 small dwlg houses. I shall then sell all the personal property [except the negroes] now on the Glen Ross estate. –Nathan Lufborough, exc of the last will & test of Richd Rose

Negroes wanted: highest cash prices will be paid for from 25 to 30 negroes, of both sexes, if immediate application be made to the subscriber, at Brown's Hotel, Wash. –Harris Edmondson

THU SEP 28, 1843
Dr Henry Ware, jr, D D, died at Framingham, near Boston, on Fri last, at the age of 49. As a Prof in the Divinity school at Cambridge, his sphere of usefulness was enlarged. –N Y Evening Post

At Edgartown, Mass, on Thu last, Mrs Bethanah Furlong, w/o Mr Matthew D Furlong, from the Emerald Isle, was safely delivered of 3 girls at birth. They are all doing well.

The venerable pear tree, on the corner of the 3rd ave & 13th st, planted 200 years ago by Gov Stuyvessant, & of which the trunk & branches are yet in good preservation, has born a considerable quantity of fruit this year of good quality. –N Y American

The new Post Ofc on 7th st consists of 3 brick houses erected many years ago by the late Mr McLean. It has been fitted with letter-boxes, desks, tables, benches, & every other accommodation for the use of the public & the comfort of the clks & carriers.

The late coroner's inquest at Gtwn, over the body of Catharine Belzarius resulted in the jury returning the following verdict: "Catharine Belzarius came to her death from the continued ill-treatment of her husband, Adam Belzarius.' The prisoner was fully committed for trial at the next term of the Criminal Court.

On Mon, Mr Henry Holt, a mate of the ship **Thos P Cope**, lying at Phil, fell from the fore-topmast rigging on the deck, & was instantly killed.

Three boys drowned at Sag Harbor by the upsetting of a sail boat on Tue last. Two, Wm & John, 18 & 16, were sons of Mr Smith Hatfield. The other, Theodore, 16, was a son of Mr Geo Fordham, of Sag Harbor.

The man who sowed the first field of wheat in Western N Y, the venerable Mr Barlow, of Canandaiga, will be in town tomorrow. He is 92 years of age, & rooms have been provided for him at the Rochester House. -Rochester Democrat

Mrd: on Sep 26, in Wash City, by Rev Chas A Davis, Mr Thos B Entwisle, formerly of Alexandria, D C, to Miss Mary M, d/o Mr Jilson Dove, of this place.

Mrd: on Sep 26, by Rev Mr Edwards, Mr Henry Jos France, formerly of Balt, to Miss Mary Eliz Hubbard, of Wash City. [See marriage notice in Sep 29 newspaper-Henry Jos is reversed to Jos Henry.]

Mrd: Sep 11, by Rev Gary Hickman, N B Vinson, of Rockville, Md, to Mrs M W Kendall, of Gtwn, D C.

Mrd: on Sep 26, in Balt, by Rev Wm F Clarke, S J, of Gtwn College, Walter M Clarke, of Wash, D C, to Maria Amanda, y/d/o Jos Simms, of Balt.

Mrd: on Spe 20, at Staten Island, by Rev J M Wainwright, Saml Ward, of N Y, to Medora, eldest d/o John R Grymes, of New Orleans.

Died: on Sep 27, in Wash City, after a lingering illness, Mrs Harriet Armistead, formerly of Va. Her funeral will be from the residence of her sister, Mrs Dixon, opposite Brown's Hotel, this day at 3:30 p m.

Died: on Sep 25, at his residence in Hanover Co, Va, Edmund Fanning Wickham, in his 48th year, s/o the late John Wickham, of Richmond.

Died: on Sep 18, at his residence, *Hickory Hill*, in Westmoreland Co, Va, Maj Robt Beale, aged 84 years, 7 months & 18 days.

Died: on Sep 13, at Mount Vernon Arsenal, Ala, John Chas, only s/o Capt E S Hawkins, U S Army, aged 1 year & 11 months.

Wash Corp: 1-Ptn of Travis Evans: referred to the Cmte of Claims: 2-Bill for the relief of Owen McCue: ordered to lie on the table. 2-Ptn of Jas Kearney & others, for a flag footway on the south side of F st, at 14th st: referred to the Cmte on Improvements. 3-Cmte on Police, to whom was referred the ptn of Alex'r Provost & Alfred Wallingsford, reported a bill entitled "An act laying a tax on billiard tables, & to repeal all acts inconsistent with the provisions thereof," which was read twice.

Orphan's Court of Wash Co, D C. In the case of Thos Sangster, administrator of Mary Leach, dec'd, Oct 10 has been appointed for the final settlement of said estate. –Ed N Roach, Reg/o wills

A new daily Whig newpaper will be published in Wash City, on the first Mon in Nov next, to be entitled The Whig Standard. –Jno T Towers

Grate Setting: the undersigned is always prepared to set Grates & do all other kinds of brick work at the shortest notice & on the most reasonable terms. All orders left at Mr Jas Galt's, Clock & Watch Maker, between 9th & 10th sts, Pa ave, will be promptly attended to. –Thos Galt

Marble & stone-cutting work in general: for which he will take unimproved property or lumber in exchange. –Alex Rutherford, corner of 13th & D sts

Sale of very superior stock: authorized by Gov Sprigg to sell at public sale, in Upper Marlborough, on Oct 11: horses & cattle. This stock is sold because the owner has more than he wants. –Truman Belt

Geo Gibson, yeoman, brought before me a bright bay mare. The owner is to come forward, prove property, pay charges, & take her away. –R H Clements, one of the J P's for Wash Co, D C.

$100 reward for runaway negro man named Beverley, who left the plantation of John Baker, near Salem, Fauquier Co, Va. He belongs to the heirs of Henry Rose, late of said county. Beverely is about 40 years of age. -H Lufborough, Gtwn, D C

FRI SEP 29, 1843
Madame Montgolfier, the widow of the celebrated inventor of the first air balloon, called Montfolgier, is still living & has just entered her 110th year.

The Rev John Wesley, founder of Methodism, was a man of the most untiring industry. It is said that he rose every morning at 4 o'clock & labored diligently, preaching, traveling, or writing until 10 p m. In 1774, 17 years before his death, his published works amounted to 32 volumes octavo. He died on Mar 2, 1791, in his 88th year.

A most horrible murder was committed at Westfied Society, in Middletown, Conn, last Sun. Mrs Bacon, w/o Ebenezer Bacon, remained at home while the rest of her family, consisting of her husband & 2 children, went to church, a distance of 3 miles. When they returned they found her lying dead, with 7 stabs on her person. The murder is supposed to have been committed by a couple of foreigners, who had been lurking in that region some days, & who have suddenly disappeared.

to have been committed by a couple of foreigners, who had been lurking in that region some days, & who have suddenly disappeared.

From a letter dated at Harmony, Missouri, Sep 13, Saml B Wingo, sheriff of Shannon Co, Missouri, was shot on Aug 31, by a man named Moyres. Wingo had levied on Moyres' property & advertised it, & while on the way to the place of sale he was shot by Moyres, & died in a few minutes. The murderer has been arrested; also 3 other persons who are supposed to have been in the commission of the bloody deed.

Mrd: on Sep 27, by Rev A A Muller, D D, Mr Philip Kent, of Balt, to Miss Ellen Eliz Weller, of the same place.

Mrd: on Sep 26, by Rev Mr Edwards, Mr Jos Henry France, formerly of Balt, to Miss Mary Eliza Hubbard, of Wash City. [Sep 28th newspaper had Henry Jos France.]

SAT SEP 30, 1843
The Van Buren [Arkansas] Intelligencer of Sep 9 records the death of David Vann, Treas of the Cherokee Nation, who died at his residence at the Saline on Sep 2 of wounds inflicted upon him by a lawless mob on Aug 8. The Cherokee Nation generally have met with a great loss. The same paper states that John Ross is well, & that there has never been any attempt made upon his life.

Lt & Adj Mackay, of the 5th Fusileers, stationed in Ireland, was shot on parade by one of the men, & died immediately. At a previous inquest on the sldr who had died suddenly, the jury declared him to have died from excessive drill. The jury returned the verdict: that private Geo Jubee, of the 5th Fusileers, did kill & murder Adj Robertson Mackay, of the said corps.

Mrd: on Sep 28, by Rev Mr Bean, Richd J Young to Miss Sarah Eliza, eldest d/o the Rev Noble Young, late of Chas Co, Md, dec'd.

Died: on Aug 13, at Detroit, Mich, Geo Mason Hooe, aged 14 months & 20 days, s/o Lt D & Mrs Richd Etta M Ruggles.

Funeral discourse, commemorative of the death of the late Mr Geo W Stewart, will be delivered on Sun next, in the English Lutheran congregation, City Hall. The friends & acquaintances of the dec'd, & of his father W H Stewart, are respectfully invited.

Jos Carter, jr, who was recently tried at Belvidere, N J, for the murder of John Castner, has 4 other indictments, one of which was for assault upon the boy, Jesse Force, with intent to kill. –Newark Adv off. Her body passed between the bed & the wall through an aparture not big enough to admit her head, & she remained suspended by the chin until life was extinct.

The following are the Whig Candidates who have been put in nomination for seats in the Leg of Md:

Anne Arundel Co:
John Johnson	Dr Stevens Gambrill	Robt Garner
Nich B Worthington	Reuben Warfield	

Montg Co:
Alex'r Kilgour	David Trundle	
Saml d Waters	Lyde Griffith	

Harford Co:
Wm J Polk	Colemen Yellott	
Dr Thos C Hopkins	Dr Francis Butler	

Balt City:
John L Carey	Jas Curley	G W Lurman
Aaron R Levering	W H Watson	

Fred'k Co:
David W Naill	Wm Lynch	Otho Thomas
Edw Buckey	John Barthelow	

Alleghany Co:
John Pickell	Henry Bruce	
Saml P Smith	Geo McCulloh	

St Mary's Co:
John M S Causin	Wm H Thomas	Jas R Hopewell

Calvert Co:
Saml Turner	J J Dalrymple	Jas S Morsell

Prince George's Co:
Col Wm T Wootton	Robt Ghieselin	
Chas B Calvert	Benedict I Semmes	

Cecil Co:
Thos C Crockshank	Abraham Chandler	
John Simpers	John B Yarnall	

Kent Co:
Chas B Tilden	Geo S Holliday	Geo W Spencer

Queen Anne's Co:
Matthias George	Jas Tilghman	Saml T Harrison

Talbot Co:
Theo R Lockerman	John Harper	

Caroline Co:
Zabdiel W Potter	Robt H McKnett	Wm M Hardcastle

Dorchester Co:
Dr Jos Nichols	Dr Francis P Phelps	J Bond Chaplain

Levin Richardson
Somerset Co:
Levin Phillips   Benj Lankford
Wm S Waters   Robt J Dennis

MON OCT 2, 1843

Letter to John Ross, Principal Chief of the Cherokee Nation: dated Cape Cottage, Cape Elizaeth, Me: Sep 10. Friend & Brother: The papers announced your re-election to the ofc of Principal Chief of your Nation; & Lowery, I see, is by your side as Second Chief. I mourn over the sad event that has consigned Isaac [is it?] Busheyhead to the grave, & Hicks, as some of the papers state; & that our old friend Vann should be severely wounded. Write to me, & settle the contradictory statements made by the papers on the subject of these butcheries. [The letter continued: subject-It is high time that relations of a permanent sort should exist between us & you.] Address me to the care of Ed C Biddle, Publisher, Phil. And now with friendly regards to Maj Lowery, & my red brothers generally, & prayers for their peace, preservation, & prosperity, I shake hands with you as a friend & brother. –Tho L McKenney P S. Just as I was folding this letter it occurred to me to send it to you printed through the Nat'l Intell; & I have obeyed that impulse.

P H Brooks will canvas the city for subscriptions to the Whig Standard. –Jno T Towers

C Eckloff, Merchant Tailor: opposite Brown's Hotel. A suit can be finished at 24 hours notice.

$5 reward for a bay horse that strayed from the premises of the subscriber, near Rock Creek Church. -Robt A Beall

Public Sale: by virtue of 2 writs of fieri facias issued by R H Clements, sale on Oct 7, on the premises, on 2nd st east, near B st north, the following described property, viz: 60 vests, 20 pairs pantaloons, 34 plaid caps, 38 shaving boxes, 4 pink stocks, 4 pair drawers, earthenware & corkery, store fixtures, candles & soap, cigars, jar of snuff, spices, starch, thread, tape, scales, tobacco, mantel clock, 12 chairs, 2 cupboards, 2 bureaus, looking glass, feed bin, ironmongery, stove, & cord of wood, seized & taken in execution as the property of Philip Reilly, & will be sold to satisfy executions in favor of Edw Reilly, for cash. –H R Maryman, Constable

NOTICE: By virtue of a writ of fieri facias, issued by B K Morsell, one of the justices of the peace for Wash Co, D C, I shall offer for sale, on Oct 9, on the premises, all the right, title, & claim of Benj Johnson to the following property, to wit: one small frame or wooden house, with his leasehold to the half of lot #2 in sq 79, on F st, near the corner of 22nd, in the First Ward, for cash, to satisfy a judgment due Ulysses Ward.
–Lambert S Beck, constable

NOTICE: By virtue of an order of distress from Jos L Scholfield, I shall offer at public sale, on Oct 10, the following property: one center or tea table, a bureau, a walnut table, a mantel clock, 2 small looking glasses, 5 chairs, a pine leaf table, 1 pair Iron Dogs, one brass candlestick, a lot of old carpeting, one pair shovel & tongs, one feather bed, one lot of bed clothes, one bolster & pillows, seized & taken as the property of Geo St Clair & Eliz Law, or the property found on the premises, to satisfy house rent.
–Lambert S Beck, Bailiff

Dreadful steamboat explosion on the 19th ult at Bayou Sara, on the Mississippi river, on board the steamboat **Clipper**, one of the regular packets between that place & New Orleans. She was under the command of Capt Laurent, backing out from Bayou Sara to proceed to Tunica, where her boilers exploded, causing the almost total destruction of the boat, & killing or wounding 2/3^{rds} of the people-only 16 escaping injury, 14 killed, 10 missing, & 9 wounded, some dangerously. Bodies diverged like the jets of a fountain in all directions, falling to the earth & upon the roofs of houses, some 250 yards away. The passengers were *L Thomas, missing; P B Montamat, commission merchant, New Orleans. Capt Laurent escaped unhurt. Mr Bessy, chief clerk, missing, 2nd clerk killed. John Tyson, chief engineer, badly wounded. Wm Sumter, 2nd engineer, killed. Wm Nelson, 3rd engineer, killed. Arnault J Lavaud, pilot, missing. Eight dead bodies have been found, among whom are the carpenter, Mr Pool, the 2nd engineer, Mr Sumter, & Mr Wall, pilot. Of the wounded there are Mr Montemat, of New Orleans, Mr Tyson, chief engineer, & Mr Pierson, mate. *Mr Thomas, a grocer of Bayou Sara, had but just taken leave of his wife & family & stepped on board when the explosion occurred.

Wm A Butler, late U S Consul at Nicaragua, Central America, died on the 26th ult, on board the schnr **Ursula**, on his passage home from St Juan.

On Wed the Court of Gen Sessions of Phil passed sentence upon the several persons who have been concerned in the recent firemen's & weavers' riots in that city. The sentences were as follows: Mahlon Graham, 9 months in prison; Saml McReynolds, the same; Jacob Sailor & Mas McMinn, 6 months; Peter Fox & Edw Ennis, 2 months; John Stewart, alias Baltimore Bill, & Jos Springer, 30 days; John Johnson, 1 year.

The Boston Courier announces the death, at his residence in Newton, of Saml Trowbridge, a Revolutionary pensioner, aged 86. Mr Trowbridge was one of the Newton company of minute-men which was in the battle of Lexington, & the last survivor but one. Solomon Richards yet lives, & is nearly 92 years old.

Bela Badger appointed to represent the third Congessional District of Pa in the Whig Nat'l Convention which is to be held at Balt in May next.

Balt, Sep 30. Shocking murder on Thu last in one of our public streets, on the person of Miss Ann Maria Burk, a young woman of irreproachable character. The dec'd, age about 28 years, left the dwlg of Randall H Moale, in Franklin st, in whose family she lived as a nurse, to go the dwlg of Mr Poultney, in Mulberry st, to bring home Mr Moale's dght, who had been spending the afternoon at Mr Poultney's. She left Mr Poultney's and went ot the milliney store of Miss Clarke, in Chas st. When in Mulberry st she was suddenly approached by a man; who struck her a powerful blow with a club, which felled her to the ground, & he then fled. She lingered in great agony until yesterday, when she died. The Mayor has issued a proclamation offering a reward of $500 for the apprehension of the murderer. –American

Stodart, Worcester, & Dunham piano for sale: supply just received from N Y. –F A Wagler, Piano ware-room on H st.

The cars from Balt last Fri night did not reach Wash City until nearly 10 o'clock. It seems, that when the train reached that part of the track nearly opposite Mr Calvert's, about 8 miles from Wash, the locomotive engine came in contact with a cow, which the former passed over & still kept on the track. The passenger cars were thrown off the railway. No person was injured. The cow was, of course, killed upon the spot.

Thos, the eldest s/o Jas Adams, last Sat, in the fields not far from the residence of D Carroll, was seated on a fence loading a gun, & while the ramrod was in the barrel of the piece, the latter suddenly went off, & the ramrod passed through his thigh; the shot in the gun entered his breast & came out at the back near the shoulder. Thos, not more than 14 years of age, should recover from his wounds.

Shoplifting: last Sat, Jas Hammet, alias Martin Nowrski, stole a fur cap, the property of Edw G Handy, for which [the thief being caught & committed to jail by Justice Morsell,] he will have to answer at the next Criminal Court.

New Currying Shop: on High st, Gtwn, D C, a few doors from Linthicum's corner: intend keeping an assortment of superior harness, sole, & other leather, tanned in their own yard, Loudoun Co, Va, under the immediate care of Abraham Young. –Sangston & Young

For sale or exchange, for good productive property in Washington, a very productive Farm of 160 acs of land, with a roomy house, on the Little River Turnpike, 7 miles from Alexandria. Particulars at the ofc of J H Bradley, Wash, or inquire of S Scott, Anandale Post Ofc, Fairfax Co, Va.

TUE OCT 3, 1843
New Book: "Memoirs of the Court of England, from the Revolution in 1688 to the death of George II, by John Heneage Jesse, Phil. Lea & Blanchard, 3 vols 12 mo."

Marshal's sale: virtue of 2 writs of fieri facias, issued in the Clk's Ofc of the Circuit Court of Wash Co, D C: sale on Oct 28, before the courthouse door of said county, the following property, viz: Lot 1 in sq 54, in Wash City, with 2 frame tenements thereon; lot 3 in sq 86, in Wash City. Also, all the residue of that part of lot 3 in sq 118, in said city, which was conveyed to the late Wm P Gardner by the late John Ott, in the year 1808-serving & reserving from the operation of the indenture now in recital 16 feet front & breadth, & containing those dimensions to the rear of the said part of said lot, being the eastern side thereof, adjoining the dwlg house of Thos Munroe, & which said excepted part belonged to Robt Leckie, & the said part intended to be thereby conveyed was then in the occupancy of Joel Wright, with the improvements thereon, being an old frame house occupied as a drug store. Seized & levied upon as the property of Lazare Kervand, & sold to satisfy judicials 153 & 154 to Nov term, 1841, in favor of John Marbury, trustee. –Alex'r Hunter, Marshall of D C

Appointments by the Pres: 1-Greenbury Dorsey, Collector of the Port of New Orleans, in place of Thos Gibbs Morgan, resigned. 2-E W Smallwood to be a Justice of the Peace in Wash Co, D C.

New Haven, Conn, Sep 28. A young man, 16 years of age, Julius M Welch, was crushed to death this morning under the canal bridge in Temple st. He was a clerk in the store of A M Welch & Co, of Bristol, Conn, & came to the city on a visit in the canal boat **Ceres**, with his brother of the above firm. Welch laid down upon the deck. The boatmen cautioned him of his danger, but it was now too late to retreat. He was pushed along about 10 feet until he came to the swell of the deck, when he was caught, he gave but one shriek. It was found impossible to extricate him until he was entirely dead. -Palladium

The Norfolk Beacon states that Com Wilkinson took command of the U S Navy Yard at Gosport on Thu, vice Com Shubrick, whose term of command expired last week.

Mrd: on Oct 2, by Rev S B Southerland, Mr Albert H Beecett to Miss Susan C Huntt, both of Wash City.

Died: on Oct 2, at his residence on Md ave, in Wash City, of typhus fever, after an illness of 12 days, Mr Henry Grieb, aged 31 years, 2 months & 11 days.

Died: on Sep 28, at his residence, near Newport Mills, Montg Co, Md, after a short sickness, Mr Erasmus Perry, leaving a large family & a numerous circle of acquaintances to mourn his irreparable loss.

Died: on Sep 20, at Springfield, Ill, Wm Gallaway, jr, formerly of Wash City, aged 30 years.

Died: on Sep 29, in Wash City, Wm Henry, s/o Ann Sophia & Nelson R Robertson, aged 2 years, 9 months & 21 days.

Died: on Sep 22, at *Contentment*, the residence of his mother, near Port Tobacco, Henry G Brawner, s/o Catharine Brawner, in his 13th year. This most promising youth had endeared him to all who knew him.

Died: on Oct 2, in Gtwn College, in his 16th year, Master Eugine N Picot, of Richmond, Va, a youth of fine talents & high promise, who returned from home after the late vacation quite sick, in the expectation of soon recovering. The advanced stage of his disease, bilious fever, obliged him to retire to the infirmary, where he lingered until death marked him, by a melancholy distinction, for its first victim among the students since the foundation of Gtwn College. R J P

A colored woman, Catharine Taylor, about 30 years of age, died very suddenly last Sun at the house of a respectable lady, residing on Louisiana ave. Jury verdict: Catharine Taylor died in consequence of cancer in the throat & breast.

WED OCT 4, 1843
Edw Warner, Atty at Law, ofc 33, East wing of the City Hall.

Henry Clay, jr, & John J Jacob, jr: Attys & Counsellors at Law, Louisville, Ky. Collections entrusted to their care will be promptly attended to.

Anthony S Chew, Thos Corwin: Law Ofc, Cincinnati, Ohio.

Private Teacher wanted: to engage the services of a Lady capable of teaching all the branches of an English education, together with French & Music. A letter, with references, addressed to me at Aquasco, PG Co, Md, will receive immediate attention. –Saml C Moran

Miss Hanson, in Rochester, N H, about 10 days ago, was murdered by And'w F Howard, who confessed his crime. Finding Miss Hanson alone in her house, he tried to get money he knew she & her brother had. As she refused, he shot her through the neck, causing instant death. He found only about $30. Howard has been committed to Dover jail, with his brother, who is detained as a witness.

Geo Herrick, of Charleston, mate of the emigrant barque **Renown**, [shipwrecked off the Cape de Verds,] & Wm Luce, Albert F Lambert, Seth Crowell, & John Johnson, seamen of the barque, died of bilious fever on their passage to New Bedford from the Cape de Verds in the whaling brig **Emeline**, in which they had taken passage for New Bedford.

Mrd: on Aug 1 last, by Rev Mr Rairol, Saml C McPherson, formerly of Chas Co, Md, to Mary Virginia, d/o Capt Wm H Bassett, of Wash, La.

Died: at the residence of her son-in-law, Wm Allen, Mrs Mgt Turner, in her 76th year. Her funeral will take place at 10 o'clock this morning from her late residence, Pa ave, between 9th & 10th sts. [No date-recent.]

Died: on Sep 22, at the residence of her father, in Chas Co, Md, after an illness of 3 days, of congestive fever, Ellen Hall, 3rd d/o Saml C & Mary M Moran, aged 4 years, 6 months & 19 days.

Handsome furniture at auction: on Oct 11, at the residence of Mrs Bowen, on the northwest corner of 6th & D sts. –Wm Marshall, auctioneer

For rent: a new brick dwlg house & back bldg, fronting on H st, between 11th & 12th sts. Apply to Michl O'Brien, corner of E & 9th sts, or next door.

THU OCT 5, 1843
The claim laid by the Corp of Bowdoin College, [Me,] against certain real estate of the late Jas Temple Bowdoin, including the island of Nauchon, one of the Elizabeth islands near the entrance of New Bedford harbor, & a valuable property in Beacon st, Boston, has been amicably adjusted, seven-tenths of the property being awarded to the surviving son of the dec'd, now a resident in Europe, & the remaining three-tenths to the College.

The Wheeling Times says that a Mrs Mitchel died in that town last week, who had been supposed to be very poor, & partially subsisted on charity for several years past. In her house were found 1,100 Spanish dollars, & it appears that she also owned a valuable farm in Pa.

Mrd: on Oct 3, by Rev Jas H Brown, Henry L Northup, formerly of Louisville, Ky, to Mary Frances Dodds, formerly of Winchester, Va.

Mrd: at Centreville, Md, by Rev Jas Allen, Mr Jas Brown, Special Agent of the Post Ofc Dept, of Springfield, Ill, to Miss Sarah Julia, d/o the late Thos Martin, of Talbot Co, Md. [No date-current item.]

Died: on Oct 3, in Wash City, the Rev Zachariah Jordan, of the Balt Conference of the Meth Episcopal Church. His funeral will take place this afternoon from Mrs Friend's, his late residence, near the Navy Yard gate.

Died: on Oct 4, Martha Seawell, 2nd d/o Richd & Ann Jane Cruikshank, in her 4th year. Her funeral will be today, at 10 a m.

Wash Corp: 1-Ptn from N W Fales & others: referred to the Cmte on Improvements. 2-Ptn from Jos Swigart: referred to the Cmte of Claims. 3-Ptn of Geo Grimes & Geo T McGlue, praying to be reimbursed certain additional expense incurred in repairing streets in the First Ward: referred to the Cmte of Claims.

Orphan's Court of Chas Co, Md. Letters of adm de bonis non on the personal estate of Jas D Mitchell, late of said county, dec'd. –Henry L Mitchell

Sale of Lands for Canal scrip: the undersigned, trustees for the C & O Canal Co, will offer at public sale the following lands: in Frederick on Oct 18: a piece of land containing 18 acs, being part of **Mine Bank Farm**, lying between the canal & the river Potomac, at the **Point of Rocks** in Fred'k Co, Md.
At the ofc of the collector of Tolls, in Gtwn, D C, on Oct 23:
An island in the Potomac, called **Cupid's Bower**, containing about 12½ acs.
Piece of land adjoining the 22nd section, containing about 25 acs.
Part of a tract of land called **Long Acre**, & part of a tract called **Variation**, both containing abou 67 acs, about 2½ miles below Seneca
Part of a tract of land called **Mount Nebo**, containing about 18 acs, 2½ miles below **Edward'd ferry**.
Piece of land near **Conrad's ferry**, containing about 7 acs, purchased of Joshua Chilton. A vacant lot of ground in Gtwn, D C, fronting 47 feet on Cherry st, & the same on the canal, suitable site for a warehouse, having the privilege of landing from the canal free of wharfage.
-Clement Cox, Wm A Bradley, John P Ingle, trustees The undersigned is authorized to dispose of any of the above mentioned property at private sale. –John P Ingle

FRI OCT 6, 1843

Washington. Loss of the steam frig **Missouri**, Capt John T Newton: left Gibraltar bay, on Aug 26. This ill-fated ship left this port on Jul 31 for the Mediterranean, with Mr Cushing, Minister to China, on board. On Aug 26, by some means unexplained, took fire, & in 3 hours was totally destroyed. Letter dated Gibraltar, Aug 28, 1843 to Hon David Henshaw, Sec of the Navy, Wash, from John Thos Newton, Capt. The Hon Mr Cushing & myself came on shore to pay our respects to our Consul, Mr Sprague, who accompanied us to the Govn'r, Sir Robt Thos Wilson. We received a message at 8 o'clock that the **Missouri** was on fire: every assistance was rendered, as well as from Sir Geo Sartorius, commanding Her Britannic Majesty's 74, ship **Malabar**. The ship **Rajah** of 600 tons of Boston has been chartered for the purpose of conveying the crew & Ofcrs to the U S. Enclosed is the testimony of 3 coal-heavers, John Sutton states: I went in the starboard Engineer's store-room, with a globe lantern, to get a pair of beam scales to weigh coal, which they were at that time taking in; in getting down the scales a wrench fell & broke a glass demijohn containing spirits of turpentire; I wiped up as much as I could; I then went down to the cylinder where they were at work to see how much of the spirits had run down; I had not reached the spar deck when I head the cry of fire. Wm J

Williams states: I heard something dripping down; I heard Clum sing out fire. Afred Clum states: I saw something like water dripping down & I sung out to Sutton; flames blazed up. –J T N

We learn from Jefferson City, Mo, that the jury in the case of Dr Prefontaine, one of the robbers of Charvis, the Santa Fe trader, has returned a verdict of guilty. The law requires that he should pay a fine of $1,000 & be imprisoned in the common jail for 12 months. The jury recommended him to mercy.

Orphan's Court of Wash Co, D C. Letters of adm on the personal estate of J N Nicollet, late of Wash County, dec'd. –Geo Thomson, adm

Norfolk, Oct 4. The man of war anchorage off the Naval Hospital presents an imposing & quite a warlike appearance. First in view is the splendid ship **Pennsylvania**, of 120 guns, Capt Zantzinger, bearing the broad pennant of Cmdor E Pendleton Kennedy. Near her lie moored the sloop of war **Vandalia**, Cmder Chauncey, the sloop of war **Warren**, Cmder Hull, of 20 guns each; brig **Bainbridge**, Cmder Mattison, Lt Commanding Johnson having been detached; brig **Dolphin**, Cmder Knight, of 10 guns each, & brig **Oregon**, Lt Commanding Porter; schnr _____ Lt Commanding Bisphan, & schnr **Wave**, Lt Commanding Shubrick. The **Vandalia**, Cmder Chauncey, & Warren, Cmder Hull, will, it is expected, shortly proceed to sea. Cmder Bruce has been ordered to the **Dolphin**, & will probably take command of her immediately. A U S brig of war, on a cruise, was spoken off Cape Canaveral by Capt Harvey, of the brig **Kanawha**, at N Y, from New Orleans. The U S ship **Columbus**, Cmder Turner, & schnr **Enterprise**, Lt Commanding Wilson, the latter arriving from Montevideo, were at Rio de Janeiro on Aug 23; all well. Cmder L M Powell has been ordered to ordnance duty. Passed Midshipman B F B Hunter, from the **Wave**, to be acting master of the **Vandalia**, & Passed Midshipman J C Williamson, detached from the **Vandalia** & waiting orders.
-Beacon

From Europe. Capt Sir John Ross had just returned from his voyage of exploration of the South Seas. He was in excellent health & spirits, & expressed the greatest satisfaction at the result of his voyage.

Mrs Christina Gilmour arrived at Liverpool in the N Y packet ship **Liverpool** in custody of Geo McKay, a Scotch ofcr. She was confined in Bridewell during the night, & on Tue took her departure for Glasgow. She is represented as a fine young woman, not more than 25 years of age.

Mrd: on Sep 26, at Alexandria, by Rev Elias Harrison, J H Lathrop, Collector of the port of Buffalo, N Y, to Miss Mariana Bryan, eldest d/o Danl Bryan, P M, of Alexandria.

Mrd: Oct 3, by Elder Trott, Mr Wm Langfitt, of Prince Wm Co, Va, to Miss Ann Bonthorn, of Wash City.

Died: on Oct 2, at *Fairview*, the residence of her father, Saml Lane, in Franklin Co, Pa, of pulmonary consumption, Mrs Juliana Hayman, relict of the late Wm Hayman, of Wash, leaving a disconsolate family of small children. Mrs Hayman had been in declining health for several years. She was a highly intelligent & pious woman, of retiring manners, & beloved by all who knew her. Her children have by this visitation of death been bereft of a kind & devoted mother, her aged father of an affectionate dght, & her sisters & brother of an attached sister.

Died: on Sep 24, at the residence of Dr Kearney, U S Navy, Marlborough, PG Co, Md, after an illness of 10 days, Thorawgood S Stith, in his 27th year, eldest s/o the late Griffin Stith, formerly merchant in Smyrna, Asia Minor.

Died: on Oct 3, Louis Napoleon, s/o Wm & Martha Ann Kelly, in his 2nd year.

Died: on Oct 5, Ann Cecilia Theresa, d/o John & Claudia Cummiskey, aged 16 months & 9 days, after a protracted illness of 4 months. Her funeral is this evening, at 4 o'clock, from Mrs Arguelles'.

Grand Lodge of D C will pay the last tribute of respect to the remains of our R W brother Wm W Billing, dec'd, on Oct 8, from his late dwlg, at 1 o'clock. –Robt Keyworth, R W Grand Master -Wm Greer, Gr Sec

SAT OCT 7, 1843
The Hon David Sterigere, Judge of the Ninth Judicial Circuit of the State of Missouri, died at his residence near Washington, in Franklin Co, on Sep 24.

The Leipsic Gazette announces the death at Warsaw of the Count de Braincki, leaving a fortune of 120 millions of Polish florins, [75 millions of francs.]

A rare chance to any one wishing to engage in a large Boarding-house. In consequence of the ill health of his wife, a gentleman wishes to dispose of the entire stock of furniture & carpeting, & will sell the whole on a liberal credit. The house can be leased for 1 ot 5 years. It contains 23 rooms & all in complete order. Apply to Geo Mattingly.

Mrd: on Oct 4, at the residence of Mrs Saml Keyser, in Balt, by Rev John M Duncan, Henry J Drayton, of Louisiana, to H Jane, y/d/o the late Saml Keyser, of Balt.

Mrd: on Oct 4, at the residence of Mrs Saml Keyser, in Balt, by Rev John M Duncan, Worthington G Snethen, of New Orleans, Solicitor of the General Land Ofc, to Virginia, only d/o the late Dr Morris Polk, of Balt.

Died: on Oct 5, of consumption, Wm W Billing, in his 43rd year. His funeral will be from his late residence, corner of 14th & L sts, on Sabbath afternoon at 2 o'clock.

For the last 2 weeks, L B Ward & Co have been hammering out, at the Hammersley Forge, N Y, the largest wought iron gun in the world. It is 14 feet long, 3 feet in diameter at the breech, & weighs 30,000 pounds, or 15 tons. It is made for the Gov't, & will be placed on board the steamer **Princeton**, Capt Stockton, now at Phil. When finished, it is calculated that it will carry a ball of one-third greater weight, & one-fourth increased distance, than the best cast iron guns.

Extensive robbery was committed recently in Maxstawney township, Berks Co, Pa. Mrs Maria Sassaman, an aged widow, was robbed of gold & silver from a locked chest. It is supposed the robbery was committed on Sun while the family were attending divine services. The amount taken was about $1,200.

The Rev Dr Moriarty, of Portsmouth, Va, will preach in St Peter's Church, Capitol Hill, tomorrow, Sun, at 11 a m.

Improved Fairfax land for sale or exchange: the subscriber offers 244 acs of land in Fairfax Co, Va, having on it 2 tenements, & it is susceptible of division to suit purchasers. The stock & implements, &, if desirable, the furniture, will be sold with the land. –A B Fairfax

For Kingston, Jamaica: the brig **Temperance** will sail on or about Oct 16. For freight to the extent of 200 barrels, or passage, having good accommodations, apply to Clement Smith, Gtwn.

J H Gibbs, having just returned from N Y, will open this day at his Fancy Store, Pa ave, between 8th & 9th sts, a beautiful assortment of Fringes, Gimps, silk, cord, buttons, etc.

For sale of rent, the house & lot lately occupied by P McKenna, on Pa ave. Please inquire of Mr Thumlert, next door, who occupies a part of the same property. Persons wishing to purchase will call on the subscriber at his Lumber Yard, Water st, Gtwn, D C. –John Pickrell

For sale: the house in which I now live, on Fayette st, Gtwn, recently built, 2 stories, & arranged into 10 apts. 2 doors from the Ladies' Academy, within a short walk of the College & Trinity Church, convenient to places of public worship. For terms apply to Mr Sabret E Scott, on Water st, in Gtwn, or on the premises to P H O'Reilly, Gtwn.

For rent, a house on Capitol Hill: a 3 story house on N J ave, south of B st. Apply to J Hand, Patent Ofc, or to the present occupant.

Fishery. The subscriber has for rent a Fishery on the Potomac river, opposite Mount Vernon, on accommodating terms to a good tenant. –Mary Webster, Abingdon, Harford Co, Md

MON OCT 9, 1843
Convention of the Protestant Episcopal Church: extracted from the N Y papers: Sep 28. Convention took up the election of the following for the ensuing year: Rev Drs Berrian, Lydell, McVickar, & Taylor, clerical. Messrs Thos L Ogden, Floyd Smith, Murray Hoffman, Gulian C Verplanck, lay. Delegates to General Conventions: Rev Drs Brown & Sheerwood, & David B Ogden. Substitutes: Rev W L Johnson & Rev Dr Creighton. Missionary Cmte: Rev Wm Richmond, B I Haight, Lot Jones, Jos H Price, Edw N Meade, clerical. Messrs C N S Rowland, John H Swift, Cornelius Oakley, Floyd Smith, Alex L McDonald, lay. Fri, Sep 29. Bishop Onderdonk in the chair. Resolutions of Judge Oakley taken up. Mr John Duer supported the resolutions in a speech of upwards of an hour. Debate was continued by Thos L Ogden, Chief Justice Jones, David B Ogden, Judgle Oakley, John Anthon, & Rev Dr Wainwright. Speech by Mr Jno Anthon. John Duer offered a document when Bishop Onderdonk rose under great excitement, & said he would not receive such a document. These remarks were received with great applause. Mr Duer rose to explain, but the Bishop refused to hear a word, saying, "Sit down, sir! Take your seat-I won't hear a word!" The convention adjourned sine die.

Wm Goddard, of Petersham, Mass, whose recent forgeries on the Ware & other banks have been noted, pleaded guilty to 3 indictments preferred against him, & has been sentenced to 2 days solitary confinement & 2 years hard labor in the State prison on each indictment, making in all 6 days solitary confinement & 6 years at hard labor.

Gentlemen nominated to attend the Whig Nat'l Convention, at Balt, on May 1 next:

Newcastle County:
John M Clayton	Geo Platt	Chas Tatman
Dr J W Thomson	Chas I Dupont	Arnold S Naudain
Dr Robt McCabe	Henry Dupont	
Robt M Black	John C Clark	

Kent County:
Robt Frame	Wm Shaw	Dr Wm W Morris
Presley Spruance	Dr Wm Burton	Jos Hill
Chas Marim	Peter F Causey	
Thos Wainwright	Jas S Buckmaster	

Sussex County:
John A Hazzard	Jos S Barnard	Thos Fooks
Dr Wm Harris	Robt Houston	Chas G Ridgeley
Gardiner H Wright	Peter N Rust	
Henry Dunning	Jeremiah F Kinney	

Joshua Vansant appointed Naval Ofcr for the Port of Balt, vice Carr, promoted, & Jas P Heath, Weighmaster in the Custom-house, in place of R D Milholland, removed. Both the appointees are Locofocos.

Died: on Fri last, in Wash City, Jas Leander Cathcart, in his 77th year. At age 10 years he entered the Continental Navy, & served as midshipman on board the vessels **Confederacy** & **Tyranicide** during the Revolutionary struggle, & soon after the peace was captured by the Algerimes off the coast of Spain. He remained 11 years in captivity, returned bearer of dispatches to Pres Washington, & ever since held & faithfully discharged public trusts abroad, when his country was seeking a place among the nations of the earth, & for the last 20 years in the ofc of the Second Comptroller of the Treasury. It is hoped that the numerous family of the deceased will not have cause to say that "Republics are ungrateful." 40 years ago Mr C's services were useful in aiding the heroic sloop **Preble** & other choice spirits in the Mediterranean, & very few have met with & suffered more than the reverses of fortune in the same spirit that he has done.

Died: on Thu last, at *Hatton Hill*, PG Co, Md, Henry D Hatton, of that county.

Died: on Sep 30, in Alexandria, John Adam, aged 62 years. He was a native of Va, but for the last 30 years a resident of Alexandria. If strong sense, scorn of meanness, & quick warm feelings be manly qualities, nature might stand up and say to the world, this was a man.

Died: on Oct 5, at Alexandria, Capt Ignatius Allen, late master of the steamboat **Joseph Johnson**.

The venerable Clarkson Crolius, for some years a member of the Leg & Speaker of the House, died at his residence last evening. He has been ill for some weeks of a disease of the heart. –N Y Tribune

Boston Journal: Nathl Greene appointed Postmaster of that city in the place of Geo Wm Gordon, who goes Consul to Rio Janeiro. Appointment to take effect on Oct 15.

Ran away from the subscriber, in Wash City, negro slave Ben Brown, the property of F X Hall. $50 reward upon his being safely lodged in Wash co jail, so that I get him again. S R Gawronski, Agent for F X Hall, *Greenleaf's Point*.

Lime of the best quality daily arriving at the Railroad depot in Wash City, & can be had cheap for cash of Jas B Phillips, Plasterer.

$5 reward for recovery of strayed black colt. –Alfred Heitmiller, 2nd st, near McLaine's Row

Rev Septimus Tuston, of Wash City, to preach the opening sermon at the approaching meeting of the Presbytery of Balt.

Masonic Funeral. The remains of the late W W Billing were followed to the grave in Congress Burial Ground yesterday by a numerous procession of the ancient brotherhood, preceded by the German band playing a solemn dirge. A great number of citizens also attended the funeral services in the Protestant Methodist Church.

Howard Society meeting on Tue last & the following gentlemen were elected ofcrs for the ensuing year:
Pres-Wm W Seaton
V P: Archibald Henderson
V P: Jas L Edwards
Treas-Jas Adams
Sec-Geo M Phillips

Managers:
John McLelland	Andrew Coyle	Saml Byington
Gen Gilliss	J W Maury	Griffith Coombe
Chas A Davis	Jacob Gideon	Thos Blagden
Danl Haskel	Jos Ingle	Jas Coombe
Jas Larned	John P Ingle	Geo A Adams
N B Van Zandt	Wm Brent	Peter N Pearson
Thos Mustin	Wm J McDonald	Marmaduke Dove
Lewis Johnson	John Underwood	Wm E Howard

Nat'l Institute meeting at the Hall, this evening, at half past 7 o'clock. –Jno K Townsend, Acting Rec Sec

Attention, Mechanical Riflemen! A stated meeting of the Company will be held at your Armory, in the City Hall, this evening, at 7 o'clock. –Geo H Boyd, Sec

Repeal Association: regular meeting this evening at 8 o'clock, in the Hall of the Wash Benevolent Society. -F McNerhany, Sec

Circuit Court of Wash Co, D C. Wm M Pringle has applied to be discharged from imprisonment, under the act for the relief of Insolvent Debtors: hearing on the first Mon in Nov next. –Wm Brent, clk

Orphan's Court of Wash Co, D C. Letters of adm on the personal estate of John B Cutting, late of the U S Navy, dec'd. –Landon N Carter, adm

TUE OCT 10, 1843

Three days from Europe. 1-The ship **Great Western** brought out 135 passengers, among whom were the Rev Bishops Chubert & Hughes, & Mr Ogilby, British Vice consul for the port of Charleston. 2-Miss Georgiana Bagot, y/d/o the late Sir Charles, was married on Sep 22, to Lt Col Frazer, Assist Quartermaster General in Canada. 3-Ex-Pres Boyer, of St Domingo, his wife, & suite, are among the passengers by the ship **Dee**, from Jamaica, arrived at Falmouth on Sep 19. We had accounts from Jamaica, a short time since, that Madame Boyer was dead. Can the Ex-Pres have got another wife already? 4-Mr Stewart, the British Minister at Bogota, died there about the middle of August. 5-Queen Victoria & her party arrived at Autwerp on Sep 19, by railway, accompanied by King Leopold & his Queen. Her first visit was to the cathedral; after this came a grand procession, a visit to the recently erected statue of Rubens, & finally dinner at the palace. The town was illuminated at night. The Queen embarked on board the royal yacht, which preceded her to Antwerp, & arrived at Woolwich on the 21st, & proceeded to Windsor. She left a 1,000 guineas at Eu for the servants alone, besides diamond snuff-boxes & other costly cadeauz to personages of higher standing. 6-Henry L Bulwer, brother of the celebrated novelist, proceeds to Madrid, to succeed Arthur Aston as the British rep at that Court.

Robt Wickliffe, jr, of Ky, the unsuccessful competitor of Mr Garrett Davis for Congress, has received from the President the appointment of Charge d'Affaires to Sardinia.

Nestorians of the Plain. Mr Perkins & his wife, who, after a residence of 7 or 8 years among the Nestorians as missionaries, lately made a visit to this country, accompanied by Mar Yohannan, a native Bishop, & who left here in Mar last on their return, arrived at their former residence, Oroomiah, in Jun last, in good health.

Navy Orders. –Cmder Jos Mattison to command of brig **Bainbridge**, vice Lt Z F Johnston detached. Cmder L M Powell ordnance duty. All midshipmen within the U S whose warrants bear date in 1838 are ordered to attend the naval school at Phil.

It is a fact that the Rev Danl Parsons, curate of Harden, Wilts, long know as a tractarian, had seceded to the Church of Rome. Private reasons will for the present prevent his becoming a priest, but he is to assume, as we are informed, the ofc of teacher in some Catholic establishment.

Albany Argus: iron steam vessels. U S Gov't: bldg for the Revenue service, under the direction of Capt Howard, 6 iron rev cutters, 4 to be propelled by Lt Hunter's submerged wheel, & 2 by Ericsson's propellers. One vessel on Ericsson's plan being built for the Atlantic by R L Schuyler, of N Y. There is also being put up at Erie an iron steam frig of 700 tons. Vessels designed & built under the direction of Mr Hart, U S Naval Constructor. Engines designed by Chas W Copeland, principal engineer U S Navy.

The Montreal Courier states that at the recent fire in that city in St Paul & Com'rs sts, a man, Jas Gibbons, a vender of pastry, & had formerly belonged to the King's Dragoon Guards, was burnt to death.

Mr Jas Orr, of Hollidaysburg, Pa, left home on Sat week with his dog & gun, to shoot wild pigeons, & was found dead on Sun, about 5 miles from town. It appears his gun accidentally discharged the load into his head, tearing off part of the skull, & causing instant death. His faithful dog continued with him.

Mrd: on Sun last, by Rev Jas Donelan, Mr Andrew J Joyce to Miss Frances Marion, d/o the late Wm Norris, all of Wash City.

Mrd: on Oct 9, at St Peter's Church, by Rev Mr Van Horseigh, Jas Broom to Eliz H, d/o Ernest Guttslich, all of the District.

Mrd: on Oct 5, at Bel Air, PG Co, Md, the residence of Benj Ogle, by Rev Mr Marbury, Chas G Wilcox, of Gtwn, to Anna Maria, d/o the late Julius Forrest, of PG Co, Md.

Mrd: on Oct 5, by Rev Dr Laurie, Mr Bland Hall to Miss Mary Brown, all of Wash City.

Died: on Sep 3, at the villa d'Eleie, near Florence, Tuscany, Mary Lawrence, w/o Lt Wm Preston Griffin, of the U S Navy, & only d/o the lamented Capt Jas Lawrence, who fell defending the American flag on board the ill-fated ship **Chespeake** in 1813. Mrs Griffin was well known in the social circles of N Y, New England, & Washington. During the last few years she had been much in the south of Europe. On Wed she was in the full bloom of health. On Sunday she was numbered with the dead. An only dght, only 4 days old when she died, is the only living representive of herself & her gallant father. Her death bed was cheered by the presence of a devoted husband & mother, & of her early & constant friend, Mrs Dix, of Albany. On Sep 4 her remains were deposited in the Protestant burial ground without the walls of Florence: the heights of Frosole look down upon it. –Albany Argus

At the late commencement of Jefferson College, Pa, the honorary degree of D D was conferred on the Rev Wm Peddie, of Edinburgh, Scotland.

Died: on Sep 26, at Princeton, Indiana, after a brief but severe illness, Miss Susannah Hood Snethen, d/o Rev Nicholas Snethen & the late Susannah Hood Snethen. She was a woman who held the first place in the hearts of her doting parents & of her fond brothers. When "Death had seated himself down by the doors of her trembling heart," her father was lifted from his sick bed & led, with tottering steps, by one of her brothers to the couch on which the dying Christian lay. In the same house lay the prostrate forms of her brother-in-law & her niece, suffering from disease. May the Lord of Grace sustain her afflicted parent & brothers & sisters, is the earnet prayer of an absent brother who adored her.

Circuit Court of Wash Co, D C. John P Van Tyne, a bankrupt, has filed his ptn for his discharge & certificate: hearing on Dec 18. –Wm Brent, clk

Local News: election for Police Magistrates to serve for the ensuing year in Wash City was held yesterday: the results are as follows:
1st Ward-Saml Drury & H C Williams
2nd Ward-Jesse E Dow & John D Clark
3rd Ward-Wm Thompson & B K Morsell
4th Ward-Jos W Beck & R H Clements
5th Ward-Nathl Brady & Saml Byington
6th Ward-Geo Adams & Jas Marshall
Brd of Alderman & Brd of Common Council. B B French appt'd Chairman & E J Middleton appt'd Sec of the Joint Meeting. Tellers, Messrs E W Clarke & S Bacon. [The new police magistrates elected are H C Williams, Jos W Beck.] E W Clarke declared himself no candidate just before the ballot box went round.

Mr F C Labbe informs that his Dancing Academy will re-open on Oct 17, at his dwlg-house, on Pa ave.

Bridge Wanted: sealed proposals will be received by the Leesburg Turnpike Road Co until Oct 24 to build a wooden bridge over Goose creek: covered with a cypress roof. –L M Boss, Sec of the Board of Dirs.

Farm for sale, on the premises, on Oct 21, containing 241 acs, situated in Montg Co, Md, & on the Bladensburg road from Rockville & near the village of Leesborough, distant only 10 miles from Wash City. The farm is a present tenanted by Mr Jas Fling. The bldgs are adapted for a manager & servants, & the preservation of tobacco & other crops, & there are handsome sites on the land for a family dwlg. –Jas J Bowden, at Wm Morton's, Gtwn. N B-Some servants, reared on the farm, may be had with it, but not to be sold out of the State of Md.

For sale: valuable 3 story brick house, one of the Seven Bldgs, with a lot of ground on which it stands. It was occupied by the Hon Mr Van Buren during his V P term, & more recently by the Hon R J Walker, is next east of the residence of Capt Forest, U S Navy. Title unquestionable. -Robt W Dyer & Co, aucts

WED OCT 11, 1843
Paris, Sep 20, 1843. Count Toreno died on Sat last in his noble mansion near the Champs Elysees. An abscess formed in his mouth, & is said to have caused cerebral fever. He was robust, & only 56 years of age. He has left seven millions of francs for his youthful

wife & 2 children. The corpse was embalmed by Gannal. The church of the Roule was hung in black, & the escutcheon of the grandee of the first class figured every where.

Orphan's Court of Wash Co, D C. Letters of adm on the personal estate of Henry Grieb, late of said county, dec'd. –F Grieb, adm

Orphan's Court of Wash Co, D C. Letters of adm on the personal estate of Jas Greenleaf, late of said county, dec'd. –D A Hall, adm

$50 reward: lost on Oct 9, between Gtwn & the Bank of Wash, $510 in notes. The finder, by leaving it with Capt Goddard, of the 'Watch," or at the ofc of the Nat'l Intell, will receive the above reward.

Letter to F Markoe, jr, Corr Sec of the Nat'l Institute: from John Parrott, Consul of the U S at Mazatlan. Wash, Sep 13, 1843. Adding to the numerous collection 2 boxes of very valuable mineral specimens of gold & silver procured in the Mexican Republic. They are deposited in the Navy Dept in charge of my brother W S Parrot, who will deliver them to you.

Mr Elliott Higgins, aged about 60 years, was killed in N Y on Fri when taking a ride in a barouche drawn by 2 horses, who became frightened and dashed off at top speed, throwing him over the dasher in such a manner that his body hung for a time suspended with his head close to the heels of the horses. He fell to the ground & death ensued in a few minutes.

New Haven Chronicle states that a young woman, the wife of Isaac Loveland, of Durham, Conn, was so badly burned a few evenings since by her clothes taking fire while she was asleep, that she expired the next day, after enduring the most severe physical & mental suffering.

Letter to F Markoe, jr, Corr Sec of the Nat'l Institute from Jas B Murray, enclosing a letter of Wm Railton, Architect of the Admr Nelson Monument: N Y, Sep 21, 1843. Monument in progress of completion in Trafalgar Sq, requesting the acceptance of a model of the structure, & a fac simile in miniature dimension corresponding with the model of the scaffolding by means of which it was reared. Memory of him who was "first in peace, first in war, & the first in the hearts of his countrymen."

Mrd: on Oct 5, at Valley View, Fauquier Co, Va, by Rev Geo Lemmon, Dr E D Foree, of Newcastle, Ky, to Miss Flora Virginia, y/d/o the late Hon Edw B Jackson.

Mrd: on Oct 3, at Waverley, Culpeper Co, Va, Mr John Howison, of Fredericksburg, to Miss Ann M, d/o the late Hancock Lee.

Mrd: on Oct 10, by Rev Mr Van Horseigh, Mr Zachariah Mattingly to Miss Jane Eliza Brown, all of St Mary's Co, Md.

First rate farm for sale: his farm called **Burgundy**, about 2 miles from Alexandria, in the neighborhood of Gen John Mason, John J Frobles, & others. It contains about 400 acs: bldgs are good. Possession immediately. [The above will be divided into 2 farms if desired.] –Saml Lunt

Circuit Court of Wash Co, D C. John H Mullins has applied to be discharged from imprisonment under the act for the relief of Insolvent Debtors: hearing on the first Mon in Nov next. Same for John Hamilton. –Wm Brent, clk

THU OCT 12, 1843
$5 reward for my bank book, containing a check, lost between 7th st & Good Hope, PG Co, Md; marked good by S B Boarman, bookkeeper, & made to the order of Henry Tolson. –John F Clarke

The Nashville Banner of Oct 2 notices the late visit of the distinguished veteran to that place, Marshal Bertrand who arrived on Fri, accompanied by his son, Col Napoleon Bertrand & his aid M Mangel. He visited Gen Jackson of the Hermitage: also visited Mr Justice Catron. Bertrand is a fine old French gentleman, combining the high courtesy of the anceient noblesse the spirit & ardor of the "Empire."

The Marengo Patriot states that the w/o Mr John Burgler went to obtain water out of the cistern of a neighbor, in Demopolis, Ala, at night, & accidentally fell in. The husband descended by a rope, seized his wife in his arms, & while persons above were raising them, the rope broke, & both the husband & wife perished in 7 feet of water. The dec'd parents left an only child about 8 months old.

Died: Sep 25, at Locust Hill, King Geo Co, Va, of bilious pleurisy, Dr Robt Stith Parsons, in his 38th year.

Died: on Oct 5, at Cincinnati, aged 63, Mr Jas H Looker. For 40 years he was an inhabitant of that city, & during that time had been engaged in active business. He established the first paper in Cincinnati, [the Liberty Hall,] in connexion with John W Brown, & was one of the oldest printers in the West.

The ships **Erebus & Terror**. London, Sep 19, 1843. Capt Jas Ross, the commander of the Antartic Expedition, landed at Folkstone on Sep 4: he has 2 ships under his command, the **Erebus & Terror**, Capt Crozier & Cmder Bird being the principal ofcrs. They left England in Sep, 1839, & reached St Helena in Jan 1840.

Wash Corp: 1-Ptn from Jas A Breast: referred to the Cmte on Improvements. 2-Act authorizing John Pettibone to erect scales for the weighing of hay, straw, & fodder: passed. 3-Bill for the relief of Jas E Thumlert: referred to the Cmte of Claims. 4-Ptn of P H Moreland, praying remission of a fin: referred to the Cmte of Claims.

For rent: that large Boarding house corner of 7th st west & Market space, & over the stores of Messrs Pittman & Phillips & W M Perry. For terms apply to J J Dermott, near the premises, or to the subscriber, north B st, Capitol Hill. –Anne R Dermott

For rent: 4 new brick houses, each containing 9 rooms, situated on 9th st, between N Y ave & L st, recently erected by Col Wm Doughty. Apply to A P Skinner, Agent, on La ave, between 9th & 10th sts.

Men's fine, cheap, & elegant clothing, the property of D Barnett, late of Balt, will be for sale on Tue, at Mr D S Waters' Auction Store, east side of 7th st, opposite Messrs Pittman & Phillips' dry goods store, who is well know here for selling good & cheap clothing, & has sold for years in Mr McIntire's, afterwards Capt Blake's, & late at Mr Dyer's. Superior coats at $12 & $14. Fine black satin vests at $2.25, worth $4.

FRI OCT 13, 1843
Mr Nathl Willis has sold the Boston Recorder to the Rev Martin Moore, formerly of Cobasset. Mr Willis retires from the paper altogether, having been editor for 25 years.

Mrd: on Oct 9, at Alexandria, by Rev Jas T Thornton, Wm S Peachy, of Williamsburg, Va, to Virginia, y/d/o the late Bathurst Daingerfield, of that place.

Mrd: on Oct 10, in St Peter's Church, by Rev Jas T Johnston, Littleton Dennis, of Worcester Co, Md, to Anne Caroline, d/o Wm Fowle, of Alexandria.

Mrd: on Oct 10, in St Paul's Church, by Rev Jas T Johnston, Geo D Fowle to S Ellen, d/o Bernard Hooe, all of Alexandria.

Died: on Oct 9, at the residence of her father, Amos Burr, at Bridgeport, Conn, Mrs Sarah A, w/o W R Symons, of Savannah, Ga, leaving an infant 4 days old.

Died: on Oct 5, at his late residence, **Hatton's Hills**, near Piscataway, PG Co, Md, Henry D Hatton, in his 55th year: of congestive bilious fever, after a short but severe illness of only 3 days' duration. He leaves his bereaved wife, with whom he had happily lived for more than 30 years & his devoted children; & his numerous slaves, to whom he was ever a friend & benefactor. -S

The Rev Wm T Eva, [aged 16] of Pipe Creek Crct, will preach in the 9th st Methodist Protestant Church, this Fri at 7 o'clock. –S B Southerland, Pastor

CAUTION: All persons, & particularly gunners, are warned not to trespass on my property purchased of the estate of John S Dodson, as the law will be enforced. –John F Clark

For rent, house #5 in Franklin Row. Inquire of John France, near 12th st, or to the subscriber. –R France

Navy Yard Bridge: dividend of 1½% has been declared, payable at the Bank of Wash. –Wm Gunton, Treas

Orphans Crt of Fred'k Co, Aug Term, 1843. Oct 9. Ordered that Joshua Dill, adm d b n, with the will annexed, of Eliz Seiver, late of Fred'k Co, dec'd, cause to be inserted once a week for 6 weeks in succession: the distributees entitled to the personal estate of Eliz Seiver, dec'd, are notified that the Court will proceed to make a distribution of the assets in the hands of the adm d b n, on the 2nd Tue in Jan, 1844. -G M Eichelberger, Reg/o wills, Fred'k Co, Md

SAT OCT 14, 1843
In the city of Phil John M Scott [Whig] has been re-elected Mayor by a majority of 2,609 votes. Morton Mc Michael is elected Sheriff of the city & county of Phil by 1,770 majority. In the Congressional districts: Edw Joy Morris [Whig] elected; Jos R Ingersoll [Whig] re-elected. John T Smith [Loco] elected; Chas J Ingersoll [Loco] re-elected. Jacob S Yost [Loco] elected. Michl H Jenks [Whig] elected. Abraham R McIlvaine [Whig] elected. Jeremiah Brown [Whig] re-elected to Congress by 915 votes over the competitors. John Ritter [Loco] elected. Gen Henry Frick [Whig] elected over Mr Snyder. Alex'r Ramsey [Whig] elected. Dr Henry Nes [Independent] elected. Jas Black [Loco] elected. Andrew Stewart [Whig] elected. Judge Wilkins [Loco] elected. He was opposed by Henry M Brackenridge [Whig] & Neville B Craig, supported by the Antimasons.

The subscriber has just opened an assortment of single & double barrel guns, of fine quality, made to order. Also Patent Safety-top Powder Planks, a very superior article, made by Dixson & Sons; together with shot belts, game bags, etc. –E Lindsley

Inscription on the tomb of Napoleon. The following is to be inscribed on the socle of his tomb at the Invalides: Born on the 15th of August, 1769; captain of a squadron of artillery at the siege of Toulon in 1793, at the age of 24; commander of artillery in Italy in 1794, at 25; general in chief of the army in Italy in 1796, at 27; general in chief of the expedition of Egypt in 1798, at 29; first consul in 1799, at 31; consul for life after the battle of Marengo, 1800, at 32; emperor of the French 1804, at 35; abdicated the throne after the battle of Waterloo Jun 18, 1815, at 46; died in exile at St Helena May 5, 1821, at 52.

On Sat week P W Maxey was elected Mayor of Nashville by a majority of 199 over Dr Boyd McNairy, both Whigs.

On Sat week Wm E Butler, bar-keeper at the Western Exchange, New Orleans, committed suicide by drowning himself in the Mississippi.

Died: on Mar 29, at Hong Kong, China, of small pox, after a week's severe illness, Theodotia Ann, w/o the Rev Wm Dean, of the American Baptist mission.

Died: on Oct 8, suddenly, at his residence, *Vaile Verde*, PG Co, Md, Notley Maddox, in his 75th year.

Thos Caldwell was killed about 12 miles from Fayetteville, a few days since, by a man named Young, in defence of his wife, against an attack of Caldwell whilst in a state of inebriety.

On Oct 15, Mr Benj Vore, his wife, & a traveler, Mr Stevens, citizens of the U S, were murdered at the residence of Mr Vore upon the military road, in the Cherokee Nation, & the house burned to the ground to destroy all evidence. Mr Vore was a licensed trader in the nation. Mr Stevens, a carpenter, was expected at Fort Smith about this time. Mrs Vore was killed a short distance from the house, & her corpse was dragged to the house to be destroyed in the fire. A large party have gone in pursuit of the perpetrators.

The trial of Jacob West, John West, & Ogeese [or Augustus] Choteau, for the murder of Isaac Bushyhead & an attempt on the life of D Vann, will commence next week, in the Saline District, Cherokee nation. [Mr David Vann has recovered beyond all danger from his late wounds.]

Headquarters Nat'l Blues. You are hereby ordered to meet at the Armory for parade on Oct 16, at 6 o'clock, in winter uniform, with knapsacks. –John Brannin, Sergeant

Washington Light Infty to meet at the Armory on Oct 16, at 7 o'clock, in full winter uniform, with knapsacks, canteens, etc. By order: H Richey, First Sergeant

A Jefferson farm for sale or exchange. I wish to sell a valuable farm in Jefferson Co, Va, containing, by a recent survey, 576½ acs: lies on the Shenandoah river, about 5 miles from Charlestown; 2 dwlgs on the farm, with out-bldgs. For the terms apply to the subscriber at Mount Vernon, near Alexandria, or R B Washington, near Charlestown, Jefferson Co, who will show the premises. I will sell on accommodating terms, or exchange for other property on the tide water of Va or Md. –John A Washington

Farmers of the North, look here! The subscribers are authorized to negotiate the sale of several tracts of land in the country adjacent to the Dist of Col: one near the Little River Turnpike, in Va, . Four tenements: about 700 acs; plenty of water. For particulars apply to Hampton & Son, F st, Wash.

Orphan's Court of Wash Co, D C. Letters of adm d b n on the personal estate of Michl Farrell, late of said county, dec'd. –Tho Carbery, adm d b n

Houses to rent: adjoining the Railroad Ofc, on Pa ave, with accommodations for a family. Possession on Oct 25. Apply to Mr Slater, on the premises. A 2 story brick dwlg on 12th st, between G & H sts, lately put in good repair. Possession on Nov 1. –S Burche

Valuable house on C st for sale: in reservation #10, fronting north on C st, owned & recently occupied by Rev Mr Rich, is for sale: It is 2 stories high with a good basement & attic rooms, built of brick, with slated roof: with a good brick stable with a slated roof. Desirable residence for a private family. For terms of sale apply to H L Ellsworth, Com'r of Patents, or to the subscriber, at his ofc over Todd's Hat Store, Pa ave. -D A Hall

MON OCT 16, 1843
A Convention of persons interested in the production & manufacture of silks was organized in N Y on Thu. Gen Jas Tallmadge was chosen Pres.

Trustee's sale: virtue of a decree of the Chancery Court of the State of Md, we will sell at public sale, at the court-house in Port Tobacco, Chas Co, Md, on Nov 7 next, all the real estate of the late John Haislip of Robt, containing, by recent survey, 697 acs 3 roods & 13 perches, divided into 4 convenient lots. This estate is 6 or 7 miles from Port Tobacco. The several lots will be shown by Mr Lawson, who resides on the land. –W H Tuck, Wm B Stone, Trustees

The Hon Lewis F Linn, Senator in Congress from Missouri was found dead in his bed, at his residence in Ste Genevieve, on Oct 3. For some time previous his health had been feeble. He leaves an interesting family & the State as his mourners.

Mrd: on Oct 10, at Middletown Point, N J, by Rev Chas Webster, Nicholas Halter, of Wash city, to Miss Agnes, d/o John A Vanderbilt, of the former place.

Died: on Oct 14, at his residence on north I st, in Wash City, near St John's Church, after a long & painful illness, Thos Baker Johnson, only s/o Joshua Johnson, dec'd, formerly American Consul at London, & brother of Mrs John Quincy Adams. His funeral will be on Oct 17, at 3 o'clock, from his late residence.

Died: on Oct 8, at Newark, Dela, Maj Richd Bennett, late of Wash City, after a long & distressing illness, which he bore with Christian patience & resignation. He was a native of Somerset Co, Md, & although a beardless boy at the commencement of the last war with Great Britain, he was among the first to volunteer. He was in the battles of Lundy's Lane, Chrysler's Field, & others, & at Fort McHenry during its bombardment by the British. He enjoyed the confidence & friendship of Gen Brown & Gen Scott. At the close of the war he resigned his commission & retired to private life. He held an ofc in the Treas Dept; was appointed a paymaster in the army; was engaged in an arduous service in Fla & Tenn, disbursing immense sums of money, frequently having at his command hundreds of thousands of dollars, & for every cent of which he faithfully accounted to the Dept. Maj Bennett died as he lived, an honorable & honest man, deeply lamented by an extensive circle of warn & devoted friends.

Died: on Oct 13, Mr Wm Newton Croggon, a native of Cornwall Co, England, but for the last 9 years a resident of Wash City, aged 47 years.

The subscribers have just opened a Family Groceries on F st, between 14th & 15th sts. We will aim to keep on hand an assortment of hams, shoulders, shad, herring, flour, meal, corn, oats, shorts, ship stuffs, etc. –McKnight & Clephane

The Pavilion Hotel, at Saratoga, N Y, was destroyed by fire on Oct 11. It was owned by Mr Quackenbush, of N Y, & insured for $10,000: furniture insured for $3,000.

Among the passengers on the steamer **North Bend**, which arrived at St Louis, Mo, on Oct 1 from Pittsburg, were 14 ladies, Sisters of Charity, on their way to Dubuque, Iowa Territory, under the charge of the Rev C McDonahoe.

Sir Astley Cooper left a fortune of half a million sterling, Dupuytren over 3 millions of francs, & Baron Graeffe, the celebrated surgeon of Berlin, about 3 millions of dollars.

Reward for runaway, a hired slave by the name of Edward or Ned; about 22 to 25 years of age. Any person taking up said negro & returning him to Geo W Hunter, at Fairfax Court house, or to the subscriber near Drainesville, or securing him in any jail, shall receive $25 & expenses if found in this State, or $50 & expenses if found in any other State or Terr, by applying to Eliphalet Miller, Drainesville, Fairfax Co, Va.

Capitol Hill Institute-a literary association: meeting last Thu at the Engine-house of the Columbian Fire Co. Annual election of the ofcrs: Dr Fred'k May, Pres; John P Ingle, 1st V P; Jas Adams, 2nd V P; Simon Brown, Sec; Benj B French, Treas; J G Proud, Loring B True, & John M Brodhead, Exec Cmte.

Josiah Hamilton, a young mechanic, a journeyman coachmaker, residing on C st, near 12th, on some slight acquaintance with a man called John Eagan, permitted him, while out of work, to live in the house of the former, who not only gave him lodging but victuals & clothing. Eagan remained upwards of 2 months and one day robbed Hamilton of his clothing & some money: loss about $70. Eagan is a native of Ireland, about 23 years of age. Mr Hamilton will give $5 reward for the arrest of the thief.

Wash Corp: An Act authorizing John Pettibone to erect scales for the weighing of hay, straw, & fodder, on the corner of C & 14th sts west, brought to be sold in Wash City; & that Pettibone shall enjoy the privilege of weighing same, during the pleasure of the Corp, & be allowed the same fees & be liable to the same penalties as are prescribed by the acts of this Corp regulating the weighing of same. Pettibone shall keep the said scales & their appurtenances in complete repair at all times for weighing, & shall be in all respects subject to the same regulations & penalties as other weighers of the same, within Wash City.

For rent: a 3 story brick house in the Six Bldgs, at present in the occupation of Wm Gordon. Possession can be had, as early as it may be wanted, on application to Mr Gordon, or John C Vowell, Alexandria.

Circuit Court of Wash Co, D C. Jos Richards has applied to be discharged from imprisonment under the act for the relief of Insolvent Debtors: hearing on the first Mon in Nov next. –Wm Brent, clk

TUE OCT 17, 1843
Richd S Evans, Atty at Law, Wash, D C: ofc #2, west wing of City Hall. References: Hon W C Rives, Levi Woodbury, & Thos H Benton, of the U S Senate.

John Waters invites the attention of the public to his present stock of Fall & Winter Goods: Pa ave, north side, 3 doors east of 10th st.

For rent: well-finished 2 story brick house, on N Y ave, between 9th & 10th sts. Apply to Jos Bryan, near the premises. Possession to be had by Nov 1.

A Voice from the Past: copy of a reply of Fisher Ames to an application for leave to print his speeches, having for its subject the present Constitution, then newly formed. It is dated Dedham, Dec 1, 1800:

The Whigs of the 7th Congressional district of Mass have unanimously renominated the Hon Julius Rockwell as their candidate for Congress, & appointed Wm C Plunkett Delegate to the Whig National Convention.

Destructive fire at Newbern, N C, on Oct 5 in the store of Mr T Williams, on Craven st, destroyed 13 storehouses. Amongst the sufferers are: T Williams, E Clark, J Brissington, John R Green, Lewis Phelps, Mrs Blaney, M A Osten, T Hall, S Simpson, S B Forbes, John Osgood, John Charlotte, & Jacob Gooding.

Intelligence brought by the last arrival of Santa Fe traders places beyond doubt the safety of the party which went out in the spring under the escort of the U S dragoons: reached S F in about 20 days from the time of their separation from the escort, at the crossings of the Arkansas; route is now entirely clear of Texians, & has been ever since Capt Cooke disarmed a portion of the expedition under Col Snively's command. This news seemed to have a powerful influence over the Mexicans when it reached S F, as they treated the Americans with hospitality, instead of the ill will which had previously marked their intercourse.

St John's Church, Gtwn, D C, will be reopened this morning at 11 a m, by the Rt Rev W B Wittingham, D D, Bishop of this Diocese, with a special service provided for the churches that have been repaired & enlarged. At the same time & place the Rev Philip Berry, Deacon, will also be ordained by him to the priesthood.

Died: on Sabbath evening, John H, eldest s/o Sylvanus Holmes, of Wash City. His funeral will be this afternoon, at half past 2 o'clock.

Letter from Rufus Welsh, now on a Mediterranean tour in his own ship, is with one of the finest circus companies in the world. Mr Alvah Mann, the partner of Mr Welsh, sets sail this day with an immense troupe, such as Cadwallader, Gienroy, & other of that ilk, for Demarars. Welsh & Mann have more than $100,000 invested in their business.
--N Y Plebeian

Geo Bowden, with his wife, child & Emma Keeler were crossing the river at Castine, Maine, on Mon week, the boat was suddenly upset & the women & child were drowned. Mr B was saved in a exhausted state.

The Wash Light Infty left Wash City yesterday for Old Point, Norfolk, & Richmond, in the steamer **Chesapeake**, under command of Capt Nevitt. The parade of the Wash Light Infty & the Nat'l Blues was witnessed by a great number of citizens. Capt France, the commander of the Wash Light Infty, was presented a splendid sword by the members of his corps, & it was given to him by Mr Tate, a member of the corps. Capt France has been connected with the corp for 8 years.

On Fri last, as Mr Gannon, of the Steamboat Hotel, was riding near Capitol Hill, he was thrown from his horse, & afterwards received a severe kick from the unruly animal. Mr Gannon's hurt was at first considered very serious by the attending physician, but hopes are now entertained of his recovery.

WED OCT 18, 1843
A son of Mr Andrew Graham, of Pittsburg, was shot dead last week by a playmate, who snapped a pistol at him in sport, under the impression it was not loaded.

Book for sale at the bookstore of R Farnham, corner of 11th st & Pa ave. Lives of the Presidents of the U S, with biographical notices of the signers of the Declaration of Independence, sketches of most remarkable events in the history of the country; by R W Lincoln, embellished with a portrait of each of the Presidents & 45 engravings.

Land for sale on Dec 19 next, the subscribers, excs of Mrs Julia A Wilson, will proceed to sell at public auction, on the premises, the farm below Goose creek, the residence of the late Maj W B Harrison, known by the name of *Soldiers Repose*, containing 500 acs, adjoining the lands of C Stoven, Chas Gulatt, & others; also 25½ acs adjoining the lands of Mrs Sarah Ellzey. On the first tract are the usual farm bldgs. Mr Bradshaw, the present tenant, or either of the subscribers, will show the lands. The subscribers will also sell on Dec 21, the interest of the late Julia A Wilson in the Tanyard & bldgs connected therewith, situated upon the suburbs of Middleburg, Loudoun Co, Va. All the bldgs are of stone & the whole premises in good condition. –Burr W Harrison, Wm H Gray, excs

For sale: in pursance of the last will & test of Wm Vinson, late of Montg Co, a tract of land containing about 180 acs, a portion of which lies immediately on Big Seneca Creek, the residue of the tract is high land. Dr W B Vinson, living near the same will show it, or Chas Vinson, residing in Gtwn, D C. The title is clear of all incumbrance.
–Chas Vinson, Wm B Vinson, excs

Cottage Farm for sale: the subscriber having an opportunity to extend his Piano business, & finding it impossible to combine it with farming, offers for sale this desirable country residence, 500 yards north of the Little River Turnpike Road, 5 miles from Alexandria: tract contains about 150 acs; improvements consist of a commodious frame dwlg house, containing 11 rooms, pantries, kitchen, servants' house, brick smoke-house, corn-house, & a large brick bars, granary, & stables, a well & a pump of excellent water. Terms may be known of the subscriber who may be found at his Piano Store, in Alexandria, or on the premises. –Richd Davis N B-A further supply of superior German Pianos is expected shortly.

Mrd: on Oct 10, at *Cedar Grove*, Fishkill Landing, N Y, by Rev Dr Dewey, Christopher Pearse Cranch, s/o Judge Cranch, of Washington, to Eliz, d/o J P Dewindt.

Mrd: on Oct 10, at *Chestnut Hill*, near Sperryville, by Rev Barnett Grimsley, Middleton Miller, of Washington, to Ann C, 2nd d/o the late John H Wood, all of Rappahannock Co, Va.

Died: on Sep 29, at Rockville, Md, in his 34th year, Mr Jos Braddock A M, Principal of the Rockville Academy. Mr Braddock was a native of Rockville. His knowledge of the Latin & Greek languages, of the higher mathematics, & of science generally, was profound & discriminating. The whole community feels that a grievous loss has fallen upon them, & do most tenderly sympathize with his bereaved family. -Senex

Died: on Oct 16, A H Quincy. The friends of the dec'd are requested to attend his funeral, from his late residence on N Y ave, this afternoon at 2 o'clock.
On Oct 6, Mr Thos H Pratt, of Bibb Co, Ga, was accidentally shot by a pistol while walking out a short distance from his house by himself. He was able to reach a house near by, but died a few hours after.

Instruction in Vocal Music at Mrs Fleischmann's Seminary. The Principal having secured the kind services of a gentleman recently from France. Seminary on E & 6th sts.

The New Orleans papers have lately announced the demise of 2 gentlemen connected with the newspaper press of that city-the one, Mr Robt L Brenham, associate editor of the Tropic, & formerly of the Southern Sportsman; & the other, Chas R Alexander, of the Diamond, formerly a resident of Alexandria, in this District. They both died of the prevailing fever.

THU OCT 19, 1843
Died: on Oct 17, Wm Gale, only s/o Benj F & Ellen E Dyer, aged 3 years & 5 months. His funeral will be from the residence of his father, on 13th st, near N Y ave, this day, at 10 a m.

On Sun last, in Gtwn, a child between 2 & 2½, s/o a Mrs Williams, near the market, was left alone in a room where accessible to fire. The lady first absented herself, giving leave to a servant to do the same, & when she returned, some time after, found the child lying upon the fire horribly burnt & dead. Persons in the neighborhood heard the screams of the child, but dreaming of nothing unusual no assistance was rendered. A smaller child in an adjoining room remained unharmed. -Advocate

The Rt Rev Dr O'Connor, late pastor of St Paul's Church, Pittsburg, Pa, was consecrated Bishop of the new See, on the feast of the Assumption, Sep 13, in the church of St Agatha at Rome. The consecration was performed by his Eminence, Cardinal Fransoni, assisted by 2 other prelates. The See of Pittsburg will embrace all of Western Pa.
--Phil Chronicle

Mr Henry J Raymond, who has been connected with the N Y Tribune as assistant editor, has relinquished his position in view of entering upon another sphere of usefulness. The Tribune remarks that as a reporter & critic, he has hardly a superior in the editorial ranks.

Mrd: on Oct 17, at Rockville, by Rev Mr Gilliss, Mr John P Wheeler, of the Treas Dept, to Miss Ann Mary, d/o the late Col T F W Vinson, of Montg Co, Md.

Died: on Oct 16, Judson Washburn, s/o Lewis T & Antoinette C Fales, aged 5 years & 10 months. His funeral will be from their residence on 9th st, near N Y ave, this afternoon, at 3 o'clock.

Household furniture at auction: on Oct 25, at the residence of Mrs Fred'k Keller, corner of Md ave & 12th st, opposite Gunnell's lumber yard, her household & kitchen furniture. –Robt W Dyer & Co, aucts

$5 reward for a strayed or stolen heavy built bay Mare; & also, a small dark Bay Horse. The horses are terribly old. Reward for either of them if brought to me near the Canal, between 10th & 11th sts, opposite Cazanave's wood-yard. –Thos M Milburn

In the last Albion we find the following: "Should this meet the eye of Mr Wm R Glassbrooke, who left England about 8 years ago, & settled somewhere in the Western Territories, if he will write to his old family atty he will hear of something to his advantage; his old uncle being death Jun 4 last, leaving him the said W R G, L47,000 sterling & the old paternal estate, Lincombe Hall, 236 acs of freehold, all free of expense, payable to him on his coming to the age of 42, which is May 6, 1842. Mr Wm R Glassbrooke, of Westmoreland, in this country, answers to the above description, & we doubt not he is the fortunate man. -Rome [N Y] Citizen

$100 reward for runaway young yellow woman, Matilda Hammon, about 18 or 20 years of age. I feel confident she will make for Gtwn, D C, where she has a mother named Priss Hammon, belonging to Jenkin Thomas, & an uncle by the name of Henry Contee, belonging to the heirs of Clement Smith; she also has some connexions in Wash. –Nicholas Brooke, on his farm in Montg Co, Md

Wash Corp: 1-Memorial of Josiah Essex & others interested, praying that the interest on the stock issued for the bldg of the Almshouse may be made payable quarterly, as the other stocks of the Corp: read & laid on the table. 2-Cmte of Claims, to whom was referred the ptns of D W Oyster, Francis Selden, & Ransdale Pegg, asked to be discharged from their further consideration. 3-Memorial from Z Jones & others, remonstrating against the manner in which 9th st west is being graduated between K & M sts: referred to the Cmte on Improvements. 4-Bill for the relief of Wm Cunningham: referred to the Cmte of Claims.

FRI OCT 20, 1843
Col John Millen, a Rep elect to the next Congress from the State of Ga, died on Sun last at his residence near Savannah. He was a native of that city, where he had successfully practiced the profession of law for many years, & had frequently represented the county in the State Legislature.

The ship **Rajah** arrived at Boston on Mon, having on board the materials which were saved from the wreck of the war-steamer **Missouri**, & bring as passengers most of her ofcrs & crew. The following are the names of the ofcrs: S B Bissell, G R Gray, T T Hunter, Lts; F Alexander, Acting Master; A J Bowie, Assist Surgeon; A S Taylor, Lt of Marines; J Farrow, Chief Engineer; J M Wainwright, D McN Faifax, C S Throckmorton, Passed Midshipmen; A C Wakeman, Purser's Clk; J S Bohrer, J Fry, H Davidson, J H March, Midshipmen; W Scott, Assist Engineer; H Hunt, A S Palmer, S Archbold, T Zeller, do; R Dixon, Boatswain; N Barton, Gunner; C Jordan, Carpenter; J D Freeman, Sailmaker; & 275 men & boys. Capt Newton remained behind to look after the wreck, & kept with him one Lt, the Purser, 2 Midshipmen, 2 Engineers, & 40 men, who would be kept at work in recovering as much of the property as they could.

We regret to learn that the Ware river packet **Mary Eliza**, Capt Wm Williams, sr, which left Norfolk on Fri, was capsized off Back river on the night of the same day, & it is supposed all on board perished. Capt Williams was found dead, being lashed to the mast. The schnr was towed into Back river on Mon. -Beacon

Appointments by the Pres: Wm H Bassett, to be Marshal of the U S for the Western District of La, in place of Gervais Fontenot, resigned. Consuls: Wm Hogan, of Ga, for Nuevitas, in Cuba, in place of Wm H Freeman, resigned. A Follins, for Omoa & Truxillo, in Honduras. Hooper C Eaton, of Md, for Lyons, in France, in place of N Berry, resigned. Pedro de Regil y Estrada, for Merida & Sisal, in Yucatan, in place of C Thompson, jr, resigned.

Obit from the Burlington [Vt] Free Press. Died: on Oct 3, at the residence of his son, Dr J P Russell, Army Surgeon, while on a visit at Governor's Island, N Y, another sldr of the Revolution, David Russell, of this town. Mr Russell, after leaving the army of the Revolution, in which he had been early engaged, came to this State previous to its being admitted into the Union. In 1783 he entered into the printing business at Bennington with Anthony Haswell, under whose auspices during that year the Vermont Gaz was established. In 1784 the Leg of this State established 5 post ofcs-at Bennington, Rutland, Brattleboro, Windsor, & at Newbury. Mr Haswell, the senior partner, was appointed Postmaster Gen, Mr Russell discharging its duties; upon the admission of Vt into the Union in 1791 these post ofcs became a part of the establishment under the control of the Genr'l Gov't, & Mr Russell was appointed paostmaster at Bennington; he contined until he was appointed collector of customs for the district of Vt, when, in 1797, he removed to Burlington, & entered upon the duties of his ofc, until superseded by Dr Jabez Penniman. He has lived beyond the usual time allotted to man, & died before life became a burden. His pilgrimage on earth closed in his 86th year-leaving a widow & a large circle of relatives & friends to mourn his loss.

Died: on Tue last, Judson Washburn Fales, s/o Lewis T & Antoinette C Fales, aged 5 years & 10 months. And on Thu following, Lewis McDonald, infant s/o the same, aged 1 year. The funeral of the elder brother, which was notified for yesterday, has been postponed in consequence of the younger, & will take place this afternoon, from the residence of their bereaved parents in 9th st, near N Y ave, at 3 o'clock.

Died: on Sep 30, at Fort Jesup, La, Helen Jackson, d/o Capt R S Dix, U S Army, aged 3 year & 4 months.

Excx sale of furniture, stock, & negroes: on Nov 1, by order of the Orphan's Court of Wash Co, D C, for cash, at the late residence of John Burrows, dec'd, of said county, on the river road, about a half mile above Tennallytown, all the personal estate of the dec'd: beds, bedsteads, tables, chairs, bureaus, andirons, desk, bookcase, china & glass ware, kitchen furn, etc: farming stock & utensils, included 3 horses, 7 cows, 3 hogs, & a lot of chickens, 4 beehives, cart, & harness, cutting-box, cradles & scythes, etc. Also, the crops of corn, oats, potatoes, etc, of the present year, with 6 likely young slaves-2 men, 2 women, & 2 children. -Edw S Wright, auct

Notice: by virtue of a writ of fieri facias, issued by B K Morsell, one of the justices of the peace for Wash Co, D C, & to me directed, I shall sell on Oct 27, on the public square opposite the Centre Market-house, in Wash City, the following property, to wit: one center or tea table, one bureau, one walnut table, one mantel clock, 2 looking glasses, 5 stick back chairs, pair iron dogs, lot of old carpeting, tongs, feather bed, bed clothes, seized & taken as the property of Eliz Lowe, & will be sold to satisfy a judgment due Dr Thos Sewall. -Lambert S Beck, Constable

Mrd: on Sep 28, by Rev Robt T Nixon, Mr Wm W Franck to Miss Frances Hoye, all of Port Royal, Caroline Co, Va.

Mrd: Oct 12, by Rev Robt T Nixon, Wm B Hall to Mrs Mary M Omohundro, all of Westmoreland Co, Va.

Notice: by virtue of a writ of fieri facias, issued by B K Morsell, one of the justices of the peace for Wash Co, D C, & to me directed, I shall sell on Oct 27, on the public square opposite the Centre Market-house, in Wash City, the following property, to wit: one center or tea table, one bureau, one walnut table, one mantel clock, 2 looking glasses, 5 stick back chairs, pair iron dogs, lot of old carpeting, tongs, feather bed, bed clothes, seized & taken as the property of Reazen St Clair, & will be sold to satisfy a judgment due Dr Thos Sewall. -Lambert S Beck, Constable

SAT OCT 21, 1843
Maj G Tochman, of Poland, begs leave to announce that he will deliver 2 Lectures on the subject of Poland & Russia in Gtwn, at the Protestant Methodist Church, Congress st, on Oct 23 & 26, at 7 p m. Tickets of admission to be had at the Apothecary Store of Dr O M Linthicum, of Gtwn: 25 cents.

Dentist: Dr Humphreys has rented the house of Chas Lee Jones, on the east corner of 3rd st & Pa ave, & is now prepared to attend to such ladies & gentlemen as have engaged his professional services.

Bargains! Boots & Shoes. –John Sexsmith

Marshal Bertrand spent the whole of Sat, Oct 7, with Mr Clay, at Ashland, & left the following morning for Cincinnati.

Canton papers to May 30th have been received at N Y. The most prominent item of news is a report that Cmdor Kearney had received a communication from the Emperor informing him that the U S would be allowed to trade at all the ports open to the English.

The American noticed the arrival in the N Y harbor of the U S steamer **Princeton**, on Wed. Capt Stockton came in upon us like a flash, to the admiration of all who saw her. She came into the Narrows under sail, but when abreast of Robbin's Reef took in her canvass, & then, against a strong ebb tide, without any apparent moving cause, went ahead more rapidly than he ever seen a vessel move before. She is driven by submerged propellers at the stern.

Van Buren [Ark] Intell: 1-Arch Saunders is another accomplice in the late outrage in the Cherokee nation. 2-Also, that the Starrs murdered Mr Kelly, the white man mentioned in our last. 3-Lovely Rogers, who gave himself up to the authorities of Saline district, Cherokee nation, when suspected being concerned in the murder of Isaac Bushyhead, has, after an examination, been released. 4-The authorities of the Cherokee nation are using every exertion to apprehend the murderers of Mr Vore & family. Mr W S Coodey, with about 200 men, is scouring the country. There are also about 200 men in arms on our side of the line. Their apprehension is inevitable. 5-Gen Taylor left on Sep 25 for Fort Gibson, with a view of settling the existing difficulty in the Cherokee nation.

Naval. The U S ship **Dale**, in 79 days from Valparaiso, with the remains of the late Com Alex Claxton on board, arrived at Phil on Thu last. 2-The store-ship **Erie** had arrived from the U S with provisions for the Pacific squadron. Cmdor Jones had gone in the ship **Madedonian** to the Sandwich Islands.

Washington College, Pennsylvania, is on the National Road, 32 miles from Wheeling. The College is in a flourishing condition, having numbered on its catalogue for the last year 183. Winter session will commence on Nov 1. –A W Acheson, Sec of the Board

Notice to Benj Jopling & Wm Jopling, who formerly lived in Amherst, Nelson, or Albemarle Co, Va, & who were the children of Ralph Jopling, dec'd, or their heirs, excs, or adms: You are hereby informed that, by a decree of the Circuit Superior Court of Law

& Chancery for the county of Nelson, in Va, you are entitled to a distributive share of the estate of Sarah Ball, dec'd, formerly Sarah Jopling; & by communicating to us as Com'rs in the case of Bill against Jopling, by letter directed to us at Lovington, Va, or in person, such information & facilities will be afforded as may be desired. –Chas Perrow, Henry T Harris, Comrs

Virginia Iron Works for Sale. John Alexander, plntf, against S S Baxter, administrator of John Irvine, dec'd, & John Jordan & others, dfndnts. Pursuant to a decree in this cause by the Circuit Superior Court of Law & Chancery for Rockbridge Co, on Sep 23, 1843, we shall proceed, on the premises, on Dec 20 next, to sell by public auction that extensive Iron Establishment in Alleghany Co, Va, known as the works of the late firm of Jordans & Irvine, consisting of a Forge & Furnace, with everything attached. The forge is on the Jackson's river, one mile above its confluence with the Cowpasture, which form the James River. The furnace is about 6 miles from the Forge. The real property consists of about 50,000 acs of land. Further information can be obtained by addressing the undersigned, at Lexington, Va. –A T Barclay, John Ruff, Wm C Lewis

Mrd: on Oct 17, at the residence of Wm A Bradley, by Rev Dr Laurie, Mr Ashton S H White to Miss Amie G, d/o the late Abraham Bradley.

Died: on Sep 25, in Grand Coteau, of the congestive fever, Mr Jos A Gardiner, aged 57 years, a native of Md, but for the last 6 years a resident of Louisiana. He was as much beloved for amiable qualities in Md as he was in La, where he was known for his kindness & affiability to all.

Died: on Oct 19, Sarah Josephine, y/d/o Jos & Sarah Ann Sessford, aged 21 months. Her funeral will take place this Sat, at 10 a m.

MON OCT 23, 1843

We understand that the Hon Abraham Rencher, late a Rep in Congress from N C, has been appointed Charge d'Affaires of the U S to Portugal, vice Mr Barrow, who has applied for permission to return home.

John H Pendleton, U S Charge d'Affaires to Chili, was at Santiago, the seat of Gov't, in good health.

Circuit Court of Wash Co, D C. Wm Sawkins has applied to be discharged from imprisonment under the act for the relief of Insolvent Debtors: hearing on the first Mon of Nov next. –Wm Brent, clk

Died: yesterday, aged 3 years & 3 months, Mgt Emma Newton, d/o Mr Ignatius Newton. Her funeral is this afternoon at 3 o'clock, from their residence on Mass ave, between 5th & 6th sts.

Chas A Newmayer, Miniature Painter, has removed to the house of Dr Van Patten, on Pa ave, next door west of Todd's Hat Store, where he respectfully invites the public to call & examine his specimens.

For rent: a neat & convenient 2 story brick dwlg, with back bldgs attached, containing in all 10 rooms. It is situated between 9th & 10th sts, on N Y ave. Apply to John C Harkness, next door east.

Handsome furniture at auction: on Oct 27, at the residence of Mr W H Lowrey, on E st south, between 11th & 12th sts, near the steamboat wharf: his household & kitchen furniture. -Robt W Dyer & Co, aucts

Navy Orders: Capt C W Skinner to command of frig **Potomac**; Capt G W Storer to command of Navy Yard, Portsmouth, N H; Capt F H Gregory to command of frig **Raritan**; Capt J Percival to command of frig **Constitution**; Capt B Dulany to command receiving ship **New York**.

For rent: the house & lot just vacated by Dr Lawson, Surgeon Genrl U S Army, near the Navy Dept, at the corner of N Y ave & 17th st west, first corner south of Gen Towson's. Inquire of Jas Carrico.

Wash Corp: 1-An act for the relief of Henry Thomas: penalty imposed on Thomas as security for Chas Turner, on a certain prison bounds' bond, in which the Corp of Wash is a party, be & the same is hereby remitted, provided the said Thomas pay the costs of prosecution.

Editors: You will confer a favor by allowing space for a brief notice of 3 oil-paintings by Mr Henry J Brent, now exhibited at the studio of Mr Bingham, Pa ave: they are a marine view, called "Too much wind, or taking in sail," "A view of the Ruins of Jamestown," & "A Ruined English Castle," & are each replete with interest, & well worthy of the attention of amateurs. Each one is worth the prices asked for the whole. -Wash, Oct 19

TUE OCT 24, 1843
Handsome furniture at auction: on Oct 27, at the residence of Mr W H Lowrey, on E st, between 11th & 12th sts, near the steamboat wharf. -Robt W Dyer & Co, aucts

The case of the State of Georgia vs Canatoo, a Cherokee Indian, committed to jail upon a charge of digging gold in that part of the Cherokee nation not as yet ceded, but attached to the county of Grinnett for the purposes of civil & criminial jurisdiction. The prisoner was brought up by habeas corpus, & his discharge moved for upon 3 grounds: 1-Defect of commitment; 2-There was no law making the offence criminal; & 3-If there was, it was contrary to existing treaties, & therefor contrary to the U S Constitution.

A new Orphan Asylum is to be opened in a few days on 10th st, corner of G, for the education of orphan boys. The premises, formerly Mr McLeod's Central Academy, have lately been put in complete order for the purposes, & are to include a day school for boys upon the plan of the St Vincent's Female Orphan Asylum in F st. The institution is under the gov't of the Trustees of St Vincent's Orphan Asylum, of which it s a part, who have procured Sisters of Charity to take charge of the whole establishment.

At Louisville, Ky, on Mon week, Mr Wm G Benham was stabbed by Talbot Oldham, s/o Judge Oldham, of Jefferson Co. Oldham stabbed Benham on the arm near the shoulder, severing a large artery, & once in the back. Mr Benham died that night. Young Oldham immediately mounted a horse & fled from the city.

Edw R Brinckerhoff & T W Beecher left Albany a few days since on a shooting excursion in Hamilton Co. In struggling through a swamp, Brinckerhoff's rifle discharged by coming in contact with a tree. The ball struck Mr Beecher, just over the right eye, passed through the brain, & came out between the eyes. He expired in about 8 minutes expired. Mr Beecher was lessee of the Albany Bath, & leaves a young wife.

W Henry Russell announces he intends giving Vocal Entertainment on Oct 26, at Carusi's Saloon, which will be his last. Cards of admission 50 cents, to be obtained at Dr Patterson's Drug Store, & Anderson's Bookstore. Performance to commence at 7½ o'clock. [Oct 25 newspaper: The Pres & his family, with several members of his Cabinet, attended the concert.]

Boarding-house. Mr J B Morgan informs Members of Congress & others that she is prepared to accommodate those who may favor her with a call with board or furnished rooms. Location next door to the corner of 3rd st, a few doors west of the Railroad Depot.

WED OCT 25, 1843
Nashville, Oct 11, 1843. Members of the Tenn Leg, of the inhabitants of Nashville, & other citizens of Tenn, invite the Hon John J Crittenden to a public dinner. Signed:

J M Anderson	Adam R Alexander	Thos R Jennings
Danl L Barringer	Francis F Fogg	G W Martin
John Cocke	Edwin H Ewing	Thos L Bransford
J W Harris	John Bell	Terry H Cahal
A P Maury	Ephraim H Foster	A R Humes
Richd Cheatham	Donald McLeod	-Cmte

Reply to Messrs J M Anderson, D L Barringer, & others, Cmte: from J J Crittenden, Nashville, Oct 12, 1843. Circumstances will not permit me to accept.

Whigs of the 8th Congressional district of Ky assembled in Lexington on Oct 16, & appointed Richd Pindell a delegate to the Nat'l Whig Convention to be held in Balt in

May next, & Thos B Stevenson his alternate. Following gentlemen appointed as delegates from this district to said Convention: A M Rigg, Gibson Simpson, John B Mussey, of Owen; S F Gano, R F Ford, D Howard Smith, of Scott; Orlando Brown, B B Sayre, W G Talbot, of Franklin; Geo B Kinkead, Jos A Peters, Wm P Hart, of Woodford; Robt E Woodson, Jos C Price, Saml Moseley, of Jessamine; Wm O Smith, W B Arnold, Jacob Spears, of Bourbon; Wm R Hervey, Edw A Dudley, & John F Leavy, of Fayette.

Mrd: by Rev Mr Bean, Mr Wm Thomas, of St Louis, Mo, to Miss Jane M, 2nd d/o Mr Jas Tucker, of Wash City. [No date-current item.]

Circuit Court of Wash Co, D C. John H Ford, [colored,] has applied to be discharged from imprisonment under the act for the relief of Insolvent Debtors: hearing on the first Mon in Nov next. –Wm Brent, clk

The books of John C Cook & Wm M Moran, trading under the firm of Cook & Moran, at Gallant Green, Chas Co, Md, have been placed in my hands for collection. The interest of Cook in these books was transferred to Moran on Apr 15, 1842, for a valuable consideration. –Robt S Reeder, Atty for Wm M Moran, Port Tobacco, Md

THU OCT 26, 1843
Thanksgiving Day. Early as 1623, 3 years after the landing of the Pilgrims at Plymouth, from the happy termination of a severe drought which threatened the entire destruction of the colony & the abundant crops which succeeded that season, a day was set apart for public thanksgiving, which was devoutly observed. In 1630, 7 years after, a day was simultaneously observed throught out all in the colonies, in obedience to their continued prosperity, which, among other blessings, included the arrival of Govn'r Winthrop & his fleet, which was of incalculable importance to the colonists, & since which time, as we learn by "Holmes' American Annals" & other authority, a thanksgiving day has been annually set apart & religiously kept by their descendants.

Two lots for sale, in square 76, [18 & 23,] 40 feet front & 115 feet deep. For particulars, inquire of Mr John Sioussa, at his residence, on N Y ave, between 12th & 13th sts.

New store for rent: now in the course of erection adjoining the store of Messrs Boteler & Son, & 3 doors east of D Clagett's dry goods store. Application may be made between this & Nov 1 to Mr Jas Dixon, F st, opposite Corcoran & Riggs, or to the undersigned, living in Montg Co, Md. –Thos Connelly

Gen Ebenezer Elmer, Pres of the New Jersey Cincinnati Society, & the last surviving ofcr of the New Jersey line of the Revolutionary army, died on Wed last, having attained the great age of 91 years.

The following are ofcrs attached to the U S ship **Independence**, flag ship of the Home & West India squadron: Cmdor, Chas Stewart; Capt, Isaac McKeever; Lts: S Smith Lee, J F Schenck, J S Palmer, F Huger, A Attwood Holcomb, A S Baldwin; Fleet Surgeon, Jas M Greene; Purser, F B Stockton; Chaplain, Jos Stockbridge; Acting Master, Jas S Biddle; Assist Surgeons, J Madison Minor & C H Wheelwright; Cmdor's Sec, Chas T Stewart; Capt's Clk, Wm A Poor; Cmdor's Clk, A B Ashton; Passed Midshipmen, Foxhall A Parker, jr, C Benham, B N Westcost, C M Morris, A J Drake; Midshipmen, A V Fox, Edw Allen, F W Colby, A Barbot, J B Bankhead, Robt Milligan, Wm S Cushman, And F Monroe, Alex J Mitchell, H H Geo Hunter; Boatswain, M Hall; Carpenter, John Rainbow; Gunner, Wm B Brown; Sailmaker, Jas Frazer

Newburyport Herald: fatal explosion of the boiler in the Patent Cordage manufactory of Michl Wormsted & Son, on South & Marlborough sts, on Fri last. Mr John Green, the engineer, was instantly killed, & Mr Lorenzo Ross, was badly scalded, & his body completely blackened. He revived & may recover.

Died: on Oct 21, Mrs Anna T, consort of Dr John Hunter, of Wash City. Her bereaved & sorrow stricken family have sustained an irreparable loss, & regret the sudden departure from life of one who was eminently endowed with all the virtues which adorn the female character.

During the review of the troops at Hartford by Col Richd M Johnson, he lost one of his shoe strings, but did not discover his loss at once. The relic was picked up by some devoted patriot, who at once [as Col Johnson had left the place] dispatched a special messenger with it to this city, with instructions to deliver it to some member of the cmte appointed to receive him on his arrival. A day or two since, this messenger called on Alderman Woodhull of the Second Ward, one of the cmte, & gave into his keeping the precious shoe string, at the same time vouching most solemnly that it was the identical one worn by Col J at Hartford. It will of course be delivered to him when he arrives. In the meantime Woodhull will cheerfully exhibit the relic to the curious. -Courier

Jas I Dickins, Atty & Counsellor at Law: ofc #4, west wing of City Hall. [Local ad.]

The undersigned has been appointed agent of Saml Lucas, of Balt, for the sale of his Porter, Ale, Cider, & Brewers' Yest, so justly celebrated for their respective superior qualities. All orders left at his residence, Railroad Hotel, Pa ave, will receive prompt attention. –P Moran

Christian Eckloff, Merchant Tailor, opposite Brown's Hotel, having now a complete assortment of Fall & Winter Goods. J W Eckloff, Cutter at the above, being agent for Mahan's Protractor & Proof systems of garment Cutting. -Capitol

$5 reward: strayed or was driven away from the Commons, near the Capitol, on Thu, 3 cows & 2 calfs. Any person returning them to the subscriber on B st north, near the western gate of the Capitol square, shall receive the above reward. –A M E O'Gannon

$50 reward for runaway, my negro man Wm Oliver, about 22 or 23 years of age: ran away from Mr Henry D Hatton's. The said negro has a father belonging to Mrs Lyles, near Tenallytown, about which he may be lurking. –Edw H Edelin, PG Co, Md

NOTICE: by writ of fieri facias, issued by B K Morsell, a J P for Wash Co, D C, I shall offer at public sale, for cash, on Nov 2, opposite the Centre Market-house, in Wash City, D C, 1 roan Horse, seized & taken as the property of Jas Fugett, & will be sold to satisfy a judgment due Sampson Simmes. –Lambert S Beck, Constable

Crmnl Crt, Wash, D C: Oct 23. Grand Jury:

Peter Force, foreman	Geo W Riggs	Wm B Thompson
John Kurtz	Hamilton Lufborough	Jos Forrest
John P Ingle	Thos Brown	R C Weightman
Geo Watterston	Andrew Coyle	Lewis Carbery
Thos Blagden	Saml McKenny	Francis Dodge, sr
Geo W Young	Philip T Berry	W Gunton
John F Cox	Danl Kurtz	Abner C Pierce
Otho M Linthicum	John Boyle	John Dixon

Oct 24: 1-Jas Curtis, free negro, indicted for stealing from Geo Knott a $5 bill: found guilty. Oct 25: 2-Jas Evans, alias John Evans, & Geo Hall, guilty for a riot at gtwn on Jun 1, 1843. 3-Thos J Fletcher found guilty of keeping a disorderly house in Wash City. 4-Augustus Lucas found not guilty for an assault on Everard Krouse. 5-Saml Gassaway & Chas Coates [slaves] were indicted under the old law of Md [passed in 1728] for burglariously entering the store of Jas & Henry Thecker, of Gtwn, & stealing from them 3 pairs of boots & a box of cigars, being of the value of $15. Jury found them guilty. This verdict subjects the prisoners, under the law, to the punishment of death. We understand they will be recommended to the clemency of the Executive. 4-Lydia Green, free negress, found not guilty of stealing 2 one dollar notes, the property of Sarah Brown.

For rent: the commodious 3 story dwlg-house at the corner of E & 5th sts, for some years past the residence of the Rev Mr Stringfellow. Also, 2 other large dwlgs on the square west of the Gen Post Ofc. Apply on 10th st west, to John Boyle.

For rent: a spacious 2 story brick dwlg, on N Y ave, between 13th & 14th sts. For terms inquire of Mrs Thaw, N Y ave, between 12th & 13th sts.

Sale of household furniture, farming utensils, etc, by order of the Orphan's Court of Wash Co, D C: all the personal effects of the late Jas Greenleaf, dec'd, at his late residence on Capitol Hill, 1st st east. -Robt W Dyer & Co, aucts

Capitol Hill Institute: meeting to be held at the Hall of the Columbia Fire Co this Thu at 7 p m. A Lecture will be delivered by A H Lawrence, upon "The adaptation of external nature to the physical & intellectual nature of man." The chair will be taken precisely at the hour. –Simon Brown, sec

Excellent household furniture at auction: on Oct 31, at the residence of Mr J Z Harton, 10th st, south side of Pa ave, all his household & kitchen furniture. -Robt W Dyer & Co, aucts

FRI OCT 27, 1843
Mr Jas F May, a much respected citizen of Davidson Co, Tenn, was killed about 7 miles from Nashville on Sat week, in attempting to escape from a barouche with which his horse was running off. –Whig

A young & promising son, aged 14, of John R Nelson, a State Senator from Knox Co, fell from a tree near Knoxville, Tenn, a few days since, & was instantly killed. -Whig

Among the passengers in the packet-ship **Argo**, arrived at N Y from France last week, were Mr Aaron Vail, late Charge d'Affaires to Spain, & Mrs Scott, [the lady of Maj Gen Scott,] & 4 dghts.

One hundred dozen country knit half hose: for sale very cheap by John Allen, Pa ave, between 9th & 10th.

Appointments by the Pres: 1-Geo Mohr to be Consul of the U S for Dresden, Saxony, in the place of E F Rivinius, resigned. 2-Jos C Luther, of N Y, to be Commercial Agent of the U S at Port au Prince, in the Island of St Domingo, in the place of F D Cummins, declined.

The circumstances attending the death of Senator Linn: he was up to Oct 2, in unusually good health. He was preparing some business, intending on the next day to visit St Louis. In the afternoon, when stooping to search for some papers in a trunk, he raised his head suddenly, & asked Mrs Linn if his face appeared flushed, as he felt dizzy & when a painful sensation soon passed off, & he resisted the suggestion that he should be bled. He continued employed in correspondence throughout the evening and later retired. He asked Mrs Linn in the morning, if he might not be disturbed, as he would endeavor to sleep an hour or two. When visited 2 or 3 times he was still found in the state of slumber. At 12 o'clock on Oct 3 Mrs Linn approached his bedside to awaken him. She attempted to do so, but in vain. Three or four hours later there was a profuse bleeding from the mouth & nostrils. –St Louis New Era

Criminal Court-Wash: Oct 26, 1843. 1-Jas Hammel, alias Martin Nowiski, indicted for stealing a fur cap, value of $3, the property of E G Handy, was found guilty. The prisoner was defended by C S Wallach. 2-John Bohlay, jr, found guilty of an assault upon J G Hempler. He was also found not guilty of another assault upon J G Hempler. The defence of Bohlayer was conducted by Jas Hoban. 3-Jim Chesley, free negro, indicted for an assault on Isaac Carrington, free negro, was found guilty. 4-Jas Ellis, indicted for an assault on Susan Mattingly, at Gtwn, was found guilty. The defence was conducted by W Woodward. Prisoner was sentenced to pay a fine of $20, to give security to keep the peace for one year, & to stand committed until the security be given. The security was immediately given, & the dfndnt was discharged.

Mrd: on Oct 19, at *Twiford*, the residence of her father, by Rev B F Stewart, Jos F Harvey to Miss Ann Washington, eldest dght of Col John W Hungerford, all of Westmoreland Co, Va.

Vocal & Instrumental Concert. Julius Knop's Benefit Concert will take place at Apollo Hall on Mon next, on which occasion he will be assisted by members of the Apollo Association, & the entire force of the German Band. The Concert will be under the direction of Mr Hewitt, & Mr Scheel will preside at the piano forte. Tickets, 50 cents, admitting a gentleman & a lady. Tickets may be had at Fischer's Stationers' Hall, O Fish & Co's Hat Store, Ritter's, Tobacconist, between 11th & 12th sts, Pa ave, & at the door.

Wash Corp: 1-Nominated for Chimney Sweeps: W M Robinson, for the First Ward; Geo Y Bowen, for the Second Ward; John E Keenan & Jas A Breast, for the Third Ward; & N H Wilkinson, for the Fourth, Fifth, & Sixth Wards. Nominations were confirmed. 2-Ptn from Alexander Provost & Alfred Wallingsford: referred. 3-Ptn of D Clagett & others for grading & gravelling: referred to the Cmte on Improvements. 4-Cmte of Claims asked to be discharged from its further consideration of the ptn of Geo Grimes & Geo T McGlue. 5-Cmte of Claims asked to be discharged from further consideration of the ptns of Francis Selden & Ransdell Fegg: taken up & agreed to.

Household furniture at auction, on Oct 31, at the residence of Mr Francis Mechelin, on 1st st, near Pa ave. -Wm Marshall, auctioneer

Sale of household furniture, on Oct 27, at the late residence of Jos E McNear, on 7th st, a lttle south of Md ave, & near the residence of Wm A Bradley: & a patent mahogany Beehive. -Robt W Dyer & Co, aucts

SAT OCT 28, 1843
The St Louis Republican states that David R Atchinson has been appointed by the Govn'r Senator in Congress to supply the vacancy occasioned by the death of Mr Linn. It is not known whether he will accept the appointment.

By a letter from Claiborne, Mr Dellet, Rep in Congress from the Mobile district, is prostrate with an attack of disease from which there is little or no hope of his recovery.

Mrd: on Oct 10, in Louisiana, at the country seat of her father, Miss Anna Maria Hennen to N R Jennings, both of the city of New Orleans.

Mrd: on Oct 12, at Henderson, Ky, Capt P N Barbour, U S Army, to Miss Martha Isabella, y/d/o J B Hopkins, of that place.

Mrd: on Oct 17, in N Y, Maj Washington Seawell, U S A, to Susan Amelia, y/d/o the late John M Bloom.

Mrd: on Oct 19, Lt Robt E Johnson, U S N, to Annie T, d/o Jos P Norris, of Phil.

Died: at Newnan's, East Florida, of fever, Chas Wm Cushing, Atty at Law, formerly of N Hampshire. [No date-current item.]

Died: on Oct 27, in Wash City, John Byrne, aged 60 years, a native of the county of Wesford, Ireland. His funeral will be from the residence of Martin Renehan, on F st, between 14th & 15th sts, on this day, at 3 p m. The members of St Matthew's Male Sodality, of which Mr Byrne was a member, are requested to attend the funeral from his late residence to St Matthew's Church.

Fashionable Tailoring Establishment-Jos H Daniel, Merchant Tailor, a few doors west of Brown's Hotel, next to Todd's Hat Store.

NOTICE: The subscribers have opened a Conveyance Ofc at the corner of 8th & L sts south, near the Navy Yard. They will draw all kinds of deeds, leases, & contracts. –Geo Adams & Son

$150 reward for runaway yellow man named Jim Orme, about 26 years of age; has a wife living at Mr Wm Hilliary's & a father on Mr Thos B Crauford's land near the ***Long Old Fields***, where he may be lurking. –Thos E Berry, near Queen Anne, PG Co, Md

MON OCT 30, 1843
Private letters received at Augusta give accounts of a most destructive fire which occurred at Monticello, Ga, on Oct 22. The stores of Messrs Loyall, Edmondson, T J Smith, & Chas Norton, were all consumed.

The Govn'r of the State of N Y has pardoned Chas F Mitchell, who was under confinement in the State prison for forgery. He has been confined nearly a year. The cause that prompted the pardon was his rapid decline by consumption, which it is supposed will soon terminate his days.

Earthquake in Massachusetts on Tue. The houses in the towns of Canton, Sharon, Stoughton, Easton, & South Dedham, were shaken, the doors were jarred open, & dishes on the breakfast table rattled.

Carlilse [Pa] Herald & Expositor. Rev Wm T Sprole, Pastor of the First Presbyterian Church of this borough, has retired from his charge, having accepted a call from the first Presbyterian Church in Washington. The pulpit of this town has lost one of its brightest ornaments.

Mrd: on Oct 8, by Rev John Davis, Mr Hamilton McHenry to Miss Mary Jane, eldest d/o Mr Franklin Edmonston, all of Washington.

Died: on Oct 14, at Barnaby, PG Co, Md, Henry Garland Callis, s/o Henry A & Eleanor H Callis, in the 10th year of his age.

LOOK HERE. John D Boteler has again commenced his old business of Gun & Locksmithing & Bell-hanging on Pa ave, between 4½ & 6th sts, next door to the Athenuaeum Bldg, where Lane & Tucker carry on Merchant Tailoring.

The burglary at Alexandria was of a most audacious & successful character. The villains on last Thu night entered the dwlg of Cassius F Lee, which is on one of the most public streets, & stole cloaks, coats, hats, & plated articles in value to $150. They cut a piece out of the front door large enough to put a hand through & open the lock inside by turning the key. Since writing the above we learn that the dwlg of Mr Michl Shanks, in the First Ward of Wash City, was feloniously entered last Fri night, in the same manner, & several articles were stolen.

Criminal Court-Washington, Oct 27, 1843. 1-John Brown, free negro, was charged with grand larceny, in stealing $31 on Sep 5, 1843, the property of Saml Stettinius. Robbery was committed at the Railroad Depot where Mr Stettinius was an agent. The prisoner restored the money to Mr Stettinius. Verdict-guilty. 2-Wm Gray, alias McManus, found not guilty of stealing, on Oct 8, 2 coats of the value of $13, the property of Wm Goulder. The prisoner remains in custody for trial under the charge of burglariously entering Mrs Owner's boarding-house on Oct 8, 1843. Oct 30, 1843: 1-Eliz Hall charged with riot & an assault upon Susan & Mary Creamer, was called up. The assault on Mary Creamer-11 years of age, was taken up first: verdict-guilty.

TUE OCT 31, 1843
From the Terre Haute [Indiana] Express. Barbarous murder was perpetrated on Oct 17 in that county; at the residence of Mrs Brady, where it appears, some company had assembled, amongst them, Geo Brock & Saml Dias. Offensive words by Brock & Dias

procured an axe and killed Brock. He almost severed his head from his body. The murderer was secured & is now in the county jail.

Exeter [N H] New Letter: on Oct 17, Alfred Hill was arrested on a complaint against him for the violation & murder of a child not yet 9 years old, whom but a few weeks before he had taken from the poorhouse in Newmarket. She died on Fri & Hill was committed to jail to await the action of the grand jury in Feb next.

Horrible murder committed at Middle Brook Mills, Montg Co, Md, on Oct 18. Geo Dunn, traveling with a woman supposed to be his wife, is the perpetrator of the deed & the woman the victim. They were seen together about 200 yards from the dwlg of Mr House, in conversation; the man was last seen hastily leaving the spot. The body of the woman was found horribly mutilated. A book found close by had a card showing that during the summer he had at some time boarded with Michl Conolly, in Balt, who said the man called himself Thompson. It was ascertained that he had another wife living in Virginia with 2 or 3 children.

Maj Gen Gaines has obtained leave of absence, & Col Kearney, of the dragoons, has assumed command of the third military dept.

The remains of the late Cmdor Alexander Claxton, of the U S Navy, having been conveyed to Balt, were yesterday interred at Green Mount Cemetery with appropriate funeral honors. Cmdor Claxton died in Jun, 1841, while in command of the Pacific squadron, & was buried at Valparaiso, but that his body has been recently disinterred under direction of the Gov't, & taken to his native place for interment.

The trial of Mr Palmer C Ricketts, editor of the Cecil Whig, for shooting Amos T Forwood, in Aug last, commenced at Elkton, Md, on Thu, & concluded on Sat: verdict of acquittal-the evidence in his behalf going to prove that the act was committed in self defence.

Criminal Court-Wash: Oct 30. 1-U S vs John B Manley, indicted for an assault & battery upon Anna Maria Balzell/Baltzell, in Wash City, on Aug 4, 1843: verdict-guilty. 2-Isaiah H Stewart, found guilty of an assault & battery upon Jas Goddard, on Jun 19, 1843. 3-Henrietta Butler, free negress, found guilty of stealing 2 bank notes of the value of $10, the property of John T Devaughn. 4-Aloysius Cole, free negro, found guilty of stealing a hat the value of $6, the property of Wm F Seymour. 5-Lewis Hewitt, found guilty for an assault & battery on Geo W Wren. 6-Jas Mitchell, free negro, found not guilty of stealing a pair of boots of the value of $5, the property of John C Krofhiser, of Gtwn.

Alden Bradford, a very prominent citizen of Massachusetts, & long Sec of the Commonwealth, is no more. He died at Boston, Thu, aged 78 years.

Mrs Susan Frederick, of Haverstraw, arrived in N Y on Tue with an infant about 8 weeks old, & started from the steamboat for the house of a friend. She held the child to her bosom as she passed through the street. On arriving at her destination she discovered it was dead, having no doubt been suffocated. She saw it alive, & apparently well, 10 minutes before.

Pomonkey for sale: Having removed some time since, to reside permanently in Balt, I am desirous to dispose of the above beautiful & valuable residence at private sale. It is situated about 4 miles below Mount Vernon, upon the Potomac river, in Chas Co, Md: property is in good farming order: dwlg-house is large & possesses every convenience & it has the necessary out-bldgs. The celebrity of this ancient seat is well known to a large protion of the community. The farm offered for sale contains about 800 or 900 acs. The title is indisputable, & it will be sold clear of all incumbrances. Col Wm L Brent, of Wash City, or the subscriber in Balt, will show the premises. The steamer **Augusta** passes the farm twice every day, & will land passengers who may request the Captain. –Robt J Brent, Balt, Md

Mrd: on Oct 26, by Rev Mr Edwards, Mr Saml M Herbert to Miss Sarah Ellen, 3rd d/o Mr Simeon Matlock, all of Wash City.

The funeral of Susan H, w/o John P Ingle, will take place from her late residence, Capitol Hill, this afternoon, at 3 o'clock. The friends of the family are respectfully invited to attend.

Recent meeting of the citizens of Wash Co, residing east of the Eastern Branch, held pursuant to public notice, at "*Good Hope*," Zachariah Walker called to the chair, & Jos L Smith appointed sec. Cmte appointed: Alex'r McCormick, Benj P Smith, David Barry, G M Dove, Geo W Tarlburtt, Henry Naylor, John L Brightwell, S B Scaggs, Robt Nevitt, & John Suratt. Cmte to obtain information in regard to the affairs of this county to be laid before this body at its next meeting; & to make recommendations in relation to the extension of the powers of the Levy Court & a reorganization of it.

WED NOV 1, 1843
The Mayor of the city of Charleston has set apart Tue next for the performance of the ceremonies in honor of the late Hugh S Legare. The eulogium is to be pronounced by the Hon Wm C Preston.

Army & Navy Chronicle: Lt Addison R Taliaferro, who was recently tried by court martial at Norfolk, has been sentenced to be cashiered.

On Sat week, during a military drill in the village of Bristol, Vt, 2 respectable residents of that place, John F Bloss & Wm Haskins, were engaged in charging a six pounder; they had rammed home the cartridge, & were withdrawing the ramrod, when the man stationed at the breach of the piece taking his thumb off the vent, it immediately discharged, carrying away the right arm of Mr Haskins & shivering his left arm that it will doubtless have to be amputated; his eyes were both put out, & his right shoulder broken to pieces. There is little hope of the recovery of either.

Mr John Bowers, of Addison, Vt, recently sold his farm, & in a few days after learned that if he had waited he might have obtained $200 more for it. This made him melancholy, which increased upon him until he committed suicide by hanging himself.

Circuit Court of Wash Co, D C. Francis Benne has applied to be discharged from impisonment under the act for the relief of Insolvent Debtors. –Wm Brent, clk

Lt Geo J Wyche, of the U S Navy, committed suicide at Boston on Wed last. He was attached to the receiving ship **Ohio**, & is supposed to have been laboring under derangement of mind at the time he committed the act, aggravated, perhaps, by the use of opium.

Robt Munford, M D, formerly of Richmond, Va, now a resident practitioner of Med & Surgery at Havana, in the Island of Cuba, offers his professional services to invalids visiting that Island from the U S.

Orphan's Court of Wash Co, D C. Letters of adm on the personal estate of Mgt A Culver, late of Wash Co, dec'd. -Geo S Coe, adm

Mrd: on Oct 26, by Rev Mr French, John T Knowles, of Wash City, to Marcelia, y/d/o the late Jas Ager, of Gtwn.

Criminal Court-Wash: Oct 31. Eliz Hall & Emma Reed, indicted for an assault with intent to kill Susan Creamer, in Wash City: jury returned a verdict of guilty against both dfndnts. They were conveyed in a hack back to jail. [Nov 2 newspaper: moved for a new trial.]

Died: on Oct 31, Mrs Amelia Wilson, in her 65th year, a native of PG Co, Md, & for the past 16 years a resident of Wash City. Her funeral will take place at her son-in-law's, Mr Thos Macgill, on 7th st, between G & H sts, at 10 o'clock this morning.

Died: on Mon, in Wash City, after 2 weeks' illness, perfectly resigned to the will of her Maker, Mrs Juliet Weston, d/o the late Edw Day, of Balt Co, aged 52 years, leaving 2 dghts to lament their loss.

Died: on Oct 13, in King Geo Co, Va, at ***Mount Chem***, the residence of her grandfather, Geo N Grymes, Medora Everard Stith, only child of Everard Meade Stith, late of Northumberland Co, Va, aged 13 years, 2 months & 22 days.

Died: on Oct 15, at Onancock, Accomac Co, Va, from congestive brain fever, Henry Pearce, eldest s/o Gideon & Eliza Pearce, of Gtwn, D C, aged 23 years. In Aug, 1841, the dec'd graduated at the Norwich Univ, Vt.

THU NOV 2, 1843
Elisha Whittlesey, late Auditor of the Post Ofc Dept, has been elected Pres of the Ohio Life Ins & Trust Co in Cincinnati, in place of Micajah T Williams, resigned.

Thos Donoho appointed by the Pres to be a Justice of the Peace in Wash Co, D C.

On Thu of last week, says the Carlisle [Pa] Volunteer, as the train of cars from the East was passing near Smith's warehouse, about 5 miles above Newville, a young man named Danl Finsfrock, who was standing outside the passenger car, on the platform, was precipitated across the track & both his legs were severed above the knees. He was taken to his residence in Shippensburg, where he expired in about 3 or 4 hours. He had been married but a few months.

Centerville [Md] Times. There was a burial a few days ago of a faithful servant, the aged & infirmed female, the property of Judge Earle. She had for years been domesticated with the family of the Judge, & as age & infirmity approached, was supplied with those comforts which are peculiar privileges of the aged servants of the South. At the funeral, which took place on the farm of Richd Earle, the ceremony was attended by nearly all the male members of the family, & the corpse borne by Col John Tilghman, clerk of the county, Chas C Tilghman, Pere Tilghman, Jas T Earle, Richd T Earle, & Saml Earle.

Mrd: on Oct 31, by Rev Mr Stringfellow, Chas F Wood, of the U S Revenue service, to Miss Sarah Catherine, only d/o the late John S Compton, of Gtwn, D C.

The Albany Argus states that Henry B Gibson, of Canandaiga, is about establishing a private bank in Buffalo City, to be owned & managed by himself in person, the bills already ordered through the Comptroller.

We hear, from good authority, that Monroe Edwards, the convict, made an effort to escape, by firing one of the rooms in the State Prison at Sing Sing. It was discovered & the fire was put out. Edwards received 100 lashes on his bare back, & the Colonel was suffering severely from the discipline. –N Y American

Died: on Oct 23, at Bremo, the residence of Gen John H Cocke, Carter H Harrison, in his 52nd year.

Died: on Oct 17, of paralysis, Mrs Sarah Macon, in her 79th year. Mrs Macon was the w/o the late Thos Macon, of Orange, & last surviving sister of Jas Madison.

Died: yesterday, in Wash City, Gertrude Mgt, y/d/o Col Jos G Totten, Chief Engineer, U S Army. Her funeral will be from the resieence of her father, in Gadsby's row, this afternoon at 2 o'clock.

Died: on Oct 27, at Balt, John Babcock, printer, in his 91st year. He was the head of the once celebrated publishing house of Babcock & Son, of New Haven, Conn, of which State he was a native. He was a fellow workman of Benj Franklin, & at the time of his death was supposed to be the oldest surviving printer in the U S.

Died: on Oct 17, in Fred'k, Md, Mr John Lipp, in his 100th year. He was born near Frankfort, Germany, in 1744, & emigrated to the U S when in the 17th year of his age.

Letter received on Sat night from Westbrook, [formerly a part of Saybrook,] on Connecticut river, telling of a fearful tragedy that occurred in that town on Fri. Mr John Stannard, jr, a wealthy farmer in that town, about 50 years of age, who had a wife & 2 children, was deliberately shot at the supper table by his own son, Alpheus Stannard, about 24 years of age. When John, the younger son, saw the gun, he left the room. Alpheus seemed quite unconscious of the tragedy in which he was engaged, & was sent to the Retreat at Hartford. The unfortunate father was an estimable man, deacon of the Congregational Church in that town, & himself & family have always lived in the most affectionate manner. –New Haven Courier of Mon

Criminal Court-Wash: Nov 1. 1-Jas O'Brien found guilty for an assault & battery on Bernard O'Brien, at Gtwn, on Jul 18, 1843. 2-Henry Lacy, free negro, found guilty for an assault & battery on Dennis, the slave of John Hopkins. 3-Richd R Crawford indicted & tried for an assault & battery upon Teresa Sweeny. The jury had not rendered a verdict & were still in the room. 4-John Barney Manly found guilty for an assault & battery upon Eliza Mattingly. 5-John Brown, free negro, found guilty for stealing an engraved copper plate of the value of $20, the property of John B Morgan.

I have received from Messrs Langhorn & Armstead, of Lynchburg, a supply of their Natural James River Leaf Chewing Tobacco, put up expressly to my own order from the best inspections in the State of Va of the growth of 1842. –Jas M Dorsett, Snuff, Tobacco, & Fancy Store, Pa ave, #11 east of Gadsby's Hotel.

A WET NURSE. A young married woman, who has lost her first child at its birth, will take a child to nurse, if immediate application be made to Wm Clark, near the Navy Yard Gate.

Tobacco Agency. Wm Laird, formerly partner in the late firm of John Laird & Son, of Gtwn, D C, has established himself at #2, Light st wharf, Balt, as Genr'l Commission Merchant, especially as agent for Planters in the sale of their tobacco.

Wash Corp: Oct 31, 1843. List of the ordinaries & taverns in Wash City, the names of the persons to whom licenses have been granted, the names of those who have certified that the acts to regulate them have been complied with.

By whom the premises were examined & certified	By whom recommended
Henry Rochat, square 74, Pa ave	
Patrick Magee	Partick Magee
J Douglass	J Douglass
J Roberts	J Roberts
John Mullikin	John Mullikin
John Fister	John Fister
Elias Barnes	Elias Barnes
Benedict Jost, square 168, Pa ave	
Hugh Haney	Hugh Haney
Saml Redfern	Saml Redfern
Matthew Bouvet	Matthew Bouvet
John C Roemile	John C Roemile
Thos Smith	Thos Smith
Jacob Brodback	Jacob Brodback
Agricole Favier, square 119, 19th st	
Saml Redfern	Saml Redfern
Geo Krafft	Geo Krafft
A Hoover	A Hoover
Chas A Schneider	Chas A Schneider
F Schneider	F Schneider
Thos Smith	Thos Smith
Chas Borremans, square 74, Pa ave	
Thos Lundy	Thos Lundy
John Fister	John Fister
Barney Kelly	John Mullikin
John Mullikin	John Douglass
John Douglass	F Schneider
F Schneider	Barny Kelly
Jas B Freers, square 86, 20th st	
Henry Walker	Henry Walker
Elias Barnes	Elias Barnes
Thos Lundy	Thos Lundy
A Hoover	A Hoover
Saml Stott	Saml Stott
Francis Godfrey	Francis Godfrey
W Crutchfeldt, square 292, Pa ave	
Jas McColgan	C Eckloff

P Kinchy	Jas McColgan
C F Sengstack	P Kinchy
A Noerr	C P Sangstack
A Carothers	A Noerr
C Eckloff	A Carothers
Peter Jones, square 355, 11th & Water st	
T R Riley	T R Riley
John Foy	John Foy
Jas E Thumlert	Jas E Thumlert
Lewis Thomas	K H Lambell
K H Lambell	R Wimsatt
R Wimsatt	Lewis Thomas
Lewis Gallabrun, square 225, Pa ave	
Jas McColgan	Jas McColgan
John H Eberbach	John H Eberbach
John France	John France
Abraham Butler	Abraham Butler
Allison Nailor	Allison Nailor
E Simms	E Simms
Jas Maher, square 256, E & 13½ sts	
Thos Y Connelly	Thos Y Connelly
Wm T Dove	Wm T Dove
Wm Orme	Wm Orme
R E Kerr	R E Kerr
John France	John France
Jas McColgan	Jas McColgan
John H Eberbach, square 291, Pa ave	
John France	John France
Nicholas Traverse	Nicholas Traverse
C P Sengstack	C P Sengstack
L H Schneider	L H Schneider
P Kinchy	P Kinchy
Michl Sardo	Michl Sardo
Michl Ward, square 324, 12th & D sts	
Jas McColgan	Jas McColgan
Nicholas Callan	Nicholas Callan
C P Sengstack	C P Sengstack
Wm Dowling	Wm Dowling
Jas Fitzpatrick	Jas Fitzpatrick
Abraham Butler	Abraham Butler
Geo St Clear, 11th & Water sts	
Jas Mitchell	Jas Mitchell
Lewis Thomas	Lewis Thomas

K H Lambell	K H Lambell
T R Riley	T R Riley
Geo W Kendrick	Geo W Kendrick
W H Gunnell	W H Gunnell
Abraham Butler, square 254, F st north	
Chas F Bihler	Chas F Bihler
E Simms	E Simms
Allison Nailor	Allison Nailor
Wm Buist	Wm Buist
R E Kerr	R E Kerr
Jas Clephane	Jas Clephane
John C Stewart, sq 267, 13½ st & Md ave	
J S Harvey	J S Harvey
Wm Evans	Wm Evans
Dearborn Johnson	Dearborn Johnson
Wm B Walker	Peter Cazanave
Peter Cazanave	Jas H Collins
Jas H Collins	Wm B Walker
Wm Thomas, square 192, 13th & E sts	
John France	John France
Grafton Powell	Grafton Powell
E Simms	E Simms
Abraham Butler	Abraham Butler
Allison Nailor	Allison Nailor
C P Sengstack	C P Sengstack
A Fuller & Co, square 225, Pa ave	
Wm T Dove	Wm T Dove
Allison Nailor	Allison Nailor
W W Corcoran	W W Corcoran
John C Rives	John C Rives
Jas McClery	Jas McClery
Geo M Davis	Geo M Davis
Andrew Hancock, square 292, Pa ave	
Jas McColgan	Jas McColgan
R E Kerr	R E Kerr
E Simms	E Simms
John France	John France
C P Sengstack	C P Sengstack
John Ward	John Ward
Thos J Fletcher, square 224, F st north	
John H Eberbach	John H Eberbach
A Fuller	A Fuller

Wm Dowling	Wm Dowling
Abraham Butler	Abraham Butler
E Simms	E Simms
N Travers	N Travers
Edw Fuller, square 225, Pa ave	
Geo Lamb	Geo Lamb
Allison Nailor	Allison Nailor
M St Clair Clarke	M St Clair Clarke
Jas M Caustin	Jas M Caustin
W W Corcoran	W W Corcoran
John France	John France
Wm Dowling, square 2544, F st north	
E Simms	E Simms
Jas McColgan	Jas McColgan
Nicholas Callan	Nicholas Callan
Jas Fitzpatrick	Jas Fitzpatrick
Jas Maher	Jas Maher
John Ward	John Ward
John Purdon, square 226, Pa ave	
Isaac Goddard	Isaac Goddard
Chas F Bihler	Chas F Bihler
John France	John France
N Travers	N Travers
Abraham Butler	Abraham Butler
Michl Ward	Michl Ward
Jas Davis, square [blank]	
Edw Simms	Edw Simms
Abraham Butler	Abraham Butler
John France	Joh France
Jas Clephane	Jas Clephane
Wm Orme	Wm Orme
Grafton Powell	Grafton Powell
H W Sweeting, square 490, C st	
S Hyatt	Seth Hyatt
Alex'r Lee	Alex'r Lee
Edw Simms	Edw Simms
John P Pepper	John P Pepper
Jas P McKean	Jas P McKean
Levi Pumphrey	Levi Pumphrey
Jos Boulanger, square B, Pa ave	
E Lindsley	E Lindsley
Wm C Orme	Wm C Orme
Geo Stettinius	Geo Stettinius

R G Briscoe	R G Briscoe
Jas T Clarke	Jas T Clarke
Jos S Clarke	Jos S Clarke
Eva Kleindienet, square 455, 7th st	
J W Uttermuhle	J W Uttermuhle
Jos Straub	John A Donohoo
Bernard Giveny	Bernard Giveny
John A Donohoo	Jos Straub
Christian Weber	Christian Weber
Jacob Syfferly	Jacob Syfferly
John Foy, square 378, D st	
John T Towers	John T Towers
Chas F Bihler	Chas F Bihler
Philip Mohun	Philip Mohun
B F Middleton	B F Middleton
Robt Keyworth	Robt Keyworth
Caleb Buckingham	Caleb Buckingham
Jas Cuthbert, square 490, Louisiana ave	
R Burdine	R Burdine
B F Middleton	B F Middleton
Jas Fossett	Jas Fossett
Levi Pumphrey	Levi Pumphrey
Jos H Bradley	Jos H Bradley
Chas Bell	Chas Bell
A Rupert, square 408, 9th st	
Peter F Bacon	Peter F Bacon
John Emerick	John Emerick
Wm Uttermuhle	Wm Uttermuhle
Raphael Jones	Raphael Jones
Saml Bacon	Saml Bacon
Michl Talty	Michl Talty
John H Clarvoe, square 461, 7th st	
I T Ellwood	W G W White
Peter F Bacon	Saml Bacon
W G W White	Peter F Bacon
Saml Bacon	R G Briscoe
R G Briscoe	Jos S Clarke
Jos S Clarke	Jas T Clark
Andrew R Jenkins, reservation 10, Pa ave	
T F Semmes	T F Semmes
Jas Fossett	Jas Fossett
Alex'r Lee	Alex'r Lee
Alex'r Provost	Alex'r Provost

John P Pepper
Jas P McKean

Ann Powers, square 461, 7th st
John A Donohoo
B O Sheckell
W G W White
B F Middleton
Michl McDermott
I T Ellwood
Jas Long, square 466, 6th st
Thos Cookendorffer
Alex'r Provost
Alex'r Lee
Seth Hyatt
John P Pepper
Jas Fossett
Lucy A Laskey, square 461, 7th st
B F Middleton
B O Sheckell
W G W White
M McDermott
Peter F Bacon
Martin Murphy
Geo St Clear, square 458, 7th st
B O Sheckell
Peter F Bacon
Saml Bacon
J A Donohoo
Theodore Harbaugh
Michl Talty
Wm Benter, square 491, Pa ave
Alex'r Lee
B F Middleton
J P Pepper
Jas Fossett
S P Franklin
John Brown
Jesse Brown, square 460, Pa ave
W C Orme
G C Grammer
A H Young
Wm M Morrison

John P Pepper
Jas P McKean

John A Donohoo
B O Sheckell
W G W White
B F Middleton
M McDermott
I T Ellwood

Thos Cookendorffer
Alex'r Provost
Alex'r Lee
Seth Hyatt
John P Pepper
Jas Fossett

B F Middleton
B O Sheckell
W G W White
M McDermott
Peter F Bacon
Martin Murphy

B O Sheckell
Peter F Bacon
Saml Bacon
J A Donohoo
Theodore Harbaugh
Michl Talty

Alex'r Lee
B F Middleton
J P Pepper
Jas Fossett
S P Franklin
John Brown

G C Grammer
A H Young
Wm M Morrison
W B Todd

R G Briscoe	Wm C Orme
W B Todd	R G Briscoe
John Douglass, square 490, Louisiana ave	
T F Semmes	T F Semmes
E G Handy	E G Handy
Levi Pumphrey	Levi Pumphrey
John M Young	John M Young
R Burdine	R Burdine
Peter F Bacon	Peter F Bacon
Wm Gadsby, square 491, Pa ave	
Edw Simms	Edw Simms
Alex'r Lee	Leonidas Coyle
Leonidas Coyle	Alex'r Lee
Danl Campbell	Danl Campbell
John W Maury	John W Maury
Jas Lusby	Jas Lusby
Jas P Gannon, square 461, 7th st	
Saml Bacon	Saml Bacon
Peter F Bacon	Peter F Bacon
W G W White	W G W White
R R Burr	R R Burr
Thos Pursell	Thos Pursell
B O Sheckell	B O Sheckell
B O Sheckell, square 461, 7th st	
Saml Bacon	Saml Bacon
Peter F Bacon	Peter F BAcon
W G W White	W G W White
R R Burr	R R Burr
Thos Pursell	Thos Pursell
D S Waters	D S Waters
Wm Feeney, square 432, 7th st	
Bernard Giveny	Bernard Giveny
Theodore Harbaugh	Theodore Harbaugh
John A Donohoo	John A Donohoo
Owen Connelly	Owen Connelly
David S Waters	David S Waters
Thos Jarboe	Thos Jarboe
Jas McGrath, square 320, P ave	
Jas W Haliday	Jas W Haliday
Jacob Gideon	Jacob Gideon
Stephen P Franklin	Stephen P Franklin
Alex'r Provost	Alex'r Provost
Caleb Buckingham	Caleb Buckingham

Walter Lenox	Walter Lenox

Signs because Mr McGrath promises to keep his house closed on the Sabbath.

Patrick Moran, square 573, Pa ave	
B F Middleton	John Foy
John Foy	B F Middleton
Michl McDermott	Michl McDermott
Jas Kelcher	Jas Kelcher
T F Semmes	T F Semmes
Jas Fitzgerald	Jas Fitzgerald
Thos Baker, square 431, 8th & D sts	
Leonard Harbaugh	Leonard Harbaugh
Jos Harbaugh	Jos Harbaugh
Theodore Harbaugh	Theodore Harbaugh
Raphael Jones	Raphael Jones
David S Waters	David S Waters
John Foy	John Foy
Jas Davis, square 431, 7th & E sts	
John Ellis	John Ellis
R R Burr	R R Burr
Thos Jarboe	Thos Jarboe
Henry Hay	Henry Hay
Jos Borrows	Jos Borrows
Geo Parker	Geo Parker
Michl Talty, square 433, 7th st	
Jas Fitzgerald	Jas Fitzgerald
Stans Murray	Stans Murray
Raphael Semmes	Raphael Semmes
John A Donohoo	John A Donohoo
Bernard Giveny	Bernard Giveny
E M Preston, jr	E M Preston, jr
John West, square 461, Pa ave	
Thos Cookendorffer	Thos Cookendorffer
Jas B Phillips	Jas B Phillips
R G Briscoe	R G Briscoe
Jas T Clark	Jas T Clark
Jas Fossett	Jas Fossett
Seth Hyatt	Seth Hyatt
Patrick H King, square B, Pa ave	
Jas Fossett	Jas Fossett
Alex'r Lee	Alex'r Lee
Benj Bell	Benj Bell
E M Preston, jr	E M Preston, jr
John Fleming	John Fleming

Saml Bacon	Saml Bacon
Martin Murphy, reservation 10, Pa ave	
Peter F Bacon	Peter F Bacon
John Fleming	John Fleming
Stanislaus Murray	Stanislaus Murray
Wm H Upperman	Wm H Upperman
John A Donohoo	John A Donohoo
John T Ryon	John T Ryon
Peter A De Saule	
J H Eberbach	J H Eberbach
John Ellis	John Ellis
John Richd Hendley	John Richd Hendley
John Foy	John Foy
Robt Keyworth	Robt Keyworth
John T Sullivan	John T Sullivan
Alfred Burdine, square 923, K & 8th sts	
Adam Gaddis	Adam Gaddis
C O'Neale	C O'Neale
G Sherman	G Sherman
John F Tucker	John F Tucker
Geo Hartman	Geo Hartman
R M Combs	R M Combs

<u>Fourth Ward</u>

Jas Haligan, square 729, East Capitol st	
D Homans	D Homans
Henry Gooding	Henry Gooding
Peter McCaffrey	Peter McCaffrey
Jas Lynch	Jas Lynch
John A Lynch	John A Lynch
Wm Magill	Wm Magill

<u>Sixth Ward</u>

Christopher O'Neale, square 930, L st	
Philip Inch	Philip Inch
R H Harrington	R H Harrington
Thos Bayne [as written]	Thos Payne [as written]
R M Combs	R M Combs
Geo Duckworth	Geo Duckworth
Adam Gaddis	Adam Gaddis
Francis Reilly, square 928, 8th st	
John H Bohlayer	John H Bohlayer
Thos Thornley	Thos Thornley
Jas Gordon	Jas Gordon
John Howe	John Howe

Stephen Henning	Stephen Henning
Fred'k Speiser	Fred'k Speiser
R H Harrington, square 930, 8th st	
Philip Otterback	Jas Tucker
Jas Tucker	Fred'k Speiser
Andrew Forrest	Philip Otterback
Fred'k Speiser	Jas Rhodes
Jas Rhodes	Jas Owner
Jas Owner	[blank]

The partnership under the firm of John Foy & Thos Baker, restaurants at the Capitol, is dissolved from Nov 1, 1843. Persons indebted will please pay the same to John Locke, collector, or Thos Baker. –John Foy

Home-made cheese of excellent quality. The undersigned, living in Balt Co, Md, [opposite to Elk Ridge Landing] has in the Washington Market this morning, & intends hereafter to bring here on the first day of every month, HOME MADE CHEESE. –Saml Sutton

PUBLIC DISPENSARY: During the ensuing winter the consultations at the Dispensary will be held in the hall of the Medical College, daily, Sundays excepted, between 10 & 11 a m. The poor who may desire advice & medicine should be punctual in their attendance. –W P Johnston, sec

The undersigned has removed from the Glass-house near the steamboat wharf, next to the old Mansion House, & of 10th st, where he is better established to continue to manufacture his Improved Patent Lead Holders, patented Aug 12, 1843. –Jos Nock, Machine & Lock Manufacturer, formerly of Phil.

FRI NOV 3, 1843
The Van Buren [Ark] Intelligencer of Oct 14 states that the trial of Jacob West & others, for the murder of Isaac Bushyhead & attack upon Mr David Vann, commenced on Sep 25. Jacob West has been convicted, & was sentenced to be hung on the 11th. The jury recommended West to the Chief for pardon, & that it was supposed that the sentence would be remitted.

Boston, Oct 31. Inquest held Oct 30th, by Coroner Pratt, at the house of Chas Everett, Bussey Pl, on the body of Henry J Mould, a teacher of music, formerly of Cleveland, Ohio, who shot himself through the head with a pistol, literally blowing out his brains. Mr Mould was of excellent character & habits, & about 27 years of age. He has left a wife, who resides at Utica, N Y. He has been in the city 3 months. -Atlas

Yellow Fever. The brig **Linden** cleared at Mobile on the 23rd ult for Providence, R I, but before reaching the bar, lost the entire crew with the fever. Another crew having been obtained, the brig sailed a second time; when 3 days out, Capt Collins sickened & died, & the 2nd mate soon followed. She arrived off our coast some day since in charge of the first mate, who had also become disabled. She was passed by several vessels, all of whom neglected or refused assistance. She was finally boarded by Mr S Matthews, mate of the barque **Ann Reynolds**, of Boston, & by him conducted into Newport, where she arrived on Fri last.

Washington Allston-from the North American Review. Our thoughts are drawn to the loss we recently suffered in the death of Washington Allston, an artist in the highest sense of the word. For many years he held undisputed pre-eminence among the American painters. Some of his published poems are not surpassed by any thing in American literature. We have always felt, in the presence of Allston's pictures, that they were stamped with a sublime genius & all nobleness of soul.

House for rent: the subscriber offers for rent his dwlg house, on Pa ave, between 1st & 2nd sts: house is 3 stories high, & contains 9 rooms, besides back bldgs. –Gregory Ennis

On Sep 24, the Galveston steamer **Sarah Barnes** crossed the Galveston bar for New Orleans. On Sep 25, a considerable leak was discovered in her hold: the water ascended to the fires & engines: orders were given to cast off the boat's painter, & while doing this she sunk. There were on board altogether 30 souls-of these 18 went on the rafts & 12 took the boat. Of the former but 5 were saved; of the latter but 3 perished-who were passengers, 2 males & a female-& they were lost in the breakers in landing from the boat on the 26th. Saved: A G Abell, bearer of dispatches; B P Hartshorn, of Galveston; F Pinkard & servant, of Galveston; Thompson Riley, clerk; Chas Cloud, mate; ____ Matthews, first engineer; Henry Stewart, steward; Thos Green, cabin boy; Jas Lochlin, deck hand; Peter O Gorman, barkeeper; Peter Carlton, deck hand; Homan Farmer, deck hand; John Johnson, deck hand. Lost: Capt Chas Franklin, of Galveston; Jas Potter, Houston; H S Daggett, New Orleans; J Boyd, ____ Martin, Matagorda; Dr Cosgrave, Brazos; Judge Blair, Galveston; female, [name unknown,] Houston; 2 deck passengers, [names unknown;] Wm Mehin, J McDonough, firemen; Wm Mure, ____ Eubanks, deck hands; Alex'r Isbel, cook, J Dean, second engineer.

Jonathan Heyworth, a native of England, & lately from N Y, who has been for some time lecturing about the country on temperance, gave an impressive lecture on board the steamboat **Empress**, on the 17th ult, on her passage from Louisville. It appears he got drunk & jumped overboard, & drowned. –Aurora

Died: on Oct 28, at his late residence in Sussex Co, Dela, Hon Thos Robinson, late Member of Congress from Delaware, after an illness of 4 years, which he bore with Christian fortitude.

Died: on Tue last, in Newbern, N C, of bilious fever, Hon Chas Shepard, formerly a Rep in Congress from that district.

Died: on Oct 28, at Phil, Susan Shippen Roberdeau, wid/o the late Col Isaac Roberdeau, of the U S Topographical Engineers.

Died: in Loudoun Co, Va, Mr John Swigart, in his 64th year. His funeral will be at the residence of Mr Edw Hawkins, his son-in-law, on F st, between 13th & 14th sts, in Wash City, on Nov 3, at 3 o'clock. [No death date.]

Died: on Oct 16, after a lingering illness, at the residence of her son, Dr John Edwin Craig, in Warren Co, Va, Mrs Henrietta Burgess, for several years a resident of Gtwn, D C, aged 56 years. She was the d/o the late John Wilson, of Henry, of PG Co, Md, & the sister of the late John A Wilson, of Wash City.

NOTICE: Was committed to the jail of Fred'k Co, Md, on Oct 30 last, as a runaway, a black girl who calls herself Martha Jane. She is about 19 years of age & says she belongs to Mr Gibbons, of Montg Co, Md. The owner, if any, is hereby requested to come & have her released. She will otherwise be discharged according to law. -Geo Rice, Sheriff of Fred'k Co.

Daring robbery at Alexandria: 3 old convicts taken: Jas Sims & ___ Scott, from Gtwn, & another man named German, from Balt; robbery committed at Wise's Hotel, on Thu: all the money was taken out of the drawer in the bar room.

Criminal Court-Nov 2. 1-Wm Grey alias McManus, found guilty of burglariously entering the dwlg of Mrs Catharine Owner, on Captiol Hill, & stealing a piece of soap. 2-McKendrick Deans found guilty of stealing 3 flutes & a coat, the property of C Schwartz, near Gtwn. 3-Thos Butler found guilty for an assault on Eliz Miles. 4-Robt Graham found not guilty for an assault & battery on T J Bell.

A Jullien announces he has taken the house formerly occupied by Mr Louis Vivan as a boarding house, where he can accommodate a couple of gentlemen or a small family in genteel style. A J can likewise furnish dinners, parties, suppers, at the shortest notice. Jellies, Creams, & Pastry of all kinds made to order.

SAT NOV 4, 1843
MAGUIRE'S Hat & Cap Store, on 7th st. Thank you for your past patronage, I rely with confidence on the generous support of the citizens of Washington & the public to keep my humble bark afloat near shore, as I am not ambitious of venturing in deep water.
--John Maguire

Mrs R A Beck has returned from the North with her Winter Fashions of Millinery & Dress Patterns, which are open this morning, Sat, Nov 4, for inspection. Residence Pa ave, opposite Gadsby's Hotel.

NOTICE. This is to inform that Mary Heffley has obtained in the Court of PG Co, Md, sitting as a Court of Equity, Oct term, 1843, a decree of divorce a vinculo matrimonii from her husband, Fred'k Heffley, & a copy of the decree, certified by the clerk of the said Court, is in possession of the subscriber. –Mary Heffley

The Queen of Spain:the people have beheld her birth & growth, have seen her encompassed with all the tenderness of a mother's care, & then an orphan & an object of contention to the ambition of parties. The people took her under their protection & rallied round her throne. Isabella II will attain her 13th year Oct 10. Those persons who see her in private speak most favorably of her gayety & open disposition.

Appointment by the Pres. Edmund F Brown, to be a Justice of the Peace, Wash Co, D C.

A bill has passed the N J Leg to divorce Mrs Appleton from her husband, Dr Chas W Appleton, late the agent of the N J State Temperance Society, & who figured in the papers some time since as a polygamist. His last wife is an estimable lady of New Brunswick, whom he married some time since. He had at least 2 former wives still living, & children by both, & figured by turns as a doctor, preacher, temperance lecturer, & last a professor of science of Animal Magnetism.

The Hon Chas A Wickliffe, Postmaster General, returned to Wash City on Thu from his visit West.

About 20 of Sir Wm D Stewart's men left him & a portion of them reached St Louis on the 23rd ult. They quitted him on Oct 1 near Platte river. A fracas had occurred between a Mr Smith & a Mr Walker, in which the former had been injured. A Frenchman, too, belonging to the party, had been accidentally killed.

Circuit Court of Wash Co, D C. Ephraim S Sawyer had applied to be discharged from imprisonment under the act for the relief of Insolvent Debtors: hearing on the 2nd Mon in Nov inst. –Wm Brent, clk

Mrd: on Nov 2, in Wash City, by Rev Mr Brown, Mr Ceylon S Houghton, formerly of Vt, to Miss Eliz E Bennett, of Wash City.

Mrd: on Nov 2, in Leesburg, Va, by Rev Geo Adie, Thos W Edwards to Sarah E, only d/o the late Geo M Chichester.

Notice to our Subscribers. Mr C W James is our traveling agent for the States of Ohio, Indiana, & Michigan, assisted by Moses Meeker, Jas R Smith, J B Humphreys, J T Dent, G H Comstock, & E Y Jennings.

Mr E Dryer, Fresco Painter, has arrived in Washington to paint St John's Church, where a specimen of his art may be seen as soon as executed. In the mean time it can be examined at the Odeon in Gtwn. Mr Dryer painted the celebrated Odd Fellows Hall, Barnum's City Hotel, & several other public & private bldgs in Balt with the entire approbation of his employers

MON NOV 6, 1843
Funeral Rites on the interment of the remains of the late Comm Claxton on Oct 30 at *Green Mount Cemetery*, were truly solemn, beautiful, & imposing. Environing the grave was a group of mourners, relatives, friends, brother sldrs & a numerous body of the sons of Neptune; & the reverend Clergy.

The New Orleans papers of Sat week have accounts of the loss of the ship **Don Juan**, of N Y, & the ship **United States**, of Phil, while on their way to the port of New Orleans- both having been lost on the Bahama Islands in a violent gale on Sep 30. The passengers & crews of both vessels were saved, as well as the principal part of their cargoes. The ships are a total loss.

Austin Moss, an inhabitant of Raleigh, N C, was handling a loaded pistol on Mon last, when it went off, & lodged the whole load in his abdomen. He lingered until Tue, when he died.

Mrd: on Oct 27, in Wash City, by Rev Mr Brown, Mr Isaiah Burtley to Miss Ann C Blair.

Schroeder, who ran away with a young girl from Wilmington, Dela, a few days since, has been examined & committed in default of bail in $500 to answer to the charge of abduction. The girl is only 15 or 16 years old, & the man 30 or 35, & has a wife & family in Fred'k, Md.

Savannah, Oct 31. On Sun last, an open skiff boat, about 20 feet long arrived in our harbor from Phil. She is owned by 2 fishermen, Uriah M Thompson & John Friend, who came out in her accompanied by a lad of about 12 years of age, named Saml Thompson. They intend fishing in our river during the coming winter for shad. The boldness of this undertaking is only equaled by its success, & the true love of adventure.

Died: on Sep 24, at *Oak Hill*, PG Co, Md, after a short but severe illness, Julius Eversfield, in his 8th year. The family have sustained a great loss; for he was a child of uncommon talents.

Criminal Court-Wash: Nov 3. 1-Hugh McCormick found not guilty for stealing driftwood during the late freshet, the property of Thos & Eben Brown. 2-Edw Hilton found not guilty for an assault upon a slave belonging to Jos Radcliffe.

Michl German, who said he was from Wash, is known to be from Balt. He was convicted of stealing coffee & suffering imprisonment for that offence in the Md pen, from which he was discharged about 6 months ago. He has been loafing about this city for some time past. –City Reporter

Sale of china & glass ware, & store fixtures, on Nov 8, at the residence of Mrs Hammond, on the corner of 9th & I sts. -Robt W Dyer & Co, aucts

Two furnished rooms to let in the second story over Mr Gahan's shoe store in E st, near 7th, handsomely furnished for a parlor & bed room. Apply 2 doors east of Mr J F Callan's drug & seed store.

Cheap house for rent: 2 story brick house on C st, between 13½ & 14th sts; for $110 per annum. –Hampton & Son, F st, near the Treas bldg

For rent, 2 story brick house on N Y ave, between 9th & 10th sts. For terms apply to Jos Bryan.

For rent, a 2 story frame dwlg house on I st, near 7th. Apply to Mr Steer, the present tenant, or to the subscriber. –Thos Blagden

The recent death of Mrs John P Ingle obliges us to mourn the loss of one who had endeared herself to a large circle of friends by all those noble qualities which are the characteristics of a Christian. As a wife, dght, mother, & sister, her loss is only the more keenly felt that it can never be repaired. Death had been approaching her with rapid steps for months. –M S

TUE NOV 7, 1843
Letter from an ofcr of the U S ship **St Louis**, dated Rio Janeiro, Sep 6, says: we arrived here just in the nick of time to witness the festivities on the occasion of the young Emperor's marriage to the Princess Theresa, of Naples. They arrived here on Sun in the Brazilian frig, that was sent with 3 other ships of war to escort her, & were married on Mon. The Princess is about 25 years old & the Emperor is just 18. He resembles in picture his sister, the Queen of Portugal. Another sister, the Princess Francesca, was taken from here by the Prince de Joinville not long before our arrival in Jul. The Princess Januaria, another of the family, is still here, & by far the prettiest young lady I have seen in Rio.

Mr John M Batchelder, of Saco, Maine, was recently married to Mrs E C Beardsley, of N Y. About a year & a half ago Mr Batchelder, the groom aforesaid, was married to a lady whose health was so delicate that they set sail for Vera Cruz, for her health. Mrs E Constantia Beardsley was a fellow passenger. Mrs Batchelder & Mr Beardsley both went the way of all flesh. The bereaved widower, as soon as propriety would admit, addressed himself to the disconsolate widow, & proposed. Mrs Beardsley declined. Mr Batchelder & his new flame were duly published in the parish church, & all was going on merrily, when, on the Sat preceding the Tue on which the marriage was published to take place, Mr Batchelder received a letter from the relenting widow Beardsley in which she withdrew her declination of his offer of marriage. Mr Batchelder had to pay the disappointed bride to be $2100 for breach of his promise to her.

Louisville Journal of Mon week records the death of Miss Isabel B Keats, in that city. On Sat she was accidentally killed by the discharge of a gun in the parlor. The first impression was that she had committed suicide, but she assured her mother that she did not mean to kill herself. She lingered until morning.

Mrd: on Sun last, by Rev Mr Brown, of the Navy Yard, Mr Jas B Smull to Miss Mary Ann, only d/o Benj Kinsley, all of Wash City.

Died: on Sun last, at the Female Orphan Asylum in Wash City, Sister Claudia [Ringe] in her 24th year. Her funeral will be at 8 o'clock when holy mass & requien will be chanted.

Died: yesterday, in Wash City, Mrs Hannah Serena Slater, w/o Mr Wm Slater, in her 86th year. Her funeral will be from the residence of Mr P Finegan, 9th st, next to D, at 2 o'clock.

Died: on Oct 21, of intermittent fever, Anna, oldest d/o Mr John A Young, formerly of Balt.

Died: on Wed last, at Leonardtown, Md, after a short illness, Mrs Amanda F Howard, eldest d/o Matthias Jeffers, of Wash City, leaving a disconsolate husband & 4 small children & many relatives to mourn their irreparable loss.

Jas R Vineyard was tried at the late term of the U S Dist Court, for Green Co, Wisc, for the murder of J P D Arndt in the Council Chamber of the Territory some 18 months since, & acquitted. The jury were out but a few minutes.

The U S Marshal for the Dist of Missouri offers a reward of $150 for the apprehension & confinement, in any jail of the U S, of Thornton H Freeman, late Postmaster at Carrollton, in that State, who was under arrest for robbing the mail.

On Sun last as some persons were playing at ball on 8th ave, N Y, the bat slipped from the hand of one of the players & struck the head of Wm Hicks, 8 or 9 years old, injuring him that his life is in great danger.

Trustee's sale of valuable lands: acting under a deed of trust, executed by Julia A Wilson, on Jul 9, 1838, to Richd H Henderson, trustee, [I being substituted in the place of said Henderson, he being dec'd,] I shall sell at public auction in Leesburg, Loudoun Co, Va, on Jan 22, the real estate as follows, to wit: One moiety of the tract late the residence of Maj Wm B Harrison, the father of said Julia, now dec'd, called *Soldier's Repose*, in Loudoun Co, the moiety of said Julia, containing between 400 & 500 acs. It descended to Julia from her mother, late Mrs Penelope Harrison, w/o said Wm B Harrison. Also, one moiety of another small tract in said county, adjoining *Soldier's Repose* & the land of Chas Lewis, containing about 25½ acs. Also, one undivided moiety of 550 acs, in Clinton Co, Ohio. Also, one undivided moiety of the tract called *Xenia* tract in Green Co, Ohio. All which lands descended to the said Julia A as one of the heirs at law of said Mrs Penelope Harrison, dec'd. Also, six-tenths of a house & tannery in Middleburg, Loudoun Co, now rented to Weeks & Newman, & purchased by Wm B Harrison from Jacob Mann. Also, six-tenths of a tract of 556 acs, in Madison Co, Ohio; which 2 last pieces of property were devised to the said Julia by her late father, the said Wm B Harrison, dec'd, by his last will & test, of record in Loudoun Co court. –Saml M Edwards, Trustee [The Cincinnati Gaz & Washingtonian, Leesburg, Va, will insert the above.]

For rent, that convenient 2 story frame dwlg on 7th st, near Md ave, now in the occupancy of Jas H Birch. Apply to C W Boteler.

WED NOV 8, 1843
The Hon Edw P Livingston, late Lt Govn'r of the State of N Y, died in N Y C on Fri.

Rev Prof Joel S Bacon, of Mass, has accepted the Presidency of the Columbian College, D C.

Carriages, barouches, etc. The subscriber, who wishes to dispose of his stock of Carriages, Barouches, etc, offers for sale, at great bargains, the following: a splendid new Barouche. A new superior finished Buggy, with top. One second-hand Buggy, with top, only used a few weeks. Two new square Barouches, for family use. Also, 2 second-hand hacks, 2 second-hand Sulkeys, & one market Carryall, for cash or good paper. –Chas Rosenthal, Gtwn, rear of Union Hotel.

Report of Mr J P Kennedy, from the Cmte on Commerce, to whom was referred the memorial of the friends of African colonization, assembled in Wash City in May last. During the Administration of Mr Jefferson the State of Va made an application to the Genr'l Gov't for aid in making provision for the colonization & settlement of the free colored population of this country. That State desired to originate some measure; at length the Gov't was directed, in 1816, when Dr Finley was employed at Wash, to correspond with the Pres for the promotion of that design. The American Colonization Society was founded in Dec, 1816. One of its most valuable results of its labors was the adoption by Congress for the suppression of the slave trade: denounced as piracy, & subjected to the penalties of such an offence. Foreign States were invited to co-operate in the effort to destroy this trade. Mr Monroe, in reference to recaptured Africans demanded that due provision should be made for their shelter, sustenance, & defence, temporarily at least, after their arrival in Africa. The colony of Liberia rose, both as a home for recaptured Africans restored by the humanity of our Gov't to their own country, & as a well organized community of free colored men, prepared & disposed to extend their useful arts, civilized laws, & Christianity, both along the coast & into the interior of Africa.

Mrd: on Nov 7, by Rev S B Southerland, Mr Douglass Moore, formerly of Balt, to Miss Eliz Ann Kirk, of Wash.

Mrd: on Oct 31, in Owego, N Y, by Rev Alfred Louderback, Ben Johnson, Atty & Counsellor at Law, of Vicksburg, Miss, to Miss Maria Louisa, eldest d/o E E Smith Sweet, of the former place.

Died: on Oct 27, at Savannah, Mrs Sarah M Gates, w/o Lt Col Gates, U S Army, of a disease of the heart, after a long & painful illness of many months, which she suffered with astonishing patience & resignation up to the last moment of her existence.

Just arrived, direct from England, a choice lot of the newest styles of Fancy Cashmere & Thibet Shawls, suitable for ladies wear. –Miss A Pilling, Pa ave, near 11th st

THU NOV 9, 1843
Dr J Turner Barclay, a graduate of the Univ of Pa, may be consulted in every branch of the medical profession, & will practice Dental Surgery upon principles & terms that must ensure satisfaction. Ofc adjoining his residence, on the east side of N J ave, 12 doors south of the Capitol.

Last Jun a Nonpareil escaped from the aviary of Dr A McWilliams, near the Navy Yard. It disappeared & Dr McW gave it up as lost. The weather becoming cool, he discovered to his surprise that the little wanderer had returned, & was endeavoring to get into its former habitation; as soon as he opened the door it flew into the aviary, & rejoined its companions. This bird is never seen, in its wild state, further north than the Carolinas.

Mr W W Wallace announces that he will give a Concert of Vocal & Instrumental Music, assisted by Mrs Bailey, at Carusi's Saloon, on Nov 10. Tickets 50 cents each, to be had ar the usual places.

Balt, Nov 7. The splendid barque **Latrobe**, under command of Capt John E Allen, sailed yesterday, from Bond st wharf, with between 70 & 80 emigrants destined for the Md colony on the coast of Africa, under the patronage of the Md Colonization Society. Mr Goodwyn who liberated 31 of the emigrants was present on the occasion. Impressive address was delivered by the Rev H V D Johns; prayers by the Rev Mr Aldrich, of the Bapitst Church; after which J H B Latrobe gave them a parting farewell, in behalf of the Society, as its presiding ofcr.

Albert Clark, alias Smith, was tried in Balt City Court on Mon last, & found guilty of obtaining goods under false pretences.

Died: on Nov 7, in her 62nd year, Eliz, wid/o Danl McPherson, late of Gtwn. Her funeral will be at 1 o'clock today, from her late residence on 10th st, between F & G sts.

Meeting of the subscribers to stock in the Temperance Hall will be held this evening at the Medical College. By order of the Pres: -Z K Offutt, Sec

Criminal Court-Wash: Nov 8. 1-Chas Gates found not guilty for an assault & battery upon his wife, Eliz Gates, on Oct 31, 1843. 2-Wm Ford, free negro, found guilty of obtaining under false pretences, on Aug 31, 1843, one pair of boots of the value of $7, the property of Walter Clarke & Son.

Wash Corp: 1-Ptn from Jas Fossett: referred. 2-Ptn from Wm Wallis & Silas Moore, police ofcrs of the 3rd Ward: referred to the Cmte of Claims. 3-Ptn from Alfred Jones: referred to the Cmte of Claims. 4-Bill for the relief of Wm Creutzfeldt: referred to the Cmte of Claims & passed. 5-Bill for the relief of John West: referred to the Cmte of Claims & passed. 6-Ptn of Wm Gunton & others that was referred to the Cmte on Improvements: read twice. 7-Bill for the relief of C P Zackman: referred to the Cmte of Claims.

Meeting of the Cmte appointed at the late Military & Firemen's Convention will be held on Fri at the Union Engine-house. –J Mason, jr-Capt Potomac Dragoons, Chairman

The Capitol Hill Institute will hold a meeting on Nov 9 at the room of the Columbia Fire Co. A dissertation, limited by rule to 20 minutes, will be read by B B French, upon the Writings of Bulwer, & one by L B True, upon the Writings of Danta & Petrarch. The public are invited. –J G Proud, jr, Sec

Orphan's Court of Wash Co, D C. Letters testamentary on the personal estate of Delia Tudor, late of said county, dec'd. -Chas Saml Stewart, exc

FRI NOV 10, 1843
The robbers of the Quincy Stage, John W & Richd Rand, who were arrested on suspicion of having stolen the $4,000 in bills from the stage, were examined before the Police Court at Boston on Sat, & committed for further examination in default of bail in $8,000. A mold for casting counterfeit Spanish dollars, & another for casting American quarters, were found on John, which form the grounds of another complaint against him.

It is supposed that Mr Chas Baldwin, a smelter, has been murdered at St Louis. He was about to start for Wisconsin. He had $1,000 in gold on his person, which he had been foolishly displaying.

Miss Eliz Thompson, a deaf & dumb girl, of Jefferson Co, Mo, lately recovered damages to the amount of $3,000 against Henry H Porch, of the same county, for a breach of the marriage contract. After affecting her ruin, Porch deserted her.

The late Thos L Lindsay, at St Chas, Mo, bequeathed upwards of $5,000 to the American Bible Society. All his 21 slaves are to be sent to Liberia, to do which he left his executors ample means, not only for sending them out, but for providing liberally for their wants after they get there.

Trenton State Gaz: the bedroom of Mr Amos Williamson, keeper of a tavern at Ringoes, Hunterdon Co, was entered last Sat by some burglars, under the impression that Mr W had $3,000 in his possession, & seemed disappointed to learn that he had only $40. They struck him with a pistol & injured his wife. They made their escape.

Cheese! 6,000 prime New Cheese, just arrived per schnr **Washington**, Capt Barber, & for sale low. Apply to Capt on board, or to Henry Thecker, Agent, Water st, Gtwn.

Mrd: on Nov 7, by Rev Mr Adie, Col Wm Worsley to Virginia G, d/o Dr Chas G Edwards, all of Loudoun Co, Va.

I O O F-The Grand Lodge of D C will hold its Annual Communication on Mon next, when an election for ofcrs for the ensuing year will take place. –Urias Hurst, Grand Sec

SAT NOV 11. 1843
Though the first frigs **Constitution & United States**, & one or two others, were built in 1797, the existence of the American Navy should be dated from the war of 1812. Up to that time the few ships owned by the U S were not generally considered as protectors in peace or as defenders in war.

The Govn'r of Ga has appointed the first Mon in Jan next for the election of a member of Congress to fill the vacancy occasioned by the death of Col John Millen.

To let, a 2 story brick house on Pa ave, near the Railroad Depot. Apply to M Adler, Agent, at Gtwn.

On Sat, as one of the students, a s/o Rev Dr Snodgrass, of Troy, N Y, was going out on a shooting excursion, his gun was accidentally discharged, sending the whole charge of shot into the breast of a student by the name of Lord, of N Y, whose life is considered to be in great danger.

Mrd: on Thu last, by Rev Septimus Tunton, Mr Wm R Lownds to Miss Serena Taylor, all of Wash City.

Mrd: on Nov 8, at Weverton, Md, by Rev Mr Hoover, Wm O Collins, Atty at Law, of Hillsborough, Ohio, to Miss Catharine Willis, d/o Mr Caspar W Wever, of the former place.

Mrd: on Oct 24, near Piscataway, PG Co, Md, by Rev Dr Marbury, Mr John A Coe to Miss Susan E, d/o the late Dr Wm McPherson, of Chas Co, Md.

Died: on Nov 3, at Balt, at the residence of Maj Lendrum, Miss Lucy E Lendrum, of Westmoreland Co, Va.

Died: on Oct 24, at the residence of his brother, Thos J Marshall, near Piscataway, PG Co, Md, of haemorrage from the lungs, Dr Wm Marshall, in his 58th year. In his professional career his reputation was wide spread. As a son, husband, brother, father, friend, & neighbor, he was an example which all might follow with advantage. He leaves his bereaved family. The Vestry of Christ's Church, St John's Parish, Md, on Oct 31, 1843, resolved that by the death of the late Dr Wm Marshall, this Board has been deprived of one of its most zealous members. Members of this board will wear crape on the left arm for 30 days. That the sympathies of this Board be tendered, through the Register, to the afflicted family of the dec'd. -Alex M Marbury, Rector
-Philip King, Register

Nat'l Blues to meet at the armory this evening, at 6 o'clock, in full winter uniform with side-arms, for the purpose of attending Maj Tochman's lecture. By order of Capt Tucker: John Brannan, Sergeant

Orphan's Court of Wash Co, D C. Letters testamentary on the personal estate of Wm W Billing, late of said county, dec'd. -Rebecca K Billing, excx

Rev Jas Knox will preach in the Second Presbyterian Church, N Y ave, tomorrow at 11 a m & 3 p m.

Public sale of negroes: by an order of the Orphans' Court: sale on Nov 29, at the late residence of Geo R Spalding, dec'd, near Port Tobacco, Chas Co, Md, all the personal property of which he died possessed consisting of likely & valuable negroes-house servants & farm hands-horses, mules, oxen, & stock generally, farming utensils of various kinds, straw & fodder, corn, & household and kitchen furniture.
-Geo Brent, John F Spalding, Adms of G R Spalding, dec'd.

MON NOV 13, 1843
The venerable Col John Trummell died in N Y C on Fri last, at the age of 87 years. Thus fades away another of the illustrious band of Revolutionary men. Col Trumbull, as a soldier, an artist, a diplomatist, & a Christian gentleman, was, through many generations, honored & respected in life, to be honored & lamented in death. Col Trumbull, after serving with his regt in the field, became a member of Gen Washington's military family. After the Revolution he went to Europe to perfect himself in his favorite art of painting. He has, by his historical pictures, forever united his fame with that of the great period & events he has commemorated. While in England he became, by the choice of Mr Pinckney & Christopher Gore, the 5th Com'r under the Jay treaty, for the settlement of American claims upon England.

Mr P Burgheim, Prof of Music at Balt, has composed, & by permission dedicated to Mr Clay, a grand march, with the title of "The Ashland March." It is published by Mr F D Benteen, of Balt, & is for sale by Mr Fischer of Wash City.

N Y papers: news of the death of S V Clevenger, on board the packet ship **Duc d'Orleans**, on her passage from Leghorn to N Y. He was a citizen, & we believe a native, of the State of Ohio; a self-taught artist, who went to Italy 3 years ago, [following the track of Powers] to cultivate his talents in the midst of the great works of antiquity. He died at sea on Sep 23, leaving a wife & children to mourn over the loss they have sustained.

Mr Thos Baldwin, of Bladensburg, deserves great credit for the zeal with which he has pursued the burglars who lately robbed the store of Messrs Isaacs & Brother at Bladensburg. He had visited Wash City, Alexandria, & Phil, for the purpose of ferreting out all the parties concerned in the burglaries. Arrested was the old convict Caleb Bladen, the master-spirit of the gang, & Mortimer, the keeper of the stolen goods. Mr Baldwin left Wash City last Sat to receive Bladen from the Mayor of Phil. [From the Alexandria Gaz of Sat: Bladen lived with, or was constantly about the premises occupied by a family named Mortimer, about a mile west of Mr Custis' residence, Arlington. Mr Thos Baldwin, late Sheriff of PG Co, Md, set himself to work to ferret out the affair. Bladen made a full confession regarding the robberies in Bladensburg, at Mrs Mason's, & Mr C F Lee's, in Alexandria, & we believe, at Mr Michl Shank's.] [Nov 27 newspaper: Bladen, the famous rogue, found guilty on 3 indictments-2 for burglary & 1 for larceny. Mortimer, the confederate of Bladen, found guilty. –Gaz]

N Y, Nov 10. Court of Sessions, before the Recorder & Aldermen Tillon & Martin. Michl Walsh, Editor of the Subterranean, was called upon for sentence. For the libel on John S Magnus the prisoner was sentenced to pay a fine of $25; for libel on Levi D Slamm, fined $100; for the assault & battery on Abitha B Millard, fined $50; for gross libel on Jos Southard, to be imprisoned in the penitentiary 2 months, & stand committed till the fines be paid. Mr Walsh then, with a smile, was escorted to prison. The sentence of Geo Wilkes was suspended, & Lorenzo D Cummings was fine $50 for the assault & battery on Millard. –Courier & Enquirer

Norfolk Herald states that on Fri week the premises of Mr Saml Brittingham, near New Town, Worcester Co, on the eastern Shore of Md, were invaded by 3 ruffians, who seized all his colored servants, 4 in number, consisting of a woman 50 years of age, & her 3 children, a boy about 16, & a girl 8 & the other 5 years old. Mr Brittingham [who is an aged man] & his wife attempted to call for help, but were stopped when the villains presented firearms at them. Mr Brittingham recognized the robbers as persons who had been for several weeks sojourning about New Town. They names they went by were Benj C Dickson & Rowland H Vail, & both reported to be from Ky. The third was unknown.

Newark Daily Adv: on Thu a fire broke out in the house of Mr Gersham Chadwick, [near Newark,] which was entirely consumed, & most distressing was that Mrs Chadwick & her 2 children, a girl & boy, perished in the fire. Mr Chadwick jumped from an upper window & burnt in the attempt. Mr Chadwick had just removed into the house from Rahway. Nothing could be save & Mr Chadwick is left completely destitute.

Cincinnati Messenger: from Little Rock, Ark, a saddler living near that place, named Doyle, murdered his wife on the 20th ult and the following day he committed suicide by cutting his throat from ear to ear.

Criminal Court-Wash: Nov 10. 1-Owen Clark guilty of an assault & battery on John F Dunnington: sentenced to pay a fine of $10 & to give security in the sum of $100 for his good behavior & to keep the peace for 1 year. 2-Chas Brown, free negro, guilty of stealing on Oct 31, 1843, one counterpane of the value of $5, the property of Hewel Fulcher: 2 years in the pen. 3-Wm Gray, alias McManus, convicted of burglary: 3 years in the pen. 4-Jas Curtis, free negro, convicted of grand larceny: 18 months in the pen. 5-Wm Ford, free negro, convicted of obtaining a pair of boots under false pretences: 18 months in the pen. 6-Geo Dean, alias McKendree Dean, convicted of grand larceny: 18 months in the pen, to take effect from Nov 18th instant. 7-John Brown, free negro, convicted of grand larceny: 2 years in the pen, to take effect one day from & after the rising of the next term of the Circuit Court. 8-Aloysius Call, free negro, convicted of grand larceny: 2 years in the pen. 9-Henrietta Butler, free negress, convicted of grand larceny: 18 months in the pen. 10-Jas Hammet, alias Martin Nowiski, convicted of petit larceny: 3 months in the county jail. 11-Jas O'Brien, convicted of an aggravated assault upon Bernard O'Brian, at Gtwn on Jul 18, 1843: fined $20 & to be imprisoned 1 month in the county jail. 12-Jim Chisley, free negro, convicted of an assault on Isaac Carrington: fined $5 & costs. 13-Henry Lacy, free negro, convicted of an assault upon Dennis, the slave of John Hopkins: fined $5 & costs. 14-T F Sloan, convicted of an assault upon Jas Maguire: fined $20 & costs. 15-John Barney Manley, convicted of an assault upon Eliza Mattingly: fined $20 & to give security in the sum of $200 for his good behavior & to keep the peace for 2 years. 16-John Barney Manley, convicted of an assault upon Anna Maria Baltzell: fined $20 & to give security in the sum of $200 for his good behavior & to keep the peace for 2 years. 17-No sentence was passed upon Eliz Hall & Emma Reed, convicted of assault with attempt to kill Susan Creamer. New trial is expected.

Mrd: Nov 9th, at Albany, by Rev Dr Sprague, Gen Rufus King to Susan, d/o Col Robt Elliot, all of Albany.

Sale of household furniture, by order of Orphan's Court of Wash Co, D C: sale on Nov 15, at the residence of the late Francis S Key, on C st, between 3rd & 4½ sts, part of the household furniture, personal effects of the dec'd, such as: mahogany hair-seat sofa, Brussels carpet & rug; mahg center, pier, & dining tables, lot glass; Spanish chair, brass andirons, shovels, tongs, & fenders; hat rack, hall lamp, high & French-post bedsteads & beds; mattresses, bedding, mahg bureaus & toilet glasses; wardrobes, chamber carpets & chairs, washstands, & chamber sets, with some good kitchen effects.
-Robt W Dyer & Co, aucts

Valuable Washington & Gtwn property at auction: by virtue of 2 deeds of trust to us, the one executed by Walter Smoot, & the other by said Smoot & wife: sale on Nov 25, all the valuable water property in Gtwn held by said Walter Smoot, situated on the south side of Water st, including lots 19 & 20 & parts of lots 18, 21, 22, & 23, all of the water lots on the south side of said st. This property has a front of about 120 feet on Water st; improvements include 2 valuable 2 story brick warehouses, another of 2 stories, partly of brick & partly of frame, & an extensive frame warehouse, besides several valuable wharves, one of which is the landing or the several steamboats that ply to the town. The property has been lately occupied in several parcels by Messrs Walter Smoot, Jno Hedges, & C Hogmire, & is well known. On the same day, also in front of the premises, a valuable bldg lot in Wash City, being lot 7 in square 41. Title of all this propery is believed to be perfectly good & free from all emcumbrance. The sale will be positive, & without restriction. –Thos J Davis, Jos Smoot, Trustees. -E S Wright, auct for Gtwn.
-Robt W Dyer & Co, aucts

TUE NOV 14, 1843
Sudden death at Andover, on Thu, just before the train of cars started on its return to Boston, Geo Gay, of the city of Boston, was found dead in one of the cars. It was

supposed he died of apoplexy. Mr Gay was of the firm of Gay & Simmons, counselors at law, & much respected by the profession & his friends.

Criminal Court-Wash: Nov 13. 1-Thos J Fletcher, convicted of keeping a disorderly house in Wash City: fined $20 & to suffer one month's imprisonment in the county jail. 2-John Bohlayer, jr, convicted of an aggravated assault & battery upon John G Hempler at the Navy: fined $20 & to suffer 20 days in the county jail. 3-J B B Wilson, of Gtwn, was admitted as an atty & counsellor of the Court.

Public meeting of the Tavern-keepers of Wash City to be held at the house of Mr Thos Baker, on 8th st, corner of D, on Nov 16, at 7 o'clock. By order of the Chair.

Sale of groceries: the subscriber, intending to discontinue the grocery business at the Navy Yard, designs all to whom he may be indebted to present their bills during the present week for payment, & those indebted to him-that he will expect an early settlement of their accounts. –Jno Costigan -Robt W Dyer & Co, aucts

Supreme Court reports for 1843, by B C Howard, Reporter of the Supreme Court of the U S, just published, & this day received for sale by F Taylor.

WED NOV 15, 1843
A Classical Teacher wanter. I wish to engage immediately an experienced Teacher to instruct 3 youths from 18 to 20 years of age in Latin, Greek, & the higher branches of Math; & 6 females in the ordinary branches of English. To a suitable person a salary of $300, with board, washing, & fuel, will be given. Satisfactory evidences as to qualification & character will be expected. –Th Goode, Hot Springs

For sale: the undersigned, proprietor of the Dranesville Tavern, in the town of Dranesville, lately incorporated by the Leg of Va, offers for sale the whole premises, consisting of 116 acs of land attached thereto. It is at the junction of the Falls Bridge & Middle Turnpike Road, about 17 miles from the District. The house is a large frame bldg in good repair & long used as a public house: store-house attached, & a good blacksmith shop on the premises. For further information apply to H W Thomas, Fairfax Court-house, or to the undersigned, who resides on the premises.
–Ann M Farr, Dranesville, Fairfax Co, Va

$150 reward for runaways from the neighborhood of Upperville, Fauquier Co, Va: the following negroes: Aclus, about 35; Austin, about 28; & Sam, about 25. They are all accustomed to working on a farm. –John A Carter, administrator of H N Dulany, Upperville, Va

Eight now Catholic Bishops appointed at Rome for the U S: Rev Dr Reynolds fills the place of the late Bishop England. Rev Mr Quarters is Bishop of Chicago. Rev Andrew

Byrne is Bishop of Arkansas. Rev Mr McCluskey is Coadjutor Bishop for N Y. The three last are now of N Y C. Rev Wm Tyler is Bishop of the new See, Hartford, Conn. Rev John Fitzpatrick Coadjutor Bishop of Boston. These gentlemen are of Boston.

The packet ship **Sheffield**, Capt Chas W Popham , from Liverpool, Oct 8, with a valuable cargo of dry goods & hardware, arrived off Fire Island & took a pilot on Nov 10; while in the act of hauling on the wind, she went ashore on the east Bank, north of Romer; the sea made a complete breach over her, she striking very hard. The steamboat **Wave**, Capt Vanderbilt, from Staten Island, took off all the passengers & all the crew, except the captain & 4 seamen, who remained with the ship. No hopes are entertained of saving the ship. [Nov 16 newspaper: passengers in the **Sheffield**: Rev B F Cutler, D D & lady, of Brooklyn; Mr Sanderson, lady & servant, of N Y; Mr & Mrs Spreckelson, child, & servant, of Balt; Mrs Maxwell, of N Y; Rev Mr Kerfoot, of Hagerstown, Md; Erastus Brooks, of N Y; Mr Sherwood, of Fishkill; & 93 in the steerage. They all joined in a unanimous card of acquittal from all blame to Capt Popham.]]

Circuit Court of Wash Co, D C. Robt Grant has applied to be discharged from imprisonment under the act for the relief of Insolvent Debtors: hearing on Nov 23. –Wm Brent, clk

A letter dated Reistertown, Md, on Nov 12, states that a man named Storick, a witness in the case of Adam Horn, alias Hellman, indicted, & to be tried on Mon in Balt Co Court for the murder of his wife, committed suicide near Reistertown yesterday by cutting his throat with a shoe knife. Storick gave testimony before the grand jury last week in Horn's case, which evidence is said to have been of little importance. He was subsequently arrested in the county in consequence of some confessions made relative to the murder.

Mrd: on Nov 7, by Rev J H Wingfield, Mr John N Ashton, jr, formerly of King Geo Co, Va, to Miss Ellen T E, eldest d/o John Cocke, of Portsmouth, Va.

Died: on Nov 6, at Raleigh, N C, of ulceration of the stomach, Mrs Rebecca Cameron, the beloved consort of the Hon Duncan Cameron.

Died: on Oct 22, near Selma, Ala, Col Thos Kenan, in his 73rd year. The dec'd was a native of N C, & s/o a worthy Revolutionary patriot. He was for a number of years, & as long as he would consent to serve in that capacity, a member of Congress from that State.

Died: last week, at Portland, Maine, Gen Joshua Wingate, jr, in his 71st year. He was for many years engaged in public life, & for several years Chief Clerk of the War Dept in Wash City. Subsequently he was appointed Collector of Bath, & always sustained a high character for intelligence & integrity. His father is still living in Hallowell, aged nearly 100 years.

Died: on Nov 14, after a lingering illness, Mrs Frances Eliz Gibbs, consort of John H Gibbs, in her 22nd year. Her funeral will be from her late residence on Pa ave, between 8th & 9th sts, today, at 2 p m.

Died: on Oct 31, at his planation, near St Martinsville, La, John Palfrey, aged 77 years, a native of Boston, & a lineal descendant of one of the first settlers of New England in 1620.

Died: on Oct 4, at sea, on board the barque **Sarah Hand**, from New Orleans to Phil, Wm W Ringgold, late a passed midshipman in the U S Navy.

Died: on Nov 5, at Pottsville, Pa, in her 23rd year, Henrietta Virginia, w/o Lt W A Nichols, U S Army, & d/o Col John Garland, U S Army.

Burlington [Vt] Free Press: 3 miles south of that village on Nov 7, 3 sons of Mr Peter Culbert, Thos, Wm, & Geo, aged 12, 10, & 8 years, resorted to the mill pond near their father's residence to enjoy the newly-formed ice. Hardly had they ventured upon it when it gave way & the elder brother went down. The 2 other brothers soon followed in their vain attempt to rescue the elder brother. The bodies were recovered.

THU NOV 16, 1843
Col Richd M Johnson, Ex-V Pres of the U S, arrived in Wash City from a tour in the Northern States. He is at his friend, the Rev O B Brown's house. We are glad to learn he is in good health, & will remain several days.

The Rev Mr J Carbery, of St Inigoes, Md, has sent to the Institute, for inspection of the curious, a deformed claw of a crab caught in St Mary's river in Jun last; & a sweet-potato of a growth resembling a reptile.

The dead body of Col John Colburn was found in one of the docks at N Y on Sunday. He was formerly of Tennessee or Louisiana, & during the last war was a Lt Col in the Army. For the last few years he has been employed as agent for the U S for the removal of the Indians to the far West. He was a man of exceedingly temperate habits, but for the last few months, which time he has spent in N Y, he has appeared somewhat deranged. He has left wife & children in Oneida Co, N Y.

The beautiful new U S frig **Cumberland**, Capt Breese, is about to sail from Boston to the Mediterranean, with Cmdor Jos Smith, to relieve Cmdor Morris of the squadron there. Intoxicating drinks are to excluded from the wardroom & steerage during the long cruise, & between 200 & 300 of the crew refuse their grog.

A distressing accident occurred on board the steamboat **Rowena** on Nov 4, as she was going into St Louis, by the bursting of her cannon, which caused the death of a young man, Wm Whitehead, a deck passenger, & a black man, who fired it off. Another young man, Wm Yarnall, was badly wounded. Both of the young men were from Jersey, Licking Co, Ohio.

Tribute of friendship to the memory of the late Danl Hale Haskell, of Wash, who died of pulmonary consumption on Oct 20, 1843, after a confinement to his bed of about 2 weeks. He was a native of New England, [Maine] & for upwards of 25 years a resident of Wash City, & for the last 7 years of his life in the employment of the Gov't on duties which he discharged faithfully & commendably. –M

Obit-died: on Aug 23 last, at his residence near Front Royal, Warren Co, Va, Mr Jas Sinclair, in his 87th year. He was by birth a Scotchman, & was born Dec 28, 1756, near Forres, Morayshire, Scotland, where he spent his early youth. About the close of the Revolutionary war he emigrated to America, first stopping at Gtwn, D C, where he remained some time with a relation, who had previously come over to this country. He finally settled in Warren, [at that time Fred'k Co,] to which place he became strongly attached, & remained to the day of his death. Mr Sinclair's ancestors were all members of the Presbyterian Church, in which he was early instructed, but soon after coming to America he joined the Methodist Episcopal Church. For the last 18 years the old gentleman's mind has become very frail; indeed he was regarded by his family & neighbors an idiot on all subjects save religion, of which he appeared to retain much that was valuable. He had been one of the most active & industrious farmers in Fred'k Co.

From Jamaica: The collector of Customs at Nevis, Henry Harding, was drowned in Sep by the accidental upsetting of a boat.

Died: on Nov 14, in Wash City, Mrs Jane Doyne, in her 73rd year. Her funeral will be from the residence of Mrs Dove, on F st, between 11th & 12th sts, this day, at 2 p m.

Died: on Nov 14, Jos W Bittinger, in his 22nd year. His friends & acquaintances are requested to attend his funeral this day, at 2 o'clock, from the residence of his father, corner of Bridge & Jefferson sts, Gtwn.

NOTICE: Application has been made to the Pres & Dirs of the Bank of the Metropolis for the renewal of a certificate of 50 shares of stock in said Bank of $10 each, #22, issued on or about Aug 15, 1815, in favor of the subscriber, which certificate has been lost or mislaid. –Ann Hedglie

Trustee's sale of valuable real estate in Fauquier Co, Va: by virtue of a deed of trust, executed by John Carter & Eliza F, his wife, to the subscriber, for the purpose of securing the payment of a bond for $3,000, with interest, due from said John Carter to Hamilton

Lufborough, guardian of Mary Jane & Ann H Rose: sale on Jan 9, of 300 acs of land in the upper northern part of said county, being a part of the estate conveyed by said deed; which estate is the same on which said John Carter, now dec'd, lately resided. The tract of 300 acs, which is advertised for sale, is the upper part of that estate commonly known as the "*Number Six Estate*," & adjoins the lands of W Rust, Danl Hitt, Dr Smith & Geo Calvert. It contains 55 or 56 acs of woodland. The deed under which I shall sell was admitted to record in the Clk Ofc of Fauquier Co Court on Apr 5, 1836.
–Jas H Lufborough

$5 reward for a small red cow that strayed from the residence of the subscriber, on 9th st, near E st, opposite the Radical Methodist Church. She was lately obtained from Mr Alex'r Shepherd, a short distance from Rock Creek Church. –Geo Stettinius

Wash Corp: 1-An Act for the relief of John West: that the penalty incured by John West, as security for the late Alex'r C Hall, in a fine incured by said Hall, be & the same is hereby remitted: Provided, that West pay the costs of prosecution.

The Presbytery of D C, according to appointment, proceeded last evening to the installation of the Rev Jas Knox, called to the pastoral charge of the Second Presbyterian Church on N Y ave. An eloquent sermon was preached by the Rev J G Hamner, of Balt. Rev John C Smith, of this city, presided. Rev J N Danforth, of Alexandria, delivered a charge to the pastor.

FRI NOV 17, 1843
From the late Paris Journals: The King of France yesterday entered on his 71st year, having been born Oct 6, 1773. He is the first of his race who has arrived at so advanced an age.

Jos Rosati, Bishop of St Louis, in North America, died in Rome on the 25th ult. He was the founder of the first establishment of Lazarists in the New World, & passed 25 years in his apostolical ministry, although he was only 53 years of age. He was a native of Sora, in the Kingdom of Naples.

Cologne, Sep 22. Lt Pelzer, who lately, in consequence of a dispute at a ball, fought a duel with M Hain, a bookseller, & shot him, was sentenced by a court martial to be beheaded. The King has commuted this sentence to 15 years' imprisonment in a fortress; & Lt Pelzer has been conveyed today to the fortress of Ehren Vreitstein, as well as the 2 seconds, who are condemned to 10 years imprisonment.

Alexandria Gaz: Benj C Dickson & Rowland H Vail, 2 of the persons who lately abducted a negro family from Worcester Co, Md, have been arrested. On Sat night, Jas Chatham, Jas Cole, & Thos Javins, in pursuit of them, found the men in a house just beyond Dranesville. The negroes were in the same house & seemed much rejoiced at being rescued from the kidnappers.

Mrd: on Nov 7, in Gtwn, by Rev Littleton F Morgan, Henry L Carlton, of PG Co, Md, to Miss Ann W Clark, of the former place.

Died: on Nov 5, at St Mary's Seminary, in Balt, Rev Jas Hector Nicholas Joubert, in his 67th year.

The Freedmen's Vigilant Total Abstinence Society will meet this evening at the Medical College, until the Temperance Hall is completed. –Edmund Brooke, sec

SAT NOV 18, 1843
Florida: Pilatka is the best position for persons with pulmonary affections. I mention that Surgeon Elwes died of congestive fever in the summer of 1842. St Augustine: The first death from yellow fever occurred on Oct 10, & between this & the 31st, 8 men died of the disease. Capt Garner, of the 3rd Artl, contracted the disease in St Augustine, & died at Picolata on the 23rd, & Maj Jacob Brown died here on the 24th; Col Downing died on the 24th or 25th; Lt Gannett contracted the disease here, & died at Pilatka on the 30th; Mrs Forward died on one of the last days of the month. [The undersigned physicians, residents of the city of St Augustine, believe that false & exaggerated reports have been circulated abroad as to the existence of a malignant epidemic. –Chas Byrne, Wm H Simmons, S F Jones]

On Oct 10, 1843, the sentence of the Marine Gen Court Martial in the case of 1st Lt Thos T Sloan was commuted by order of the Pres of the U S, & he suspended for 6 months without pay from Sep 1, 1845. On Oct 20, 1843, the sentence of the Marine Gen Court Martial in the case of Maj & Brvt Lt Col Wm H Freeman was commuted by order of the Pres, & he suspended from rank & duty for the period of 2 years, with pay & allowances, from Jul 18, 1843, & to be restricted to the State of Massachusetts during that time, in lieu of the sentence of the Court before which he was tried. –Army & Navy Chronicle

A few days ago, Mr Harvill J Arnold, a very respectable citizen of Cumberland Co, N C, late Deputy Sheriff, was accidentally shot through the heart with his own gun, & died instantly.

Windsor, the residence of Mrs Eliz Pleasants, in Powhatan, 25 miles from Richmond, on the James river, was consumed by fire on Sun, with a total loss of every species of property in the house. The venerable widow, more than 90 years of age, was saved with difficulty, being conveyed on a bed literally through the flames. The fire originated in a room the key of which had been carried away by its occupant. Mrs Pleasants found shelter under the hospitable roof of John Gilliam, at *Maiden's Adventure*. –Richmond Whig

Public sale of very valuable negroes & stock: at my residence, near Bladensburg, PG Co, Md, on Dec 20: 45 or 50 valuable young negroes, consisting of men & women, boys, girls, & children. At the same time & place I will offer my entire stock of blood horses, together with some farm stock. –Saml Sprigg

NOTICE: By virtue of a writ of venditioni exponas, issued by B K Morsell, a J Ps for Wash Co, D C, I shall offer at public sale, Nov 25, on the premises, one frame or wooden bldg, with the lesse to the freehold, on the west half of lot 2, in square 79, fronting on G st, near 21st st, in Wash, D C. Seized & taken as the property of Benj Johnson, & will be sold to satisfy a judgment due Ulysses Ward. –L S Beck, Constable

We learn that John West has not been hung; but, on the contrary, a respite was granted him until the 25th inst. In the mean time an effort was made by his friends to get him a reprieve. We are assured that there is no doubt but the Chief will grant it.

New Haven Register: announces the death of Robinson S Hinman, Judge of the Court of Probate for the district of New Haven, & a member of the bar of this county. He died at the house of Wm H Ellis, in this city, on Nov 10, at the age of 42.

Mrd: on Nov 9, at Augusta, Ga, by Rev Mr Ford, G H Talcott, Lt Ordnance Corps, U S Army, to Miss Catharine Jane Starke, d/o Maj W W Starke, of that city.

Died: on Nov 16, Mary P Nourse, eldest d/o Col M Nourse. Her funeral is today at 2 o'clock.

Died: on Nov 19, of scarlet fever, Mary Olympia, only child of John O'Neale, aged 2 years & 9 months. Her funeral will be from the residence of Geo Savage, this morning, at 10 o'clock.

Died: on Nov 12, at her residence in Chas Co, Md, Miss Mary McConchie, in her 58th year. Her name needs not the language of eulogy to endear it to those who knew her.

MON NOV 20, 1843
A German named Augustus Miller was arrested at Phil on Thu last, on a charge, based on his own confession, of having murdered old Mr Parke, John Castner, his wife & child, in Warren Co, N J, May 1st.

Judge Edw Livingston, an old & respectable citizen & farmer of Franklin Co, Ohio, was thrown from his horse Tuesday, between the town of Columbus & his house, & was killed.

Died: on Nov 6, at the Infirmary in Balt, in her 89th year, Mrs Mary Ann Pic, a native of Paris, France, but for many years a resident of Gtwn, D C.

Mrs W McCauley, having removed her residence from F st to Pa ave, 4th door from the corner of 3rd st, is prepared to accommodate a Mess of Members of Congress or others, who may desire comfortable boarding by the day, week, or year.

For rent: a large frame house with brick basement, on B & 10th sts, fronting the mall. Apply to J H Howell, Engraver, Pa ave, near 4½ sts.

Brown's Indian Queen Hotel has recently been fitted up in a style of elegance & convenience: an addition fronting on C st has been newly built; that part of the Hotel fronting on Pa ave has undergone a vast improvement. The bar has been removed to the rear, & the liquors reduced one-half in price. Board per week $10. –Jesse Brown

Fifth Annual meeting of the Female Union Benevolent Society of Washington: was held in the First Baptist Church, 10th st, on Nov 14: opening prayer by Rev Dr Laurie. Meeting was addressed by the Hon Mr Penrose & Pishey Thompson.

Directresses:

Mrs Laurie	Mrs M St Clair Clarke	Mrs C A Webb, Sec
Mrs O B Brown	Mrs Mills	Mrs S C Ingle, Treas

Managers:

Mrs T P Jones	Mrs John Davis	Mrs Gilliss
Mrs W A Bradley	Mrs Tucker	Mrs Morton
Mrs Anderson	Miss Auchmuty	Mrs Conly
Mrs C S Fowler	Miss Moore	Mrs Bulfinch
Mrs Powell	Mrs S Brown	Miss Bingham
Mrs Cox	Mrs Purdy	Mrs Milburn
Mrs Stelle	Mrs Easby	Mrs Fred Hall
Mrs J L Edwards	Mrs Lyons	Miss Paris

Thos Marsh was arrested in N Y on Fri on suspicion of having last week purposely fired the house of Mr Chadwick, at Newark, N J, by which Mrs C & her 2 children were burnt to death. It is said that he sold to Chadwick the premises destroyed, & then had a dispute with him about the price, which was decided against Marsh by the referees, & that on hearing this decision he vowed that Chadwick should never enjoy the property. The house was burnt the very night Chadwick moved into it.

Lemon Hill: this property has been purchased by the city of Phil: price was $75,000: consists of 42 acs, & has been valued as high as $200,000. The property is a valuable acquisition to the city.

TUE NOV 21, 1843

Washington High School: second quarter will commence on Nov 27. –Arnold & A N Girault

References:

Wm Linton	Capt H N Crabb	Rev Septimus Tuston
Maj T L Smith	Edw H Cabell	Dr John M Brodhead
Rev Dr Hawley	J Hoover	Gen Roger Jones
Col W W Seaton	Hon Chas A Wickliffe	Dr Bailey Washington
Wm Hunter	John D Barclay	Gen T S Jesup
Maj Jas N Barker	J Michard	

Found, in my wood-yard, a large Carpet, from appearance a little used, which was probably stolen from some house in the neighborhood. The loser can have it by describing the same & paying for this advertisement. Call at Canal st, near the Market house. –Isaac Hill

For rent: the brick house on the corner of Missouri ave & 4½ st, now occupied by Mr Jos C Daws. Possession on Dec 1. Inquire of the subscriber, next door, on Missouri ave. –Ulysses Ward

Fire broke out in the upper part of a brick bldg occupied by Mr W H Harrover, tinner, on the east side of 7th st. How is started, we are unable to learn.

At the late Annual Communication of the Grand Lodge of the Independent Order of Odd Fellows for D C the following ofcrs were elected to serve for the year ending in Nov, 1844, to wit:

John Sessford, of Wash Lodge, Grand Master
Geo Grant, of Harmony Lodge, Grand Warden
A G Herold, of Eastern Lodge, Deputy Grand Master
Chas Calvert, of Friendship Lodge, Grand Sec
Wm W Moore, of Central Lodge, Grand Rep to the Grand Lodge of the U S

Mrd: on Nov 7, at Jacksonville, Ill, by Rev Dr Todd, Col John A McClernand, Rep in Congress, to Miss Sarah F Dunlap, d/o Col Jas Dunlap, of Jacksonville.

Mrd: on Nov 16, by Rev Mr Vanhorseigh, Mr John J White to Miss Ann Beall, both of Wash City.

Mrd: on Oct 6, near Moorestown, Burlington Co, N J, by Friends' ceremony, Jas M Walker, of Loudoun Co, Va, to Eliza, d/o Caleb Hunt, dec'd.

Died: on Sun, at his residence in Wash City, after a protracted illness, Capt Elijah Lyon, of the 3rd Regt U S Artl. His funeral is this morning at 11 a m, from his late dwlg on F st, west of the Navy Dept.

Died: on Nov 5, at Mount Vernon, Ohio, Dr John Ridgely, a native, &, during the greater part of his life, a resident of Annapolis, Md.

WED NOV 22, 1843
Great Whig Convention in Ky, at Louisville, on Nov 13 & 14. The Hon Chilton Allan was chosen Pres. Nominating cmte presented the name of Judge Wm Owsley, of Boyle Co, as their choice for the ofc of Govn'r, & that of Archibald Dixon, of Henderson Co, for the ofc of Lt Govn'r. The following were chosen the Whig Electors for the State of Pres & V P of the U S in 1844:
Benj Hardin, Joel Underwood, for the State at large
Robt A Patterson, of Caldwell Co   Green Adams, of Knox
Philip Triplett, of Daviess Co   Wm J Graves, of Louisville
B Mills Crenshaw, of Barren   Leslie Combs, of Fayette
John Kinkead, of Lincoln   Landaff W Andrews, of Fleming
Wm R Grigsby, of Nelson   Wm W Southgate, of Kenton
The following were chosen Delegates to the Nat'l Whig Convention which is to be held at Balt in May:
Thos Metcalfe, Squire Turner, for the State at large
A Harpending, 1st dist   A G Stevenson, 6th dist
Alfred Allen, 2nd dist   Thos P Wilson, 7th dist
Benj H Reeves, 3rd dist   Richd Pindell, 8th dist
Bryan Y Owsley, 4th dist   Chas Eginton, 9th dist
Jno B Thompson, 5th dist   Wm K Wall, 10th dist

John W Rand has been convicted of having been concerned in the robbery from the Quincy [Mass] stage of a package of $4,000 on Oct 31. The jury could not agree on a verdict with reference to his brother Richd.

An alarming calculation: Maj Long, of the U S Topographical Corps, whose attention has lately been directed to the action of the water on the Illinois shore of the Mississippi, opposite the mouth of the Missouri, has informed the editor of the St Louis Era that the river has within the last year cut away about 200 yards of the bank, leaving only about 1,000 yards to connect the Mississippi with the low grounds of Long Lake.

Furnished rooms to let: a handsomely furnished Parlor & Chamber can be had on pleasing terms on application at Krafft's bakery, on Pa ave, near the corner of 18th st. Also, a comfortable 2 story frame house, with back bldgs attached, on K st north, near 18th st. Possession can be had immediately, on application to Mr Roemmele, on the premises, or to –Geo Krafft

$5 reward: for Buffalo Cow that strayed from the subscriber, on Capitol Hill, on Nov 12. --Michl Dooley

Handsome household furniture at auction: on Nov 27, at the residence of Thos T Barnes, on 6th st, nearly opposite the Unitarian Church, his household & kitchen furniture. -Robt W Dyer & Co, aucts [Also, the house is for rent to a good tenent & the rent will be moderate. Apply to Thos T Barnes.]

Mr Hassler, for many years at the head of the Coast Survey of the U S, died at Phil on Mon. He had some time since been attacked with pleurisy. We believe he attained the age of nearly 80 years, & was much enfeebled previous to his last illness.

Mr Oliver P Tilden, of Balt, a single man aged about 28 years, who, while on a gunning excursion, threw the but of his loaded gun down with so much force as to cause an explsion. The whole load entered his mouth, killing him instantly.

Augustus Miller, alias Auguste Jacobi, who was arrested at Phil last week on his own confession of having been concerned in the N J murder, now denies having had any thing to do with it. He has been detained for further examination.

Among the passengers who sailed from N Y for Liverpool in the packet ship **Hottinguer**, was Mr Cmdor Stewart, lately a resident of Washington.

Naval: the frig **Raritan**, Capt Francis H Gregory, was placed in commission on Nov 15, with 200 of her crew on board; her complement will be 500.

Barre Gaz: Mrs Harriet Smith, a native of the town, of a respectable family, the w/o Mr Josiah Smith, one of the best citizens, a member of a church, & a mother, had been detected of shoplifting during the last 3 years, of various kinds of dry goods to the amount of several thousand dollars. The forgeries of Wm Goddard, says the Gaz, did not create a deeper sensation than this disclosure.

Orphan's Court of Wash Co, D C. Letters of adm on personal estate of Danl H Haskell, dec'd, be granted to Alex'r McIntire, unless cause to be contrary be shown on or before Dec 12. –Ed N Roach, Reg of Wills

Mrd: on Nov 21, at Honesty, Montg Co, Md, by Rev Dr John Mines, Mr John B Wiltberger, of D C, to Miss Mary Eliz, d/o Jacob Bohrer.

Died: on Nov 20, Mrs Charlotte W Galt, in her 19th year, w/o Thos Galt. Her funeral will be this morning at 10 a m, from the residence of Mr J L Clubb, on 9th st above H st.

A CARD: the undersigned takes this method to return to the Firemen & Citizens his thanks for their kind attentions at the fire last evening, & for rescuing his stock from the devouring element. He announces to the public that his assortment of Stoves, Tin & Sheet Iron Ware, & also his Manufacturing Shop, remain uninjured, & that he is now as before open & ready to wait upon his friends. –Wm H Harrover

Died: Nov 20, of paralysis, Mr Geo Miller, in his 75th year. His funeral is this morning at 11 a m, from his late residence on the alley east side of 7th st, between G & H sts.

THU NOV 23, 1843

Winter Fashions: Mrs S Parker, having just returned from the North, will open, on Nov 24, an elegant assortment of French Millinery & Fancy Goods.

Naval: the U S frig **Cumberland**, bearing the broad pennant of Cmdor Jos Smith, sailed from Boston on Mon morning for the Mediterranean.

Liberty [Missouri] Banner of Nov 3: Mr Wm Spencer, of this county, was accidentally shot by one of his neighbors, being mistaken in the woods for a wild turkey. Mr Spencer was an amiable citizen, & his death will be deeply felt by all of his acquaintances.

The schnr **Thos Dail**, from Norfolk bound to New Smyrna, put into the port of St Augustine, Fla, on Oct 29. While there the mate & 3 men, in attempting to go ashore in a yawl, were drowned. They were: Henry Gray, mate, a native of Phil; seamen Wm Ennis, of Md, John Jews, of Va, & Backus, of Va.

Died: yesterday, at Brown's Hotel, Pettus Harman, of England. His funeral will take place from the residence of Henry L Ellsworth, on C st, this day, at half past 3 o'clock p m. [The dec'd arrived on Thu last, accompanied by his lady, on a visit of curiosity; visited some of the Public Bldgs on Fri; was seized with inflammatory rheumatism on the following day, which terminated his life yesterday morning. They were to have embarked on their return to England on Dec 1. The distress of the bereaved wife may be imagined.]

Died: at Washington Arsenal, aged 1 year, Ann Blackburn, d/o Maj John Symington. [No date-current item.]

Died: on Sat last, after a short illness, in his 4th year, Norman L, 2nd s/o Geo Macleod, Highlands, near Bladensburg, Md.

Wash Corp: 1-Cmte of Claims asked to be discharged from the further consideration of the ptn of Alfred Jones: they were discharged accordingly. 2-Bill for the relief of A F Zackman: read a 3rd time & passed. 3-Cmte of Claims: asked to be discharged from further consideration of the ptns of Edw Hawkins, of John M Johnson, of Wm Markwood, & of P H Moreland.

NOTICE: the creditors of Jos C Dawes are notified that the subscriber will attend at the Washington Hotel, in Rockville, Montg Co, Md, on Dec 5, for the purpose of making a final distribution of the assest of said Dawes among the creditors entitled, under an order of said county court, to receive the same. –Walter Magruder, jr, Trustee of Jos C Dawes

FRI NOV 24, 1843
Cardinal Alexander Guistiniani died at Genoa on the 11th ult. He was born in that city in 1778, & was raised to the purple in 1832.

Col Rampon, the Cmder of the corps of Dromedaries in the army of Egypt, died at Toulon, on Oct 22nd, at a very advanced age.

Dr Thos Feinour respectfully informs the citizens of Wash that he has taken up his residence in this city, with the intention of devoting his whole attention to his profession. His residence is on 4½ st, a few doors south of Pa ave, where he will be ready at all times to attend to business in his profession.

Mrs E Scott has opened a Boarding house in the large 3 story bldg opposite the eastern wing of the City Hall, the same in which Mr Archer & Col Preston, with his family, resided throughout the last long session.

From the N Y Tribune: U S Dist Court-before Judge Betts in Equity. U S vs Jesse Hoyt, Lorenzo Hoyt, Jesse Oakley, Thos Oakley, Geo B Kissam & others. The bill alleges that the dfndnts were sureties on the bond of Jesse Hoyt, late Collector of the Customs, against whom a judgment has been obtained by the U S for $221,083.29; that the said Jesse Hoyt was possessed of large estates in N Y, Md & Ill, all of which, with other assets, were assigned to the dfndnts, Jesse Oakley & Geo B Kissam, in trust for the parties who are surety on the bond; that said dfndnts have given no security for the faithful performance of their trust, & have violated that trust by discharging large sums of money for the personal use of Mr Hoyt. The object of the application is for an injunction against Jesse Oakley & Geo B Kissam, prohibiting them from disposing of the estate, & also for the appointment of a receiver. The Court stated that the District Judge has no power, in the vacation of the Circuit, to make any further order than to lay the parties under temporary injunction till the merits of the case have been passed upon the Circuit Court. Ordered accordingly.

Florida: in Jul, 1841, the assistant surgeon, Dr Noyes, was attacked with fever, &, with barely strength enough to embark, was only able to reach St Augustine [on Jul 26th,] & soon died.. His place at New Smyrna was supplied by Assistant Surgeon Weightman, who remained scarcely a month before he too became prostrated with the fever, of the place, & early in Sep left for St Augustine, where, with this & other maladies of which he complained, he soon after died on Oct 30th. [Weightman died of malaria.] Tampa: at this place is one of the permanent posts-Fort Brooke: in 1839 the yellow fever prevailed, when Capts Barker, Peyton, & Griffin died, & several sldrs & citizens. At Cedar Keys, was a large depot for the supply of the army: established in 1839; in 1841, Mr Hambaugh, sutler of the 1st Infty died. Fort Clinch is a perfect grave yard, & like Tallahassee, in a short time the grave yard contained more inhabitants than the settlement. A company [says an ofcr of the 3rd Artl] under Capt [now Brvt Lt Col] Childs arrived at Black creek in Jul or Aug, & marched to Micanopy in perfect health. In less than a month one-half the men in this company were sick. –Physician Second -Fort Trumbull, Conn, Nov 8, 1843

On Wed last the great estate of the late Isaac Lawrence was brought to auction, under Austen, Wilmerding & Co, at the Merchants Exchange. 123 lots were sold on the 33rd to 35th sts, between Bloomingdale & Middle road, that is to say, on the plain between the House of Refuge & Murray Hill, at an aggregate average of $370 each. These prices are twice as great as could have been attained a year ago. Some of the lots were immediately worth a profit at private sale. –N Y Journal Com

Piracy. On Nov 20, 1843, the brig **Maria Theresa** was lying in the Potomac river, near the bridge at Washington, 5 of the crew, who were left at night with charge to keep watch, stole the launch from alongside & other property belonging to the vessel. Their names are: Silas Howard, John Chase, John Sutten, Lucas Sparrow, & John Brown. The names that they went by on board the brig were Frederick, Johe, Martin, Nelson, & Chas. They are all young men, between 20 & 34 years of age. Johe is an Indian of Chili, or that way; 2 are Swedes or Dutch & 2 are Irish or English. Reward is $50 for their delivery, & any reasonable expenses in addition thereto I will pay. –Wm F Clark, Master of brig **Maria Theresa**

Trustee's sale of valuable improved property: by virtue of a deed of trust to the subscriber, executed by Perez Packard, dated Jul 11, 1836: sale of all that tract or parcel of land in Wash City known as square 485, together with bldgs & improvements thereon: frame dwlg houses & out-bldgs. –David A Hall, trustee -Robt W Dyer & Co, aucts

Circuit Court of Wash Co, D C. Edw L Hamilton has applied to be discharged from imprisonment under the act for the relief of Insolvent Debtors: hearing on Dec 5. –Wm Brent, clk

Mrd: on Nov 21, at Medical Hall, Harford Co, Md, by Rev Mr Pinney, Dr Chas T Chamberlain, of Jefferson Co, Missouri, to Pamelia H, d/o the Hon Stevenson Archer.

Died: Wed last, of scarlet fever, Sarah Rose, y/d/o Geo & Susan Savage, aged 1 year, 2 months & 12 days.

Died: on Nov 18, at Annapolis, Maj Henry Hobbs, Examiner General of the Western Shore, aged about 40 years, universally esteemed & respected.

Bldg lot at private sale: lot 11 in sq 220, fronting on H st; nearly adjoining St Matthew's Church, & the residence of Mrs Ann Hill: a most beautiful site for a private residence. -Robt W Dyer & Co, aucts

SAT NOV 25, 1843
Mr Everett, our estimable resident Minister to the Court of St James, has met a severe affliction in the death of his eldest dght.

Mrd: on Nov 22, by Rev O B Brown, Mr Wm H Jones, of Va, to Miss Mary Q Force, d/o Col Peter Force, of Wash City.

Mrd: on Thu, by Rev Septimus Tuston, Mr Richd M Potter to Miss Mary Ann Mandon, all of Wash City.

Public sale: By order of the Orphans' Court, I will sell, at Benedict, Chas Co, Md, on Dec 15, 8 likely negroes. –G Stone, administrator of C S Locke

The Augusta [Ga] Chronicle of Nov 14: Since Oct 25, the Western mail, to & from this city, has been several times robbed of amounts ascertained to be $1,800 to $2,000. Suspicions have settled upon the Postmaster at Camac, E A Crandle, & a man by the name of Wm Butler, who had charge of the mail on the Georgia railroad. They have both been arrested.

Family Groceries, next to the corner of 3rd & Pa ave. –J B Morgan [Also, a furnished house for rent, the entire upper part, with a large kitchen, of the 3 story house where he keeps store.]

Household furniture, wines, sale, by order of the Orphans' Court: at the residence of the late Capt Lyons, on F st west, between 18th & 19th sts, near the War Dept, his household & kitchen furniture. -Robt W Dyer & Co, aucts

MON NOV 27, 1843
Mrs Tschiffely would be pleased to accommodate several gentlemen with board at her residence on I st, between 9th & 10th sts, 5 minutes' walk to any of the public Depts.

Orphan's Court of Wash Co, D C. Ordered this day, on application, that letters of adm de bonis non, with will annexed, on personal estate of Henry Thompson, dec'd, be granted to Richd Dement, unless cause to the contrary be shown. –Ed N Roach, Reg o/wills

Report from Special Agent Alexander to the Postmast General. Milledgeville, Ga, Nov 18, 1843. Hon C A Wickliffe, Postmaster General: A few day since I had arrested & prosecuted E A Crandall, Postmaster at Camak, Ga, for taking money from a letter directed to Jess Rickelson, Camak, Ga. I now inform you that said Crandall was on Nov 17, tried, convicted, & sentenced to 10 years' hard labor in the State prison of Georgia.

Mr M Allen, of Providence, was thrown from his carriage on Tue & instantly killed.

Mademoiselle Calve [says the New Orleans Crescent of Nov 15th] met her death by poisoning herself. It was but a few weeks ago it was publicly stated that she was to be married to a notability of this city, & that she had renounced the stage. What has been the cause of this sad change in her destiny is not yet clearly revealed. She was one of the greatest favorites of those who love to frequent the French Opera that ever visited the U S.

The funeral of Ferdinand Rudolph Hassler, late Chief of the U S Coast Survey, took place at Phil on Thu, from the Hall of the Philosophical Society. The remains of the dec'd were interred at Laurel Hill. Rev Dr Ducachet was the officiating clergyman.
–North American

Ball for the benefit of the poor to be given in Wash City on Nov 30, at the Wash Assembly Rooms.
Managers:

Hon A P Upshur	Thos H Blake	Alex'r Lee
Hon David Henshaw	Mj Wm B Scott	Wm H Topping
Gen A Henderson	Edw Simms	Saml T Ashby
Gen r C Weightman	John H Hewitt	John F Coyle
Gen Walter Jones	Stan Murray	Walter M Clarke
Maj A A Nicholson	W W Seaton	J D Hoover
Maj Geo A Walker	John W Maury	L C Browne
Maj P G Howle	Walter Lenox	Jos B Tate
Col Peter Force	John T Towers	John S Cunningham
Col Wm Hickey	S Masi	J B Phillips
Jos Gales	D Fister	Geo W Phillips
John C Rives	John P Pepper	F A Harry
M Young	Jesse E Dow	

Tickets $2, to be had at Mr Fischer's Music Store, Franck Taylor's, Messrs Patterson's, Delany's, Stott's, & Gilman S Drug Stores, Washington, & at Linthicum's Drug Store, Gtwn.

Died: on Nov 20, John Iredell, of Horsham township, Montg Co, Pa, aged 81 years, 7 months & 12 days.

Died: on Nov 11, Mrs Ann Yost, w/o the Hon Jacob S Yost, a Rep in Congress from the 5th Congressional district of Pa.

Lost or mislaid, a note drawn by Richd H Clagett in favor of A B Berry for $423 & some cents, dated PG Co, Mar, 1843, with a credit of $20, in Oct. The finder will be liberally rewarded. –A B Berry, PG Co

Miss F Y Godefroy, from 349 Broadway, N Y, having just returned from Paris with a complete assortment of silks, cloaks, ball dresses, begs leave to call attention to her millinery & dress making establishment.

Orphan's Court of Wash Co, D C. Letters testamentary on the personal estate of Elijah Lyon, late of the U S Army, dec'd. -Z Lyon, exc [Mr Jas Eveleth, of Wash, is authorized to receive all moneys due, & to pay all debts against the estate of E Lyon. –Z Lyon]

Circuit Court of Wash Co, D C. John T Berger has applied to be discharged from imprisonment under the act for the relief of Insolvent Debtors: hearing on Dec 5. –Wm Brent, clk

TUE NOV 28, 1843
Christopher Lilly, who killed McCoy in a prize fight in the vicinity of N Y in Sep, 1842, has been arrested at New Orleans, where he lately arrived from Liverpool.

Wm Wyman, late Pres of the Phenix Bank, in Massachusetts, charged with embezzling the funds of the bank, had a 2nd trial [the jury not having agreed in the first instance] at Lowell last week, which resulted in the verdict of guilty. It is said he was sentenced to 7 years' confinement in the State prison. [Dec 1 newspaper: Wyman sentenced to 7 years confinement in the State prison. Sentence was suspended, to await the decision of the Supreme Court of Massachusetts on the exceptions taken to certain opinions of the Court before which he was tried. The dfndnt's bail has been increased to $60,000.]

The Rev L Reed, late Pastor of the Presbyterian Church in the village of Plattsburg, N Y, was convicted on all the charges & deposed from the ministry. The victim of seduction was a girl only 17 years of age, & a member of his church. –Plattsburg Republican

Died: on Nov 6, at Portsmouth, N H, Gen Joshua Wingate, jr, in his 71st year. He was born in Haverhill, Mass, & completed his education at Harvard Univ, when he removed to Hallowell, where he became engaged in business as a merchant. Having married a d/o the late Maj Gen Henry Dearborn, he accompanied that gentleman to Wash when he was appointed Sec of War in 1801, & was for several years chief clerk in the War Dept; but his health having been impaired by the deleterious influence of a Southern climate upon a Northern constitution, he returned to Maine & was soon appointed Collector of Bath, which ofc he filled until 1822, when he resigned & has since resided in Portland, except for a few years in Hallowell.

Died: on Nov 24, Edwin, infant s/o Rachael & Veltere Willett, aged 5 months.

For rent, on moderate terms, the beautiful House & grounds fronting the Mall, formerly the property of E Porter. Apply to Mr Catlett, of the firm of Estep & Catlett, or to the subscriber. –Marcus C Buck

Accident resulted in the death of Mr M W Campbell, of Nashville, Tenn, at Maysville, Ky, on Nov 18. Mr C was a passenger on board the steamboat **Ben Franklin**, Capt J Summons, & designed to land at Maysville. On reaching that town, in spite of the remonstrances of Mr C, the captain of the **Ben Franklin** insisted on putting him ashore in the yawl, in order to save the wharfage tax. While Mr C was in the yawl, preparing to start, the **Ben Franklin** came in contact with a steamboat lying at the wharf, which crushed the yawl to pieces, & so mangled Mr Campbell that he died in a few minutes. The jury of inquest held over the body censure in strong terms the conduct of the captain of the steamboat. [Dec 4 newspaper: The Grand Jury of Mason Co, Ky, found an indictment against J Blair Summons, the captain of the steamer, for manslaughter.]

Harrison Lindley, s/o the Sheriff of Orange Co, Ind, accidentally shot himself on Nov 9 & died instantly; as did J Newton Francis, a worthy young man, & one of the publishers of the Springfield Journal, on Nov 10.

Wm S Chrise, the murderer of Abraham Frey, was executed at Cumberland, on Fri last; from seven to ten thousand persons are supposed to have been present. Negro Danl was also hung on Fri, in PG Co, Md, for the murder of Mr John Smith. He made a confession of the murder, & also that he had killed some years ago a fellow servant in Alleghany Co.

The late Horace Appleton Haven, of Portsmouth, N H, left by his will, which was proved a few days since:
To Harvard College-$3,000
To Portsmouth Athenaeum-$2,000
To N H Bible Society-$1,000
To American Peace Society-$1,000
To Alfred W Haven, in trust for the Seaman's Friends' Society of Portsmouth-$500
To Portsmouth South Parish Sunday School Society-$500
Besides $800 to the town of Portsmouth, to be invested by the selectmen in some safe manner, for the purpose of producing by the interest premiums to meritorious boys attending the High School of the town.

A colored woman named Charlotte, the servant of Mr J S Essex, of Gtwn, threw herself from Dodge's wharf into the Potomac & was drowned. What instigated this dreadful act we have been unable to ascertain. Coroner Woodward held an inquest over the body yesterday.

On Sat last a fire broke out in a frame dwlg belonging to Mr Solomon Drew, on the south side of Louisiana ave, between 6th & 7th sts. The roof was burnt & the house otherwise damaged. The property is insured.

Circuit Court of Wash Co, D C. Gustavus Hegdon has applied to be discharged from imprisonment under the act for the relief of Insolvent Debtors: hearing on Dec 5.
–Wm Brent, clk

Orphan's Court of Wash Co, D C. Letters testamentary on the personal estate of Thos B Johnson, late of said county, dec'd. –J O Adams

WED NOV 29, 1843
Furnished rooms to let: the subscriber has comfortable & well furnished apartments to let. Her house is on F st, between 13th & 14th sts. Terms moderate. –Mrs M Byrne

In the Criminal Court of New Orleans, Chas P A Lennon, found guilty of stealing a slave, was sentenced to 6 years of hard labor in the pen.

John W Rana convicted at Boston a few days since of robbing the Quincy stage of $4,000 belonging to the Quincy Bank, has been sentenced to 4 years' hard labor in the pen.

Died: on Mon, after a lingering illness, Benj Trott, artist. He was a native of Boston, & it was his proud boast that he had been the intimate friend of the celebrated Gilbert Stuart. He has died far from the land of his birth, but here he has found friends who can mourn over the fate of poor Trott. His funeral will take place today, at 1 o'clock, from Mr Clary's, on H st, between 10th & 11th sts.

Died: on Nov 18, at New Orleans, the Hon Armand Beauvois, in his 60th year.

Died: on Nov 1, at St Francisville, La, of yellow fever, Robt U Hyatt, of Louisiana Bar, in his 25th year. Mr Hyatt was a native of Wash, D C–a respectable Member of the Bar, & highly esteemed for many excellencies of private character.

Died: on Nov 20, at Washington, Pa, Mr Hugh Workman, at the advanced age of 85 years. He was the oldest citizen of that borough, having lived there uninterruptedly from 1777 to the time of his death, a period of near 66 years. He was a sldr of the Revolution, & served his country faithfully in the campaigns of McIntosh & Crawford.

Died: a fortnight since, at his residence in Somerset township, Pa, Mr Martin Barkhammer, sen, in his 86th year. The dec'd was a sldr of the Revolution, & had resided in the township in which he died, uninterruptedly, during a period of some 56 or 57 years.

Died: on Nov 22, in Queen Anne's Co, Md, the Hon Richd Tilghman Earle, formerly chief judge of the 2nd judicial district of Md, a post which he resigned several years ago on account of impaired health. His practice, before his elevation, was probably more extensive than that of any member of the profession at that time on the Eastern Shore. –Kent News

For sale: that well known farm, the property of Jas Greenlease, dec'd, lying in Loudoun Co, Va, bordering upon & in full view of the Leesburg & Snickers' Gap Turnpike Road, containing 295½ acs: improvements are a 2 story stone dwlg; large barns; corn & wagon-house, dairy, & all other necessary bldgs. –The Heirs

Trustee's sale of valuable real estate: virtue of a decree of Wash Co Court, as a Court of Equity: sale on Jan 3, on the premises, that fine farm, the late residence of Peter Miller, dec'd, in Pleasant Valley, Wash Co, Md, adjoining the tract of land called **Weaverton**, containing 237 acs of land: large brick dwlg, spring house & a dairy, a large Swisser bars, stabling, corn crib, blacksmith shop, & all other necessary out bldgs. Also, a smaller farm adjoining the above farm, containing 56 acs. Also, another valuable farm, adjoining the above, containing 180 acs: with a neat weather boarded dwlg, convenient to which are a good spring & stone dairy, a log barn, & smoke house. Also, a small farm adjoining the above, containing 53 acs; with a comfortable log dwlg, with stone basement. Also, another small farm bounded in part by the above, containing 80 acs; with a log dwlg, stable, & spring house. Also, will be offered, several half-acre lots, one mile from Harper's Ferry. -John Miller, trustee

The Hon Wm S Fulton, U S Senator from Arkansas, was dangerously ill at his residence in Little Rock at the last advices.

Col R M Johnson left Hagerstown for his home in the West on Fri morning.

Terrible fatalities at N Y; on Sat, an aged man, John Colbert ran suddenly from behind an omnibus & was knocked down by the horses to the railroad car, crushing his legs. They were amputated the same evening & he died the next morning. On Sun Edw Curry was run over by the train & died during the night.

NOTICE: by virtue of 2 writs of fieri facias, issued by Jas Marshall, a J P in & for Wash Co, D C, at the suits of Razious Arnold & Rebecca Bright, against the good, chattels, lands, & tenements of John G Berger, to me directed, I have seized & taken in execution all the right, title, & claim of said John G Berger, in & to a lot of oak wood, & I hereby

give notice that on Dec 5, 1843, in front of Jas Marshall's ofc, near the engine house, Navy Yard, I will off for sale the said propery so seized, by public auction.
—H R Maryman, cnstbl

Great Bargains-at C B Thornton's cheap cash store, west of Brown's Hotel: beaver cloths; cassimeres; cassinets; brocade; velvet; flannels, sheeting, plaids, & lace.
—C B Thornton

THU NOV 30, 1843
The Augsburg Gaz states, from Florence, Oct 10, that the Count de Survilliers [Jos Bonaparte] has recently had several attacks of apoplexy, & that fears were entertained for his life.

Kennebec Triumphant! The Hallowell [Maine] Cultivator announces that Mrs A F Trufant, of Winthrop, gave brith on Tue last, to two boys & one girl. Mother & children doing well.

Mr Edw Moody, of Springfield, a brakeman on the Western Railroad, was suddenly killed, on Wed week. In an unguarded moment, as the cars were going under the bridge, he probably stood up, & was knocked off between the cars. Mr Moody was aged 31, a man of good character, & has left an afflicted widow & one child to mourn their loss.

Madison [Indiana] Banner, of Nov 22, states that the most destructive fire which ever occurred at that place broke out on Nov 21 at Mr Payne's Pork Warehouse on West st, & 5 of the finest warehouses in the city, occupied by Mr T L Payne, E D Payne, Barber & Branham, & Washer & Wharton, were entirely destroyed.

The Hague, Oct 18. The ceremony of the baptism of the infant s/o his Royal Highness the Prince of Orange was solemnized today. The young Prince received the names of Wm Fred'k Maurice Alexandre Henry Charles.

Died: on Nov 29, at his residence, on Greenleaf's Point, in Wash City, John Wheat, in his 67th year. He was a kind husband & affectionate father, & with a firm reliance on Christ he left this world of sorrow for a better & happier home. His funeral is today at his late residence, at 12 o'clock.

Died: yesterday, Mr A G Tebbets, of Wash City, tavern keeper. The dec'd has left a numerous family to lament his loss. He was much respected by his friends & neighbors.

Died: on Sep 7 last, near Matagorda, Texas, Mr Henry C Slade, formerly a resident of Wash City. He was endeared to a large circle of relatives & friends during his life, the remembrance of which is embalmed in their hearts now that he is departed.

Two valuable houses at private sale: one on 13th st, between G & H sts, a 2 story brick house with 12 rooms; with stable, carriage-house, & wood-house, attached. Also, the frame house called "the *Cottage*," on the corner of 14th st west & L st north: with milk-house, wash-house, wood-house, & stable. It contains 10 rooms. For further particulars inquire at the Cottage, or of Jas A Kennedy.

Lots for sale: lots 14 & 15 in square 127, on 18th st, between H & I sts, & may be divided into 5 good lots. Lots 10 in square 142, fronts on G st, between 18th & 19th sts. Several handsome bldgs have erected this season. The subscriber will sell these lots on favorable terms. –J Guest, N Y ave, near 14th st

NOTICE. By virtue of 2 writs of fieri facias, issued by John H Goddard, a J P for Wash Co, D C, at the suit of J Fugitt & Co, against the goods, chattels, lands, & tenements, rights & credits of John Bush, Jas Grimes, Wm Bush, & Patrick Goings, & to me directed, I have seized & taken in execution all the right, title, claim, & interest of the said Bush, Grimes, Bush, & Goings, in & to one hackney carriage, & on Dec 2, on the green opposite the center Market-house, I will offer for sale the said hackney carriage, so seized & taken in execution, [if not redeemed] by public auction. –S Moore, constable

Alexandria Criminal Court-Nov 29. Sentences passed by Judge Dunlop on the following who had been tried & found guilty. 1-Caleb Bladen, for larcenies & burglaries: 14 years in the pen of D C. 2-Albert Mortimer, for larcenies & burglaries: 14 years in the pen. 3-Sarah Marstin, larceny: 18 months in the pen. 4-Jas Tate, larceny: 2 years in the pen. 5-Jas Thomas, larceny: 3 years in the pen. 6-John Carr, larceny: 1 year in the pen. 7-Chas Richardson, larceny: 18 months in the pen. 8-Geo Parrish, larceny: 2 years in the pen.

The installation service of the Rev Wm T Sprole, Pastor elect of the First Presbyterian Church, took place on last Mon. Sermon was by Rev Dr Dewitt, of Harrisburg. The Rev Chas Rich, late much-loved Pastor of this people, was obliged due to ill health to relinquish the charge.

Wash Corp: An act for the relief of C F Zackman, that the fine imposed on him for a violation of the law in relation to hogstyes, be & the same is hereby remitted, provided he pay the costs of prosecution.

FRI DEC 1, 1843
A beautiful monument to the memory of Cmder Ralph Voorhees, of the U S Navy, has been erected in the burying ground of New Haven by "the ofcrs & crew of the U S ship **Preble**, in testimony of their respect."

Mr Peleg Noyes, of Albany, N Y, whose mysterious disappearance some days since caused much anxiety, has been heard from, by a letter, postmarked New Orleans, Nov 17. He states that a friend invited him to go with him as far as the Narrows, in a ship bound to New Orleans. He complied, but he remained too long in the cabin, & when he came on deck he found the steamboat he was going to take back, had left. He was forced to make the whole voyage. He will return as soon as he can accumulate the means to do so.

Bangor Gaz ofc, dated Sat, states that a large English ship went ashore at Gouldsborough on the Tue previous: 22 persons were on board, 18 of whom were lost. The four who were saved report that at the time of the disaster the capt, ofcrs & crew were all drunk; that they saved themselves. The ship was the barque **Caroline**, of Greenock, & was from Granada bound to St Johns, N B. Lost: John Crawford, master; Matthew Daugle, 1st ofcr; David Pettycrew, 2nd ofcr; John Payne, carpenter; John Spendlow, boatswain; John Sinclair, Hugh Card, Chas Green, Wm Williams, Jos Roberts, David Griffiths, John Nelson, John Imanuel, John Scot, & John Wilson, seamen; Edw Wilson, cook; Chas Steward & John Jemison, apprentices. Saved: Fred'k Smith, Wm Moore, & Francis Williamson, seamen; Geo Williams, steward

Watterston's New Guide to Washington: strangers visiting this city will find this little volume of great use. The following is an extract in relation to our Navy. At the commencement of the Revolutionary war there was not a single armed vessel belonging to any of the Colonists. In 1775 Rhode Island fitted 2 small schnrs to defend the coasting trade, & Connecticut had 2 small vessels. In the spring of 1776 Massachusetts fitted out several armed vessels, the flage of which bore a figure of the pine tree, & the motto "Appeal to Heaven," which is thought to be the old Colonial flag. The first naval battle took place about 3 weeks after the battle of Lexington. A British schnr, with four 6 pounders & swivels, with 2 sloops, was attacked by about 30 young men, commanded by Capt O'Brien & Jos Wheaton, & captured, & all on board made prisoners. Wheaton had the honor of being the first to pull down the enemy's flag. In Dec, 1775, Congress commissioned several other vessels, amounting to 13. And thus commenced our gallant navy, which now consists of 11 ships of line, 74 & 120 guns; 1 ship razeed, 54 guns; 14 frigs first class, 44 guns; 2 frigs second class, 36 guns; 18 sloops of war, 16 to 20 guns; 8 brigs of war, 10 guns; 3 receiving vessels, & 5 small schnrs, making in all 71 vessels. There are 2 dry docks, one at Norfolk & one at Charlestown, constructed of hewn granite. The former cost $872,220 & the latter $652,482. The above work is for sale at R Farnham's Bookstore, 11th & Pa ave, where can also be had a few copies of the last edition of Mr Watterston's Gallery of American Portraits.

Alfred Schucking will give instruction to a select class of gentlemen in the German Language & Literature. Apply to him at his residence on E st, between 9th & 10th sts, between the hours of 3 & 7.

Benj Groves, s/o Mr Henry Groves, came to his death by suffocation, on board the ship **Emerald**, lying in the dock at New Bedford, Mass, on Sun. The ship was "smoking out," by means of sulphur & charcoal, to destroy rats. Groves died from the noxious gases which filled every part of the vessel. -Register

Mr Dominic Von Malder, of Nova Scotia, received information lately that he had become entitled to a fortune of L17,000 per annum by the decease of a relative in Europe. Mr Von Malder earned his livelihood as a journeyman printer.

Died: on Nov 30, Mrs Tabitha Lambright, in her 63rd year. For more than 35 years the dec'd sustained the character of a pious & devoted member of the Methodist Episcopal Church. Her funeral will be held today, at 3 o'clock, from the residence of her son-in-law, John C Harkness, on N Y ave, between 9th & 10th sts.

Circuit Court of Wash Co, D C, Nov Term, 1843. In Chancery. Juliana Williamson & others vs Geo W Williamson & others. Chas A Williamson, the trustee in the above cause, having reported the following sales, made pursuant to the decree, to wit:
Lot #1, being a ground rent of $77.50 per annum, secured upon 53 feet front, part of lot #22, on High st, in Beatty & Hawkins addition to Gtwn, to Mrs Ann H Hyde for $580.
Lot #2, being a rent of $30, secured upon 30 feet front, part of lot #13, in same addition, to Benj S Bohrer for $220.
Lot #3, being a rent of $27.50, secured upon 26 feet front, part of lots #127 & 128, to Henry Kengla for $265.
Lot #4, being a rent of $22, secured upon 22 feet front, other part of same lots, to Henry G Wilson for $175.
Lot #5, being a rent of $40.50, secured upon 36 feet 9 inches front, other part of same lots, to Henry Kengla for $405. And further part of the same lots adjoining the last lot on the north & fronting 16 feet 18 inches, to Henry Kengla for $118.25.
Lot #6, being a rent of $51.70, secured upon 47 feet front, part of lot #157, in said addition, to Geo A Bohrer for $517.
Lot #7, being a rent of $19.80, secured upon 18 feet front, part of the last lot, to Henry Kengla for $155.
Lot #8, being part of said lot 157, fronting 46 feet, with the frame tenements thereon, to Geo A Bohrer for $400.
Lot #9, being part of lot #19, fronting 25 feet on High st, to Noble Hurdle for $225.
Lot #10, being lots #6 & 7, in square 291, in Wash City, with the brick house thereon, to Dr Thos Lawson for $4,300.
And the said trustees having further reported that all the said purchasers had complied with the terms of sale, & that Ann B Hyde & Geo A Bohrer had paid to him the full amount of their respective purchase moneys. –Wm Brent, clk

Mrd: on Tue last, by Rev Mr Pinkney, Mr Jedadiah Gettings, of Montg Co, Md, to Miss Ann Virginia, 2nd d/o Robt Clarke, of PG Co, Md.

Mrd: on the 23rd ult, in St Paul's Church, by the Bishop of New Jersey, Capt Edmund Schriver, Assist Adj Genr'l of the Army, to Harriette Louise, only d/o the late Nathan Warren, of Wash City.

Public sale: on Jan 3, 1844, by virtue of a deed of trust to the subscriber, dated Jun 3, 1841: sale of lot 4 in square 317 in Wash, with the dwlg house & bakery thereon.
–David P Shoemaker

SAT DEC 2, 1843
Jas A B Watson, charged with being concerned in the great robbery of Treas notes in the Custom-house at New Orleans, by the decision of the Circuit Court of Wash Co, D C, will be conveyed in the custody of Jas O'Neil, Deputy Marshal for the eastern district of Pa, to New Orleans, to depart today.

The Greenville [S C] Mountaineer says: we were informed that there is a man living in the neighboring mountains of N C, by the name of Blackwell, who has reached the age of 136 years. At the time of Braddock's defeat, he was about 45 years old, & had a wife & 5 children. He enjoys good health & is quite active, frequently galloping his horse several miles. He has outlived several wives, & the one he has now has been his partner for some years; but he remarks that he expects to survive her, & marry another.

Died: on Jul 18 last, at his residence in Clermont Co, Ohio, [Judge] Ambrose Ransone. He was born in Cumberland Co, Va, Jul 12, 1765, emigrated to Ohio [then Northwestern Terriroty] in 1798. With his own hands he assisted in laying the corner stone of the great commonwealth of Ohio, & contributed in the forming of the character of the people of the Miami Co. He was a member of the first court organized in his county. In his youth he was associated with Patrick Henry, Wythe, & others, fathers of the great Republic.

Situations wanted, by a Cook & Coachman, who come well recommended by their last employers; also, each can give city references. Apply to John Donovan, next to the Railroad Depot.

NOTICE: is given to all interested that the subscribers will meet at the residence of the late Thos Scott, in Montg Co, on the first Mon of Feb next, at 11 o'clock, & proceed to lay off the widow's dower in the real estate of said dec'd, & divide the residue thereof among the heirs of said dec'd, according to the directions of a commission issued out of Montg Co Court at the instance of Oratio Clagett & others.
–E Gatton, T S Watkins, & B Willett

MON DEC 4, 1843
Beef of superior quality may be procured at the subscriber's Stall, Centre Market, at the low price of 6 cents per lb. Cone, one & all, give me a call. –P Crowley

Union Hotel, Gtwn: subscriber had taken possession of the above house: thoroughly repaired & the rooms are furnished with new beds, bedding, & furniture; the bar supplied with the choicest Liquors & Wines, at moderate prices. –Chas Gordon [Also to let, my house on I st, near the residence of Mrs [Gen] Macomb. The house is large & in Wash City. –Chas Gordon]

Matthew Nelson, of Monroe Co, has been elected Treas of the State of Tenn for 2 years from the expiration of the term of the present incumbent.

Metropolitan Hotels: Boulanger's Hotel, on the south isde of Pa ave, nearly in front of the National Hotel, is a very respectable establishment. Mr Boulanger is well known as an old citizen & hotel keeper. Maher's [Globe] Hotel, also on the south side of Pa ave, opposite the National Theatre, is a very good house & well kept. Mrs Maher keeps an excellent table, & is highly spoken of for the attention which she uniformly pays to her numerous guests & boarders. There are many other smaller but very respectable hotels & taverns, kept by Messrs Sweeting, Butler, Gannon, King & Hall, De Saule, Moran, Thomas, Connolly, Baker, McGrath, & others. The Union Hotel, of Gtwn, lately fitted up in very superior style, by Mr Chas Gordon, is an excellent & spacious establishment. It contains about 80 rooms, has a large dining room & splendid ball room. Mrs Lang also keeps a very good house in Gtwn.

Police Intelligence: on Thu last 2 warrants were issued against John Bush, charging him with stealing slaves the property of Mr W J McDonald & Mrs Young of Wash City. He is now bound in 3 cases in the sum of $500 each. On the same day, Geo Slatford was arrested under the charge of having 4 times fired a double-barrelled gun among a party of colored persons who were assembled at a dance in a house on Camp Hill, in the First Ward of Wash City. Several of the colored persons were severely wounded in the firing. The prisoner not having found the required bail, was committed by the justice for trial at the next Court.

For rent, the Brick House which I have nearly completed on the corner of 6th st & Louisiana ave: contains 9 rooms, including garrets, with a kitchen. Inquire of S Drew, or G & T Parker, opposite the Centre Market.

The dwlg of Basil D Mullikin, in PG Co, Md, was destroyed by fire on Fri night last. Loss $5,000-no insurance.

Mrs Bradford, w/o David Bradford, drowned herself on Sun last in the forge pond in Plymouth, Mass. Her husband observed her shoes upon the bank of the pond, & in a moment after her lifeless body rose to the surface of the water.

An action was brought in the U S Circuit Court at N Y, on Tue last, by Wm Wm E Millet against Mr Wm W Snowden, editor of the Ladies' Companion, to recover the penalty of $1 per sheet for violation of the plntf's copyright of a musical composition. The Jury rendered a verdict in his favor of $625.

At the recent session of the Oyer & Terminer, held at White Plains, N Y: 1-Henry Townsend was convicted of an assault with intent to kill the Rev Mr Dickinson. He was one of a party that attacked the house of Mr Dickinson, in revenge for a complaint before the Court of Sessions which he had made against them. He was sentenced to the State prison for 4½ years. 2-Jas Knapp was convicted of arson in the 3rd degree for setting fire to the jail on Nov 14, with a view to escape. He was sentenced for 9 years.

Albany papers: two ofcrs of that city, Jas H Burnham, a city constable, & Edw Guthrage, a private watchman, have been arrested, charged with the commission of a number of burglaries.

Wash Corp: 1-Ptn of Jas Dixon: referred to the Cmte of Claims. 2-Ptn of Jas Laurie & others, praying the opening of an alley in square 226: referred to the Cmte on Improvements. 3-Ptn of Wm W Moore & others, praying for certain flag footways in the Third Ward: referred to the Cmte on Improvements. 4-Cmte of Claims reported a bill for the relief of Nicholas Ferreton: which was read twice.

Valuable lot for sale: lot 3 in square 374, on H st west of 9th, & lying between the residences of Messrs Straham & Duncanson. Apply to Rev Thos M Flint, at Mrs W W Billings', corner of 14th & L sts.

C G Seippel, from Germany, now a resident citizen of the U S, informs that he has located himself in Wash City for the purpose of excercising Hydrophatic or Water Cure, according to the system of the famous Vincent Priessnitz at Grafenberg.

House on C st for sale, & a house for rent. The house lately occupied by Rev Chas Rich, on C st, near 3rd, is offered at private sale. The house lately occupied by the subscriber is for rent. Inquire of D A Hall.

For rent, the large house & grounds attached, the former residence of Col Bomford, on I st west, near the dwlg of the Hon Danl Webster. Also for rent, the house & lot, late the residence of Dr Lawson, Surgeon Genr'l of the U S Army, nearly opposite the Navy Dept. Inquire of Jas Carrick.

TUE DEC 5, 1843
Jas A Ratcliff, a bankrupt, has filed his ptn for his discharge & certificate: hearing on Feb 19, before the Circuit Court of the U S for D C, sitting in Bankruptcy. –Wm Brent, clk

Land for sale: by virtue of a decree of Chas Co Court, sitting as a Court of Equity: sale at public auction, at *Hill Top*, on Dec 28, all the lands of the late Middleton Garrett & Catharine Garrett, dec'd, containing 350 acs more or less: situated near Durham Parish Church, Chas Co, Md. Improvements: a comfortable dwlg, kitchen, corn-house, barn, & stables. –Frs E Dunnington, Trustee

Mrd: on Nov 30, at N Y, by Rev Dr Anthon, Jos B Varnum, jr, to Susan M, d/o the late N B Graham, all of that city.

Mrd: on the 30th ult, by Rev Wm N Ward, John Hooff, Cashier of the Farmers' Bank of Alexandria, to Martha J, 2nd d/o the late Samson Blincoe, of Leesburg, Va.

Mrd: on Nov 30, in Wash City, by Rev Mr Biewend, Mr Paul Kinchy to Miss Magdalene Hitz, both fom Switzerland, but for many years residents of Wash.

Died: on Nov 22, in Lexington, Va, after a long & painful illness, in her 70th year, Mrs Mgt R Chapin, wid/o the late Gurden Chapin, of Alexandria. Mrs Chapin was a native of Chas Co, Md, but in early life removed to Alexandria, where nearly 40 years ago she united herself with the Episcopal church, of which she continued a member until her death.

Died: on Nov 16, suddenly of apoplexy, in King George Co, Va, Dr Lawrence T Dade, the brother of the gallant Major who perished in Florida.

Died: on Nov 11, at Clay Hill, the residence of her son-in-law, Francis B Whiting, Mrs Lucy Burwell, relict of the late Col Nathl Burwell, of Carter Hall, in Clarke Co, Va, at the advanced age of 84 years.

Died: on Nov 20, at Newbern, N C, Mr Robt G Moore, for many years past an instructor of youth in that town, & formerly joint proprietor & editor of the Newbern Spectator.

Died: on Dec 4, in Wash City, at the residence of T F Semmes, Mary Eugenia, in her 12th year, 2nd d/o Dr B J & Emily Semmes, of Piscataway, PG Co, Md.

WED DEC 6, 1843
The Canal which connects the town of Alexandria with the *C & O Canal* at Gtwn was formally opened on Sat. On Jul 4, 1831, the first spadeful of earth on the canal was thrown up, & on Dec 2, 1843, the first canal boat reached town. The locks bringing the canal into the river are now in the course of construction, & will be finished next year. The day has at last arrived when the canal boats could float across the Potomac, over a splendid & permanent aqueduct, & be brought to Alexandria along a canal 7 miles long.

Mrd: on Nov 28, by Rev Mr Stringfellow, Mr Lewis Thomas to Miss Margaret Lewis, all of Wash City.

Mrd: on Dec 4, by Rev Chas A Davis, Mr Chas W Pettit to Miss Gertrude Croggon, both of Wash City.

Mrd: on Dec 3, by Rev Mr Edwards, Mr Fred'k P Sioussa to Miss Harriet L Sloan, both of Wash City.

House in 9th st for rent: four 2 story basement houses at 9th & L sts. –Jas Mankin, 9th, between H & I sts.

The Sisters of St Vincent's Orphan Asylum & the Ladies of the Board of Managers present their sincere thanks to Mr C B King for a most excellent portrait of the Very Rev Fr Matthews, the benevolent founder & patron of the Institution. By order of the Board: Janet M C Riggs, Sec.

To the Ladies: for sale at Mr McKean's, upstairs, formerly Mrs Ronckendorf's, on Pa ave, between 6th & 4½ sts, a large assortment of goods from Madame Payon's, Phil. –Rachael Jackson

Wash Corp: 1-Cmte of Claims asked to be discharged from the consideration of the ptn of David S Waters: they were discharged accordingly. 2-The cmte to which the ptn of Jas Fossett was referred, reported a resolution in relation to a billiard license to Jas Fossett: on the third reading it was decided in the negative. 4-Cmte of Claims, to whom was referred the ptn of Wm & Hiram Jennings, asked to be discharged from its further consideration. 5-Bill for the relief of Nicholas Ferreton was taken up & passed.

Circuit Court of Wash Co, D C. Thos J Fletcher has applied to be discharged from imprisonment under the act for the relief of Insolvent Debtors: hearing on Dec 12. –Wm Brent, clk

Orphan's Court of Wash Co, D C. Letters of adm on the personal estate of Jas N Tubman, late of said county, dec'd. –Mary E Wilmer, John H Bayne, adms

THU DEC 7, 1843
Superior Beef & Mutton: at the Centre Market, first stall in the old market, next the Engine house. -Henry Walker, Victualler

Willard Hawes, a respectable citizen of Genesee Co, N Y, was found dead, with his head & face frozen into a pool of mud & water, in the road near Warsaw, a short time since. He was subject to fits, & while returning from the house of a neighbor is supposed to have been attacked by one.

On Nov 28, Mr Sands Furman, a farmer & estimable citizen of Nichols, Owego Co, N Y, met almost instant death by falling through a trap door in the store of Messrs L Turman & Brothers, Owego, striking his head against the stone wall in his descent, & thence falling to the bottom of the cellar.

Died: on Dec 6, of scarlet fever, after a short illness, Lewis Benjamin, infant s/o Eliz & Jas S Hall. His funeral will be from his residence on Pa ave, at 11 o'clock this morning.

Trustee's sale: on Jan 5, at public auction, by a deed from Duff Green, dated Aug 11, 1835, all that piece of land in Wash City, D C, being part of square 377; upon this property there are 4 dwlg houses, all in good order & under reasonable rent to good tenants. The whole must be sold together. –A Coyle, Trustee
-Robt W Dyer & Co, aucts

Gen Santa Anna re-elected Pres of the Republic. He lately visited Vera Cruz & remained there a week.

Valuable estate for sale: the subscriber's plantation known as *Bowieville*, in PG Co, containing 754 acs of land: the dwlg built at great cost & out of the best materials, stands on a commanding eminence, overlooking a beautiful country. This plantation lies in the region known as the *"Forest of Prince George's."* -Robt Bowie, Good Luck P O, PG Co, Md

FRI DEC 8, 1843

Circuit Court of Wash Co, D C. Benj Thompson has applied to be discharged from imprisonment under the act for the relief of Insolvent Debtors: hearing on the first Mon in Jan. –Wm Brent, clk

Noble Charity: Wm Appleton, of Boston, has placed in the hands of the Trustees of the Massachusetts Genr'l Hospital $10,000, the income of which is to be applied in aiding such patients in the McLean Asylum for the Insane, as, from straitened means, might be compelled to leave the institution without a perfect cure. –Mercantile Journal

Johnathan Wheeler, of Grafton, in this State, a highly respectable citizen of that town, committed suicide on Sat last by hanging himself in his own granary. He was nearly 78 years old. He had no children.
–Boston Atlas

The trial of Capt Nicholson, of the Harkaway, which has been in progress for several days in the Federal Court, resulted in his acquittal. Public opinion had pronounced his innocence of the criminal violence charged long before the verdict of the Jury was announced. –Richmond Whig

Thos Taylor, s/o Mr Francis Taylor, residing at Goochland Court-house, Va, met with a most melancholy accident on Nov 15, which caused his death on the Fri following. He was accidentally shot while turkey-hunting with a party engaged in pursuit of game.

The Hse/o Reps: completed its organization yesterday by electing Newton Lane to be Sergeant-at Arms; Jesse E Dow to be Door-keeper; & Blair & Rives to be Printers to the House.

Sailing of Missionaries. The Rev T D Hunt & lady, Rev E Whittlesey & lady, Rev C D Andrews, Rev John F Prague & Miss Whitney, from the American Board of Com'rs for Foreign Missions, sailed from Boston on Mon last for the Sandwich & Society Islands.

Died: on Dec 6, at his residence in Gtwn, D C, Lt Alex'r H Marbury, of the U S Navy, in his 36th year, after a short & severe illness. His funeral is today, from his late residence, on West st, Gtwn, at 3 p m.

Circuit Court, Dec 7. 1-The case of the U S vs Justice Mattingly, convicted in the Criminal Court of taking illegal fees, to hear the argument in favor of a new trial on Dec 16. 2-In the case of the U S vs W S Wright, convicted at the Criminal Court of obtaining money from Edw Dyer under the false pretence that he was the brother of Hon Silas Wright, U S Senator from N Y, the Court agreed to pospone their decision on the motion for a new trial.

SAT DEC 9, 1843
The Potomac Dragoons state that their Sixth Annual Ball will take place at the Pomplan Hall, Union Hotel, Gtwn, on Dec 26. Tickets $2: to be had in Gtwn at the different drug stores; in Washington at the drug stores of Fauquhar & Morgan, 1st Ward; at Patterson's, 9th & Pa ave; at J P McKean's, near Gadsby's Hotel, & at Mr C Neal's Hotel, Navy Yard. –Sergeants Cunningham, Miller, Moxley, Cpt Knott, & Private Newman, Cmte

Household furniture at auction: by order of the Orphan's Court of Wash Co, D C, all the effects of Augustine G Tebbets, dec'd, at his late residence on Louisiana ave, adjoining the Assembly Rooms. Also, the bar, counter, & fixtures of the establishment. The furniture is nearly new. –Hannah Tebbets, admx -Wm Marshall, Auctioneer

Female teacher wanted: to take charge of a small female school & teach the usual branches of an English education, French, & music on the piano. Salary is $300 & board. All communications, post paid, addressed to the subscribers at Scotland Neck, Halifax Co, N C, will be attended to. –Whitmel J Hill, Whitmel H Anthony

Land for sale: decree of the Circuit Superior Court of Law & Chancery for Loudoun Co, rendered on Sep 25, 1843, in the suit of Walter Smith, surviving partner of Clement Smith, against Jas L McKenna & others: sale on Feb 12, 1844, of the tract of land in said decree mentioned. It lies in Loudoun Co, by the lands of Mrs Muse, Wm Greenlease, & Dr Geo Lee. It contains about 2,000 acs: has upon it 5 dwlg houses, with the usual out-houses & stabling. –B W Harrison, John Janney, Com'rs

Trustee's sale of very valuable land in Westmoreland Co: by deed of trust executed by Henry Hazel & wife, dated Jun 10, 1841, for the purpose of securing a debt therein mentioned, due to John P Mastin: sale on Jan 6, 1844, of a certain tract of land in said county, containing 1,142 acs one rood & 28 poles. The title to this tract is unquestionable. –John P Davis, trustee

NOTICE: by virtue of a writ of fieri facias, issued by Wm Thompson, a J P for Wash Co, D C, I shall expose to public sale, on Dec 16, 1843, in Wash City, the following goods & chattels, to wit: 8 brooms, 4 large stone jugs, 3 Demijohns, 1 barrel of bottles, 1 barrel of cider, 2 empty barrels, 1 box of soap, 1 box of candles, 1 box of mustard, 1 box tea, part of a box of prunes, 3 show glasses, 18 pieces of crockery ware, 2 doz stockings, 6 pair of suspenders, 1 lot of tobacco, 10 pair scissors, needles, pins, buttons, tapes, nails, & 2 glass lamps: seized & taken as the property of John D Inbrod, & will be sold to satisfy a judgment in favor of Semmes & Murray. –R R Burr, Constable

Meeting of the Friends of the Lord's Day, held in Balt, Nov 16, 1843. Cmte: B Kurtz, A M Carter, R J Breckinridge, J G Hamner, E J Richardson, F Israel, T E Bond, jr

$50 reward for runaway negro boy Henson Noaks, 22 or 23 years of age, who ranaway from the canal, in Wash City. Address me, at Occoquan Post Ofc, Prince Wm County, Va. –Redmond Selecman

The Army.
Dragoons-The resignation of 2nd Lt Chas F Ruff has been accepted, to take effect on Dec 31, 1843.
Rifles-Resignation of 2nd Lt Bayard Clarke accepted, to take effect Dec 15, 1843.
2nd Artl-Maj J Erving transferred from the 3rd to the 2nd Artl, & assigned to duty in N Y harbor.
3rd Artl-Maj W L McClintock transferred from the 2nd to the 3rd Artl.
The following promotions have been made, to fill the vacancy occasioned by the death of Capt E Lyon:
1st Lt John A Thomas to be Capt
2nd Lt Stewart Van Vliet to be 1st Lt
Brvt 2nd Lt R W Johnson to be 2nd Lt

Died: on Dec 7, in her 17th year, of consumption, Caroline Shoemaker, only d/o the late David Shoemaker, of the Genr'l Land Ofc. Her funeral will be at the residence of her uncle, Abner E Peirce, on Rock Creek, on Sat at half past 2 o'clock.

Died: on Nov 17, Mr Thos A Wyatt, a resident of the neighborhood of Walnut Grove, Kanawha Co, Va, in his 33rd year. The dec'd was an honest, truthful, &, in every sense of the word, a most respectable man. He was a good son, a good brother, a most humane master, & had been from his youth the main stay of his father's family.

Died: on Dec 3, suddenly of croup, Robt Goldsborough, aged 1 year & 1 month, s/o T J & H Dorsett, of Anne Arundel Co, Md.

MON DEC 11, 1843

Balt, Dec 9. A short time back Henry Linker arrived in this city from Ohio, from whence he had fled to escape a love affair in which he was involved. Information of that fact having been forwarded to this city, he was arrested upon a charge of breach of promise, &, in default of security, was committed to jail. The deluded object of his plighted vows- she to whom he had knelt in moments of impassioned love, & swore fidelity, also arrived in this city a few days since, & was yesterday joined in the holy bands of matrimony within the prison walls of our county jail. -Clipper

The Cherokee Council has provided by law for the publication of a newspaper to be called the "Cherokee Advocate," to be printed in the English & Cherokee languages. Mr Wm Ross will be the editor.

Tragedy occurred in Chenango township, Beaver Co, Pa, on Thu week, which resulted in the death of Mr Saml Wilkinson, for many years a resident of that township. Mr Rutter, constable of Slipperyrock township, had an execution against dec'd, & was accompanied to his residence by a young man, Irvin, as agent for the plntf, to show property upon which to levy. Irvin pointed out a colt, which the constable attempted to take into possession, but was resisted by a son of dec'd, who claimed it as his property, & between them a scuffle ensued. Irvin going to the assistance of the constable, was caught by the dec'd, whom he immediately stabbed in the left breast with a pocket knife, causing his death in 10 to 15 minutes. Irvin is in prison, & will probably have his trial at the Mar term. –Beaver Argus

Bowling Saloon: fashionable & healthy amusement: bldg is on Missouri ave, near 6th st. –John M Farrar

Wm Wilson was convicted last Aug before the Hartford Conn County court of the crime of incest. The charge was founded on the fact that he had married the dght of his dec'd wife by a former husband-the same being, as charged by the judge, in violation of the law; & the jury returned a verdict accordingly. The case was carried to the Supreme Court, where the decision of the lower court was since reversed, the court deciding that the affinity between the plntf in error & his wife's dght ceased on the death of his wife.

To all gentlemen in want of good, cheap, fashionable, & substantial articles for their own use. –Jos H Daniels, regular Merchant Tailor, a few door west of Brown's Hotel, Pa ave. [I was bred a tailor.]

Cow Lost. $30 reward for the return of the cow to the stable from which she was taken, or on her delivery at my farm, near Beltsville Post Ofc, Md. –Thos T Hunter

$15 reward for runaway negro man Chas Cole, about 60 years of age. I will give the above reward if delivered at my residence, **Mount Juliet**, D C. –Chas Scrivner

Died: on Sat, aged 45, John Kincart, a native of Comonaghan, Ireland. The members of the Wash Benevolent Society, of which the dec'd was a member, are to meet at their hall on G st, this afternoon, at 2 p m, to attend his funeral.

TUE DEC 12, 1843
The Duke of Sutherland gave his dght a dowry of 80,000l on her marriage with Lord Blantyre.

Died: on Nov 23, at his residence, in Fauquier Co, Va, Mr Thos Fitzhugh, in his 82nd year. He was an old & highly respected citizen, & was at the time of his death, & had been for many years before, the presiding Justice of the Court of his county. He has left a very large number of relations, connexions, & friends to cherish & respect the memory of his many virtues.

Died: on Oct 6, 1843, at the residence of his Aunt Lynn's, near Aldie, Va, Mr Jas C Williams. He was the s/o Notley C & Frances D Williams, then of Loudoun Co, Va. He was a dutiful son & much endeared to his parents, & brothers & sisters. He was a student at Augusta College, Ky, where he obtained his degreeof A M, & afterwards for several years held a professorship at St Chas College, Missouri. Having private business to attend to in Va, he resigned his seat at the college & went to Va, in Oct 1842, for that purpose, & intended soon to have returned to his father's in Missouri, but in the latter part of Aug last he contracted a severe cold, which settled on his lungs, from which he never recovered.

Died: on Dec 6, of scarlet fever, Jaried Bagan, aged 10 years & 2 months.

WED DEC 13, 1843
Valuable lot & warehouse at public auction: sale on Dec 16, on the premises, an undivided moiety of the lot at the corner of 7th & B sts, on square 461, on which is erected a warehouse, fronting on the canal. –Rd Smith, Jno A Smith, Excs of the late Dr H Hunt. -Robt W Dyer & Co, aucts

Senate: 1-Deepest regret of the death of the late Senator Linn, who died on Oct 3 last, at age 48 years. He laid down to sleep & awoke no more. It took place in his own house, & his unconscious remains were surrounded by his family & friends. Lewis Field Linn was born in Ky in 1795, in the vicinity of Louisville. His grandfather was Col Wm Linn, one of the favorite ofcrs of Gen Geo Rogers Clark. At age of 11 he had fought in the ranks of men, in the defence of a station in Western Pa, & was seen to deliver a deliberate & effective fire. He was one of the first to navigate the Ohio & Mississippi from Pittsburg to New Orleans & back again, in 1776*. He was killed by the Indians at an early period, leaving a family of young children, of whom the worthy Col Wm Pope [f/o Govn'r Pope,] became the guardian. The father of Senator Linn was among these children; &, at an early age, with 3 other boys, was taken prisoner by the Shawnee Indians, carried off, & detained captive for 3 years, when all 4 made their escape & returned home, by killing their guard. The mother of Senator Linn was a Pennsylvanian by birth, her maiden name Hunter, born at Carlisle. Tradition preserves the recollection of her courage at Fort Jefferson, at the Iron Banks, in 1781, when the Indians attacked & were repulsed from that post. The father of Senator Linn died young, leaving this son but 11 years of age. At an early age he was qualified for the practice of medicine, & commenced it in the then Territory, now State, of Missouri. He was called into political field by an election to the Senate of his adopted State. Among his private virtues, the love which he bore to that brother, the half-brother only-who, only 13 years older than himself, had been to him the tenderest of fathers. For 29 years I had known the depth of that affection. He had traveled a thousand miles out of his way to see that brother; & his name was still the dearest theme of his conversation. *The next effort at this perilous navigation was made by Cols Gibson & Linn, the latter the grandfather of the present Dr Linn, of St Louis, now in the U S Senate from Missouri. John Smith, now or lately of Woodford Co, in this State, was, in 1776, engaged in reconnoitering this country, with Jas Harrod, so eminently distinguished in the history of Ky difficulties & dangers. –Butler's History of Ky, Pages 155-56.

Wash Co, D C. I certify that Wm Smith, 8th st, Wash, brought before me a stray gray gelding. -B K Morsell, J P

Furniture at auction at the Navy Yard: on Tue next, at the residence of Mrs Queen, nearly opposite the Anacostia Engine-house, Navy Yard, her household & kitchen furniture. -Robt W Dyer & Co, aucts

Circuit Court of Wash Co, D C. Peyton Collier has applied to be discharged from imprisonment under the act for the relief of Insolvent Debtors: hearing on Dec 19. –Wm Brent, clk

In Eliz City, N C, Mrs Jane Saunders, w/o Mr T Saunders, was burnt to death, from grease falling on the hearth & taking fire, while she was preparing breakfast; the flame communicated to her dress. She died in 24 hours.

Martha Butler, colored, late an inmate of the workhouse, was found dead the day before on old Bladensburg road, near the farm of Mr Enoch Tucker. It appeared she died from exposure to the cold.

Wash Corp: 1-Ptns from Geo T McGlue, praying remission of fines: referred to the Cmte of Claims. 2-Bill for the relief of Wm Cunningham: passed.

Mr Alfred B Norton, hospital steward at Fort Pike, La, came to an untimely death on Nov 10, while out on an excursion for game. Having killed a duck, he waded out to recover it, & was drowned.

Six persons found guilty a few days since in the Qrtr Sessions of Columbia Co, Pa, for conspiring together & destroying property belonging to 3 citizens of that county. They cut off the tails of 2 horses belonging to Abraham Labor, tore down & destroyed the dwlg house of Philip Dodder, & cut down 23 apple trees, the property of Andrew Crivelin. Their names are Wm McHenry, Henry J Yable, Thos Yable, Alex'r Yable, Jeremiah Yable, & Cyrus Fox. Each were fined $1 and costs with Henry J Yable also to serve at hard labor in the Eastern Penitentiary at Phil for 18 months. Thos Yable to serve 17 months; Jeremiah Yable to serve 16 months; Cyrus Fox to serve 19 months; Wm McHenry to serve 18 months. Alex'r Yable to serve 6 months in the county jail.

Died: on Tue, in Gtwn, Helen Maria, d/o Cmdor Chas Morris. Her funeral will be on Thu at 2 o'clock.

Great Temperance Mass Meeting on Dec 14, at the Methodist Protestant Church, on 9th st. Jas Hoban, Henry J Drayton, & R M Harrison will address the audience.
–Edmund Brooke, John C Harkness, J L Henshaw, cmte

THU DEC 14, 1843
Having engaged as a Tutor for my own children a gentleman who is eminently qualified to be an instructor of youth, I have determined to take into my family a few boarders. References may be made to the Rt Rev Wm Meade, the Rev Wm G H Jones, Millwood, Clarke Co, Va; the Rev Alex Shinas, Berryville, & the Rev Wm Williamson, Warrenton, Va. All letters addressed to these gentlemen must be post paid. –J A Williamson, Janeville, near Berryville, Clarke Co, Va

To let: large frame house containing 9 rooms, on the corner of 8th & E sts. Inquire of Jas A Williams, on 5th, between H & I sts.

I have bought the splendid room on the corner of 4½ & Pa ave, formerly Fossett's Billard Room, & wish to make it known to my friends & public that I have opened it for the amusement of those who feel disposed to give me a call. –John Waters, jr

Orphan's Court of Wash Co, D C. Letters of adm on the personal estate of Alex'r H Marbury, late of said county, dec'd. –Fra Dodge, adm

The ship **Birmingham**, Wm J Robinson, master, which sailed from N Y on Nov 8, bound to Mobile, was totally wrecked on the 16th, on Ellson's reef, near Harbor Island, Bahamas, the wind at the time blowing fresh, with a heavy sea. Those lost were Chas Williams & John Hamilton, crew, & Wm Thompson, steward, all belonging to N Y. The capt & crew were taken to Nassau, in a sloop, having lost all their clothes & effects, & some of them being cut & bruised by the breakers, while swimming to the shore. The American consul at Nassau furnished them with clothing, & they were comfortably provided for.

The U S frig **Congress** arrived at Mahon on Oct 17, after a most delightful cruise of nearly 6 months, during which time she visited the coast of France, Italy, Greece, Turkey, & in fact every port of interest & importance in the Mediterranean. Our beautiful frig was the admiration of every one that has seen her. The following is a correct list of the ofcrs now attached to her, all in good health:
Capt-Philip F Voorhees
Lts-Robt L Browning, Thorton A Jenkins, Richd Bache, David D Porter, Wm Rockendorff.
1st Lt Marines, Benj E Brooke; 2nd Lt, John C Grayson; Surgeon, Thos L Smith; Purser, Benj J Cahoone; Chaplain, Wm G Jackson; Acting Master, Benj S Gantt; Prof of Math, John Pierce, jr; Assist Surgeon, Saml Jackson; Passed Midshipman, Wm H Caldwell
Midshipmen: Edw R Calhoun, Robt C Rodgers, Edw Simpson, J Q A Crawford, Edw Brinley
Wm Riley, Thos C Eaton, A W Habersham, David P McCorkle, Watson Smith, Stephen B Luce, Thos S Fillebrown, Wm W Holmes, Wm G Hoffman, Lehman P Ashmead, John H Upshur, Jos L Friend, Chas C Bayard, Wm R Mercer, John D Langhorne
Capt's Clk, Francis H Fleming; Purser's Clk, Henry B Walker; Boatswain, Wm Black; Gunner, Saml G City; Carpenter, Jas Magill; Sailmaker, Geo D Blackford

Child's nurse is wanted to take to the country a middle-aged white woman, who would find it a comfortable & permanent home. None need apply unless they came well recommended. Also, wanted to purchase, a negro woman, who understands house-work generally. Good character will be indisputable from the person selling. Apply to Mrs E Peyton, corner of 4½ st & Pa ave.

Charleston, on Dec 4: while Mr Saml Webber was engaged in arranging the cornice of a 3 story bldg in Hasell st, he suddenly fell, head foremost, from the scaffold. On his descent, Mr Dangerfield, at work on the 2nd story scaffold, reached forth his hand, touching Mr W on the shoulder, causing the body to turn, & thus avoid instant death. Mr Webber sustained such injury as to render his recovery doubtful. -Courier

Singular Disappearance. A trunk was opened last week by the Superintendent of the Tonawanda Rail Road, which had been there since Sep, & some papers showed it belonged to a clergymen from Massachusetts, by the name of White. A letter of inquiry was written to the Rev Dr Woods, through whose means it was discovered that the trunk probably belonged to a son of Mr Aaron White, of Boylston, Mass, who left his friends there for the west on Sep 20, & has not been heard of since.

Second-hand Piano Fortes for sale, of 5½ & 6 octaves, warranted in good order. –J P Kahl, Piano Forte Maker, Pa ave, between 12th & 13th sts.

Col John M Taylor died in Phil on Dec 6, at age 92 years. In the prime of his manhood he rendered distinguished services to his country. At the siege of Quebec, in 1775, he discharged the very arduous duties of Commissary of the American army under Genr'l Montgomery, during the whole period that army lay before Quebec. Col Taylor continued in the service & in the commissary dept till 1779, always an upright man & a very meritorious ofcr. –Phil Gaz

Jas F Drake was convicted in N Y last week of illegal voting. He was sentenced to 3 months confinement in the penitentiary.

Mrd: on Dec 12, in Wash City, by Rev G W Samson, Mr Simon Frazer to Mrs Hannah Davis, all of Wash City.

Mrd: on Dec 7, at Marietta, S C, by Rev Mr Glennin, Capt Lloyd J Beall, U S Army, to Miss Fanny D, d/o Col Arthur P Hayne.

Died: Nov 27, at *Woodlawn*, King George Co, Va, Mrs Tabitha Johnson, w/o Y Johnson, in her 76th year.

Spectacles, Jewelry, Spoons, Watches, & Clocks of all description. –Jas Galt, Pa ave between 9th & 10th sts

FRI DEC 15, 1843
Senate: 1-Ptn from M M Quackenboss & others, asking that a compromise may be made with them as sureties of Saml Swartwout, late collector of N Y. 2-Ptn from Wm De Peyster & Alfred M Cruge, asked to be remunerated for a slave lost in Florida. 3-Papers in the case of John Grant taken from the files & referred. 4-Papers of Noah Miller, ditto. 5-Ptn from Jos Warring, asking additional compensation for services in the Solicitor's ofc. 6-Ptn from the wid/o Qrtrmaster Weed, of the Marine Corps, asking to be allowed half the monthly pay of her late husband. 7-Ptn from Stephen Steele & Jas Daniel, asking confirmation of certain tracts of land. 8-Ptn from Duncan L Clinch & J H McIntosh, praying indemnification for losses sustained in Florida. 9-Ptn from Gen J H Hernandez, also asking for indemnity for losses in Florida. 10-Ptn from Jane Gordon, asking a pension. 11-Ptn from Gideon & Shadrach Bachelder, asking compensation for stone furnished at Sandy Bay breakwater, in Massachusetts. 12-Ptn from Harriet H Saunders, for a pension. 13-Ptn from Eliz Lomax, asking to be allowed commutation pay due to her

father for Revolutionary services. 14-Ptn from Eugene Smith, an ofcr in Florida war, asking an increase of pension. 15-Ptn from Chas Morgan, asking to be allowed for the services of his father in the Revolution. 16-Ptn from Mrs Mary McCall, for a pension. 17-Ptn from Susan McCulloh, asking for a pension. 18-Ptn to remove from files certain papers of Jno Martin & refer them. 19-Resolved that the Pres of the U S be requested to cause to be communicated to the Senate all the information of the War Dept on "mountain howitzer" obtained by Lt Freemont from the Arsenal at St Louis in May last, & taken by him on the expedition to the Oregon.

Mr Jas T Swindler, s/o Capt Jas Swindler, on Fri last, while returning from Charleston, Va, to his father's residence, about 9 miles below, on the other side of the Kanawha, was thrown from his horse & instantly killed. His body was found shortly after by the stage driver & conveyed to his father's house.

Mrd: Nov 24, at Barnstable, Mass, by Rev J Gates, Mr John Poor to Miss Sophia Rails. –Louisiana Chron

Hse/o Reps:: 1-Notice of the death of Barker Burnell, late an active & efficient member of the 27th Congress. He was a native of Nantucket, a small island of the ocean appendant to the State of Mass, long renowned as the mother of a race of men, for umblemished integrity, etc. The panegyric of Edmund Burke upon the Nantucket whalemen of his age has resounded in every corner of the earth. Two years from May last Barker Burnell came to serve his county as a trusty councilor. He was disabled a great part of the last session of Congress. On Jun 15th of last Jun he expired.

Died: on Dec 13, after a severe illness of several months, Miss Virginia Costin, aged 23 years & 6 months.

Died: on Wed, in his 10th year, Chas, s/o Chas & Margaret Fisher, of Wash City. His funeral will be from the residence of Mr Fisher, on G st, between 12th & 13th sts, this morning, at 11 o'clock.

Died: on Dec 12, in Montg Co, Md, Mrs Eliz Peerce, in her 83rd year, after a long & painful illness, which she bore with Christian fortitude from the earliest stage of her affliction till death.

NOTICE. By order of distrain, & to me directed, I shall offer for sale on Dec 19, the following goods & chattels, to wit: 12 chairs, 2 rocking chairs, crockery, china, glass ware, pine tables, 3 washstands, 2 bureaus, 2 pair andirons, 1 safe, 3 tubs, carpet, tin ware, brass fender, table cover, pots, skillets, a 10 plate stove & pipe, complete, furniture, etc, seized & taken as the property of Mrs Hungerford, & will be sold to satisfy house rent due & in arrears to John C McKelden. –J A Ratcliff, Bailiff

SAT DEC 16, 1843
Senate: 1-Ptn from E Appleton & a great number of booksellers & publishers, asking the establishment of a copyright law. 2-Ptn from Mary J Babbitt, asking a pension. 3-Ptn from G F Pearson, asking to be promoted to his legitimate rank. 4-Ptn from the heirs of Henry de la Francia, asking compensation for arms furnished under convention with Gov't in 1810. 5-Ptn from David Currier. 6-Additional testimony in the case of Jos Veasie. 7-Mr Morehead, asking to take from the files of the Senate the papers of Francis A Harrison, & have them referred. 8-Tribute of respect to the memory of Col John Millen, a member elect from the State of Georgia: a native Georgian; the city of Savannah was the place of his birth & his death: his parents died when he was young; he was bred an orphan; died Oct 15 last, aged about 40 years. He was never married; left a lone single sister.

Orphan's Court of Wash Co, D C. Letters of adm on the personal estate of John Kincart, late of said county, dec'd. –Mary Ann Kincart, admx

For sale or rent: spacious 3 story brick house at the corner of I & 16th sts, near St John's Church. For terms apply to me at my residence on north G st, at the west end of the city. –Nathl Frye, Atty for the proprietor

Mrd: on Dec 14, by Rev G W Samson, Mr Edw Woolls to Miss Mary C Essex, d/o Mr J Essex, all of Wash City.

Died: on Dec 14, Chas W Goldsborough, Chief of the Bureau of Provisions & Clothing of the Navy Dept, & one of the oldest & most respected residents of Wash City. His funeral will be from his late residence on G st west this day, at 12 o'clock. [Dec 29 newspaper: he was a native of Md, highly educated, & in the employ of the Gov't nearly half a century.]

Died: Nov 28, at Baton Rouge, La, Mrs Susan Amelia Seawell, w/o Maj Washington Seawell, U S Army.

Hon G W Summers, one of the Reps elected to Congress in Va, writes that he has been confined by severe indisposition all the Fall, though he has been steadily recovering.

For rent, a parlor & chamber, at Mrs Shield's, on 5th st, near the Trinity Church, opposite the City Hall, in a pleasant neighborhood, & within a few minutes' walk of the avenue.

Wm Hough has been arrested on suspicion of having committed the late mail robbery at Hudson.

MON DEC 18, 1843
Constable's sale: by virtue of 2 executions, issued by Jas Marshall, & to me directed: sale on Dec 22, in front of Mr Williams' jail, near the intersection of 7th st west & Md ave, negro boy Rozier Payne, aged about 11 years. Seized & taken in execution as the property of John E Derment, & will be sold to satisfy judgments due Geo Hartman & Stanslaugh Tench. –Saml Scott, Constable [Same as above, to satisfy debt due Jas Shreve. –S Moore, Constable]

Year & Month Clocks for sale: Wm Blanchard, Pa ave, between Fuller's & Galabrun S Hotels.

Inquest was held on Wed in N Y over the body of Dr Stephen N Naudin, a native of France, aged 75 years, who, it appears, died of an effusion of the chest, hastened by an attempted suicide. He attempted to commit sucide by taking laudanum, but the stomach pump being used the poison was drawn off. On Sat he cut his throat with a razor. He had been affluent, but became reduced in circumstances & was dejected.

Masonic: meeting of the Grand Lodge in Nov last, the following ofcrs for the ensuing year were duly chosen:
Wm M Ellis, Grand Master
Joel Downer, Deputy Grand Master for Washington
John Meyer, Deputy Grand Master for Gtwn
H N Steele, Deputy Grand Master for Alexandria
Thos Smith, Grand Senior Warden
Robt Coltman, Grand Junior Warden
H C Williams, Grand Sec
Philip Inch, Grand Treas
Saml Walker, Grand Tyler
Rev A A Muller, Grand Chaplain
Robt B Boyd, Grand Senior deacon
Robt Clark, Grand Junior deacon
Dr W B Magruder, Grand Marshal
B M Deringer, Grand Sword Bearer
John Robinson, Grand Pursuivant

Alex'r Dallas Bache, L L D, has been appointed by the Pres to fill the vacancy occasioned by the decease of Mr Hassler, late Superintendent of the coast survey.

Saml Boothby, of Buxton, Maine, considered the wealthiest man in town, committed suicide Dec 3, in consequence of some perplexity in business.

Hon Abram Rencher, his wife & children, of N C, Charge d'Affaires of the U S at the Court of Lisbon, sailed from N Y on Dec 11, in the packet-ship **Toronto**, for London.

The Cleveland Herald mentions the death in that city of Ralph Granger, a member of the Ohio Bar, s/o the late Hon Gideon Granger, & elder brother of the Hon Francis Granger.

The 4 year old dght of Mrs Gow, on Dec 13, at New Orleans, was attacked by a large bear that had been reared as a pet in the yard of Messrs Stone & Kennedy's hospital. The beast had been made furious by stones being thrown at it, & struck the child with its paws & ripped her bowels quite out. She expired.

Hse/o Reps:: 1-Ptn of Harriet Carter, of Newton, Mass, for the renewal of her pension. 2-Ptn of Wm Neilson,of Balt, Md, for reimbursement of medical expenses while in the service of the U S. 3-Ptn of Jos W Newcomb, for a claim, under a resolution of Congress, in favor of children of Gen Warren. 4-Ptn of Lemuel Williams, for commissions as a disbursing agent in bldg a custom-house. 5-Memorial of Mary Reeside,of Phil, sole excx of the last will & test of Jas Reeside, dec'd, setting forth that her late husband was for many years in the service of the P O Dept of the U S, as a mail contractor; that the U S became heavily indebted to him; that a suit was brought against the U S, &, after a prolonged trial, the jury found the verdict for the said Jas Reeside, & certified that the U S were indebted to him in the sum of $188, 496.06; that the verdict was, upon a motion for a new trial & argument, confirmed by the court & a writ of error sued out by the U S has been disposed of, & the verdict stands in full force & unsatisfied. The memorial suggests, that the U S are bound in justice & good faith to provide the payment of the debt so found to be due. 6-Following gentlemen were nominated in the election of Chaplain: F T Tiffany, Episcopal; Wm Al Daily, Methodist Protestant; Henry W Dodge, Baptist; Isaac Ketchum, German Reformed; Isaac S Tinsley, Baptist; S G Bulfinch, Unitarian; A A Muller, Lutheran. On the first vote there was no choice. On the second ballot, the Rev J S Tinsley, having received a majority of all the votes polled, was declared to be duly elected Chaplain to this House.

Letter from an American gentleman in Constantinople, dated in that city Oct 17, 1843, gives an account of the disinterment of the remains of Cmdor Porter: On the 14th instant, we brought up in the Yence Downia the remains of Cmdor Porter to the city, they were taken on board the U S brig **Truxton**, Capt Upshur, sent out to take the body to America, which vessel is to sail tomorrow. After his death, he was buried at his residence at St Stephano, 10 miles below the city. The coffin was enveloped in a U S flag, with the hat & sword of the late Cmdor placed on the top, & was raised by the sailors of the **Truxton**, & a long procession formed with the band playing the dead march. The relations of the dec'd, many members of the diplomatic corps, merchants, & sailors followed. On board the steamer, a guard of honor was stationed over the coffin, & the steamer left St Stephano. The steamer came to anchor near the **Truxton**, & the body was removed on board. Thus ended this imposing ceremony, well worthy of him who was its object.

On Dec 8 the remains of the Hon Barker Burnell, the late Rep in Congress from Nantucket, were taken from the vessel which conveyed them home, & carried to their final rest. A solemn feeling pervaded the whole town, & it was truly a solemn scene.

Isaac Aly, living beyond Harrisville, Harrison Co, Ohio, murdered his wife on Fri week, by striking her several blows on the head with an axe. They had lived together happily for some time. He was considered insane at times, but harmless. He is now in Cadiz jail.

Confectionary, on Bridge st, Gtwn. –Em Emmert

Two sons of Mr Matthew Macguire drowned on Nov 28. Four of his sons were crossing ice that had become thin, & 2 fell in. Their mother, sister, & father tried to rescue them, but the two boys were not recovered till they were dead. –St John's Caledonian

Thos McGrowan, one of the deck hands on board the steamer **Montezuma**, on her passage to New Orleans from Cincinnati, fell into the fly-wheel & was instantly killed.

Four men drowned. Drake Thompson, well known in N Y as a carrier of periodicals, was drowned in the East river on Sun last, along with 3 companions, while hunting ducks, when the boat upset.

Died: yesterday, Mrs Mary T Dixon, wid/o the late Col John Dixon, of Gloucester Co, Va. Her remains will be conveyed this morning from her late residence in Wash City, to be entombed in the family burying ground at Williamsburg, Va.

TUE DEC 19, 1843
Obit-died: on Nov 30, at his seat in Rappahannock Co, Va, Maj John Roberts, of Culpeper, in his 86th year. Born in Apr, 1758, he had just attained his 17th year when the breach of the Royal Govn'r into the magazine at Williamsburg aroused to arms the virtue of his countrymen. The removal of the colonial gunpowder by Dunmore provoked the first act of arms in Va; & within 48 hours from then the tidings reached Culpeper Co & her sturdy men were on their march to the theatre of this aggression. Young Roberts was one of this gallant band. In the minute service of Sep, 1775, Maj Roberts was chosen lt of riflemen, & in Dec of 1775, he was appointed a lt of the Va line on the continental establishment. In 1778 he was promoted to capt, & on Mar 5, 1779, he was commissioned a major of infty in the same line. The duty of arranging & executing an exchange for the convention prisoners captured at Sarotoga in Oct, 1777, was a task he performed with signal propriety at East Windsor, Conn, near the close of Sep, 1781. He was then ordered to the South, in the expectation that his assistance might be given in the army with Gen Nathl Greene. This hope perished in the diminished number of sldrs in that dept of the war, which denied to the commanding Gen the indulgence of a wish for his services. In 1783 the war closed, & Maj Roberts returned to his native state. In Apr, 1796, he was called into the Leg Councils of the Commonwealth, continuing for 13

sucessive years. In 1798 he was a prominent member of that Democratic party which passed the resolutions presented by John Taylor, of Caroline. In private life the cardinal virtues were the lamp to his footsteps.

Hse/o Reps:: 1-Memorial of the heirs of Capt Wm Evans, dec'd, for an invalid pension. 2-Memorial of Mrs Ann Scott, wid/o Maj Saml Scott, dec'd, for Revolutionary bounty land or commutation pay. 3-Ptn of Messrs Jas R Whitehead, Wm Walker, John Daniel, Wm Watson, & others in Prince Edward, Va, praying for the establishment of a post route. 4-Ptn of Reuben Taylor, a sldr of the Revolution, asking for an additional pension. 5-Ptn of W W Browning & J S Skinner, praying the confirmation of the location of certain lands made to satisfy the claim of Alabatcha, by virtue of the 14th article of Dancing Rabbit Creek. 6-Ptn of Robt O Kelly, of Richmond, Ky, praying an increase of his pension. 7-Ptn & vouchers in the case of the claim of Col Francis Vigo, late of Indiana. 8-Ptn & vouchers of Cornelius Bogard, praying compensation for 2 horses lost during the last war. 9-Ptn of John J Beck, of Missouri, praying compensation for a horse lost in the battle of Tippecanoe. 10-Ptn of Gideon Walker, of Indiana, praying compensation for services rendered as an enlisted sldr from 1792 to 1785. 11-Ptn of L Millander & others, for the confirmation of certain entries of land in the New Orleans land district. 12-Ptn of Lewis Janin, for confirmation of the sale of a tract of public land in the New Orleans land district. 13-Ptn of Bernard Haskin, for the confirmation of the sale of a tract of land in the district north of Red river, Louisiana. 14-Ptn of F Denon & others, for the confirmation of certain land entries in the New Orleans land district. 15-Ptn of Peter Philibert & others, for a directory law for the issuing of patents for confirmed land claims. 16-Ptn of B Manging & others, praying for legislation on the subject of contested land claims in Louisiana. 17-Ptn of L Deletra & others, for the allowance of additional compensation to the deputies & clerks of naval ofcrs at New Orleans. 18-Ptn of Henrietta Barnes, d/o Capt Lathrop Allen, for the commutation & bounty land of her father.

Senate: 1-Ptn from Jacob Mitchell & others, asking indemnification for French spoliations prior to 1800. 2-Ptn from Peyton King, of Alabama.
3-Mr Atchison asks that the papers in the case of Chas E Sherman be taken from the files & referred to.
4-Ptn from John Fraser & Co, praying that a sum of money exacted for a supposed violation of the revenue laws may be refunded. 5-Ptn from the heirs of Elihu Hall, asking confirmation of titles to certain lands in Louisiana, Mississippi, & Florida. 6-Mr Archer-asking to withdraw from the files of the Senate the papers in the case of Robt Mayo, representative of Geo Mayo. 7-Mr Huntington-asking to withdraw from the files the papers of Eneas A Munson. 8-Mr Woodbridge-asking to withdraw from the files the papers of Asa Weeks & Stars, & Jos Campau. 9-Mr White-that the excx of Wm B Cheever have leave to withdraw papers from the files of the Senate. 10-Bill for the relief of Chas E Sherman, introduced. 11-Bill for the relief of Caroline E Clitherall, wid/o Dr Geo Clitherall, late a surgeon in the U S Army, introduced. 12-Mr Hubard asked leave to

withdraw the papers in the cases of Mrs Mary Crafton, wid/o Thos Crafton, & of Mrs Mary Gafford, wid/o Jos Gafford, which are now on file in the Clerk's ofc, & were improperly referred last Congress to one of the standing cmtes, instead of being forwarded to one of the Depts. Ordered accordingly.

Private teacher wanted: a lady capable of teaching all the branches of an English education, together with music. Address me at Pomonkey P O, Chas Co, Md.
–Robt Brawner

The following persons who were injured by the late explosion of the steamboat **Warren**, on the Alleghany river, have since died of their wounds: Wm H Bates, of Freeport; Jas Williams, of Brady's Bend; John Lewis, of Brady's Bend; Saml Weaver, of Red Bank Furnace; John Jennings, of Brady's Bend.

Valuable farm for sale: the subscriber offers at private sale his Farm, purchased recently of the Silk Company. It is about 2½ miles north of the Capitol. It contains 180 acs of land: the dwlg is 40 feet square, 2 stories high, built of brick, pebble dashed, & covered with slate, & having a splendid portico the whole length. It has a large barn, stables, cow house, ice house, poultry house, servants & overseer's houses. For terms inquire of R France, Athenaeum Bldg, Pa ave, near 4½ st.

Ptn in writing, to me the subscriber, Chief Judge of the Orphans' Court of Chas Co, [it being in the recess of the County Court of said county,] from Jas L Cony, praying for the benefit of the act of Assembly, passed at Nov session, 1805, & the several supplements thereto, a schedule of his property & a list of his creditors on oath, as far as ascertained, being annexed to his ptn; & the said Cony having satisfied me, by competent testimony, that he had resided in Md 2 years immediately preceding the time of his application; it is ordered that Cony be discharged; provided a copy of this order be inserted in some newspaper published in D C, once each week for 2 months prior to the 3rd Mon in Mar next, notifying the creditors of the said Jas L Cony to be & appear in Chas Co Court on the 3rd Mon in Mar next. Given under my hand this 13th day of Dec, 1843.
–Richd Barnes -John Barnes, jr

Wanted, by a man who has none but his wife, situation as Overseer on a Farm or Laborer, who is willing to work & study the interest of his employer. His wife is a perfect country housekeeper. Application to be made at Mr Martin Murphy's, corner of 4½ st & Pa ave.

Mrd: on Dec 5, in Dumfries, by Rev Mr Towles, Dr Francis C Fitzhugh, of Bedford, King George Co, Va, to Rosa, only d/o the late Dr John Spence, of Dumfries.

Died: on Dec 18, after a long & painful illness, Mrs Eliz Gardner, consort of David A Gardner, in her 45th year. Her funeral is tomorrow, at 2:30 p m, from her late residence on G, between 14th & 15th sts.

Died: on Dec 13, at *Norwood*, [his residence in Powhatan Co, Va,] Wm H Kennon, in his 43rd year, leaving behind him a wife & 3 children to lament his untimely end. Mr Kennon was an ofcr in the Navy until about 3 years ago, having attained the rank of lt. He was induced to resign his commission for a high consideration, which, as he conceived, was due his family. He retired in 1840 to his farm in Va. The rush of his afflicted slaves to the side of his deathbed offerd a most conclusive proof of his kindness.

Died: on Oct 13, at Church Hill, Jefferson Co, Miss, John Steele, in his 64th year, a native of PG Co, Md.

Died: on Nov 24, at Charlottesville, Albemarle Co, Va, after a severe illness of a few days, Mrs Mary A Jackson, in her 30th year, w/o the Rev Wm M Jackson, of that county.

In Chancery. Somerset Co Court, Nov Term, 1843. Jas Bounds, vs, Peter O Skinner & Jane L Skinner, his wife, Thos Bounds, & others. The object of the Bill filed is to obtain a decree for the appointment of a trustee to make sale of the real estate which Wm Bounds by his last will & testament directed to be sold. The bill states that Wm Bounds, of Jas, died in 1828, having made his will, by which he appointed his wife, Zipporah Bounds, & his son, John Bounds, his excs, who accepted the trust, & the said Wm devised his real estate to his wife during her life, & after her death he directed the same to be sold by the surviving exc on a credit of 1 & 2 years, & the proceeds of sale to be equally divided between his children, to wit: John Bounds, Jas Bounds, Biddly Lowe w/o Ralph Lowe, Geo W Bounds, Eliz Mitchell w/o John Mitchell, Jane L Skinner w/o Peter O Skinner, Thos Bounds, Marcellus Bounds, Emmarellus Bounds, Mannellus Bounds, Levin Bounds, Zipporah Bounds, & Wm Bounds. That said John Bounds, one of the excs, died in the lifetime of Zipporah Bounds, the life tenant, who also died in 1843. That John Bounds, dec'd, left the following children: Biddly L Bounds, of full age, Jas Bounds, Mary Ann Bounds, Eleanor E J Bounds, Rachael W Bounds, John Bounds, infants. That Biddy Lowe, w/o Ralph Lowe, died, leaving her said husband & the following children, to wit: Wm Lowe, Mgt Lowe, Rachael Lowe, & Zipporah Lowe, all infants, her heirs at law. That Levin Bounds, Wm Bounds, jr, & Zipporah Bounds, children of the said testator, are dead intestate, with children, leaving their brothers & sisters & their descendants aforesaid their heirs at law. That John Mitchell & Eliz conveyed their interest in said real estate to Zipporah Bounds, wid/o Wm, & that said Zipporah died intestate, leaving Geo W Bounds, Eliz Mitchell, Jane L Skinner, Thos Bounds, Marcellus Bounds, Emmarellus Bounds, who intermarried with Chas V Crockett, & Mannellus Bounds her heirs at law. That the said Chas V Crockett & wife have conveyed their interest under the will of the said Wm Bounds to Marcellus Bounds. That the said John Mitchell is dead, & all the dfndnts reside in Somerset Co, except Peter O Skinner & Jane L Skinner his wife, & Thos Bounds, who reside out of Md. And the bill prays for a decree appointing a trustee to make sale of the real estate devised to be sold by the will of the said Wm Bounds, & for further relief.
True copy: Test: Levin Handy, Clk

WED DEC 20, 1843
On Dec 9, the w/o Mr John Chamberlain, of Fulton, Ohio, stepped into a neighbor's, leaving 2 infant children playing with a silk handkerchief, in front of a coal fire. Mrs C returned in a few moments & found one of her children enveloped in fire. The little sufferer lingered until Sunday noon, when it expired.

A P Bagby will attend faithfully to any business confided to his professional care in the U S Supreme.

Senate: 1-Ptn from Cmder Jas McIntosh, asking that compensation may be made him for extra services, in performing the duty of ofcrs belonging to a higher grade. 2-Ptn from Eliz Young, asking for a pension. 3-Ptn from Geo Wilson & others, workmen lately employed in the Wash Navy Yard, representing the exhaustion of the appropriation for construcion & equipment, & their consequent sudden discharge from employment; & praying an early appropriation for the resumption of the work on the vessels begun in said yard, & that they may be restored to employment, by the unexpected loss of which they are suffering great hardships during the inclement season of winter. Many had incurred considerable expense in removing their families & furniture to this city from distant parts of the country.

Matthew St Clair Clarke was on Mon nominated by the Pres for the ofc of Auditor of the Post Ofc Dept, made vacant by the resignation of Mr Whittlesey; & the Senate confirmed his resignation yesterday. The Senate also confirmed the nomination of Alex'r G Penn to be Post-master for the City of New Orleans.

Visitor in Wash City is the Hon Henry St George Tucker of Va, in greatly improved health. –Globe

Mr Putnam R Rea, the founder, & for many years senior editor of the New Orleans Bulletin, died in that city on Dec 5, after an illness of several months.

Newark Post of Thu. Yesterday Augustus Van Houton, aged 12 or 14 years, & s/o Mr Van Houton, of this city, fell off from the front part of a wagon loaded with bones, & the wheel passed over his neck & breast. He survived the accident but a few minutes.

Rev Danl Ostrander, an aged & highly esteemed minister of the Methodist Episcopal Church, died at Plattskill, Ulster Co, N Y, on Fri last.

The Pensacola Gaz of Dec 9: The U S ship **Vincennes**, Capt Buchanan, received orders to proceed down the Gulf on a cruise, & will sail next week. The U S brig **Falmouth**, Cmder J R Sands, was at Key West at the last accounts, & expected here. The U S ship **Vandalia**, Capt Chauncey, & brig **Somers**, Lt Commanding West, when last heard from were at Havana.

The St Augustine herald of Dec 6: Lt J E Blake, U S Topographical Engineers, returned on Fri last, having completed the survey of the Haulover, between Indian river & Mosquito Lagoon. The distance to be cut through is about 725 yards, & the level 7½ feet. The expense of cutting is estimated at about $3,000.

The five year old d/o Mr Wm Davis, of Zanesville, Ohio, died of hydrophobia last week. The child was bitten severely by an infuriated cat last Jun.

Mrd: on Dec 13, at the Mount Savage Iron Works, Alleghany Co, Md, by Rev Mr Wall, J B Staples, counsellor at law, of N Y, to Eliz, d/o Wm Young.

Mrd: on Dec 13, by Rev Mr Stringfellow, Mr S D Castleman, of Clarke Co, Va, to Miss Jane, only d/o Thos Cookendorfer, of Wash City.

Died: on Dec 13, at the residence of his grandfather, Thos Summerville, in PG Co, Md, Jas Forbes, eldest s/o Col John H Sothoron, aged 4 years, after an illness of 3 days of scarlet fever. He was intelligent beyond his years, & more than ordinarily devoted to his affectionate parents.

The hot-house of Mrs Gen Wade Hampton, at Columbus, S C, with an extensive collection of choice foreign plants & shrubbery, was entirely consumed by fire on Dec 14.

Two white men named Robt Curtain & John Murry, have been arrested at Balt by ofcrs Campbell & Shack, charged with the murder of Mr John Selby, which took place in Berry's district, Montg Co, Md, on Oct 6, 1842. Mr Selby was hit on the head & robbed of about $70, in his house, after Mrs Selby had prepared supper for the men. [Dec 21 newspaper: Mr Selby was still alive, & there is no doubt as to the assault & robbery by the above, who Mr Selby can identify. Mr Murray/Murry-note spelling.]

Hse/o Reps:: 1-Ptn of Mrs Salome Meyers, of Pa, for compensation on account of the Revolutionary services of her late husband, Peter Meyers. 2-Ptn of Philip R Rice, of Ky, praying to be paid the value of a vessel impressed into the service of the U S in the Revolutionary war & lost. 3-Ptn of Alex'r Connelly, late Postmaster of Covington, Ky, praying for the passage of a law to refund to him certain moneys collected of him by the Post Ofc Dept. 3-Ptn of Saml Thompson & 64 others, citizens of Muskingum Co, Ohio, praying that a pension may be granted to Jos Watson, of said county, for services rendered as a sldr of the late war. 4-Ptn & papers of David Alspach, praying for relief, & that a judgment against him in favor of the U S may not be enforced. 5-Ptn & papers of the heirs of Dennis Pursel, praying compensation for a boat taken for the use of the army of the U S during the Revolutionary war. 6-Ptn of Susannah Carpenter. 7-Additional documents of Reuben Taylor, a sldr of the Revolution. 8-Memorial of Ann M Dornback, wid/o a sldr of the Revolution.

Frederic Clitch, store on Pa ave, between 9th & 10th sts:. Fancy Work, Paper Boxes, Embroidery, Toys of all kinds, Plays, Vases, & other articles.

THU DEC 21, 1843
Senate: 1-Papers of Wm A Weaver be taken from the files of the Senate & again referred. Also, the papers of Jas Runet. 2-Ptn from Thos Cutts & 24 others, asking indemnification for French spoliations prior to 1800. 3-Ptn from John Washington, in relation to military service. 4-Ptn from Geo Harrison & others, praying to be allowed a claim. 5-Cmte on Commerce, made an adverse report on the claim of Enoch Baldwin.

Gtwn Classical & Scientific Academy: Jas McVean, Principal. Winter examination of the pupils will commence today. Parents & patrons of education are invited to attend.

On or about Feb 18, 1841, Caroline Clark Barnes & her husband John Barnes, entered into an agreement with John Wilson, atty at law, then of Fayette, Howard Co, Missouri, but now of N Y C, which provides for the execution of a power of atty, which was shortly afterwards executed to said Wilson; & whereas by said power of atty the said Caroline Clark Barnes & John Barnes constituted the said Wilson their atty in fact, to settle the effects belonging to the estate of Mary Clark, dec'd, late of Pennsylvania, who was the sole testamentary heir of Danl Clark, dec'd, late of the city of New Orleans, who was the sole testamentary heir of Thos Wilkins, dec'd, late of Mississipi, the property of which estates is situated or held in Louisiana, Mississippi, Missouri, & elsewhere; & whereas the said Wilson has totally neglected & failed to comply with his covenants in said agreement, which were the consideration for the execution of said power of atty. We, the undersigned, give notice that we have annulled, recalled, & countermanded said power of atty; & shall refuse to ratify any contract made by said Wilson concerning any part of the property belonging to either of said estates, 1/4th of which was & is claimed by said Caroline Clark Barnes, as one of the testamentary heirs of the said Mary Clark, dec'd. –John Barnes, Caroline Clark Barnes -St Louis, Mo, Dec 7, 1843

About Mar 20, 1841, Eleanor Macniff, by her atty in fact, Peter Macniff, & the said Peter Macniff, her husband, for himself, entered into an agreement with John Wilson, atty at law, then of Fayette, Howard Co, Mo, now of N Y C, which agreement provides for the execution of a power of atty, which the said Eleanor & Peter constituted said Wilson their atty in fact to manage & settle the estate of Mary Clark, dec'd, late of Pennsylvania, who was the sole testamentary heir of Danl Clark, dec'd, late of the city of New Orleans, who was the sole testamentary heir of Thos Wilkins, dec'd, late of Mississippi, which estates consisted of property situated or held in Louisiana, Mississippi, Missouri, & elsewhere, 1/4th of which property was & is claimed by the said Eleanor Macniff as one of the heirs of said Mary Clark, dec'd. And whereas the said Wilson has totally failed to comply with his covenants in said agreement, we the undersigned have revoked, annulled, & countermanded said power of atty; & will absolutely refuse to ratify any contract made by said Wilson. –Peter Macniff, Eleanor Macniff. –St Louis, Mo, Dec 7, 1843

Hse/o Reps:: 1-Memorial of Mary Ann Symmes, praying Congress to authorize the Treas Dept to audit & settle, upon principles of justice, the accounts of her late husband, Capt John Cleves Symmes, an ofcr during the last war to the U S Army. 2-Ptn of Wm Saunders, of Bedford Co, Va, for relief as a surety for Wm Estes, a post-master. 3-Ptn of Richd Pollard, late Charged'Affaires of Chili, asking for remuneration for losses sustained by him while a public ofcr in the negotiation of certain bills. 4-Ptn of Jas Blair & 256 others of Indiana, asking that Congress grant the said State the vacant land lying in the Vincennes land district for continuing the Wabash & Erie Canal from Terre Haute to Evansville, Ind, on the Ohio river. 5-Memorial of Jas S Campbell, praying for compensation for property of his father, Col Saml Campbell, lost in the service of the Gov't in the Revolutionary war; & also for services rendered in that war. 6-Ptn of Seth Sweetser, American Consul at Guyaquil, for compensation for services rendered by him in negotiating the ratification of the treaty of Jun 13, 1839, between the U S & Ecuador.

Negro man for sale-a likely negro man about 24 years of age. Inquire of Thos Young, Coachmaker, near the Railroad Ofc.

Judge Smith Thompson died on Mon last, at Russ Plaas, his country seat, near Poughkeepsie, we believe in his 77th year. He was born in Dutchess Co, N Y, his life having begun & where it ended. He studied law under Gilbert Livingston, of Poughkeepsie, whose dght he married, & with whom he became associated at the Bar. In 1819 he acceped the Secretaryship of the Navy, tendered him by Pres Monroe.

Died: on Dec 20, Mrs Catharine Williams, in her 44th year, consort of Jas Williams. Her funeral will be from her late residence, on 5th st, between G & H sts, on Dec 22.

Judge Wells, of the U S District Court of Missouri, was lying dangerously ill at Jefferson city on Dec 7.

FRI DEC 22, 1843
The Chilicothe advertiser says that the following ofcrs of the Legislature of Ohio are all practical printers: John M Gallagher, Speaker of the House; Chas Borland, Clerk of the lower House; D Robertson, Clerk of the Senate.

From Mexico: 1-Mr Alas, Minister of the General National Treas died on Nov 11. 2-The U S ship **Constellation**, Cmdor Kearney, & the British frig **Carysfort**, Lord Geo Paulet, arrived at Monterey, Calif, about the middle of Nov.

The trial of David Babe, alias Wm Brown, & Geo Matthews, for murder & piracy on board the schnr **Sarah Lavinia**, late of Alexandria, was commenced before the U S Circuit Court at N Y on Mon. Babe was first put on trial: verdict-guilty.

Mr Weir's picture of the Embarcation of the Pilgrims was last evening raised to its assigned place in one of the 2 southeastern panels of the Rotundo of the Capitol & is open to the public view this morning, being the anniversary of the landing on this Continent of the intrepid company whose embarcation from Holland the painting is designed to commemorate. The Picture of the Embarcation of the Pilgrims from Delft-Haven, in Holland, painted by Robt W Weir, was in conformity to an act of Congress for filling the vacant panels in the Rotunda of the Capitol. The painting represents part of the congregation of Mr John Robinson, who, having been driven from England by persecution, had resided in Holland for 11 years, & are now gathered upon the deck of the vessel **Speedwell**, at the moment of embarkation for America. The historical text may be found in Morton's New England Memorial. Those represented in the painting are, the Pastor, Mr John Robinson, Gov Carver, his wife & children, Elder W Brewster, his wife & sick child, Wm Bradford & his wife, Saml Fuller & wife, Wm White & his wife, Edw Winslow, wife, & 2 boys under their care, Capt Miles Standish, & his wife Rose. Near the mast are a domestic & child, Capt Reynolds & sailor, with the cradle in which Peregrine White was rocked; on the wharf are some spectators. The embarkation took place at Delft-Haven, Holland, on Jul 21, 1620, on board the **Speedwell**, a small vessel of 60 tons, which proceeded to Southampton, & sailed from thence in company with the ship **Mayflower**. The vessel proving leaky, they were obliged to put into Dartmouth, where, after repairing, they again started, but were soon obliged to put back into Plymouth. There they abandoned the **Speedwell** as unseaworthy, & they were received on board the **Mayflower**. About one half the number who came out in the **Mayflower** died the first year. The difficulties which the **Speedwell** encountered were owing to the treachery of Capt Reynolds, who was hired by the Dutch merchants either to frustrate the voyage or carry them to some place remote from their own settlements. This deceit, aided by a storm, caused the subsequent settlement at Plymouth, the destination of the colony having been Hudson's river. They landed at Plymouth on Dec 11, 1620; "and here being number about 20, they rendezvous this evening; but a storm rising, it blows & rains hard all night-continues so tempestuous for 2 days that they cannot get on board, & having nothing to shelter them." Their Pastor, Mr Robinson, did not accompany then, but remained with the great number of his flock in Holland, intending to come, yet ever unable to accomplish his desire. He died at Leyden, 1625, in his 50th year. His widow & children came over to Plymouth colony, & his son Isaac lived to the age of 90, who is mentioned by Prince as "a venerable man." Govn'r Carber is described as a man of great prudence, integrity, & firmness of mind. He had a good estate in England, which he spent in the emigration to Holland & America. He was taken sick in the field, while they were engaged in their planting, & died in Apr, 1621. His affectionate wife, overcome by the loss, survived him but 6 weeks. One of his grandsons lived to the age of 102 years; and, about the middle of the last century, 1775, that decendant, with his son, grandson, & great grand-son, were all at the same time at work in the same field, whilst an infant of the 5th generation was in the house at Marshfield. Wm Brewster's reputation was high in the church. He lived to the age of 84, & was eminently useful to the colony in many ways. Wm Bradford was the 2nd Govn'r, & was a sensible man, of strong mind, & sound judgment, & a good memory, & much inclined to study & writing. He wrote "A History of Plymouth People & Colony." His wife was lost overboard the day after the vessel came to anchor. This happened while her husband was absent, upon an expedition to examine the coast. Mr Saml Fuller & his wife are represented in the painting to be on the point of taking leave of each other, as she did not come over at this time. Mr & Mrs White are kneeling in the painting. Mr White died the following Feb; Mrs White was the mother of Peregrine White, the first English child born in the colony, a few days after their arrival, & before the landing. Peregrine lived to be over 83. He was vigorous, & of a comely aspect to the last. Mr & Mrs Winslow were recently married, & were persons of fortune. Mrs Winslow died soon after their arrival, & in the following spring he married Susanna, the wid/o Wm & mother of Peregrine White, which was the first marriage solemnized in the colony, May 12, 1621. Mr Winslow was the 3rd Govn'r. Capt Miles Standish & his wife Rose: this intrepid soldier, the hero of New England, as John Smith was of Virginia, was descended from the younger branch of a family of distinction, & was heir apparent to a large estate, fraudulently detained from him. After the landing at Plymouth, he was made their military commander. He lived to an advanced age. Belknap says his coat of mail was known to have been in the possession of his grandson, & is now supposed to be lost, but his sword is preserved in the cabinet of the Historical Society. Rose died in Jan.

Malicious Prosecution: this case was tried before the U S Court now in session in Salem, Mass, in which the jury returned a verdict of $356. This action was brought by Miss Sarah Blanchard, of Marblehead, against John Lovett, of Beverly, to recover damages for having procured a warrant & causing the plntf's house to be searched for stolen money, which was taken from the Salem Depot some time last spring. -Salem Obs

Chas A Clinton, of N Y, the s/o the late Govn'r, is engaged in arranging the papers of his father preparatory to publication. –N Y American

The Montrose [N Y] Star of Dec 14 announces the death of Mr Ira Gregory, of Bridgewater, a few days before. Mr G's head was caught at his saw mill, between the saw-gate & a large beam connected therewith, producing instant death. He has left 5 children, the first not more than 12 or 14 years of age, the mother having died very suddenly but a few months since.

Mrd: on Dec 19, by Rev Mr Atkinson, Mr Jos Kennedy, late of Washington, to Miss Sarah B Meng, d/o Chas Meng, of *Moss Hill*, Prince Wm Co, Va.

Died: on Dec 20, after a painful illness of consumption, Mrs Eliz R Davis, consort of Mr John A Davis, & y/d/o the Rev John B Ferguson, of Wash City. Her funeral will be this Sat at 10 o'clock, from her late residence on N, between 3rd & N J ave, near Mr Thos Blagden's wharf.

Died: on Dec 21, Mr Wm Radcliff, in his 38th year. His funeral will be from his late residence on Md ave, near the Potomac bridge, this afternoon, at 2 o'clock.

Died: on Dec 21, Jos Delos, s/o Wm H & Frances E Griffith, aged 9 months & 18 days.

Senate: 1-Ptn from John McDonnell, asking that the payment of certain duties made by him which had been illegally exacted may be refunded. 2-Ptn from Geo W Cummings, asking for a pension. 3-Mr Bayard: asking that the papers of Geo F Pearson be removed from the legislative files to the executive files of the Senate. 4-Ptn from Geo Taylor, asking to be indemnified for French spoliations prior to 1800. 5-Cmteon Revolutionary Claims: bill for the relief of Eneas Munson was ordered to a 2nd reading. 6-Cmte of Claims: asking to be discharged from the further considerationof the ptn of Geo B Adams: referred to the Cmte on Finance.

Negroes for sale: a blacksmith, a woman & 2 children, 2 negro men, a woman & 4 children, -4 girls 8 to 10 years of age, all likely & valuable negroes. They are not sold for any fault, but for the want of money. Inquire of Thos Williams, 7th st, or Mr R Butt, at the Washington Poor-house.

A poor miserable inebriate, Shadrach Hawkins, was found dead, with his face downwards, in a ditch not far from the residence of Mr Henry Walker, in the First Ward of Wash City. The dec'd was a colored man of intemperate habits.

Hse/o Reps:: 1-Ptn of Seth Adams, of Zanesville, Ohio, praying for indemnity for French spoliations prior to the year 1800. 2-Ptn of Jas Butler,of Phil, praying a pension for injuries received while in the service of the U S on board the ship of war **Independence** in 1816. 3-Ptn of Jonas D Platt, of Troy, N Y, a sldr in the war of 1812 with Great Britain, praying for a pension.

SAT DEC 23, 1843
Orphan's Court of Wash Co, D C. Letters of adm on the personal estate of Chas W Goldsborough, late of said county, dec'd. –W S Parrott, T Fillebrown, jr, admx

Hse/o Reps:: 1-Ptn from Isaac Winslow & Sons, of Boston, claiming a return of duties paid under mistake. 2-Ptn of Maria Babbitt, of Charlestown, Mass, for the continuance of her pension. 3-Ptn of Sarah Hildreth, heretofore presented Dec 20, 1838. 4-Ptns of Eliz Gardner, Emma Hartford, Eliz Elmon, Eliz Peck, Mary McClanning, Sally C Sparks, Eliza Root, Ruth Black, widows of Revolutionary widows, praying for the continuance of their pensions. 5-Ptn of Catharine Johnson, wid/o William, for a pension in cosideration of the services her said husband. 6-Ptn of Tappan & Dennet & 22 other firms, of Boston, engaged in the book trade, asking the adoption of an international copyright law. 7-Ptn of Mary Colburn, for military services of her husband during the last war with Great Britain. 8-Ptn of Elbridge G Woodman, for the purchase by the Gov't of his invention of a new mode of constructing forts, principally with iron. 9-Ptn of Israel D Goodridge & others, for payment of a fishing bounty. 10-Ptn of Saml Watson, of Giles Co, Tenn, a sldr of the Revolution, paying a pension for his services. 11-Ptn of John Everly, of Giles Co, Tenn, a sldr of the Revolution, praying for a pension. 12-Ptn of Alethea Allen, of Lawrence Co, Tenn, wid/o Danl Allen, praying a pension on account of the Revolutionary services of her husband. 13-Ptn of J W Seymour & 126 other citizens of Licking Co, Ohio, praying for a reduction of the present rates of postage. 14-Ptn of Alpheus Plummer, of Barre, Mass, praying for relief for losses sustained in the depreciation of Continental money. 15-On motion of Mr Harper, the ptn & papers of Solomon Sturgis, of Muskingum Co, Ohio, praying for relief, was taken from the files of the House & referred to the Cmte on Private Land Claims. 16-Ptn of Amos Hunting, of Shrewsbury, in Franklin County, Mass, praying for a pension.

Musicians wanted: 2 drummer & 1 fifer are wanted at the Virginia Military Institute, Lexington, Va, to whom the pay allowed in the U S Army will be given. Boys about 15 years of age would be preferred. -Francics H Smith, Superintendent Va Military Institute

Died: on Dec 10, in Raleigh, N C, in her 60th year, Mrs Sarah Polk, relict of the late Col Wm Polk. The dec'd was the d/o Col Philemon Hawkins, of Warren Co, who was one of the patriarchs of the Revolutionary period, & for many years subsequent thereto a prominent character in the councils of the State. In early life the dec'd became the w/o Col Wm Polk, whose name is identified with the Revolutionary history of North Carolina. Mrs Polk enjoyed in an eminent degree the affectioante respect of the community in which her life was passed.

Senate: 1-Bill for the relief of Isaac Ilsley, with a report: ordered to be printed. 2-Resolved, that the Pres of the U S be requested to communicate to the Senate a copy of the proceedings of the court-martial in the case of 2nd Lt D C Buell, 3rd Infty, & of all orders & papers in relation thereto, from the original order for assembling the court to the final order for the dispersion of its members.

Orphan's Court of Wash Co, D C. Sale at auction on Dec 27, by order of the Court, at the residence of the late D H Haskell, dec'd, on 16th st, adjoining St John's Church, his household & kitchen furniture. -Robt W Dyer & Co, aucts

Variety Store: cutlery, baskets, brushes, hollow ware & a general assortment. Bell-hanging & locksmithing attended to expeditiously & at moderate prices.
–J D Boteler, Pa ave, between 4½ & 5th sts

Columbia Typographical Society meeting this evening, at the usual place.
–Jas Wimer, Rec Sec

Rev Mr Colquitt, of Ga, will preach at the Foundry Methodist Episcopal Church on 14th st, on Sabbath morning next at 11 o'clock.

MON DEC 25, 1843

Obit-died: on Dec 13, at **Marshall Hall**, Chas Co, Md, Thos H Marshall, in his 46th year. His widow & the orphan have been deprived of their counsellor, their friend, & support, & the church of an efficient & zealous member. For 10 long years the dec'd was sorely afflicted. His suffereings were intense, springing from the character of his disease, which in its progress defied the best medical skill of the country. He died a Christian, & a Christian hope is his.

Wash Corp: 1-Ptn of Saml Hoover & others, praying remission of a fine: referred to the Cmte of Claims. 2-Report of the Cmte of Claims, made on Jul 11 last, adverse to the ptn of Z Hazel, was taken up & agreed to. 3-Communication fro High McCormick, Principal of the Eastern Free School, inviting the Board to attend an examination of the pupils of the school on Thu next, at 10 o'clock. 4-Bill for the relief of Jas Dixon: passed. 5-Act for the relief of Wm Cunningham: that the fine imposed upon him, for a violation of the act in relation to licenses for carts, be & the same is remitted: Provided, the said Cunningham pay the costs of prosecution. 6-Chas A Davis, Ignatius Mudd, & Geo H Fulmer were appointed the cmte on the part of the Board of Common Council. John W Maury, Jas Adams, & Saml Byington, appointed the cmte on the part of the Board of Aldermen.

The undersigned propose, with the approval & co-operation of Congress, to make Pa ave the most beautiful street & the most agreeable & magnificent promenade on the continent. –Jas Maher, Public Gardener, Wash, Dec 20, 1843.

Norfolk Herald: Jas T Soutter, on Tue last, resigned the Presidency of the Bank of Va, at Norfolk, in consequence of his intended removal to N Y.

Jos Artot is of French parentage, & was born in Brussels in 1815. His father was an artist of great talent, & was employed in the orchestra of the theatre of that city. His parents did not intend that he should become a musician, & he who is at present the European king of violinists was near being prevented from learning that instrument. At age 6 years he broke his arm; it was badly set. At the age of 7 he was called to the Court of the King of Holland where he played a concerto of Vioti to the astonishment of all. His father took him to Paris & put him under the care of the Director of the Conservatoire Rodolph Kreutzer. Cheubini predicted that he would become one of the greatest artists of the age. At age 11 years he obtained the great prize against 18 competitors, the youngest of whom was 19. In 1841, Haspodar, a passionate admirer of music, invited Artot to Wallachia. He was returning when his carriage was upset through the imprudence of a postillion, & he received an injury from which he yet suffers. The last winter he made, through Belgium & Holland, in company with Madame Cinti-Damoreau, a tour of uninterrupted triumphs. Artot is tall, his features are expressive, his air is graceful & melancholy, his manners are elegant.

The marriage of the Earl of Shelburne, eldest s/o the Marquis of Lansdowne, with the d/o Count de Flahault, French Ambassador at the Court of Vienna, took place in that city on Dec 1.

On Wed, while the great bell of the cathedral of Notre Dame was being rung, the clapper gave way, & the enormous mass fell down through 2 floors of the tower, & lodged at the 3rd. A ringer named Mazarin, was so injured in the head, by a splinter from the scaffolding, that it was necessary to carry him immediately to the hospital of the Hotel-Dieu.

The consecration of the Cathedral of Versailles took place on Sun last. The bldg was commenced 100 years ago.

English news: the London papers announce the death of Mr Wrench, the popular comedian; of Mr Rees, also a comedian, formerly of this country; of Miss Ellen Pickering, the novelist; of the Marquis of Winchester; of Chas Brinsley Sheridan, s/o the celebrated orator & dramatist, & of Francis C Sheridan, his grandson; of Sir Francis McNaughton, brother of the envoy who was murdered at Cabul; of the Countess of Cork; of Mrs Holmes, d/o Gen Sir Robt Sale; of the Countess of Mayo, lady in waiting upon the Queen Dowager; of the Countess of Roscommon; & of Mary, the w/o Sharon Turner, the eminent historian.

On Dec 3 the Judge of the Prerogative Court gave his decision on the long-disputed question of the ex-Sheriff Parkins' will, by which he bequeathed all his property to Mr Geo Best, of N J, with whom he resided for some time before his death. The will was disputed on the ground of insanity, by Mrs Finlay, only surviving sister of Mr Parkins, & since her death by her husband. The Judge pronounced in favor of the will. The property within the jurisdiction of the British court was between L20,000 & L25,000 sterling.

An extraordinary, large, & splendid beautiful White Owl was shot, in the neighborhood of Washington, at Pomonkey, by Edw C Brent, on Dec 19, & presented to the Nat'l Institute. It is the first bird of that description which has been seen in this part of our country.

Downed in Crown Point, on Dec 2, Mr Ambrose Nowell, aged 23 years, while skating on the lake, when the ice broke. Mr Goodwin & son [a lad of 14 or 15 years] were drowned in Willsborough on Nov 20, while crossing a pond on the ice.

Dr Jos Nichols, a member elect of the Leg of Md from Dorchester Co, Md, died on Mon last.

Mrd: on Dec 19, at Carter Hall, by Rev Mr Jones, John Page to Miss Lucy M, eldest d/o Geo N Burwell, all of Clarke Co, Va.

Mrd: on Nov 29, by Rev L F Morgan, of Gtwn, D C, Arthur M Payne to Miss Mary Hume, eldest d/o Jacob Hume, all of Fauquier Co, Va.

Mrd: on Dec 5, in N Y, Lt Bayard Clarke, U S Army, to Aletta Remsen, d/o the late Thos R Lawrence.

Mrd: on Dec 5, in New London, Conn, Lt Jas Totten, U S Army, to Miss Julia H, d/o Anthony Thatcher.

Mrd: on Oct 7 last, at Darmstadt, Germany, Mr Levin Schucking, one of the Editors of the Augsburg Gaz, to Joan Louisa, Baroness de Gall, of the former place.

Mr P Jones was killed near Cincinnati a few days ago by the accidental discharge of a gun in the hands of a companion, in company with whom he was hunting. A twig caught the trigger of the gun.

Circuit Court of Wash Co, D C. Humphrey Snow has applied to be discharged from imprisonment under the act for the relief of Insolvent Debtors: hearing on the first Mon of Jan next. –Wm Brent, clk

WED DEC 27, 1843
Orphan's Court of Wash Co, D C. In the case of John D Thomas, administrator of Col Jas Thomas, dec'd. Jan 12 next appointed for the settlement of said estate.
–Ed N Roach, Reg o/wills

Pres appointments: Albert Davy, of Pa, Consul at Leeds, England. Louis Marks, of N Y, Consul at Bavaria & the Prussian Provinces of the Rhine.

Mr Senator Merrick, of Md, was called home yesterday by information of the dangerous illness of one of his children.

On Wed an inquest was held at Boston on the body of Celia McDevitt, w/o Wm McDevitt, found dead in a cellar in Cross st. The jury returned a verdict that she came to her death from exposure, & want, & from the neglect & abuse of her husband. While she was lying dead in one part of the room he was lying drunk in another. They had 2 young children.

A young man named Lewis File, in the employ of Mr Evans of the glue factory at Lansingburgh, on Sun last fell head foremost into a large caldron of boiling glue, & died in a few hours. –Albany Daily Adv

Senate: 1-Ptn from Joel M Smith, asking compensation for his services as a pension agent. 2-Same for John Dawson. 3-Pt from citizens of Brookfield, N Y, asking that John Keith, a Revolutionary sldr, may be allowed a pension. 4-Ptn from Philip Allen & others, citizens of R I, praying indemnification for French spoliations. 5-Mr Sturgeon: asking to take from the files the papers of Henry Newingham. 6-Ptn from Edw Kennard, asking reimbursement of a fine for an unintentional violation of the revenue laws.

The undersigned deem it highly important to organize a Colonization Society for D C.

John Davis	John P Ingle	R T Berry
R Fendall	R Farnham	Wm Hawley
Michl Nourse	W M Morrison	S G Bulfinch
P Bradley	Pichey Thompson	Geo Savage
D A Hall	W B Edwards	S B Southerland
Jas Adams	A Coyle	J P Moore
Richd S Coxe	W R Abbot	Geo W Samson
C B Penrose	S G Gassaway	J W Hand
Jas Larned	Anthony Hyde	J T Johnston
Jno M Moore	C M Butler	Edw Kingsford
J H Offley	Vinal Luce	Elizs Harrison
W G Ridgely	Jas McVean	Joshua N Danforth
Ashbel Steel	L F Morgan	W M Fowle
Rd Smith	Saml McKenney	H C Smith
Jos H Bradley	S A Roszel	John McCormick
W Redin	Jeremiah Orme	A Griffith
John Marbury	David English	John Lanahan
Clement Cox	Septimus Tuston	Cassius F Lee
John Underwood	J F Polk	Chas B Dana
A Rothwell	J W French	Washington Roby
Jas Hoban	Horace Stringfellow	
Thos L Smith	Jas Laurie	

Died: on Dec 24, John Henry, only s/o Benj D & Margaret Klopfer, aged 3 months.

Died: in Tarboro, N C, Maj Jas W Clark, in his 65th year. He was born in Bertie Co, educated at Princeton College, married & settled in Edgecomb, where he had resided about 40 years. He served several years in the Leg of his State in both branches, both from Bertie & Edgecomb Counties, & represented that district in Congress in the years 1815 & 1816. [No date-current item.]

Hse/o Reps: 1-Ptn of Jas B Cooper & citizens of the State of N Y, to separate the people of N Y from slavery. Laid on the table. 2-Ptn of Geo Brinckerhoff & citizens of Albany, N Y, to remove the overslaugh: referred to the Cmte of Ways & Means. 3-Ptn of Hannah Bacon, wid/o Capt Judah Bacon, claim-French spoliations before 1800: referred to the Cmte on Foreign Affairs. 4-Ptn of Theophilus Somerby, of Dover, N H, arrears of pension: referred to the Cmte on Revolutionary Pensions. 5-Ptn of Thos L Ragsdale, statement for illuminating & ventilating the Hse/o Reps: referred to the Cmte on the Public Bldgs. 6-Ptn of Jas Frame & others, of Clark Co, Ohio, abolition of slavery & slave trade in D C: excluded by the rule. 7-Ptn of David Horten & others, of Clark Co, Ohio, against the annexation of Texas: referred to the Cmte on Foreign Affairs. 8-Ptn of Seth Linton & others, people of Ohio, to abolish all laws sanctioning slavery in the U S: excluded by the rule. 9-Ptn of Mrs Ann Royall, for a pension: referred to the Cmte on Revolutionary Pensions. 10-Ptn of Abraham G Gibson, for compensation as Charge d'Affaires: referred to the Cmte on Foreign Affairs. 11-Ptn of D C Lansing & citizens of the State of N Y, to reject the annexation of Texas: referred to the Cmte on Foreign Affairs. 12-Ptn of David Ravintree & inhabitants of McKean Co, Pa, & vicinity, to rescind 21st rule: referred to the Cmte on the Revisal of the rules. 13-Ptn of Jos Mann & 36 citizens of McKean Co, Pa, against the annexation of Texas: referred to the Cmte on Foreign Affairs. 14-Ptn of F Ducoing, for arrears of pension for disability caused by wounds received in the battle of Jan 8, 18_5. 15-Ptn of Carlos de Villemont, praying for confirmation of title to a tract of land in Arkansas. 16-Ptn of J Riley Knight, for compensation for losses sustained by him when keeper of the lighthouse at the mouth of the Mississippi, by hurricanes. 17-Ptn of J H Caldwell & others, to be released from payment of certain duty bonds for iron imported for the use of the New Orleans & Nashville Railroad Co. 18-Ptn of Jas Dixon for settlement of his account for extra work done on the Alexandria courthouse. 19-Ptn of John P Ingle & others, for Govn't to buy additions to the Congressional Burying Ground. 20-Ptn of Wm W Seaton & others, for a public clock. 20-Ptn of Geo Selden & 230 citizens of Erie Pa, praying an appropriation for the harbor at Erie. 21-Ptn of Jos Brown, a pensioner, asking for back pension. 22-Ptn of Franklin Whitney, of New Bedford, for a patent. 23-Ptn of A Allen, of Fairhaven, to be paid for a boat built for the Revenue service. 24-Ptn of Jas Emison & 350 other citizens of Knox Co, Ind, asking a donation of lands to improve the Grand Rapids of the Wabash river. 25-Ptn of Saml Drew, of Muskingum Co, Ohio, praying for a pension. 26-Ptn of Benj Thompson & 70 others, of Charlestown, Mass, for the discontinuance of the spirit ration in the Navy. 27-Ptn of Moses Noyes, for 7 years' half pay on account of the services of his father during the Revolutionary war. 28-Ptn of Maria Babbit, for a pension on account of services of her husband in the naval service. 29-Ptn of Jos R Willet, son & legal rep of Gen Augustine Willet, for advances & supplies for the Revolutionary army. 30-Ptns of Mary Green & Gertrude Thomas, of the State of N Y, the widows of dec'd Revolutionary sldrs, praying severally for pensions by the extension of the provisions of the act of Congress of Jul, 1838, to the widows of such Revolutionary sldrs as were married after Jan 1, 1794.

Just arrived & for sale, 5 head of Mules well broke to harness. To be seen at the Franklin Stables on 8th st, Washington. –Nicholas Rowles, Proprietor

$100 reward for runaway negro man Ned-Edward Henson, about 23 years of age. –Anthony C Page

THU DEC 28, 1843
Household furniture at auction, on Jan 2, at the residence of Mr J Shaw, 13th & F sts; his household furniture nearly new & in good order. -Robt W Dyer & Co, aucts

Desirable residence for sale or rent, at the east end of Gay st, Gtwn, north side: contains 2 parlors on the first floor, besides kitchen & 2 small rooms, 4 chambers, & a good cellar. There is a smoke house, milk house, & pump of good water. Also, a stable & cow house. Also for sale, adjoining the above, 2 small frame houses, occupied by good tenants. Apply on the premises, or to the Rev Jas McVean, of Gtwn.

Hse/o Reps: 1-Ptns of S B Ruck, S B Folger, & E M Jones, for pay for supplies furnished Lt Prescott for U S dredging machine: referred to the Cmte of Claims. 2-Ptn of John Kinney, for bounty on fishing schnrs **Florilla** & **Garnet**: referred to the Cmte on Commerce. 3-Ptn of Levi Eldridge, for bounty on fishing schnr **Harriet**: referred to the Cmte on Commerce. 4-Ptn of P L Parsons & Co & 160 citizens of Buffalo, N Y, praying an appropriation for continuing the work on the harbor at Michigan city, on Lake Michigan, Indiana. 5-Memorial of Wm Wright, of Boston, setting forth that a gross fraud has been committed upon the U S in the settlement of its claim upon the late Commonwealth's Bank at Boston. 6-Ptn of Geo W Manypenny & 34 other citizens, of Muskingum Co, Ohio; of Adam Peters & 89 citizens of same county: for the erection of a bridge across the Ohio river at Wheeling. 7-Mr Paterson, of N Y, on Dec 22, presented the ptn of Henry Ely, of Rochester, N Y: it sets forth that, in 1838 & 39, upon being advised by the Collector of the port of N Y that he would be entitled to a drawback of the duties upon flour imported for export, he imported 2 lots of flour from Canada, one of which was re-shipped to Canada, the other sent through the N Y canal to N Y C, & shipped thence to the island of St Thomas, the duties upon which he had paid; & asks that they may be refunded to him. 8-Mr Paterson, of N Y, also presented the ptn of Everard Peck & about 3,000 other citizens of Rochester, N Y, composing nearly 2/3rd of the male population in that city over 21 years of age, asking that the uniform postage of .05 on all single letters be adopted in place of the present rates. 9-Cmte of Claims: made an adverse report upon the ptns of Gilbert Stalker & Lewis B Willis. 10-Cmte of Claims: discharged from the consideration of the memorial of the Leg of Ky in behalf of Christopher Miller, & it was referred to the Cmte on Revolutionary Pensions.

Auction on Jan 3, at the residence of Mr C Laurie, on Indiana ave, east of 4½ st, a large handsome assortment of mahogany & other furniture, whole of which is nearly new, having ben purchased within the last 6 months. –Wm Marshall, auctioneer

Senate: 1-Ptn from Nicholas Thomas, asking for a pension. 2-Mr Bates: asking that the papers of Catharine Haywood may be taken from the files & again referred. 3-Ptn from Jacob Follansby, asking for arrears of pension. 4-Mr Woodbury: asking to take from the files the papers of Malachi Hagan & refer them. 5-Ptn from Erastus S Brown & others, citizens of Illinois, asking a confirmation of their titles to certain lands.

Annapolis Herald: the Govn'r has appointed Lyde Goodwin McBlair, to be Examiner Genr'l of Md, vice Henry Hobbs, dec'd.

Died: on Dec 25, Jeremiah A, infant s/o Wm & Anna Maria Orme, aged 18 months.

We understand that the house of Capt Housman, of the schnr **Whig**, who arrived here this morning from Va, situated at Staten Island, north side, near Port Richmond, was burned to the ground last night. The wife & child of Capt Houseman perished in the flames. Money & property in the house is supposed to have led to the horrid crime.
–N Y American of Tue

FRI DEC 29, 1843
Cotillion Party to be given at the Union Hotel in Gtwn on Jan 1. No tickets for admission can be procured except by application to some one of the Managers. Managers:

Washington	Gtwn
Dr O M Linthicum	Dr Wm Plater
J H Hager	Peter Wilson
Howard Diven	Robt Ould
Le Dran Brown	Albert Noyes
Fitzhugh Coyle	L J Anderson
Henry B Foster	Geo B Balch, U S N

Cadiz Galleons: Her Catholic Majesty's Gov't has granted a license & royal order to A Mackemot to recover the treasures of certain plate ships, among which were the galleons sunk by part of Admiral Blake's squadron on Sep 19, 1656, off this port. He has triumphed at last over some of the gigantic obstacles opposing the success of undertaking in limine. The contract of M Auvedo, of London, in 1670, & that of Don Arturo O'Brien, a Spanish ofcr, from 1688 to 1699 or 1700, having terminated in an utter failure. Cadiz, Oct 8. The Cadiz galleon enterprise, mentioned last packet, has since discovered a galleon fully laden, but owing to the lateness of the season & its divers, Messrs Abbinett & Son, having engaged in the recovery of the American steamer **Missouri**, which lies in only 5 fathoms of water off Gibraltar, & can be worked at all the winter, the recovery of this galleon must be postponed till spring. Labors will resume on May 1 with greater power & effect

At Garey's Ferry, on Dec 2, Mr Geo M Galpin accidentally shot & killed Mr John C Loper, his most intimate friend. It was truly an unfortunate & deplorable occurrence. –St Augustine News

Mr Wm Taliaferro, a most amiable & respected young man, s/o the late Wm F Taliaferro, of Westmoreland Co, Va, came to an untimely death when he was thrown from his horse on Dec 9, & was so injured by the fall that he expired in a few hours after. –Alex Gaz

Died: on Dec 27, in Wash City, Armsted G Dulin, in his 29th year.

Senate: 1-Ptn from Cmder Jas McIntosh, asking pay for services performed while acting in a rank superior to his own. 2-Ptn from Eliz B Scott, wid/o the late Alex'r Scott, asking to be remunerated for sums advanced by her late husband. 3-Ptn from the heirs of Philip Barbour, asking a law to confirm titles to lands granted to their father. 4-Mr Benton: asking that the papers in the case of the heirs of Gen Eaton be taken from the files & again referred.

Hse/o Reps:: 1-Mr Grider gave notice of his intention to offer at some future day a bill for the benefit of the devisees of Jas Rumsey, dec'd, or their heirs. 2-Ptn of J M Pumphrey & 46 other citizens of Guernsey Co, Ohio, praying for the erection of a bridge across the Ohio river at Wheeling. 3-Mr Jenks asked leave to withdraw from the files the ptn & papers of Adam Serrel, an old sldr, asking some relief for the loss of his military land, sold for taxes while he was in the service of the U S.

Obit-died: at Glasvar, the residence of his father, in Chas Co, Md, Wm D, s/o the Hon Wm D Merrick, aged 7 years, 8 months & 10 days, with inflammation of the brain. He leaves a devoted father & mother, brothers & sisters. [Dec 27 newspaper: Mr Senator Merrick, of Md, was called home yesterday by information of the dangerous illness of one of his children.] [No date on the obit notice.]

John H Hewitt, Professor of Music: pupils to meet as usual at Apollo Hall.

SAT DEC 30, 1843
Senate: 1-Ptn from Jas A Wilson, gate keeper at the Capitol, asking an increase of compensation. 2-Ptn from John Millikin, asking indemnification for French spoliations prior to 1800. 3-Mr Clayton: asking that the papers in the case of the claim of the heirs of Francis Cazenove may be withdrawn from the files. 4-Mr Fulton: to take from the files of the Senate the papers of Benj Crawford.

Furnished rooms to rent: on G st, between 14th & 15th sts. –D A Gardner

Obit-died: on Dec 24, near Aldie, Va, Mrs Rebecca Skinner, [formerly Bronaugh,] w/o Usher Skinner. She is survived by her husband & numerous relatives & friends.

Hse/o Reps:: 1-Unfinished business was the memorial presented yesterday by Mr Giddings from one Wm Jones, representing himself to be a prisoner in the U S jail of Washington City, born free, & now of right free, who had been seized in this city without cause, & was now advertised to be sold as a slave. [A very long discussion followed. The memorial was referred to the Cmte on the Judiciary.]

The U S brig **Truxton**, Lt Commandant Geo P Upshur, arrived at Hampton Roads on Wed, & the next day proceeded to the Naval Anchorage below Norfolk. The **Truxton** had on board the remains of Cmdor Porter, originally destined for interment near Phil; but, in consequence of the earnest desire of his family [now at Constamtinople] that they should be interred at Washington, Lt Upshur has thought it most advisable to put into Norfolk, & await the further orders of the Navy Dept. -Herald

The President's House will, as usual, be open on New Year's day, for the reception of such of his fellow-citizens & strangers as may be disposed to exchange salutations with the Chief Magistrate of the U S. -Madisonian

A

Aaron, 389
Abat, 115
Abbey, 84
Abbinett, 572
Abbot, 362, 418, 569
Abbott, 96, 183, 259, 275, 296, 317, 362, 384
Abell, 13, 104, 251, 308, 404, 498
Abercrombie, 60, 403
Abernethy, 247, 387
Abert, 249, 323
Accord, 217
Acheson, 472
Ackerman, 90
Acosta, 19
Adair, 282
Adams, 8, 15, 37, 41, 42, 53, 61, 70, 87, 102, 105, 116, 146, 164, 209, 216, 222, 225, 229, 255, 257, 261, 272, 279, 309, 320, 325, 362, 372, 391, 403, 415, 418, 424, 436, 444, 454, 457, 463, 464, 481, 521, 530, 564, 566, 569
Adamson, 242
Addison, 15, 68, 179
Adelmare, 200
Adie, 162, 500, 507
Adison, 101
Adkins, 205
Adler, 406, 508
Ager, 485
Agnew, 273
Aiken, 276
Ailer, 172
Aitken, 182
Alas, 562
Albany, 333
Albright, 280
Aldrich, 506
Aldworth, 55
Aler, 273

Alexander, 62, 90, 175, 216, 286, 352, 356, 358, 468, 470, 473, 475
Alford, 364
Allan, 74, 381, 521
Allemong, 369
Allen, 7, 27, 72, 77, 79, 86, 91, 101, 113, 114, 123, 133, 137, 177, 179, 194, 216, 223, 252, 270, 282, 311, 339, 350, 377, 418, 435, 447, 453, 477, 479, 506, 521, 527, 555, 565, 569, 570
Allinson, 120
Allison, 161, 304, 316, 396
Allspach, 14
Allstan, 167
Allston, 316, 498
Allwood, 91
Almy, 334
Alsop, 207
Alspach, 559
Alvord, 109, 110
Aly, 554
Ambler, 278
Ames, 61, 294, 465
Ammen, 226
Amos, 80
Amsden, 410
Anderson, 4, 42, 64, 71, 90, 101, 114, 124, 145, 167, 195, 211, 215, 247, 252, 283, 297, 301, 381, 387, 390, 402, 426, 475, 519, 572
Andrae, 418
Andre, 84, 115, 144
Andrew, 189
Andrews, 17, 18, 31, 38, 167, 185, 368, 436, 521, 542
Andross, 324
Angel, 319
Angus, 22, 56, 65, 108
Ankerstroem, 372
Annable, 254
Ansley, 262
Anthon, 452, 539
Anthony, 310, 542

Appelgate, 397
Appleton, 37, 330, 500, 541, 551
Arando, 249
Arbuckle, 225, 285, 286
Archbishop of York, 304
Archbold, 470
Archer, 133, 232, 233, 340, 524, 525, 555
Archibold, 353
Arguelles, 62, 390, 450
Argyle, 377
Arkwright, 241
Armand, 340
Armigo, 249
Armistead, 278, 333, 404, 438
Armstead, 24, 487
Armstrong, 6, 43, 91, 92, 96, 171, 174, 189, 234, 334, 376, 385, 428
Arndt, 503
Arnold, 32, 46, 124, 139, 220, 299, 349, 394, 410, 412, 476, 517, 531
Arny, 348
Arrowsmith, 237
Arthur, 91, 242
Artot, 566
Arundel, 201
Asa, 555
Asberry, 113, 157
Asbury, 45
Asey, 248
Ashby, 527
Ashdown, 231, 250
Ashmead, 32, 548
Ashmun, 182
Ashton, 334, 477, 513
Ashworth, 24
Aston, 455
Astor, 182, 183
Atchinson, 480
Atchison, 555
Atherton, 35
Athey, 266
Atkinson, 266, 564

Atler, 96
Attempt, 118
Atterbury, 237
Atwater, 68
Atwood, 343
Atz, 24
Auble, 213
Aubrey, 372, 400
Auchmuty, 519
Audubon, 155, 207
Augar, 322
Augerman, 139
Augur, 54
Aukward, 206
Aulick, 51, 122, 123, 362
Austen, 525
Austin, 133, 209, 279, 311
Auvedo, 572
Avery, 272, 305
Axe, 394
Axson, 392
Ayler, 305
Aymer, 434
Ayres, 184

B

Babbit, 570
Babbitt, 170, 259, 551, 564
Babcock, 209, 487
Babe, 355, 370, 562
Bache, 31, 32, 226, 368, 548, 552
Bachelder, 549
Backus, 523
Bacon, 30, 60, 260, 293, 329, 359, 391, 439, 457, 492, 493, 494, 496, 504, 570
Badger, 444
Bagan, 545
Bagby, 1, 60, 558
Baggott, 304
Bagot, 101, 148, 245, 251, 455
Bailey, 69, 88, 91, 146, 183, 390, 402, 505
Baillie, 381

Bailly, 87
Baily, 177, 204, 210
Bainbridge, 238, 312
Baird, 192, 212
Baker, 56, 73, 90, 108, 136, 183, 238, 245, 259, 290, 337, 367, 375, 396, 415, 439, 495, 497, 512, 537
Balch, 296, 297, 572
Balcknall, 246
Bald Eagle Island, 217
Baldwin, 18, 24, 44, 121, 209, 234, 251, 380, 385, 388, 477, 507, 509, 560
Ball, 54, 75, 88, 121, 146, 159, 401, 418, 473
Ballard, 53, 106, 115, 197
Ballestier, 395
Ballinger, 112
Baltimore, 130, 394
Baltzell, 55, 121, 483, 511
Balzell, 483
Bancroft, 392
Bankhead, 248, 297, 298, 477
Banks, 381
Bapet, 133
Barber, 38, 91, 133, 167, 507, 532
Barbett, 417
Barbot, 477
Barbour, 124, 238, 334, 481, 573
Barclay, 12, 24, 260, 272, 293, 473, 505, 520
Bargamin, 311
barges **Mary Eliza & Antoinette**, 151
bark **Parthian**, 72
Barker, 28, 164, 166, 349, 386, 387, 520, 525
Barkhammer, 531
Barksdale, 235
Barlow, 80, 237, 438
Barnaclo, 338
Barnard, 399, 453
Barnert, 407
Barnes, 38, 53, 67, 110, 121, 200, 413, 488, 522, 555, 556, 560

Barnett, 92, 296, 460
Barney, 32, 91
Barns, 91
Barnum, 178
Baroness de Gall, 568
barque **Alert**, 350
barque **Anita**, 245
barque **Ann Reynolds**, 498
barque **Caroline**, 534
barque **Diana**, 277
barque **Latrobe**, 506
barque **Margaret Hugg**, 163
barque **Renown**, 446
barque **Sarah Hand**, 514
Barranco, 338
Barratt, 17
Barret, 368
Barrett, 33, 292
Barringer, 475
Barrington, 252
Barron, 84, 301, 318
Barrow, 52, 86, 473
Barry, 12, 28, 57, 58, 81, 108, 231, 314, 484
Bart, 259
Barter, 166
Barthelow, 441
Bartlett, 52, 74, 114, 145, 170, 216, 309, 371
Barton, 46, 53, 160, 225, 380, 403, 470
Bartow, 100
Bass, 265
Bassert, 51
Bassett, 149, 261, 293, 362, 447, 470
Batchelder, 503
Batchelor, 27, 180
Bates, 107, 180, 204, 226, 231, 250, 348, 556, 572
Bathurst, 119
Battie, 54
Batts, 378
Baxter, 32, 303, 473
Bayard, 32, 140, 148, 312, 388, 548, 564

Baylies, 219, 223
Bayliss, 373
Baylor, 434
Bayne, 400, 496, 540
Baynes, 406
Bazinet, 182
Beach, 179, 380
Beadel, 246, 377
Beal, 91
Beale, 32, 133, 171, 368, 438
Beall, 72, 106, 123, 149, 162, 173, 175, 359, 370, 442, 520, 549
Beall,, 248
Beall's Pleasure, 374
Bealle, 426
Bean, 5, 292, 302, 376, 418, 440, 476
Beard, 75, 90
Beardsley, 239, 503
Beattie, 340, 341
Beatty, 118, 187
Beatty's Plains, 117
Beaty, 116
Beauchamp, 29
Beaulieu, 182, 183
Beauvois, 530
Beck, 3, 12, 15, 24, 41, 83, 115, 134, 153, 196, 210, 219, 260, 261, 293, 373, 412, 443, 457, 471, 478, 500, 518, 555
Becker, 103
Beckham, 405
Beckwith, 308, 403
Bedinger, 241
Beecett, 445
Beecher, 223, 307, 361, 475
Beechler, 32
Beeler, 93, 360
Beers, 93, 97, 184, 215, 334, 342, 424
Beesely, 168
Behler, 164
Belam, 288
Belger, 135, 321
Belknap, 247, 563

Bell, 13, 28, 31, 36, 55, 70, 91, 95, 107, 121, 130, 182, 229, 254, 263, 300, 319, 368, 475, 492, 495, 499
Bellanger, 182
Belt, 211, 239, 261, 439
Belton, 138, 313
Beltzhoover, 299
Belzarius, 437
Belzer, 381
Bemo, 423
Ben Lomond, 404
Bend, 422
Bender, 53, 292, 346, 418
Bene, 319
Benedic, 243
Benedict, 209
Benguerel, 86
Benham, 129, 296, 361, 475, 477
Benjamin, 278, 313
Benne, 352, 485
Benner, 91
Bennett, 102, 216, 303, 354, 369, 381, 403, 463, 500
Benning, 242
Benny, 90
Benson, 336, 377, 378
Bent, 226, 328
Benteen, 509
Benter, 493
Benthall, 247
Bentley, 59, 105, 228, 282, 435
Benton, 23, 465, 573
Berage, 15
Bereman, 410
Berg, 416
Bergen, 365
Berger, 528, 531
Berges, 370
Bergh, 290
Berkeley, 233, 373
Berkett, 182
Berls, 343
Bernard, 133, 221, 233

578

Berrian, 452
Berrien, 23, 436
Berry, 120, 133, 197, 199, 201, 208, 233, 239, 329, 330, 383, 418, 428, 466, 470, 478, 481, 528, 569
Bertrand, 422, 429, 459, 472
Bertus, 428
Besse, 266
Bessy, 443
Best, 178, 567
Bestor, 214, 296, 297
Bethune, 396
Betsinger, 336
Betts, 25, 58, 285, 524
Beuhler, 331
Bevan, 72, 126, 193
Beveridge, 241
Beverley, 262, 285
Beverly, 336
Bickley, 232, 280, 418
Bicknell, 115
Biddle, 46, 376, 442, 477
Bier, 31, 350
Biewend, 539
Big Spring Mills, 77
Bigelow, 32, 209, 236, 284, 391
Bihler, 296, 490, 491, 492
Bilisoly, 340, 344
Bill, 443
Billie, 380
Billing, 87, 450, 451, 454, 508
Billings, 23, 52, 538
Billups, 337
Binda, 348
Bingey, 418
Bingham, 50, 105, 305, 474, 519
Bingley, 397
Binney, 219, 391
Birch, 95, 120, 231, 261, 326, 407, 504
Birchard, 391
Bird, 104, 195, 340, 341, 344, 459
Birdsall, 92, 247
Birkey, 60

Birmingham, 358
Biscoe, 38, 196, 236
Bishop, 3, 155, 163, 246
Bispham, 388
Bisphan, 449
Bissel, 178
Bissell, 352, 470
Bittinger, 515
Bizourd, 337
Black, 110, 120, 134, 199, 302, 318, 356, 373, 452, 461, 548, 565
Blackburn, 54, 91, 523
Blackford, 32, 196, 364, 548
Blacksmith, 24
Blackstone, 348
Blackwell, 198, 536
Bladen, 509, 533
Blagden, 105, 186, 214, 307, 413, 454, 478, 502, 564
Blair, 102, 206, 339, 437, 498, 501, 542, 561
Blake, 50, 175, 225, 226, 228, 277, 285, 287, 387, 460, 527, 559, 572
Blakeslee, 209
Blakiston, 14
Blakmore, 110
Blanc, 115
Blanchard, 201, 356, 445, 552, 563
Blaney, 465
Blantyre, 545
Blatchfond, 40
Blatchford, 182
Bleecker, 246, 298, 306
Blincoe, 539
Blinn, 67
Bliss, 82, 112, 201
Blodgett, 7
Blonto_, 90
Bloom, 481
Bloomsbury, 99
Bloss, 484
Bloyce, 414
Blue, 335

Blue Plains, 34
Blunt, 352
Bluse, 92
Blythe, 120, 158
Boardman, 304
Boark, 90
Boarman, 206, 337, 459
boat **Ann**, 105
boat **Ceres**, 445
boat **John Fitch**, 78
boat **Ohio Belle**, 70
boat **Savannah**, 77
Bobo, 91
Bock, 32
Bodisco, 340, 400, 423
Boerum, 141, 148
Bogan, 353
Bogard, 555
Bogardus, 246
Boggs, 134, 267
Bogue, 348
Bohlay, 480
Bohlayer, 480, 496, 512
Bohomon, 1
Bohrer, 291, 318, 348, 353, 470, 522, 535
Boisaubin, 370
Boiseau, 407
Boisseau, 53
Bold, 64
Boles, 245
Bolivar, 26
Bolton, 63, 224
Bomford, 190, 234, 242, 538
Bominger, 216
Bonaparte, 532
Bond, 341, 434, 543
Boneville, 180
Bonga, 183
Bonney, 70
Bonnissant, 189
Bonsall, 110, 228
Bonson, 228

Bonthorn, 450
Book, 363
Booker, 322
Boon, 91
Boone, 5, 34, 172, 329
Bootes, 81, 173, 187
Booth, 3, 148, 270, 382, 400
Boothby, 552
Boothe, 139
Borden, 310
Borg, 147
Borland, 184, 561
Borremans, 488
Borrows, 20, 495
Borston, 367
Borup, 182, 183
Bosley, 356
Boss, 28, 418, 457
Bosseron, 178
Bossier, 289
Bossing, 162
Bostwick, 242
Boswell, 91, 205
Bosworth, 31, 41, 104, 164
Boteler, 1, 12, 24, 87, 128, 329, 476, 482, 504, 566
Bottemly, 418
Bottomley, 237
Botts, 186, 340
Boucher, 340
Boucherville, 336
Boudinot, 246
Bouissant, 190
Boulanger, 491, 537
Bounds, 557
Bourdon, 249
Bouvet, 488
Bowden, 457, 466
Bowdoin, 120, 447
Bowen, 334, 377, 447, 480
Bower, 117
Bowers, 485
Bowes, 267

Bowie, 30, 71, 140, 183, 231, 239, 352, 370, 426, 470, 541
Bowieville, 426, 541
Bowlegs, 353
Bowlen, 56
Bowles, 204, 319
Bowling, 57, 426
Bowling-Green, 323
Bowman, 91, 198, 238
Bowyer, 232, 253
Boyd, 11, 15, 23, 25, 42, 73, 168, 311, 358, 363, 380, 395, 454, 498, 552
Boyden, 391
Boyer, 205, 455
Boyle, 32, 154, 162, 193, 196, 200, 225, 261, 268, 305, 337, 385, 397, 418, 478
Brackenridge, 461
Bradbury, 402
Braddock, 274, 425, 467, 536
Bradford, 31, 166, 299, 313, 368, 395, 483, 537, 562, 563
Bradley, 18, 81, 83, 107, 167, 177, 206, 227, 242, 256, 261, 268, 283, 292, 307, 343, 367, 400, 432, 444, 448, 473, 480, 492, 519, 569
Bradshaw, 467
Bradstreet, 56
Brady, 72, 143, 169, 198, 260, 293, 333, 348, 415, 418, 457, 482
Brainard, 86, 95, 113, 136
Braincki, 450
Brambly, 167
Bramfield, 84
Branch, 45
Brand, 216
Branham, 532
Brannan, 410, 508
Brannin, 462
Brannon, 90
Bransford, 475
Brant, 96, 428
Brant's Mills St, 117
Brashears, 74

Bratt, 356
Brawner, 35, 446, 556
Bray, 212, 290
Brayton, 334, 351
Brazell, 92
Breakiron, 132
Breast, 460, 480
Breck, 324
Breckenridge, 252, 253, 269, 410, 418
Breckinridge, 232, 543
Breedlove, 228
Breese, 248, 514
Bremmer, 392
Brenah, 370
Brengle, 116
Brenham, 90, 468
Brent, 1, 26, 38, 52, 114, 118, 129, 149, 153, 167, 199, 207, 217, 283, 313, 332, 340, 341, 398, 404, 418, 454, 474, 484, 509, 567
Brentano, 237
Brereton, 321
Brevoort, 215
Brewer, 71, 118
Brewerton, 248
Brewster, 182, 183, 562, 563
Brey, 90
Brice, 116, 356
Briceland, 296
Bridges, 185
Bridgman, 178, 179
Bridyn, 90
Brien, 253, 338, 369
brig **Abigail Richmond**, 197
brig **Amphitrite**, 49
brig **Antelope**, 366
brig **Argus**, 85
brig **Atlantic**, 186
brig **Bainbridge**, 387, 449, 455
brig **Boxer**, 166, 365
brig **Delaware**, 184
brig **Dolphin**, 449
brig **Emeline**, 447

brig **Excel**, 285
brig **Falmouth**, 558
brig **Kanawha**, 449
brig **L'Orient**, 157
brig **Linden**, 498
brig **Maria Theresa**, 525
brig **Mary**, 205
brig of war **Truxton**, 281
brig **Ohio**, 343
brig **Oregon**, 449
brig **Pecounic**, 272
brig **Perry**, 135, 407
brig **Pilgrim**, 197
brig **Porpoise**, 316, 387
brig **Raymond**, 80
brig **Samson**, 198
brig **Savannah**, 393
brig **Somers**, 2, 4, 12, 34, 51, 73, 169, 234, 559
brig **Statira**, 198
brig **Temperance**, 451
brig **Truxton**, 553, 574
brig **Union**, 148
brig **Warrior**, 14, 25
Briggs, 72, 221, 380
Brigham, 294
Bright, 427, 531
Brightwell, 112, 346, 484
Brinckerhoff, 475, 570
Brinley, 548
Briscoe, 18, 44, 51, 213, 236, 387, 492, 494, 495
Brisette, 182
Brissington, 465
Brittingham, 510
Britton, 14, 65, 113, 143, 180
Broad Run tract, 404
Broadstreet, 73, 108
Brobston, 366
Brock, 482
Brockenbrough, 23, 55
Brockesby, 216
Brocks, 63

Brockway, 183
Brodback, 488
Brodhead, 464, 520
Brodie, 238
Broke, 85
Bromwell, 271
Bronaugh, 8, 41, 107, 169, 261, 276, 574
Bronowski, 433
Bronson, 46, 78, 162, 310
Brooke, 5, 30, 31, 32, 37, 59, 64, 97, 159, 162, 173, 215, 225, 244, 248, 275, 278, 340, 346, 374, 390, 399, 418, 469, 517, 547, 548
Brookes, 212
Brooks, 89, 124, 180, 196, 198, 209, 238, 255, 295, 297, 354, 442, 513
Broom, 418, 456
Broughton, 216, 378
Brown, 1, 14, 15, 23, 27, 31, 41, 44, 49, 51, 54, 57, 68, 70, 75, 82, 91, 103, 104, 108, 120, 121, 123, 126, 129, 135, 147, 149, 159, 172, 178, 197, 198, 199, 200, 205, 209, 212, 226, 229, 234, 243, 251, 258, 264, 297, 310, 313, 319, 321, 332, 333, 341, 356, 358, 361, 362, 368, 370, 371, 375, 377, 398, 415, 424, 447, 452, 453, 456, 459, 461, 464, 476, 477, 478, 479, 482, 487, 493, 500, 501, 502, 503, 510, 514, 517, 519, 525, 526, 562, 570, 572
Browne, 24, 326, 382, 400, 527
Browning, 4, 32, 166, 422, 548, 555
Bruce, 33, 68, 275, 368, 382, 433, 441, 449
Bruen, 70, 121
Bruff, 24, 295
Bruin, 103, 433
Brum, 31
Brush, 57, 92
Bryan, 31, 35, 48, 52, 135, 148, 159, 198, 266, 312, 350, 358, 380, 432, 450, 465, 502

Bryant, 261, 294, 296, 334
Bryce, 50
Bryson, 296, 334
Buchanan, 30, 50, 73, 266, 558
Buchhofer, 132
Buck, 35, 209, 302, 373, 401, 529
Buck's Bones, 118
Buckey, 441
Buckingham, 8, 89, 93, 112, 207, 292, 312, 492, 494
Buckley, 219
Buckmaster, 452
Budd, 349
Buel, 251
Buell, 238, 565
Buexestine, 367
Buffalo King, 181
Buffington, 116
Bugh, 116
Bugher, 200
Buist, 264, 269, 397, 410, 418, 490
Bulfinch, 8, 77, 226, 277, 342, 394, 519, 553, 569
Bull, 84
Bullit, 16
Bullus, 418
Bulow, 79
Bulwer, 455, 506
Bunce, 57
Bunt, 400
Bunting, 337
Burch, 94, 232, 253, 351, 418
Burche, 12, 87, 97, 123, 220, 463
Burchel, 383
Burdine, 32, 161, 492, 494, 496
Burford, 21
Burger, 71
Burgess, 499
Burgham, 286
Burgheim, 509
Burgler, 459
Burgoyne, 254
Burgundy, 459

Burk, 117, 444
Burke, 91, 95, 316, 319, 340, 341, 370, 422, 550
Burl, 433
Burne, 436
Burnell, 277, 550, 554
Burnett, 261
Burnham, 286, 538
Burns, 159, 396
Burnside, 389
Burr, 11, 25, 49, 113, 228, 292, 305, 327, 367, 371, 436, 460, 494, 495, 543
Burriss, 60, 104
Burrouges, 221
Burroughs, 78
Burrows, 291, 297, 471
Burt, 259
Burtiss, 177
Burtley, 501
Burton, 353, 452
Burwell, 539, 568
Busby, 90
Bush, 90, 203, 533, 537
Busheyhead, 442
Bushnell, 388
Bushyhead, 462, 472, 497
Buster, 90
Busvine, 334
Bute, 228
Butler, 44, 64, 66, 96, 167, 183, 191, 193, 220, 222, 226, 241, 275, 295, 321, 322, 349, 376, 382, 418, 441, 443, 462, 483, 489, 490, 491, 499, 510, 526, 537, 546, 564, 569
Butt, 267, 292, 564
Butterfield, 182
Butts, 397
Buxenstein, 207
Byan, 287
Byerly, 184
Byington, 261, 454, 457, 566
Byng, 160
Byrd, 100

Byrne, 154, 337, 427, 481, 513, 517, 530
Byron, 90

C

C & O Canal, 539
Ca_h, 223
Cabaniss, 75
Cabell, 27, 520
Cable, 27
Cadotte, 182
Cadwalder, 368
Cadwallader, 31, 88, 259, 466
Caesar, 200
Caesarino, 201
Cahal, 475
Cahill, 187, 225, 337
Caho, 241
Cahoone, 32, 548
Cairns, 88
Calder, 211
Calderon, 237, 248
Caldwell, 31, 48, 57, 92, 237, 256, 283, 303, 307, 380, 419, 462, 548, 570
Calhoon, 108
Calhoun, 32, 59, 113, 151, 160, 170, 237, 548
Call, 510
Callan, 33, 65, 211, 231, 250, 260, 261, 268, 269, 292, 293, 327, 374, 489, 491, 502
Callen, 116
Callender, 124
Calligan, 411
Callis, 482
Calve, 527
Calvert, 36, 91, 300, 399, 441, 444, 516, 520
Cam, 216
Camack, 215
Cameron, 90, 178, 513
Cammack, 11, 97, 269, 410
Camp, 332
Campau, 555

Campbell, 30, 52, 54, 65, 70, 75, 85, 96, 116, 139, 200, 227, 237, 243, 250, 257, 262, 337, 381, 382, 494, 529, 559, 561
Campo, 370
canal boat **Little Western**, 256
Canatoo, 474
Candler, 414
Canfula, 90
Canning, 275
Cannon, 184, 222, 255, 303
Canter, 14, 25, 48, 114
Carber, 562
Carbery, 181, 211, 216, 243, 261, 267, 305, 463, 478, 514
Card, 534
Carder, 298
Carey, 64, 299, 441
Carleton, 118
Carley, 188
Carlin, 268, 389
Carlisle, 7, 36, 44, 134, 295
Carlton, 295, 498, 517
Carmack, 47
Carman, 1, 396
Caro, 64
Carondelet, 142
Carothers, 109, 489
Carpender, 400
Carpenter, 68, 95, 347, 560
Carpentier, 182
Carr, 210, 228, 274, 340, 377, 453, 533
Carrick, 538
Carrico, 340, 474
Carrington, 46, 311, 480, 511
Carroll, 38, 40, 55, 59, 93, 163, 220, 312, 332, 356, 369, 370, 394, 444
Carson, 78, 400
Carter, 8, 153, 178, 186, 208, 226, 258, 261, 273, 280, 285, 295, 377, 378, 387, 401, 405, 440, 454, 512, 515, 543, 553
Cartwright, 83

Carusi, 279, 409
Caruthers, 35, 54
Carvallo, 249
Cary, 67, 100, 274
Casanave, 436
Case, 136, 428
Casey, 435
Cash, 91
Caskie, 311
Cassady, 410
Cassedy, 208
Cassin, 49, 340, 348, 376
Castellanos, 340, 344
Castleman, 559
Castner, 213, 401, 440, 518
Caswell, 362
Cathcart, 78, 453
Cathedral of Versailles, 567
Catlett, 96, 101, 262, 432, 529
Caton, 22, 154, 214
Catron, 18, 121, 459
Catts, 133, 161
Caughman, 278
Causey, 452
Causin, 20, 195, 305, 307, 441
Causine, 147
Caussin, 344
Caustin, 356
Cavendy, 51, 362
Cayce, 241
Cazanave, 469, 490
Cazenove, 314, 573
Cecil, 377
Cecily, 237
Cedar Grove, 467
Cedar Point Plantation, 218
Centine, 67
Chadbourne, 322
Chadeyne, 255
Chadwick, 250, 510, 519
Chaffee, 95
Challenge, 48

Chamberlain, 110, 233, 258, 428, 525, 558
Chamberlayne, 161
Chambers, 53, 178, 179
Champlain, 114
Champlin, 15, 23, 39, 42, 52, 73, 98
Chance, 116
Chandler, 14, 27, 81, 101, 113, 116, 144, 174, 433, 441
Chandonai, 6
Channing, 316
Chanunard, 216
Chapel, 59
Chapin, 235, 238, 304, 405, 539
Chaplain, 382, 442
Chapman, 128, 130, 146, 187, 301, 306, 406, 418
Chapron, 50
Charette, 182
Charles, 532
Charleston, 262
Charlotte, 465
Charlton, 177
Charvis, 226, 239, 343, 366, 449
Chas, 525
Chase, 246, 336, 350, 377, 525
Chassaing, 337
Chatard, 368
Chateline, 420
Chatham, 516
Chaullier, 247
Chauncey, 240, 246, 349, 428, 449, 559
Chaupes, 237
Chauvenet, 224
Cheatham, 475
Cheesebrough, 274
Cheeseman, 96
Cheever, 555
Chenet, 20
Chenoweth, 31
Chenowith, 368
Cherokee, 48, 53, 68, 440, 442, 462, 472, 474, 544

585

Cheshire, 212, 233, 367
Chesley, 480
Chester, 116
Chestnut Hill, 467
Cheston, 255
Cheubini, 567
Chew, 12, 87, 95, 140, 273, 285, 437, 446
Chichester, 500
Chick, 93, 334
Child, 228, 343, 406, 416
Childs, 54, 525
Chillum Castle Manor, 332
Chilton, 186, 396, 448
Chilton Castle Manor Resurveyed, 123
Chipman, 119
Chippewa Indians, 182
Chisholm, 415
Chisley, 511
Chladni, 208
Choate, 329, 366, 371
Choctaw nation, 175
Cholmondet, 251
Choteau, 462
Chouteau, 177, 178, 239, 269
Chrise, 529
Christian, 311
Christie, 403
Chrony, 359
Chubert, 455
Chumesero, 79
Church, 416
Churchill, 321
Chutkowski, 71
Cingefield, 118
Cipriant, 230
Cisalpine, 43
Cisil, 148
Cissel, 308, 399
City, 32, 548
Clagett, 189, 258, 268, 299, 370, 378, 400, 418, 476, 480, 528, 536
Clapham, 334

Clapp, 369, 377, 378
Clark, 17, 59, 76, 91, 113, 173, 175, 178, 191, 211, 232, 234, 240, 243, 259, 273, 278, 293, 337, 368, 388, 391, 424, 452, 457, 461, 465, 487, 492, 495, 506, 510, 517, 525, 545, 552, 560, 569
Clarke, 31, 59, 65, 90, 117, 118, 162, 199, 231, 234, 254, 258, 260, 283, 292, 296, 297, 322, 327, 340, 363, 386, 388, 409, 436, 438, 444, 457, 459, 491, 492, 506, 519, 527, 535, 543, 558, 568
Clarvoe, 319, 339, 431, 492
Clary, 530
Clatsop Indians, 372
Clautice, 337
Claxton, 472, 483, 501
Clay, 10, 56, 81, 114, 145, 163, 171, 289, 371, 425, 446, 472, 509
Clayton, 116, 237, 452, 573
Cleaveland, 303
Clements, 128, 131, 333, 439, 442, 457
Clemson, 163
Clendening, 68
Clephane, 351, 464, 490, 491
Clerc, 67
Cleveland, 207
Clevenger, 509
Clifford, 213
Clifton, 330, 332, 340
Clinch, 39, 61, 96, 106, 549
Clinton, 237, 247, 563
Clitch, 560
Clitherall, 555
Clitz, 296
Clopton, 90
Closey, 304
Cloud, 498
Clubb, 522
Clum, 449
Coad, 234, 337
Coakely, 161

Coakley, 262
Coal & Iron Banks, 117
Coalburn, 348
Coates, 478
Cobb, 31, 224, 234, 368, 388, 391
Cobell, 262
Cochran, 22, 285, 302
Cochrane, 275
Cock, 351
Cocke, 90, 191, 223, 383, 409, 475, 486, 513
Coddington, 348
Coddy, 91
Coe, 308, 485, 508
Coffee, 188
Coffin, 84, 159, 345, 354, 391, 395, 396
Coffman, 91
Cogdale, 415
Coghill, 401
Coghlin, 369
Cogswell, 394
Cohen, 171, 181, 396
Cohn, 6
Coke, 42, 114, 145
Colbert, 531
Colborn, 51
Colburn, 514, 565
Colby, 477
Colclazer, 74, 132
Coldwell, 340
Cole, 335, 346, 483, 516, 545
Coleman, 31, 47, 126, 166, 208, 213, 368
Colemen, 324
Coles, 237
Colgate, 88, 108
Collard, 22
Collars, 377
Collier, 546
Collins, 4, 32, 59, 87, 177, 185, 200, 224, 257, 371, 377, 402, 490, 498, 508
Colquhoon, 216
Colquhoun, 206

Colquitt, 566
Colston, 164
Colt, 216, 418, 436
Coltman, 243, 552
Colton, 22
Colville, 91
Colvin, 356
Combe, 293
Combs, 14, 337, 411, 496, 521
Comegys, 31
Commercial Mart, 118
Compton, 161, 191, 486
Comstock, 214, 501
Condict, 293
Cone, 216
Conley, 348
Conly, 519
Connard, 400
Connell, 144
Connelly, 3, 476, 489, 494, 559
Conner, 83, 116, 118, 127
Connolly, 5, 154, 537
Connor, 81, 182
Conolly, 377, 415, 483
Conrad, 83, 121
Conrad's ferry, 217, 448
Conroy, 347
Constable, 254
Constantine, 230
Contee, 76, 127, 334, 469
Contentment, 446
Converse, 417
Conway, 15, 246, 343, 365, 377
Cony, 556
Coodey, 472
Cook, 24, 31, 70, 86, 95, 113, 116, 134, 150, 157, 166, 205, 208, 211, 224, 226, 237, 260, 298, 328, 363, 377, 476
Cooke, 165, 168, 286, 366, 373, 466
Cookendorfer, 559
Cookendorffer, 493, 495
Cookman, 319
Cooley, 247

Coolidge, 216
Coomb, 367
Coombe, 38, 140, 287, 454
Coombs, 220, 364, 431
Coon, 222
Coone, 343
Cooper, 83, 97, 202, 225, 230, 292, 293, 294, 296, 334, 346, 368, 377, 395, 416, 464, 570
Cope, 140
Copeland, 18, 39, 455
Coplan, 90
Copway, 182
Corbin, 11, 32, 182, 399
Corby, 192
Corcoran, 83, 197, 300, 308, 325, 418, 433, 476, 490, 491
Core, 14, 100, 113, 138, 170
Cornelius, 57
Cornell, 48, 111, 203, 260
Corner, 99
Corning, 17
Cornings, 422
Cornwallis, 359, 381
Cornwalllis, 224
Corry, 81
Corson, 417
corvette **Cyane**, 23
corvette **Heroine**, 395
Corwin, 446
Cosay, 339
Cosgrave, 498
Coskery, 195
Coskey, 343
Costello, 275
Costigan, 195, 218, 512
Costin, 550
Cotesworth, 224
Cottage, 533
Cotti, 182
Cottingham, 95, 96, 270
Cotton, 198, 238
Couch, 82, 108

Coulter, 116
Coumbe, 305
Countess of Cork, 567
Countess of Denbigh, 72
Courtney, 96
Courts, 413
Coutan, 369
Couteau, 182
Couts, 322
Couveillion, 182
Covent Garden, 118
Cover, 174
Cowan, 83, 223
Cowardin, 311
Cowdry, 382
Cowper, 364
Cox, 13, 29, 76, 90, 97, 108, 149, 154, 190, 201, 211, 233, 242, 249, 261, 262, 292, 299, 308, 331, 340, 344, 347, 348, 391, 448, 478, 519, 569
Coxe, 31, 49, 172, 269, 344, 357, 569
Coyle, 126, 231, 418, 454, 478, 494, 527, 541, 569, 572
Cozzens, 197
Crabb, 436, 520
Crafton, 67, 89, 556
Crafts, 41
Craig, 33, 42, 318, 399, 461, 499
Crain, 200, 262, 399
Cranch, 141, 149, 426, 467
Crandall, 527
Crandell, 11, 260, 261, 293
Crandle, 526
Crane, 95, 188, 259, 321, 333
Crauford, 481
Craufurd, 248
Craven, 333, 334, 335, 417
Crawford, 27, 62, 101, 105, 114, 137, 148, 184, 237, 277, 344, 487, 530, 534, 548, 573
Cray, 7
Creamer, 482, 485, 511
Crebassa, 182

Creek chief, 202
Creighton, 452
Crenshaw, 521
Cressman, 150
Creutsfeldt, 205
Creutzfeldt, 346, 506
Crews, 45
Cripps, 78, 287
Cristy, 401
Crittenden, 39, 90, 475
Crivelin, 547
Crocker, 199, 237, 309
Crockett, 557
Crockshank, 441
Crockwell, 280
Croggon, 464, 539
Croghan, 177
Crolius, 453
Cromebee, 216
Cromwell, 2, 4, 25, 51, 58
Crook, 228
Crosby, 32, 359, 399
Cross, 50, 384, 406, 412, 436
Crossan, 246
Crosswell, 413
Crow, 8, 24, 58, 250, 303
Crowell, 446
Crowley, 536
Crown, 167, 318, 321, 418
Croxall, 116
Crozer, 366, 389
Crozet, 322
Crozier, 459
Cruge, 549
Cruger, 14, 39, 64, 334
Cruikshank, 448
Cruit, 3, 199, 293
Cruitzfeldt, 374
Crump, 258, 265, 387
Crusselle, 76
Crutchfeldt, 488
Cruzat, 95
Cudlipp, 38, 211

Cugir, 377
Culbert, 514
Culbertson, 88
Culbreth, 253
Cull, 261, 293
Culver, 383, 485
Cummin, 340
Cummings, 30, 159, 324, 348, 510, 564
Cummins, 204, 430, 479
Cummiskey, 340, 344, 450
Cunard, 350
Cunningham, 116, 135, 160, 288, 361, 376, 469, 527, 542, 547, 566
Cupid's Bower, 217, 448
Curley, 441
Curran, 327, 384, 407
Currie, 105
Currier, 551
Curry, 185, 216, 531
Curson, 96
Curtain, 559
Curtis, 73, 291, 294, 510
Cushing, 7, 36, 218, 219, 239, 391, 448, 481
Cushman, 422, 477
Custis, 154, 344, 509
Cutbush, 299, 314
Cuthbert, 492
Cutler, 513
Cutter, 200
cutter **Hamilton**, 393
cutter **Woodbury**, 42
Cutting, 178, 313, 454
Cutts, 74, 115, 261, 269, 318, 560
Cuyler, 32, 171

D

D'Hauteville, 278
D'Wolf, 70
Dade, 10, 47, 96, 362, 539
Daggett, 335, 498
Daily, 365, 381, 553
Daingerfield, 460

Dairy, 344
Dakes, 319
Dale, 161, 226, 347
Daley, 430
Dallam, 133, 233
Dallas, 74, 234, 326
Dalrympl, 324
Dalrymple, 382
Dalton, 105, 293, 327
Daly, 330
Damarine, 41
Damon, 294
Damoreau, 567
Damp, 80
Dana, 7, 34, 185, 210, 316, 345, 569
Dandridge, 134
Danforth, 278, 516, 569
Dangerfield, 139, 237, 548
Daniel, 46, 81, 161, 220, 295, 481, 549, 555
Daniell, 129, 228
Daniels, 31, 236, 544
Danigerfield, 435
Dannehower, 364
Dant, 38
Danvers, 265
Daracott, 79
Darden, 111
Dardenne, 339
Darlin, 105
Darnall, 79
Dashiell, 63
Daugle, 534
Daunas, 20
Davenagh, 406
Davenport, 178, 241, 323, 396
David, 177, 396
Davidson, 51, 106, 170, 285, 353, 356, 406, 419, 424, 434, 470
Davies, 104, 105, 133, 232, 297, 298, 349, 425
Davis, 12, 15, 32, 35, 42, 71, 86, 88, 90, 91, 100, 111, 116, 117, 120, 148, 159, 166, 167, 170, 180, 195, 200, 213, 219, 226, 247, 248, 254, 256, 258, 260, 263, 267, 281, 293, 295, 306, 314, 344, 351, 353, 354, 380, 384, 386, 387, 390, 396, 400, 402, 409, 417, 424, 438, 454, 455, 467, 482, 490, 491, 495, 511, 519, 539, 543, 549, 559, 564, 566, 569
Davlin, 114, 155
Davy, 15, 568
Dawes, 223, 395, 524
Dawkins, 27, 61, 107
Dawley, 120
Daws, 520
Dawsing, 81
Dawson, 108, 194, 212, 224, 255, 288, 367, 569
Day, 92, 228, 485
Dayton, 54
De Blanc, 340
De Buys, 60, 98, 114
De Camp, 364, 365
De Generes, 115
De Groot, 345
De Kalb, 38, 381
De Kraft, 32
De Lusser, 138
De Peyster, 39, 64, 549
De Puy, 327
De Russey, 163
De Russy, 6
De Saule, 496, 537
De Saules, 224, 367, 411
De Sisser, 114
De Vaughan, 3
Deakins, 80
Deale, 292
Dean, 407, 462, 498, 510
Deans, 499
Dearborn, 128, 355, 365, 490, 528
Debuys, 21, 194
Decatur, 58, 83, 242
Decker, 226, 351

Deckey, 101
Dee, 31, 368
Deeble, 153, 233, 424
Deer Park, 116
Degges, 397
Dejaddon, 182
DeKraft, 399
Delancy, 351
Delande, 12
Delano, 22
Delany, 44, 48, 114, 167, 288, 527
Delap, 173
Delaplane, 30
Delarge, 191
Delassus, 82
Delavan, 70
Delecarlia, 261
Deletra, 555
Delft, 47
Dellet, 381, 481
Dellon, 90
Delong, 102
Delvigne, 150
Dement, 526
Denby, 340
Denham, 117, 164, 384, 432
Denison, 356
Denneale, 231
Dennet, 565
Dennis, 389, 414, 442, 460
Dennison, 287, 417
Denny, 35, 246
Denon, 555
Denson, 345
Dent, 59, 167, 251, 322, 346, 348, 394, 501
Depeyster, 14
Dequindre, 112
Derby, 379, 411
Deringer, 552
Derment, 552
Dermott, 239, 419, 460
Desaussure, 172

Deshler, 160
Deshon, 321
Devaughn, 483
Dever, 68
Devereux, 35, 370
Devlin, 126, 172, 215
Devoe, 100, 181
Dew, 426
Dewey, 45, 48, 84, 209, 225, 243, 467
Dewindt, 467
Dewing, 50
Dewis, 91
Dewit, 73
Dewitt, 533
Dexter, 43, 44, 109, 168, 228, 371, 391
Dias, 482
Dibrell, 161
Dicey, 35, 57
Dick, 134, 217, 269, 409
Dickerson, 4
Dickey, 150, 200, 289
Dickins, 280, 307, 477
Dickinson, 17, 209, 350, 538
Dickson, 33, 67, 133, 366, 510, 516
Dicy, 43, 82, 113
Diehl, 184
Diffenderffer, 68
Digges, 45, 83, 126, 332, 399
Dill, 461
Dillard, 396
Dille, 88
Dillet, 244
Dilmore, 216
Dimock, 28
Dingley, 183
Disbrow, 95
Diven, 572
Dix, 100, 299, 428, 456, 471
Dixon, 25, 84, 94, 209, 261, 279, 293, 353, 389, 424, 438, 470, 476, 478, 521, 538, 554, 566, 570
Dixson, 461
Dobbin, 64

Dobbins, 198, 238
Dod, 32
Dodd, 361
Dodder, 547
Dodds, 447
Dodge, 59, 110, 261, 344, 347, 424, 478, 547, 553
Dodson, 123, 461
Dohrman, 27, 133, 170
Doll, 159
Donavoe, 130
Donelan, 20, 45, 61, 78, 103, 244, 348, 399, 408, 412, 430, 456
Donelly, 403
Doniphan, 201, 261
Donn, 1, 24, 87, 92, 173, 188, 306, 329
Donnelly, 340, 344
Donoghoe, 348
Donoho, 154, 486
Donohoe, 415
Donohoo, 41, 103, 167, 170, 177, 233, 492, 493, 494, 495, 496
Donovan, 536
Doods, 173
Dooley, 154, 243, 415, 522
Doolittle, 409
Doran, 24, 369, 370
Dornback, 560
Dorrance, 67
Dorsett, 284, 487, 544
Dorsey, 30, 37, 107, 120, 128, 129, 195, 200, 224, 314, 401, 413, 426, 445
Doty, 170
Dough, 54
Dougherty, 91
Doughty, 30, 43, 161, 460
Douglas, 52, 269, 351, 409, 410
Douglass, 90, 93, 246, 261, 292, 414, 488, 494
Dove, 261, 262, 284, 293, 438, 454, 484, 489, 490, 515
Dow, 148, 211, 312, 457, 527, 542
Dowden, 154, 224, 312, 372

Dowling, 121, 126, 154, 214, 232, 241, 415, 489, 491
Downer, 102, 552
Downes, 57, 63, 246, 276, 296, 347, 350, 377
Downing, 25, 38, 247, 517
Downs, 90
Dowson, 391, 419
Doyer, 369
Doyle, 42, 225, 270, 340, 344, 510
Doyne, 515
Drain, 340
Drake, 50, 60, 82, 231, 250, 296, 477, 549
Drayton, 51, 324, 362, 450, 547
Drew, 48, 114, 170, 311, 530, 537, 570
Drewry, 68, 72
Drill, 22
Driver, 238
Drummond, 29, 56, 100, 125, 186
Drury, 76, 222, 231, 250, 286, 292, 293, 457
Dry Hill, 118
Dryden, 23
Dryer, 501
Drysdale, 39, 113, 144
Du Barry, 175, 334
Ducachet, 527
Ducatel, 337
Duckworth, 496
Ducoing, 570
Duconge, 50
Dudley, 476
Duer, 452
Duffield, 35
Dugan, 92, 337
Duke of Wellington, 282
Dulaney, 14
Dulany, 25, 64, 89, 115, 128, 135, 376, 378, 474, 512
Dulau't, 182
Duley, 419
Dulin, 573

Dumbleton, 92
Dun, 397
Dunbar, 91, 133, 233
Duncan, 18, 296, 362, 450, 451
Duncanson, 538
Duncomb, 357
Dunderdale, 403
Dunham, 14, 162, 223, 393, 444
Dunhan, 91
Dunlap, 252, 520
Dunlop, 431, 533
Dunmore, 554
Dunn, 92, 173, 258, 282, 338, 483
Dunning, 453
Dunnington, 510, 538
Dunscomb, 128
Duplantier, 142
Duplesses, 168
Dupont, 407, 452
Dupuy, 53
Duralde, 31, 399
Durham, 348
Durkee, 270, 337
Durmitt, 36
Dusenbery, 91
Dushane, 385
Dutch, 370
Dutton, 314
Duval, 108
Duvall, 8, 24, 40, 205, 330, 342, 415, 424
Duvernay, 182
Dyer, 12, 37, 119, 132, 168, 180, 262, 318, 329, 361, 457, 468, 522, 542
Dyes, 403
Dykers, 340, 344
Dyson, 393

E

Eaches, 129
Eader, 67
Eagan, 464
Earl, 141
Earl of Denbigh, 72
Earle, 427, 486, 531
Early, 356
Earthquake, 482
Easby, 26, 351, 519
Eastland, 90, 223
Eastman, 7, 26, 259
Easton, 11, 436
Eaton, 32, 38, 60, 259, 265, 470, 548, 573
Eberbach, 489, 490, 496
Eccleson, 419
Eccleston, 431
Eckel, 12
Eckford, 129
Eckloff, 193, 346, 419, 442, 477, 488, 489
Eddes, 219
Eddy, 177, 228, 310
Edelin, 88, 262, 340, 478
Eden Island, 364
Eden's Paradise Regained, 116
Edgecomb, 57
Edgecombe, 39, 94
Edgerton, 396
Edgington, 380
Edmands, 110
Edmonds, 50, 114, 117, 151, 209
Edmondson, 437, 481
Edmonston, 349, 482
Edson, 41
Edward'd ferry, 448
Edwards, 16, 19, 24, 29, 75, 91, 120, 158, 163, 174, 180, 184, 204, 205, 234, 279, 300, 334, 377, 417, 438, 440, 454, 484, 486, 500, 504, 507, 519, 569
Edwards' ferry, 217
Edwards' Ferry, 77
Egan, 348
Egbert, 226
Egerett, 52
Eggleston, 385

Eginton, 521
Eichelberger, 67, 337, 461
Eights, 210
Elder, 86, 108, 337
Elder Spring, 118
Eldredge, 108
Eldridge, 73, 571
Elgin, 303
Eliot, 256, 257, 376
Elk Island, 57
Ellery, 56, 73, 108, 113, 152
Ellet, 194
Ellicott, 116, 159
Ellington, 260
Elliot, 25, 104, 169, 283, 292, 381, 419, 511
Elliott, 127, 283
Ellis, 97, 194, 231, 245, 250, 311, 480, 495, 496, 518, 552
Ellison, 248
Ellsworth, 62, 166, 254, 256, 352, 463, 523
Ellwood, 492, 493
Ellzey, 467
Elmemdorf, 385
Elmer, 476
Elmes, 367
Elmon, 565
Elting, 322
Elton, 381
Eltonhead, 343
Elwes, 341, 375, 517
Ely, 182, 376, 571
Emanuel, 237
Emerick, 492
Emerson, 86, 113, 138, 210
Emison, 570
Emmerson, 82
Emmert, 198, 554
Emmons, 53, 210, 330, 399
Emory, 123, 125, 225
Empie, 153
Enders, 185

Engel, 101
Engle, 343
English, 190, 216, 237, 298, 385, 569
Enni, 154
Ennis, 126, 147, 154, 214, 415, 443, 498, 523
Enos, 309
Entwisle, 196, 438
Erb, 126
Ericsson, 455
Erind, 32
Ernst, 123
Erskine, 259, 434
Erving, 177, 396, 543
Erwin, 426
Esk, 91
Espey, 64, 115, 284
Espy, 48, 210
Essex, 469, 530, 551
Estep, 432, 529
Estes, 561
Estko, 189
Estrada, 470
Etting, 334, 419
Etz, 223
Eubanks, 498
Eustis, 78, 300, 304, 306, 312, 321, 322, 396
Eutew, 118
Eva, 460
Evans, 22, 25, 56, 108, 118, 119, 159, 265, 375, 394, 419, 438, 465, 478, 490, 555, 569
Evans' Purchase, 118
Eveleth, 35, 57, 73, 114, 528
Evens, 186, 188
Everett, 108, 120, 210, 218, 219, 386, 497, 526
Everhart, 264, 397
Everly, 96, 107, 116, 565
Eversfield, 362, 501
Everson, 47
Evinger, 271

Evrit, 96
Ewen, 91
Ewing, 273, 396, 475
Ewrey, 91
Eyeleth, 143
Eyers, 366
Eyre, 237

F

Fabre, 15, 113, 136, 171
Faherty, 154
Fahnestock, 313, 356
Faifax, 470
Fair Hill, 117
Fairfax, 118, 210, 296, 353, 451
Fairview, 450
Falconer, 228
Fales, 163, 448, 469, 470
Fallon, 97
Falls, 210
False, 100
Fanning, 268
Fansill, 386
Farmer, 498
Farnham, 65, 108, 127, 149, 164, 181, 467, 534, 569
Farnnam, 391
Farnum, 21, 151
Farquhar, 8, 276
Farquharson, 116
Farr, 42, 512
Farragut, 135
Farrar, 286, 544
Farrell, 463
Farrington, 39
Farron, 352
Farrow, 75, 470
Fatherty, 415
Faulkner, 186
Fauntleroy, 377
Fauquhar, 542
Faut, 15
Favier, 47, 488

Favro, 192
Fay, 64
Fearing, 64
Fearson, 4, 284, 424
Feast, 356
Featherstonhaugh, 228
Feddeman, 427
Feeney, 494
Fegg, 480
Fegur, 354
Feinour, 524
Felger, 116
Fell, 181
Fenby, 68
Fendall, 227, 302, 367, 569
Fenton, 15, 396
Fenwick, 6, 195, 261
Feodorouna, 230
Fergeson, 368
Ferguson, 31, 54, 97, 105, 231, 233, 240, 250, 261, 292, 293, 356, 564
Fergusson, 68
Fernwaldt, 354
Ferral, 122
Ferrall, 134
Ferreton, 429, 538, 540
Ferris, 134
Fessenden, 363, 374
Fibreman, 49
Ficklen, 55, 291
Field, 104, 207, 397
Fields, 96
File, 569
Fill, 375
Fillebrown, 31, 548, 564
Fillebrowne, 32
Fillmore, 185, 436
Finch, 110, 216
Findlay, 291
Findley, 278, 385
Finegan, 154, 503
Finlay, 567
Finley, 40, 133, 233, 505

Finn, 228
Finney, 10
Finsfrock, 486
first Bank, 376
Fischer, 36, 253, 480, 509, 527
Fish, 97, 480
Fisher, 43, 57, 63, 75, 81, 90, 95, 113, 143, 171, 235, 294, 352, 417, 550
Fisk, 112, 125
Fiske, 396
Fister, 488, 527
Fitch, 10, 143
Fitzgerald, 90, 154, 162, 196, 207, 258, 495
Fitzhugh, 22, 116, 127, 161, 209, 370, 377, 383, 545, 556
Fitzpatrick, 1, 261, 293, 489, 491, 513
Fitzsimmons, 369, 378
Fix, 232
Flagler, 209
Flahault, 567
Flanagan, 16, 112
Fleischmann, 468
Fleming, 154, 495, 496, 548
Flemming, 32, 337
Fletcher, 7, 8, 44, 139, 243, 284, 347, 348, 373, 396, 419, 478, 490, 512, 540
Flicher, 229
Fling, 457
Flint, 59, 206, 209, 391, 538
Flood, 63, 209
Floors, 380
Flores, 370
Florida, 185
Florida Indians, 123, 124, 128
Floris, 249
Flower, 366
Flowers, 381
Flowery Meads, 117
Floyd, 5, 47
Fogg, 299, 475
Folger, 571
Follansbee, 180

Follansby, 572
Follins, 470
Fontenot, 470
Fooks, 453
Foot, 15
Foote, 154, 298, 423, 431
Forbee, 69
Forbes, 171, 225, 228, 317, 328, 465
Forble, 393
Force, 12, 330, 440, 478, 526, 527
Ford, 14, 31, 55, 100, 113, 130, 136, 146, 220, 349, 382, 418, 476, 506, 510, 518
Fordham, 102, 311, 438
Foree, 458
Forest, 278, 457
Forest of Prince George's, 426, 541
Forrest, 32, 255, 261, 264, 346, 390, 404, 426, 456, 478, 497
Forrester, 32
Forstall, 340
Forsyth, 9, 12, 138, 140, 216
Fort Adams, 225, 422
Fort Brooke, 138, 525
Fort Clinch, 525
Fort Deposite, 356
Fort Du Quesne, 16
Fort Edward, 270
Fort Gibson, 286, 472
Fort Hamilton Narrows, 416
Fort Jefferson, 546
Fort Jesup, 471
Fort King, 271
Fort McHenry, 259, 339, 464
Fort Monroe, 312, 333
Fort Moultrie, 333
Fort Ontario, 178
Fort Pike, 547
Fort Smith, 21, 333, 462
Fort Snelling, 125
Fort Towson, 286
Fort Trumbull, 525
Fort Washita, 175, 286, 359

Fortier, 340
Fortress Monroe, 306
Forward, 120, 136, 166, 398, 432, 517
Forwood, 483
Fossett, 419, 492, 493, 495, 506, 540, 547
Foster, 1, 19, 54, 62, 66, 123, 265, 475, 572
Foulkes, 419
Fountain Inn, 181
Four Mile Tree, 383
Fourquet, 237
Fowle, 212, 460, 569
Fowler, 47, 49, 57, 59, 75, 94, 111, 117, 124, 130, 177, 180, 243, 259, 264, 297, 310, 385, 402, 519
Fowler's Lot, 117
Fox, 21, 86, 177, 331, 361, 431, 443, 477, 547
Fox Chase, 118
Foxes, 178
Foy, 154, 263, 325, 415, 489, 492, 495, 496, 497
Frailey, 32, 399
Frame, 452, 570
Francais, 115
France, 8, 41, 76, 79, 123, 130, 227, 281, 438, 440, 461, 466, 489, 490, 491, 556
Francia, 551
Francis, 58, 203, 218, 529
Francisco, 376
Franck, 415, 471
Frank, 200
Franklin, 69, 115, 185, 231, 250, 321, 379, 396, 487, 493, 494, 498
Fransoni, 468
Frary, 160
Fraser, 363, 555
Frasure, 86
Frazer, 13, 216, 455, 477, 549
Frederick, 191, 484, 525
Freelon, 378

Freeman, 86, 96, 108, 124, 215, 248, 257, 269, 273, 278, 332, 353, 395, 470, 503, 517
Freemont, 550
Freers, 488
Frelinghuysen, 223
French, 7, 10, 38, 45, 106, 154, 183, 254, 255, 288, 310, 322, 348, 376, 380, 457, 464, 485, 506, 569
Frensley, 90
Freshfield, 409
Frey, 165, 529
Frick, 461
Friedenberger, 139
Friend, 278, 447, 501, 548
Friendship, 118, 176
Friendship Enlarged, 370
frig **Belle Poule**, 301
frig **Boston**, 58
frig **Brandywine**, 46, 187
frig **Carysfort**, 562
frig **Columbia**, 182, 301
frig **Congress**, 31, 32, 548
frig **Constellation**, 33
frig **Constitution**, 80, 85, 187, 474
frig **Cumberland**, 514, 523
frig **Macedonian**, 127, 175, 296, 331, 387
frig **Missouri**, 135, 227, 352, 448
frig **Potomac**, 474
frig **Raritan**, 474, 522
frig **Savannah**, 376
frig **Spartan**, 159
frig **United States**, 23, 58, 314
frig **Warspite**, 245, 247, 251
Fritz, 256, 377
Frobles, 459
Frost, 226, 380
Froste, 228
Frothingham, 88, 391
Fry, 162, 353, 431, 470
Frye, 216, 394, 551
Fugett, 478

Fuggittt, 367
Fugitt, 9, 130, 168, 214, 292, 533
Fulcher, 510
Fullalove, 253
Fuller, 194, 199, 209, 391, 419, 490, 491, 552, 562, 563
Fullerton, 70
Fulmer, 261, 293, 347, 348, 566
Fulslove, 8
Fulton, 81, 93, 94, 340, 531, 573
Furlong, 437
Furman, 540
Futler, 436

G

Gaddis, 496
Gadsby, 49, 134, 230, 295, 494, 542
Gadsden, 166, 175, 234
Gafford, 89, 556
Gage, 120
Gagely, 4
Gahan, 502
Gaines, 225, 240, 273, 333, 366, 406, 483
Gainnie, 341
Gainnis, 340
Gaither, 117, 292, 295, 326
Galabrun, 113, 412, 552
Gale, 113, 145, 247, 377
Gales, 127, 387, 527
Gallabrun, 58, 489
Gallagher, 31, 173, 262, 297, 298, 399, 561
Gallaher, 23, 107, 146
Galland, 282
Gallant, 45, 126
Gallant Green, 314
Gallatin, 19, 192, 385
Gallaudet, 235, 259, 375
Gallaway, 397, 446
Gallay, 237
Gallia, 17
Galloway, 116

Gallup, 255
Galpin, 573
Galt, 124, 312, 415, 439, 522, 549
Gamble, 232, 253, 403
Gambrell, 388
Gambrill, 357, 382, 441
Gana, 22
Gandford, 23
Gannabrantz, 17
Gannal, 458
Gannett, 330, 391, 517
Gannon, 58, 148, 466, 478, 494, 537
Gano, 476
Gansevoort, 4, 12, 25, 58, 83, 246, 377
Gant, 36
Gantt, 7, 239, 548
Gantts, 122
Gardiner, 23, 167, 168, 292, 314, 326, 347, 473
Gardner, 32, 79, 92, 135, 148, 160, 165, 166, 168, 171, 268, 322, 348, 356, 357, 373, 410, 445, 556, 565, 574
Garey, 271
Garland, 8, 514
Garlick, 379
Garnage, 390
Garner, 341, 357, 375, 382, 441, 517
Garnett, 205
Garrard, 59, 241
Garret, 276
Garrett, 8, 117, 205, 538
Garrison, 129
Garty, 2, 4
Gary, 295, 302, 319
Gassaway, 130, 354, 388, 393, 478, 569
Gassett, 391
Gatchell, 299
Gates, 266, 339, 381, 505, 506, 550
Gatewood, 95
Gattias, 133
Gatton, 536
Gauthier, 182
Gawronski, 24, 38, 453

Gay, 511
Gaymont, 221
Gebbard, 210
Gebhard, 313
Geddy, 278
Gedney, 226, 327
Gee, 44, 54
Geinzler, 378
Geisinger, 135
Geisler, 412
Geisse, 225, 323
Gen Duff Green's iron & ore lands, 117
Gensang, 117
George, 335, 413, 441
George II, 445
German, 63, 499, 502
German National Gaz, 171
German silver, 55
Germantown, 333
Germond, 229
Gerrity, 345
Gettings, 535
Gettis, 91
Getty, 296, 313
Gettys, 347
Ghieselin, 441
Ghiselin, 203
Gibbon, 296
Gibbons, 67, 314, 389, 456, 499
Gibbs, 147, 180, 207, 280, 361, 451, 514
Giberson, 173, 228, 373
Gibson, 7, 36, 90, 91, 227, 252, 277, 439, 486, 546, 570
Giddings, 574
Gideon, 12, 94, 130, 221, 231, 250, 261, 346, 454, 494
Gieig, 160
Gienroy, 466
Giesey, 10
Gilbert, 67, 95, 130, 133, 232
Gilchrist, 377, 410
Giles, 409
Gill, 32, 299, 396

Giller, 74
Gillespie, 385
Gillet, 40
Gilley, 7
Gilliam, 517
Gillis, 356, 399
Gilliss, 32, 299, 340, 454, 468, 519
Gilman, 10, 212, 285, 527
Gilmer, 186
Gilmore, 285
Gilmour, 449
Gilpin, 126, 428
Gilson, 14, 31, 100, 113, 138, 170
Girard, 60, 210
Girault, 54, 169, 394, 520
Gittings, 337, 339
Giveny, 492, 495
Givison, 419
Gizor, 176
Glasgow, 249
Glass, 216
Glassbrooke, 469
Glasson, 362
Gleason, 90
Glen Ross, 437
Glendy, 247, 387
Glenn, 62, 99, 167, 181
Glennin, 549
Gloninger, 337
Glover, 279, 402
Glymont, 352
Goddard, 53, 107, 149, 155, 206, 220, 228, 261, 262, 292, 293, 302, 339, 405, 415, 429, 452, 458, 483, 491, 522, 533
Godefroy, 528
Godey, 188
Godfrey, 17, 231, 259, 488
Godon, 368
Goell, 61, 101
Goggin, 53, 186
Goings, 533
Gold, 49, 161, 408

Golden, 62, 290
Goldenham, 12
Golder, 39
Goldin, 290, 306
Golding, 155, 164
Goldsborough, 31, 348, 368, 436, 544, 551, 564
Good Hope, 484
Goode, 39, 166, 167, 186, 404, 437, 512
Goodel, 178
Goodhue, 397
Gooding, 465, 496
Goodman, 90
Goodrich, 118, 166, 325, 430
Goodridge, 37, 565
Goodwin, 568
Goodwyn, 506
Gookin, 215
Gorcas, 339
Gordon, 22, 40, 64, 73, 96, 114, 128, 145, 154, 156, 178, 198, 238, 283, 315, 353, 391, 395, 403, 453, 465, 496, 536, 537, 549
Gore, 224, 509
Gorid, 216
Gorman, 498
Gormley, 165
Goshen Farm, 77
Goslin, 182
Gosnell, 337
Gotha, 431
Gott, 255
Goudimel, 227
Gough, 94, 107, 139, 218
Gould, 47, 104, 294, 346, 377
Goulder, 482
Goulding, 222
Gow, 553
Gracie, 324
Grafley, 248
Grafton, 31, 368, 436
Graham, 18, 31, 130, 144, 191, 225, 231, 275, 287, 305, 368, 443, 466, 499, 539

Graig, 238
Grain, 83, 292
Grammer, 75, 131, 244, 268, 291, 293, 307, 433, 493
Granger, 351, 553
Grant, 23, 48, 104, 180, 322, 513, 520, 549
Grasin, 216
Gratiot, 229
Grattan, 27
Graves, 74, 188, 279, 521
Gray, 13, 56, 61, 75, 113, 143, 200, 247, 295, 352, 378, 387, 406, 467, 470, 482, 510, 523
Grayson, 32, 201, 211, 383, 548
Greele, 383
Greely, 63
Green, 8, 12, 15, 17, 27, 70, 82, 90, 99, 114, 117, 120, 135, 234, 247, 337, 348, 365, 376, 380, 381, 387, 388, 389, 403, 465, 477, 478, 498, 534, 541, 571
Green Mount Cemetery, 483, 501
Greenan, 203
Greenchilds, 216
Greene, 33, 249, 453, 477, 554
Greenfield, 271, 378
Greenhow, 251
Greenleaf, 98, 396, 419, 426, 458, 478
Greenleaf's Point, 424, 435, 453, 532
Greenlease, 531, 542
Greenough, 23, 95, 327, 328
Greenwood, 359, 385
Greer, 21, 264, 450
Greeves, 360
Gregg, 88, 385
Gregory, 18, 189, 311, 361, 474, 522, 563
Greiner, 398
Grelaud, 290, 321
Grenin, 92
Grenon, 59
Gresham, 22, 56, 86, 114, 142

Grey, 362, 499
Grice, 164, 238, 245
Grider, 380, 573
Grieb, 193, 445, 458
Grier, 83
Griffin, 31, 154, 183, 405, 456, 525
Griffith, 6, 66, 104, 109, 158, 413, 441, 564, 569
Griffiths, 534
Grigsby, 521
Grigsly, 419
Grimes, 177, 448, 480, 533
Grimsley, 467
Grindage, 117
Grinder, 325
Griner, 191
Grinnel, 407
Grinnell, 84
Griswelt, 166
Griswold, 162
Groc, 55
Grogan, 96
Grosh, 410
Gross, 205, 340, 425
Grouard, 372
Ground, 256
Grove, 116
Groves, 534
Groyceau, 91
Grub, 243
Grubbs, 162
Grubs, 91
Grun, 2
Grymes, 438, 485
Guerrant, 24
Guest, 56, 94, 296, 381, 533
Guie, 18
Guile, 349
Guista, 169
Guistiniani, 524
Gulatt, 467
Guliand, 79
Gummere, 268

Gunby, 117
Gunnell, 169, 269, 307, 309, 338, 410, 469, 490
Gunsolve, 400
Gunton, 131, 375, 461, 478, 506
Gurley, 197, 367
Gustavus III, 372
Guthrage, 538
Guthridge, 56
Guthrie, 25, 101, 113, 137, 166
Gutierrer, 249
Guttslich, 456
Guy, 205, 244
Guyther, 302
Gwathmey, 336
Gwinn, 63, 224, 376
Gwynn, 88, 117, 356
Gyngell, 228

H

Haas, 39
Haberhsam, 10
Habersham, 31, 62, 548
Hackett, 403
Hagan, 161, 279, 365, 404, 572
Hager, 572
Haggerty, 226
Hagner, 186
Hahnemann, 361
Haight, 209, 452
Hain, 516
Haines, 79
Hairing, 365
Haislep, 413
Haislip, 173, 463
Haldeman, 210
Hale, 247, 270
Haley, 25, 101
Haliday, 164, 183, 260, 293, 494
Haligan, 324, 496
Halkerson, 117
Hall, 13, 20, 21, 73, 92, 99, 112, 113, 116, 133, 140, 143, 180, 209, 210,

228, 233, 264, 265, 268, 269, 276,
277, 283, 284, 291, 295, 319, 320,
321, 329, 336, 354, 356, 361, 364,
379, 389, 391, 393, 394, 412, 419,
422, 423, 425, 447, 453, 456, 458,
463, 465, 471, 477, 478, 482, 485,
511, 516, 519, 525, 537, 538, 541,
555, 569
Halliday, 271, 419
Halloway, 322
Hallowell, 87, 90, 356, 389, 513
Halsey, 382
Halter, 463
Haly, 21
Hambaugh, 341, 525
Hambleton, 18, 39, 65, 114, 170
Hambright, 41, 86, 114, 136
Hamburg, 375
Hamersly, 149
Hamilton, 5, 8, 40, 62, 84, 129, 149, 224, 255, 278, 322, 358, 365, 381, 411, 419, 459, 464, 525, 548
Hammack, 257
Hammel, 480
Hammersley, 296
Hammet, 444, 510
Hammett, 204
Hammill, 86, 116
Hammon, 247, 469
Hammond, 19, 24, 46, 65, 90, 118, 124, 175, 377, 502
Hammond's corner, 118
Hamner, 133, 233, 516, 543
Hampton, 167, 181, 463, 502, 559
Hamtramck, 347
Hancock, 177, 490
Hand, 452, 569
Handley, 154, 214
Handy, 24, 32, 33, 39, 50, 71, 129, 342, 356, 393, 399, 403, 419, 422, 444, 480, 494, 558
Haney, 488
Hanly, 8, 26, 89, 93, 94, 122, 132, 319

Hanna, 215
Hannahan, 67
Hanne, 90
Hansbrough, 164
Hanscom, 368
Hanson, 21, 159, 241, 353, 362, 446
Haraway, 96
Harbard, 222
Harbaugh, 49, 262, 346, 352, 493, 494, 495
Hard, 209
Hardcastle, 413, 441
Harden, 120
Hardesty, 414
Hardie, 321
Hardin, 396, 521
Harding, 169, 174, 278, 289, 515
Hardiso, 434
Hardison, 188, 434
Hardy, 325, 348
Hare, 130, 257, 355
Harkness, 122, 132, 299, 308, 326, 474, 535, 547
Harman, 523
Harmer, 227
Harney, 286
Harpending, 521
Harper, 58, 65, 102, 211, 294, 379, 441, 565
Harring, 393
Harrington, 248, 261, 423, 496, 497
Harrington's, 208
Harris, 6, 28, 42, 54, 75, 78, 86, 91, 108, 123, 128, 160, 223, 226, 239, 298, 324, 343, 356, 361, 376, 414, 422, 452, 473, 475
Harrison, 31, 32, 57, 63, 68, 81, 90, 94, 96, 102, 108, 134, 236, 260, 293, 302, 315, 368, 388, 398, 413, 441, 450, 467, 486, 504, 542, 547, 551, 560, 569
Harrod, 546
Harrott, 268
Harrover, 520, 523

Harryman, 388
Hart, 60, 141, 144, 148, 163, 225, 256, 337, 455, 476
Hartford, 565
Harthan, 401
Hartman, 120, 496, 552
Harton, 479
Hartshorn, 498
Harvey, 8, 146, 247, 281, 449, 480, 490
Harvy, 90
Harwood, 225, 297, 299
Haskel, 454
Haskell, 31, 100, 114, 137, 515, 522, 565
Haskin, 555
Haskins, 484
Hasler, 397
Haspodar, 567
Hassinger, 272
Hassler, 522, 527, 552
Hastings, 31, 159, 267, 368
Haswell, 470
Hatch, 102, 229
Hatchee Lustee, 128
Hatfield, 369, 370, 438
Hathaway, 70, 416
Hathway, 162
Hatton, 180, 453, 460, 478
Hatton Hill, 453
Hatton's Hills, 460
Haumer, 133
Haven, 210, 529
Havener, 407
Havenner, 254
Hawes, 540
Hawk, 91
Hawkins, 8, 29, 54, 76, 117, 148, 222, 265, 347, 394, 438, 499, 524, 564, 565
Hawks, 233
Hawley, 49, 74, 174, 206, 209, 233, 295, 318, 436, 520, 569
Hawsey, 255

Hay, 90, 495
Hayden, 422
Hayes, 44, 91, 128, 210, 212, 355
Haymaker, 18, 75
Hayman, 264, 267, 308, 347, 396, 399, 450
Hayne, 549
Hays, 4, 12, 15, 133, 355
Hayward, 81
Haywood, 572
Hazard, 225, 362
Hazel, 83, 543, 566
Hazell, 293
Hazle, 327
Hazlehurst, 354
Hazlitt, 322
Hazzard, 452
Head, 231
Headley, 299, 300
Heard, 45
Heath, 20, 215, 253, 367, 409, 453
Heath's Neglect, 118
Heaton, 21, 155
Hebard, 178, 179
Heberton, 78, 154, 174
Heckman, 354
Heddenburg, 91
Hedge, 343
Hedges, 241, 511
Hedglie, 515
Heffley, 500
Hegdon, 530
Heiden, 162
Heigerty, 83
Heiste, 346
Heitmiller, 454
Heively, 77
Hellen, 344
Hellman, 203, 513
Heltmiller, 214
Hempler, 480, 512
Henart, 109

Henderson, 15, 17, 33, 34, 49, 50, 82, 127, 320, 332, 401, 454, 504, 527
Hendley, 9, 415, 496
Hendren, 13
Henley, 258, 418
Henn, 417
Hennen, 481
Henning, 373, 497
Heno, 368
Henry, 20, 200, 238, 296, 390, 407, 425, 536
Henshall, 274
Henshaw, 225, 309, 323, 354, 386, 419, 432, 448, 527, 547
Hensly, 92
Henson, 426, 571
Hepburn, 27, 89
Herard, 205
Herbert, 126, 415, 484
Hercas, 243
Hernandez, 53, 144, 348, 400, 549
Herndon, 275, 433
Herness, 246
Herold, 520
Heron, 246
Herrick, 446
Herron, 8
Hersch, 85
Hervey, 476
Hervy, 256
Hess, 273, 385
Hettick, 118
Hewitt, 20, 409, 480, 483, 527, 573
Hews, 40
Heyberger, 56, 67, 114, 152
Heyworth, 498
Hibbard, 21
Hibbs, 419
Hickelthorn, 300
Hickey, 28, 527
Hickman, 438
Hickory Hill, 438
Hicks, 35, 45, 113, 144, 337, 442, 504

Hickskell, 4
Hield, 313
Hieskeil, 4
Hieskell, 12, 234
Higbee, 436
Higby, 70
Higdon, 164
Higgins, 458
Higginson, 120, 228
Hildreth, 391, 565
Hildt, 253
Hill, 7, 8, 36, 40, 90, 91, 133, 154, 168, 175, 228, 276, 287, 305, 340, 370, 390, 391, 398, 415, 435, 452, 483, 520, 526, 542
Hill Top, 538
Hilleary, 122
Hilleman, 75
Hillen, 402
Hilliard, 235
Hilliary's, 481
Hills, 192
Hillyard, 380
Hilton, 216, 292, 294, 502
Himes, 347
Hinch's Discovery, 118
Hinchman, 160
Hindman, 216
Hines, 189, 387
Hinger, 298
Hinman, 216, 518
Hinton, 220, 348, 353
Hirst, 267
Hitchcock, 78, 202, 203, 238
Hitchens, 315
Hitchings, 315
Hite, 339
Hitt, 516
Hittinger, 237
Hitz, 292, 539
Hoban, 131, 154, 167, 247, 387, 480, 547, 569
Hobbie, 277, 347, 348

Hobbs, 526, 572
Hobby, 1
Hoblitzell, 262, 432
Hoburg, 45, 126
Hodge, 193
Hodges, 108
Hodgkin, 53, 57, 95, 113, 151, 171
Hodgkins, 244
Hodgson, 381
Hoff, 377
Hoffman, 31, 43, 57, 74, 94, 105, 203, 349, 357, 452, 548
Hogan, 18, 369, 470
Hogmire, 511
Hohns, 358
Hoisington, 223
Holbrook, 84
Holcomb, 317, 477
Holder, 16, 112
Holderman, 90
Holffer, 91
Holiday, 183, 314
Holland, 15, 163, 228
Hollander, 149, 169
Hollenback, 252
Holliday, 441
Hollidge, 292
Hollingsworth, 227
Hollister, 138
Holloway, 216
Holman, 127, 146
Holmead, 85, 127, 195, 284, 417, 429
Holmes, 31, 32, 100, 114, 137, 166, 180, 221, 248, 283, 315, 378, 388, 391, 434, 466, 476, 548, 567
Holohan, 94
Holt, 75, 120, 183, 437
Holtzclau, 44
Holtzman, 288
Homans, 56, 231, 243, 250, 496
Homer, 395
Honeywood Mills, 405
Hooe, 247, 440, 460

Hooff, 539
Hook, 118
Hooker, 74, 266
Hooper, 337
Hoover, 25, 346, 397, 419, 488, 508, 520, 527, 566
Hopatte-Hadjo, 47
Hopetoun, 380
Hopewell, 441
Hopkins, 30, 54, 84, 94, 117, 126, 209, 265, 369, 377, 379, 382, 385, 404, 405, 428, 441, 481, 487, 511
Hopkinson, 45
Hopper, 95
Hopping, 187
Hopson, 180
Horer, 101
Horn, 194, 203, 219, 372, 513
Hornor, 199
Hornung, 3
Horsey, 419
Horsford, 210
Horten, 570
Horton, 337
Hoskin, 228
Hotley, 182
Hough, 81, 551
Houghton, 210, 500
Hourie, 91
House, 14, 31, 359, 483
Houseman, 572
Housman, 572
Houston, 119, 154, 177, 220, 381, 453
Hover, 29, 113, 137
How, 143, 232
Howard, 14, 17, 117, 139, 292, 386, 446, 454, 455, 503, 512, 525
Howe, 1, 83, 87, 223, 322, 339, 496
Howell, 24, 32, 68, 368, 377, 519
Howie, 172, 367
Howison, 8, 228, 234, 458
Howitt, 353
Howle, 128, 340, 344, 347, 348, 527

Hoye, 471
Hoye's coal, 117
Hoyle, 374
Hoyt, 79, 195, 255, 524
Hubard, 555
Hubbard, 366, 438, 440
Hubbell, 428
Hubler, 268
Hudgins, 252
Hudson, 6, 234, 297, 298, 391
Hueston, 388
Huff, 241
Huger, 477
Hughes, 17, 96, 133, 225, 287, 308, 334, 347, 377, 455
Hugunin, 246
Hulbert, 182
Hull, 80, 84, 88, 127, 138, 449
Hume, 568
Humes, 475
Humphrey, 51, 84
Humphreys, 90, 224, 226, 238, 393, 472, 501
Hun, 275
Hungerford, 18, 39, 73, 363, 480, 550
Hunt, 14, 31, 60, 61, 100, 113, 138, 159, 233, 244, 246, 303, 343, 353, 385, 407, 419, 434, 470, 520, 542, 545
Hunter, 6, 7, 32, 36, 58, 89, 94, 125, 174, 179, 227, 232, 242, 244, 245, 250, 300, 327, 334, 347, 352, 360, 381, 400, 445, 449, 455, 464, 470, 477, 520, 545, 546
Hunter's Art, 117
Hunting, 565
Huntington, 8, 30, 162, 237, 334, 371, 377, 555
Huntt, 58, 348, 445
Hurdle, 284, 535
Huron, 116
Hurst, 83, 273, 356, 507
Hust, 77
Hutchenson, 343

Hutchings, 338
Hutchins, 25, 59, 149, 310
Hutchinson, 19, 120, 180, 206, 362
Hutchison, 236
Huthwaite, 185
Hutmuller, 220, 259
Hutton, 392
Hyatt, 44, 74, 354, 381, 491, 493, 495, 530
Hyde, 129, 198, 206, 221, 311, 535, 569

I

Iardella, 26
Ickes, 176
Iglehart, 220, 340
Illaley, 89
illegitimate, 175
Ilsley, 565
Imanuel, 534
Improvements, 117
Inbrod, 543
Inch, 496, 552
Ing, 405
Ingalls, 322
Ingersoll, 64, 461
Ingham, 436
Inginac, 205
Ingle, 212, 218, 231, 268, 292, 293, 387, 448, 454, 464, 478, 484, 502, 519, 569, 570
Ingram, 266
Ington, 116
Inman, 134
Inskeep, 54
Iowas, 181
Iredell, 528
Ireland, 381
Irminger, 237
Irvin, 73, 544
Irvine, 312, 436, 473
Irving, 325, 356
Irwin, 120, 196, 238
Isaacs, 509

Isabella Furnace, 196
Isabella II, 500
Isbel, 498
Isett, 30
Isom, 90
Israel, 43, 110, 159, 543
Iverson, 140
Ives, 237
Izard, 306

J

Jackson, 17, 18, 21, 25, 28, 32, 35, 36, 39, 52, 65, 68, 91, 99, 103, 114, 120, 127, 133, 155, 202, 209, 210, 219, 224, 228, 329, 331, 371, 387, 390, 400, 401, 458, 459, 471, 540, 548, 557
Jacob, 287, 414, 446
Jacobi, 522
Jacobs, 410
Jakelsen, 377
James, 39, 68, 91, 109, 161, 228, 231, 313, 501
Jameson, 160, 163, 200, 206, 356
Jamesson, 376
Jamestown, 333
Jamieson, 212
Jamison, 62, 182
Janin, 555
Janney, 161, 212, 542
Jaquett, 381
Jarboe, 337, 494, 495
Jardine, 185
Jarves, 226
Jarvis, 88, 280, 322, 385
Jatem, 91
Java Resurveyed, 117
Javins, 35, 113, 151, 516
Jay, 19, 192, 509
Jeancy, 91
Jeffers, 503
Jefferson, 174, 175, 190, 309, 336, 504
Jeffrey, 246
Jemison, 534

Jenifer, 145, 319
Jenison, 148
Jenkins, 2, 32, 33, 50, 64, 67, 82, 84, 94, 95, 114, 130, 147, 152, 161, 226, 337, 340, 348, 492, 548
Jenks, 461, 573
Jennings, 15, 39, 42, 47, 52, 56, 57, 64, 73, 96, 98, 105, 113, 114, 151, 185, 475, 481, 501, 540, 556
Jennison, 310
Jernigan, 82
Jesse, 445
Jesuits, 274, 294
Jesup, 47, 170, 367, 436, 520
Jeter, 221
Jett, 84, 96, 99
Jewell, 52, 81, 97, 125, 198, 228
Jewelry, 117
Jewet, 396
Jewitt, 117
Jews, 523
Jirdinston, 411
Job, 21
Johe, 525
Johns, 198, 238, 385, 506
Johnson, 5, 7, 26, 36, 37, 53, 68, 73, 74, 76, 79, 90, 93, 108, 112, 116, 118, 134, 173, 182, 192, 208, 238, 252, 257, 260, 261, 283, 287, 291, 292, 301, 302, 305, 309, 319, 329, 331, 357, 358, 362, 370, 377, 382, 385, 396, 397, 401, 407, 431, 432, 441, 442, 443, 446, 449, 452, 454, 463, 477, 481, 498, 505, 514, 518, 524, 530, 531, 543, 549, 565
Johnston, 8, 14, 31, 56, 82, 113, 155, 164, 171, 182, 219, 225, 247, 308, 364, 368, 377, 455, 460, 497, 569
Johnstone, 321
Johonnot, 396
Jolly, 371
Jonathan, 323

Jones, 7, 8, 23, 24, 30, 36, 43, 50, 72, 75, 82, 83, 89, 91, 96, 116, 119, 120, 125, 127, 128, 133, 150, 159, 161, 166, 180, 192, 206, 223, 226, 228, 231, 233, 237, 246, 248, 249, 252, 253, 265, 267, 270, 281, 288, 304, 305, 308, 336, 342, 357, 358, 375, 377, 385, 396, 406, 408, 414, 419, 433, 434, 452, 469, 472, 489, 492, 495, 506, 517, 519, 520, 523, 526, 527, 547, 568, 571, 574
Jongh, 296
Jonny, 90, 91
Joops, 90
Jopling, 472
Jordan, 154, 178, 238, 406, 447, 470, 473
Jorden, 38
Jordinson, 110
Jordon, 178
Jost, 132, 488
Joubert, 517
Jouett, 362
Jourcay, 90
Joyce, 172, 317, 456
Joye, 177
Joyslin, 430
Jubee, 440
Judah, 322
Judd, 256
Judik, 337
Judkins, 216
Judlin, 198
Judson, 436
Jullien, 499

K

Kahbege, 182
Kahl, 272, 549
Kaigler, 91
Kamalenoski, 430
Kane, 246
Karl, 10
Kas, 181
Katzenback, 162
Kauffman, 150
Kavanagh, 301
Kavanaugh, 182
Keach, 435
Kean, 381
Kearney, 7, 36, 97, 269, 438, 450, 472, 483, 562
Kearny, 78
Keats, 503
Kedglie, 410
Keech, 13
Keefer, 105
Keeler, 466
Keely, 92
Keen, 67
Keenan, 252, 480
Keese, 203
Keeve, 133
Kehoe, 97, 290
Kehue, 91
Keighler, 330
Keith, 67, 125, 133, 172, 246, 263, 569
Kelcher, 495
Kell, 333
Keller, 31, 53, 105, 139, 147, 348, 420, 469
Kelley, 91, 92, 118, 261
Kellog, 387
Kellogg, 31, 336
Kelly, 10, 35, 77, 89, 107, 114, 154, 156, 170, 171, 290, 295, 369, 450, 472, 488, 555
Kelso, 299
Kelty, 368
Kemble, 215
Kemp, 163, 420
Kenan, 513
Kendall, 27, 52, 61, 68, 110, 111, 251, 297, 367, 436, 438
Kendrick, 196, 220, 344, 490
Kenedy, 14, 25

Kengla, 318, 535
Kennard, 296, 334, 358, 569
Kennedy, 48, 94, 114, 116, 117, 135, 221, 238, 258, 299, 364, 378, 449, 504, 533, 553, 564
Kennon, 122, 127, 557
Kenny, 369
Kent, 53, 77, 428, 440
Kenton, 84
Keon, 54
Kepler, 159
Kerby, 34
Kerfoot, 513
Kernan, 154, 337
Kerr, 75, 87, 142, 200, 299, 420, 489, 490
Kerrigan, 369
Kervand, 445
Ketchum, 553
Kevan, 347
Key, 26, 28, 45, 51, 54, 72, 77, 149, 236, 305, 370, 511
Keyes, 289
Keyser, 450, 451
Keyworth, 188, 305, 340, 348, 450, 492, 496
Kid, 133
Kidd, 129
Kidston, 216
Kidwell, 8, 276, 318
Kiernan, 139
Kilbourn, 225
Kilbourne, 178
Kilfoile, 92
Kilgore, 258
Kilgour, 413, 441
Kilman, 292
Kilty, 31
Kimball, 47, 57, 86, 113, 157
Kimmel, 281
Kimmell, 61, 202, 347, 352
Kincaid, 76, 213, 223
Kincart, 545, 551

Kinchey, 333
Kinchy, 26, 489, 539
Kinduck, 374
King, 4, 22, 23, 25, 31, 41, 79, 86, 90, 91, 104, 115, 117, 118, 119, 122, 134, 136, 153, 158, 161, 168, 197, 220, 223, 244, 253, 285, 295, 308, 348, 356, 359, 368, 393, 396, 405, 407, 429, 495, 508, 511, 537, 540, 555
King Charles I, 376
King Leopold, 455
King of France, 516
King-ford, 239
Kingham, 391
Kingsbury, 359
Kingsford, 569
Kingsland, 70
Kingsley, 21
Kinkead, 476, 521
Kinlock, 31
Kinne, 50, 82
Kinney, 60, 453, 571
Kinsley, 298, 503
Kinzer, 109
Kinzie, 46, 162
Kirby, 54, 93, 420
Kirchivell, 153
Kirk, 68, 75, 108, 262, 354, 505
Kirkham, 135, 321
Kirkpatrick, 315, 340, 344
Kirkwood, 381
Kissam, 50, 524
Kitcham, 74
Kitts, 366
Kleiber, 272, 292
Kleindienet, 492
Klimkiewiez, 189
Klopfer, 295, 570
Knapp, 245, 296, 297, 391, 538
Knight, 62, 82, 197, 347, 373, 382, 449, 570
Knop, 278, 480
Knott, 56, 68, 478, 542

Knowles, 56, 73, 108, 244, 261, 355, 415, 426, 485
Knox, 7, 508, 516
Koontz, 118, 178
Koren, 246
Kosciusko, 190
Koy, 216
Krafft, 71, 488, 521
Kraft, 337
Krazen, 228
Kremer, 276
Kreutzer, 567
Krofhiser, 483
Krug, 35
Krum, 18
Kuhn, 391
Kurtz, 183, 420, 423, 478, 543
Kuykendall, 91, 133

L

La Mauna, 20
Labbe, 231, 457
Labor, 547
Labranche, 288, 388
Lacoste, 341
Lacy, 91, 262, 302, 319, 487, 511
Ladd, 391
Ladebauche, 182
Lafayette, 202, 381
Lafitte, 337
Laforge, 91
Laird, 487
Lakeman, 310
Lalanne, 38
Lamar, 106, 367, 373, 426
Lamb, 237, 491
Lambell, 121, 489, 490
Lamberson, 331
Lambert, 4, 81, 84, 334, 427, 446
Lambright, 11, 535
Lanahan, 569
Lancaster, 348
Land, 329

Land Flowing with milk & honey, 118
Lander, 204
Landois, 252
Lane, 23, 88, 450, 482, 542
Laney, 266
Lang, 204, 537
Langdon, 50, 134, 184, 263
Langfitt, 450
Langhorn, 487
Langhorne, 32, 186, 548
Langley, 163
Langtree, 223
Langtry, 95
Lanham, 87
Lanham's Delight, 37
Lanier, 32, 399
Lankford, 271, 442
Lannahan, 158
Lansdale, 99, 353
Lansdowne, 215
Lansford, 359
Lansing, 570
Laplace, 412
Laplant, 178
Lapon, 268
largest steamboat, 41
Larned, 49, 140, 293, 454, 569
Larner, 294
Larrabee, 42
Larzelere, 102
Lascelle, 210
Lashapel, 335
Laskey, 493
Latent Worth, 116
Lathrop, 450
Latimer, 336
Latrobe, 506
Lattimer, 237
Laub, 193, 214
Laubacher, 349
Lauck, 8, 48, 115
Laue, 310
Laughan, 262

Laughton, 396
Laurason, 246
Laurence, 360
Laurens, 224, 247
Laurent, 443
Laurie, 49, 64, 111, 207, 216, 297, 456, 473, 519, 538, 569, 572
Lauxman, 110
Lavaud, 443
Lavergne, 101
Law, 166, 299, 334, 420, 443
Lawrence, 185, 192, 297, 315, 343, 381, 456, 479, 525
Lawrenson, 154, 363, 410
Lawry, 336
Laws, 25, 73, 108, 150, 191
Lawson, 20, 97, 101, 463, 474, 535, 538
Lawwell, 366
Lay, 367
Layton, 107, 114, 156, 307
Lazarists, 516
Lazenby, 384
Le Blanc, 63, 81
Le Clare, 179
Le Roy, 336
Lea, 17, 58, 174, 184, 356, 445
Leach, 201, 231, 240, 439
Leakin, 116
Lear, 49, 190, 198, 238
Leatherwood Bottom, 117
Leavitt, 7, 237, 245
Leavy, 476
Lebar, 97
Leckie, 63, 228, 445
Leclair, 178
Lecor, 100
Lecroix, 340
Leddy, 420
Lee, 16, 38, 39, 90, 114, 135, 145, 171, 200, 206, 226, 232, 236, 244, 257, 284, 298, 334, 345, 356, 391, 420, 458, 477, 482, 491, 492, 493, 494, 495, 509, 527, 542, 569

Leech, 63
Leechan, 90
Leecock, 4, 12, 17, 169
Leffler, 160, 355
Legare, 3, 28, 97, 199, 218, 219, 284, 286, 288, 294, 484
Leibert, 49, 113
Leibey, 5
Leigh, 32, 142, 168, 200, 376
Leland, 402
Lemmon, 278, 458
Lemon Hill, 519
Lendrum, 508
Lenman, 243
Lennig, 337
Lennon, 530
Lenox, 26, 110, 268, 293, 495, 527
Lenthall, 238
Leonard, 259, 348, 378
LeRoy, 83, 228
Lery, 216
Leslie, 316, 372
Lester, 354
Letson, 432
Levely, 238
Leven, 372
Levenseller, 80
Levenselter, 166
Leveridge, 30, 104
Levering, 441
Levine, 219
Levins, 218
Levy, 87, 237
Lewis, 14, 24, 25, 39, 48, 57, 63, 69, 90, 96, 100, 113, 114, 120, 158, 171, 193, 226, 234, 246, 252, 263, 316, 319, 326, 344, 348, 362, 374, 377, 381, 383, 388, 404, 422, 473, 504, 539, 556
Lienberger, 14
Lightfoot, 55, 221
Lightner, 70
Ligon, 423
Lilly, 340, 345, 528

Limestone, 117
Lincoln, 64, 223, 279, 381, 467
Lindley, 99, 529
Lindsay, 384, 409, 507
Lindsey, 310
Lindsley, 307, 387, 396, 461, 491
Lindsly, 20, 166, 177, 293, 326
Liney, 343
Link, 6
Linker, 544
Linn, 23, 463, 479, 480, 545, 546
Linnard, 124, 225
Linthicum, 261, 471, 478, 527, 572
Linton, 215, 520, 570
Lionberger, 25, 49, 114, 170
Lipp, 487
Lippitt, 88
Lipscomb, 110, 119, 126, 325
Lispenard, 300
List, 120
Littell, 340
Little, 225, 292, 323, 341, 355, 374, 415
Littlefield, 120, 294, 402
Livergood, 91
Livingston, 89, 154, 370, 504, 518, 561
Lloyd, 81, 88, 308, 332, 392, 396
Lobdell, 269
Lochlin, 498
Locke, 15, 154, 219, 415, 497, 526
Lockerman, 91, 133, 441
Lockett, 174, 184
Lomax, 50, 65, 74, 108, 549
Lombard, 131
Long, 137, 296, 297, 345, 361, 493, 521
Long Acre, 217, 448
Long Meadows, 242
Long Old Fields, 481
Longacre, 420
Longdon, 148, 314
Longfellow, 330
Longford, 56
Longston, 62
Looker, 459

Loomis, 45
Loper, 573
Loras, 244
Lord, 90, 113, 143, 166, 195, 218, 293, 508
Lorillard, 245, 408
Loring, 391
Lossell, 220
Lost Glove, 118
Louallier, 35
Louderback, 505
Loughborough, 70
Louis Philippe, 56, 240
Love, 75, 88, 246, 267
Lovejoy, 367
Loveland, 458
Lovely, 118
Lovett, 563
Lowber, 230
Lowe, 27, 101, 138, 170, 229, 239, 292, 327, 362, 374, 394, 406, 420, 471, 557
Lowell, 56, 391
Lowers, 401
Lowery, 442
Lowndes, 20, 160, 325, 326, 351
Lownds, 355, 508
Lowrey, 183, 474
Lowry, 171, 233, 260, 351, 361, 385, 424
Loyal, 246
Loyall, 234, 481
Lozier, 361
Lubin, 154
Lucas, 477, 478
Luce, 32, 49, 436, 446, 548, 569
Luckett, 33, 97
Lucky Discovery, 176
Ludeke, 318
Ludlow, 420
Ludwigh, 346
Lufborough, 437, 439, 478, 516
Luff, 149, 196
Lufkin, 259

Lukens, 28
Lukins, 95
Lumpkin, 68, 121, 415
Lumsden, 206, 216
Lundy, 488
Lungeford, 433
Lunt, 459
Lurk, 90
Lurman, 441
Lusby, 494
Lusser, 82, 138
Luther, 227, 385, 479
Lutz, 276, 420
Lydane, 56
Lydell, 452
Lyle, 10, 50
Lyles, 478
Lyman, 315
Lynch, 1, 58, 154, 195, 242, 251, 261, 293, 304, 308, 415, 441, 496
Lynn, 376, 406
Lyon, 1, 521, 528, 543
Lyons, 91, 102, 161, 234, 243, 255, 330, 388, 410, 519, 526

M

M'Crackin, 118
Mabson, 81
Macartney, 158
MacDaniel, 19
Mace, 182, 258
Macgill, 420, 485
MacGregor, 228
Macguire, 554
Machen, 269, 390
Machine, 303
Mack, 59, 138
Mackall, 199, 420
Mackay, 440
Mackemot, 572
Mackenzie, 2, 4, 12, 25, 51, 58, 66, 73
Mackey, 7
Macleod, 523
MacLeod, 329
Macniff, 560
Macolla, 287
Macomb, 39, 42, 52, 73, 97, 98, 114, 537
Macomber, 96
Macon, 385, 486
Macoule, 427
Macrae, 15
Macready, 433
Madden, 304
Maddox, 149, 236, 261, 275, 462
Maddux, 191
Madigan, 399
Madis, 95
Madison, 141, 175, 229, 309, 326, 371, 423, 486
Madrigan, 33
Maffit, 75, 336
Maffitt, 226, 269
Magar, 292, 333
Magee, 488
Magie, 367
Magill, 111, 496, 548
Maglathlin, 391
Magnus, 510
Magoon, 274, 311
Magrew, 88
Magruder, 116, 127, 128, 133, 192, 233, 261, 269, 293, 314, 323, 324, 355, 358, 375, 382, 524, 552
Maguire, 154, 193, 499, 511
Mahan, 298
Maher, 91, 154, 223, 410, 415, 489, 491, 537, 566
Mahler, 120
Maines, 96
Maison Rouge, 273
Maison Rouge grant, 274
Malby, 91, 133
Mallon, 91
Malvern Hills, 255
Man of Fire, 181

man of the house, 203
Manahan, 166
Mandon, 526
Mangel, 459
Manger, 117
Manging, 555
Mangum, 7, 36
Mankin, 540
Manley, 483, 511
Manly, 339, 487
Mann, 50, 82, 94, 297, 337, 400, 466, 504, 570
Manning, 83, 262, 337
Mansfield, 364
Mantz, 302
Manypenny, 571
Marberry, 116
Marblehead, 320
Marbury, 34, 199, 288, 314, 340, 445, 456, 508, 542, 547, 569
March, 353, 470
Marchand, 246
Marche, 150
Marim, 452
Marin, 309
Marion, 266
Markness, 423
Markoe, 49, 458
Marks, 568
Markward, 111
Markwood, 524
Marlow, 262
Marquis of Winchester, 567
Marr, 163, 334
Marrin, 402
Marsh, 27, 53, 101, 268, 519
Marshall, 5, 10, 42, 52, 72, 97, 134, 149, 164, 168, 173, 193, 198, 205, 238, 240, 261, 278, 292, 293, 335, 340, 344, 355, 358, 394, 447, 457, 480, 508, 531, 542, 552, 566, 572
Marshall Hall, 566
Marstin, 533

Martin, 34, 50, 51, 56, 73, 87, 90, 114, 136, 143, 229, 237, 314, 362, 381, 447, 475, 498, 510, 525, 550
Martina, 189
Marvell, 282
Maryman, 359, 374, 442
Masi, 265, 348, 527
Masicot, 340
Mason, 8, 17, 22, 97, 102, 117, 118, 124, 140, 197, 221, 226, 239, 261, 314, 383, 408, 459, 506, 509
Massachusetts Spy, 323
Massar, 149
Massey, 266, 304
Massie, 265
Masson, 341
Masterson, 64, 67, 86, 108
Mastin, 543
Mather, 60
Mathews, 3, 45, 91, 195, 355, 414
Mathieu, 47
Mathiot, 114, 158
Matlock, 61, 350, 484
Maton, 133
Matson, 258
Matthew, 200
Matthews, 13, 196, 269, 348, 358, 370, 498, 540, 562
Mattingly, 136, 209, 450, 459, 480, 487, 511, 542
Mattison, 79, 449, 455
Mattoon, 422
Maury, 61, 246, 260, 261, 293, 305, 342, 349, 399, 454, 475, 494, 527, 566
Mauvais, 350
Maverick, 180, 206
Maxcy, 118, 294
Maxey, 420, 462
Maxwell, 91, 513
May, 7, 20, 36, 97, 135, 138, 147, 228, 230, 247, 277, 293, 348, 378, 387, 399, 413, 464, 479
Mayer, 118

Mayers, 237
Mayfield, 39, 64, 114, 137
Mayhew, 311
Maynard, 31, 280, 368, 414
Mayo, 27, 89, 127, 296, 331, 334, 555, 567
Mazarin, 567
Mc Michael, 461
McArthur, 388
McAtee, 8
McBlair, 225, 385, 572
McCabe, 64, 416, 452
McCady, 133
McCaffrey, 351, 496
McCall, 550
McCalla, 285
McCalmont, 321, 322
McCann, 35
McCarthy, 214
McCartney, 252
McCarty, 154, 168, 214, 370
McCaughan, 277
McCauley, 8, 189, 261, 292, 293, 327, 519
McClanahan, 247
McClanning, 565
McClean, 51, 386
McClellan, 11, 87
McClelland, 91, 101, 214, 231, 250, 295, 311, 322
McClenachan, 389
McClenahan, 352
McClernand, 520
McClernin, 427
McClery, 268, 490
McClintock, 25, 321, 543
McCluney, 171, 234, 341, 388
McClung, 281
McClure, 207, 238, 291
McClurg, 70
McCluskey, 513
McCobb, 63, 261
McColgan, 488, 489, 490, 491

McCollom, 92
McComb, 3, 15
McConchie, 518
McConkey, 79
McConnell, 381
McCorkle, 32, 548
McCormich, 250
McCormick, 37, 226, 243, 334, 390, 484, 502, 566, 569
McCoskry, 298, 331
McCoull, 358
McCouly, 91
McCown, 313
McCoy, 95, 528
McCready, 120
McCreary, 243
McCreery, 246, 377
McCubbin, 154
McCue, 41, 231, 438
McCulloch, 64
McCulloh, 118, 412, 441, 550
McCutcheon, 91
McDade, 90
McDaniel, 226, 359, 366
McDaniels, 277
McDermot, 208
McDermott, 154, 169, 384, 420, 493, 495
McDevitt, 569
McDonahoe, 464
McDonald, 175, 179, 266, 268, 307, 337, 356, 363, 452, 454, 470, 537
McDonaluo, 91
McDonnell, 51, 360, 362, 564
McDonough, 498
McDougald, 27
McDougall, 31, 368
McDowell, 102, 125
McDuffie, 31, 294, 368
McElhenny, 287
McElwee, 401
McEmery, 67
McEvers, 89, 305

Mcfall, 90
McFarland, 362
McFerran, 322
McGahey, 106
McGarr, 169
McGary, 234, 388
McGaughey, 258
McGee, 76, 105, 114, 156
McGehee, 291
McGill, 14, 114, 152
McGinnis, 16, 67, 101, 114, 158
McGlue, 448, 480, 547
McGonagle, 76
McGordes, 377
McGovern, 403
McGowan, 370
McGrath, 24, 205, 415, 494, 495, 537
McGraw, 209
McGregor, 37, 370
McGrew, 51
McGrowan, 554
McGuire, 44, 57, 86, 108, 313, 327, 420
McGunnigle, 240
McGurly, 91
McHenry, 70, 337, 482, 547
McIlhenny, 96
McIlvaine, 461
McIlwaine, 298
McInerny, 335
McIntire, 12, 75, 260, 391, 410, 460, 522
McIntosh, 51, 246, 281, 362, 378, 530, 549, 558, 573
McIntyre, 347
McKay, 211, 449
McKean, 8, 97, 189, 272, 276, 283, 291, 420, 491, 493, 540, 542
McKee, 12, 17, 265
McKeen, 263
McKeever, 63, 258, 477
McKelden, 302, 346, 417, 550
McKeldon, 250
McKendree, 256
McKenna, 97, 125, 279, 451, 542

McKennan, 288, 381
McKenney, 10, 71, 246, 377, 442, 569
McKenny, 478
McKenzie, 201, 381
McKeon, 15
McKibbin, 195
McKinley, 2, 4, 12, 17
McKinne, 94
McKinnel, 91
McKinnell, 133
McKinnon, 216
McKnett, 413, 441
McKnew, 420
McKnight, 83, 464
McKoun, 6
McLain, 398, 402
McLane, 5, 246, 403
McLasky, 337
McLaughlin, 67, 91, 108, 118, 160, 227, 246, 287, 303, 348, 349, 386, 387
McLean, 5, 18, 70, 241, 289, 336, 356, 357, 400, 437, 541
McLeges, 133
McLellan, 59
McLelland, 454
McLeod, 106, 154, 161, 237, 351, 380, 381, 475
McLocky, 337
McMahan, 91
McManus, 482, 499, 510
McMichae, 188
McMichen, 90
McMinn, 443
McMoth, 90
McMullin, 91
McNair, 159
McNairy, 462
McNaughton, 100, 186, 394, 567
McNeal, 78, 209, 363
McNear, 480
McNeer, 244
McNeil, 58
McNeill, 396

McNerhany, 193, 454
McNichol, 303
McNulty, 338
McPeak, 268
McPhail, 392
McPherson, 15, 88, 96, 120, 146, 180, 257, 424, 447, 506, 508
McRae, 54, 296, 311
McReynolds, 443
McRhea, 96
McRoberts, 165
McThompson, 223
McVean, 198, 560, 569, 571
McVickar, 452
McVikar, 297
McWilliams, 20, 47, 85, 96, 269, 505
Mead, 106
Meade, 83, 275, 452, 547
Meadow Mountain, 116
Means, 391
Mechelin, 480
Mecklenburg, 118
Meduna, 370
Meehan, 332, 429
Meeker, 378, 501
Meekins, 410
Meeks, 29
Mehegan, 8
Mehin, 498
Melbourne, 364
Meley, 116
Mellen, 109
Mendenhall, 182
Meng, 564
Menter, 317
Mercer, 32, 43, 78, 174, 361, 381, 548
Merchant, 322
Meredith, 96, 116, 315, 428
Meriwether, 24
Merrick, 59, 62, 132, 242, 568, 573
Merrit, 260
Merry Oaks, 425
Mesick, 13

Metcalf, 53, 99
Metcalfe, 148, 198, 387, 521
Methot, 340
Metoyer, 340
Metteregger, 57
Meyer, 552
Meyerbeer, 230
Meyers, 559
Micanopy, 353
Michard, 325, 520
Michaux, 96
Mickelberry, 29
Mickum, 71
Middleton, 8, 90, 93, 162, 173, 218, 232, 272, 354, 379, 420, 457, 492, 493, 495
Mifflin, 224
Milbanke, 364
Milburn, 78, 161, 243, 261, 469, 519
Milburne, 107
Miles, 167, 183, 265, 499
Milford, 122
Milholland, 453
Millander, 555
Millandon, 48
Millard, 140, 337, 510
Millen, 90, 291, 469, 507, 551
Miller, 20, 38, 39, 57, 90, 94, 103, 107, 129, 146, 166, 169, 179, 191, 212, 214, 215, 227, 234, 256, 267, 272, 290, 309, 313, 326, 328, 354, 356, 372, 378, 382, 400, 411, 424, 464, 467, 518, 522, 523, 531, 542, 549, 572
Miller's Chance, 118
Miller's Island, 256
Millet, 537
Millier, 228
Milligan, 477
Millikin, 573
Mills, 7, 79, 90, 118, 219, 302, 303, 337, 362, 375, 406, 483, 519
Millsten, 396
Millstone Point, 217
Mill-stone Point, 217

Milne, 381
Milnor, 243, 349
Milton Hill, 392
Minchin, 429
Mine Bank farm, 217
Mine Bank Farm, 448
Minerals in anticipation, 117
Mines, 522
Minge, 30, 268
Minor, 278, 342, 386, 408, 477
Minshall, 377
Mitchel, 146, 447
Mitchell, 35, 57, 88, 91, 97, 111, 121, 178, 193, 246, 264, 293, 305, 312, 373, 377, 392, 408, 448, 477, 481, 483, 489, 555, 557
Mitteregger, 339
Mix, 348
Moale, 444
Modecai, 342
Moffet, 178
Moffitt, 393
Mohawks, 181
Mohr, 479
Mohum, 218
Mohun, 263, 344, 492
Mollard, 150
Mo-nee, 87
Monkur, 320
Monlin, 335
Monroe, 21, 47, 53, 83, 175, 181, 229, 309, 477, 505, 561
Monspey, 150
Montamat, 443
Montefiore, 307
Montemat, 443
Montgolfier, 439
Montgomery, 80, 117, 216, 296, 357, 389, 435, 549
Montrinat, 216
Moody, 532
Moon, 57, 405

Moore, 53, 56, 62, 72, 73, 75, 77, 90, 91, 104, 113, 142, 146, 152, 154, 163, 170, 192, 194, 211, 216, 228, 230, 234, 235, 247, 251, 289, 292, 312, 324, 325, 327, 334, 345, 378, 388, 419, 426, 460, 505, 506, 519, 520, 533, 534, 538, 539, 552, 569
Moore's Farm, 117
Mooreland Farm, 77
Moran, 24, 147, 314, 377, 415, 431, 446, 447, 476, 477, 495, 537
Morange, 369, 370
Moravians, 353
Mordecai, 248
Morden, 84
Morehead, 91, 551
Moreland, 14, 25, 48, 114, 395, 460, 524
Moresson, 79
Morfit, 13, 367
Morgan, 8, 14, 25, 31, 92, 103, 114, 117, 139, 147, 158, 170, 216, 227, 228, 229, 276, 337, 368, 377, 381, 445, 475, 487, 517, 526, 542, 550, 568, 569
Moriarty, 451
Mormon, 134, 246
Morphy, 54
Morrell, 391
Morrill, 21
Morrin, 256
Morris, 4, 30, 46, 54, 92, 117, 130, 184, 187, 238, 254, 296, 312, 366, 407, 420, 452, 461, 477, 514, 547
Morrison, 7, 182, 198, 209, 224, 290, 493, 569
Morrow, 38, 82, 420
Morse, 105, 121
Morsel, 276
Morsell, 15, 83, 243, 262, 382, 441, 442, 444, 457, 471, 478, 518, 546
Morson, 31, 433
Morss, 24
Mortimer, 509, 533
Morton, 128, 226, 239, 457, 519, 562

Morus, 90
Moseley, 162, 476
Moser, 91
Moss, 56, 501
Moss Hill, 564
Motter, 221
Moul, 316
Mould, 497
Moulder, 148, 317
Moulton, 1, 25
Mount, 82
Mount Airy, 116, 176, 399
Mount Chem, 485
Mount Juliet, 545
Mount Nebo, 217, 448
Mount Stuart, 383
Mountz, 126, 261, 420
Mourse, 176
Mower, 238, 298
Moxham, 381
Moxley, 408, 542
Moyres, 440
Mudd, 3, 45, 260, 293, 348, 417, 566
Muhlenburg, 145, 407
Muiller, 91
Mulford, 260
Mullady, 344, 347
Mullany, 234
Mulledy, 294
Mullen, 37, 370, 420
Muller, 192, 250, 291, 415, 440, 552, 553
Mullhall, 300
Mullikin, 8, 13, 30, 249, 415, 488, 537
Mullin, 48
Mullins, 459
Mumford, 128
Munden, 275
Munford, 311, 485
Munkittuck, 237
Munn, 39, 57, 82, 108
Munro, 349, 420

Munroe, 28, 65, 113, 123, 445
Munson, 555, 564
Murdaugh, 246
Murdoch, 385
Murdock, 117, 303, 356
Mure, 498
Murphy, 14, 32, 38, 61, 63, 88, 97, 258, 279, 378, 493, 496, 556
Murray, 31, 64, 90, 166, 167, 169, 226, 234, 242, 272, 312, 356, 368, 370, 407, 458, 495, 496, 527, 543, 559
Murrey, 77
Murry, 559
Muruaga, 341, 344
Muse, 74, 246, 542
Mussey, 476
Mustin, 454
Myers, 12, 112, 126, 163, 175, 179, 198, 417
Myrick, 377

N

Nague, 392
Naill, 441
Nailor, 420, 489, 490, 491
Nalle, 362
Nalley, 244
Nally, 115
Napoleon, 171, 175, 422, 461
Nash, 284, 362
Nason, 330
Natkinson, 105
Naudain, 452
Naudin, 552
Naylor, 106, 189, 211, 232, 277, 314, 318, 484
Neal, 168, 188, 542
Neale, 39, 57, 76, 89, 97, 100, 237, 261, 293, 337, 420
Neely, 45, 90, 91, 108, 346
Neill, 23, 322
Neilson, 105, 114, 156, 420, 553

Nelson, 32, 54, 70, 90, 100, 104, 118, 135, 136, 309, 321, 322, 336, 399, 400, 425, 443, 458, 479, 525, 534, 537
Nes, 461
Nesbit, 356
Nestorians, 455
Neufoille, 171
Nevera, 17
Nevin, 223
Nevins, 340, 348, 422
Nevitt, 304, 466, 484
Nevius, 226, 340
New, 385
Newbold, 78, 140
Newburg, 174
Newbury, 43
Newcomb, 94, 366, 553
Newell, 358
Newhull, 378
Newingham, 569
Newman, 70, 100, 287, 396, 504, 542
Newmayer, 474
Newmeyer, 243
Newton, 8, 135, 175, 186, 239, 352, 353, 448, 470, 473
Nicholas, 51, 341, 362, 385, 406
Nicholl, 365
Nicholls, 15, 247, 420, 429
Nichols, 1, 31, 70, 351, 382, 402, 442, 514, 568
Nicholson, 32, 228, 234, 236, 420, 527, 541
Nicodemus, 433
Nicollet, 210, 411, 449
Niles, 40, 387
Nimblett, 41, 113, 151
Nimmo, 216
Nixon, 46, 54, 109, 159, 408, 471
Noaks, 543
Noble, 53
Nock, 105, 409, 497
Noell, 344
Noerr, 489

Noggle, 178
Nokes, 66, 115, 249
Noland, 133, 147, 373, 377
Nonpareil, 505
Nordin, 46
Norman, 310
Normand, 384
Norris, 1, 53, 63, 71, 83, 111, 181, 298, 456, 481
North, 82, 114, 160
Northup, 117, 297, 447
Norton, 398, 481, 547
Norvell, 131, 225, 323, 408
Norwood, 55, 557
Nourse, 31, 35, 60, 64, 85, 117, 189, 238, 342, 388, 425, 518, 569
Novel, 91
Novoscoski, 433
Nowell, 568
Nowiski, 480, 510
Nowlan, 369, 370
Nowrski, 444
Noye, 325
Noyes, 347, 415, 524, 533, 570, 572
Noyrit, 10
Null, 263
Number Six Estate, 516
Nutt, 80, 406
Nye, 68

O

O'Berry, 226
O'Brien, 17, 154, 251, 313, 338, 404, 447, 487, 511, 534, 572
O'Connell, 227, 246
O'Conner, 66
O'Connor, 154, 348, 468
O'Day, 184, 222
O'Donnell, 290, 396
O'Donoghue, 340
O'Driscoll, 340
O'Flannagan, 74
O'Hara, 369

O'Harra, 83
O'Kelly, 197
O'Neal, 16, 318
O'Neale, 126, 255, 373, 496, 518
O'Neil, 536
O'Reilly, 369
Oak Grove, 186
Oak Hill, 501
Oakes, 182
Oakland Mills, 220
Oakley, 24, 94, 107, 237, 247, 425, 452, 524
Oakville, 113
Oaky, 216
Oats, 90
Ochiltree, 403
Ochterlony, 395
Odell, 194
Oden, 250
Odia, 62
Oeconomos, 241
Offley, 198, 569
Offutt, 506
Ogden, 25, 47, 63, 92, 137, 145, 223, 452
Ogg, 21
Ogilby, 455
Ogle, 456
Ogleby, 118
Ohe, 110
Olaro, 249
Oldham, 90, 226, 475
Oliver, 118, 216, 478
Olly, 380
Olmstead, 396
Olmsted, 219
Omelveny, 389
Omohundro, 471
Onderdonk, 57, 436, 452
Oneida Indian, 158
Orange Island, 256
Orendorff, 96

Orme, 25, 44, 118, 129, 165, 197, 261, 282, 292, 293, 369, 379, 481, 489, 491, 493, 494, 569, 572
Ornden, 216
Orr, 456
Orsbourn, 194
Ortereger, 139
Osages, 181
Osborn, 210
Osbourn, 5, 248, 252
Osburn, 201
Oseola, 423
Osgood, 465
Osten, 465
Ostrander, 242, 558
Oswald, 192, 194
Otis, 89
Ott, 116, 445
Otterbach, 276
Otterback, 21, 497
Ottowa Indian, 138
Ould, 3, 267, 572
Ously, 154
Overstreet, 71
Overton, 90
Owen, 84, 90, 210, 219, 228, 258, 358
Owens, 55, 135, 193, 227
Owner, 175, 208, 231, 250, 394, 482, 497, 499
Owsley, 521
Oxnard, 236
Oyster, 41, 469

P

Paca, 118, 337
Packard, 11, 420, 525
packet **Mary Eliza**, 470
Padgett, 22, 161, 265
Page, 28, 31, 63, 94, 140, 167, 179, 224, 333, 361, 362, 368, 401, 403, 568, 571
Pageot, 340
Paine, 224
Paley, 116

Palfrey, 514
Palmer, 56, 241, 329, 353, 377, 417, 470, 477
Palmerston, 364
Panet, 340, 344
Pangborn, 283
Pannill, 50
Papanti, 236
Papineau, 249, 301
Paradise, 295
Parage, 150
Pardy, 71
Paris, 519
Park, 223
Parke, 206, 213, 401, 518
Parker, 31, 62, 91, 117, 120, 173, 187, 241, 246, 277, 290, 296, 305, 306, 308, 349, 367, 368, 391, 477, 495, 523, 537
Parkes, 297, 298
Parkin, 192
Parkins, 567
Parkman, 99
Parks, 388, 391
Parmelee, 317
Parment, 62
Parnell, 118
Parr, 201
Parris, 54, 277
Parrish, 533
Parrott, 237, 420, 458
Parrs, 201
Parry, 70
Parson, 425
Parsons, 198, 237, 315, 353, 455, 459, 571
Parthemore, 192
Partridge, 422
Pascault, 187
Paschal, 10
Paschall, 251
Pascoe, 189, 302
Paterson, 108, 161, 254, 571

Patrick, 39, 113, 145, 170, 179
Patten, 27, 30, 33, 56, 73, 105, 108, 109, 113, 138, 171, 373, 425
Patterson, 8, 44, 57, 75, 214, 216, 273, 276, 343, 381, 419, 475, 521, 527, 542
Pattison, 95, 228, 230
Pattrick, 341
Patullo, 291
Paul, 279
Paulding, 31, 399
Paulet, 562
Paulien, 149
Paullen, 161
Paullin, 49
Pavey, 245
Pawley, 210
Pawnee, 181
Pawnees, 335
Paxton, 366
Payne, 61, 68, 93, 101, 207, 258, 321, 339, 340, 348, 381, 423, 496, 532, 534, 552, 568
Payon, 540
Peabody, 308
Peachy, 460
Peacock, 90
Peak, 101
Peake, 25, 27
Peale, 76, 189, 326
Pearce, 287, 429, 486
Pearce's Mill, 429
Pearson, 89, 232, 292, 294, 454, 551, 564
Peck, 289, 321, 336, 565, 571
Peddie, 456
Pedru, 48
Peel, 100, 186
Peeple, 243
Peerce, 550
Peet, 349
Pegg, 47, 429, 469
Pegram, 23, 161
Pegraw, 246

Peilicer, 73
Peirce, 40, 393, 543
Pell, 120
Pelletier, 86
Pellicer, 108
Pellier, 52
Pelton, 177
Pelzer, 516
Pemberton, 343, 410
Pendergast, 340
Pendergrast, 407
Pendleton, 208, 233, 352, 473
Penfield, 433
Penhallow, 104, 113, 155
Penn, 558
Penniman, 165, 470
Pennock, 420
Penny, 377
Penrose, 38, 519, 569
Pepper, 10, 72, 113, 317, 491, 493, 527
Percival, 224, 316, 376, 474
Perient, 201
Perin, 201
Perkins, 112, 259, 310, 360, 391, 396, 402, 455
Perrault, 28
Perrico, 327
Perrie, 314
Perriman, 382
Perrine, 268
Perrow, 473
Perry, 2, 4, 12, 17, 27, 41, 107, 127, 133, 136, 155, 163, 170, 178, 237, 246, 334, 377, 433, 445, 460
Peters, 21, 60, 62, 67, 85, 101, 113, 114, 151, 152, 170, 244, 352, 476, 571
Peterson, 206
Petit, 370
Petronilla, 360
Pettes, 424
Pettibone, 3, 460, 465
Pettigrew, 323
Pettigru, 294

Pettit, 244, 258, 348, 539
Pettycrew, 534
Peyton, 48, 50, 525, 548
Phagan, 62
Phelps, 8, 31, 33, 90, 159, 172, 178, 207, 313, 368, 382, 399, 442, 465
Phenix, 247, 387
Philibert, 555
Philips, 1, 90, 97
Phillips, 3, 35, 99, 153, 167, 259, 262, 360, 420, 442, 453, 454, 460, 495, 527
Phister, 179
Pic, 519
Picard, 182
Pickell, 441
Pickering, 51, 362, 567
Pickett, 145, 433
Pickler, 398
Pickman, 379, 411
Pickney, 224
Pickrell, 52, 112, 253, 347, 423, 424, 451
Picot, 344, 446
Pier, 338
Pierce, 22, 32, 70, 114, 156, 211, 259, 261, 269, 277, 295, 348, 422, 478, 548
Pierson, 90, 219, 443
Pike, 57, 294, 306, 391
Piland, 133
Piles, 33, 37
Pilgrims, 476
Pilgrims at Holland, 350
Pillart, 91
Pilley, 91
Pilling, 253, 505
Pilsbury, 334
Pinckney, 278, 509
Pindell, 475, 521
Piner, 377
Piney Plains, 118
Piney Point, 317
Piney Woods, 374
Pink of Alleghany, 116

Pinkard, 498
Pinkham, 341
Pinkney, 98, 377, 535
Pinney, 525
Pioneer, 276
Pitnam, 324
Pittman, 3, 436, 460
Pitts, 147, 299
Pius, 91
Plant, 191, 292, 326
Plater, 94, 107, 139, 572
Platt, 39, 108, 169, 174, 182, 183, 209, 289, 328, 452, 564
Pleasant Hill, 393
Pleasant Hills, 307
Pleasants, 72, 161, 167, 244, 278, 517
Pleasonton, 38
Plowden, 199, 348
Plumer, 366
Plummer, 100, 565
Plumsell, 110
Plunkett, 465
Plymouth, 333
Pocahontas, 202
Poindexter, 27, 101
Point of Rocks, 217, 448
Poisien, 431
Poiteaux, 311
Polb, 298
Polenesky, 54
Polerecsky, 157
Poleresky, 113
Political Emancipation, 117
Polk, 166, 200, 296, 382, 441, 451, 565, 569
Polkinhorn, 75, 85
Pollard, 11, 132, 241, 310, 561
Pollen, 88, 108
Pollerescky, 35
Pomeroy, 284
Pomert, 54
Pomonkey, 484
Pook, 164

Pool, 56, 443
Poole, 263
Poor, 135, 307, 309, 334, 348, 477, 550
Pope, 5, 201, 379, 416, 546
Pope Gregory XIV, 240
Popham, 513
Poplar Hill, 399
Porch, 507
Porche, 340
Portch, 392
Porter, 16, 32, 45, 54, 91, 98, 121, 122, 196, 209, 219, 248, 253, 258, 281, 288, 290, 309, 401, 420, 449, 529, 548, 553, 574
Porterfield, 65, 93, 103
Portsmouth, 333
Posey, 399
Postlethwaite, 89
Poston, 216, 292
Pottawatamies, 87
Pottawatomie, 145
Potter, 5, 71, 84, 169, 234, 322, 388, 392, 413, 441, 498, 526
Potts, 118, 328
Poultney, 444
Powell, 48, 246, 252, 283, 449, 455, 490, 491, 519
Power, 204, 319, 340, 341
Powers, 17, 22, 56, 86, 113, 144, 212, 493, 509
Powhatan Mansion, 119
Prague, 542
Prather, 75, 233, 326
Pratt, 10, 42, 84, 96, 214, 237, 239, 468, 497
Pravis, 249
Preble, 78, 246
Prefontaine, 226, 239, 449
Prentiss, 23, 73, 225, 386
Pres of the U S, 390
Prescott, 289, 392, 571
President's House, 574
Presstman, 430

Preston, 113, 214, 221, 229, 357, 385, 484, 495, 524
Pretty Prospect, 117, 176
Prettyman, 86
Prevost, 271
Price, 73, 105, 178, 323, 352, 389, 452, 476
Priessnitz, 538
Prieur, 139
Primrose, 378
Prince, 289, 395
Prince Albert, 230
Prince Augustus, 230
Prince de Joinville, 301
Prince of Orange, 532
Princess Clementine, 56
Princess Francesca, 502
Princess Januaria, 502
Princess Theresa, 502
Pringle, 146, 163, 353, 454
Pritchett, 396
Proctor, 306
Proffit, 403
Prophet Francis, 202
Proud, 464, 506
Proudfit, 196
Prout, 26, 264, 276
Provost, 438, 480, 492, 493, 494
Pruden, 376
Pryor, 84
Pugh, 109, 110, 416
Pulvermacher, 191
Pumpelly, 194
Pumphrey, 371, 387, 491, 492, 494, 573
Purcell, 96, 201
Purdon, 110, 181, 276, 491
Purdy, 92, 327, 394, 519
Purnell, 331
Purrell, 149, 170
Pursel, 560
Pursell, 494
Purviance, 364
Push, 101

Putman, 53
Putnam, 209, 381
Pye, 45, 329, 337, 352

Q

Quackenboss, 549
Quackenbush, 361, 464
Quanto, 118
Quarles, 82
Quarters, 512
Quastoff, 247, 387
Quavre, 84
Queen, 5, 19, 206, 318, 326, 420, 546
Queen Dowager, 567
Queen of Portugal, 431
Queen Victoria, 230, 247, 455
Queenault, 381
Quigley, 393
Quin, 425
Quinby, 321
Quincy, 307, 468
Quinn, 370
Quynn, 358

R

Rabbit's Walk, 118
Radcliff, 80, 292, 564
Radcliffe, 329, 502
Ragge, 410
Ragsdale, 73, 570
Rails, 550
Railton, 458
Rainbow, 477
Raines, 14
Rainey, 347
Rains, 313, 323
Rairol, 447
Rambo, 79
Ramorny, 9
Rampon, 524
Ramsay, 113, 135, 155, 232, 354
Ramsey, 31, 44, 117, 309, 461
Rana, 530

Ranault, 17, 28
Rand, 507, 521
Randall, 14, 31, 100, 114, 137, 171, 310, 370, 406, 428, 432, 435
Randolph, 38, 50, 55, 91, 119, 120, 167, 224, 255, 436
Rankin, 301
Ranson, 83, 422
Ransone, 536
Rapalye, 285
Rapp, 237
Ratcliff, 15, 173, 306, 538, 550
Ratcliffe, 66, 424
Rathbone, 362
Rathburn, 115
Raub, 163, 171, 430
Ravesies, 50
Ravintree, 570
Rawlings, 209, 414
Rawls, 396
Rawson, 7
Ray, 22, 80, 147, 377
Raymond, 7, 50, 59, 81, 104, 128, 224, 379, 468
Raynolds, 322
Rayseau, 237
razee **Independence**, 258
Rea, 558
Read, 63, 195, 224, 296, 386, 403
Ready, 348
Reaver, 338
Reber, 6
Reckless, 42, 107
Rector, 19
Red Hill, 75
Red Springs, 24
Redd, 273
Reddall, 310
Reddin, 173
Reddish, 275
Redfern, 12, 122, 132, 319, 488
Redfield, 210
Redgate, 356
Redin, 77, 252, 319, 354, 429, 569
Redwood, 311
Reed, 59, 111, 167, 170, 177, 259, 341, 355, 367, 402, 485, 511, 528
Reeder, 36, 192, 476
Reedy, 348
Rees, 567
Reese, 90, 91, 117, 375, 389, 414
Reeside, 553
Reeves, 319, 347, 521
Reid, 30, 102, 242, 416
Reilly, 8, 14, 35, 110, 113, 157, 237, 340, 442, 451, 496
Reily, 430
Reimbursement, 118
Reines, 228
Reinhart, 71, 130, 195, 403
Reintzel, 407
Reiss, 191, 409
Relf, 273
Rell, 377
Remick, 294
Remsen, 568
Renahan, 415
Renault, 14, 43
Rench, 421
Rencher, 473, 552
Reneham, 154
Renehan, 481
Renshaw, 70, 385
Renwick, 323
Reommele, 269
Republican Bonum, 116
Request, 118
Res, 91
Resurvey, 176
Resurvey on Cillur's Discovery, 217
Retirement, 36
Revere, 165
Revolutionary Pensioners, 147
Reynolds, 14, 133, 228, 233, 299, 313, 321, 356, 370, 378, 396, 512, 562
Rhind, 334

Rhinevault, 47, 57, 114
Rhoades, 209
Rhoads, 366
Rhodes, 139, 164, 238, 287, 349, 497
Ribbing, 372
Rice, 47, 91, 105, 132, 182, 209, 328, 361, 369, 391, 409, 431, 499, 559
Rich, 33, 43, 53, 57, 74, 166, 212, 226, 305, 324, 334, 367, 463, 533, 538
Richadrson, 382
Richards, 3, 107, 208, 209, 311, 338, 342, 359, 361, 443, 465
Richardson, 77, 198, 216, 221, 238, 254, 292, 299, 312, 356, 373, 391, 421, 442, 533, 543
Riche, 108, 113, 142
Richey, 165, 173, 462
Richmond, 452
Rickelson, 527
Ricketts, 398, 483
Riddle, 105, 114, 156, 366, 421
Ridgeley, 453
Ridgely, 31, 52, 117, 198, 199, 299, 368, 377, 393, 428, 521, 569
Ridgeway, 228, 327
Ridgway, 8, 210, 365
Riding, 383
Riely, 397
Riffort, 199
Rigden, 198
Riggles, 292
Riggs, 287, 300, 356, 410, 478, 540
Right, 24
Righter, 21
Rights of Man, 116
Riley, 32, 90, 166, 261, 276, 302, 421, 489, 490, 498, 548
Ringe, 503
Ringgold, 123, 257, 259, 268, 279, 283, 332, 514
Riordan, 140
Ripley, 22, 91, 133, 321
Ritchie, 70, 118, 228, 311, 347, 348

Rittenhouse, 403
Ritter, 234, 320, 333, 341, 461, 480
Rives, 215, 244, 465, 490, 527, 542
Rivieres, 340
Rivinius, 479
Roach, 9, 29, 133, 170, 172, 297, 341, 348, 367, 379, 522
Roan, 91
Roane, 281
Roatch, 211
Robb, 100, 403, 436
Robbins, 20, 396
Roberdeau, 499
Roberts, 33, 90, 91, 126, 158, 159, 171, 223, 237, 247, 259, 268, 330, 387, 488, 534, 554
Robertson, 66, 115, 140, 153, 234, 292, 446, 561
Robeson, 211
Robey, 68, 108
Robinett, 280
Robinson, 21, 24, 35, 56, 60, 109, 115, 165, 168, 185, 204, 209, 216, 228, 274, 292, 402, 480, 498, 548, 552, 562
Robo, 133
Roby, 569
Rochat, 488
Roche, 334
Rochford, 340
Rockendorff, 548
Rockeyfellow, 91
Rockwell, 134, 267, 465
Roddy, 39, 42, 48, 52, 98, 114
Rodella, 149
Rodgers, 4, 12, 17, 68, 219, 296, 548
Rodman, 17, 362, 363
Rodrigues, 377
Rody, 15, 64
Roe, 167
Roemile, 488
Roemmele, 521
Roezel, 158
Rogan, 374

Rogers, 2, 23, 24, 47, 52, 53, 77, 91, 102, 113, 157, 170, 210, 228, 242, 279, 288, 361, 372, 388, 472
Rohr, 159
Rolando, 31
Rolland, 340
Rollings, 429
Rollins, 260, 319, 368, 377
Rolls, 373
Rolph, 357
Roman Catholic, 428
Ronckendorf, 540
Ronckendorff, 32, 180, 243, 272, 336
Rondthaler, 400
Rooker, 166
Roosevelt, 141
Root, 209, 366, 565
Roper, 53, 274, 337
Rosas, 274
Rosati, 516
Roscoe, 231
Roscommon, 567
Rose, 6, 84, 130, 136, 373, 398, 437, 439, 516
Rose Hill, 398
Rosencrans, 321
Rosenthal, 504
Rosewell, 382, 400
Ross, 23, 226, 421, 437, 440, 442, 449, 459, 477, 544
Rosser, 278
Rosson, 55
Roszel, 110, 569
Rother, 372
Rothfritz, 139, 147
Rothschilds, 222
Rothwell, 12, 121, 209, 232, 243, 296, 297, 329, 418, 569
Rouge, 240
Rousha, 301
Roushe, 101
Roussain, 182
Rousseau, 164

Rowan, 241, 331
Rowe, 185
Rowland, 178, 452
Rowles, 273, 356, 571
Rowlet, 42
Rowlett, 16
Roy, 233
Royal, 108
Royall, 42, 570
Royer, 96
Royster, 54
Rozier, 421
Ruck, 571
Rucker, 331
Rudd, 376
Ruff, 179, 473, 543
Ruffin, 86
Ruffner, 103
Ruggles, 56, 440
Rumsey, 96, 573
Runet, 560
Runyan, 91
Rupert, 422, 492
Rush, 59, 113, 143, 170, 211, 314, 407
Rushworth, 263
Russ, 170
Russel, 391
Russell, 35, 52, 56, 73, 79, 84, 108, 125, 146, 209, 215, 348, 391, 470, 475
Russy, 6
Rust, 77, 453, 516
Rutherford, 311, 439
Rutledge, 83
Rutter, 334, 360, 432, 544
Ryan, 237, 372, 377
Ryder, 344
Ryon, 90, 496
Rypma, 208

S

Sac, 21, 86, 177, 181
Sacs, 178
Sadler, 282

Sage, 171
Sailor, 443
Sale, 567
Sample, 258
Sampson, 237
Samson, 297, 388, 392, 549, 551, 569
Samuel, 120
Sanders, 83, 113, 138, 170, 225, 370
Sanderson, 513
Sandford, 26
Sandrue, 249
Sands, 11, 31, 153, 297, 303, 368, 378, 421, 559
Sanford, 92, 187, 353
Sangstack, 489
Sangster, 439
Sangston, 444
Santa Anna, 9, 541
Santamarina, 221
Santburg, 91
Sapping, 88
Sardo, 274, 354, 423, 489
Sargeant, 391
Sargent, 91, 158
Sartain, 287, 326
Sartorius, 448
Sassaman, 451
Saunders, 4, 25, 91, 101, 119, 293, 400, 407, 409, 472, 546, 549, 561
Savage, 7, 25, 51, 73, 93, 97, 108, 129, 154, 208, 215, 353, 362, 417, 518, 525, 569
Savary, 402
Sawkins, 473
Sawyer, 1, 7, 402, 500
Sayre, 476
Scaggs, 484
Scasscar, 24
Schannal, 377
Scheel, 53, 480
Scheibler, 208
Schenck, 184, 281, 477
Schley, 31, 368

Schmuck, 337
Schneider, 237, 488, 489
Schnierle, 408
schnr **Betsey**, 43
schnr **Blooming Youth**, 37, 79
schnr **Buffalo**, 23
schnr **Byron**, 434
schnr **Cod Hook**, 73
schnr **Codhook**, 108
schnr **Cordelia**, 298
schnr **Credit**, 56, 73, 108
schnr **Dolphin**, 137
schnr **Edward Burley**, 316
schnr **Enterprise**, 182, 449
schnr **Florida**, 76
schnr **Florilla**, 79
schnr **Frances Kennedy**, 272
schnr **Francis Jane**, 271
schnr **Francis Thomas**, 410
schnr **Garnet**, 56, 73, 108
schnr **Grampus**, 15, 57, 169, 246, 275, 276, 377, 378
schnr **Harriet**, 571
schnr **Joanna**, 23, 52
schnr **Joseph**, 64
schnr **Lark**, 365
schnr **Lilly**, 23
schnr **Louisa**, 317
schnr **Lucy Ann**, 56, 73, 108
schnr **Lurana**, 52
schnr **Martha**, 23, 52
schnr **On-ka-kye**, 388
schnr **Only Son**, 56, 73, 114, 143
schnr **Privado**, 64
schnr **Robin Hood**, 130
schnr **Samuel Phillips**, 86
schnr **Sarah Lavinia**, 355, 370, 562
schnr **Seppican**, 79
schnr **Sevo & Ida**, 73
schnr **Thomas**, 146
schnr **Thos Dail**, 523
schnr **Three Brothers**, 73, 108
schnr **Twin**, 79

schnr **Two Sons**, 114, 145
schnr **Union**, 56, 73, 108
schnr **Ursula**, 443
schnr **Washington**, 507
schnr **Wave**, 86, 449
schnr **Whig**, 572
schnr **William**, 56
schnr-of-war **San Antonio**, 194
schnrs **Florilla & Garnet**, 571
schnrs **Savo & Ida**, 56
schnrs **Sevo & Ida**, 108
Scholfield, 443
Schooley, 7, 110
Schriver, 535
Schroeder, 356, 501
Schucking, 534, 568
Schultz, 348
Schuyler, 84, 95, 107, 455
Schwartz, 499
Scollay, 308
Scot, 534
Scott, 17, 29, 31, 39, 48, 91, 94, 110, 122, 125, 133, 182, 194, 228, 231, 232, 248, 249, 284, 289, 292, 295, 313, 318, 337, 345, 348, 353, 377, 392, 399, 421, 444, 451, 461, 464, 470, 479, 499, 524, 527, 536, 552, 555, 573
Scovel, 47
Scovell, 403
Scranton, 251
Scrivener, 384
Scrivner, 545
Scroggins, 333
Scruggs, 215
Scudder, 223
Seal, 166
Seaman, 403
Searcy, 226
Sears, 48, 113, 170, 391
Seat Pleasant, 330
Seaton, 127, 150, 154, 227, 269, 297, 311, 367, 436, 454, 520, 527, 570

Seaver, 180, 264, 284, 367, 402
Seawell, 123, 448, 481, 551
Sedgwick, 8, 391
Sedwick, 300
Seebars, 11
Seeger, 194
Seekamp, 195
Sefiora, 9
Seibert, 25
Seippel, 538
Seitz, 421
Seiver, 461
Selby, 559
Selden, 43, 73, 75, 77, 88, 159, 253, 258, 286, 322, 327, 364, 383, 405, 429, 469, 480, 570
Seldon, 237
Selecman, 543
Sellers, 91, 430
Seminole, 14, 47, 62
Seminoles, 423
Semmes, 8, 83, 127, 167, 233, 242, 273, 328, 334, 341, 347, 348, 421, 441, 492, 494, 495, 539, 543
Semple, 54, 60, 148, 393
Senabough, 90
Seney, 216
Sengstack, 489, 490
Sergeant, 276, 428
Serrel, 573
Serrin, 292, 354
Servant, 148
Servier, 377, 378
Sessford, 164, 292, 473, 520
Settle, 8
Settles, 177
Sevegne, 395
Sewall, 20, 166, 180, 218, 391, 399, 421, 471
Seward, 1, 219
Sewell, 74
Sexsmith, 472
Seymour, 483, 565

Shaaf, 140
Shack, 559
Shaefe, 421
Shaeffer, 110
Shafer, 79, 96
Shaffer, 245
Shakspeare, 265
Shamrock Hill, 193
Shandy Hall, 89
Shank, 509
Shanks, 19, 236, 482
Shannon, 14, 25, 31, 49, 114, 179, 216, 315, 363, 387
Shanton, 32, 368
Sharp, 391
Sharpe, 421
Sharrets, 167
Sharretts, 166
Shaw, 138, 165, 176, 216, 360, 369, 412, 421, 452, 571
Shawnee Indians, 155, 546
Sheckell, 493, 494
Sheehan, 369, 370
Sheerwood, 452
Sheffer, 380
Shelburne, 567
Shelton, 188, 191, 195, 323
Shemwell, 236
Shepard, 251, 257, 499
Shepherd, 53, 90, 127, 132, 212, 234, 238, 253, 257, 317, 385, 388, 516
Sheppard, 194, 267, 356
Shepperd, 83, 223, 297
Sherburne, 226, 363
Sheridan, 409, 567
Sheriff, 261, 374
Sherman, 94, 330, 496, 555
Sherwin, 207
Sherwood, 331, 513
Shield, 551
Shields, 50, 295, 393
Shiles, 177
Shillito, 110

Shilt, 93
Shinas, 547
Shinn, 71
ship **Alabama**, 44
ship **Alkmar**, 24
ship **Arcadia**, 285
ship **Argo**, 479
ship **Austin**, 212
ship **Birmingham**, 548
ship **Bonhomme Richard**, 226
ship **Boston**, 361, 407
ship **Brandywine**, 239, 246
ship **Cabot**, 393
ship **Caledonia**, 433
ship **Caroline**, 247
ship **Chespeake**, 456
ship **Columbia**, 148, 297, 313, 343
ship **Columbus**, 244, 368, 449
ship **Columbus 74**, 31, 236
ship **Comet**, 171
ship **Concord**, 148, 216
ship **Constellation**, 562
ship **Dale**, 472
ship **Decatur**, 362
ship **Dee**, 455
ship **Delaware**, 387
ship **Dolphin**, 4, 382
ship **Don Juan**, 501
ship **Duc d'Orleans**, 509
ship **Emerald**, 534
ship **Empress**, 254
ship **Encomium**, 171
ship **Erie**, 83, 238, 304, 472
ship **Fairfield**, 32
ship **Flavius**, 254
ship **Gen Williams**, 146
ship **George**, 92
ship **Glasgow**, 343
ship **Great Western**, 455
ship **Herald**, 263
ship **Hibernia**, 216, 315
ship **Hottinguer**, 522
ship **Imaun 74**, 159

ship **Independence**, 66, 263, 477
ship **Iowa**, 328
ship **Iris**, 205
ship **John Adams**, 2, 148, 162, 163, 296
ship **Levant**, 403
ship **Lexington**, 387, 399
ship **Liverpool**, 449
ship **Loo-Choo**, 409
ship **Lowell**, 277
ship **Lucy**, 270
ship **Macedonian**, 334
ship **Madedonian**, 472
ship **Malabar**, 448
ship **Margaret**, 315, 343
ship **Maria Theresa**, 141
ship **Marseilles**, 301
ship **Mary Carver**, 316
ship **Mayflower**, 562
ship **Memphis**, 350
ship **Missouri**, 242
ship **Montezuma**, 230
ship **New York**, 474
ship **North Carolina**, 34, 63
ship of the line **Franklin**, 316
ship of war **Independence**, 564
ship of war **Vandalia**, 171
ship **Ohio**, 400, 485
ship **Orient**, 149
ship **Pennsylvania**, 13, 135, 309, 376, 378, 449
ship **Potomac**, 2
ship **Preble**, 32, 533
ship **Rajah**, 448, 470
ship **Robert Bruce**, 49
ship **Rothschild**, 181
ship **Samuel Hicks**, 213
ship **San Bernard**, 194
ship **Scotland**, 56
ship **Sea Gull**, 30
ship **Sharon**, 298
ship **Sheffield**, 513
ship **Silvie de Grasse**, 237
ship **St Louis**, 239, 246, 502

ship **St Matthews**, 78
ship **Stephen Whitney**, 235
ship **Thos P Cope**, 437
ship **Thunder**, 365
ship **Toronto**, 552
ship **Union**, 245
ship **United States**, 501
ship **Valparaiso**, 227
ship **Vandalia**, 341, 388, 559
ship **Vincennes**, 206, 558
ship **Vindictive**, 341
ship **Yorktown**, 362, 407
Shipley, 44, 88
Shipman, 17, 90, 216, 227, 424
ship**Rienzi**, 316
ships **Congress & Fairfield**, 387
ships **Erebus & Terror**, 459
Shiras, 339
Shirley, 51, 362, 405
Shockley, 270
Shoemaker, 12, 251, 269, 536, 543
Shone, 367
Short, 39, 121
Short Island, 217
Shorter, 147
Shortridge, 372
Shove, 310
Shreve, 55, 63, 109, 552
Shreves, 406
Shriver, 10, 88
Shryock, 12
Shubrick, 63, 135, 182, 301, 400, 445, 449
Shucking, 214
Shultz, 354
Shumway, 209
Shuster, 210
Shyne, 18, 20, 186, 197
Sibley, 17, 171
Sickles, 32
Sidebotham, 421
Sikes, 198
Silk Farm, 427

Silliman, 210
Simmes, 172, 380, 478
Simmons, 284, 421, 512, 517
Simms, 31, 111, 132, 173, 306, 387, 410, 438, 489, 490, 491, 494, 527
Simnard, 252
Simonds, 262, 319, 399
Simons, 91
Simpers, 441
Simpler, 265
Simpson, 32, 56, 134, 166, 212, 252, 297, 299, 368, 421, 465, 476, 548
Sims, 368, 499
Sinclair, 234, 515, 534
Sinkler, 226
Sinnickson, 90
Sinnott, 314
Sinon, 200
Sioussa, 476, 540
Sioux, 181
Sioux Indians, 170, 335
Sister Claudia, 503
Sister Frederika, 424
Sister Mary Doloris, 49
Sister of Charity, 424
Sisters of Charity, 351, 464, 475
Sisters of St Vincent, 540
Sitgreaves, 225
Skaggs, 413
Skidder, 70
Skidmore, 75, 88
Skillman, 76
Skinner, 15, 27, 50, 59, 82, 106, 113, 114, 135, 142, 193, 229, 254, 269, 343, 371, 402, 410, 460, 474, 555, 557, 574
Skirving, 56, 57, 67, 81, 105, 113, 142, 151, 154, 170, 171
Slack, 36
Slacum, 6
Slade, 7, 216, 241, 532
Slamm, 510
Slater, 9, 281, 398, 463, 503

Slatford, 537
Slaughter, 278, 283
Slaymaker, 109
Slidell, 288
Sligworth, 401
Slingerland, 209
Sloan, 175, 511, 517, 540
Sloat, 63
Slocum, 416
sloop **City**, 121
sloop **Decatur**, 225, 226
sloop **Fairfield**, 31, 236, 247, 387
sloop **Falmouth**, 378
sloop **General Lewis**, 57
sloop **Levant**, 225
sloop of war **Austin**, 194, 251
sloop of war **Concord**, 141, 163
sloop of war **John Adams**, 141
sloop of war **Levant**, 333
sloop of war **Marion**, 296
sloop of war **Preble**, 399, 411
sloop of war **Vandalia**, 234, 449
sloop of war **Warren**, 449
sloop **Preble**, 31, 236, 387, 453
sloop **Vandalia**, 225
Small, 2, 4, 12, 17, 51
Smallwood, 11, 139, 388, 445
Smart, 77, 355
Smiley, 209
Smith, 1, 6, 8, 11, 15, 17, 25, 32, 35, 38, 39, 43, 44, 47, 49, 52, 53, 57, 60, 63, 64, 67, 72, 73, 77, 83, 86, 90, 91, 94, 95, 103, 108, 113, 114, 115, 117, 120, 128, 130, 142, 143, 148, 153, 161, 163, 171, 175, 176, 177, 178, 185, 186, 189, 197, 201, 202, 207, 209, 210, 212, 214, 216, 224, 225, 226, 228, 230, 231, 232, 233, 234, 236, 238, 241, 243, 244, 247, 255, 257, 258, 261, 268, 269, 272, 274, 276, 291, 294, 300, 308, 315, 330, 337, 338, 340, 352, 355, 356, 358, 362, 364, 365, 367, 368, 369, 370, 373,

375, 377, 378, 380, 382, 388, 391,
399, 405, 408, 410, 411, 412, 421,
426, 433, 436, 441, 451, 452, 461,
469, 476, 481, 484, 488, 500, 501,
506, 514, 516, 520, 522, 523, 529,
534, 542, 545, 546, 548, 550, 552,
563, 565, 569
Smitha, 196
smoking, 165
Smoot, 122, 135, 167, 212, 253, 261,
295, 302, 308, 376, 379, 384, 424,
431, 511
Smull, 503
Smyth, 392
Snassey, 68
Snead, 113, 313
Snearley, 185
Sneed, 51, 57, 144
Snethen, 451, 456
Snively, 328, 366, 466
Snodgrass, 102, 508
Snow, 227, 356, 568
Snowden, 370, 537
Snowdon, 324
Snyder, 8, 461
Soldier's Repose, 504
Soldiers Repose, 467
Solomon, 158
Somer, 289
Somerall, 25
Somerby, 570
Somers, 209, 295
Somerville, 81, 99, 246
Sommers, 400
Soper, 5
Sothoron, 8, 18, 276, 415, 559
Soule, 74, 102, 369
Southall, 42, 114, 145
Southard, 39, 510
Southerland, 291, 415, 445, 460, 505, 569
Southey, 204
Southgate, 167, 320, 521

Southworth, 294
Soutter, 566
Spalding, 97, 186, 404, 509
Spangler, 278
Sparks, 392, 565
Sparrow, 525
Spaulding, 368
Spear, 27, 101, 363, 415
Spears, 476
Speed, 409
Speedwell Forges, 196
Speiden, 77, 247, 387
Speiser, 497
Spelman, 260, 370, 396
Spence, 95, 114, 152, 247, 556
Spencer, 2, 4, 12, 17, 24, 30, 31, 32, 51,
66, 88, 96, 104, 120, 122, 135, 148,
163, 202, 209, 218, 236, 245, 270,
290, 309, 377, 408, 441, 523
Spendlow, 534
Spenser, 347
Spicer, 126
Spotts, 296
Spottswood, 31
Sprague, 124, 291, 306, 391, 448, 511
Spreckelson, 513
Sprigg, 167, 221, 330, 360, 439, 518
Springer, 443
Springstead, 313
Sprole, 482, 533
Sproul, 146
Spruance, 452
Spurr, 401
Squirrel Range, 116
St Aurelia, 240
St Clair, 120, 396, 443, 471
St Clear, 489, 493
St Jean, 183
St Mary's, 333
St Romes, 392
St Vrain, 328
Stabler, 341
Stacy, 242

Stafford, 40
Stainback, 165
Stairs, 315
Stalker, 571
Stallings, 97, 193, 205, 291
Stanard, 162
Standish, 562, 563
Stanford, 109, 306
Stanhope, 232
Stanley, 259
Stanly, 404
Stannard, 487
Stansbury, 186
Stanton, 364
Staples, 294, 559
Stapp, 90
Stark, 126, 306
Starke, 518
Starks, 333
Starrs, 472
Stars, 555
Staub, 68, 121
steam packet **Hibernia**, 248
steamboat **Anna Calhoun**, 151
steamboat **Belle**, 247
steamboat **Belle of Pittsburg**, 433
steamboat **Ben Franklin**, 529
steamboat **Cinderella**, 380
steamboat **Clipper**, 443
steamboat **Columbia**, 302
steamboat **Cutter**, 177
steamboat **Empress**, 498
steamboat **Harry of the West**, 207
steamboat **Joseph Johnson**, 453
steamboat **Levi Welch**, 430
steamboat **New Albany**, 136
steamboat **Ohio**, 396
steamboat **Osceola**, 193
steamboat **Oseola**, 219
steamboat **Phenix**, 25, 71
steamboat **President**, 139
steamboat **Pulaski**, 222
steamboat **Rainbow**, 252

steamboat **Rowena**, 515
steamboat **Swan**, 139
steamboat **Union**, 171, 302
steamboat **Warren**, 556
steamboat **Wave**, 513
steamer **Admiral**, 429
steamer **Augusta**, 484
steamer **Ben Franklin**, 238
steamer **Britania**, 204
steamer **Chesapeake**, 356, 466
steamer **Cincinnati**, 180
steamer **Columbia**, 153, 315
steamer **Hibernia**, 236, 343
steamer **J M White**, 350
steamer **Lexington**, 386
steamer **Meteor**, 238
steamer **Missouri**, 470, 573
steamer **Montezuma**, 554
steamer **North America**, 287
steamer **North Bend**, 464
steamer **Pegasus**, 380
steamer **Princeton**, 385, 451, 472
steamer **Sarah Barnes**, 498
steamer **Splendid**, 399
steamer **Tennessee Valley**, 371
steamship **Great Western**, 228, 306, 328
steamship **President**, 319
steamship **Princeton**, 407
steamship **Union**, 300
Stean, 242
Stear, 129
Stearns, 21, 259
Steedman, 226
Steel, 198, 569
Steele, 237, 322, 549, 552, 557
Steenberger, 197
Steer, 502
Stegar, 194
Stehley, 13
Stein, 188, 236
Steinberger, 308
Steiner, 189

Stelle, 519
Stellwagen, 5, 316
Stembel, 226
Stene, 388
Stenson, 296
Stephen, 5
Stephens, 221, 323
Stephenson, 405
Steptoe, 201, 339
Sterigere, 450
Stern, 99
Sterrett, 421
Sterrit, 159
Stettinius, 38, 302, 307, 394, 482, 491, 516
Steuart, 169, 270
Stevens, 20, 39, 45, 51, 54, 68, 79, 86, 140, 184, 270, 322, 362, 365, 377, 378, 462
Stevenson, 71, 132, 139, 334, 476, 521
Steward, 534
Stewart, 4, 30, 50, 74, 84, 125, 129, 185, 192, 207, 215, 216, 225, 239, 262, 297, 298, 300, 301, 302, 303, 310, 319, 321, 339, 393, 406, 425, 428, 440, 443, 455, 461, 477, 480, 483, 490, 498, 500, 506, 522
Stickle, 388
Stillwell, 88, 218
Stimpson, 126
Stimson, 391
Stiner, 103, 302
Stinnecke, 238
Stith, 383, 450, 485
Stockbridge, 114, 477
Stocking, 291
Stockton, 27, 28, 61, 272, 385, 407, 451, 472, 477
Stodart, 444
Stoddard, 112
Stoddert, 15
Stokes, 27, 301

Stone, 15, 49, 234, 264, 318, 380, 391, 463, 526, 553
Stony Ridge, 116
Storer, 63, 474
storeship **Lexington**, 247
Storick, 513
Storm, 96
Storms, 234, 263, 430
Stott, 231, 250, 269, 488, 527
Stout, 33, 399
Stoven, 467
Stowell, 170
Straham, 538
Strain, 403
Strais, 296
Strammer, 17
Strang, 79
Straub, 492
Strayhorn, 271
Street, 25, 43, 57, 63, 98, 104, 113, 171, 174, 178
Stretch, 230, 421
Stricker, 121
Striker, 6, 55
Stringfellow, 44, 165, 199, 367, 378, 478, 486, 539, 559, 569
Stringham, 258, 315, 417
Strobia, 396
Strong, 209
Stroube, 180
Strout, 19
Strudwick, 50
Stryker, 23, 82, 114, 345
Stuart, 182, 186, 215, 530
Stubbs, 154, 287, 415
Stubss, 196
Stull, 189, 238, 375
Sturdivant, 6
Sturgeon, 569
Sturgis, 393, 565
Stuyvesants, 323
Stuyvessant, 437
Suit, 398

Sullivan, 12, 17, 45, 114, 154, 157, 238, 282, 340, 344, 363, 381, 415, 496
Sully, 386
Sulphur Springs, 252
Summers, 31, 69, 186, 365, 373, 402, 435, 551
Summons, 529
Sumner, 393
Sumter, 385, 443
Suratt, 484
Survilliers, 532
Suter, 269, 410
Sutherland, 32, 54, 126, 368, 545
Sutten, 525
Sutton, 178, 261, 365, 432, 448, 449, 497
Swank, 372
Swann, 112, 113, 236, 246, 357, 377
Swanston, 281
Swart, 179
Swartwout, 129, 549
Swasey, 102
Sweat, 82
Sweeney, 209
Sweeny, 291, 487
Sweet, 505
Sweet Pink, 118
Sweet Spring Tract, 24
Sweet Springs, 252
Sweeting, 491, 537
Sweetman, 41, 113, 151
Sweetser, 64, 67, 561
Sweetzer, 234
Swett, 422
Swift, 1, 248, 349, 452
Swigart, 448, 499
Swindler, 550
Swink, 112
Switzer, 40
Swords, 298
Sydnor, 235
Syfferly, 205, 492
Sykes, 238, 375

Sylvester, 66, 435
Symington, 523
Symmes, 561
Symons, 460

T

Tabb, 96
Tabler, 384
Taft, 102
Taggart, 379, 406
Talbertt, 231
Talbot, 85, 287, 311, 476
Talbott, 99
Talcott, 124, 518
Taliaferro, 89, 164, 334, 376, 484, 573
Tallmadge, 463
Tallmadge, 306
Talty, 335, 492, 493, 495
tame horses, 255
Taney, 18, 70, 125, 129, 406
Tanner, 228
Tappagnes, 335
Tappan, 23, 56, 73, 89, 108, 565
Tarlburtt, 484
Tarleton, 381
Tasche, 340
Tascoe, 258
Tastett, 401
Tate, 97, 360, 466, 527, 533
Tatman, 452
Tatnall, 32
Tattnall, 387
Taulioni, 241
Taunton, 224
Tayloe, 56, 111, 221, 252, 261
Taylor, 10, 13, 53, 59, 74, 83, 89, 96, 97, 106, 110, 112, 124, 129, 131, 134, 140, 153, 195, 203, 208, 231, 281, 282, 295, 297, 309, 323, 333, 339, 352, 366, 389, 390, 403, 446, 452, 470, 472, 508, 512, 527, 541, 549, 555, 560, 564
Tayman, 212, 257

Teasdale, 230
Tebbets, 532, 542
Tellkampf, 313
Temegnio, 370
Temple, 44
Templeman, 117, 118, 348
Tench, 552
Tenney, 204
Tenure, 86, 108
Terrett, 286
Terry, 49, 396
Thacher, 101
Thatcher, 246, 377, 568
Thaw, 478
Thaxter, 391
Thayer, 277, 391
Theabold, 117
Thecker, 131, 478, 507
Theobald, 410
Thiers, 227
Thoams, 228
Thom, 228
Thomas, 7, 16, 19, 20, 36, 41, 48, 76, 78, 82, 96, 102, 107, 113, 115, 121, 124, 126, 166, 168, 169, 231, 237, 240, 241, 242, 243, 251, 261, 271, 282, 319, 323, 326, 356, 362, 365, 371, 386, 402, 409, 415, 421, 428, 433, 441, 443, 469, 474, 476, 489, 490, 512, 533, 537, 539, 543, 568, 571, 572
Thomas & Ann, 118
Thomasson, 380
Thompson, 4, 12, 18, 42, 47, 48, 55, 59, 82, 90, 97, 100, 104, 106, 110, 114, 120, 128, 131, 133, 157, 171, 180, 193, 206, 220, 226, 233, 256, 269, 270, 296, 305, 334, 368, 385, 397, 407, 421, 457, 470, 478, 483, 501, 507, 519, 521, 526, 541, 543, 548, 554, 559, 561, 569, 570
Thomson, 449, 452
Thorawgood, 450
Thorn, 133, 164, 227
Thorne, 29, 241
Thornley, 250, 496
Thornly, 101, 231
Thornton, 145, 246, 367, 369, 418, 460, 532
Thorpe, 110
Threlkeld, 211
Throckmorton, 84, 296, 353, 470
Throop, 255, 266
Thruston, 20, 67, 113, 242, 261, 288, 343, 374
Thumb, 140
Thumlert, 181, 374, 451, 460, 489
Thurston, 101
Thyson, 172
Tibbatts, 380
Tibbets, 7, 22
Ticknor, 284
Tidball, 196, 273
Tiffany, 47, 129, 553
Tilden, 40, 441, 522
Tilghma, 224
Tilghman, 188, 413, 441, 486, 531
Tillan, 72
Tilley, 131
Tillon, 510
Tillotson, 12
Tilton, 32, 236, 368
Timberlake, 38, 199
Timms, 183
Tims, 231, 243, 250
Tingey, 58
Tinsley, 553
Tipen, 216
Tipton, 367
Titus, 328
Tobey, 102
Tochman, 471, 508
Todd, 14, 31, 39, 114, 129, 152, 244, 368, 369, 390, 399, 412, 425, 463, 474, 493, 494, 520
Toland, 377
Tolbert, 226

Toler, 186
Toles, 285
Tolkenton, 328
Tolman, 177
Tolson, 122, 123, 459
Tombul, 223
Tomkinson, 368
Tomlinson, 67
Tompkins, 31, 123, 199
Tompson, 91
Tonge, 226
Topping, 527
Toreno, 457
Torrence, 343
Torrey, 223
Torry, 381
Totten, 27, 101, 113, 137, 219, 362, 487, 568
Tough, 240
Touro, 205
towboat **Phenix**, 254
Towers, 23, 133, 154, 261, 293, 439, 442, 492, 527
Towle, 195, 261, 427
Towles, 556
Townley, 261, 426
Townsend, 259, 296, 396, 454, 538
Towsan, 239
Towson, 226, 436, 474
Tracy, 65, 211, 391
Trader, 133
Trapnell, 285
Trask, 391
Travers, 491
Traverse, 489
Travis, 434
Tree Hill, 253
Trenchard, 32
Trenor, 21
Trenton, 228
Tretler, 133, 172
Tricott, 149
Tricotti, 169

Trimble, 101, 247
Trio, 118
Tripler, 238
Triplett, 167, 521
Trippe, 399
Tristoe, 93
Trook, 41
Trott, 450, 530
Trowbridge, 443
Troy, 228
True, 375, 464, 506
Trueheart, 206
Trufant, 532
Truheart, 35
Truman, 15
Trumbull, 90, 224, 227, 407, 509
Trummell, 509
Trundle, 413, 441
Truscott, 248, 326
Truslow, 54, 142
Tschiffely, 526
Tubman, 337, 540
Tuck, 5, 14, 42, 108, 285, 334, 463
Tucker, 5, 13, 25, 47, 49, 65, 76, 77, 93, 188, 218, 246, 302, 387, 476, 482, 496, 497, 508, 519, 546, 558
Tuckerman, 219
Tudor, 204, 425, 431, 506
Tunton, 508
Tupper, 260
Turman, 540
Turnbull, 237, 386
Turner, 47, 54, 63, 90, 116, 141, 142, 160, 247, 292, 334, 357, 369, 382, 399, 447, 449, 474, 567
Turpin, 191
Turton, 301
Tuston, 108, 248, 277, 318, 454, 520, 526, 569
Tutt, 208, 233
Twiford, 480
Twiggs, 285, 333
Twitchell, 242

Tyler, 24, 43, 77, 109, 134, 154, 178, 183, 190, 207, 215, 227, 242, 247, 259, 266, 275, 297, 364, 513
Tyson, 356, 443

U

Udall, 422
Underwood, 101, 294, 454, 521, 569
Uoulle, 182
Updegraff, 21
Upperman, 8, 71, 296, 297, 496
Upshaw, 30
Upshur, 4, 32, 84, 135, 175, 275, 281, 309, 335, 376, 386, 434, 527, 548, 553, 574
Upson, 377
Upsur, 286
Urahem, 91
Urquhart, 237, 348
Usher, 91, 101
Utermuhle, 193
Uttermuhle, 492

V

Vail, 309, 479, 510, 516
Vaile Verde, 462
Vaks, 133
Valient, 187
Valnier, 249
Van Alen, 255
Van Allen, 216, 403
Van Alstine, 163
Van Bokkelen, 322
Van Brunt, 15, 17, 109
Van Buren, 203, 221, 247, 260, 301, 346, 405, 457
Van Coble, 421
Van Cortland, 421
Van Horn, 51, 362
Van Horne, 90
Van Horseigh, 456, 459
Van Houton, 558
Van Loon, 88

Van Ness, 50, 86, 206, 250, 277, 305, 318, 344, 421
Van Orsdallan, 57
Van Patten, 474
Van Renesselaer, 141
Van Rensselaer, 182, 294
Van Riswick, 115
Van Schaack, 209
Van Sinderen, 392
Van Twillers, 323
Van Tyne, 457
Van Velson, 17
Van Vichten, 91
Van Vliet, 543
Van Zandt, 336, 454
Vance, 168, 340
Vanderbilt, 463, 513
Vanderlyn, 316
Vanderpool, 80
Vandiver, 116
Vandyke, 90
Vanhorn, 100, 312
Vanhorne, 238
Vanhorseigh, 520
Vann, 440, 442, 462, 497
Vansant, 453
Vansittart, 166
Vanstanberg, 362
Vanstenburg, 51
Vantyne, 9
Vanuxem, 210
Variation, 217, 448
Varnum, 385, 539
Vasques, 83, 104
Vass, 64, 115
Vaux, 428
Veasie, 551
Velsor, 17
Venable, 385, 421
Venables, 303
Vendenberg, 279
Verguson, 59
Vermillion, 155

Verplanck, 452
Verren, 436
Very, 391
Vesey, 120
vessel **Emma Isadora**, 112
vessel **Saratoga**, 136
vessel **Speedwell**, 562
vessels **Confederacy & Tyranicide**, 453
Vevans, 126
Vidal, 60
Vienne, 35, 57, 82, 113
Viets, 40
Vigers, 409
Vigo, 555
Vila, 391
Villalba, 328
Villard, 241, 421
Villemont, 570
Vineyard, 503
Vinson, 414, 438, 467, 468
Viomenil, 381
Visser, 131
Vivan, 499
Vleit, 52, 73, 113, 156
Voisins, 241
Von Malder, 535
Vonesson, 58
Vonsson, 204
Voorhees, 32, 105, 110, 162, 200, 533, 548
Voorhies, 115, 158
Voorrees, 198
Vore, 462, 472
Vowell, 176, 465

W

Waddell, 70, 216, 234, 294, 388, 421
Waddle, 113, 157, 262
Wade, 18, 123, 337
Wager, 334
Waggaman, 139, 165, 277, 334
Waggoner, 68, 260
Wagler, 44, 409, 419, 444
Wagner, 242
Wagoner, 73
Wahusly, 67
Wailes, 139
Wainwright, 165, 216, 296, 353, 406, 438, 452, 470
Wait, 209, 269
Wake, 121, 196
Wakefield, 100
Wakeman, 307, 353, 470
Walbach, 312, 333
Walcutt, 395
Waldenses, 29
Waldo, 29
Waldron, 10, 56, 81, 113, 143, 171, 278, 377
Walen, 108
Wales, 2, 4, 12, 17
Walker, 5, 30, 42, 44, 55, 61, 75, 87, 90, 184, 202, 215, 261, 278, 281, 346, 347, 352, 354, 361, 391, 398, 413, 421, 457, 484, 488, 490, 500, 520, 527, 540, 548, 552, 555, 564
Wall, 234, 251, 260, 282, 320, 321, 396, 443, 521, 559
Wallace, 79, 91, 109, 118, 160, 252, 258, 327, 362, 421, 505
Wallach, 7, 36, 46, 295, 480
Walland, 228
Waller, 399
Wallingsford, 438, 480
Wallis, 21, 292, 312, 506
Walls, 415, 421
Waln, 87
Walsh, 226, 231, 299, 362, 377, 408, 510
Walters, 28
Waltham, 4
Walton, 220, 278
Wand, 362
Wa-pil-lo, 178
War of Independence, 117

Ward, 28, 51, 186, 230, 237, 250, 293, 308, 362, 386, 421, 438, 443, 451, 489, 490, 491, 518, 520, 539
Warder, 423
Wardlaw, 381
Ware, 282, 308, 391, 437
Warfield, 24, 105, 328, 357, 366, 382, 441
Waring, 3, 10, 87, 98, 118, 172, 183, 206, 212, 257, 262, 282, 350
Warley, 51
Warner, 17, 161, 285, 428, 446
Warnock, 330
Warren, 143, 182, 209, 280, 299, 319, 449, 535, 553
Warrenton, 362
Warring, 549
Warrington, 7, 36, 51, 277, 403, 413
Warry, 101
Washburn, 229, 294, 469
Washer, 532
Washington, 7, 19, 23, 29, 33, 46, 49, 54, 57, 64, 66, 69, 88, 93, 95, 100, 103, 115, 131, 142, 162, 199, 208, 224, 230, 274, 308, 314, 344, 352, 359, 362, 367, 381, 407, 425, 432, 453, 462, 480, 509, 520, 560
Washington Directory, 407
Waskey, 362
Wasson, 158
Watchman, 356
Water, 397
Waterman, 21
Waters, 3, 52, 85, 90, 118, 120, 121, 228, 283, 292, 318, 358, 374, 384, 413, 428, 441, 442, 460, 465, 494, 495, 540, 547
Watkins, 358, 536
Watkinson, 156, 170
Watson, 31, 39, 48, 64, 86, 162, 233, 249, 250, 267, 281, 368, 434, 441, 536, 555, 559, 565

Watterston, 62, 261, 269, 340, 344, 374, 410, 478, 534
Watterton, 261
Watts, 40, 78, 90, 96, 120, 158, 232, 253, 297, 343, 359
Waugh, 8, 276
Wayland, 178, 298
Wayne, 21, 325
Wear, 177
Weaver, 56, 67, 75, 109, 114, 152, 164, 167, 187, 210, 246, 279, 315, 556, 560
Weaverton, 531
Webb, 27, 95, 109, 116, 129, 133, 135, 170, 226, 230, 246, 247, 278, 296, 300, 327, 376, 378, 387, 391, 519
Webber, 177, 548
Weber, 492
Webster, 7, 36, 42, 106, 178, 183, 192, 210, 218, 219, 254, 366, 370, 371, 427, 452, 463, 538
Wechter, 373
Weed, 62, 287, 549
Weeden, 195
Weeks, 91, 102, 504
Weems, 404
Weightman, 247, 261, 269, 478, 524, 527
Weir, 298, 350, 562
Weisiger, 311
Welch, 115, 158, 203, 294, 445
Weldon, 7
Weller, 64, 95, 113, 440
Wellford, 387
Welling, 107
Wellman, 88, 402
Wells, 38, 43, 102, 184, 218, 371, 403, 415, 561
Welsh, 61, 106, 118, 307, 374, 403, 466
Wentworth, 391
Werden, 361
Wernwag, 384
Wesley, 353, 439

West, 3, 31, 93, 234, 246, 247, 368, 399, 415, 462, 495, 497, 506, 516, 518, 559
Westcost, 477
Westcott, 296
Western Connexion, 116
Westlake, 107
Weston, 54, 84, 402, 485
Westover, 405
Wetherall, 143
Wethered, 356
Wetherell, 113
Wetmore, 349
Wever, 23, 73, 75, 98, 114, 170, 508
Wey, 133
Weyanoke, 30
Weymouth, 382
Whalen, 421
Whaling, 90, 223
Whann, 108
Wharney, 27
Wharry, 113, 137
Wharton, 428, 532
What you please, 118
Wheat, 161, 410, 532
Wheatly, 74
Wheaton, 534
Wheeler, 146, 159, 173, 198, 238, 338, 468, 541
Wheelock, 247, 441
Wheelwright, 391, 396, 477
Whelan, 44
Whetter, 118
Whetton, 96
Whillow, 377
Whimpster, 381
Whipple, 10, 39, 97, 128
Whistler, 286
White, 10, 32, 40, 43, 55, 56, 74, 91, 95, 113, 133, 137, 147, 149, 159, 167, 211, 236, 258, 261, 288, 304, 333, 337, 347, 348, 363, 380, 387, 391, 430, 435, 473, 492, 493, 494, 520, 548, 555, 562, 563

White Bear, 181
Whiteford, 216
Whitehead, 99, 216, 343, 555
Whitehouse, 330
Whitehurst, 91
Whitely, 124
Whiteman, 75, 108
Whithead, 515
Whiting, 96, 313, 334, 539
Whitlock, 204
Whitmore, 17, 210, 283, 417
Whitney, 27, 163, 330, 542, 570
Whittel, 228
Whittemore, 28
Whittingham, 183
Whittle, 86
Whittlesey, 277, 352, 412, 486, 542, 558
Whitton, 361
Wickham, 162, 438
Wickliffe, 63, 108, 110, 126, 170, 237, 256, 286, 290, 309, 356, 357, 455, 500, 520, 527
Wier, 246
Wight, 162
Wiklinson, 368
Wilber, 92
Wilbur, 272, 294, 402
Wilburn, 8
Wilcox, 88, 297, 337, 375, 456
Wilde, 21, 42, 48, 72, 432
Wilder, 172, 210
Wildey, 326
Wilds, 146
Wiley, 5, 41, 113, 151
Wilkes, 6, 238, 336, 510
Wilkeson, 138
Wilkins, 77, 121, 356, 385, 461, 560
Wilkinson, 43, 57, 70, 108, 296, 315, 347, 400, 445, 480, 544
Willard, 47, 254
Willet, 571
Willett, 117, 529, 536
William, 208

William's Discovery, 116
Williams, 3, 8, 9, 10, 18, 21, 27, 57, 59, 67, 79, 81, 84, 91, 93, 101, 102, 106, 107, 109, 111, 113, 114, 115, 121, 130, 134, 136, 137, 144, 147, 153, 161, 182, 203, 204, 207, 208, 212, 215, 230, 234, 251, 263, 270, 286, 295, 313, 319, 332, 338, 368, 371, 374, 378, 391, 396, 398, 406, 449, 457, 465, 468, 470, 486, 534, 545, 547, 548, 552, 553, 556, 561, 564
Williamson, 41, 45, 52, 59, 62, 82, 166, 195, 274, 318, 319, 334, 340, 369, 382, 388, 400, 421, 428, 449, 507, 534, 535, 547
Williman, 237
Willink, 421
Willis, 90, 234, 373, 460, 508, 571
Willis Grove, 373
Willmer, 162, 237
Willoughby, 90, 177
Wilmer, 540
Wilmerding, 525
Wilson, 2, 4, 14, 17, 25, 31, 39, 48, 56, 57, 68, 81, 89, 90, 91, 107, 111, 112, 113, 114, 126, 151, 170, 177, 182, 227, 230, 236, 237, 250, 260, 284, 285, 293, 325, 340, 341, 367, 376, 386, 399, 403, 424, 432, 435, 437, 448, 449, 467, 485, 499, 504, 512, 521, 534, 535, 544, 558, 560, 572, 573
Wilson's Risk, 118
Wilt, 43
Wiltberger, 269, 292, 522
Wimer, 22, 112, 566
Wimsatt, 136, 209, 292, 489
Winchester, 367
Winder, 381, 386
Windsor, 517
Winebrener, 436
Winfree, 324
Wing, 90, 427
Wingall, 270
Wingate, 513, 528
Wingfield, 513
Wingo, 440
Winn, 223
Winship, 370
Winslow, 11, 25, 49, 57, 81, 113, 114, 142, 171, 242, 352, 562, 563, 564
Winston, 95, 162, 334, 341
Winter, 250
Winters, 85
Winthrop, 349, 408, 476
Wise, 38, 68, 106, 172, 291, 378, 499
Wiseman, 28
Wism, 91
Wisson, 161
Withers, 98
Witherspoon, 362
Withington, 177
Witt, 318
Wittingham, 466
Wm the Conqueror, 29
Wolcott, 162
Wolf, 278, 391
Wolfenden, 84, 88, 102, 113, 145
Wolffy, 362
Wolford, 46
Woll, 57
Womack, 120
Wonderful Dwarf, 140
Wonn, 385
Wood, 25, 64, 97, 117, 220, 297, 322, 403, 406, 421, 434, 467, 486
Woodal, 268
Woodberry Forest, 371
Woodbourne, 433
Woodbridge, 555
Woodbury, 366, 436, 465, 572
Woodferd, 103
Woodhull, 226, 336, 477
Woodland, 91
Woodlawn, 549
Woodman, 259, 565
Woodruff, 155

Woods, 66, 135, 166, 321, 549
Woodside, 102
Woodson, 96, 162, 476
Woodville, 405
Woodward, 85, 110, 287, 480, 530
Wool, 207, 333
Wooley, 403
Woolfolk, 274
Woolls, 551
Woolsey, 328, 399
Wooster, 234
Wootton, 441
Worcester, 444
Workman, 530
Works, 209
Wormley, 8, 39
Wormsted, 477
Worrall, 111
Worsley, 507
Worth, 45, 151, 225, 291, 333
Worthington, 20, 66, 74, 110, 183, 210, 252, 357, 379, 382, 429, 441
Wren, 483
Wrench, 567
Wright, 1, 8, 24, 81, 83, 90, 107, 113, 124, 130, 164, 176, 183, 209, 219, 238, 250, 258, 261, 262, 271, 281, 288, 318, 329, 331, 349, 361, 373, 375, 421, 445, 452, 471, 511, 542, 571
Wroe, 11, 384
Wyandotts, 335
Wyatt, 90, 133, 233, 263, 543
Wyche, 485
Wyckoff, 365
Wyeth, 237
Wyman, 63, 296, 371, 528
Wynn, 73, 337, 348
Wythe, 536

X

Xenia, 504

Y

Yable, 547
yacht **On-ka hye**, 86
Yager, 196
Yarnall, 441, 515
Yates, 14, 22, 40, 96, 107, 148, 170, 173, 210, 254, 347, 383
Yeates, 107
Yeatmen, 66
Yellott, 382, 441
Yelvert, 245
Yohannan, 112, 310, 455
Yorktown, 51
Yost, 461, 528
You, 246, 275, 377
Young, 20, 30, 35, 39, 41, 50, 60, 71, 73, 75, 90, 95, 99, 107, 114, 116, 142, 149, 176, 195, 231, 242, 244, 246, 250, 293, 304, 332, 348, 352, 356, 373, 388, 393, 400, 403, 412, 421, 422, 440, 444, 462, 478, 493, 494, 503, 527, 537, 558, 559, 561
Younge, 88
Younglove, 96

Z

Zackman, 506, 523, 533
Zane, 187
Zantzinger, 30, 86, 107, 135, 276, 449
Zeller, 353, 470
Zellers, 422
Zeltner, 189, 190
Zevala, 397
Zevely, 166
Zieber, 92
Zimmerman, 126, 372
Zumalt, 90

www.ingramcontent.com/pod-product-compliance
Lightning Source LLC
Chambersburg PA
CBHW071215290426
44108CB00013B/1186